Beginning Visual C++ Components

with MFC Extensions & ActiveX Controls

Matt Telles

Wrox Press Ltd.®

Beginning Visual C++ Components

with MFC Extensions & ActiveX Controls

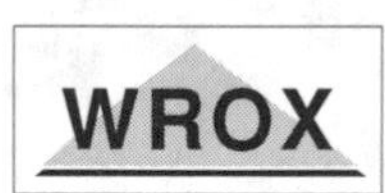

Published by Wrox Press Ltd. 30 Lincoln Road, Olton, Birmingham, B27 6PA , UK.
Printed in Canada
1 2 3 4 5 TRI 99 98 97 96

Library of Congress Catalog no. 96-61219
ISBN 1-861000-49-9

Trademark Acknowledgements

Credits

Authors
Matt Telles

Editors
Alex Stockton
Julian Dobson
Jon Hill

Technical Reviewers
Ian Carbaugh
Glenn Clarkson
Duane Helmuth
Ariel Katz
Mark Kilpatrick
Lynn Mettler
Justin Rudd
Marc Simkin
Julian Templeman
Dan Vallejo
Gerry Whelan

Managing Editor
John Franklin

Operations Manager
Gina Mance

Design/Layout
Neil P.J Gallagher
Andrew Guillaume

Proof Readers
Pam Brand
Simon Gilks
Robin Morris

Index
Simon Gilks
Robin Morris

Cover Design
Third Wave

For more information on Third Wave, contact Ross Alderson on 44-121 236 6616
Cover photograph supplied by The Image Bank

About the Author

Matt Telles is a professional programmer working in Visual C++ for anyone that will pay him. He has 12+ years professional programming experience working in Visual C++, MFC, C, MS-DOS, MS-Windows, Visual Basic, Delphi, Java, and anything else that happens to be needed. Matt spends his 'copious' spare time with his wife, kids, cats, and beer, not necessarily in that order. He can be reached via email at **7044.432@compuserve.com**

Dedications

This book is dedicated to my mother, Edna Telles, for putting up with me.

Also, my wife, Dawnna, and kids (hi, Jenny and Rachel!) requested some sort of mention in this one.

Special thanks to the nice people at Wrox who turned my illiterate scribbles into the book you now hold.

Visual
C++

Beginning
Visual C++ Components

Summary of Contents

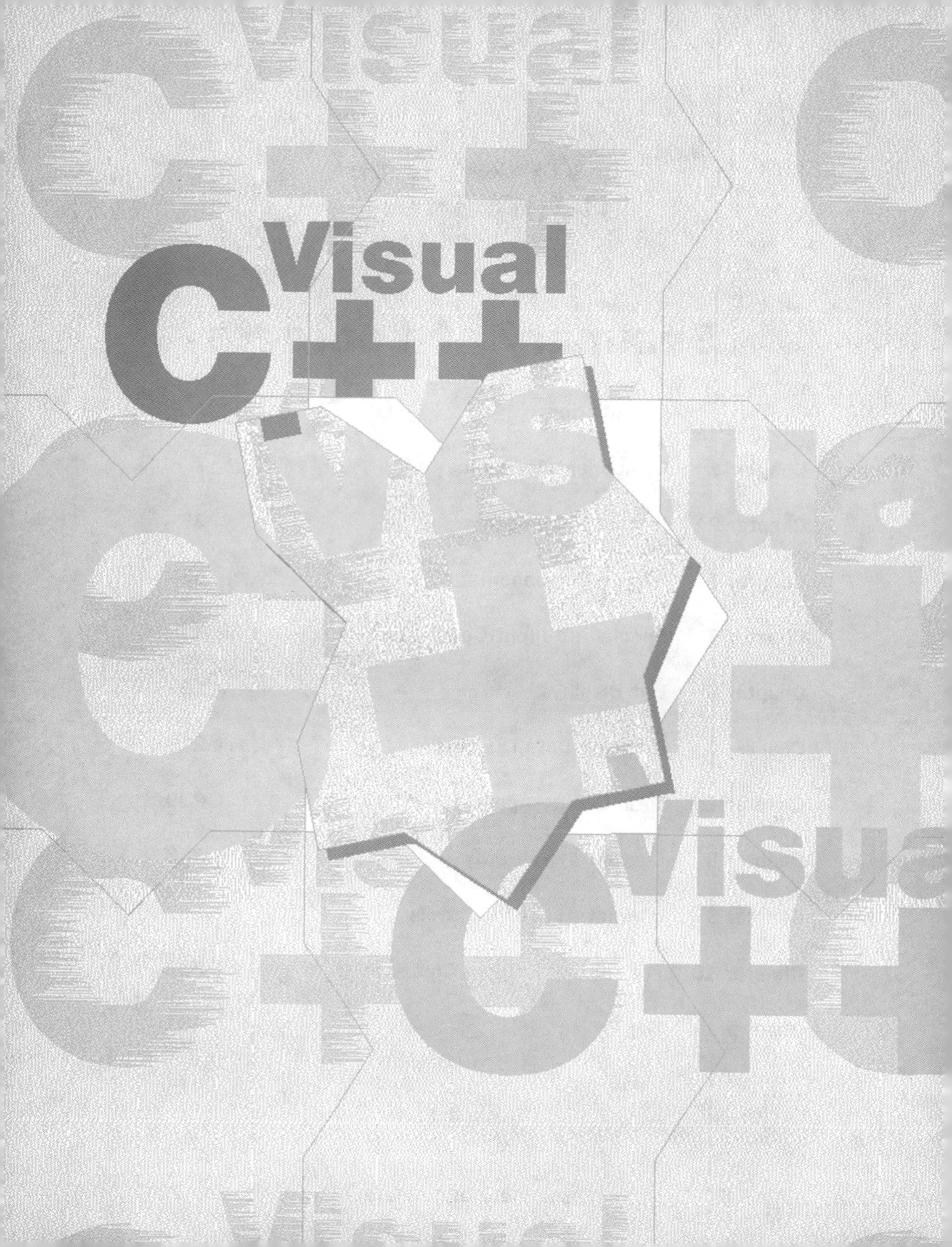
Visual
C++

Beginning
Visual C++
Components

Table of Contents

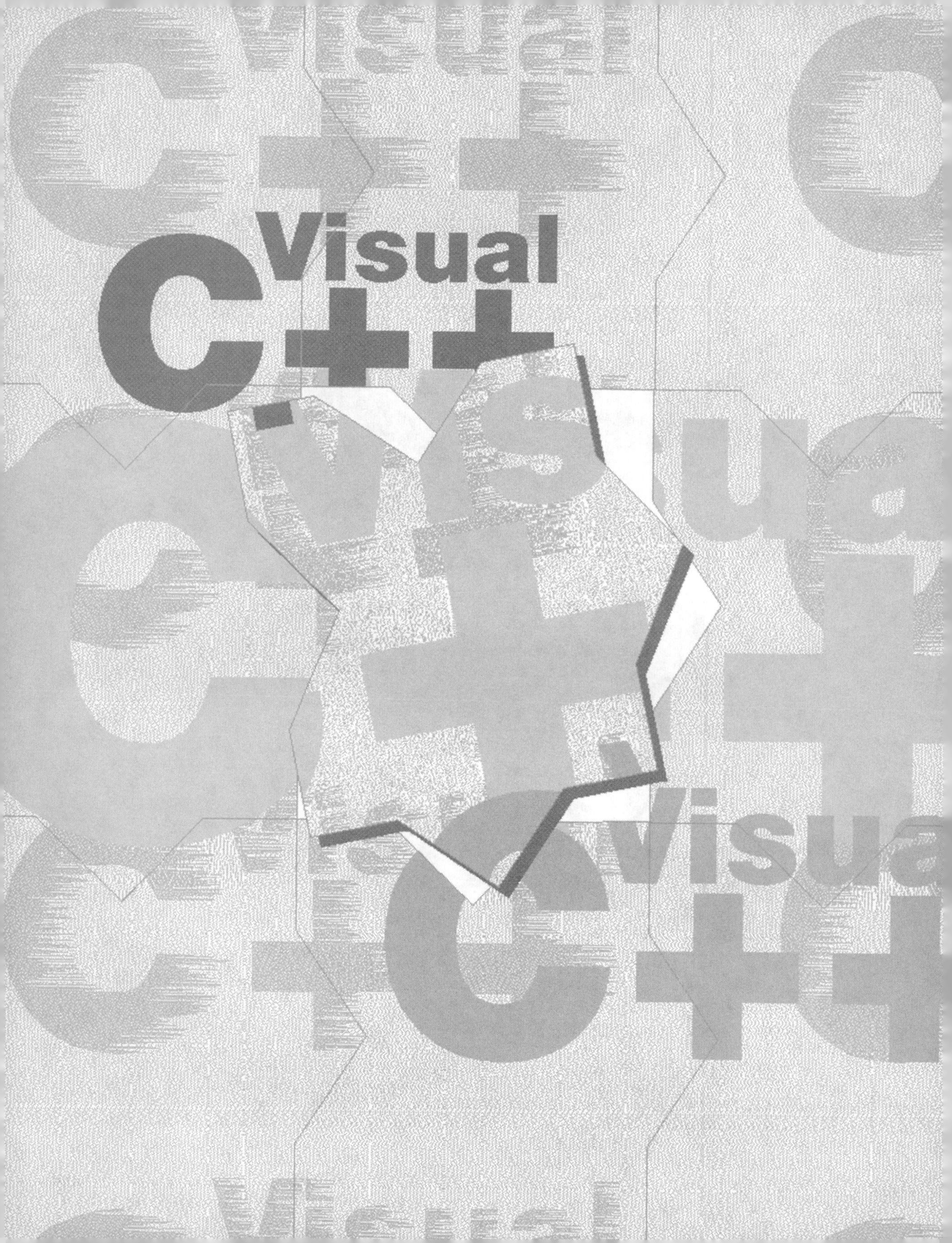
Visual
C++

Introduction

Welcome to **Beginning Visual C++ 4.x Component Programming with MFC Extensions and ActiveX Controls**. A bit of a mouthful, you think? Well, in spite of the long-winded title, this book is all about *saving* time! With all of the demands for time that programmers face in today's fast-paced world, this should come as a relief.

What, exactly, is an MFC extension? What is an ActiveX control? These are just two of the topics we will be examining in this book. Along the way, you will be treated to some industrial strength components that can be dropped straight into your applications. Somebody wants to do your work for you! Who are you to complain?

Who this Book Is For

In general, this book was written for programmers. To use the book effectively, you should have an understanding of Windows programming concepts, a firm grasp of the C++ programming language, and some exposure to Visual C++. Programming managers may also gain from this book in understanding what components are really capable of and what the overhead involved with developing components will be.

The audience for this book is considered to be moderate to advanced Visual C++ programmers who have worked previously on Visual C++ applications for Windows. If you've worked your way through Ivor Horton's **Beginning Visual C++ 4** (also from Wrox Press) then this book is a great next step.

Have Your Component Cake...

Although the concepts discussed in the book are not entry-level, the book can also be used as a 'cookbook' for beginning programmers who would like to include more advanced components in their applications. Using the book as a cookbook requires no real advanced training in Windows development, nor does it require the same level of programming expertise.

If you're a beginning Windows programmer and simply want to use the components developed in this book to make your own applications look more professional, please feel free to do so.

One of the basic tenets of the book is that component reuse should be as simple and easy as possible. While you are using the components, however, keep an eye out for ideas and techniques that you can use in your own applications as well. It is only by studying other people's programs and designs that you can improve your own coding techniques.

...and Eat It

Although the components in this book are presented for use in Visual C++ applications, they will appeal to users of other development environments as well. Any development environment which can use ActiveX controls can use the controls developed in this book. Visual Basic, Delphi, and Internet Explorer are just three of the environments which offer support for ActiveX controls.

The MFC extensions we will talk about can be bundled into dynamic link libraries (DLLs) and wrapped with C functions or COM interfaces to make them accessible from other environments (such as Visual Basic or Delphi) as well. Don't think that the only place that components are necessary is in object-oriented languages such as Visual C++. All languages require component technology to some degree.

Leaf through the chapters and look for components that can help you in your own applications. Read the design specifications for the components to see how they work. Type them in, grab them from the Wrox web site or send for the code disk and use them!

> *All the code for this book (and many other Wrox titles) is available for free download from* **`http://www.wrox.com/`**, *or you can send off for a disk. See the offer in the back of the book for details.*

Consider for a moment what an average programmer is paid for an hour of work. In that hour, programmers must write memos, go to meetings, design enhancements and applications, and then create some code. If a single component in this book were to take you, as a programmer, a few hours to implement (and many would take considerably longer than that), you will be saving many times the cost of this book! If you learn nothing else from this book, learn that writing and reusing components will save you money in the short and the long term.

Make no mistake, there is nothing wrong with using this book to further your own applications. You needn't learn any more than you want or need in order to use the components in this book. Further, if you don't have the time to read the book, please feel free to use the code herein without even understanding how it works! Although this is rarely a good idea in the long run, all programmers are quite accustomed to the idea of having not enough time to do it right, but plenty of time to fix it!

What You'll Learn from this Book

The main aim of this book is to introduce programmers to the idea of designing and developing custom components. Read through the book to see what kinds of problems are solved within. Look at each component design to see what sorts of problems we are solving and what interfaces we are exposing to the end user. Try out the exercises at the end of each chapter to further your understanding of how to work with components and how they can be extended.

You will learn how to generate a set of requirements from a problem statement. You will learn how to design components given a set of requirements. Once you have a design, you will learn, in a step-by-step manner, how to implement components using cutting-edge technologies —MFC extensions, ActiveX controls (using MFC or ATL), and even custom AppWizards—to solve the problems. Hopefully, you will see that the technology used is not nearly as important as the thought process that goes behind creating a new component.

If you choose to create the components as you read through the book, please take note of the design process and read the descriptions fully. Even though it is a lot more fun to write code than to read books, the reading will help you gain a fuller understanding of the code you are writing. Take note especially of highlighted sections, as these will help you in the creation of your own components in the future.

What You'll Need to Use this Book

Components developed in this book are written in Visual C++ 4.*x* and use the Microsoft Foundation Classes (MFC) to implement the technology behind the components. This means that you'll need a copy of Visual C++ 4.0 or greater (at the time of writing, Visual C++ 4.2 was the latest version available).

Later in the book, we develop some controls using the ActiveX Template Library (ATL). To develop ActiveX components using the ActiveX Template Library, you'll need to download a copy of the ATL from Microsoft's web site. In addition to the ATL, you will of course need the ActiveX SDK (available from the aforementioned web site or on the MSDN CD-ROM). Later in the book, we will get into the new Internet Control Pack from Microsoft, currently available in Beta format on the Microsoft web (or FTP) site. Finally, depending on the version of Visual C++ you're using, you may need some tools from the Win32 SDK (also available on the MSDN CD-ROM). It certainly seems like a lot of stuff, doesn't it? The gain will be worth the pain, I assure you.

Of course, to run Visual C++, you'll need a computer running Windows 95 or Windows NT. All of the code for this book was developed using a 486/66 and a Pentium/133. To get the best use out of the development environment and the operating system, it is recommended that you have at least 16 megabytes of memory and at least a VGA monitor. Note that these are the requirements for using Visual C++ itself, *not* for the components developed here.

To test the ActiveX controls that you develop, you can use Visual C++ and the Test Container. However, it's always a good idea to test your controls in as many containers as possible, so if you've got Visual Basic (4.0 or later) or Internet Explorer (3.0 or later) then all the better. Internet Explorer is freely available for download from Microsoft's web site.

> *You can download the ActiveX Template Library from*
>
> `http://www.microsoft.com/visualc/v42/atl/default.htm`

Internet Explorer from

`http://www.microsoft.com/ie/download/`

and the Internet Control Pack from

`http://www.microsoft.com/msdownload`

What is an ActiveX Control anyway?

There seems to be some confusion among developers about what precisely ActiveX controls are and how they relate to OLE controls. The ActiveX Control specification says that ActiveX controls are simply creatable COM objects (the only interface they *must* support is **`IUnknown`**). This means that a huge swathe of components that people have already written as COM objects are actually ActiveX controls. Maybe you've already written some ActiveX controls yourself without realizing it?

This, of course, means that all OLE controls *are* ActiveX controls (although not all ActiveX controls are OLE controls, since an ActiveX control doesn't have to support some of the interfaces required for OLE controls). Throughout this book, we'll be referring to 'ActiveX controls' but, most of the time, you can mentally replace this term with 'OLE controls' if that makes you feel more comfortable.

Conventions

We use a number of different styles of text and layout in the book to help differentiate between different kinds of information. Here are examples of the styles we use and an explanation of what they mean:

TRY IT OUTS - How Do They Work?

1. These are examples that you should work through.
2. Each step has a number.
3. Follow the steps through.

FYI **Extra details, for your information, come in boxes like this.**

- **Important Words** are in a bold type font.
- Words that appear on the screen, such as menu options, are a similar font to the one used on screen, e.g. the File menu.
- Keys that you press on the keyboard, like *Ctrl* and *Enter*, are in italics.

- All filenames are in this style: **StdAfx.cpp**.
- Function names look like this: **GetLength()**

```
// Code listings look like this if it's code you need to add yourself
// Or this if you've seen the code before or it's something added by one
// of the wizards.
```

Tell Us What You Think

We've worked hard on this book to make it useful to you. We've tried to understand what you're willing to exchange your hard earned money for, and tried to make the book live up to your expectations. But we're only human, and we sometimes make mistakes. We rely on you to help us find those errors and correct them through the errata pages that we keep on our web site.

If you do find a mistake, please have a look at the errata page for this book on our web site first. If you can't find an answer there, tell us about the problem and we'll do everything we can to answer promptly!

Aside from mistakes, we'd also like to know what you think about this book in general. Tell us what we did wrong and what we did right. This isn't just marketing flannel—we really do all huddle around the e-mail to find out what you think. If you don't believe it, send us a note. We'll answer and we'll take whatever you say on board for future editions. The easiest way to get in touch is to use e-mail:

feedback@wrox.com
CompuServe 100063,2152

You can also find more details about Wrox Press on our web site. Here you'll find the code from our latest books, sneak previews of forthcoming titles and information about the authors and editors. You can order Wrox titles directly from the site or find out where your local bookstore carrying Wrox titles is located. Look at the advert in the back of this book for more information. The address of our site is:

http://www.wrox.com

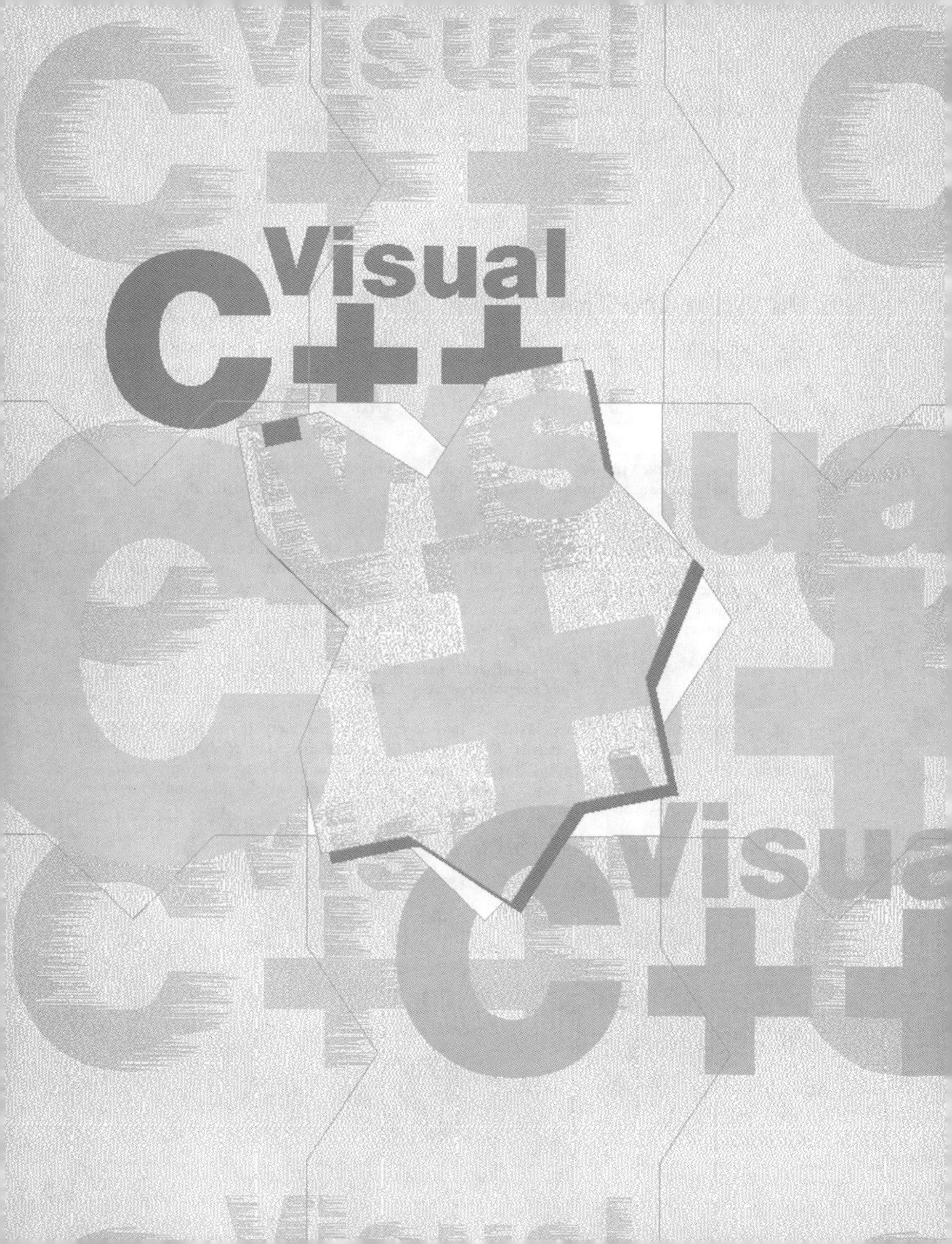
Visual
C++

Component Technology

Today's software development field is buzzing with new terms and exciting ideas. Among the oldest of those new ideas and the newest of those terms is component technology. Components are being credited with everything from cutting development time in half to curing the common cold. While it seems obvious that components can't do everything that they claim, it's equally obvious that they are the wave of the future. It would be helpful, therefore, to know just what we're talking about in this new field.

What is Component Technology?

Put simply, component technology is the process of implementing components. A component is a discrete piece of software that can be used to perform a task. Another way of looking at it is that a component is a 'black box' that takes certain forms of input and uses a 'magic' process to transform that input into a given set of functionality and, possibly, output. While the term is new, the idea of components is quite old. Consider the following function, written in standard C++:

```
int EncodeString(char* string, char* password, int len)
{
   int p = 0;

   for (int i = 0; i < len; ++i)
   {
      string[i] = string[i] ^ password[p];
      p++;
      if (p == strlen(password))
         p = 0;
   }
   return i;
}
```

Most programmers will recognize this function as one uses an extremely simple algorithm to encode a string for protection. While most people would refer to it simply as a *function*, another term for it would be a *component*. After all, it fits all the criteria for a component. It takes a set of inputs (input string, password string, and length of string) and uses a 'black box' (the algorithm for encoding in this case) to produce an output (the encoded string). Shown in a pretty diagram form, the process goes something like this:

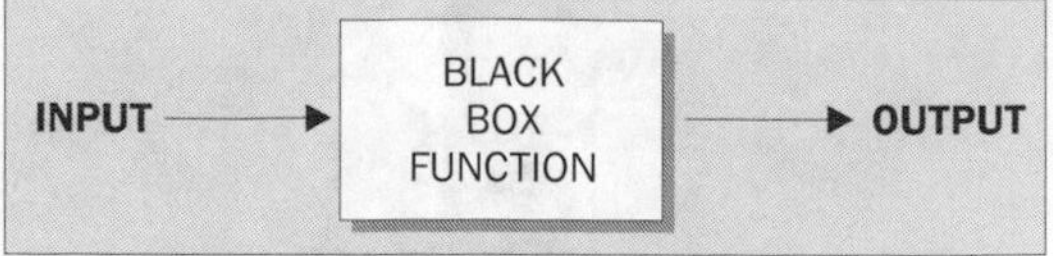

In this simple case, the input is just a couple of character strings and an integer representing the length of one of those strings. The black box function is just an algorithm which uses the second input string to transform the first into an output string, which represents the output of the function. This component, while simple, does the job.

The Component Development Cycle

Component technology is more than simply writing functions. It encompasses several other important steps:

- Design
- Implementation
- Documentation
- Testing
- Reuse

Let's take a quick look at what each of these means. We will also look at them in some depth in the next chapter.

Design

In the 'good old days', programmers often wrote modules, small programs, and even large-scale applications without ever thinking about what they were doing. They just 'knew' how to get from the beginning to the end of the application. Since one programmer was most often responsible for an entire project, there was little need for design specification, user interface issues or other arcane documentation. Instead, the programmers happily turned out reams of code and produced applications for users who had little or no say in the matter.

Fortunately, the good old days are behind us now. Today's programming environment requires that programs work the way the user wants them to work, not the way the programmer 'knows' they should work. This is really the way it should be, since in most cases it's the user that needs to use the application, not the programmer. Today's Windows applications are a case in point. Not only do Windows applications need to perform the basic functionality expected by users, but they are also expected to conform to certain user interface standards that users have come to expect of Windows programs.

Because of the complexity and variety of techniques now required in Windows programming, it has also become normal for large-scale applications to be implemented by teams of programmers, rather than the traditional single program/single programmer model. A single programmer can't be expected to be an expert in all fields.

All of these issues lead to the need for program design. In an application, design can specify the user interface, database format, 'look and feel', and other issues in which the various programming team members should remain consistent. It's disconcerting for the user to move between screens and be faced by different user interfaces. For this reason, teams often design complete user interfaces for the application they're developing before writing a single line of code. Standards such as database interfaces, error handling, and utility functions, are also handled during the design phase. A properly designed application can cut both development time and user dissatisfaction.

What does all of this have to do with components? You can think of a component as a small application that is used by larger applications. In fact, a better definition of a component is a 'building block'. Applications are built with and upon components. For this reason, it's most important that a component does a specific job, and that it does it well.

Consider for a moment a component which is intended to manipulate data in a specific database. An application might have several similar components which work on various tables in a single database. One solution would be to create a new C++ class (which is a simple form of component itself) for each database table needed in the application. This class could have fields (and methods) which represent each unique field in each database table.

A better suggestion would be to consider a more broad-band solution. We could, for example, define a single C++ class which knows how to 'talk' to the database and request records. Each field in the database could then be retrieved by using its name, or its index, or both. This solution (which is nicely represented by the MFC classes **`CRecordset`** and **`CDaoRecordset`**) would work across all databases which use records and fields.

In fact, our first solution is the one most often used by programmers today. It isn't portable across applications, it isn't reusable (unless one is dealing with the same table in the same database in another application) and it's prone to error. Why is it error prone? Because each time you cut and paste a block of code from one module to another, you have a chance to make a mistake. In most cases, those mistakes are simple textual errors which are caught by the compiler. At other times, however, they can lead to long searches through the code and late nights with the debugger trying to find them.

The second solution works much better for our database problem. It leads to a single code base which can be shared (reused) among many applications. It also provides a single component (class) which can be used in many places. If an error is discovered, it can be fixed by making the appropriate changes to the base class. Other applications using the object won't be adversely affected by the change unless the **interface** to the class changes. With a good design of the interface, this is unlikely to occur.

The purpose of writing components is to create reusable code that will be used by other people. The only reason for someone else to use one of your components is if that component does what it's supposed to do. To determine what a component is supposed to do, it's necessary to perform at least rudimentary design on the problem that you're trying to solve. We'll talk about the kinds of design you should consider in Chapter 2.

Implementation

Once you know what it is that you're going to create, the next step is to actually create it. Although this seems like a rather obvious statement, you would be surprised at how many companies never get to this step. The importance of actually getting to the implementation phase can't be overemphasized. Too many companies continue to design and design and design a project (whether it be an application, a component, or a simple function) until the project is canceled. This process, regardless of its path, leads to a single end: bankruptcy for the company and unemployment for the programmer. Don't let this happen to you!

The important thing to understand about the design and implementation stages of development is that, to be useful, the process must be iterative. It's not unusual for a component to be half-completed in implementation and then go back through another design phase. This can occur for a variety of reasons: perhaps the initial design was wrong, or the project simply grew in scope. What is important, however, is that the two phases can't occur simultaneously.

The developer or manager is responsible for making sure that while a component is designed, there's no implementation going on. Similarly, when the implementation phase is going on, designs can't change for the portion of the work being done. This isn't to say that future work can't be designed. Programmers will tell you horror stories of writing code that does a specific job, only to come in the next day and find that the entire scope of the project has changed (without any alterations to the final deadline, of course).

Since the software development process is in the real world, we can't stop the constant change (only in the software world could you have an expression like 'constant change'). We can, however, reduce the stress by planning for changes at the outset. This planning and the work that goes behind it falls into the realm of component implementation.

Prepare for Change

If you knew up front that you were writing a spreadsheet application, such as Lotus 1-2-3 or Microsoft Excel, you would probably make certain assumptions about the implementation of the product. One of those assumptions, for example, would be that the end result would be made up of rows and columns. Imagine though, that the spreadsheet that you started working on in January had turned into a word processor application by June (don't laugh, it really does happen!). Word processors, as you might imagine, don't have rows and columns. They tend to lean more towards blocks of text. How could you possibly plan for such an event?

The answer is that changes such as going from a spreadsheet to a word processor don't happen overnight. Your manager doesn't wake up one morning and decide "Today we'll create a word processor out of the spreadsheet project!" Well, maybe yours does, but it doesn't generally happen that way. What does happen is that a marketing person comes along and sees the spreadsheet application in its initial prototype. You did remember to create a prototype, didn't you? Of course you did! The prototype is the bridge between design and implementation. Anyway, this marketing person takes the product out into the field and shows it to some users. These users then give feedback to the marketer concerning their needs and problems. The marketing person throws away all this feedback and gives you a completely different set of requirements from the users. Or at least, that's how it feels sometimes.

The initial requirements for a project rarely match the final design. What is important for you to know as a component writer is that the same applies to components. Consider our hypothetical spreadsheet/word processor application. If you had written the entire application using a monolithic Visual C++/MFC model, you would be completely out of luck. Had you designed the application to be a modular group of components, on the other hand, you might very well be able to make the transformation possible.

Imagine that you had written a single text entry component. Spreadsheet applications could take advantage of it to store data for text cells. Word processor applications could take advantage of it to edit their text. Mail applications could take advantage of the component to enter new messages and display existing messages. In each case, however, the basic component doesn't change. If you had built the component in such a way as to allow the programmer to specify the way to load text into it and get text out of it, you could use that single component in multiple applications.

Before you start thinking that we are in an old Saturday Night Live commercial (it's a floor wax *and* a dessert topping), it should be pointed out that a component can't be all things to all people. The wider the scope of the component, the narrower the band of applications that can use it. If, for example, you were to create a data-aware component that could read fields out of a certain kind of database, you would be unable to use that component in another application that used a different kind of database. These are the decisions that you must make at implementation time.

In Chapter 2, we'll discuss how you can move back and forth between design and implementation. In addition, we'll examine the need to keep each component from growing into a Swiss Army knife.

Documentation

If there's a single thing that prevents code reuse in the software development community, it's the lack of documentation. There are probably tens of thousands of modules, functions, and components that exist in the world but remain hidden away on hard drives, networks, and floppy disks on shelves because no-one knows how to use them.

Consider for a moment the ActiveX (formerly OLE) Grid Control, **`Grid.ocx`**, that ships with Visual C++ 4.*x*. It seems like a nice control. It's capable of displaying rows and columns with varying text or bitmaps. It supports horizontal and vertical scrolling, and can be used in nearly any application that requires a row and column display. It is, however, rarely used in applications. Why is this?

The grid control that ships with Visual C++ 4.*x* is a ported version of the original **`Grid.vbx`** that was shipped with Visual Basic (the updated control still ships with Visual Basic 4). Someone at Microsoft apparently thought that it would be a good idea to ship an example of an ActiveX control with Visual C++, since that's the platform that Microsoft recommends for the development of new ActiveX controls. This seems like a good idea, since we have stressed that code reuse is important. Unfortunately, whoever made this decision seems not to have communicated to anyone else that documentation was necessary for the grid control. As a result, the only documentation available for the control is a rather cryptic help file that is obviously written for Visual Basic programmers. What does all of this lead to? No reuse of the grid component.

Fortunately for you, though, we'll implement a grid control in this book and give you not only documentation on how to use it, but also the source code for the component itself. Aren't you lucky?

What does documentation mean? It isn't that silly a question, since documentation can come in one of several forms. At its most basic, documentation for a component can be as simple as a fully commented header file, along with the original basic design specification for the control. Components written for programmers should include a complete help file for the control, listing all of the available functions and the various parameters accepted by those functions. The 'functions' for any given component are really just the functionality exposed by that component to the outside world. For a C++ class, the exposed functionality consists of the **`public`** methods and variables defined in the class. For an ActiveX control, the exposed functionality is the set of properties and methods which has been defined to be available to the outside user. The type and range of the data is different, but the end result is the same. The functionality is whatever is available for the user to use.

We'll take a more in-depth look at documentation and what you as a programmer or manager should expect (and should provide) in the next chapter.

Testing

After inadequate documentation, the most certain way to ensure that programmers don't use your component is to make it buggy, or leave it buggy. While most programmers are accustomed to a certain level of bugs in any product, that level varies as the complexity of the software increases. Where a programmer might be willing to use a buggy component in a simple utility, the programmer is much less likely to use it in a commercial product. Bugs are a fact of life in the software development world, but it doesn't mean we have to like it.

The best way that you can avoid bugs in your software is through testing. Testing is more than just hacking away at a screen until it breaks (although that is one of its forms). Testing must be approached in a methodical and logical fashion. If you expect that your user will use your component in a certain way, you should test that way exhaustively. However, testing a component in the manner in which it's expected to be used isn't enough. A component must be tested in ways that it's not expected to be used to ensure it can handle errors robustly.

Testing is intended to find two kinds of bugs: physical bugs and logical bugs. Physical bugs are the sort Windows programmers are most used to. General Protection Faults, resource leaks, memory overwrites, and other spectacular bugs are all examples of physical bugs. Logical bugs are far more insidious. A logical bug means that the program continues to execute but produces incorrect results. Logical bugs are generally much harder to track down than physical bugs, and are also much more dangerous to the end user.

For an example of a logical bug which causes the user (in this case, the programmer) grief and heartache, consider a simple calculator such as the one found in Windows 3.*x*. A calculator component might easily emulate the calculator found in Windows 3.*x*, and would probably be patterned after it. If you wrote such a control and entered an equation like:

```
3 + 4 + 5 - 6 =
```

you would probably expect the result to be 6. It would be very puzzling to you, therefore, if the calculator came up with another result, such as 18. This is an example of a logical error. It doesn't crash the system or overwrite memory, but it causes problems nonetheless.

Reuse

To be effective, a component has to be reused. Reuse is what makes code valuable to a company, because it reduces the effective cost of developing the software. If you spend two weeks writing a piece of software that is used once, it costs the company you're working for (or yourself if you're independently employed) *n* dollars. Each time that code is reused in a project, you save *n* dollars on the new project. If you reuse the component enough times, the effective cost of the original work drops to near zero.

The lure of object-oriented programming was that it would reduce the price of software development. Instead, most companies found that the cost increased. The reason? Lack of reuse of developed components. If you develop a component (or a block of code for that matter) a hundred times, you'll certainly get better at writing it. The real question, though, is why you are writing it a second (or third or fourth) time to begin with. Why aren't these components simply reused?

The answer lies in the design, development, and documentation of the components in the first place. Unless you lay a firm foundation, even the strongest skyscrapers will fall. So it is with component technology.

At this point, we understand the benefits and risks of component technology. We'll find that the benefits to a company far outweigh the risks involved if, and only if, the process is followed logically and methodically. The problem is that most companies (and individuals) stop at this point. They look at the risks and benefits and decide that component technology (or before that object-oriented technology) is the way to go. Full steam ahead and damn the torpedoes! There's only one little problem. We have yet to define exactly what a component is!

What is a Component?

In its simplest form, a component is a block of software. Unfortunately, this is a lot like saying that, in its simplest form, a car is a block of metal. It's important that you, as a programmer or manager, understand exactly what components are, so that you can understand their strengths and limitations.

For the purposes of this book, we'll define a component as a black box of software which takes input, performs whatever work it needs to do, and then accomplishes a specific set of functionality. Components have a defined interface to the outside world. Finally, components perform only the set of tasks necessary to accomplish a single related set of goals. Let's look at each of these points individually.

A Component is a Black Box of Software

Components aren't intended to have their internal workings viewed. This is to prevent users from modifying internal structures or settings that may be necessary to the workings of the component. It's also important from another viewpoint, that of future enhancements. If a component is to grow with the software it supports, it's often necessary to modify the internal algorithms used for the support of the functions the component supports. As an example, consider the following C++ class method:

```
int CSearchComponent::Search(TCHAR* pszWord)
{
   // Get a list of words
   GetWordList(m_StringArray);

   // See if the word is found
   for (int i = 0; i < m_StringArray.GetSize(); ++i)
      if (m_StringArray[i] == pszWord)
         return 1;

   // Not found, indicate error
   return 0;
}
```

This method searches through an internal list of words to see if a given word is found. It's probably used to indicate keywords for a compiler, parser, or other tool. It works by simple brute force searching through a list.

Consider what would happen if you wanted to port this particular component class to a new environment, one with thousands of possible keywords. Perhaps the keywords actually vary by the type of input you're parsing. In this case, you would be very unlikely to want to store thousands of strings in memory. Even if there's enough memory to work with, it would be difficult to keep the strings correct in each case and to make changes in many different places. A better choice would be to store the strings in a database and use some sort of internal setting to determine which word to search for. In this case, you might modify the above method as follows:

```
int CSearchComponent::Search(TCHAR* pszWord)
{
   // Assume the first two characters define the database
   TCHAR db[3];
   _tcsnccpy(db, pszWord, 2);
   db[2] = 0;

   // Open the database
   CMyDb database(db);

   // See if we can find the word
   if (database.FindKey(pszWord))
      return 1;

   // Not found, indicate error
   return 0;
}
```

Notice that, even though the internal structures have completely changed (going from a simple internal list of terms to a complete database system), the interface to the method remains the same. This means that existing applications which are using the component don't need to change either. This behavior, often called **backwards compatibility**, is an important consideration for companies. If a change can be localized to a single component or even a set of components, the impact on the overall structure of the system is reduced and so the time (and therefore cost) of the change is minimized.

A Component Implements a Specific Set of Functionality

In order to be successful, a component has to do something for the programmer using it. If the component does too little, it will be rejected because it doesn't do the job it's needed for. If, on the other hand, the component does too much, it will be rejected because it's impossible to understand and to test. For this reason, the set of functionality which needs to be implemented by a component should be carefully selected.

If you were writing a component that implemented a zip code lookup, for example, you might consider the following functions:

- Determine if a zip code is valid.
- Determine the city for the zip code.

- Determine the state for the zip code.
- Given a city and state, validate an input zip code.

These are all reasonable things for a zip code component to do. If the component was unable to give back the state for a given zip code, it would be unlikely that it would be used. What would be the advantage to the programmer in using it? Now, consider adding the following list to the supported functionality of the zip code component:

- Determine the senators for a given zip code.
- Determine the number of addresses in a given zip code.
- Given a full zip code (zip+4), determine the name of the person living there.

Are these valid extensions to our zip code component? For most programmers, these functions would have little use, but few would object to their presence. After all, you might very well need political or demographic data later on. There's more to the component, however, than just these simple additions. To determine the name of the person living at a zip+4 number, for example, would require an immense database for any given area. Would you really want to have to ship a simple address book application on five CD-ROMs because of the existence of this component? Probably not.

When you're creating components, give some thought to the probable uses of the component by its users (generally programmers). If the programmer would use the function nearly all of the time, by all means include it. In our zip code example, it will require a certain amount of data to support the city and state information. For most programmers, though, using a zip code validation component indicates that they're willing to make this allowance, since they would otherwise not be interested in doing the validation at all. Except for a few applications, such as mailing list vendors, adding the complete zip code database is probably massive overkill.

A Component Implements a Defined Interface

As mentioned previously, the interface for a component has to be defined in a fixed way so that clients of the component won't need to be changed when enhancements are made to it. We examined that interface in a simple way for a C++ class structure. Components can be vastly more complex than simple C++ classes. In this book, we'll examine not only C++ classes (MFC extensions) that implement components, but also more cutting-edge component technology, such as ActiveX controls.

While it's annoying when a C++ class header file changes, it leads to a fairly simple set of changes in the component. The compiler detects the change in the header file and recompiles all modules which depend on it. If the change adds, deletes or modifies an existing class interface (method), it may very well generate an error at compile time. The programmer will then move to fix the errors by modifying the source code so that it conforms to the new interface. While this can be a tedious and annoying job, it's really not very hard to do.

For new technologies, such as ActiveX controls, changes to the interface can have more serious and wide-reaching impacts. One of the biggest problems with using ActiveX controls in Visual C++, for example, is that the compiler is unaware of changes to the control itself. Once an ActiveX control has been added to a project, Visual C++ adds a **wrapper class** around the control, in order to give the programmer easy access to the functionality provided by it. This wrapper class, however, isn't regenerated each time the ActiveX control file changes. This can lead to intermittent or difficult-to-trace problems, caused by a faulty interface between what the C++ wrapper class 'thinks' is the correct calling sequence and what the ActiveX control itself 'knows' is the right way to be called. A fixed interface is more than simply a nicety in cases such as these.

Once again, documentation is necessary to keep track of what the defined interface is for a component. If you make a habit of always sending out documentation updates whenever your component changes, you may annoy some programmers who have to make changes, but you'll keep a lot of other programmers from days of difficult debugging. In general, when you make changes you should try to support the existing interface, at least for long enough to be able to notify others that they should migrate to the new one.

A Component Performs Only the Tasks Necessary to Accomplish a Goal

This statement seems rather odd. Why would someone want to perform more than the tasks necessary to complete a given goal? Why do more work than is necessary to get the job done? The answer often lies in the programmer. Many programmers are proud of their creations. They want others to use those creations and so try to make those creations (components) everything to everybody. What this usually leads to is making the component into something that's unusable by the vast majority of potential users.

Consider, for example, a calendar component such as the one shown opposite. This component allows the user to select a month, day, and year in a simple, intuitive manner. It could be used in virtually any application that needs to input dates from the user and respond to date changes.

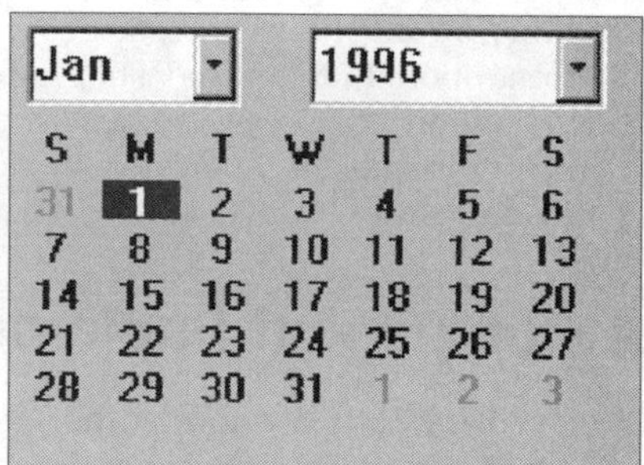

When the user selects a new date in the component, you would expect to be notified of this event. You could then do whatever processing you might want to do with that notification. For example, a scheduling program might look up all open time slots for a given date. A personal information manager might use the date as input to another field (such as a birthday or anniversary). In this way, the component is open-ended and not program-specific.

Now consider the same calendar component, but with a few 'enhancements'. When a date is selected, the component looks in a database to validate that the selected date is usable. Only usable dates are stored in the database. Months and days must be supplied to the program for dates that will be selectable.

Who would be likely to use such a component? Probably not the scheduling program (although it might). Certainly not the personal information manager application. Most general programmers don't want to create a separate database for each date range they want to allow the user to enter. By making the component capable of handling restricted dates (a requirement that was probably requested by a specific user), the programmer has made the component useless to the rest of the world.

A Brief History of Components

In the beginning, there was assembler. And the programmer looked upon the assembler and said "It is good". The only real problem was that the assembler made you do the same things over and over again in order to accomplish the same jobs. It got rather boring repeatedly writing the same pieces of code.

After assembler came COBOL (COmmon Business Oriented Language). COBOL was a vast improvement over assembler, because it allowed programmers to write in a higher level language. Programs could be written in a more modular style, and pieces of code copied from one program to another. Eventually, the programmers got so used to copying code that the language itself developed 'copy libraries' which could share code segments between different programs. The age of components was beginning.

Around the same time as COBOL came a language called FORTRAN (FORmula TRANslation), which, by the time of its fourth incarnation (FORTRAN IV), allowed programmers to write separately compiled subroutines. These subroutines could be collected together into a library which was then linked into applications. Libraries were probably the first real examples of components, but unfortunately they suffered from a number of problems. They were rather limited in scope and type of variable passing. They did little error checking, because there was no way to tell the compiler what the return types or parameters for library subroutines were. In many cases, although libraries advanced the software development world, they were a step backwards for component technology because of the new problems they introduced.

Circa 1970, the C language made its first appearance in the software development community, and had an immediate and major impact on it. Because C was closer to machine language than FORTRAN or COBOL, it was widely used for writing operating systems, utility applications and, finally, large-scale applications which required access to the lower levels of the machine. Because it was popular among programmers, C eventually became the language of choice among software development houses. More importantly to the story of components, however, C gave us the first truly standard library. The standard C library remains a consistent method for calling parameters, return types, and function naming. Programs written in the C language using the standard library in 1975 will, for the most part, still compile today and work the way they're supposed to.

In addition to adding the standard library, C also added the notion of cross-platform compatibility. Even when FORTRAN and COBOL programs could be ported from one machine to another, the process was often imperfect and caused many headaches for applications developers. C introduced the preprocessor to compilers, a method of modifying the code before the compiler ever saw it. The C notions of **`#ifdef`**, **`#else`** and **`#endif`** are still available today in modern C++ compilers. This preprocessing support allowed the programmer to write code that could be conditionally compiled, allowing operating system- and application-specific code to be segregated into meaningful areas. Only code which was intended for a specific operating system or application version would actually be compiled.

The next stage of component technology took place with the second release of the ANSI committee's standard C document. In this document, they created something called a **function prototype**. Function prototypes are standard in C++, but their presence in C was something very new. Programmers of the day (of which I was one) rued prototypes for requiring them to do more work to write even simple applications. Prototypes are simply declarations of the calling sequence and return type of functions in programs. They are used to let the compiler know how a function should be called, before the compiler actually finds the real definition of the function. In this way, the compiler can catch errors in calling sequences. Consider the following function, written in simple C:

```
int aFunction(int arg1, char* arg2, float arg3, double arg4,
        struct someStructure* x)
{
    // Do some things with the arguments
    x->someMember = 3;
    x->somePointer = &y;

    // Copy a string
    strcpy(arg2, "This is a test");

    return 0;
}
```

Now, consider a hypothetical piece of code somewhere else in the application which calls this function:

```
    // setup variables
    char buffer[10];
    float x;
    double y;
    struct someStructure* z;

    aFunction(1, x, y, z, buffer);
```

It's obvious, from looking at the function and the calling sequence, that the programmer has placed several of the arguments in the wrong order. In the early days of C, the compiler would simply generate code to push the arguments on the stack in the order they were given with no complaint. This would lead to probable errors (if you were lucky) and very strange symptoms that occurred much later in the application (if you weren't so lucky). Problems like this were quite common in C applications, since there was no guarantee of what a function stored somewhere in a library looked like. If the documentation was wrong (which happened often enough), or the programmer simply misread it (which also happened frequently), the program would crash.

Once function prototypes began to have an impact, however, there was a drop in the number of bugs reported in programs. Programmers began to look on prototypes less as a burden and more of a godsend (at least I did). Prototypes were the first true interface contracts. They specified what the interface of a function looked like to the programmer, and required (contracted with) the compiler to enforce that calling sequence. Component technology took a big leap forward and began to pick up speed.

In the mid-1980s, the C++ language was introduced. C++ was a so-called object-oriented language. This meant that it supported such things as encapsulation (or data hiding) and levels of protection for member data (**`public`**, **`private`**, and **`protected`** support). These new concepts allowed programmers, really for the first time, to require that users go through interface methods to set new values in objects. Before this, using C, programmers were supposed to use access methods to work on structures, but were still permitted by the compiler to manipulate data members of structures directly. This allowed programmers to introduce errors into code, rather than waiting for the component writers to create their own problems!

With C++ came a whole new generation of programmers. These programmers were taught to create separate modular interfaces for applications, and to build these applications out of prefabricated components wherever possible. It's possible that, had these programmers been left alone, they would have taken programming to new heights. Unfortunately, they had the rest of us to deal with. Many older programmers are not willing to make the effort to do the up-front design necessary to create quality components. Component technology leaped forward briefly, but was then dragged, kicking and screaming, back down into the development morass.

And then we saw the Light. Well, not exactly a light, but a new way of creating controls. Microsoft Visual C++ 4.0 was released in mid to late 1995, and immediately began having an impact on the way programmers wrote code. The new, integrated ControlWizard made it an easier task to write true ActiveX controls that could be easily shared between applications written in different languages. The Component Gallery made it easier to publish new controls where people could see them (although it's still unable to share over a network, a major failing in corporate environments). Finally, Microsoft allowed programmers to write their own custom AppWizards for generating new applications. These features made creating reusable components easier than not creating them. Programmers have always been a rather practical bunch. When faced with writing controls that could be shared (and admired!) by our peers, or continuing to write single applications from scratch, we generally bowed to the inevitable. Component technology was born again.

The next stage in the evolution of components came in early 1996 with the release of the ActiveX Template Library (ATL) in beta form from Microsoft. The ActiveX Template Library allowed the programmer to begin creating 'lightweight' components that could be used in Internet applications. As the world seems to be moving more and more towards a unified Internet community, the ability to create new controls for use in HTML forms seems like a large step in the right direction.

What does the future hold for component technology? It's rather hard to look into the future or make accurate guesses about the coming development world, but it's certain that some set of standards will emerge triumphant in the upcoming component wars. If you review the components provided in this book, you'll find that they all have something in common: none of the controls is application- or even industry-specific. This allows you to begin working on application-specific controls for your own industry while using the general components created here.

It's not hard to imagine that some day companies will have their own complete suites of components created especially for them by their own corporate (or even contract) programmers. These suites, combined with the generic components available here and on the market, will make programming more of a 'drag-and-drop, change some properties and go' sort of world.

Then again, maybe not. Regardless of the future of software development, it seems unlikely that programmers will ever be replaced by people clicking here and there to create applications. Still, you never know. It's in your best interest, therefore to learn to use and understand components.

Why Use Components?

It seems that everyone is talking about components and component technology these days. Components are the hot-selling software packages, and every development environment loves to promote its ability to create reusable components. Since components are so hot, there must be some reason why everyone wants them, mustn't there? Well, hula-hoops were hot, and pet rocks, and multimedia, and... you get the idea. What reasons are there for using components?

The first big reason that management at major companies is going for component technology and developing reusable components internally is cost. Most companies dedicate a considerable amount of time and resources to developing applications, but few devote either to testing. Because of this, bug fixing and version enhancements are a major money loser. Although an application can be developed in six months, it doesn't mean it can be delivered in six months. Often, applications develop new bugs between releases due to new enhancements.

Components can reduce both the initial cost of development and the ongoing cost of bug fixes and enhancements. Since components can be written to be used across multiple development sites (projects), they can save money by reducing the number of times a given piece of software needs to be written. This often has the added side-effect of making the look and feel of disparate applications similar, which makes life easier for users.

In addition, once a component has been thoroughly tested in a single application, the internal workings of that component can be safely assumed to work across other applications, freeing up the testers to work on the actual application functionality. If the same component is reused in many different applications and application versions, problems which are found in one application and traced back to the component, can be automatically fixed across all applications which use that component. All of these factors lead to quicker software development and lower costs.

The second biggest reason for developing components is time savings. While saving time is often coupled with cost, it has other effects as well. If a component is reused between two applications, the time that would have been used to create that component in the second application can be used to add extra functionality or for additional testing instead. A project which might have been doomed by a lack of certain critical features can instead be improved by the addition of newer functionality and features that users want. More importantly, a project that would have had to leave out secondary 'wish list' features because time had to be devoted to creating components, would instead be 'fleshed out' and appeal to a wider group. Time is often equated to money in software development, but it can mean much more than that.

Another important reason for component development centers around the reduction of programmer and manager frustration. There's little good that can be said about developing the same piece of software for the third or fourth time. Programmers often get annoyed when their skills begin to erode due to a lack of challenge. Managers turn to the same people again and again to develop the same products because those people are 'good at it'. While it's true that programmers will often learn better ways to do things by redoing them, it's also true that there are diminishing returns. Shortcuts and bad programming techniques are often implemented because a programmer no longer wants to work on a given project.

If component technology is used to implement reusable components, the frustration level of programmers drops. Once a component is written and shared across a company, that piece of software need never be written again. New components can be added to the company repository, and programming can again become fun. Rather than deciding how to rewrite the accounting software, the programmer can pick and choose between components to implement a given strategy. You'll find that once a company begins to use a software repository, the number of bugs found drops significantly, and programmer morale begins to rise.

All of this assumes that the components you create are reusable. If you create components that no one else wants to use, they won't be reused and the whole process is for naught. The next step, then, is to understand what makes components reusable.

What Makes Components Reusable?

That's what this book is all about. If it could be summed up in a single paragraph, what would be the point of reading the rest of the book?

What Lies Ahead in this Book?

The following chapters in this book are broken down by subject and present individual components which follow a common theme for each subject. Here's a listing of the remaining chapters in the book, and a synopsis of what you'll find in each one.

Chapter 2

In Chapter 2, we'll discuss what is involved in creating components. We'll discuss, at length, some of the subjects that were touched upon briefly in this chapter. Gathering requirements for the control, designing the component, and implementing it, will be the major segments of this chapter.

In addition, we'll talk about documentation for components, and how that documentation can affect whether the component will be reused. In addition to internal design documents, we'll look at the other kinds of documentation that can be provided by the programmers/designers, and which documentation should never be omitted.

Once you finish Chapter 2, you should find yourself ready to consider the problem of actually implementing a component. There's no real code in this chapter, but rather a groundwork for creating code, design specifications, and user documentation in the future chapters of the book. Hang in there, the code is coming!

Actually, there will be code in Chapter 2 that you can use to keep yourself from going into withdrawal. Rather than developing a full-blown Windows component, however, we'll explore the concepts behind component development using a simple C++ class. This class will allow us to develop a reusable date object which can store data in a machine-independent way.

The final part of Chapter 2 deals with the project we will be developing at the end of the book. This project is intended to accomplish two things. First, it will lend a feeling of completeness by tying together many of the myriad components we'll develop in the chapters leading up to that point. Secondly, it will serve as a test for the reuse of the components and will verify that the components we have developed are, in fact, reusable in other applications.

Chapter 3

In Chapter 3, we begin to develop components for generalized use in applications. Our theme for this chapter is 'jazzing up the user interface', and the two components we develop in this chapter reflect that idea.

Scrolling Text Field

The first component considered in the chapter is an MFC extension, that is, a component that adds new functionality by building upon the basic support supplied by the MFC framework. The MFC extension we're considering in this chapter is a marquee scrolling static text field. This field, which emulates the scrolling signs seen in stores and on Wall Street stock displays, will display a single message across a given portion of the user interface.

Shadow Text Control

The second component in Chapter 3 is the 'Shadow Text' ActiveX control. This control will display a text string in a specified color with (or without) a background shadow effect. It can be used to dress up any dialog or form and adds a three-dimensional effect to your applications without costly overheads. As this will be the first ActiveX control developed in this book, we'll discuss the way to create ActiveX controls using Visual C++ and MFC, including the addition of properties and methods to the control.

Both of the controls in this chapter are quite simple, as befits an introductory chapter. There's no user interaction with the controls, nor are there any events to watch for from the controls. At the end of the chapter, you'll find a review of the concepts covered, a comparison of the MFC and ActiveX solutions, and a short list of things you can try yourself to enhance the components you've developed.

Chapter 4

In Chapter 4, we cover the topic of specialized input controls. Here you'll learn why it's often necessary to create specialized versions of input controls that Windows provides (such as edit boxes or combo boxes) to deal with different forms of user input. In this chapter, we consider two separate MFC extensions and one ActiveX control.

Validation Edit Control

The first component considered in Chapter 4 is the validation edit control. This is a simple extension of the MFC `CEdit` class, which can be used as the basis for a set of validation controls for user input. We'll look at the kinds of user input which might require specialized input controls, such as a Social Security or telephone number. We'll consider all the requirements for a generalized form of the validation control and what sort of interface might be required before designing and implementing the control. You'll also find a specialized form of this validation control on the web site which handles Social Security numbers.

Calculator Combo Box

Once we finish with the validation control, we'll move on to another kind of user input—numbers. Numbers often require that the user make complex calculations or enter numbers in fixed formats. To solve this problem, we'll introduce the idea of a Calculator combo box control. This control, as its name implies, is derived from the standard Windows combo box control and adds drop-down calculator functionality to a user application. Users can enter numbers by simply selecting the drop-down box of the combo box and then clicking on some buttons (calculator style) to enter a numeric value. In addition to the obvious ability of the control to simplify numeric input, this control will also give the users the ability to do simple mathematical manipulation of numbers (adding, subtracting, dividing, multiplying) before the number is entered in the application.

Calendar Control

The ActiveX control developed in this chapter is a Calendar control. This component will allow the user to select dates by providing an interface which allows the selection of a month and year, and then provides a standard calendar-style selection of the day of the month desired. Besides the obvious ease of entry, this control also vastly simplifies date selection in a Windows application by removing the problems of date formatting and validation. This ActiveX control adds new complexity to the basic functionality we faced in Chapter 3, adding user interaction and program events.

The chapter concludes with a comparison of the methods used in the MFC extensions and the ActiveX controls, and a list of possible enhancements you might try yourself.

Chapter 5

In Chapter 5, we discuss the topic of list displays. List displays are simply columnar displays of textual (or other) data. In general, list displays are often used in programs to display record data such as you might find in a database. This is an important chapter, because developing really useful list display components can lead to considerable reuse by application developers. If the components are designed correctly and implemented in a programmer-friendly method, they will be used in program after program. It will be left up to you to decide if the components in this chapter succeed in this goal.

Color List Control

The first list display component developed in the chapter is a derivative of the Windows common list control. This control has many very useful features, but suffers from several glaring deficiencies that make it less than friendly (or useful) to work with in application development. Our aim for this derived control is to correct those problems while adding extra value to the component we create. The new component will allow complete control over colors and fonts for list items, as well as making it easier to add new columns, sort by column, insert and delete records, and keep track of what the user is selecting in the control. If that weren't enough to make the control more useful, we'll also add a feature that Microsoft left out entirely—the ability to select multiple items in the list.

The new component, called the **CColorListCtrl** object, will support multiple columns of varying size to allow for a 'grid-like' look. Unlike the common control, our component will support highlighting of complete lines of the list (rather than the common control's highlighting of only the first entry in the line). Additionally, the component will support storing information with each column of the grid, rather than the current ability to store information only for each row.

The new **CColorListCtrl** component is a good example of two different component building strategies. Firstly, it implements an owner-draw Windows control, which is a good way to extend existing Windows functionality while retaining the internal structures and functions supported by the Windows control. Secondly, it's a good example of extending an existing component (the **CListCtrl** class from MFC) in order to add additional functionality without giving up any of the existing functionality.

Editable Grid

The second list display component will be an ActiveX control which implements a simple, but fully functional, editable grid. This grid will allow the programmer to display text or bitmaps and to allow the end user to edit certain cells. These cells will retain their data after the user has completed the edit, allowing them to be used as a simple spreadsheet. Alternatively, the programmer may elect to simply use the grid for display purposes, allowing the user to view lists of columnar data.

The editable grid control will allow the programmer complete control over the background and foreground colors used in the grid cells (individually set for each cell, if that's so desired), as well as allowing the setting of the font to be used in displaying any text in a cell. Bitmaps may be placed in individual cells as well, with the programmer maintaining complete control over the loading, allocating, unloading, and freeing of the bitmap memory. Functionality will be added to allow the programmer to add or remove rows or columns at run time, and will allow the programmer to set the width of columns or the height of rows. Finally, the grid will, of course, be able to scroll both horizontally and vertically to allow a 'virtual' display of data.

The grid control is a good example of a simple ActiveX control that supports most of the basic functions that ActiveX controls allow. Both stock properties (**`Color`**, **`Font`**) and custom properties (row height, number of rows, etc.) are supported by the control. Methods are supported by the ActiveX control to allow adding of rows, setting of data and assigning of values. Events are supported as well, giving the programmer notification of users clicking in the control, scrolling it, modifying data in it (via the editable cells), and others.

Finally, the control shows how to create Windows components at run time within an ActiveX control, by showing how you can dynamically create an edit control and position it within the grid cell for which it was intended. The text of the edit control is set with the text of the cell it replaces, and is placed back into the cell when the user is finished.

As usual, the chapter concludes with a synopsis of what you should have learned from the chapter and a list of possible exercises you might try to enhance the components.

Chapter 6

In Chapter 6, we build on what we've learned in Chapter 5 to start working with complex data displays. These are data controls which can display or manipulate data in a more generalized fashion and can provide more feedback to the user.

Drag-and-drop List Box

The first component we consider in Chapter 6 is the drag-and-drop list box. This is a column-oriented list box which will support dragging and dropping between instances of the component. In other words, you can grab an entry in one box on a dialog with the mouse, move the pointer to another box, let go of the mouse button, and have the item moved from one list to the other. The component will also allow drag-and-drop between itself and 'normal' (non-drag-and-drop) list boxes. This powerful component is an excellent addition to any dialog box which needs to display records in a columnar fashion, and then allow the user to select some (or all) of those records and move them to another list. The list will also support intra-list dragging, i.e. dragging of items within a single list box to reposition them. This feature allows you to use the list to display records and support user sorting or prioritizing. With complete support over background and text colors, as well as display font, the drag-and-drop list box is a powerful data organizer and manipulator component.

Virtual List Control

The second component we'll consider in Chapter 6 is also an MFC extension class, the virtual list control. Unlike the previous MFC extensions we have looked at up to this point, the virtual list control is an MFC class that's built from scratch, based on the generic **`CWnd`** class. This class allows you to put an unlimited number of records on the screen using a columnar display, with complete control over the headers displayed above the list as well as the column widths of the individual columns. The user may resize the columns by dragging them to a new position, in a similar fashion to the way the Windows common list control works with a header control.

The main difference between this new component and the existing Windows common control is that this component will work in any Windows operating system (including 16-bit) and will allow you better flexibility in providing data. The component works with a 'helper' component class which provides data to it in a row/column orientation. Ideally designed for database access, the control allows the programmer to worry more about selecting the data to manipulate and less about making the display work for the user.

Color Tree Control

The final component we discuss in Chapter 6 is probably the most complex in the whole book: the Color Tree Control. This component is a replacement for the Windows common tree control (**`CTreeCtrl`** in MFC parlance) and offers much more functionality. Because it was written from scratch, and because you have the complete source code for the control, it's a much better choice for use in application development than the common tree control. The color tree control supports multiple bitmaps, multiple selection, modification of the display bitmaps for expanding and contracting (the **+** and **-** bitmaps), as well as control over the foreground and background colors of the tree and all individual nodes in the tree. Because multiple selection is allowed, you can use the tree for directory work, as well as for selection of hierarchies of data.

All properties of the control—color, font, indentation amount (distance between the bitmap and the text), and whether to display lines between nodes—are completely down to the programmer. In addition, there are predefined methods which will allow you to programmatically expand or contract the tree, select or deselect any or all of the entries, bring items into view and determine which nodes are currently selected. Notifications are supported for the selection, deselection, expansion, and contraction of nodes. As a special added benefit, the component also supports the display of text which is too wide for the node area. If the user holds the mouse over an entry whose text doesn't fit in the tree component area, a pop-up window (much like a tooltip) will be displayed showing the remainder of the text. All this and much, much more... (and, if you order right now, we'll throw in a Ginsu knife absolutely free!)

In addition to its intrinsic usefulness, the color tree component also shows how to extract useful pieces of a design and put them in separate components which can be reused on their own. In this case, we can extract the C++ classes used for holding the node information and use them in other classes which require the same sorts of functionality.

Chapter 6 also contains a complete synopsis of what should have been learned in the chapter, as well as a 'homework' list of things to try at home while reading along or working at your computer.

Chapter 7

In Chapter 7, we handle the subject of *completeness* in applications. The components developed in this chapter aren't terribly complex to implement, but offer the user a professional look and feel for applications developed with them. When a user begins to use an application, they often judge the program not by the functionality offered, but by the quality of the display and the use of components found in other applications. In this chapter, we examine the problem of implementing those 'cool' components that other programs so often use.

Contents List

The first component we examine in Chapter 7 is the 'contents list' component. This gets its name from its use in the contents screen of the Microsoft Developer Network CD-ROM. If you've ever seen this program, you'll surely have been struck by the simplicity and beauty of the contents list. The list is displayed in a splitter window and makes no attempt to wrap the information for a given table of contents entry. Instead, the text is chopped off at the side of the splitter window. When the user places the mouse over the area of a text entry which is chopped off, a pop-up window is displayed which shows the complete text for that entry. In this way, screen space is conserved until it's needed and the user is able to view those entries that they want more information about.

Although this kind of component would be useful in any list which had potentially long entries, Microsoft has chosen not to make the code (or the library) for this control available to the general programming public. Here we implement such a control, and add a few bells and whistles of our own. The contents list component is implemented as a generic MFC extension, and should work equally well in any version of Windows (16- or 32-bit).

Gradient Control

The second component we examine in Chapter 7 is a gradient control. Virtually every installation program written for Windows uses some form of color gradient as the background of the installation window, with the colors of a specific band of the spectrum smoothly changing in a particular direction across the screen. In this example, we'll build an ActiveX control which is capable of displaying the gradient effect and allows you to set the color band to use for that effect. Although most installation programs use a blue gradient for the background, there's really no reason why this needs to be true. You could, for example, use green. This would be especially nice in an application about gardening or Ireland!

This chapter deals with simple controls that provide powerful visual effects for the user. You'll find yourself coming back to these controls again and again in your own applications once you have seen the effect they have on users.

Chapter 8

In Chapter 8, we take a step into the future. While the first seven chapters showed how to develop one or more MFC extensions, followed by an MFC-based ActiveX control, this chapter does neither. We wouldn't want to get into a rut, after all. Instead, Chapters 8 and 9 introduce two new kinds of component in the Windows programming environment: custom AppWizards for Visual C++ and SDK-based ActiveX controls.

Custom AppWizard

Custom AppWizards are, as their name would suggest, customized versions of the AppWizard application generator built into Visual C++. Although documentation on how to write such custom wizards is sketchy at best, we'll endeavor to show the way towards writing a complete AppWizard. This custom AppWizard will generate skeletons for ActiveX controls, and will be used in the next chapter, where we examine a simple SDK-based ActiveX control.

When writing custom AppWizards, quite a few files need to be created that will be used for generating skeleton applications. These files will be examined in detail and their listings presented, so that you can see a real working model of a custom application.

Chapter 9

This model developed in the previous chapter will now be used to generate a custom ActiveX control, and we'll show you how that control can be used in an HTML (HyperText Markup Language) form on the Internet. With all of the excitement these days about Internet programming and the move toward distributed computing on the Internet, this chapter will be a simple introduction to what all of the hoopla is about.

ActiveX Glitz

Chapter 9 contains a complete implementation of a custom ActiveX static text control for making web pages look like Times Square. This control will be written using the custom AppWizard we generated in Chapter 8. The knowledge you'll gain by examining the individual components of the ActiveX control presented here are priceless in understanding the process of creating and using ActiveX controls in the real world.

Chapter 10

In Chapter 10, we'll examine the cutting edge of component design by extending the discussion of ActiveX technology and looking at another kind of ActiveX control development tool, ATL, the ActiveX Template Library. This library allows you to write very small controls that can be used in conjunction with web browsers to implement powerful web extensions. When you're done with this chapter, you'll be either stunned by the developing power of the Web, or worried that your computer will shortly be taking over your job. Just kidding.

Also in Chapter 10, we'll explore the idea of 'business objects'. These are objects which implement component design and technology, but use that technology to handle business information for specific industries. In our first example, we'll examine a control for the publishing industry (now, there's a surprise in a book) that allows publishers to verify ISBN numbers entered in web controls. Our second example will be an ActiveX control that allows you to drop information onto it. This could be used in any situation that requires data to be dragged and dropped, and could be used to allow more interactive information transfer from client to server in a web page.

Chapter 11

In Chapter 11, we'll present a complete application which ties together many of the pieces we have talked about in the book. The design of this application will be discussed more fully in Chapter 2.

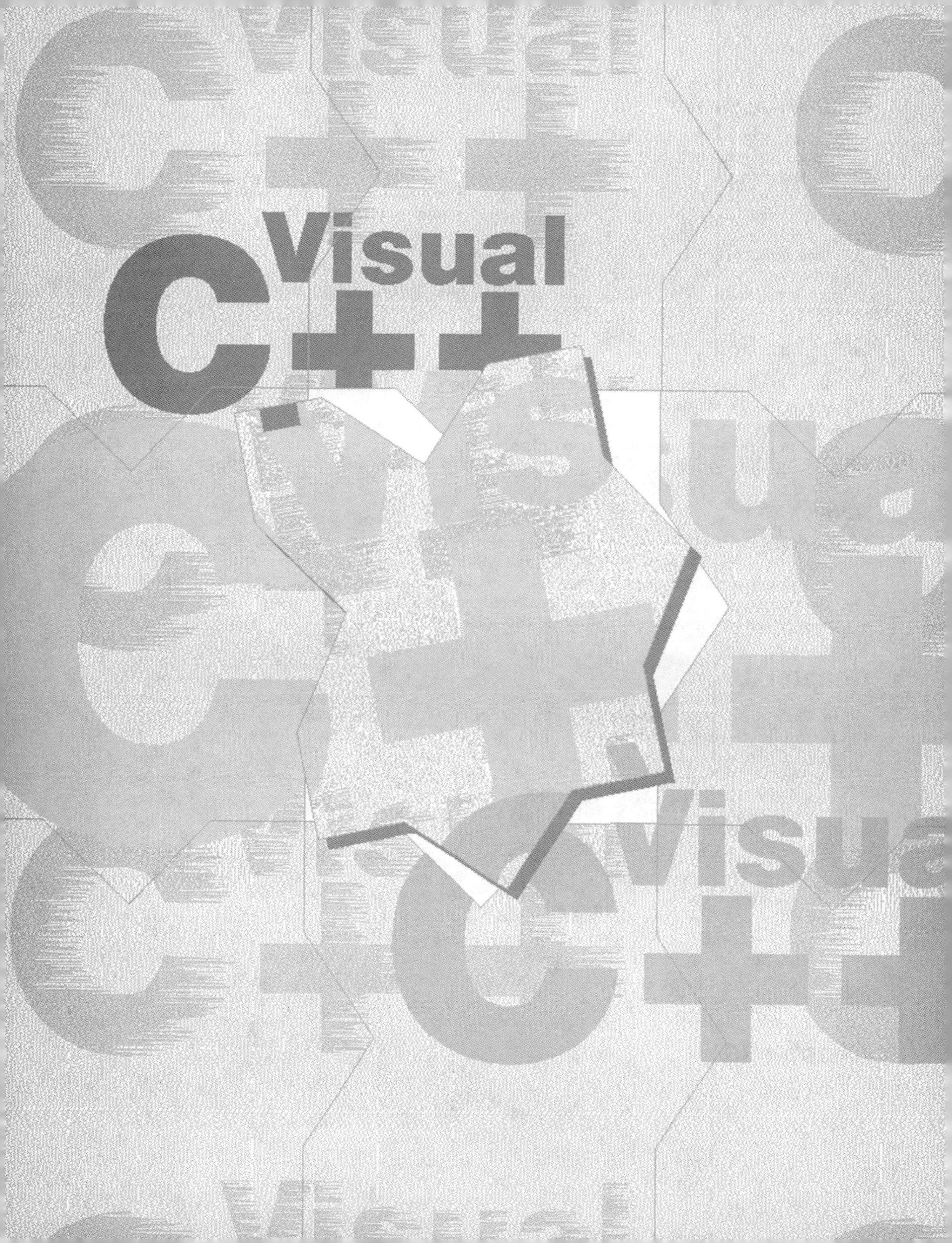
Visual
C++

Writing Components

At this point, we know all there is to know about components, don't we? Well, maybe not everything, but probably enough to start talking about how to write them, which is after all why we're here. You can't have component-based software without components.

Components, as we discovered in the last chapter, are useful only if other people use them. This concept, called **reuse**, allows companies and individual developers to cut down on the long-term cost of development by reducing the number of new pieces of software that must be developed for each new project. By reusing components from previous projects, developers can focus on the new development aspects of each project. In addition, because the components are theoretically bug-free (or so we can hope), the use of predefined components can cut down on testing and debugging times for a project, freeing up even more time for design and development of new features.

This all sounds wonderful, but if it's such a good idea, then why aren't more companies doing it? The answer is not all that simple. Although component technology *is* the best approach to developing software (not that I'm biased, of course), there are, in the early stages, certain drawbacks to developing components.

There's a buy-in cost that must be paid before any benefit can be seen. Whether that buy-in cost is time for developing new components from scratch, or actual money used to purchase pre-existing components in the marketplace, it's very real. Even the simplest form of component reuse, harvesting code from existing projects, requires the time to identify reusable pieces and move them into new projects or central repositories.

Because of the cost of developing components, many companies want to move to component-based technology, but are fearful of falling into yet another spiral of increased software costs with little end gain. Though we as developers view this as unreasonable hesitation, the reality is that upper management has been burned once too often by promises of quick results in software development to throw money into a black hole once again. (Remember the rush to CASE development? How about Artificial Intelligence?)

Although it's your skill which develops the software, it requires much more than that to actually get money into a company. Schedules still need to be met, features must be developed. In short, component development should be considered an iterative process, rather than a full-scale development assault.

Designing a Component

How, then, can you develop reusable components? The actual process is up to you, although this book will suggest some standards you should consider. As you will quickly find, the problem isn't really in developing the components but rather in making those components reusable and getting other people to use them. The road to reusability is a long one, and there are four basic bridges to cross:

- Deciding on the problem
- Listing the requirements
- Deciding how to implement the component
- Reviewing the design with users

Deciding on the Problem

Before it's possible to solve a problem, there must be some agreement on its exact nature. A few years ago, one of my projects started out as a simple utility application that I wrote to make work easier for me. One of my managers saw the utility and decided that it was exactly what our department needed to add extra usability to the software we were developing. Other managers looked at the functionality of the utility and added new requirements, changes, and features. Pretty soon, the poor little utility (which was written in about two days) became a Christmas tree, with new features hanging off it in all directions.

As each developer played with it, they added their own features, making the whole thing that much harder to understand. Eventually, a development team was assigned to the utility program and the popularity of the program itself within the company plummeted to zero. Though this might seem a rather extreme example, it was something that really happened. Furthermore, the basic philosophy that software will always need enhancing is found throughout the software development community.

In order to make something that other people want to use, you must address a need. To be really useful, the component you develop must address a specific need. It might sound contradictory, but it's true that the more specific a component is, the better are its chances of being reused. Don't think that you're the only people ever to have a very specific need. In companies that work in narrow bands of business, specific components are used over and over because each new piece of software that is developed uses the same basic processes as all the other software.

Think about a company, for example, that develops software to control devices that measure changes in temperature. Every piece of software that's developed for that company interfaces with temperature in some way. One developer at the company recognizes that they need a simple routine to convert between Fahrenheit and Celsius. This is a trivial piece of software to write, but if you look around the company then you will probably find twenty or thirty *different* routines to do this one simple job! Most will be part of larger modules which do specific tasks. One might interface to a type XY123A temperature scanner, while another retrieves satellite transmissions from Jupiter. In both cases, however, the common functionality is the basic routine to convert between different temperature scales.

If there were a single routine that converted from Fahrenheit to Celsius, and this routine was well-known and documented, it's likely that most programmers would use it. Very few people really like writing utility functions like these, and even fewer want to do it more than once. Instead of writing code in each and every program like:

```
CelsiusDegrees = (FahrenheitDegrees * 9.0) / 5.0 + 32.0;
```

which takes up a lot of room and is fraught with potential errors (all of those 'magic' numbers can get confusing), you could have a single routine that read:

```
CelsiusDegrees = FarenheitToCelsius(FahrenheitDegrees);
```

There are two advantages to this second line of code. First, there's only one copy of it. If it was suddenly found that the code that converted one temperature to another wasn't working properly, there would only be one place where it could be changed. Second, if you wanted to check for the validity of the input temperature (to allow the program to make judgment calls on the outside world, for example), you could place that code in a single place and all routines working with it would still operate successfully. In short, this is a simple, yet very useful function. So what could possibly go wrong with it?

Whether you're writing a function, a class, or an ActiveX control, you need to decide on the problem that you're solving. This problem needs to be specific, otherwise 'code creep' will take over. Imagine what our temperature conversion function could look like if it wasn't designed with a very specific purpose in mind. You could end up with a function prototype such as:

```
double FarenheitToCelsius(double Fahrenheit, int format, int
        numberOfSignificantFigures, int areaOftheWorld, int ...);
```

This function, rather than doing a straightforward conversion, attempts to determine the correct display format for the temperature, what part of the world it's probably occurring in and, for all we know, what planet the temperature was taken on. It is, hopefully, obvious to you that this function will probably never be used by another programmer unless that programmer was forced to do so by management. When designing a function, a C++ class, or an ActiveX control, always be absolutely sure that you know what problem you're solving.

This facet of component design has another, more insidious, side to it. As we've seen, it's likely that components which try to solve the entire world's problems won't be reused. On the flip side, however, components which don't completely solve the problem they're intended for won't be reused either. Consider the problem of a date class. There are probably as many classes to handle dates as there are programmers that use them. Let's look at a simple date class as an example of the 'incomplete solution' dilemma. Here's a simple header for a C++ class which implements a date:

```
class CDate
{
private:
   int m_nMonth;
   int m_nYear;
   int m_nDay;

public:
   CDate(int nMonth, int nYear, int nDay)
   {
```

```
        m_nMonth = nMonth;
        m_nYear = nYear;
        m_nDay = nDay;
    }

    int GetDay()
    {
        return m_nDay;
    }

    int GetMonth()
    {
        return m_nMonth;
    }

    int GetYear()
    {
        return m_nYear;
    }
};
```

Will this class work? That really depends on your definition of 'work'. The class is certainly complete. It implements a wrapper around a day/month/year object which represents a date. Will it be used? I think you can see that it won't be. To begin with, it adds no functionality for the programmer. It's a glorified structure that stores information and retrieves it. While it supports all the necessary pieces (day, month, year), it doesn't add any value to those pieces. In short, it doesn't really solve any problem.

To design a class properly, you need to understand both the problem and its solution. In the case of a date class, the problem could be stated simply as:

'We need a class which stores dates in a machine-independent format, verifies that the dates are correct, and allows us to convert those dates into usable forms. The date class should be able to function as a normal type and should be able to be stored and retrieved from a storage archive.'

However, this problem statement is incomplete. We would probably want considerably more out of a real date class, such as the ability to determine the day (1-365) and week (1-52) of the year, to convert to and from Julian format, and so forth. But for this example, these considerations don't really matter. The problem we want to solve is very specific. (We will be looking at other facets of component design and implementation and extending the date class later in the chapter.)

Now that we have a problem description, we can see that the class definition we started with fails on several counts:

- The date class, as given, does no verification on input, nor does it provide the capability to notify the user that the input is wrong.
- There's no way to convert the dates into anything. The class simply spits the information we give it straight back at us. Our problem statement clearly required that the class should give us the ability to convert the dates into other formats.
- The date class doesn't operate as 'a normal type'. For that matter, what does operating as 'a normal type' mean? Without understanding the problem statement further, it seems likely that we'll develop a component that no one wants.

- The problem statement clearly says that the date should be able to be stored and retrieved from a storage archive. Many C++ programmers would take this to mean that the object should be able to be 'streamed' (more on this later). Obviously, the class as given doesn't allow this.

From the above list we can determine two things. The first is that the class, as we have designed and implemented it, doesn't do the required job. Hopefully you can see this. The second point is a little less obvious but equally problematic. We know that the class should perform verification, but of what sort? This isn't clear. We also know that the class is supposed to convert itself into other formats. What other formats should be supported? We don't know that either. We could convert the date into various string formats (MM/DD/YY, or MMM DD, YYYY, for example) but that might not be what the user of the class wants. This isn't good, since the user will be unhappy with the class but we'll be unable to understand where we failed in the design and implementation process. Clearly, more work is needed on the problem statement. Let's take another crack at it.

'We need a class which stores dates in a machine-independent format, verifies that the dates are correct by validating the month/day/year combination, and allows us to convert those dates into usable forms such as output strings (MM/DD/YY, DD/MM/YY, and MMM DD,YY) and Julian formats. The date class should be able to function as a normal type and should be able to be stored and retrieved from a storage archive using the standard C++ stream operations.'

This is a better definition of what the class is supposed to do. It's not perfect, largely because some of the terms are still vague and because there are omissions. However, it's a better description of the problem. Once you've defined the problem (as best you can), the next step in the process is to list the requirements for the component.

Listing the Requirements

Many companies require a complete **functional requirements document** (**FRD**) before any work is started. When done correctly, an FRD can specify all aspects of the work that is to take place on a given piece of software (in our case, a component). Unfortunately, FRDs can be confusing and contradictory, incomplete or even too complete, specifying down to the variable names exactly how a piece of software is to be written

Each of these failings is fatal. If a document is confusing and contradictory, which often occurs when the document is written by a number of people, it will be difficult for the programmer to implement a working component. Worse, if the programmer were to follow the specification in the document, it might result in a component which was functionally complete but that didn't work!

If an FRD is incomplete, it leads to assumptions on the part of the programmer. This can be a problem when the programmer makes assumptions that turn out to be incorrect. The balance between completeness and stumbling around in the dark differs for each programmer and each piece of software, often leading to incomplete specifications.

Finally, if the document is too complete and over-specifies the project, it leaves no room for the programmer to implement something that the users might want. If the system is too closed, there's no maneuvering room for the programmer to add features that are needed by users but don't contradict the basic idea of the software. On top of that, of course, you really wouldn't enjoy writing code if you had no input as to the structure or composition of the software, and software written by unhappy programmers often contains a large number of bugs ('That's not a bug, it's in the spec!').

What, then, is the solution to the problem of specifying software? Believe me, if I had a perfect answer then I wouldn't be sitting around writing books—I would be on the lecture circuit making my fortune by explaining the solution to upper management. Since you are reading this book, you can make a fair assumption that there's no perfect solution.

For the purposes of this book, we hope to strike a compromise that will allow us to give enough information about the problem to be able to solve it, without taking up space that would be better given over to code. We'll provide a functional requirement in its minimum form, a **feature list**, which is exactly what it implies, a list of desired features for a given component. In our date class example, a feature list would look as follows:

- Validates dates in various formats.
- Converts dates into strings in several formats: MM/DD/YY, DD/MM/YY, YYMMDD, MMM DD, YYYY and Julian.
- Converts from string input (e.g. `"12/31/1996"` to an internal representation).
- Allows the programmer to check the day of the week, the week of the year and the day of the year (1-365).
- Allows the programmer to check for leap years and automatically checks leap years when validating input.
- Allows conversion using simple operators (such as `=`) using a format similar to `CDate date = "12/31/1996";`
- Allows different formats and delimiters for dates.
- Allows dates to be stored in and recalled from streams into the application, using the standard stream operators (`>>` and `<<`).
- Allows access to the pieces of the date (day, month, and year) as individual numbers, as well as retrieving the date as a string using a single method call.

This class is probably not as functionally complete as some people might like. It doesn't, for example, allow dates to be manipulated using addition and subtraction, nor does it provide date spans (the number of days between two dates). In spite of this, it's adequate for most purposes. Remember what we said about the Christmas tree effect?

The functional requirement format we've used here, the feature list, should be the absolute minimum format you should consider in your own application development. The feature list has a number of attractive properties: it's easy to read, easy to implement, and straightforward to develop from. It has its shortcomings too: it doesn't specify naming conventions, tolerances, speed of access, and so forth. For most small projects, however, a feature list may be all you need.

After the component has been described (the problem statement) and the requirements for the component defined (the feature list), the next issue is to address how the component is to be implemented by the programmer. The issue of implementation is a contract between the programmer and the user which defines what format the solution will take and what issues need to be addressed during the development phase.

Deciding How to Implement a Component

The requirements definition has specified what it is that we're going to do. Deciding how it's to be done is the next issue, and this involves working out the pitfalls of different approaches to writing a component, and balancing the advantages and disadvantages of different methods for creating a component in real code.

When you're thinking of implementing a new component, you'll ideally call a meeting for all those involved in the development process. This should include (but not be limited to) the developer, the tester(s) of the component, the users of the component, and anyone else who would be likely to need to have input into its capabilities.

When we say 'users', you should note that we're talking simultaneously about the end user (the user of the application) and the developer-user (the programmer). End users are concerned with the look and feel of the component, the speed with which it works and the methods needed to accomplish tasks when using it. Programmers, on the other hand, are concerned with the functionality of the component and the ease with which they can incorporate it within their applications. If a component does everything that the end user could ever dream of, but is implemented in a way that makes it difficult to work with, the programmer will avoid it and the end user will never have the pleasure of using it.

Developing a plan for component implementation is a lot like developing a requirements document for the component itself. You will always need to take into account certain factors during the development phase (which operating system to support, what development environments will be used, what third-party tools are needed, and so forth).

The most important thing to understand about the requirements definition and implementation phases are that they are *iterative*, by which we mean that the requirements are likely to change in response to changes both requested by users and discovered during the implementation phase. In addition, features that were omitted from requirements due to time constraints may be added back into (or removed from) the design later, when implementation reveals problems with the scheduling. Never think of a process as static. It should always be open to some form of (but not too much) change. We'll talk more about the iterative development process later.

The best way to decide on an implementation process is via a **prototype**. Prototypes are the best friends of both developers and users, and should be relied on above all else. It's all well and good to *read* about the features and capabilities of a component from a dry sheet of paper, but *seeing* the component on the screen and playing with it makes much more of an impression. Seriously consider creating prototypes of all components when questions arise during the implementation phase. Consider the following scenario:

Developer: *Yes, I think we can do that. All we need to do is* {long coding discussion}.
Manager: *Okay, we'll put it down in the implementation plan that way.*

{Two weeks later}
Developer: *We can't do it! There's a problem with the* {long coding discussion}.
Manager: *We're dead. We promised the testing people something tomorrow!*

Would you really like this to happen to you? If the developer had suggested instead that a prototype of the section of code under discussion be developed first, the problem would have been discovered sooner and testing wouldn't kill him! The figure on the following page shows the typical development process. As you can see, most companies (and programmers) believe that there's, 'no time to do it right, but always plenty of time to do it over.'

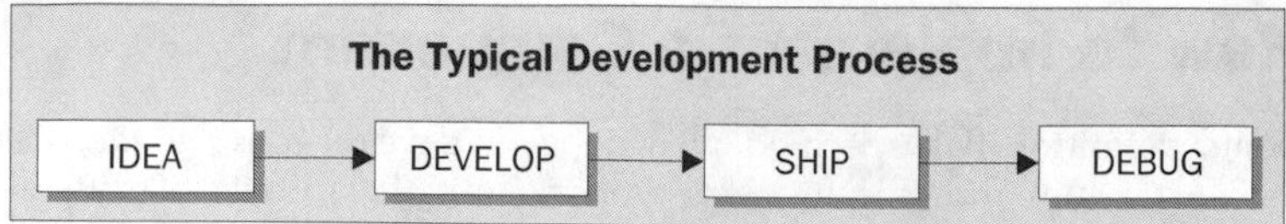

The next figure, on the other hand, shows the component development process we're advocating and discussing here. You can see it relies heavily on iteration and design rather than on debugging and fixing. The theory here is that, if you do it right the first time, you won't have to go back and fix it. You can then move on to bigger and better things. Because components are quite often used before they are completely ready, this is an even more important point. If you get most of the way through development and suddenly find a major problem with one of the features, it's hard to make changes to fix the problem when users are already embedding the control in their applications. If, on the other hand, you had developed the prototype first, you would have found the problem right away and the implementation used by applications would already reflect that issue.

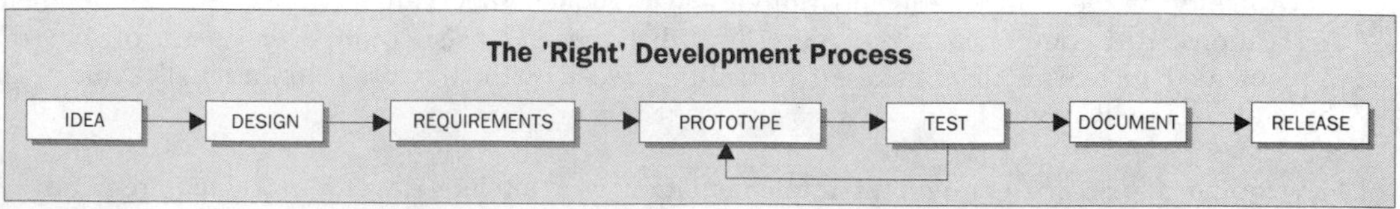

What should you consider during the implementation phase? Everything. When you've done that, go back and add all the other things you forgot during the 'everything' discussion! OK, maybe things don't quite work out that way. The important things to remember during the implementation discussion are:

- Learn from previous mistakes. When you're developing components, you'll learn a lot about the internals of Windows and how things do and don't work in that environment. If you're developing for other systems, you'll have to learn the same things there. In either case, you should take that knowledge with you when you move on to future projects. If you know, for example, that trying to do processing during a **WM_KILLFOCUS** message is strictly forbidden in Windows, don't consider implementing a validation routine in the **OnKillFocus()** routine of a component (don't worry if you think that last bit was in Greek—all will be revealed later in the book).
- Learn from others. I am a strong believer in having as many people as possible involved in the discussion of how to implement a component. The final solution, of course, belongs to the development person/team assigned the project, but if that person/team is smart, they'll listen to others that have done this sort of work before. Problems are spotted more easily when many pairs of eyes are looking for them.
- Think in terms of the abstract as well as the concrete. Concrete solutions consider the Windows messages which need to be processed, the resources needed to implement the component, and the kind of component (DLL, MFC extension, OCX, VBX, whatever) that will be built to solve the problem. Abstract thinking, on the other hand, considers the underlying data structures, the encapsulation of the algorithms, and so forth. Don't forget one when talking about the other.

- When you're absolutely sure that you have the perfect solution to a problem, find someone and explain it to them. If you can't explain the solution in simple enough terms to make the other person understand it, you don't understand it well enough to implement it yet!
- Take lots of notes. You wouldn't believe how many good ideas have gone to waste on projects because the people implementing the code forgot the suggestions made to them during project reviews and design meetings. If you keep a notebook with you whenever you're attending a design or implementation meeting, you can keep all of your ideas, potential problems and design notes together so that you can review them whenever you're getting ready to write code.

Once you've talked over with others the design strategy you've chosen for implementing the component, and created a prototype or two to see whether the design you have in mind will work, you're ready for the next step: reviewing the completed design with users.

Reviewing the Design with Users

Once you've finished the design of a component, it's important for you to review the design with the intended users of the component. There are two main reasons for this. First, it's a sanity check to be sure that everything that was supposed to be done for the component is included in the final design. If you fail to run a final review of the design, you may later be accosted by users who insist on last minute changes to the component because requested features didn't make it into the design. If you've reviewed the component design with the user then you can at least point out that the time to notice missing features was at the design meeting. It probably won't get you very far, especially if the omission is a critical one, but at least you can feel better about the whole thing.

The second important reason to review designs with users is so that users can look at the whole picture at once. The problem with design meetings, especially preliminary ones, is that they tend to focus on the minutia of the moment, rather than the component as a whole. Before early design meetings, programmers often specify the general flow and purpose of the component in advance. This leads people to assume that the overall component design is reasonable and that the highest-level features are taken care of. If you later review the component as a whole, you will often come across many useful features that were omitted in the initial design. In addition, discussing the component encourages people to think down different paths, which leads to useful additional ideas.

Reviewing the design with the users will often result in an early prototype to do 'proof of concept' work. This is a good thing. Unless you've actually implemented a component using certain concepts or algorithms, you should always do a prototype and review the results with users. If you don't do this, you can be certain that something will come up later and bite you.

This completes the development design process. At this point you'll have, at the very least, a feature list for the component you're developing, a list of ideas on how to implement the component, and a completed review with the users of the component.

There are situations, especially in small companies, when the developer and the user of a given component are the same person. This doesn't excuse you from the process described above, it just means that you can be a lot less formal about it.

Component design should then be viewed from different perspectives. First, consider the problem from the viewpoint of a programmer and throw together a quick prototype of the idea you're considering. Put together a test application and try out the idea in a real program setting. You'll often find that, as a programmer, the code strikes you as being marvelous, but as a user, you find the overall result isn't quite so spectacular. Be careful, as this scenario will often make you schizophrenic!

Once you've completed reviewing the process with the users of a system, the next step is to work on implementing the component you've so brilliantly designed. This is usually a matter of trying out your design in real code, and discovering things that don't work quite as advertised. It's normal, and in fact desirable, for you to bounce back and forth between the design and implementation processes. Let's take a look at that implementation process now.

Implementing a Component

Implementing a component is an iterative process, as we've said before. The initial phase is often not even vaguely related to the final product. This isn't necessarily a failure in design or even in the implementation process, but rather a reflection of how the world works. It isn't uncommon for a simple component to become quite complex as the person who implemented the component and the end user get together to discuss the various stages of the development process.

Rather than talk a great deal about the implementation process in the abstract, it's really a lot easier to show examples of code which do the job we're talking about. We don't really want to develop a terribly complex component here, because it's the process of implementation that's important, not the component itself. On the other hand, all components should be useful and reusable, so it makes little sense to implement an artificial component simply to prove a point. For this reason, the component we'll develop will be a simple C++ class that implements date functionality. This component can certainly be reused in any application that supports dates, but doesn't involve extraneous implementation issues, such as user interface look and feel or underlying operating system issues.

Why would anyone want to write a date class? After all, the Microsoft Foundation Class (MFC) library implements a perfectly good 'time' class which also works well with dates. It offers the ability to use dates and times and all sorts of wonderful things. What could possibly be wrong with it? Well, one thing that immediately springs to mind is that it only handles dates after January 1, 1970. While this may not be a problem if you're a child prodigy programmer, for us old folks born in the early 60s this presents something of an issue. If I want to display the first day of the year of my birth in an MFC application, therefore, I would write:

```
CTime MyBirthYear(1961, 1, 1, 12, 0, 0);
CString strFirstDay = MyBirthYear.Format("%A, %B %d, %Y");
AfxMessageBox(strFirstDay);
```

Unfortunately, running this code causes an assertion failure and ignoring the assertion still won't produce the desired results.

The **`CTime`** class would appear to have a problem with dates, wouldn't it? Well, that's a good reason to write a new one. Imagine that your boss comes to you one day and says, '<Name>, we need to be able to store Matt's birth date in our application.' Two things would immediately spring to your mind. First of all, <Name> is not your name, and secondly, who's this Matt person?

In spite of your misgivings about the whole thing, you would probably get started by writing a series of functions to manipulate the dates (that you were given) from some internal format into strings and back again. These functions would then go into the application you were writing, never to be heard of again. Well, maybe. After all, if one application at your place of employment needed to hold on to old dates (I'm really starting to feel like a relic here!), it stands to reason that future applications would also need similar functionality. This looks like a job for... a component!

Designing the date component is fairly straightforward. We can sum up the functionality we need in this simple statement:

'We need a component that can store dates with any degree of precision between the years 0 and 9999. It should allow us to input the date as a string and return the date as a string.'

We might start out by writing a functional requirements document, but honestly, how many people out there would do so for a class this simple? Go ahead, raise your hands! That's about what I thought. Instead, let's do what 'real' programmers would do: write a C++ class header that handles the requirements listed above:

```
// Listing 1 - A first cut at a date class definition
class CDate
{
// Construction
public:
    CDate(LPTSTR lpszString);
    CDate(int nMonth, int nDay, int nYear);
    CDate(const time_t* lTime);
    CDate(const CDate& date);

// Operations
public:
    LPCTSTR AsString();

// Implementation
public:
    virtual ~CDate() {};
};
```

As you can see by the above listing, we've defined a class which allows you to construct a **CDate** class out of a string, a month/day/year combination, and, as an added bonus, a **time_t** value. This **time_t** value came to me out of the blue when I thought about the **time()** function used so often by programmers. As there must be a ton of existing code that uses the **time()** function, why not allow the programmer the luxury of using that function to get the current time and convert it to use our class?

In addition to the constructors (there's also a copy constructor included for completeness), and a destructor, which doesn't do anything, the above listing provides for a function called **AsString()** which returns a pointer to a string filled with a representation of the date. This would seem to support all of the requirements we talked about in our problem statement. It's now time to start implementing the class as real code. Here's the code, broken up by a discussion of its significance:

```
// Date.h - Definition of class CDate

#ifndef WROX_DATE_H
#define WROX_DATE_H

#include <tchar.h>
#include <wtypes.h>
#include <time.h>
```

The first thing we define in the header file is the default number of days in a month. This isn't a terribly difficult thing to do, but is included for use in the application.

```
static int nDaysInMonth[] = {31, 28, 31, 30, 31, 30,
                             31, 31, 30, 31, 30, 31};
```

The first block of function declarations to add to our **CDate** class are the constructors for the class. We'll offer the user a wide choice of construction techniques and try to make our class as simple to use as possible, so that there's at least a chance that the user will reuse it!

```
class CDate
{
// Construction
public:
   CDate(LPTSTR lpszString);
   CDate(int nMonth, int nDay, int nYear);
   CDate(const time_t* lTime);
   CDate(const CDate& date);
```

The next section of any MFC class is for operations that can be performed on the class. In our case, there's only a single **public** function in this section which returns the date as a string.

```
// Operations
public:
   LPCTSTR AsString();

// Implementation
public:
   virtual ~CDate() {};
```

Once we've declared the destructor, we can provide **private** member variables and **protected** functions to help implement the class. Here we're going to include all of our internal functions that might be needed by a derived class.

```
private:
   long m_lInternalDate;
   TCHAR m_szBuffer[256];
   enum {ErrDate_NoError, ErrDate_BadMonth, ErrDate_BadDay,
         ErrDate_Incorrect_Length};

protected:
   int ExtractDate(LPCTSTR lpszString, int* nMonth, int* nDay,
                   int* nYear);
   long MakeJulian(int nMonth, int nDay, int nYear);
   int IsLeapYear(int nYear);
   void StripCharacter(LPTSTR lpszString, TCHAR chRemove);
```

```
};

#endif
```

Here's the source code for the date class. Notice that the functions are defined in the same order as the header file to make it easy to find them.

```
// Date.cpp - Implementation of class CDate

#include <tchar.h>
#include <time.h>
#include <stdlib.h>
#include <stdio.h>
#include "Date.h"

//////////////////////////////////////////////////////////////////////////////
// Constructors

CDate::CDate(LPTSTR lpszString)
{
   int nMonth;
   int nDay;
   int nYear;

   if (ExtractDate(lpszString, &nMonth, &nDay, &nYear) == ErrDate_NoError)
   {
      m_lInternalDate = MakeJulian(nMonth, nDay, nYear);
   }
   else
   {
      m_lInternalDate = 0L;
   }
}

CDate::CDate(const CDate& date)
{
   m_lInternalDate = date.m_lInternalDate;
}

CDate::CDate(int nMonth, int nDay, int nYear)
{
   m_lInternalDate = MakeJulian(nMonth, nDay, nYear);
}

// Create a date given a time value.
CDate::CDate(const time_t* lTime)
{
   // Get a date structure for this time
   struct tm* pTmPtr = localtime(lTime);

   m_lInternalDate = MakeJulian(pTmPtr->tm_mon + 1, pTmPtr->tm_mday,
                                pTmPtr->tm_year + 1900);
}

//////////////////////////////////////////////////////////////////////////////
// Implementation
```

```
void CDate::StripCharacter(LPTSTR lpszString, TCHAR chRemove)
{
   int i = 0;
   int j = 0;
   while ((*(lpszString + i) = *(lpszString + j++)) != _T('\0'))
      if (*(lpszString + i) != chRemove)
         i++;
   return;
}
```

The **StripCharacter()** function is particularly useful to the world at large. Perhaps we should extract this function and move it into a generalized function library. These are the kind of thoughts that should be running through your head when going back over code. Determining what is reusable is often a matter of writing the code for a specific purpose and then mining the code for generalized routines.

```
int CDate::ExtractDate(LPCTSTR lpszString, int* nMonth, int* nDay,
                       int* nYear)
{
   TCHAR szBuffer[256] = {0};
   TCHAR szDay[3] = {0};
   TCHAR szMonth[3] = {0};
   TCHAR szYear[5] = {0};
   int nRet = 0;

   lstrcpyn(szBuffer, lpszString, 255);

   StripCharacter((LPTSTR)szBuffer, _T('/'));

   if (lstrlen(szBuffer) >= 6 )
   {
      // Allow for MMDDYYYY
      nRet = ErrDate_NoError;

      // Extract month and verify
      lstrcpyn(szMonth, szBuffer, 2 + 1);
      if (_ttoi(szMonth) < 1 || _ttoi(szMonth) > 12)
         nRet = ErrDate_BadMonth;

      // Extract day and verify. Note we need year for leap year
      // calculation
      lstrcpyn(szDay, szBuffer + 2, 2 + 1);
      lstrcpyn(szYear, szBuffer + 4, lstrlen(szBuffer) - 4 + 1);

      if (nRet == ErrDate_NoError)
         if (_ttoi(szDay) < 1
               || _ttoi(szDay) > nDaysInMonth[_ttoi(szMonth) - 1])
            nRet = ErrDate_BadDay;
      if (_ttoi(szMonth) == 2
            && _ttoi(szDay) == nDaysInMonth[_ttoi(szMonth) - 1] + 1
            && IsLeapYear(_ttoi(szYear)))
         nRet = ErrDate_NoError;

      // If there weren't any errors, return the pieces
      if (nRet == ErrDate_NoError)
      {
         *nYear = _ttoi(szYear);
```

```
                *nMonth = _ttoi(szMonth);
                *nDay = _ttoi(szDay);
            }
        }
        else
        {
            // Invalid length, just get out of here
            return ErrDate_Incorrect_Length;
        }
        return nRet;
    }
```

MakeJulian() looks like another candidate for a generalized function library. This function takes a simple month, day, and year, and returns a **long** value representing the date.

```
long CDate::MakeJulian(int nMonth, int nDay, int nYear)
{
    long lJulianDate = 10000L * nYear;

    // Add in days for months already elapsed.
    for (int i = 0; i < nMonth - 1; ++i)
        lJulianDate += nDaysInMonth[i];

    // Add in days for this month.
    lJulianDate += nDay;

    // Check for leap year.
    if (IsLeapYear(nYear) && nMonth > 2)
        lJulianDate++;

    return lJulianDate;
}
```

And, of course, **IsLeapYear()** is a perfect candidate for inclusion in a generalized function library too. See how simple this extraction of reusable code can be?

```
int CDate::IsLeapYear(int nYear)
{
    if (nYear % 100 != 0 && nYear % 4 != 0)
        return 0;
    return 1;
}

/////////////////////////////////////////////////////////////////////////////
// Operations

LPCTSTR CDate::AsString()
{
    _stprintf(m_szBuffer, _T("%02d/%02d/%02d"), GetMonth(), GetDay(),
            GetYear());
    return m_szBuffer;
}
```

And that would be the end of the issue. The header file is published, the code entered into a library and, provided the **GetMonth()**, **GetDay()** and **GetYear()** functions are provided elsewhere, all of the users are happy. We go about our regular business and... wait a second!

Don't we need to review this with the users of the code? Of course we do. Guess what, they didn't like it. Something about not providing sufficient functionality to justify using the class. The only way to find out what the users really want is to ask them.

The next step in the procedure is to go back to the user review session and ask what is missing. Although you might assume they know what sort of functionality they want, they probably don't. The issue is not what you're missing, but that they feel there's 'not enough' in the class. Looking at it, you can probably understand what the issue is. Most companies have written dozens of routines to deal with dates: validations, manipulations and so forth. The class we have presented here does, in fact, do what it was originally designed to do: store date fields. It actually does slightly more than was required, but it fails the general test of replacing the existing functionality.

The next iteration of the class must add at least enough functionality to allow the users to use the class with their existing functions. We could provide the users with the internal value we use to store the date, but you would quickly find that no-one would understand how to use that value to manipulate as they are accustomed to doing. Rather, they would prefer to deal with dates in formats that they understand: days, months, and years. For this reason, we shall add functions to retrieve the day of the month, month of the year, and year number.

Add the following lines to the **CDate** class header:

```
// Attributes - in Date.h
public:
    int GetDay();
    int GetMonth();
    int GetYear();
```

And then add the following code to the source file containing the body of the class:

```
///////////////////////////////////////////////////////////////////////////
// Attributes - in Date.cpp

int CDate::GetYear()
{
    return (m_lInternalDate / 10000L);
}

int CDate::GetMonth()
{
    long lJulianDate = m_lInternalDate;

    // First, get the year
    int nYear = GetYear();

    // Subtract off the year part
    lJulianDate -= (nYear * 10000L);

    // For each month, subtract off the number of days
    int nDays = 0;
    for (int i = 0; i < 12; ++i)
    {
        // Account of leap years.
        if (IsLeapYear(nYear) && i == 1)
            nDays = nDaysInMonth[i] + 1;
```

```
      else
         nDays = nDaysInMonth[i];

      if (lJulianDate <= nDays)
         break;
      lJulianDate -= nDays;
   }

   return i + 1;
}

int CDate::GetDay()
{
   long lJulianDate = m_lInternalDate;

   // First, get the year
   int nYear = GetYear();

   // Subtract off the year part
   lJulianDate -= (nYear * 10000L);

   // For each month, subtract off the number of days
   int nDays = 0;
   for (int i = 0; i < 12; ++i)
   {
      // Account of leap years.
      if (IsLeapYear(nYear) && i == 1)
         nDays = nDaysInMonth[i] + 1;
      else
         nDays = nDaysInMonth[i];

      if (lJulianDate <= nDays)
         break;
      lJulianDate -= nDays;
   }
   return lJulianDate;
}
```

That must do the job, right? After all, we've provided methods to set the date, methods to retrieve the date components, and methods to create an object. What more could anyone want from a simple date class? The next user review reveals that the people working for you want quite a bit more from the class before they will be satisfied with it. They would like a way to assign a string containing a date to the date, a way to assign a date to a string, and more options in formatting the input string to the class. In our first design, you might remember, the date was allowed only in the simplest date format MM/DD/YY and no other (actually, it supported MM/DD/YYYY as well, but that's a bit pedantic). This brings up an important issue when developing components in the real world.

FYI

User reviews often lead to the modification of existing functionality as well as the addition of new functionality. In doing this, you must make a decision. Do you risk breaking existing code by modifying existing functionality, or leave the existing code alone and add new functionality to it?

Don't take this lightly. There's no better way to annoy a user (especially if that user is another programmer) than to make code that they wrote around your component break. If you're lucky, and the code they wrote simply doesn't compile anymore, you will probably just be yelled at. If, on the other hand, your change to a component produces a new and insidious error which isn't caught by the compiler, you run the risk of being lynched.

Consider for a moment what would happen if we took the constructor currently defined as:

```
CDate::CDate(int nMonth, int nDay, int nYear)
```

and modified it to the very similar:

```
CDate::CDate(int nDay, int nMonth, int nYear)
```

intending, of course, to modify the date format from MM/DD/YY to DD/MM/YY. This change can't be caught by the compiler because the signatures of the two methods are exactly the same. Existing code will compile and, in some cases, may even work (November 11th, for example, works fine, but December 13th doesn't). You're really going to make some poor programmer mad. Let's take care of the issue of adding new date formats first.

The first thing to do is to add a date format variable to the class. This variable will then be used to set the format for input and output of the date string. Since there's no one currently using the class, we don't really need to worry about how to set the format, but in this case we'll make sure that changing the format doesn't change the behavior of existing code anyway. It's good practice!

First, we modify the class header as follows:

```
// Date.h - Definition of class CDate
    ...
class CDate
{
// Enumerations
public:
   enum DateFormat {MMDDYY, DDMMYY, YYMMDD};                  // Add this

// Construction
public:
   CDate(LPTSTR lpszString, DateFormat fmt = MMDDYY);        // Note new
                                                             // parameter
   CDate(int nMonth, int nDay, int nYear);
   CDate(const time_t* lTime);
   CDate(const CDate& date);
   CDate(DateFormat fmt = MMDDYY);                           // Add this

// Attributes
public:
   int GetDay();
   int GetMonth();
   int GetYear();

// Operations
public:
   LPCTSTR AsString();
```

```
// Implementation
public:
   virtual ~CDate() {};

private:
   long m_lInternalDate;
   TCHAR m_szBuffer[256];
   DateFormat m_nDateFormat;                                     // Add this
   TCHAR m_chDelimiter;                                          // Add this

      ...

};
```

Next, we add and modify some functions, as follows:

```
///////////////////////////////////////////////////////////////////////////
// Constructors

CDate::CDate(LPTSTR lpszString, DateFormat fmt /* = MMDDYY */)
{
   m_nDateFormat = fmt;                       // Add this
   m_chDelimiter = _T('/');                   // Add this

   int nMonth;
   int nDay;
   int nYear;

   if (ExtractDate(lpszString, &nMonth, &nDay, &nYear) == ErrDate_NoError)
   {
      m_lInternalDate = MakeJulian(nMonth, nDay, nYear);
   }
   else
   {
      m_lInternalDate = 0L;
   }
}

CDate::CDate(const CDate& date)
{
   m_lInternalDate = date.m_lInternalDate;
   m_nDateFormat = date.m_nDateFormat;       // Add this
   m_chDelimiter = date.m_chDelimiter;       // Add this
}

CDate::CDate(int nMonth, int nDay, int nYear)
{
   m_nDateFormat = MMDDYY;                   // Add this
   m_chDelimiter = _T('/');                  // Add this
   m_lInternalDate = MakeJulian(nMonth, nDay, nYear);
}

// Create a date given a time value.
CDate::CDate(const time_t* lTime)
{
   m_nDateFormat = MMDDYY;                   // Add this
   m_chDelimiter = _T('/');                  // Add this
```

```
    // Get a date structure for this time
    struct tm* pTmPtr = localtime(lTime);

    m_lInternalDate = MakeJulian(pTmPtr->tm_mon + 1, pTmPtr->tm_mday,
                                 pTmPtr->tm_year + 1900);
}

// Add this constructor
CDate::CDate(DateFormat fmt)
{
    m_nDateFormat = fmt;
    m_chDelimiter = _T('/');
    m_lInternalDate = 0;
}

    ...

int CDate::ExtractDate(LPCTSTR lpszString, int* nMonth, int* nDay,
                       int* nYear)
{
    TCHAR szBuffer[256] = {0};
    TCHAR szDay[3] = {0};
    TCHAR szMonth[3] = {0};
    TCHAR szYear[5] = {0};
    int nRet = 0;

    lstrcpyn(szBuffer, lpszString, 255);

    StripCharacter((LPTSTR)szBuffer, _T('/'));

    switch (m_nDateFormat)                                  // Add this
    {                                                       // Add this
    case MMDDYY:                                            // Add this
        if (lstrlen(szBuffer) >= 6 )
        {
            // Allow for MMDDYYYY
            nRet = ErrDate_NoError;

            // Extract month and verify
            lstrcpyn(szMonth, szBuffer, 2 + 1);
            if (_ttoi(szMonth) < 1 || _ttoi(szMonth) > 12)
                nRet = ErrDate_BadMonth;

            // Extract day and verify. Note we need year for leap year
            // calculation
            lstrcpyn(szDay, szBuffer + 2, 2 + 1);
            lstrcpyn(szYear, szBuffer + 4, lstrlen(szBuffer) - 4 + 1);

            if (nRet == ErrDate_NoError)
                if (_ttoi(szDay) < 1
                     || _ttoi(szDay) > nDaysInMonth[_ttoi(szMonth) - 1])
                    nRet = ErrDate_BadDay;
            if (_ttoi(szMonth) == 2
                 && _ttoi(szDay) == nDaysInMonth[_ttoi(szMonth) - 1] + 1
                 && IsLeapYear(_ttoi(szYear)))
                nRet = ErrDate_NoError;

            // If there weren't any errors, return the pieces
```

```
            if (nRet == ErrDate_NoError)
            {
                *nYear = _ttoi(szYear);
                *nMonth = _ttoi(szMonth);
                *nDay = _ttoi(szDay);
            }
        }
        else
        {
            // Invalid length, just get out of here
            return ErrDate_Incorrect_Length;
        }
        break;                                            // Add this
    ...     // Add code for the other cases here (DDMMYY and YYMMDD)
    }                                                     // Add this
    return nRet;
}

...

///////////////////////////////////////////////////////////////////////////
// Operations

LPCTSTR CDate::AsString()
{
    switch (m_nDateFormat)
    {
    case MMDDYY:
        _stprintf(m_szBuffer, _T("%02d%c%02d%c%02d"), GetMonth(),
                  m_chDelimiter, GetDay(), m_chDelimiter, GetYear());
        break;

    case DDMMYY:
        _stprintf(m_szBuffer, _T("%02d%c%02d%c%02d"), GetDay(),
                  m_chDelimiter, GetMonth(), m_chDelimiter, GetYear());
        break;

    case YYMMDD:
        _stprintf(m_szBuffer, _T("%02d%c%02d%c%02d"), GetYear(),
                  m_chDelimiter, GetMonth(), m_chDelimiter, GetDay());
        break;

    default:
        return NULL;
        break;
    }
    return m_szBuffer;
}
```

While looking over the above changes, you'll probably have noticed that, so far, we haven't complied with the other request from the users, to add the ability to assign strings to dates and dates to strings. To do so, we need to add two new methods to the class: an **operator=()** that accepts a string, and an operator cast **LPCTSTR** which returns the date as a **LPCTSTR**. These two additions will satisfy the last known requirements of the users. Let's do that here, by adding the following highlighted lines to the header for the class:

```
// Add to Date.h
// Operations
public:
    LPCTSTR AsString();
    operator LPCTSTR();
    CDate& operator=(LPCTSTR lpszString);
```

Next, add the bodies for these two functions to the class source file:

```
// Add to Date.cpp
CDate::operator LPCTSTR()
{
    return AsString();
}

CDate& CDate::operator=(LPCTSTR lpszString)
{
    int nMonth, nDay, nYear;

    if (ExtractDate(lpszString, &nMonth, &nDay, &nYear) == ErrDate_NoError)
    {
        m_lInternalDate = MakeJulian(nMonth, nDay, nYear);
    }
    else
    {
        m_lInternalDate = 0L;
    }
    return *this;
}
```

Is there anything else we have forgotten from the user review? Actually, there isn't. The question, though, is whether or not to take what we have now constructed and return to the users with it. There are diminishing returns in repeatedly running back to the end user with a 'look at what we have *now*,' attitude. After a while, users start to begrudge the time spent looking at each new iteration, especially if all you're giving them is what they asked for. At this point, it's better for us to consider what might be missing ourselves, rather than having someone else point it out to us:

One of the advantages of implementing classes in C++ is that you can treat objects the same way that you do integers, character strings, and other first class items. This means that you can add integers to classes, subtract them, and so forth. Our class should probably offer support for some of the basic functionality involved in date manipulation as well. We'll offer several new functions to the user: the ability to add/subtract a number of days to/from an object. This takes the form of several new methods for the class. Let's add some new operators for addition and subtraction. Yes, I said *operators* plural, rather than a single operator. Remember that in C++ (as in C), you can add a number to another number by writing

```
x = x + 1;
```

or by writing

```
x += 1;
```

It only makes sense that we should allow any user to use either form of the above and get the same result. Likewise, subtraction offers the operators `-` and `-=` to accomplish the same task. Keep this in mind when creating your own components.

Always provide the user with the most likely methods to accomplish a task. This often means duplicating effort, but will result in a better-implemented and more well-used component.

Here's the code we will add to the header for the class:

```
// Operations
public:
   LPCTSTR AsString();
   operator LPCTSTR();
   CDate& operator=(LPCTSTR lpszString);
   CDate operator+(int nNumDays);
   CDate operator-(int nNumDays);
   CDate operator+=(int nNumDays);
   CDate operator-=(int nNumDays);
...
// Implementation
protected:
...
long AddDays(long lJulianDate, int nNumDays)
long SubtractDays(long lJulianDate, int nNumDays)
```

And here's the implementation for the above listed operators:

```
// Add to Date.cpp
//////////////////////////////////////////////////////////////////////////
// Operations
CDate CDate::operator+(int nNumDays)
{
   CDate date;
   date.m_lInternalDate = AddDays(m_lInternalDate, nNumDays);
   return date;
}

CDate CDate::operator+=(int nNumDays)
{
   m_lInternalDate = AddDays(m_lInternalDate, nNumDays);
   return *this;
}

CDate CDate::operator-(int nNumDays)
{
   CDate date;
   date.m_lInternalDate = SubtractDays(m_lInternalDate, nNumDays);
   return date;
}

CDate CDate::operator-=(int nNumDays)
{
   m_lInternalDate = SubtractDays(m_lInternalDate, nNumDays);
   return *this;
}

// Implementation
long CDate::AddDays(long lJulianDate, int nNumDays)
{
```

```
   // First, get the year
   int nYear = GetYear();

   // Subtract off the year part
   lJulianDate -= (nYear * 10000L);

   // Now, add the days..
   lJulianDate += nNumDays;

   int nTotalDays = 0;

   if (IsLeapYear(nYear))
      nTotalDays = 366;
   else
      nTotalDays = 365;

   while (lJulianDate > nTotalDays)
   {
      nYear++;
      lJulianDate -= nTotalDays;
      if (IsLeapYear(nYear))
         nTotalDays = 366;
      else
         nTotalDays = 365;
   }

   return (10000L * nYear) + lJulianDate;
}

long CDate::SubtractDays(long lJulianDate, int nNumDays)
{
   // First, get the year
   int nYear = GetYear();

   // Subtract off the year part
   lJulianDate -= (nYear * 10000L);

   // Now, subtract the days..
   lJulianDate -= nNumDays;

   int nTotalDays = 0;

   if (IsLeapYear(nYear-1))
      nTotalDays = 366;
   else
      nTotalDays = 365;

   while (lJulianDate < 1)
   {
      nYear--;
      lJulianDate += nTotalDays;
      if (IsLeapYear(nYear))
         nTotalDays = 366;
      else
         nTotalDays = 365;
   }

   return (10000L * nYear) + lJulianDate;
}
```

Are we done yet? (Reminds me of my small children on a car trip.) That's a good question. Are there other functions that we could add to this class? Yes, I would say that there certainly are a number of functions that could be implemented. For example, one thing that didn't come up from the user review is that there's no way, aside from in the construction of the object, to set the format of the date. This seems like a curious omission, and its implementation is left as an exercise for the reader.

Are there better ways in which the functions that we have already added could be implemented? Almost certainly. The code was written to illustrate various points, not necessarily to provide a perfect implementation of a date class. The question is, should we continue to refine the class and add functionality?

Welcome to the first big problem with component design. You can ask again and again whether a component is complete, and the answer can always be 'No'. The important thing is to realize when a component has progressed far enough to be usable by the end user and to accomplish the job for which it was intended. Knowing when to quit trying to improve something may be the hardest lesson any programmer (or indeed anyone else) will ever learn. Components could be created which solved every problem known to man, and continue to evolve, and yet those components would rarely be reused in applications for exactly that reason. Programmers believe (rightly) that components which solve many problems aren't as efficient at solving a single problem as code written specifically for that purpose.

> ***Keep components limited to solving a single problem. A problem which is complex may lead to a complex solution, but a complex solution should never be applied to a simple problem.***

At this point, we can determine that the component that we have created is probably 'ready'. In short, it's time to test it, put it into a source code control system and, of course, write some documentation on how to use it. Finally, you can turn it loose on some users. You can extend it, of course, and then redistribute the new header files, but that's an issue for another time and a later chapter.

Epilog

It would be good to say that we had just saved the world as we know it from the scourges of date problems caused by the lack of a fully functioning date class, but unfortunately we're not in this fortunate position. The only real problem with this example is that it's completely unnecessary (outside the confines of this book, anyway). The `COleDateTime` object provided by MFC actually solves this problem with considerably less effort than we just went through, and is capable of handling dates from 1 January 100–31 December 9999. It also provides many features not implemented in our class.

Let this be a lesson to you all. Always look before leaping! Had we inspected the MFC documentation, we would have known that there was already a component to do the job we needed. We would also have lost a valuable example, so it's really not all that upsetting. However, there goes our quest for world domination via the date class.

Documentation

As has been mentioned previously, components won't be reused unless there's some documentation for them. I really hate to think of how much good code and how many well designed components are sitting gathering dust on networks because no one knows how to use them. I freely admit that, when confronted with a situation in which there's no documentation about how something works, I'll often write my own version rather than using the existing code. Why, you might ask, does someone who purports to believe that components are the best thing since sliced bread not reuse them?

The answers to this and other questions related to components fall into two categories. First, a lack of time prevents most programmers from having the luxury of studying existing code and identifying the advantages and disadvantages of using it. Secondly, there's a high level of frustration associated with digging through uncommented, undocumented code to see what it does and whether it's applicable to a given situation. Because most of us have learned to work in corporate environments, we are used to having a hundred variants of a single routine, each customized for a specific purpose. If only someone would come along to write a single routine that did the job, all of that existing code could be removed and centrally located but, alas, there's never time.

For this reason, writing documentation isn't only a way to ensure that your code will be reused, but will also spread the word that you aren't merely a 'techno-geek'. Just think of the admiring looks of coworkers when they discover that, as well as slinging code with the best of them, you can actually speak English. Writing documentation is a necessary evil, even to a programmer of the highest echelon.

When you're developing documentation for a component, two key pieces must be included before it can be said to have any worthwhile purpose.

First, the documentation must describe the purpose of the component. In most cases, this takes the form of an overview and a feature list. Your documentation may be more or less complete than this, but should follow the general guidelines.

Secondly, your documentation must include a description of how to use the component. This information includes what environments the component is known to work in, and how to call it in each.

There are few things more frustrating for a Visual Basic programmer, for example, than to face a document written entirely from the viewpoint of a Visual C++ (or Delphi) programmer. In addition, since the calling conventions for the different environments are themselves different, you might leave another person wondering whether the component was ever really used in their environment, or whether it was simply put in as a selling point!

The Feature List

Basically, a feature list is just what it implies: a list of features. While simplistic, this form of design documentation has many appealing attributes. For example, a feature list can be easily generated by a combination of programmers and marketing people, creating a simple form of program definition that both groups can use to their best advantage.

How do you create a feature list for an unknown product? The best way to create any sort of list for a new product or component is to conduct a brainstorming session. Have all people concerned with the product/component sit in a room and throw out ideas as they think of them. Don't bother with filtering the ideas at this point, just write them down. Imagine that you're involved in creating a new component that's intended to be used to print bar codes for your inventory management system. A typical feature list brainstorming session might go like this:

Programmer A: *We need to be able to print '5 of 9' bar codes.*
Programmer B: *We need to be able print EINs as well.*

Marketing Person A: *It would be nice if it worked with our existing Point of Sale system.*
Marketing Person B: *How about tying it in with the bookkeeping system, letting us read in bar codes and generate instant invoices from them?*

Programmer A: *It should be able to deal with invalid bar code entries, as when someone enters 'ABCDEF%^&*(' into the application.*
Programmer B: *Yeah, and it should be able to display bar codes on the screen as well as print them.*

Marketing Person A: *How about a way to scan in bar codes?*

As you can see from the above exchange, the ideas can fly fast and furious. Some ideas (such as the concept of scanning in bar codes) probably won't be in the final list. Others (such as printing '5 of 9' bar codes) almost certainly will. At this point, however, the brainstorming session continues without concern over whether or not the idea is viable.

Following the brainstorming session, the next step is to assemble the features you talked about into a single master list. The easiest way to do this is to simply list the features in numerical order and then filter through them. Our list from the above session might read:

- Print 5 of 9 bar codes
- Print EIN bar codes
- Work with existing Point of Sale system
- Read in bar codes and generate invoices through existing bookkeeping
- Deal with invalid entries
- Display bar codes on a variety of output devices
- Scan in bar codes

This list could then be circulated to customers, programmers, marketers, and managers. The ideas would be commented upon and added to. Priorities could be set at this point to determine what must be in the component, what it would be nice to add, and what needn't be included. You could also, at this point, determine what could be included in future releases.

This is all well and good for large companies. For small shops, or individual programmers, there isn't likely to be a wide circulation of feature lists, priority planning, and so forth. What happens then? As it happens, the same thing occurs. You might be a one-man retail outlet developing a component for internal use only. In this case, you would list all of the features you need, put the list aside for a little while, and then review it later. You might find features you would like to add to the list, or features on the list which don't really need to be done, or could be done through other features. The resulting list is used to create the actual component.

Formal Design Documents

In anything but the smallest projects, there's usually some sort of formal design document process. Standards need to be followed, document styles need to be the same, and so forth. What impact does this have upon the component design process? When you're designing and documenting a component, in any format, there are several key points that need to be included:

- A description of the problem to be solved
- A description of the method to be used in solving the problem
- A description of the properties and methods of the solution
- Examples of how to use the properties and methods of the solution

Let's take a look at each of the pieces in turn. A description of the problem to be solved means just what it says. You need to describe to the reader, as simply as possible, the problem your component is intended to solve.

If you can't describe the problem in terms that will be understood by someone who isn't on the project team, you probably don't understand the problem well enough to provide a useful solution.

A description of the method to be used in solving the problem is intended to show that you understand not only the problem, but also how the problem can be solved. Once again, if you can't describe accurately the method you're intending to use, how can you possibly write code to implement that method?

A description of the properties and methods of the solution needs to be made once the component has been created, tested, and found to solve the problem. This description is intended to show the user the abilities of the component. When reading this portion of the documentation (which often takes the form of a help file), the user of the component should be able to see the purpose of each method and the availability of each property. This is important when writing MFC extensions, for example, so that users don't have to resort to reading arcane header files to see what methods are available for their use. When using ActiveX controls, it's essential to document the available properties and methods so that users of multiple environments can use the component effectively (or at all). If you fail to properly document the available properties and functionality of your component, you can be sure that they won't be used.

Finally, examples of how to use the properties and methods of the solution will do two things for the end user of the component. First, they will provide concrete examples of how something is done, something that is well appreciated by first time users of components. Second, the examples can be used to suggest uses for the component that might not be recognized at first.

The more examples you provide and the more varied those examples, the happier and more productive your component's users will be.

Help Files

Every component you write should have some sort of help file associated with it. Whether this is an actual Microsoft Windows Help file (or an HTML file, as such files will soon be implemented) or a simple text file with help text in it, this is a requirement that should never be overlooked during the development stage of components. There is really no telling how many truly excellent components are never used because the end user doesn't want to dig into the actual code or header files to figure out what is available to them.

> *If you don't want your control to be ignored, provide a well implemented Help file.*

Help files should contain two levels of information for components. First, the help file should contain an overview of the purpose of the control (the problem statement that we talked about earlier). This overview will give the user a sense of how the component is intended to be used and what sort of applications are likely to use it. Following the overview should be a detailed summary of the methods available in the component, and the properties available for use by the end user. If you're implementing an MFC extension, methods should be broken down into simple **`public`** and **`protected`** methods and **`virtual`** methods.

Below, you can see a simple overview of a help file for one of the components developed in this book. As you can see, it has a simple description of what the component is intended to do, together with a link to the detailed summary of the component. If the component had any limitations or known problems (such as only running when another component is running), these limitations would be listed here.

Component Name:	Calculator Control
Date Released:	09/09/96
Purpose:	To implement a simple calculator style drop down combo box that allows the user to enter a number.
Methods:	Create SetAssociatedWindow
Events:	None, text is automatically set in associated window.

The next figure, on the other hand, shows the detailed document for this component. As this is an MFC extension, the properties are listed first, followed by the **`public`** methods for the class. Finally, the document lists the **`virtual`** methods of the class which can be overridden by the programmer. Remember the audience when writing your help files. ActiveX controls can be used by pretty much anyone (end users, programmers, managers, even marketing folk), while MFC extensions are unlikely to be used by anyone other than a programmer. Structure the help file accordingly. If you're aiming at a C++ programmer, for example, you needn't describe what a '**`virtual`** method' is, since it can be reasonably assumed that the user understands C++.

class CCalcWnd : public CWnd

public methods:

  BOOL Create(int x, int y);

protected methods:

  void ShowCurrentValue();
  void AddDigit (LPTSTR string, LPTSTR digit);
  void DoCalculate();

virtual (overridable) methods:
None.

> *When implementing a help file, aim for the middle ground. Don't talk at such a high level as to put off entry-level programmers, but don't bore experienced programmers with common details.*

Context-sensitive Help

When you're implementing a control, consider adding context-sensitive help 'hooks' at appropriate places. These hooks will allow the programmer to add their own context-sensitive help entries to the component, so that end users can be informed of the current situation, potential pitfalls of their actions, and given 'where to go from here' information.

Context-sensitive help takes two forms. First, the addition of **tooltips** (little yellow pop-up windows that display information about specific items) allows the user to view information on a 'just in time' basis. Tooltips supply simple information about a given component on a screen. An edit field, for example, might contain a tooltip which informs the user about its intended purpose. Tooltips can be used to display error information (This is a required field), context information (You need to enter this field or the program will blow up), or just information about the purpose of an input field (Enter the Zip Code or Postal Code for this address).

The second form of context-sensitive help is the infamous *F1* key. When a user is in the scope of a component such as an edit field, pressing *F1* will often bring up a help screen tailored to the particular field in question. As an example, consider a simple dialog for inputting a customer's name and address. This dialog might contain fields for last name, first name, middle initial, address line 1, address line 2, city, state, zip code, and phone number. When the input focus is in the zip code field, for example, pressing the *F1* key might bring up a help file devoted to what valid zip codes are accepted by the application, what to do if you don't have a zip code, or how to look up zip codes for a particular city and state (if your application supported such things).

A new technology answer to this supported by Windows 95 (and the new version of Windows NT) is the 'What's this?' help message for items of the user interface that can't receive focus and thus can never have the *F1* key pressed for them.

> *Don't overlook the importance of context-sensitive help in application support. The more information you provide to the user, the less support you will need to provide.*

Writing a help file is often a project in itself. Writing a poor help file is, in most cases, worse than writing no help at all. I have an enormous amount of respect for people that can write really good technical help and documentation. It doesn't hurt that this is what my sister does for a living.

Where is all this leading? Well, since this is a programming book, it's leading to a programming project. Surprise! Programming books usually contain a project that ties together all the myriad things talked about through the text of the book, and this one is no exception. Let's take a little time to talk about that project.

The Programming Project: A HyperText Documentation Viewer

As I've been saying throughout this chapter, components aren't useful unless they have some documentation that shows how to use them. In this book, we'll develop quite a few (hopefully) useful and reusable components that can be dropped directly into your applications. To use them, however, you need to have a good idea of how those components work. In addition, the documentation needs to show you what methods and properties (for ActiveX controls) or functions and property accessors (for MFC extensions) are available. This could be done through a simple help file interface, or even with printed documentation.

The point of this book is to expose cutting edge technology to you, the programmer, that won't only give you something to use, but will also reveal to you some of the new technology available for Windows programmers. As a result, we won't write some old-style help files, nor will we use paper documentation. Instead, the controls will be documented through a HyperText Markup Language (HTML) interface that allows you to view the documentation online at any time. HTML is the future of documentation (replacing help files) for Windows, so getting used to it now is a good idea.

The screenshot below shows the basic screen for the project we will develop. The left side shows a contents list which allows the user to view wide strings in a simple non-wrapping list box format. The right side of the screen shows the Microsoft Internet HTML component displaying an HTML file containing information about the control.

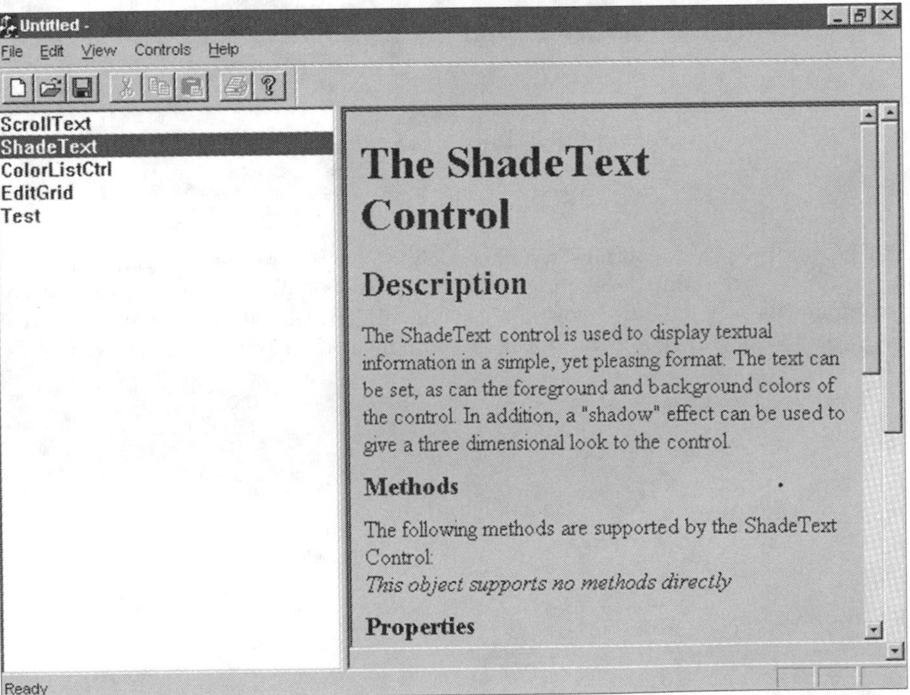

Once a component has been selected from the list box on the left side of the screen, a detailed diagram dialog can be displayed, which shows the derivation and methods available in a simple tree view. We'll develop this tree control in the book, along with the contents list and the fancy text control shown in the dialog.

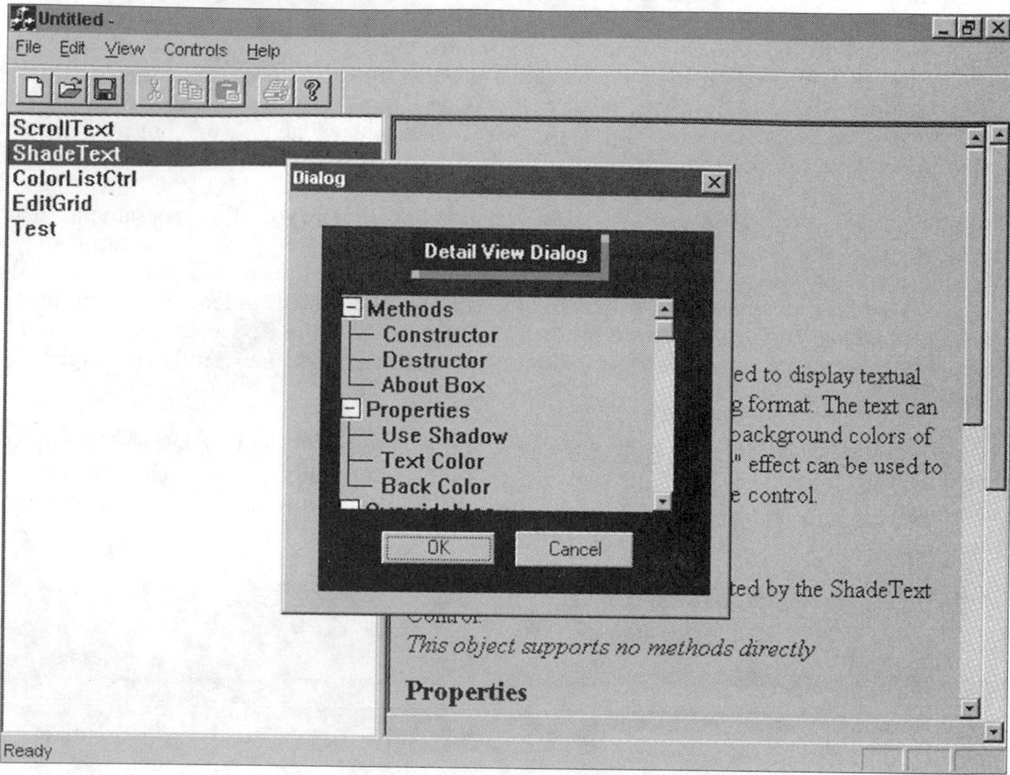

That will be the project that brings together all the components we're going to develop in this book. How do we go about developing those components? Well, that's a matter of coding. Since coding components is what this book is all about, it's probably time that we started doing it. So turn the page, and let's get into the meat of component development using Visual C++!

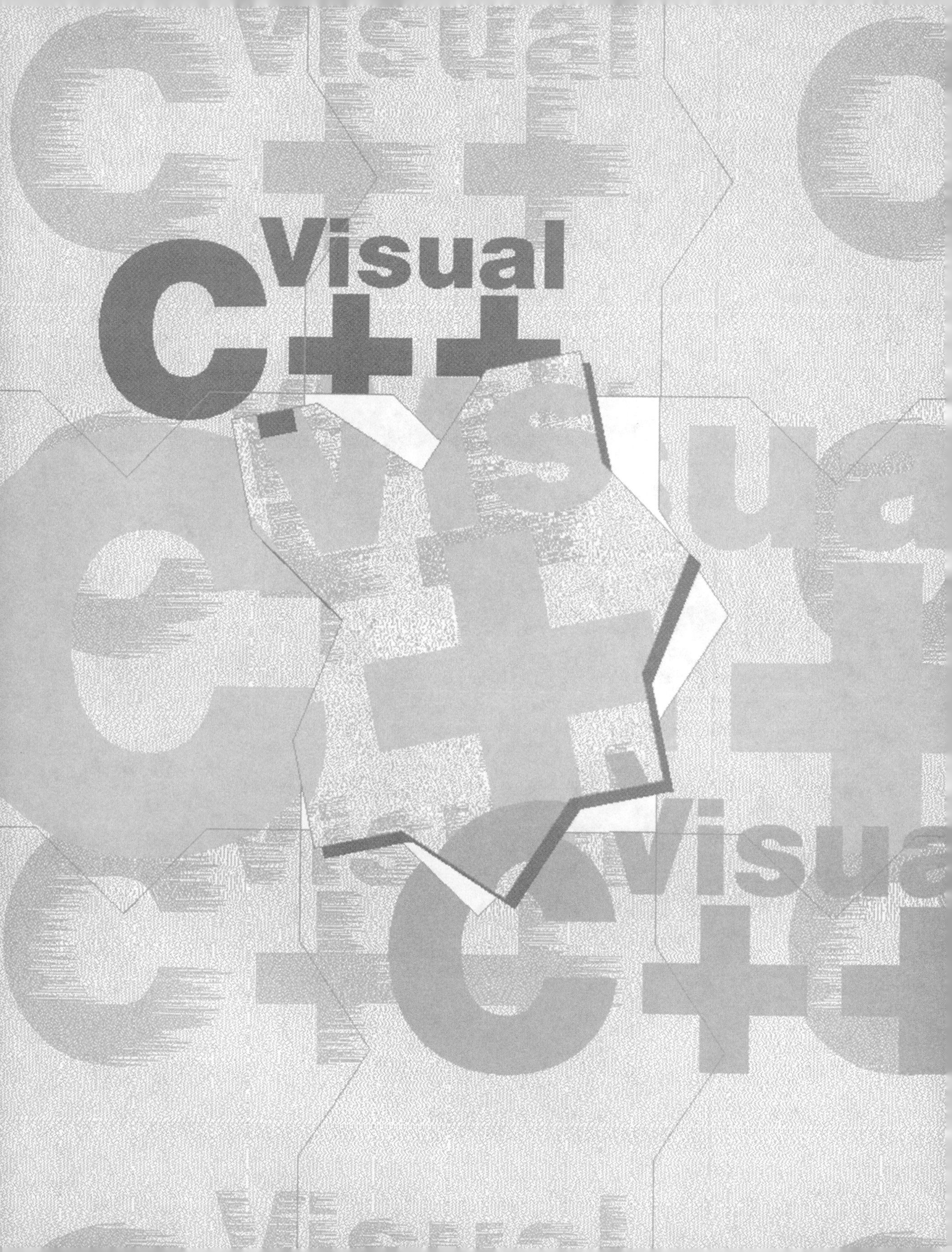
Visual
C++

Simple Components

Until now, we've considered components from a theoretical viewpoint, with little regard for their practical implementation. This is rather like designing a brand new algorithm for sorting numbers, without thinking about whether it requires an infinite amount of disk space and memory to produce results. In other words, it's time that we 'put up or shut up'.

In this chapter, we'll begin to design and implement real-world components that you can use in your own applications. The advantages are twofold. First, you can see practical implementations of the theory we discussed in the first two chapters. Secondly, even if you disagree with everything said up to this point, you'll at least end up with components worth the price of the book. Who says you can't make everyone happy?

As the previous two chapters made clear, it's first necessary to define the problem we're trying to solve and list the requirements of the components we're creating to solve the problem. Let's look at the problem definition first.

The Problem

Windows provides quite a few ways to accept data from the user. There are edit boxes, list boxes, check boxes, and so forth. However, Windows falls woefully short when it comes to displaying information for the user to view. You can really only use the static text field control to display text.

You can, of course, display text in images or icons, but that requires the definition of outside resources. What we would like to do is to come up with ways to jazz up the display of textual information on the screen; our solution shouldn't require the design and implementation of other sorts of information, such as icons or graphics. In short, what we're looking for is a better way to display text that requires nothing other than the text to display.

We're looking for a way to make the user focus on aspects of the user interface which they don't normally look at. We would prefer a solution which doesn't change the way the user works with the data (such as tooltips or property sheets); instead, we're looking to create a visual impact that the eye of the user will immediately be drawn to, so that we can indicate important information to them.

The MFC Solution: The Scrolling Text Control

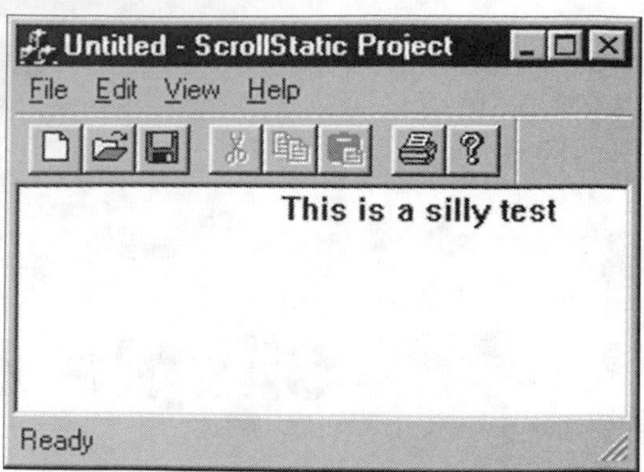

One way we can make the display more exciting to the user is to add a little motion. To provide this motion, we'll implement a control that scrolls the text across the screen. Think of it as a mini Wall Street stock ticker embedded in your application. You can see an example of the scrolling text control opposite (unfortunately, you won't be able to see it moving unless you shake the book around!).

Before we start constructing such a control, however, it would be nice if we knew *exactly* what it was that we were trying to make. To this end, we'll compose one of the feature lists (or FRDs, if you like) that we talked about in the previous chapters.

Feature List

The control should allow the client programmer to change the following aspects of its appearance:

- The text that is displayed scrolling across the control.
- The foreground color of the control (the color of the text).
- The background color of the control (the color of the control window).
- The font in which the text is displayed.
- The speed at which the control scrolls the text across the screen (including the ability to start and stop the text scrolling).

Designing the Control

Although this is a very simple control, it still requires a bit of design before we can create it. In general, when writing controls, you must first identify the functionality Windows already provides, which you will need to interface with, and then decide how to implement the portions that Windows doesn't do for you. In this case, we need to do two major things.

First, we need a way to display a text string scrolling across the screen. Windows does provide a scrolling function, **`ScrollWindow()`**, but it's not really applicable in this instance because of flicker and our need to add new text to the end. Since we need a way to change the scrolling speed, and keep track of what portions of the string are visible, we will need to display the text ourselves.

Second, we need a way to draw the text string at specified intervals. Here, Windows does provide a simple way to accomplish the task—timers. We'll create a timer and repaint the window each time the allotted interval expires.

This design, while fairly simple, will work well for this control. Since there's no user interaction with the control (besides looking at it), there's no need to concern ourselves with a more complex design.

Implementing the Control

To implement the control, we'll create a new MFC class and implement the functionality of the control within that class. In the following section, we'll describe the procedure that you need to follow to create the MFC class and implement the control.

TRY IT OUT - Create a Scrolling Text Display

1 First, we'll create a new project workspace in which we can create and test the new control. Select MFC AppWizard (exe) as the project type and call the project **ScrollStatic Project**. On Step 1 of the AppWizard, choose a Single document application.

You can leave all the other options with their default settings until you reach Step 6. Here you should take the time to rename some of the classes and files that AppWizard will produce so that your code will be more readable. The table below lists the items that you should rename:

CScrollStaticProjectApp to CScrollStaticApp
CScrollStaticProjectDoc to CScrollStaticDoc
    ScrollStatic ProjectDoc.h to ScrollStaticDoc.h
    ScrollStatic ProjectDoc.cpp to ScrollStaticDoc.cpp
CScrollStaticProjectView to CScrollStaticView
    ScrollStatic ProjectView.h to ScrollStaticView.h
    ScrollStatic ProjectView.cpp to ScrollStaticView.cpp

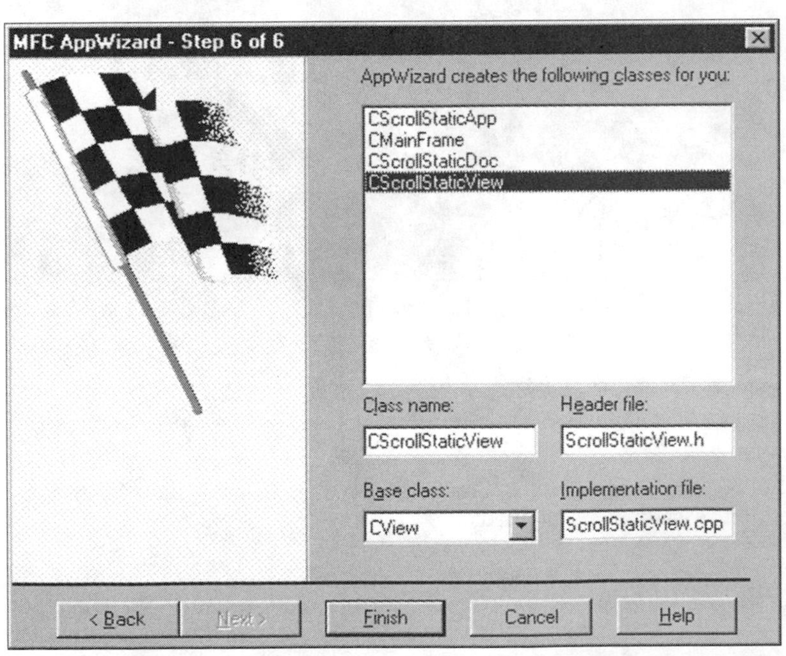

2 Once AppWizard has successfully created the project, we can use ClassWizard to create the new class that will become our scrolling text MFC extension. Bring up ClassWizard, select the Add Class... menu and choose the New... item. Call the new class CScrollStatic and choose CStatic as its Base class.

By default, the class will be saved into the file **ScrollStatic.cpp**. It's a standard naming convention for classes to be saved into **.cpp** and **.h** files with the same name as the class (minus the initial 'C') so it's good practice to follow this convention for your own code. This is the reason that we didn't use **ScrollStatic** as the name of the project: AppWizard would have created the app object in the files called **ScrollStatic.h** and **ScrollStatic.cpp** and won't allow you to change their names.

If you wish to use this component with a 16-bit version of Visual C++, you might want to rename the file to use the 8.3 naming scheme, but for readability's sake, we'll assume that you're only going to use the component with Visual C++ 4.*x* so we will use long filenames throughout this book.

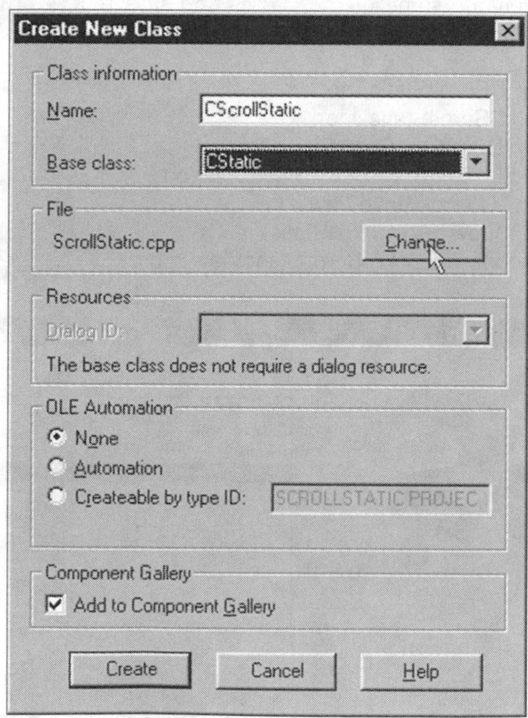

3 Now edit the **ScrollStatic.h** header file so that it looks like the listing below. The code to be added is shown highlighted.

```
// ScrollStatic.h : header file
//
```

```
#ifndef WROX_SCROLLSTATIC_H
#define WROX_SCROLLSTATIC_H
/////////////////////////////////////////////////////////////////////////////
// CScrollStatic window

class CScrollStatic : public CStatic
{
// Construction
public:
   CScrollStatic();
   virtual BOOL Create(LPCTSTR lpszText, const RECT& rect,    // Create the
                       CWnd* pParentWnd, UINT nID = 0xffff); // window

// Attributes
public:
   LPCTSTR GetText() const;              // Get the current text
   CFont* GetFont() const;               // Return the current font setting
   COLORREF GetBackColor() const;        // Get the current background color
   COLORREF GetTextColor() const;        // Get the current text color
   int GetTimerInterval() const;         // Get current display speed (in ms)

// Operations
public:
   void SetText(LPCTSTR lpszText);       // Set the current text
   void SetFont(CFont* pFont);           // Set the current text font
   void SetBackColor(COLORREF color);    // Set the current background color
   void SetTextColor(COLORREF color);    // Set the current text color
   void SetTimerInterval(int nMilliseconds); // Set display speed
   void StopScrolling();                 // Stop the text scrolling

// Overrides
   // ClassWizard generated virtual function overrides
   //{{AFX_VIRTUAL(CScrollStatic)
   //}}AFX_VIRTUAL

// Implementation
public:
   virtual ~CScrollStatic();

   LPTSTR m_lpszText;          // Current text to display
   CFont* m_pFont;             // Current font (or NULL)
   COLORREF m_clrBack;         // Current background color of rectangle
   COLORREF m_clrText;         // Current text color
   int m_nTimerInterval;       // Current display speed in milliseconds.
   UINT m_nTimerID;            // == 0 when we don't have a timer.
   int m_nOffset;              // Offset within static text field.
   int m_nTextOffset;          // Text offset when at left side.

   // Generated message map functions
protected:
   //{{AFX_MSG(CScrollStatic)
      // NOTE - the ClassWizard will add and remove member functions here.
   //}}AFX_MSG

   DECLARE_MESSAGE_MAP()
};

/////////////////////////////////////////////////////////////////////////////
#endif
```

The **#ifndef**, **#define** and **#endif** trio are probably quite familiar to you as a way to prevent a header file being included multiple times. You might feel that you don't need these directives because you'd never be stupid enough to include a header file more than once, but remember that other people will also be using your class and, if it's widely used, it may not always be obvious when it has been included already. It's always a good idea to help the users of your class avoid as many mistakes as possible.

The reasons behind the **Create()** function, the **Get** and **Set** functions and the data members of the class will become clearer as we examine the code we need to add to the **.cpp** file to get things working, but I hope you already have some idea of what they do from their names and the comments associated with each line of code. It's very important to document your classes as clearly as possible within the code itself. This includes using sensible names, commenting your code and following accepted conventions. Here you can see we've used the naming conventions, data types and code layout that will be familiar to anyone who has used MFC.

4 The first thing to do now that we have added some data members to our class is to make sure that they're properly initialized. Not initializing variables is a common cause of errors, so it's an important step. Add the code shown highlighted below to the class constructor in **ScrollStatic.cpp**.

```
CScrollStatic::CScrollStatic()
{
   // Set up member data
   m_nTimerID = 0;
   m_nOffset = 0;
   m_nTextOffset = 0;
   m_pFont = NULL;
   m_lpszText = NULL;
   m_nTimerInterval = 150; // Default to 150 milliseconds for speed

   // Default colors
   m_clrBack = RGB(255, 255, 255);   // White background
   m_clrText = RGB(0, 0, 0);         // Black text
}
```

Most of the data members are initialized to **0** or **NULL**, but the timer interval and the color variables are initialized to sensible and, more importantly, usable values. Picking usable default values is an important skill when programming components because it will save the users of your code time and effort if they don't have to assign values to properties in your objects.

5 The next step is to provide the implementation of the **Get** functions so add the following code to **ScrollStatic.cpp**.

```
/////////////////////////////////////////////////////////////////////////////
// CScrollStatic Inlines

// Get the current font setting
inline CFont* CScrollStatic::GetFont() const
{
   return m_pFont;
}

// Get the current text
```

```
inline LPCTSTR CScrollStatic::GetText() const
{
   return m_lpszText;
}

// Get the current background color
inline COLORREF CScrollStatic::GetBackColor() const
{
   return m_clrBack;
}

// Get the current text color
inline COLORREF CScrollStatic::GetTextColor() const
{
   return m_clrText;
}

// Get current display speed (in milliseconds)
inline int CScrollStatic::GetTimerInterval() const
{
   return m_nTimerInterval;
}
```

These are just very simple functions that allow access to the member variables of **CScrollStatic**. They allow the user of the class to determine through code the current settings of the class that affect its appearance.

The functions are declared with the **inline** keyword for speed. Calls to **inline** functions are replaced by the compiler with a copy of the body of the function itself. This removes the overhead of a function call at run time and allows code optimizations on the inline code that might not have been possible with normal functions.

The functions are declared as **const** to assure both the programmer using our class and the compiler that these functions don't change the state of the class. The **const** keyword is also very useful to prevent us from making mistakes in our code. We've declared that the function doesn't change the state of the class, so the compiler will make sure that we can't break that agreement. If we accidentally write code in a **const** function that does change the class's state, our code won't compile and our error will be highlighted.

6 We need to add just a little more code to handle the task of setting the colors, and font. Add the following code to the file to do these jobs:

```
/////////////////////////////////////////////////////////////////////////////
// CScrollStatic Set functions

void CScrollStatic::SetBackColor(COLORREF color)
{
   // Save the color
   m_clrBack = color;

   // Invalidate to recolor screen
   InvalidateRect(NULL);
}

void CScrollStatic::SetTextColor(COLORREF color)
```

```
{
    // Save the color
    m_clrText = color;

    // Invalidate to recolor screen
    InvalidateRect(NULL);
}

void CScrollStatic::SetFont(CFont* pFont)
{
    ASSERT(pFont != NULL);
    // Save the font
    m_pFont = pFont;

    // Invalidate to repaint screen
    InvalidateRect(NULL);
}
```

Note that when we change the font or color, we simply save the information and repaint the screen. This is a good technique to use when writing controls. Handle the implementation in a single place and call through to that handler from anything that needs to use it. In this way, we end up with a single entry point and a single place to fix when things go wrong.

7 Now we'll provide the implementation for **SetText()**.

```
void CScrollStatic::SetText(LPCTSTR lpszText)
{
    if (lpszText != NULL)
    {
        // Clear out old text and reclaim memory
        if (m_lpszText)
            delete [] m_lpszText;
        m_lpszText = new TCHAR[lstrlen(lpszText) + 1];
        lstrcpy(m_lpszText, lpszText);
    }
}
```

Essentially, what we want to do is create a new string on the heap (free store) and copy into it the contents of the string pointed to by the argument to the function. This is pretty straightforward and only slightly complicated by the fact that we need to do two things first: we need to check that we had a valid pointer passed in to the function before we use it, and we need to **delete []** any strings that we may have allocated on the heap previously. This ensures that we aren't leaking memory like a sieve.

At this point, alarm bells should be going off in your head. We've used **new []** to allocate memory for a string, and we've made sure that we don't leak memory during the life of the object by calling **delete []** on any existing strings before we allocate any more space in the free store. Great! But what happens when a **CScrollStatic** object is destroyed?

The answer, at the moment, is that it will leak any memory currently allocated to the string pointed to by **m_lpszText**. The solution to this potential problem is to use the class destructor to make sure we've deleted any memory that we allocated. We'll do that now.

8 Add the highlighted code shown below to the destructor for **CScrollStatic** in **ScrollStatic.cpp**.

```
CScrollStatic::~CScrollStatic()
{
    if (m_lpszText != NULL)         // If we allocated memory, free it
        delete [] m_lpszText;
}
```

Problem solved!

9 Now we can provide the implementation for the final **Set** function which allows the user of the class to determine how fast the text will scroll. Add the code shown below for **SetTimerInterval()** to **ScrollStatic.cpp**.

```
void CScrollStatic::SetTimerInterval(int nMilliseconds)
{
    if (m_nTimerID != 0)          // If we already have a timer, kill it
        KillTimer(m_nTimerID);
    m_nTimerID = SetTimer(1, nMilliseconds, NULL);

    m_nTimerInterval = nMilliseconds;
}
```

This function just checks to see if we already have a timer. If we do, it gets destroyed by **KillTimer()**. The function then uses **SetTimer()** to create a new timer using the argument to the function as the frequency of the timer. The ID for the timer is stored in **m_nTimerID** and the interval for the timer is stored in **m_nTimerInterval.** (The fact that the previous sentence is so obvious is a testament to the importance of sensible variable names!)

Timers, like memory, are a limited resource. Just as we were careful to ensure that objects of our class don't lose any memory when they are destroyed, we should take the same care to release any timers we may be using. However, since we're using the **CWnd** timer functions which rely on a window being present, we can't put the timer clean-up code in the destructor because the window associated with our control will be long gone by the time the destructor is called. We need to put the code in a function that will be called when the window is about to be destroyed, but before it actually happens. We'll do that now.

10 Open up **ScrollStatic.cpp** in Developer Studio, make sure CScrollStatic is selected in the CScrollStatic Object IDs list and select **WM_DESTROY** from the Messages drop-down list at the top of the window. You will be told that **WM_DESTROY** isn't handled and asked whether you'd like to add a handler. Select Yes to add **CScrollStatic::OnDestroy()** to the file. (You could also do this from the Message Maps tab of ClassWizard). Now add the highlighted code shown below.

```
void CScrollStatic::OnDestroy()
{
    CStatic::OnDestroy();
    if (m_nTimerID != 0)            // If we already have a timer, kill it
        KillTimer(m_nTimerID);
}
```

*Whenever you acquire resources for your classes, whether it's memory, timers or whatever, you should always take care to release them. You can use the class destructor to release most types of resource and a **WM_DESTROY** handler will allow you to perform any clean-up that requires the presence of a window.*

11 Now that we've looked at the destruction of the control window associated with our class, let's turn our attention back to the beginning of its life as we examine the implementation of **CScrollStatic::Create()**. Add the following code to **ScrollStatic.cpp** just below the implementation of the constructor.

```
BOOL CScrollStatic::Create(LPCTSTR lpszText, const RECT& rect,
                           CWnd* pParentWnd, UINT nID /* = 0xffff */)
{
   // Initialize text field
   ASSERT(lpszText != NULL);
   m_lpszText = new TCHAR[lstrlen(lpszText) + 1];
   lstrcpy(m_lpszText, lpszText);

   // And create the actual Windows window
   DWORD dwStyle = SS_LEFT | WS_TABSTOP | WS_VISIBLE | WS_CHILD;
   return CStatic::Create(m_lpszText, dwStyle, rect, pParentWnd, nID);
}
```

The addition of a **Create()** function means that our class follows the standard MFC model of a two-stage construction for window-based classes. The first stage is represented by the constructor which simply initializes the class and the second stage is represented by the **Create()** function which actually creates the window used by our class to display the scrolling text. Apart from setting up the text and setting the style for the window, our implementation really just relies on **CStatic::Create()** for its functionality.

12 The next thing we need to do is start the scrolling when the control is initially created on the screen. To accomplish this, bring up ClassWizard and select CScrollStatic from the Class name and Object IDs lists. Select the **WM_CREATE** message from the Messages list and click the Add Function button to add **CScrollStatic::OnCreate()** to your code. Now add to this function the code highlighted below.

```
int CScrollStatic::OnCreate(LPCREATESTRUCT lpCreateStruct)
{
   if (CStatic::OnCreate(lpCreateStruct) == -1)
      return -1;

   // Create the timer for this window. Use default speed setting
   SetTimerInterval(m_nTimerInterval);

   return 0;
}
```

We've assumed here that the user of our class wouldn't be using it unless they wanted it to scroll and that the default value we provided for the interval is adequate. If the user doesn't want the text to scroll as soon as they create the control then they can simply stop it by calling **CScrollStatic::StopScrolling()**. You can add the implementation for this function to **ScrollStatic.cpp** as shown on the next page.

```
void CScrollStatic::StopScrolling()
{
   if (m_nTimerID != 0)          // If we already have a timer, kill it
      KillTimer(m_nTimerID);
   m_nTimerID = 0;
}
```

13 Reactivate ClassWizard and select CScrollStatic from the Class name list, and again from the Object IDs. Pick the **WM_PAINT** message from the Messages box and add a new function to the class by clicking on the Add Function button. The **WM_PAINT** message is sent by Windows whenever the client area of a window needs to be redrawn. Add the following code to the new **OnPaint()** function in **ScrollStatic.cpp**:

```
void CScrollStatic::OnPaint()
{
   CPaintDC dc(this); // device context for painting

   TEXTMETRIC tm;
   dc.GetTextMetrics(&tm);

   // Make sure text fits in rectangle
   CRect rect;
   GetClientRect(&rect);

   // Reset so text doesn't run into borders
   rect.top++;
   rect.bottom--;

   // Make sure the font is selected (if one was set)
   CFont* pOldFont = NULL;
   if (m_pFont)
      pOldFont = dc.SelectObject(m_pFont);

   // And set the color for the text
   dc.SetBkColor(m_clrBack);
   dc.SetTextColor(m_clrText);

   rect.left = rect.right - m_nOffset * tm.tmMaxCharWidth;
   rect.right--;

   // Clear the background of the box
   CBrush brush;
   brush.CreateSolidBrush(m_clrBack);
   dc.FillRect(&rect, &brush);

   // And draw whatever of the text fits...
   dc.DrawText(m_lpszText + m_nTextOffset,
               lstrlen(m_lpszText + m_nTextOffset), &rect, DT_LEFT);

   if (pOldFont)
      dc.SelectObject(pOldFont);

   // Do not call CStatic::OnPaint() for painting messages
}
```

As you can see, we're simply redrawing the text in the window. The 'magic' of the function comes about through the setting of the position and offsets of the string. The position is determined via the **rect** variable (a rectangle). This variable is set by calculating where we should be drawing on the window. How does that happen?

Each time the Windows timer sends us a message, we recalculate **m_nOffset**. This variable is simply the position on the screen, in characters, where we should start drawing. When the variable reaches **0**, we've reached the left-hand edge of the screen. At this point, the **m_nTextOffset** variable begins to get incremented. This variable moves the string along (by displaying the string from that offset on) so that it appears to scroll off the left edge of the screen.

14 Our next task, once the painting has been taken care of, is to deal with clearing the background of the control to the color the programmer has selected. Windows will automatically send a **WM_ERASEBKGND** message to the control whenever its background needs to be painted. We can take advantage of that by capturing the message and clearing the background to our chosen color. Use ClassWizard to add a new handler for the **WM_ERASEBKGND** message to the **CScrollStatic** object. Add the following code to **CScrollStatic::OnEraseBkgnd()**:

```
BOOL CScrollStatic::OnEraseBkgnd(CDC* pDC)
{
   CRect rect;
   GetClientRect(&rect);

   // Clear the background of the box
   CBrush brush;
   brush.CreateSolidBrush(m_clrBack);
   pDC->FillRect(&rect, &brush);

   return CStatic::OnEraseBkgnd(pDC);
}
```

15 All right. We've processed the creation, the painting, and the setting up of the control. What other messages could we need to deal with? Oops! The most important message of all is missing! As it stands, the control creates a timer and responds to paint messages to scroll the text, but it never responds to the timer messages to force the repaints in the first place! Let's correct that right now. Use ClassWizard to add a new message handler for the **WM_TIMER** message to the **CScrollStatic** object, and add the following code to **OnTimer()**:

```
void CScrollStatic::OnTimer(UINT nIDEvent)
{
   // Determine the screen area
   CRect rect;
   GetClientRect(&rect);

   // Get the DC for the window and select the font (if any)
   // into it so we get the right sizes
   CDC* dc = GetDC();
   CFont* pOldFont = NULL;
   if (m_pFont)
      pOldFont = dc->SelectObject(m_pFont);
```

```
    TEXTMETRIC tm;
    dc->GetTextMetrics(&tm);

    // Don't forget to restore the font and release the DC
    if (pOldFont)
        dc->SelectObject(pOldFont);
    ReleaseDC(dc);

    // Does the whole string fit in the window?
    if ((m_nOffset + 1) * tm.tmMaxCharWidth < rect.right - rect.left + 1)
    {
        m_nTextOffset = 0;
        m_nOffset++;
    }
    else
    {
        // Have we reached the left side?
        if (m_nTextOffset < (int)lstrlen(m_lpszText))
            m_nTextOffset++;
        else
        {
            // Nope. Start over
            m_nOffset = 0;
            m_nTextOffset = 0;
        }
    }

    // And re-draw text
    InvalidateRect(NULL);

    // Do default processing
    CStatic::OnTimer(nIDEvent);
}
```

As mentioned above, the paint function relies on the offset values calculated here. Each time the Windows timer goes off, this function is called. It's responsible for calculating where on the screen the text will be drawn. What we're doing here is calculating the width of the screen in characters (actually, maximum character width) and then determining where our string should be displayed in terms of the number of characters across the screen. It's much the type of code that might have been written (and was) in the old DOS days. Today, though, things become more complex with the addition of fonts and kerning. In our case, we simply determine how many characters we're going to display in the line and then convert that number back into a 'real' Windows point by using the width of a character.

Congratulations! You've written (or copied, as the case might be) your first complete control for Windows.

As implemented, the scrolling text control will allow the programmer to change text, fonts, and colors, as well as the rate at which the text is scrolled across the screen. This is sufficient to satisfy all the requirements of the control which we discussed in the feature list. Now, let's go ahead and see how we might use this control in our application.

TRY IT OUT - Test the Scrolling Text Control

1 To test the control (and make sure that it actually works), switch to the **CScrollStaticView** class, which was automatically created for you, and open up the ClassWizard one last time. Select OnInitialUpdate from the Messages list and add the function to the class. Add the following code to **OnInitialUpdate()**:

```
void CScrollStaticView::OnInitialUpdate()
{
    CView::OnInitialUpdate();

    // Get the full width of the view window
    CRect rect;
    GetClientRect(&rect);

    // Make the scrolling field the top 40 pixels high
    rect.bottom = rect.top + 40;

    // Create the scrolling static field
    m_pScrollStatic = new CScrollStatic();
    m_pScrollStatic->Create(_T("This is a silly test"), rect, this);
}
```

2 You'll also need to add the declaration for **m_pScrollStatic** to the **CScrollStaticView** class header as follows:

```
CScrollStatic* m_pScrollStatic;
```

3 Now make sure that the pointer is initialized in the constructor and the associated memory freed in the destructor for the view:

```
CScrollStaticView::CScrollStaticView()
{
    m_pScrollStatic = NULL;
}

CScrollStaticView::~CScrollStaticView()
{
    if (m_pScrollStatic)
        delete m_pScrollStatic;
}
```

4 Finally, you'll need to add **#include "ScrollStatic.h"** to the beginning of **ScrollStatic Project.cpp** and **ScrollStaticView.cpp** just below the line **#include StdAfx.h**. Now you can compile and run the application. When the view is displayed, you should see the text This is a silly test scrolling across the top of the view as shown here.

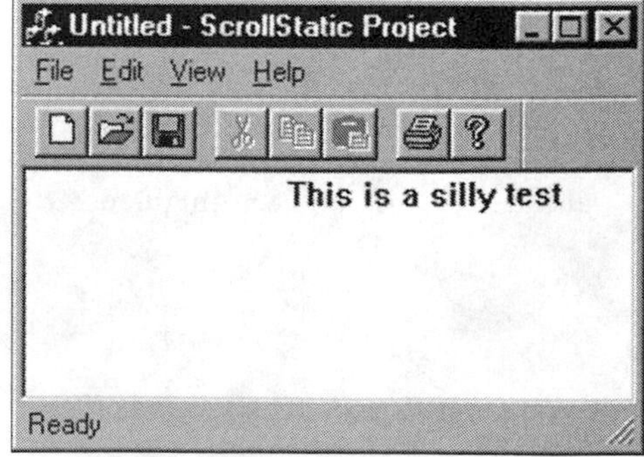

Testing the Control

Since this control supports no user interaction, it might seem that there's little we can test that hasn't already been tested in our sample program. In fact, not all of the tests are done. We haven't considered setting the text at run time, changing the colors, or changing the font. You should consider that to be your challenge for the day.

In addition, try some other things, like passing a **`NULL`** string for the text in **`SetText()`**, or providing a string longer than the width of the control. See what happens and whether the control adequately handles these scenarios (and anything else you can dream up). This is your control! Don't let it get into your code with bugs in it! For now, though, we'll move on to our next control.

The ActiveX Solution: The ShadeText Control

In trying to solve the problem of making the display more interesting and eye-catching we explored the use of motion in our MFC solution. In our ActiveX solution, we'll try adding color and shadow to make text stand out for the user.

The ShadeText control allows the programmer to define a control which displays text in a selected foreground and background color. It also allows the programmer to determine if the text should be shown with a shadow effect of the kind which was used to great advantage in the 'good old days' of DOS to create a 3D effect on text screens. As you can see here, it also has an impact on text shown in Windows.

As before, let's first consider a feature list for the ShadeText control, before we actually implement the code that creates the control.

Feature List

The shaded text control needs to allow the client programmer to change the following aspects of its appearance:

- The text that's displayed in the control.
- The foreground color of the control (the color of the text).
- The background color of the control (the color of the control window).
- The font in which the text is displayed (including size, family, pitch and emphasis).
- The alignment of the text within the control (left justified, right justified or centered).
- Whether or not the shadow effect appears.

In addition, the control needs to meet these requirements:

- We should be able to use this control in any environment which supports ActiveX controls (Visual Basic, Delphi, etc.) as well as Visual C++ itself.

- All the properties for the control must be modifiable both at compile time (a.k.a. design time) and run time.
- All the properties for the control should be **persistent**, by which we mean that the properties that are set in the design environment (Visual C++ resource editor or Visual Basic property window) must stay with the control when it's displayed.
- The control should provide a simple property sheet to display the available, configurable options for the control.

Although this seems like a lot to include in a control this simple, you'll see that the feature list we've included will make this control vastly more usable than if we had further simplified it.

Designing the Control

Designing an ActiveX control is a more complex job than designing an MFC extension class. Care must be taken to ensure that the control interface (the way the programmer 'talks' to the control) doesn't change dramatically between release versions. Although this is true of the published interfaces for MFC classes too, if you do change the interface for an MFC class, the compiler will usually point out the problem to the user of that class. There's no such protection with ActiveX controls.

This is especially important because ActiveX control **wrappers** (classes generated by ClassWizard to work with ActiveX controls imported into a project) aren't updated when the control itself changes. Later on, you'll learn how to force ClassWizard to regenerate a class wrapper for an ActiveX control, but for now you should approach the design of a control with respect for the problems you may cause later.

Another issue in designing and implementing ActiveX controls is remembering that you can use them in environments other than Visual C++. Unlike MFC extension classes, which may rely on the programmer having access to MFC classes and types, ActiveX controls may be used in Visual Basic or Delphi, which do not have access to these classes. For this reason, it's important to make sure that you only use acceptable OLE types in your design.

The `ShadeText` control needs to implement the standard OLE `IUnknown` interface. It must also register itself, save its properties in a persistent fashion, and provide a property sheet display for setting its properties. Fortunately, all of these things are provided (almost) for free by Visual C++ and the ControlWizard. For our purposes, therefore, we can simply worry about the real needs of the control in this design.

Our control needs to be able to display user-defined text and background colors. In our scrolling text control, we defined our own functions to set and get the colors. In ActiveX controls, however, we don't define our interfaces this way. Rather, we use **OLE properties** to allow the user to set the values for control. For this and all future ActiveX controls we design, we should think in terms of the properties to which we need to allow the user access. Allowing access to a property is often referred to as **publishing** it.

Properties

From our requirements list we can see that we need a number of properties:

- `Text` (for the string to display)
- `ForeColor` (the color of the text)

- **BackColor** (the color of the control window)
- **Font** (the style of the text)

All of these are known as **stock properties**. Stock properties are simply properties that are commonly used in ActiveX controls and for which a default implementation is provided by **COleControl**. Stock properties are great because we don't need to do much work to add them to our controls, as you'll see.

In addition to the stock properties, our **ShadeText** control also needs two **custom properties**:

- **Shadow** (a Boolean value indicating whether we should show the shadow)
- **Alignment** (defines the justification—left, right, or center)

When defining an interface for your controls, it's a good idea to do a bit of research on the ActiveX controls that are already out there so that you conform to the standards. Visual Basic users are still the major consumers of ActiveX Controls, so anything you can do to make your controls usable in their environment is welcome.

For example, Visual Basic comes with a couple of text controls that use an **Alignment** property to determine whether text is displayed left-justified, right-justified or centered. We could have called the property that determines the same thing in our control **Justification** (you might feel this is a more descriptive name for the property), but rather than alienate or confuse the users of the Visual Basic controls with a new property name for essentially the same thing, we chose to stick with **Alignment**.

Since our control is very simple, we won't need any methods as the properties allow us to accomplish everything we need. Now that we've established all the work we need to do, we're ready for the next stage of the development process.

Implementing the Control

We will now create a new project in Visual C++ and implement the functionality of the control within that project. The implementation breaks down into three parts:

- First, we'll create a new project and expose the properties for the ActiveX control. This will define the interface for the control.
- Second, we will implement the functions that will be used in this control.
- Finally, we will enhance the usability of the control by adding property sheets.

TRY IT OUT - Create a ShadeText ActiveX Control

1 Create a new project workspace with the name **ShadeText** using the OLE ControlWizard. You can click the Finish button right on Step 1 of the ControlWizard since we don't need to change any of the options from their defaults. This will create a project containing a single control, not derived from any existing Windows control.

2 To define the properties for the control, enter ClassWizard and select the **CShadeTextCtrl** object from the object list. Select the OLE Automation tab. Click on the Add Property... button on the page. Use this process for each property that we discuss in the following sections.

3 The first property we will add to the control is the **Text** property. This will represent the text that is to be displayed in the control at run time. To add the property, select Text in the External Name combo box. Since **Text** is a stock property (that is, it has a default implementation provided by **COleControl**) you will not need to fill in any other information.

4 Now repeat the process for the next three stock properties: **BackColor**, **ForeColor**, and **Font**. In each case, simply select the property's name from the External Name combo box and click the OK button. At the end of this step, the OLE Automation tab should like this:

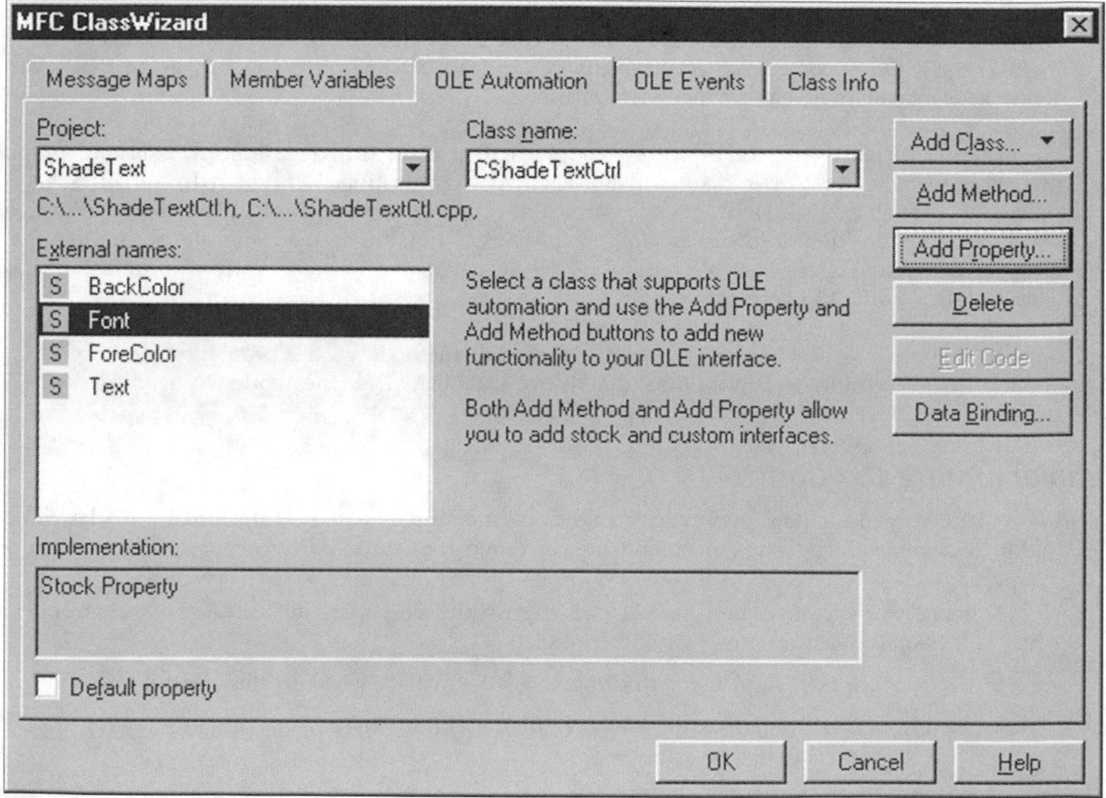

5 The next property to define is a custom property, so we'll need to provide ClassWizard with a few more details about it when we add it to our control. First type the name Shadow into the External Name field then choose BOOL as its Type. This property represents a flag set by the user to indicate whether they would like a 3D shadow displayed in the control under the text.

Change the Variable name to m_bShadow and accept the defaults for the Notification function and Implementation. This will provide us with a function called **OnShadowChanged()** that will be called whenever the **Shadow** property is changed at design or run time. The value of the **Shadow** property will be stored in a **private** variable in our **CShadowTextCtrl** class called **m_bShadow**.

6 The final property we need to define is the **Alignment** custom property. This property should be given an External Name of Alignment and a Type of long. Change the Variable name to m_lAlignment and leave the other settings at their defaults.

7 Now on ClassWizard's OLE Automation tab, highlight the Text property by clicking on it in the External Names list and make it the default property by checking the Default property checkbox at the bottom of the dialog. This allows the **Text** property to be used from a language like Visual Basic without having to state it explicitly. For example, instead of using

```
ShadeText1.Text = "Some String"
```

you could use

```
ShadeText1 = "Some String"
```

to mean the same thing.

At this stage, the OLE Automation tab will look like this:

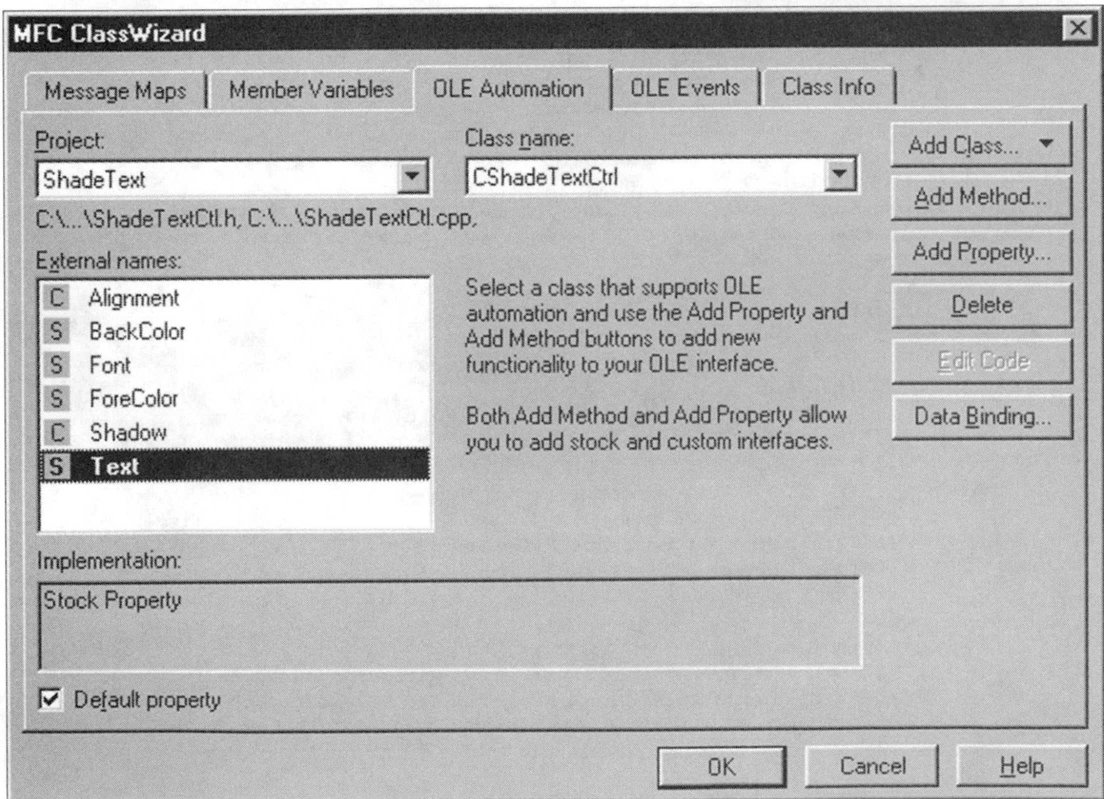

8 Now that we've defined the properties for our class using ClassWizard, it's time to get our hands dirty and tweak some of the code that ClassWizard has generated for us. Since we're just concentrating on the interface to the control at the moment, we'll just be altering some of the code generated in the **.odl** file. Remember that the **.odl** file is compiled by **Mktyplib.exe** to create a type library (**.tlb**) file. It's the type library for a control that's used by languages such as Visual C++ and Visual Basic to determine the facilities offered by a control, so it's important that we get it right.

Open up **ShadeText.odl** in the Developer Studio editor and make the changes to the file shown highlighted below. (We haven't shown the complete file here, just enough of it so that you can see where to make the changes.)

```
#include <olectl.h>
#include <idispids.h>

[ uuid(672F16C0-F9E5-11CF-AB39-0020AF71E433), version(1.0),
  helpstring("Wrox ShadeText Control"), control ]
library ShadeTextLib
{
   importlib(STDOLE_TLB);
   importlib(STDTYPE_TLB);

   typedef [uuid(672F16CF-F9E5-11CF-AB39-0020AF71E433),
            helpstring("Alignment constants")]
            enum {
                  [helpstring("Left Justify")]  wrxLeftJustify = 0,
                  [helpstring("Right Justify")] wrxRightJustify,
                  [helpstring("Center")]        wrxCenter,
                  } AlignmentConstants;

   //  Primary dispatch interface for CShadeTextCtrl
   [ uuid(672F16C1-F9E5-11CF-AB39-0020AF71E433),
     helpstring("Dispatch interface for ShadeText Control"), hidden ]
   dispinterface _DShadeText
   {

      properties:
         // NOTE - ClassWizard will maintain property information here.
         //    Use extreme caution when editing this section.
         //{{AFX_ODL_PROP(CShadeTextCtrl)
         [id(DISPID_TEXT), bindable, requestedit] BSTR Text;
         [id(DISPID_FORECOLOR), bindable, requestedit] OLE_COLOR ForeColor;
         [id(DISPID_BACKCOLOR), bindable, requestedit] OLE_COLOR BackColor;
         [id(DISPID_FONT), bindable] IFontDisp* Font;
         [id(1)] boolean Shadow;
         [id(2)] AlignmentConstants Alignment;
         [id(0), hidden] BSTR _Text;
         //}}AFX_ODL_PROP

      methods:
         // NOTE - ClassWizard will maintain method information here.
         //    Use extreme caution when editing this section.
         //{{AFX_ODL_METHOD(CShadeTextCtrl)
         //}}AFX_ODL_METHOD

         [id(DISPID_ABOUTBOX)] void AboutBox();
   };
```

The first thing that we've done here is to change the **helpstring** and the name for the type library. These will be visible to users of our control, so we need to make sure they're descriptive and readable. It's standard practice to prefix the library **helpstring** with your company name and it's more readable to have a mixed case library name.

The next thing we've done is add an enumeration to the library. This holds constants that the user of our control can pass to the **Alignment** property. We used the GUID Generator applet from Developer Studio's Component Gallery to create the **uuid** number for this enumeration. The names of the constants follow the standard convention for constants appearing in type libraries—they start with a lowercase prefix indicating the company or library that defines the constants (we've used **wrx** for Wrox) and are followed by a mixed case name describing the use of the constant.

The next thing we do is to change the data type for the **Alignment** property from **long** to **AlignmentConstants**. This forges the link between the enumeration we set up and the **Alignment** property. This is particularly useful in Visual Basic because now VB will add the constants we've defined in the enumeration into a drop-down list in the Properties window, so we have just limited the user of our class to using only sensible values for the **Alignment** property at design time. The **helpstring** that we used for each constant will also appear in the list to provide a helpful description to the user.

The next shaded line of code shows that we have added a **hidden** tag to the **_Text** property. You might be wondering how the **_Text** property got there in the first place since we never said that we'd like to add a property called **_Text**, only one called **Text**. The answer is that this line was added when we chose **Text** to be the default property for the control. When you choose a property as the default, ClassWizard will automatically use the name of the property and prefix it with an underscore and assign it to **id(0)** in the **.odl** file. The property with **id(0)** is the default property for any control.

This works fine, but it means that any type library browsers will show two properties for our control: **Text** and **_Text**. Of course, to all intents and purposes this is the same property, so we want to prevent **_Text** showing up in the browser to prevent people getting confused. The **hidden** tag will do this for us (for any type library browsers that respect this attribute, anyway).

9 Now you can compile the project and test it out. Don't expect too much in the way of functionality at the moment, but you will be able to see that the interface for the properties is there and the type library is complete. You can use the OLE Control Test Container to test the control (select Tools | OLE Control Test Container) or create a new Visual C++ project and add the control to it from the Component Gallery. You'll be able to see the header file that's created for the control based on its type library.

If you have Visual Basic, create a new project and add the ShadeText control to it. If you add a ShadeText control to the form, you'll be able to see the properties in the Properties window. Also, try pressing *F2* to bring up the Object Browser and look at the type library for the control.

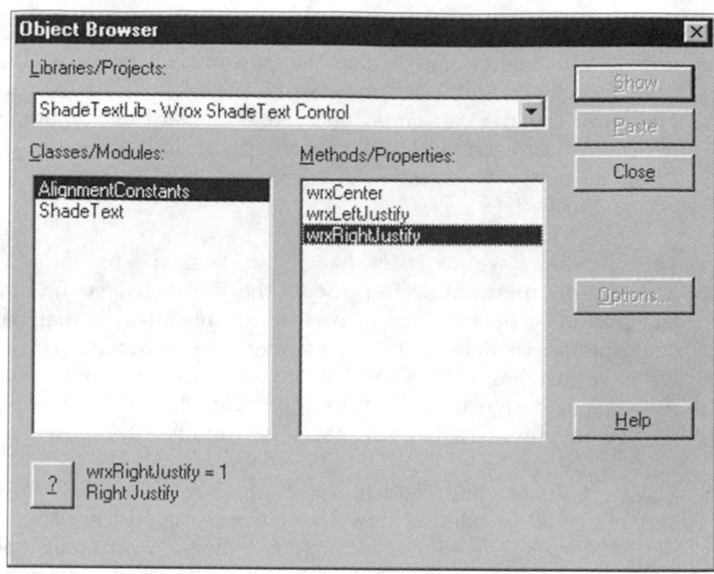

TRY IT OUT - Implement the ShadeText Control

1 Once the properties are defined in our control's interface, our next step is to provide the implementation for the control. You should modify the functions in **ShadeTextCtl.cpp** as follows:

```
void CShadeTextCtrl::OnShadowChanged()
{
   SetModifiedFlag();
   InvalidateControl();
}

void CShadeTextCtrl::OnAlignmentChanged()
{
   SetModifiedFlag();
   InvalidateControl();
}
```

The **SetModifiedFlag()** function call in the above methods simply indicates to the **COleControl** base class that this object is 'dirty' and needs to be updated. The **InvalidateControl()** method will cause the control to be repainted. Since we're changing display attributes here, this is the best way to handle the situation—by redrawing the control to reflect these changes.

2 The next step is to modify the **OnDraw()** function for the ActiveX control. **OnDraw()** is called to display the control in a dialog or other window. Enter the following code into **CShadeTextCtrl::OnDraw()**:

```
void CShadeTextCtrl::OnDraw(
        CDC* pdc, const CRect& rcBounds, const CRect& rcInvalid)
{
   const int SHADOW_WIDTH = 5;
   const int SHADOW_HEIGHT = 5;

   CBrush brBack(TranslateColor(GetBackColor()));
   CBrush brFore(TranslateColor(GetForeColor()));

   // Get the parent window
   CRect rectFore = rcBounds;

   pdc->SetBkMode(TRANSPARENT);

   if (m_bShadow)
   {
      CBrush brAmbientBack;
      brAmbientBack.CreateSolidBrush(TranslateColor(AmbientBackColor()));
      pdc->FillRect(rectFore, &brAmbientBack);
      rectFore.right -= SHADOW_WIDTH;
      rectFore.bottom -= SHADOW_HEIGHT;
   }

   // Clear the background of the window
   pdc->FillRect(rectFore, &brBack);

   // Draw the text in the rectangle centered
   CRect rect;
   rect = rectFore;
   if (GetEnabled())
      pdc->SetTextColor(TranslateColor(GetForeColor()));
   else
      pdc->SetTextColor(GetSysColor(COLOR_GRAYTEXT));

   // Get the type of justification to use
   UINT opt = DT_CENTER;

   switch (m_lAlignment)
   {
      case wrxLeftJustify:
         rect.left += 2;
         opt = DT_LEFT;
         break;
      case wrxRightJustify:
         opt = DT_RIGHT;
         rect.right -= 2;
         break;
      default:
         opt = DT_CENTER;
```

```
            break;
        }

        CFont* pOldFont = SelectStockFont(pdc);
        pdc->DrawText(GetText(), rect, opt | DT_VCENTER | DT_SINGLELINE);
        pdc->SelectObject(pOldFont);

        // Take care of shadow if necessary
        if (m_bShadow)
        {
            CBrush brShadow(RGB(128,128,128));           // Gray shadow
            CRect rectTemp = rcBounds;
            rectTemp.top = rectTemp.bottom - SHADOW_HEIGHT;
            rectTemp.left += SHADOW_WIDTH;
            pdc->FillRect(rectTemp, &brShadow);
            rectTemp = rcBounds;
            rectTemp.left = rectTemp.right - SHADOW_WIDTH;
            rectTemp.top += SHADOW_HEIGHT;
            pdc->FillRect(rectTemp, &brShadow);
        }
    }
```

The thing to watch out for when coding **OnDraw()** for ActiveX controls is that the device context passed to **OnDraw()** may represent a device context for the control's window or it may represent a **metafile**. Many environments such as Visual Basic and Visual C++'s dialog editor don't actually create a window for the control at design time, but instead ask the control to display itself via a metafile. This means that you should be careful not to assume that your control has a window in **OnDraw()** and that you don't take any actions on the device context that are incompatible with metafiles. Metafiles only support a subset of the device context class (**CDC**) functionality. You can find a list of the functions that are supported if you search for metafiles, painting OLE controls in the online help.

> *To ensure that you haven't made any assumptions about how your control will behave in a container, it's a good idea to test it in as many containers as possible. You will be able to test your controls in the Visual C++ dialog editor and the OLE Control Test Container at the very least, and it's always a good idea to test your control in Visual Basic if you have access to it.*

3 Now we'll add to the header file for our control the enumeration that defines the constants **wrxLeftJustify**, etc. Open **ShadeTextCtl.h** and add the following line to the class definition for **CShadeTextCtrl**.

```
    enum {wrxLeftJustify = 0, wrxRightJustify, wrxCenter};
```

4 The next step is to update the constructor for the class and **OnResetState()** to reset the property values to their default states when the control is first created and during run-time execution. Add the following code to the constructor **CShadeTextCtrl::CShadeTextCtrl()**:

```
    CShadeTextCtrl::CShadeTextCtrl()
    {
        InitializeIIDs(&IID_DShadeText, &IID_DShadeTextEvents);
        ResetControl();         // Set properties to default values
    }
```

Now add the same line of code to **CShadeTextCtrl::OnResetState()**:

```
void CShadeTextCtrl::OnResetState()
{
    COleControl::OnResetState();  // Resets defaults found in DoPropExchange
    ResetControl();               // Set properties to default values
}
```

5 Now we need to create **CShadeTextCtrl::ResetControl()**, so add the following code to **ShadeTextCtl.h.**

```
// Implementation
protected:
    ~CShadeTextCtrl();
    void ResetControl();
```

The implementation for this function should go in **ShadeTextCtl.cpp** as shown below.

```
void CShadeTextCtrl::ResetControl()
{
    SetText(_T(""));                     // No text
    SetBackColor(RGB(192,192,192));      // Light gray background
    SetForeColor(RGB(0,0,0));            // Black text
    m_lAlignment = wrxCenter;            // Center text
    m_bShadow = FALSE;                   // Don't show shadow
}
```

6 For the final piece of the control class, we must make sure that the settings for the custom properties are properly stored when necessary, so that the control looks the same at run time as it does at design time. This is accomplished in the **DoPropExchange()** method of the class. In this case, we have only two properties which are non-stock properties (the stock properties are stored automatically by the code in **COleControl**). Add the following code to the **DoPropExchange()** method to make them persistent:

```
void CShadeTextCtrl::DoPropExchange(CPropExchange* pPX)
{
    ExchangeVersion(pPX, MAKELONG(_wVerMinor, _wVerMajor));
    COleControl::DoPropExchange(pPX);

    PX_Bool(pPX, _T("Shadow"), m_bShadow, FALSE);
    PX_Long(pPX, _T("Alignment"), m_lAlignment, wrxCenter);
}
```

Note that the **PX_** macros are all of the same format:

- The first argument to the macro is the property exchange variable. This is used to provide an environment-independent method of storing the property values. In Visual C++, this exchange variable allows property information to be stored in the resource file. In Visual Basic, the information is stored in the **.frm** file for the form which contains the control. It's up to the control container where persistent properties are stored and it makes no difference to you as a control creator.
- The second argument is the external name we defined for the property. This corresponds to the External Name field in ClassWizard's OLE Automation Add Property... dialog.

- Next, the member variable which holds the information is used.
- Finally, the default value (if any) for the property is placed.

These macros are all 'two-way': they're used to store information during design time, and load information at run time. If you have specific functionality which you only want at load time or at save time, you can use the **pPX** object to see the state of the function as follows:

```
if (pPX->IsLoading())
   ; // Load-time code here
else
   ; // Save-time code here
```

At this point your control is complete from a functional viewpoint. You can compile and test it using the container of your choice.

> *Windows NT users should note that many versions of Windows NT 3.51 have a bug that will prevent you from recompiling the control if you've used it in a dialog of a running session of Visual C++. If this happens to you, the compiler will report that it couldn't open the* **.ocx** *file for the control (***ShadeText.ocx** *in our case) for writing. If this happens, close the Visual C++ session and restart it. You should then be able to compile and link your ActiveX control.*

However, although it might seem that we're done, there's still a bit left to do before we can call this a professional control. You'll notice that in the Test Container, selecting the control and then selecting the Edit | Properties... menu option will display the properties dialog shown opposite. Obviously, we don't want the user to see a TODO string when they use our control, so we'll have to do something about it.

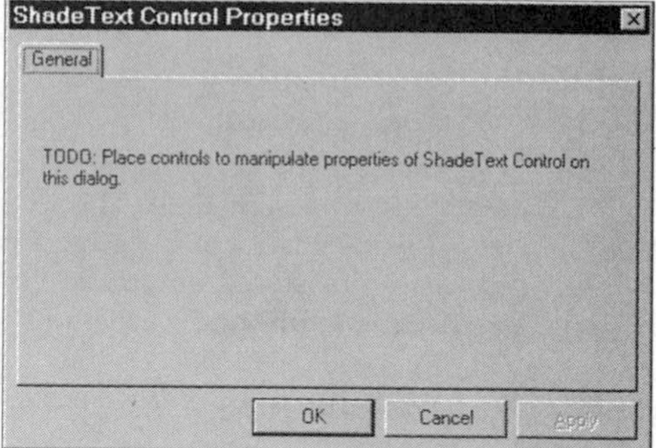

A property sheet is essentially a dialog that allows the user to set the properties for your control. You should place controls on it such as list boxes, check boxes and text fields to allow them to do this. We'll see how to do that now.

TRY IT OUT - Enhancing the ShadeText Control

1. To fix up the property sheet for the ShadeText control, select the **IDD_PROPPAGE_SHADETEXT** dialog entry from the ResourceView and open it in the resource editor. Start to modify the dialog by removing the static text field.

2. Now, add a single static text field that reads Text: and place next to it an edit box. Change the ID of the edit box to **IDC_EDIT_TEXT**.

3 Next, add a static text field that reads Alignment: and place a combo box next to it. Change the ID of the combo box to **IDC_COMBO_ALIGNMENT**. On the Styles page of the combo box's property sheet change its Type to Drop List. On the General page, add the following strings to the Enter listbox items box (you'll need to press *Ctrl-Enter* to go to a new line in the list):

0 - Left justify
1 - Right justify
2 - Center

4 Finally, add a check box with the caption Shadow and change its ID to **IDC_CHECK_SHADOW**. When you're finished, you should end up with a dialog that looks something like this:

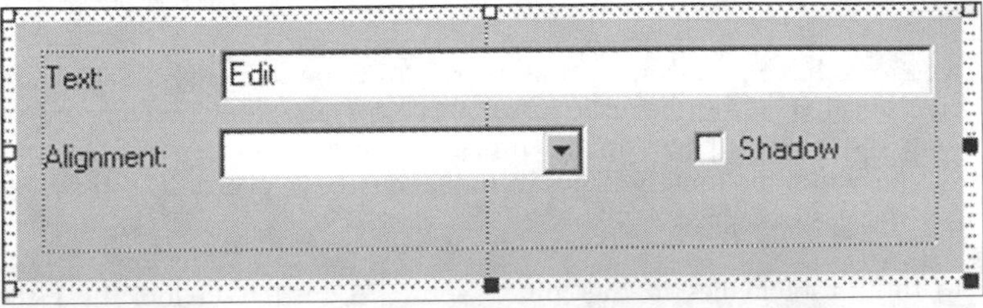

5 Enter ClassWizard and select CShadeTextPropPage from the Object IDs drop-down list box. Select the Member Variables tab and click on the **IDC_EDIT_TEXT** object in the Control IDs list. Click on the Add Variable... button. Enter **m_strText** for the name of the variable and select Text from the Optional OLE property name drop-down box. You can leave the other fields at their default settings. Click OK to close the dialog.

6 In a similar way, add a variable for the value of the **IDC_COMBO_ALIGNMENT** combo box. Call the member variable **m_nAlignment** and type Alignment as the Optional OLE property name.

7 Finally, use the same process again to add a member variable for the value of the **IDC_CHECK_SHADOW** check box. Use **m_bShadow** as the variable name and type Shadow as the Optional OLE property name.

When you've finished this process and clicked OK in ClassWizard, the wizard will add the following function to the **ShadeTextPpg.cpp** file:

```
void CShadeTextPropPage::DoDataExchange(CDataExchange* pDX)
{
    //{{AFX_DATA_MAP(CShadeTextPropPage)
    DDP_Text(pDX, IDC_EDIT_TEXT, m_strText, _T("Text") );
    DDX_Text(pDX, IDC_EDIT_TEXT, m_strText);
    DDP_CBIndex(pDX, IDC_COMBO_ALIGNMENT, m_nAlignment, _T("Alignment") );
    DDX_CBIndex(pDX, IDC_COMBO_ALIGNMENT, m_nAlignment);
    DDP_Check(pDX, IDC_CHECK_SHADOW, m_bShadow, _T("Shadow") );
    DDX_Check(pDX, IDC_CHECK_SHADOW, m_bShadow);
    //}}AFX_DATA_MAP
    DDP_PostProcessing(pDX);
}
```

This code accomplishes two things. The **DDX** macros simply do the normal MFC job of exchanging data between the Windows controls in the dialog and the member variables given to them. The **DDP** macros, however, exchange data between the associated ActiveX control properties and the member variables. In this way you needn't add any code to make the property sheet automatically assign the entered data to the ActiveX control.

8 This would appear to complete the process. We've defined the control logic, including properties and methods. We've defined the property page for the dialog, which allows the user to set the justification, text, and shadow flag properties of the control. Just a minute, though! What about those other properties we defined? **ForeColor**, **BackColor**, and **Font** are defined stock properties for the ActiveX control, but currently we have no way to access them from our property sheet. Do we need to write more property pages for them?

Fortunately, we don't have to do all of this work. MFC implements a set of stock property pages for ActiveX controls that allow the user to set the color and font. Even more importantly, by simply including those stock pages in the property sheet for the control, *all* properties which are of the proper type (color or font) will be included on these pages. The only remaining issue is how to include these stock pages.

The answer to this problem lies in the control source code. If you look near the top of the **CShadeTextCtrl** source file (**ShadeTextCtl.cpp**, unless you changed the name) you will find a macro map entitled **BEGIN_PROPPAGEIDS**. This map will define all of the property pages that will be displayed when the property sheet for the control is brought up. At present, it will look something like this:

```
// TODO: Add more property pages as needed
// Remember to increase the count!
BEGIN_PROPPAGEIDS(CShadeTextCtrl, 1)
   PROPPAGEID(CShadeTextPropPage::guid)
END_PROPPAGEIDS(CShadeTextCtrl)
```

To add the color and font pages, modify the map to look like this:

```
BEGIN_PROPPAGEIDS(CShadeTextCtrl, 3)
   PROPPAGEID(CShadeTextPropPage::guid)
   PROPPAGEID(CLSID_CColorPropPage)
   PROPPAGEID(CLSID_CFontPropPage)
END_PROPPAGEIDS(CShadeTextCtrl)
```

Congratulations! You have just written your first complete (and fairly polished) ActiveX control. Compile it in Visual C++ and test it in the Test Container (as shown on the next page) or the resource editor.

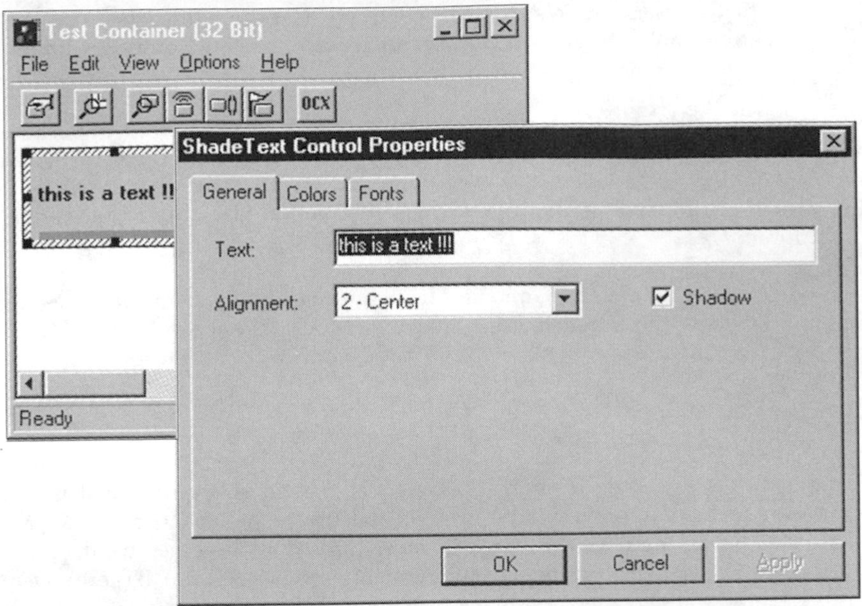

For completeness, you might want to modify the icon which is displayed when the control is added to the resource editor control palette or to the toolbar in the Test Container. To do this, edit the **IDB_SHADETEXT** bitmap in the resource editor.

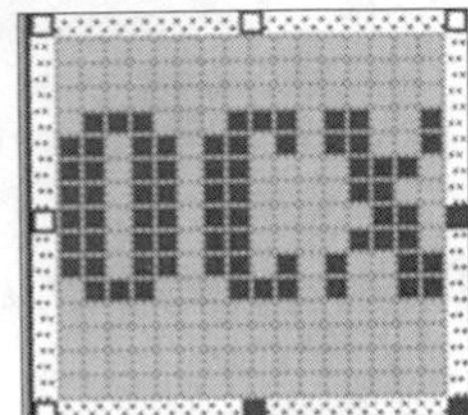

Comparing the MFC and ActiveX Solutions

After writing solutions in the form of both an MFC extension and an ActiveX control, the obvious question is: which one is better? The answer, of course, is neither. MFC extensions have benefits and drawbacks, as do ActiveX controls. The problem is deciding for a given situation whether the benefits of one solution outweigh its drawbacks, and whether the drawbacks of one solution are less significant than the benefits of the other. Let's take a look at the differences, and how those differences lead to decisions.

Distribution

The first difference is in distribution format. ActiveX controls require a separate **.ocx** file that must be registered with Windows in order to be used. MFC extensions, on the other hand, can be compiled into your application and distributed inside of the executable. This can be an advantage when installing and debugging.

If there are multiple versions of an ActiveX control running around on a system, strange errors can occur. Versioning is built into ActiveX controls, but must be maintained correctly. The flip side of this coin, however, is that changes to an MFC extension require that you ship an entirely new application to the user, whereas ActiveX controls can be modified (so long as they remain backwards compatible) and shipped to the user to replace existing controls without updating the applications that use them.

Either solution will work, but the factor to be taken into account is your application. If you're going to be updating controls on a regular basis, to work with new types of hardware for example, you would want to follow the ActiveX route. On the other hand, if you don't want to ship many files for your application, to keep the distribution size small, you would want to use the MFC solution.

All MFC-based ActiveX controls require the MFC run-time dynamic-link libraries, as do most MFC programs (at least those dynamically linked to MFC). The size of the MFC DLL is large, but doesn't help us differentiate between MFC-based controls or extensions.

Use

The next difference is in usage. If your application is written solely in Visual C++ using MFC, there's no reason to incur the overhead and speed hit of an ActiveX control. An MFC extension will certainly do the job and will be faster in most cases. On the other hand, if you have multiple applications written in different environments, such as Visual Basic or Delphi, then you will almost certainly want to use the ActiveX solution. MFC extensions can be bound into dynamic-link libraries (DLLs) and called by these other environments, but the process for users in those languages is much more difficult than with an ActiveX control. The small amount of extra effort you need to turn an MFC extension into an ActiveX control rather than a standard DLL is well worth it if Visual Basic or Delphi users are of concern to you.

Maintenance

A third consideration is maintainability. While MFC extensions can be modified (and the header files updated to accommodate these modifications) quite easily, ActiveX controls require more work to change. If you're using MFC and change the header file for an extension control, the compiler will automatically recompile all source modules which include this header file. With ActiveX controls, Visual C++ and the ClassWizard will generate a wrapper class for the control at the time the control is initially embedded in the application. This wrapper class will not be modified if the control changes. Since this is a common event during the development phase of a project, it leads to many problems. Programs that worked previously will suddenly crash or behave in an erratic or unexpected fashion without any code or linking changes. This can lead to long and frustrating debugging sessions.

Updating ActiveX Wrapper Classes

If you need to modify an ActiveX control and will be changing the interface (adding or subtracting properties or methods), follow this procedure to update your Visual C++ project.

Note that you should really only *add* new properties and methods to ActiveX controls. Removing them from released controls will break existing code and make developers using your controls very angry!

Remove the files for the wrapper class from your project. For example, if Visual C++ had generated a class of the name **CShadeText** for the ActiveX control we just developed, that class will be found in **ShadeText.cpp** and **ShadeText.h**. Remove **ShadeText.cpp** from your project and remove all references to **ShadeText.h** from all source modules in the application. Make a note of which files contain references to the header file as you do so.

Remove the source files and header files for the control (in this case **ShadeText.cpp** and **ShadeText.h**) from the project directory.

Open the project makefile (**.mak**) as a text file. Find the section which lists the name of the source module (**ShadeText.cpp**). This will be towards the bottom of the makefile in a section that contains the string **OCX**. Delete the entire section.

Enter the resource editor and select a dialog or property page which contains the ActiveX control. Delete the member variable associated with the control in ClassWizard's Member Variables page. Re-add the member variable (with the same name).

ClassWizard will now inform you that no wrapper class has been generated for this control. Allow it to regenerate the file.

Re-add the header file to all the modules that you removed it from. Recompile your source code and the control will be in sync with the wrapper class.

Design

A further consideration between the two solutions is who will do the design. If you're going to have programmers doing the majority of the design of the application and resources (dialogs), MFC extensions are as good a solution as ActiveX controls. If, however, you will have a third party (such as a GUI designer) creating the resources for the application, you have a deeper problem. In most cases, GUI designers aren't programmers. They work with the user interface and the look and feel of the application. Because of this, they would prefer to see the design as it will appear to the user. Since MFC extensions don't have the same appearance in the resource editor as they do during run time, ActiveX controls may be the preferred solution.

Consider for a moment the solution we have just presented in this chapter. In the case of the scrolling text static field we created as an MFC extension, the designer would have to place a dummy field in the place where they wanted the control to appear. Since the dummy control doesn't have the background color, text color, or font of the final extension control, it wouldn't allow the designer to see the dialog as it would be for the user. This is a problem that often leads to changes in the user interface design at a later date, which can cause grief for the developer and slips in the development schedule.

With the ActiveX solution, the **ShadeText** control, the designer will be able to specify exactly what the control will look like at both design and run time. Furthermore, the designer can save those run-time attributes (such as text color and font) at design time and be assured that the control will have those same attributes at run time. This can be an important difference when considering which solution you would like to use.

From the programmer's viewpoint, the two controls can differ greatly. In the case of an MFC extension, the programmer is assured that any display routines which are called (such as **OnPaint()** or **OnDraw()**) are guaranteed to be called only when the control actually exists on the user's screen. An MFC extension control can be used only in an active dialog or view window. ActiveX controls, on the other hand, need to concern themselves not only with the run-time active window case, but also with the design-time case. This can lead to problems—an improperly written ActiveX control can crash the resource editor in Visual C++.

Finally, we will note that if you're writing a control which is in a state of flux as to its final attributes and functionality, you would be better off using an MFC extension at first. It's not that difficult to change over from an MFC extension to an ActiveX control. The compile-time differences (changes to header files and implementation) are much simpler for extension controls than for ActiveX controls. Until this deficiency is remedied in Visual C++, it will always be easier to modify an extension control than to import a new ActiveX control into an application project.

Summary

Looking back over the chapter, let's review what we've discovered:

- Windows provides little in the way of a 'snazzy' textual display for dialogs and other windows.
- Both MFC extension classes and ActiveX controls can be used to create a new type of display object.
- Creation of MFC extension classes is done by using ClassWizard to derive a class in an existing project, while ActiveX controls are separate projects which result in **`.ocx`** files.
- ActiveX controls contain properties which may be set and saved at design time, while MFC extensions can only be completely defined at run time by the programmer.
- ActiveX controls exist in one of two states. The first state is a design time 'paint only' mode, while the second state is the full run-time control. At design time, only display functionality is valid; no window functions will work properly.
- ActiveX controls can be tested using the Test Container application which is shipped with Visual C++.
- ActiveX controls can be used in either Visual C++, Visual Basic or many other environments, whereas MFC extension classes can be used only in Visual C++.
- ActiveX controls require separate files which must be shipped for installation, while MFC extensions can be bound into the application **`.exe`** file and shipped as a single unit.

Things to Try

Here are a few 'homework' assignments that you might try to gain a fuller understanding of how ActiveX controls and MFC extensions are implemented and work.

- Add a new property for the **`ShadeText`** control which represents the highlight color. Allow the user to modify the property at design time as well as at run time.
- Implement the scrolling text control as an ActiveX control instead of an MFC extension. What are the differences in performance? How would you create a scrolling text control

in a view, as we did with the MFC extension? You will find a complete scrolling text ActiveX control on the Wrox web site. Feel free to refer to it if you get stuck on your own implementation!

- Try to implement the **`ShadeText`** control as an MFC extension as well.

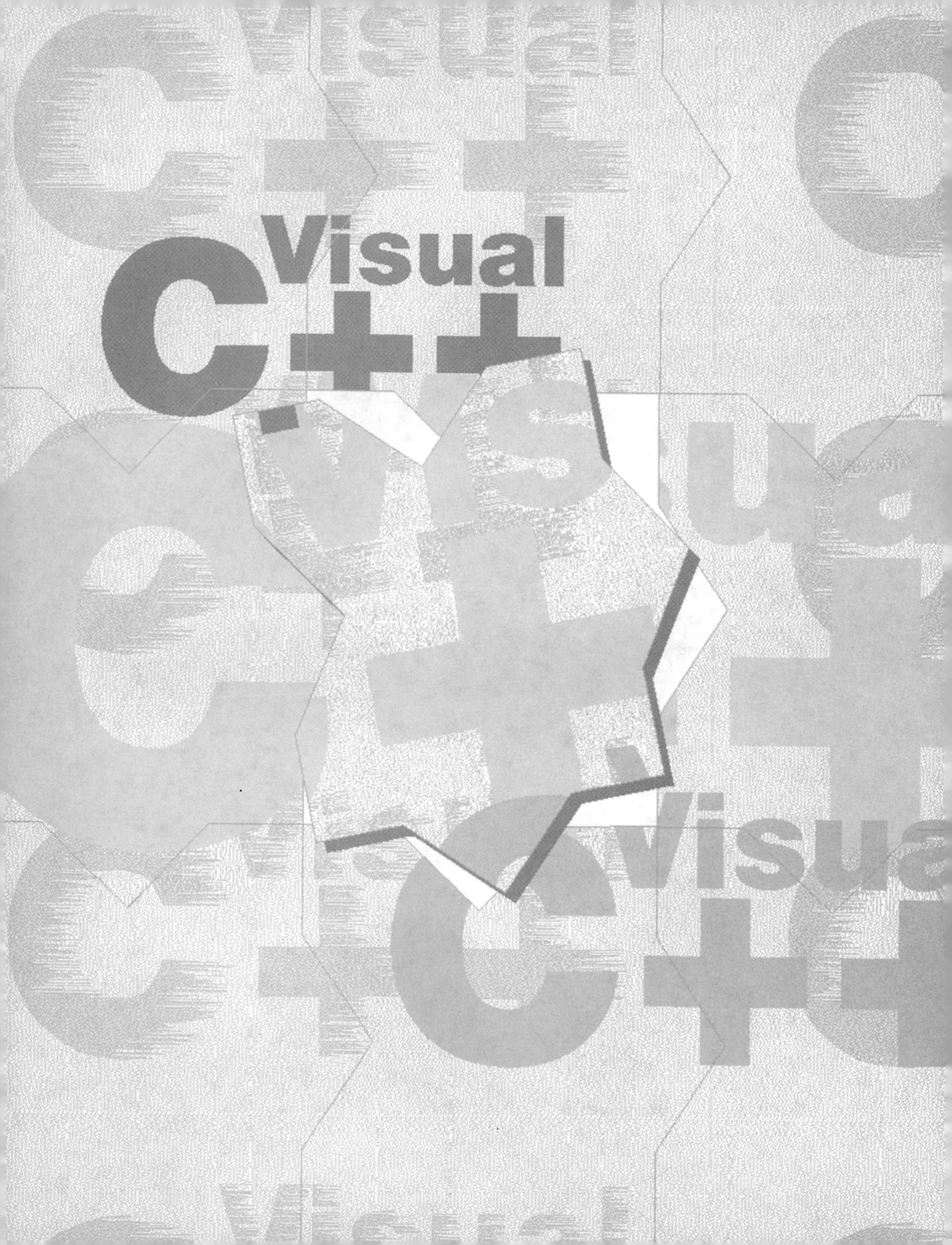
Visual
C++

Specialized Input Components

If there is one area of component technology that stands head and shoulders above the rest, it's that of user input. Components are uniquely qualified to handle specialized forms of input from the user, including validation and formatting. Components can be designed to handle specific cases, and can then be reused in any application which supports that form of input.

Consider, for a moment, the case of a standard US Social Security Number (SSN), which, for those outside the United States (or for those with very short memories inside the United States), is one of the most commonly used identification numbers in that country. The SSN has a standard format of 3 digits, a dash followed by 2 digits, another dash, and then finally 4 more digits. No SSN can have a format other than this and be valid.

Since the SSN is so common, many applications need to request an SSN from the user. In addition, it's helpful if these applications are able to verify that the number they have received from the user is valid (in form, if not in content). In other words, the SSN is a string which needs to be retrieved from the user that must follow certain clearly defined criteria. This makes SSN input a perfect candidate for component technology.

Another example, which is probably more applicable to the world at large, is the case of date input. Dates can be input in a variety of ways, but in a given application it's likely that only a single method would be appropriate.

In this chapter, we'll look at two very different ways to accept input from the user. In the first case, we'll examine how to get data via the keyboard, and then how to validate that input. Along the way, we'll develop a reusable MFC extension class that you can use for many types of validation input (such as the aforementioned SSN).

As an added bonus, we'll throw in a second MFC extension class which allows you to get numeric entries from the user in a simple calculator-style window.

Once we have examined the MFC extension cases, the next issue will be a calendar-style ActiveX control which allows the user to select a date from a familiar interface. The components have different advantages and disadvantages, and we'll examine these as we develop them. First, let's look at the overall problem which leads to the need for specialized input components.

The Problem

One of the biggest problems facing programmers writing Windows applications is a lack of support for validation. Windows provides check boxes, methods to input simple strings, radio buttons, and list boxes, but the basic Windows controls don't provide a way to get input from a user that adheres to a specific set of rules. Social Security Numbers, money, phone numbers, and other forms of input, have certain requirements that go along with them. In this chapter we'll discuss how to create reusable components that can overcome the limitations of the basic Windows controls in order to provide a set of validation objects that can be embedded in your applications.

The solutions to this problem are varied, but share a common root. We must provide a way for application programmers to ensure that the data they retrieve from the user is valid. MFC provides this functionality through **DDX** and **DDV** macros, but such methods suffer from one simple problem: they do the validation too late. There's nothing more annoying to a user than to complete a dialog and only then to find out that one of the fields at the very beginning of the dialog has invalid data in it. Users should always be informed at the earliest possible moment that a field is incorrect. In this chapter, we'll examine ways in which you can provide almost instant feedback on the validity of user input.

MFC Solution One: A Simple Input Validation Control

Imagine that you're trying to enter a Social Security Number into the dialog shown opposite. You can see from our description of SSNs at the start of the chapter, that the data entered into the SSN field is of the wrong format. In the normal course of events, the dialog would continue until the OK button was pressed, and only at that point would the dialog display an error message indicating that the SSN entered was incorrect.

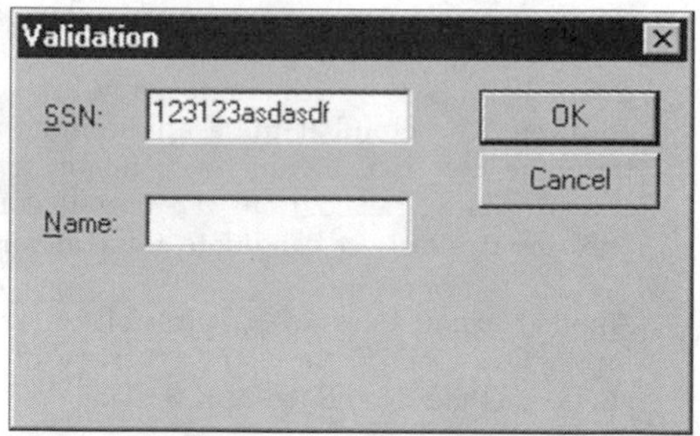

Now imagine that you have entered the data shown in the picture and then pressed the *Tab* key to move to the next field. In a perfect world, you would have a message box, such as the one shown opposite, displayed immediately. This would provide instant feedback to the user that the information entered was incorrect, and tell them what the problem was. An even better solution would be to then move the input focus back to the SSN field in order to make sure that the user corrected the problem before proceeding.

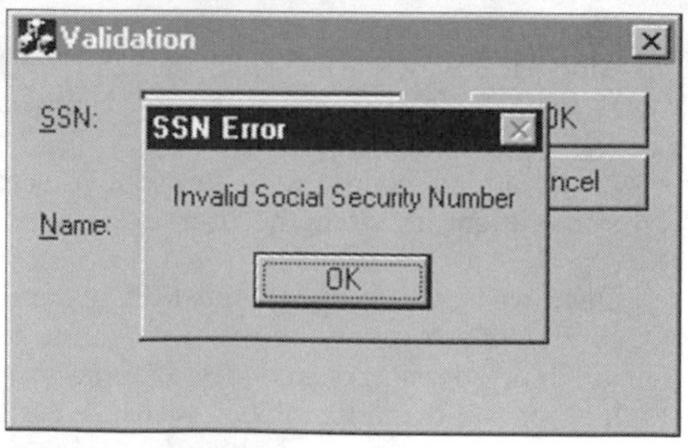

Before you finish imagining such a control, start to think about how you might implement it. Got a solution yet? Well, don't spend too much time worrying about it. This is exactly the control we will be designing in this section.

Feature List

Let's make a list of the kinds of things we would like to see in an object that validates input. Obviously, the main feature must be the ability to validate the input and reset the focus in the case of an error. Beyond this, though, we should consider the basic functionality that should be implemented in any control that will form the basic unit of display in a dialog or form view:

Ability to Turn Validation On and Off

Inevitably, a control that's supposed to validate user input should do exactly that, but sometimes the programmer will want to stop validation for reasons of efficiency. For example, you could have a batch entry system where the controls are loaded from an external function or even another program. We would have to assume that the input for these external sources was valid, since validating them field by field could easily mess up the batch entry. Perhaps we might want a sample entry form that simply displayed data for the user to view. Validation would slow down and might disrupt the process by forcing the programmer to find valid combinations of data. In either case, we don't want to make the programmer do something that they don't want or, indeed, need to do.

Ability to Set Colors

It makes sense that, if we're going to create a basic unit of display for a dialog, we allow the programmer complete control over that unit. Colors can be an interesting way to show users information about fields. If we expose the ability to set the colors for our control, we can leave it up to the user of our class to determine how they use those colors to impart information to the end user. They could, for example, use the color of the text to indicate whether the data is valid or not.

Ability to Set Formatting

It's useful to be able to display data in a set format which may vary by the field type. Money fields, for example, might be input as simple numeric entries (4.23, for example), but you would probably want to display them with an indication of the currency ($ 4.23). Similarly, an SSN without the separating dashes is just as valid as one that contains the dashes, but it's better to be able to display the data in the standard dash-delimited way, no matter how it has been input. By allowing the programmer access to this functionality, we extend the use and life of our component.

Ability to Retrieve Input

This is a more complex issue than it might seem. For simple edit fields, like a numeric one, or a standard type such as a date, the returned string might be the validated input string. For other input data, such as a Social Security Number, the input might contain extraneous information, such as the dashes that separate the three sub-fields. The programmer might not want those dashes in the version of the string they extract. Since this is a common problem, we should consider a way to filter the data before returning it to the application. This makes the component more reusable and extensible.

Designing the Control

Designing the basic validation control involves taking our feature list and examining the requirements behind each item in it. The first thing we can decide to do is base our control on

MFC's existing **CEdit** control. This gives us a basic input control on which to hang our own functionality.

Validation

For validation, we need only get the text entered into the edit control and apply a user-defined validation function to it. In our case, we want to provide flexibility to allow different forms of validation, so we must rely on the programmer using our class to do the work of writing the validation function. We'll call this validation function whenever our control loses focus, so this leads us to implement our class with a **virtual** function which determines whether the string is valid.

```
virtual BOOL IsValid();
```

The function will return **TRUE** if the text in the control is valid, and **FALSE** otherwise. Our default implementation will always return **TRUE**, effectively turning off validation.

If the function returns **FALSE**, a further **virtual** function is called to take any action that the programmer deems necessary:

```
virtual void DisplayError();
```

In our default implementation, this function will display a message box to the user, return the focus to the control and select the text.

Colors

The second item in our feature list called for us to be able to change the foreground and background color of the edit control. The prototypes for these functions are straightforward to decide upon:

```
public:
    COLORREF GetTextColor() const;
    COLORREF GetBackgroundColor() const;
    void SetTextColor(COLORREF clrText);
    void SetBackgroundColor(COLORREF clrBackground);
```

Formatting

The formatting of the displayed data will be performed by two **virtual** functions:

```
public:
    virtual CString GetFormattedData() const;
    virtual CString GetStrippedData() const;
```

The first of these, **GetFormattedData()**, is used to display the data once it has been validated and the control has lost focus. Thus, when the user enters some data and presses the *Tab* key, the validation function will be called. If the data entered is valid, the **GetFormattedData()** function will be called. This will then modify the string to its heart's content, and return it to the control, where it will be used as the text to be displayed. The default implementation will simply return the data as it was typed in.

When the control is re-entered, that is, when it regains focus, the **GetStrippedData()** function will be called to set the edit string to the 'real' version of the string. This, of course, doesn't need to be the data that was typed in originally, often it will be a stripped version, hence the name. The default implementation will simply return the data as it was typed in.

Retrieval of Data

You can see that both of the previous functions for returning data will be made **public**, so that they can be called from outside our class. They provide methods for returning the data formatted according to whatever rules the programmer requires, but it would also be a good idea to provide a function for returning the data that the user typed in originally, once validated:

```
public:
   CString GetOriginalData() const;
```

Storing the data that was typed in originally is useful if there is ever any confusion. It's often a lot easier to determine how, or whether, a mistake was made during input, if the original data is still to hand rather than just the formatted data. Again, the function is **public**, so that it can be accessed from outside the class, but it doesn't need to be **virtual**, since we're not going to provide a way for programmers to return fake data.

Rather than storing multiple versions of the data (original, formatted or stripped), we will only store the original data and pass that to the formatting functions as necessary.

Identifying Problems

Now that the overall class is defined, we need to consider some of the potential difficulties of the implementation. This planning ahead should ensure that we avoid some hurdles before getting too deep into the coding.

Focus

The most important feature of our control relies on our ability to detect the action of the user trying to exit our control. Fortunately, this is pretty easy, since the **WM_KILLFOCUS** message will always be sent when the control is losing the input focus, whether the user is tabbing away from our control or just using the mouse to click in another control.

Unfortunately, it's not as simple to deal with the **WM_KILLFOCUS** message as you might hope. One of the things that's absolutely prohibited in the processing of a **WM_KILLFOCUS** message, is to do anything that affects the focus of the control. The reason for this is logical: since you're in the middle of the **WM_KILLFOCUS** message, setting the focus to this or any other control will change the focus, leaving Windows in an unstable state (it will actually cause an infinite loop).

Since it's likely that **DisplayError()** will set the focus back to our control (in fact, our default implementation will do exactly that), we need to make sure that we don't call **DisplayError()** from within the **WM_KILLFOCUS** handler. How then are we to set the focus back to our control?

The answer is to post a message to ourselves indicating that the control validation failed (the only reason that we would be resetting the focus), and the handler for this message can then call **DisplayError()** with impunity, and reset the focus to itself.

Color

It was very easy for us to say that we'd allow the user to set the colors for our control and even to define the interface for doing this, but now we need to consider exactly how we're going to make this happen. There are two ways of doing this.

First of all, we could require that the edit control always be made owner-draw in the resource editor. This would allow us to draw the string at any time, and in whatever colors, fonts and so forth that we desired. However, this isn't a desirable solution for two reasons. If we require that the resource editor be used to modify the styles of all edit controls, we change the behavior of the design process. If a company had a designer who laid out the dialogs in the application, and a programmer who implemented the functionality for the dialog, it would force the designer to go back and change all existing dialogs for the sake of one modification. In addition, there's another more basic reason. We don't wish to do more work than necessary to implement a feature. To change an edit control to owner-draw means also handling input, selection, and all the other functionality that goes with it, which seems like a lot of hard work just to change its color!

Fortunately, there's an easier solution. There's a `virtual` function called `OnChildNotify()` already built into the MFC `CWnd` class, and this is called when a control is about to be redrawn. This method gets a `WM_CTLCOLOREDIT` message (or `WM_CTLCOLOR` in Win16) that indicates that the colors for the control are to be set. If a control responds to this message, Windows won't clear the background to the default color, nor will it modify the other color settings for the control. We can take advantage of this message to modify the colors to the settings requested for the control.

We'll use `OnChildNotify()` to set the foreground (text) color as well as the background color. The return value (`LRESULT`) for `OnChildNotify()` expected for the `WM_CTLCOLOREDIT` message is a handle to a brush, so we'll need to add members to our class for the two color settings and a background brush.

Now that we have designed, defined, and refined the control, it's time to actually get our hands dirty and write some code.

Implementing the Control

To implement the control, we'll create a new MFC class derived from `CEdit`, and implement the functionality of the control within that class. Follow this procedure to create the MFC class and implement the control:

TRY IT OUT - Create a Validating Edit Control

1 Create a new project of type MFC AppWizard (exe), call the project Validation, and choose to create a Dialog based application from Step 1 of the AppWizard. All other options can stay with their default settings.

2 Once you've created the project, use ClassWizard to add a new class by selecting the Add Class... button and selecting New... from the pop-up menu. Give the new class the name CValidationEdit, and select CEdit as the Base class. Click Create. At this point, you've created a new component that has exactly the same properties as the default **CEdit** control class. Since this isn't exactly what we had in mind, we'll now add some new functionality to the control.

3 First, we'll add new member variables to the class to hold the text and background colors, as well as the brush to use in the **WM_CTLCOLOREDIT** message processing. To do this, add the following lines to the **ValidationEdit.h** header file, just below the declaration for the destructor:

```
private:
   COLORREF m_clrText;          // Text color
   COLORREF m_clrBackground;    // Background color
   CBrush* m_pbrBackground;     // Brush object for holding background brush
```

4 In addition to defining the colors, we must also set default values for these member variables, so add the highlighted lines to the constructor for the class in **ValidationEdit.cpp**:

```
CValidationEdit::CValidationEdit()
{
   m_clrText = RGB(0, 0, 0);                    // Default text color = black
   m_clrBackground = RGB(255, 255, 255);        // Default back color = white
   m_pbrBackground = new CBrush(m_clrBackground);
}
```

5 As surely as night must follow day, **delete** must follow **new**. Add the following line to the destructor to ensure that our class is well-behaved:

```
CValidationEdit::~CValidationEdit()
{
   if (m_pbrBackground)
      delete m_pbrBackground;
}
```

6 Now we'll add the accessors for the colors. Add the following lines to **ValidationEdit.h**:

```
// Attributes
public:
   COLORREF GetTextColor() const;
   COLORREF GetBackgroundColor() const;
```

7 The implementations for these functions are extremely simple, and it shouldn't surprise you to know that they belong in **ValidationEdit.cpp**:

```
/////////////////////////////////////////////////////////////////////////////
// CValidationEdit acessor functions

inline COLORREF CValidationEdit::GetTextColor() const
{
   return m_clrText;
}
```

```
inline COLORREF CValidationEdit::GetBackgroundColor() const
{
   return m_clrBackground;
}
```

8 As well as setting defaults and allowing access to the colors, we need a way to allow the user to set the values. Add two prototypes to the **// Operations** section of the header file, as follows:

```
// Operations
public:
   void SetTextColor(COLORREF clrText);
   void SetBackgroundColor(COLORREF clrBackground);
```

9 Now add the actual member function definitions to the source file, **ValidationEdit.cpp**:

```
/////////////////////////////////////////////////////////////////////////////
// CValidationEdit Set functions

void CValidationEdit::SetTextColor(COLORREF clrText)
{
   m_clrText = clrText;
}

void CValidationEdit::SetBackgroundColor(COLORREF clrBackground)
{
   m_clrBackground = clrBackground;
   if (m_pbrBackground)
      delete m_pbrBackground;
   m_pbrBackground = new CBrush(m_clrBackground);
}
```

Note that **CValidationEdit::SetBackgroundColor()** also has the responsibility of keeping the background brush up to date, so that we can use it in response to the **WM_CTLCOLOREDIT** message.

10 The next step is to provide the code that actually changes the background and foreground colors of the control. As we mentioned previously, this is done in response to the **WM_CTLCOLOREDIT** message. We can detect this by overriding **CWnd::OnChildNotify()**.

To do this, enter ClassWizard, select CValidationEdit in the Class name and Object IDs lists, and OnChildNotify from the Messages list. Click on Add Function. This function will now be used to check for the **WM_CTLCOLOREDIT** message and to set the colors. Add the following code to it:

```
BOOL CValidationEdit::OnChildNotify(UINT message, WPARAM wParam,
                                    LPARAM lParam, LRESULT* pLResult)
{
   // If "message" is the message we're after, we handle it
   if (WM_CTLCOLOR == message ||  WM_CTLCOLOREDIT == message)
   {
      HDC hdcChild = (HDC)wParam;
```

```
        // Set the text foreground to the requested text color
        ::SetTextColor(hdcChild, m_clrText);

        // Set the text background to the requested background color
        ::SetBkColor(hdcChild, m_clrBackground);

        // Send what would have been the return value of
        // OnCtlColor() - the brush handle - back in pLResult
        *pLResult = (LRESULT)(m_pbrBackground->GetSafeHandle());

        // Return TRUE to indicate that the message was handled
        return TRUE;
    }
    // Otherwise, do default processing
    else
        return CEdit::OnChildNotify(message, wParam, lParam, pLResult);
}
```

11 At this stage, we have a control that can have its background and foreground colors set. While this may be very pretty, it isn't really the point of the exercise, so let's get started on adding the validation portions of the control. First, add a **private** data member to store the text that the user typed in:

```
private:
    COLORREF m_clrText;          // Text color
    COLORREF m_clrBackground;    // Background color
    CBrush* m_pbrBackground;     // Brush object for holding background brush
    CString m_strOriginalData; // Holds user's original data, if valid
```

12 Now add the accessor for this data member to the source file for the class. There's no need to add a function to set the value, since it will be set automatically when the control loses focus, and we don't want it to be set at any other time.

```
CString CValidationEdit::GetOriginalData() const
{
    return m_strOriginalData;
}
```

13 The next stage is to set up the **virtual** functions, which will be overridden by the programmer who uses our class. Add the following lines to the header file:

```
// Overridables
public:
    virtual CString GetStrippedData() const; // (called from OnGetFocus)
    virtual CString GetFormattedData() const; // (called from OnKillFocus)

protected:
    virtual BOOL IsValid() const;   // Override this to validate input
                                    // (called from OnKillFocus)
    virtual void DisplayError();    // Override this to take action in the
                                    // event of invalid input.
```

These functions will be used to format the control text for editing, format it for display, validate user input, and respond to invalid data. The implementation of these methods will be left up to the programmer who overrides our class, but we shall provide usable default implementations for each of these functions.

14 The default implementations, which should be added to **ValidationEdit.cpp**, are shown below. Just as we described in the design section, we return the original data when asked for formatted text, set **IsValid()** to return **TRUE** for all cases, and, in the event of invalid data, we display a message box, reset the focus to our control, and select the data in the control.

```
///////////////////////////////////////////////////////////////////////////
// CValidationEdit overridables

BOOL CValidationEdit::IsValid() const
{
   return TRUE;
}

CString CValidationEdit::GetStrippedData() const
{
   return m_strOriginalData;
}

CString CValidationEdit::GetFormattedData() const
{
   return m_strOriginalData;
}

void CValidationEdit::DisplayError()
{
   MessageBox(_T("Invalid Entry"), _T("Error"));    // Inform the user
   SetFocus();                                      // Return focus
   SetSel(0,-1);                                    // Select all text
}
```

15 After adding the validation support, it's time to do the work of trapping the focus changes. Conjure up ClassWizard, and add a new handler for the **WM_KILLFOCUS** message to the **CValidationEdit** class. Edit the code and add the following lines to the **OnKillFocus()** method:

```
void CValidationEdit::OnKillFocus(CWnd* pNewWnd)
{
   // Allow window to continue processing itself
   CEdit::OnKillFocus(pNewWnd);

   // See if valid or if they are hitting the CANCEL button
   if (!IsValid() && (pNewWnd == NULL ||
                      pNewWnd->GetDlgCtrlID() != IDCANCEL))
   {
      PostMessage(WM_COMMAND, WM_DISPERROR);
   }
   else
   {
      if (GetModify())            // If the user modified the data, save the
         GetWindowText(m_strOriginalData);    // data as the user typed it
      // Show the data in a pleasing format
      SetWindowText(GetFormattedData());
   }
}
```

So what are we doing here? First, we're allowing the **WM_KILLFOCUS** message to pass through to the underlying Windows default handling procedure. When writing your own controls, it's important to respect the underlying message handling within Windows. We don't want to do anything to break the way the control works, so we allow it to do its normal processing.

Next, we validate the control by calling the **IsValid()** method. If the input is valid, we check whether the user has modified the data. If they have, we use **GetWindowText()** to store their data in **m_strOriginalData**. The check for modification is important, since we format the string using **GetStrippedData()** when the control receives focus. Without this check, we'd soon end up with the stripped data being stored in **m_strOriginalData**, which isn't what we want. Whether the data has been modified or not, we always use **GetFormattedData()** to set the text of the control when it loses focus.

Note that there's a secondary check on the **IsValid()** line, to see whether the user's setting the focus to the **IDCANCEL** button. If this is the case, the user is asking to cancel the dialog in which this control resides, and therefore we don't bother to validate the data since the program won't be using it.

16 If the entry isn't valid, the **CValidationEdit::OnKillFocus()** routine calls **PostMessage()** with a user-defined message, **WM_DISPERROR**. Clearly, this message needs to be defined somewhere, so add this line to the top of the source file (**ValidationEdit.cpp**) in order to define the message:

```
const int WM_DISPERROR = WM_USER + 1;
```

17 This message is sent to our control to indicate that its data is invalid. To handle the message, add the following line to the header file for the control, **ValidationEdit.h**:

```
protected:
   //{{AFX_MSG(CValidationEdit)
   afx_msg void OnKillFocus(CWnd* pNewWnd);
   //}}AFX_MSG
   afx_msg void OnDisplayError();
```

Now add this line to your message map in the source file for the control, **ValidationEdit.cpp**:

```
BEGIN_MESSAGE_MAP(CValidationEdit, CEdit)
   //{{AFX_MSG_MAP(CValidationEdit)
   ON_WM_KILLFOCUS()
   //}}AFX_MSG_MAP
   ON_COMMAND(WM_DISPERROR, OnDisplayError)
END_MESSAGE_MAP()
```

Finally, add the function itself:

```
void CValidationEdit::OnDisplayError()
{
   DisplayError();
}
```

This function just calls the **virtual** function, **DisplayError()**, which can do anything that the user of our class wants to do in response to invalid data, such as displaying an error message, sounding an alarm, or formatting the end user's hard drive!

18 The final step is to trap the setting of focus to the control. To accomplish this, use ClassWizard to add a handler to the **CValidationEdit** class for the **WM_SETFOCUS** message. The handler will be called **OnSetFocus()**. Now add the following code to it:

```
void CValidationEdit::OnSetFocus(CWnd* pOldWnd)
{
   CEdit::OnSetFocus(pOldWnd);

   // Strip the data before display
   SetWindowText(GetStrippedData());
   // Set the flag for unmodified so that we don't
   // store stripped data as original data
   SetModify(FALSE);
}
```

Here we set the control's text to editable form by calling **GetStrippedData()**, and we set the modified flag of the control to **FALSE**, so that we can determine whether the user has modified the data as we discussed back in **OnKillFocus()**.

That's all there is to it. You've created a base class which can form the basis for an entire library of validation types. By way of a quick example, we'll implement a control to handle the Social Security Numbers that we talked about at the beginning of the chapter.

TRY IT OUT - Social Security Validation

1 We've already got the project which we can use as a basis to test our new class, so now we'll enhance it so that it's in a fit state to compile. First, we need to add a new class that derives from **CValidationEdit**. The easiest way to do this is to use ClassWizard to add a new class based on **CEdit**, just as we did when we created **CValidationEdit** itself. This time, give the class a Name of CSSNEdit.

2 Now that you've created the class, open up the header file **SSNEdit.h**, and alter it so that **CSSNEdit** derives from **CValidationEdit**, and not **CEdit**. Add a line to include **ValidationEdit.h**:

```
/////////////////////////////////////////////////////////////////////////////
// CSSNEdit window
#include "ValidationEdit.h"

class CSSNEdit : public CValidationEdit
{
```

You'll also need to go into the source file, **SSNEdit.cpp**, to change the message map, so that MFC knows that **CSSNEdit** derives from **CValidationEdit**:

```
/////////////////////////////////////////////////////////////////////////////
// CSSNEdit Message Map
```

```
BEGIN_MESSAGE_MAP(CSSNEdit, CValidationEdit)
    //{{AFX_MSG_MAP(CSSNEdit)
```

3 Now we can start overriding functions to provide validation and formatting capabilities appropriate for Social Security Numbers. First, copy the function declarations for the overridable functions from **CValidationEdit** into **CSSNEdit**, or just add the code shown to **SSNEdit.h** (we've left out **GetStrippedData()**, since we don't intend to override it):

```
// Operations
public:

// Overrides
public:
    virtual CString GetFormattedData() const;
protected:
    virtual BOOL IsValid() const;
    virtual void DisplayError();

    // ClassWizard generated virtual function overrides
```

4 Now we'll implement **CSSNEdit::IsValid()**. An SSN is valid if it consists of 9 digits and a number of dashes. We'll simplify our validation by not worrying about how many dashes are in the input string, or how they're positioned: we'll just remove them all. If we don't have 9 characters once that's done then we can't have a valid SSN. If we do have 9 characters, we check to make sure that all of the characters are digits. If they are, we have a valid SSN. The code to add to **SSNEdit.cpp** looks like this:

```
BOOL CSSNEdit::IsValid() const
{
    CString string;
    GetWindowText(string);

    StripCharacter(string.GetBuffer(string.GetLength()), _T('-'));
    string.ReleaseBuffer();

    if (lstrlen(string) != 9)
        return FALSE;

    for (int i=0; i < lstrlen(string); ++i)
    {
        if (!_istdigit(string[i]))
            return FALSE;
    }

    return TRUE;
}
```

5 You probably noticed that this function uses **StripCharacter()**, a function we met when we looked at the **CDate** class. To get this to work, add the declaration for this function to **CSSNEdit** in **SSNEdit.h**:

```
private:
    void StripCharacter(LPTSTR lpszString, TCHAR chRemove) const;
```

Now add the definition of **StripCharacter()** to **SSNEdit.cpp**:

```
void CSSNEdit::StripCharacter(LPTSTR lpszString, TCHAR chRemove) const
{
   int i = 0;
   int j = 0;
   while ((*(lpszString + i) = *(lpszString + j++)) != _T('\0'))
      if (*(lpszString + i) != chRemove)
         i++;
   return;
}
```

6 Now we'll implement **CSSNEdit::GetFormattedData()**. This just takes the original data, removes any extraneous dashes, and puts them back in appropriate places. The function can be this simple because we know that the original data has already been validated:

```
CString CSSNEdit::GetFormattedData() const
{
   CString string;
   string = GetOriginalData();

   // We know that the data is valid, but it may contain extraneous dashes
   // so we remove them
   StripCharacter(string.GetBuffer(string.GetLength()), _T('-'));
   string.ReleaseBuffer();

   // Now we replace dashes where we want them
   CString strFormatted = string.Left(3) + _T('-') +
                          string.Mid(3, 2) + _T('-') + string.Right(4);
   return strFormatted;
}
```

7 The final function to implement, is **CSSNEdit::DisplayError()**. This is pretty simple and just displays a message box, sets the focus to our control, and selects all the text.

```
void CSSNEdit::DisplayError()
{
   MessageBox(_T("Invalid Social Security Number"),
              _T("SSN Error"));                         // Inform the user
   SetFocus();                                          // Return focus
   SetSel(0,-1);                                        // Select all text
}
```

8 Now all you need to do to test it is add an edit box to **IDD_VALIDATION_DIALOG**. *Ctrl*-double-click on the edit box in the resource editor to bring up the ClassWizard dialog for adding member variables. Set the Category to Control and select CSSNEdit from the Variable type list. Set the Member variable name to m_SSNEdit and click OK.

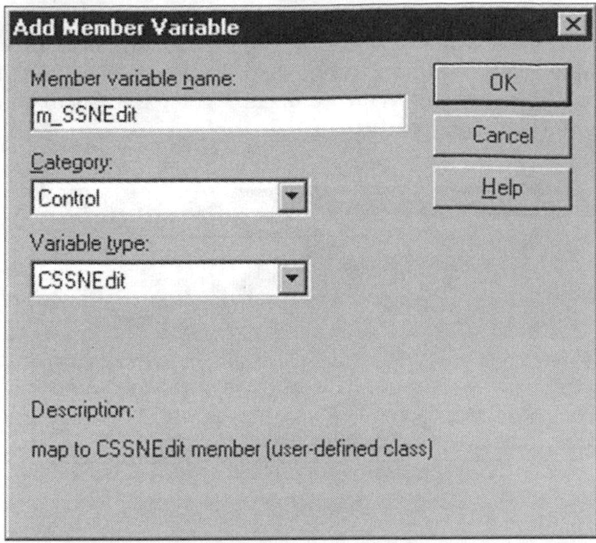

9 Compile and run the project. Try typing in the edit box and seeing what happens when you change the focus to another control.

MFC Solution Two: A Pop-up Calculator

One of the more common problems in Windows applications is that of getting numeric data from the user. One solution to this is to allow only a numeric entry in an edit box, and this is easily implemented using MFC. Unfortunately, the solution doesn't address the whole problem. Although a user may be able to enter numeric data, that doesn't mean that they can enter *meaningful* numeric data. After all, if the user needs to enter a value which represents the sum of several other numbers, the chances of getting the correct answer varies with the mathematical aptitude of the user.

A better solution is to provide the user with a control which emulates something they are already familiar with: a calculator. Since the point of creating custom controls is to give people a better means to do things, what better way could there be than to implement something that everyone has used at one time or another?

Since placing a calculator on every dialog box and for each numeric field could eat up a lot of valuable real-estate, as there will probably be multiple numeric fields per dialog, we need a solution which doesn't force dialog boxes to be twice the size of the screen. The answer to this conundrum is to use a combo box to display the final answer. The drop-down button of the combo is used to activate and deactivate the calculator portion, displayed as a 'drop-down' from the combo box. An example of this display is shown here.

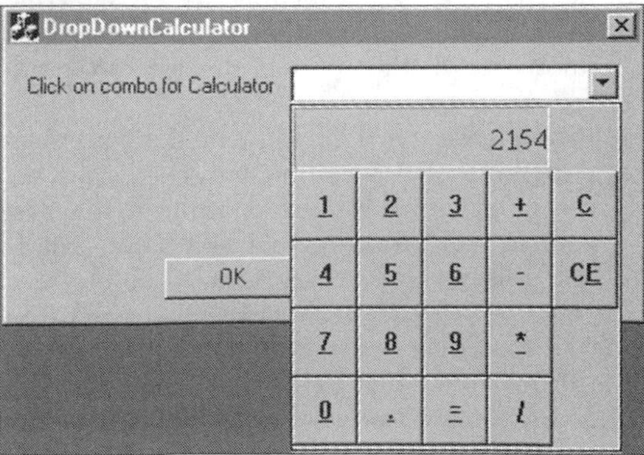

As you can see by the previous figure, the user simply enters a number by either clicking on the 'number' buttons or (as we will see later), by typing the numbers in via the keyboard. The calculator supports simple math, addition, subtraction, multiplication and division, so that the user can calculate fields easily using several numbers. When the calculations are done, the answer is displayed in the edit field portion of the combo box.

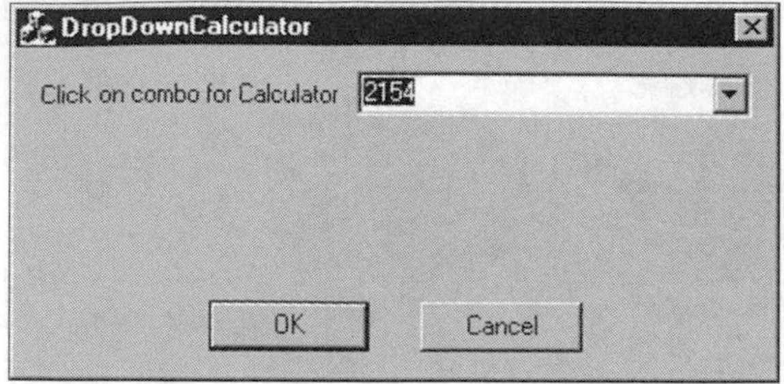

Feature List

To implement the calculator combo box, we need a list of the features we will support for the control. Let's make that list here:

- Needs to drop down a calculator window when the combo box is selected, and remove the calculator window when the combo box is closed or when the calculator window loses focus (such as by clicking on another field in the dialog box).
- Needs to support simple math functions in the calculator. For example, addition, subtraction, division, and multiplication.
- Needs to copy the entered number into the edit field of the combo box when the user leaves the calculator window.

That doesn't seem like a very long list of features. Fortunately, though, as we will see, the feature list implements a very usable and powerful control that users will truly enjoy using.

Designing the Control

Looking at the feature list, we can see that the design of the drop-down calculator will rely heavily upon the functionality of the Windows combo box. The combo box already maintains information and functionality for clicking on the button to display the combo box list, as well as knowing whether or not the list box portion is displayed.

In our case, we'll implement the control as two separate windows. The first window will be a derivative of the combo box class, and will be responsible for displaying the edit box containing the information for the control, in this case, the number entered. The second portion of the control will be the actual calculator window. This window will simply display a set of buttons, and this will allow the user to define the number using the simple math built into the control.

The first class we'll need to implement is the derived combo box. This class needs to do two things. First, it must catch the user clicking on the combo box drop-down button. This will be accomplished by watching for the **CBN_DROPDOWN** message in the class. Once the message has been caught, the class will then post a message to itself indicating that the calculator window should be displayed. The posting is necessary because it's difficult to deal with one Windows message inside of another.

The combo box class will catch the user-defined message to display the calculator window. Within this message handler, we'll create the calculator window. From that point on, it will be the responsibility of the calculator window to do all of the processing.

The calculator window needs first to create all of the child windows (the calculator buttons) for itself. Once these windows have been created, we'll simply wait until the user either clicks the equals button, or presses *Enter* (indicating that they would like to copy the current result to the combo box edit control), or clicks somewhere outside of the calculator window (indicating that they are abandoning the calculation). In either case, we'll close the window and destroy the object.

Obviously, the calculator window needs a bit of thought. Should we implement it as a simple calculator or a reverse Polish notation (RPN) calculator? Although you might want an RPN calculator, most users probably wouldn't understand it. Therefore, we'll stick with a simple version. The user will enter numbers by clicking on the buttons representing the number, and then the function buttons (+, -, *, or /) can be used to operate on the current value displayed in the calculator display screen.

We'll also want several other functions for the calculator. Clear entry and clear total keys would be nice, and a decimal point key would obviously be a necessity. Finally, we need an equals (=) key to indicate that the calculation is done and that the result should be copied to the combo box edit box. This brings up another point. How do we 'know' which combo edit box to put the result into? If we were to have multiple calculation fields in a dialog, it would be impossible to find it. We must, therefore, have an associated window with the calculator to determine where to put the information as well.

At this point, we have enough information in the design to implement the control. Let's do that now.

Implementing the Control

Implementing the control is a two step process. First, we'll implement a **`CComboBox`**-derived class that will represent the interface between the dialog box and the calculator window, and then we'll create the calculator itself. To do this, follow the procedure outlined below.

TRY IT OUT - Create the Calculator Combo Class

1 Create a new project workspace called DropDownCalculator, using MFC AppWizard (exe) as the project type. On Step 1 of the AppWizard, select a Dialog based project and leave all the other options at their defaults.

2 Once the project has been created, bring up ClassWizard and add a new class to the project. Give the new class the name **`CCalcCombo`**. Derive the class from **`CComboBox`**.

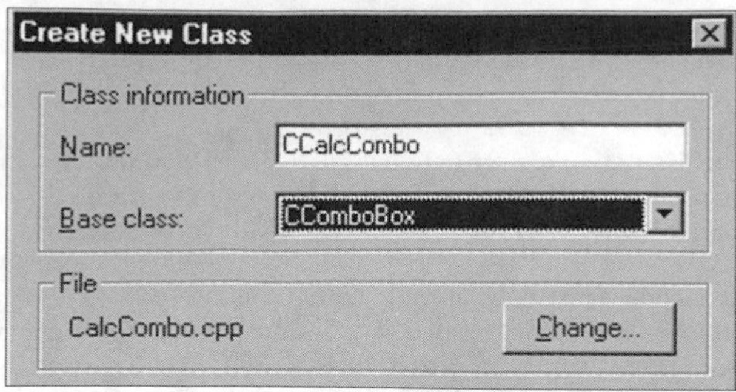

3 While still in ClassWizard, add a message handler to the **CCalcCombo** class for the =CBN_DROPDOWN message. Accept the default name of **OnDropdown()** for the message handler. Add the following code to **CCalcCombo::OnDropdown()**:

```
void CCalcCombo::OnDropdown()
{
   ShowDropDown(FALSE);
   PostMessage(WM_COMMAND, WM_DISPLAY_CALCULATOR);
}
```

4 Add the following definition for the message to the top of **CalcCombo.cpp**, just above the constructor for the class:

```
const int WM_DISPLAY_CALCULATOR = WM_USER + 1;
```

5 Now add a new message handler for the class by editing the message map in **CalcCombo.cpp** and adding the following line (highlighted here):

```
BEGIN_MESSAGE_MAP(CCalcCombo, CComboBox)
   //{{AFX_MSG_MAP(CCalcCombo)
   ON_CONTROL_REFLECT(CBN_DROPDOWN, OnDropdown)
   //}}AFX_MSG_MAP
   ON_COMMAND(WM_DISPLAY_CALCULATOR, OnDisplayCalculator)
END_MESSAGE_MAP()
```

6 Add the declaration for **OnDisplayCalculator()** to the header file for the class as follows:

```
protected:
   //{{AFX_MSG(CCalcCombo)
   afx_msg void OnDropdown();
   //}}AFX_MSG
   afx_msg void OnDisplayCalculator();
```

7 Add the following implementation for the new **OnDisplayCalculator()** function to the source file for **CCalcCombo**:

```
void CCalcCombo::OnDisplayCalculator()
{
   // Create the calculator window.  Note that it will
```

```
    // destroy itself when done.
    m_pwndCalc = new CCalcWnd(this);

    CRect rect;
    GetWindowRect(&rect);

    BOOL bSuccess = m_pwndCalc->Create(rect.left, rect.bottom);
    m_pwndCalc->SetFocus();
}
```

Note that we are leaving it up to the calculator window class to **delete** itself when it closes. This removes any need for our **CCalcCombo** class to detect when the calculator window has closed.

8 Now add the following lines to the header file for the **CCalcCombo** class:

```
    virtual ~CCalcCombo();
private:
    CCalcWnd* m_pwndCalc;
```

9 The last thing is to include the header file for the calculator class:

```
/////////////////////////////////////////////////////////////////////////////
// CCalcCombo window
#include "CalcWnd.h" // Header file for the pop-up calculator window
```

At this point, we have done everything necessary to display a new window when the drop-down button of the combo box is clicked. The **OnDropdown()** method will close the combo box (for visual impact), and post a message to itself indicating that the calculator window should be displayed. This message is handled by the **OnDisplayCalculator()** method, which creates a new window from the **CCalcWnd** class and displays it below the combo box in the dialog. All that is left is to write **CCalcWnd**, the pop-up calculator window class.

TRY IT OUT - Create the Calculator Window

1 To create the calculator window, we'll first create a new window class derived from **CWnd**, so use ClassWizard to create a new class. Give the class the Name: CCalcWnd and use a Base class of generic CWnd.

2 The class will need quite a few member variables. Let's list them here and talk a little about what they represent. Add the following lines to the **// Implementation** section of the header file for **CCalcWnd**:

```
private:
    enum {MaxDigits = 10, BaseID = 8000};
    TCHAR m_szInput[MaxDigits + 2];
    TCHAR m_szHold[MaxDigits + 2];
    TCHAR m_chOperator;
    CFont m_font;
    CWnd* m_pwndCombo;

    CButton* m_pDigit[10];
```

```
    CButton* m_pDecimalPoint;
    CButton* m_pEquals;
    CButton* m_pPlus;
    CButton* m_pMinus;
    CButton* m_pMultiply;
    CButton* m_pDivide;
    CButton* m_pClear;
    CButton* m_pClearEntry;
```

The enumeration defines two constants, **MaxDigits** and **BaseID**. **MaxDigits** is used to represent the maximum number of digits that can be displayed and manipulated by our calculator. **BaseID** represents the base control ID used for the buttons of the calculator. This will come into use when we create the buttons represented by the **CButton*** variables. The **m_pDigit** array represents the buttons for entering the digits, where **m_pDigit[0]** is the 'zero' button, **m_pDigit[1]** is the 'one' button, and so on. Hopefully, the names of the other **CButton*** members make it clear which button each variable represents.

The **m_szInput** and **m_szHold** variables will be used to display and maintain the strings which are displayed in the calculator display window. The strings are used to keep track of the current input string and the current value of the calculator, respectively. **m_chOperator** is used to store the current arithmetic operation. Its use will become obvious as you see the code to implement the calculator itself.

The **m_font** variable is simply used to hold a font for the calculator display. This variable is a standard **CFont** from MFC.

The **m_pwndCombo** variable needs a little description. This stores a pointer to the combo box associated with the calculator window. Without this pointer, we would have no way of displaying the resulting expression from the calculator in the combo box, and the entire exercise would be rather pointless. Since it seems silly to go through all of this work and not get anything out of it (which is counter to the entire concept of components), we'll hold onto the associated combo box window so that we can store the final calculated value there.

3 The next step in the process is to initialize all these variables in the constructor for the class. However, first we need to modify the constructor so that it accepts a **CWnd*** as a parameter. This will be the pointer to the associated combo box that gets passed to the calculator window from **CCalcCombo**. Modify the declaration for the constructor in **CalcWnd.h**, as shown:

```
// Construction
public:
    CCalcWnd(CWnd* pWnd);
```

Now alter the definition of the constructor in **CalcWnd.cpp** to match the declaration, and add the following code to initialize the member variables:

```
CCalcWnd::CCalcWnd(CWnd* pWnd)
{
    m_pwndCombo = pWnd;
    m_szInput[0] = _T('\0');
    m_szHold[0] = _T('\0');
    m_chOperator = _T('\0');
```

```
    for (int i = 0; i <= 9; ++i)
        m_pDigit[i] = NULL;

    m_pDecimalPoint = NULL;
    m_pEquals = NULL;
    m_pPlus = NULL;
    m_pMinus = NULL;
    m_pMultiply = NULL;
    m_pDivide = NULL;
    m_pClear = NULL;
    m_pClearEntry = NULL;
}
```

4 Now we can override the creation of the window, and create all of the child button windows that represent the functionality of the calculator. To do this, add to the **CCalcWnd** class a new message handler for the **WM_CREATE** message. Add the following code to the **OnCreate()** method:

```
int CCalcWnd::OnCreate(LPCREATESTRUCT lpCreateStruct)
{
    if (CWnd::OnCreate(lpCreateStruct) == -1)
        return -1;

    m_font.CreateFont(0, 0, 0, 0, FW_NORMAL, 0, 0, 0, 0, 0, 0, 0, 0, NULL);

    // Create a bunch of buttons
    CRect rect(0, 0, 0, 0);
    static const TCHAR DigitLabels[10][3] = {_T("&0"), _T("&1"), _T("&2"),
                                             _T("&3"), _T("&4"), _T("&5"),
                                             _T("&6"), _T("&7"), _T("&8"),
                                             _T("&9")};
    static const DWORD dwStyle = BS_PUSHBUTTON | WS_VISIBLE;

    for (int i = 0; i <= 9; ++i)
    {
        m_pDigit[i] = new CButton;
        m_pDigit[i]->Create(DigitLabels[i], dwStyle, rect, this,
                            BaseID + i);
    }

    m_pDecimalPoint = new CButton;
    m_pDecimalPoint->Create(_T("&."), dwStyle, rect, this, BaseID + 10);
    m_pEquals = new CButton;
    m_pEquals->Create(_T("&="), dwStyle, rect, this, BaseID + 11);
    m_pPlus = new CButton;
    m_pPlus->Create(_T("&+"), dwStyle, rect, this, BaseID + 12);
    m_pMinus = new CButton;
    m_pMinus->Create(_T("&-"), dwStyle, rect, this, BaseID + 13);
    m_pMultiply = new CButton;
    m_pMultiply->Create(_T("&*"), dwStyle, rect, this, BaseID + 14);
    m_pDivide = new CButton;
    m_pDivide->Create(_T("&/"), dwStyle, rect, this, BaseID + 15);
    m_pClear = new CButton;
    m_pClear->Create(_T("&C"), dwStyle, rect, this, BaseID + 16);
    m_pClearEntry = new CButton;
    m_pClearEntry->Create(_T("C&E"), dwStyle, rect, this, BaseID + 17);
```

```
    return 0;
}
```

Note that the text of each button will contain an underlined character. This character will represent the key on the keyboard which the user can press to emulate the functionality of pressing the button with a mouse click. Note that, in a dialog box, this would be an accelerator key which would be handled automatically for us. Because this is a simple **CWnd** object, however, we will need to do the work of processing these keystrokes ourselves. We will take care of that in a while. First, though, we need to deal with the clean up work for the window.

5 Add the following to the destructor for the class. This will clean up the memory allocated to the button objects for the window:

```
CCalcWnd::~CCalcWnd()
{
    for (int i = 0; i <= 9; ++i)
    {
        if (m_pDigit[i])
            delete m_pDigit[i];
    }

    if (m_pDecimalPoint)
        delete m_pDecimalPoint;
    if (m_pEquals)
        delete m_pEquals;
    if (m_pPlus)
        delete m_pPlus;
    if (m_pMinus)
        delete m_pMinus;
    if (m_pMultiply)
        delete m_pMultiply;
    if (m_pDivide)
        delete m_pDivide;
    if (m_pClear)
        delete m_pClear;
    if (m_pClearEntry)
        delete m_pClearEntry;
}
```

6 Now we'll create a new overload for the **Create()** function. Add the declaration for the function below to **CalcWnd.h** by hand.

```
public:
    CCalcWnd(CWnd* pWnd);
    virtual BOOL Create(int x, int y);
```

In addition, provide the actual **Create()** function in **CalcWnd.cpp** to register the window class and create the calculator window:

```
BOOL CCalcWnd::Create(int x, int y)
{
    static LPCTSTR lpszName = NULL;

    if (!lpszName)
```

```
    {
        lpszName = AfxRegisterWndClass(CS_DBLCLKS);
    }

    return CreateEx(WS_EX_TOPMOST | WS_EX_TOOLWINDOW, lpszName, _T(""),
                    WS_POPUP | WS_VISIBLE, x, y, 10, 10, NULL, NULL);
}
```

Note that we create the window using the **WS_EX_TOOLWINDOW** extended style, so that it won't appear in the taskbar.

7 Once the window is created, we need to resize it so that it remains a fixed size for all occurrences of this calculator window type. Use ClassWizard to add a message handler to **CCalcWnd** for the **WM_SIZE** message, and add the following code to the **OnSize()** method of the class:

```
void CCalcWnd::OnSize(UINT nType, int cx, int cy)
{
    CWnd::OnSize(nType, cx, cy);

    // Figure out how big it should be.
    CDC* dc = GetDC();
    dc->SelectObject(&m_font);
    TEXTMETRIC tm;
    dc->GetTextMetrics(&tm);
    ReleaseDC(dc);

    CRect rect;
    GetWindowRect(&rect);

    int nHeight = 2 * tm.tmHeight;        // Button height
    int nWidth = 2 * tm.tmMaxCharWidth; // Button width

    int nCalcHeight = 5 * nHeight + 3;
    int nCalcWidth = 5 * nWidth + 1;

    rect.bottom = rect.top + nCalcHeight;
    rect.right = rect.left + nCalcWidth + 2;
    MoveWindow(&rect);

    // Move the buttons as well
    m_pDigit[0]->MoveWindow(1, 4 * nHeight, nWidth, nHeight);
    m_pDigit[1]->MoveWindow(1, nHeight, nWidth, nHeight);
    m_pDigit[2]->MoveWindow(nWidth + 1, nHeight, nWidth, nHeight);
    m_pDigit[3]->MoveWindow(2 * nWidth + 1, nHeight, nWidth, nHeight);
    m_pDigit[4]->MoveWindow(1, 2 * nHeight, nWidth, nHeight);
    m_pDigit[5]->MoveWindow(nWidth + 1, 2 * nHeight, nWidth, nHeight);
    m_pDigit[6]->MoveWindow(2 * nWidth + 1, 2 * nHeight, nWidth, nHeight);
    m_pDigit[7]->MoveWindow(1, 3 * nHeight, nWidth, nHeight);
    m_pDigit[8]->MoveWindow(nWidth + 1, 3 * nHeight, nWidth, nHeight);
    m_pDigit[9]->MoveWindow(2 * nWidth + 1, 3 * nHeight, nWidth, nHeight);

    m_pDecimalPoint->MoveWindow(nWidth + 1, 4 * nHeight, nWidth, nHeight);
    m_pEquals->MoveWindow(2 * nWidth + 1, 4 * nHeight, nWidth, nHeight);
    m_pPlus->MoveWindow(3 * nWidth + 1, nHeight, nWidth, nHeight);
    m_pMinus->MoveWindow(3 * nWidth + 1, 2 * nHeight, nWidth, nHeight);
```

```
    m_pMultiply->MoveWindow(3 * nWidth + 1, 3 * nHeight, nWidth, nHeight);
    m_pDivide->MoveWindow(3 * nWidth + 1, 4 * nHeight, nWidth, nHeight);
    m_pClear->MoveWindow(4 * nWidth + 1, nHeight, nWidth, nHeight);
    m_pClearEntry->MoveWindow(4 * nWidth + 1, 2 * nHeight, nWidth, nHeight);
}
```

We're going to make the window equal to 5 lines of buttons in height, and 5 lines of buttons in width. This will provide ample space to display all of the buttons. You can certainly play with these numbers to move the buttons around, if you like. It won't affect the functionality of the window. After determining the size of the window, we move each of the buttons we created into place. It's true that the alignment of the buttons is hard-coded, but this is really to be expected. You probably wouldn't want the user defining where each button went, or you'd end up with a mess.

8 The next step is to override the painting of the window in order to display the current value of the calculator. You can do this by using ClassWizard to define a new message handler for the **WM_PAINT** message in the **CCalcWnd** class, and adding the following code:

```
void CCalcWnd::OnPaint()
{
    CPaintDC dc(this); // device context for painting

    // Setup our small font for this window
    CFont* pOldFont = dc.SelectObject(&m_font);

    TEXTMETRIC tm;
    dc.GetTextMetrics(&tm);

    // Define the pens we will use in this routine
    const int nPenWidth = 1;
    CPen penBlack(PS_SOLID, nPenWidth, RGB(0, 0, 0));
    CPen penText(PS_SOLID, nPenWidth, GetSysColor(COLOR_GRAYTEXT));
    CPen penDark(PS_SOLID, nPenWidth, GetSysColor(COLOR_BTNSHADOW));
    CPen penShadow(PS_SOLID, nPenWidth, GetSysColor(COLOR_BTNHIGHLIGHT));

    // First, paint the 3-d "border" for the control
    CRect rect;
    GetWindowRect(&rect);

    int nHeight = rect.bottom - rect.top - 2;
    int nWidth = rect.right - rect.left - 1;

    // First, do the dark outer border
    CPen* pOldPen = dc.SelectObject(&penBlack);
    dc.MoveTo(0, 0);
    dc.LineTo(0, nHeight);
    dc.LineTo(nWidth, nHeight);
    dc.LineTo(nWidth, 0);
    dc.LineTo(0, 0);

    // Next, the light inner border
    dc.SelectObject(&penShadow);
    dc.MoveTo(1, 1);
    dc.LineTo(1, nHeight - 1);
    dc.LineTo(nWidth - 1, nHeight - 1);
    dc.LineTo(nWidth - 1, 1);
```

```
    dc.LineTo(1, 1);

    // Don't forget to do the box around where the numbers will be
    rect.top = 1;
    rect.left = 1;
    rect.right = 5 * (2 * tm.tmMaxCharWidth);
    rect.bottom = 2 * tm.tmHeight - 1;

    dc.SelectObject(&penDark);
    dc.MoveTo(rect.left + 1, rect.top + 1);
    dc.LineTo(rect.left + 1, rect.bottom - 2);
    dc.MoveTo(rect.left + 1, rect.top + 1);
    dc.LineTo(rect.right - 2, rect.top + 1);

    dc.SelectObject(&penShadow);
    dc.MoveTo(rect.right-2, rect.top + 2);
    dc.LineTo(rect.right-2, rect.bottom - 2);
    dc.LineTo(rect.left+2, rect.bottom - 2);

    ShowCurrentValue();

    dc.SelectObject(pOldPen);
    dc.SelectObject(pOldFont);
    // Do not call CWnd::OnPaint() for painting messages
}
```

This code draws a border around the calculator window, then constructs a box in which to display the current input for the calculator. It finally calls **ShowCurrentValue()**, which we'll look at next, to display the current input itself, before cleaning up the device context.

Note that we're using system colors to display the information. As an example of extending controls, you might want to modify this class to use colors that you've defined yourself. Give it a shot!

9 Now we'll look at **ShowCurrentValue()**. Add the declaration for this function to the **// Implementation** section in the header file for **CCalcWnd**:

```
    virtual ~CCalcWnd();

protected:
    void ShowCurrentValue();
```

Now add the definition to the source file:

```
void CCalcWnd::ShowCurrentValue()
{
    CDC* dc = GetDC();
    CFont* pOldFont = dc->SelectObject(&m_font);
    TEXTMETRIC tm;
    dc->GetTextMetrics(&tm);

    CRect rect;
    rect.top = 2 + tm.tmHeight / 2;
    rect.left= 3;
    rect.right = 5 * (2 * tm.tmMaxCharWidth) - 3;
    rect.bottom = 2 * tm.tmHeight - 3;
```

```
    CBrush NewBrush(GetSysColor(COLOR_BTNFACE));
    dc->FillRect(&rect, &NewBrush);
    dc->SetBkColor(GetSysColor(COLOR_BTNFACE));
    dc->DrawText(m_szInput, lstrlen(m_szInput), &rect, DT_RIGHT);

    // Now we clear up our mess
    dc->SelectObject(pOldFont);
    ReleaseDC(dc);
}
```

This code really does nothing more than use **CDC::DrawText()** to draw the text for the current input value in the area bounded by the box that we drew in **OnPaint()**.

10 Along with painting the screen, we also need to handle erasing the background of the window so that it'll look right when compared to the 3D effect used to display the numbers and current value. To do this, use ClassWizard to add a message handler for the **WM_ERASEBKGND** message, and add the following code to the control:

```
BOOL CCalcWnd::OnEraseBkgnd(CDC* pDC)
{
    COLORREF clrBack = GetSysColor(COLOR_BTNFACE);
    // Erase only the area needed
    CRect rect;
    GetClientRect(&rect);

    // Make a brush to erase the background.
    CBrush NewBrush(clrBack);
    pDC->SetBrushOrg(0, 0);
    CBrush* pOldBrush = (CBrush*)pDC->SelectObject(&NewBrush);

    // Paint the Background....
    pDC->PatBlt(rect.left, rect.top, rect.Width(), rect.Height(), PATCOPY);
    pDC->SelectObject(pOldBrush);

    return TRUE;
}
```

You can use this particular piece of code to clear any window background. We're using the **PatBlt()** function to simply copy a block of colored pixels into the background of the window. This effectively clears the window to a given color. If you wish, you could substitute a bitmap into the background of the window and give your window a more interesting look.

11 At this point, we need to start hooking up the functionality for the buttons that we've created. Unfortunately, ClassWizard won't allow us to define message handlers for these buttons, because their IDs aren't stored anywhere in the resource file. We'll have to edit the message map entries by hand to hook up the methods as callbacks for the buttons.

Any Windows message can be trapped within the message map handling system, regardless of whether the message is allowed in ClassWizard. If at all possible, you should always use the message mapping system to handle messages, rather than hooking into the window procedure or OnCommand() structure.

To hook up the message handlers for the buttons to the message map in **CalcWnd.cpp**, add the following lines. As usual, we've shaded the lines you need to add:

```
BEGIN_MESSAGE_MAP(CCalcWnd, CWnd)
    //{{AFX_MSG_MAP(CCalcWnd)
    ON_WM_CREATE()
    ON_WM_SIZE()
    ON_WM_PAINT()
    ON_WM_ERASEBKGND()
    //}}AFX_MSG_MAP
    ON_COMMAND_RANGE(BaseID, BaseID + 9, OnDigit)
    ON_COMMAND(BaseID + 10, OnDecimalPoint)
    ON_COMMAND(BaseID + 11, OnEquals)
    ON_COMMAND(BaseID + 12, OnPlus)
    ON_COMMAND(BaseID + 13, OnMinus)
    ON_COMMAND(BaseID + 14, OnMultiply)
    ON_COMMAND(BaseID + 15, OnDivide)
    ON_COMMAND(BaseID + 16, OnClear)
    ON_COMMAND(BaseID + 17, OnClearEntry)
END_MESSAGE_MAP()
```

These macros link message handlers for each of the buttons (all 18 of them!) into the message map. The command messages from the digit buttons will all be handled by a single function **OnDigit()**, whereas each of the other buttons has its own handler.

12 Now we need to add the declarations for the handlers to the **CalcWnd.h** header file:

```
protected:
    //{{AFX_MSG(CCalcWnd)
    afx_msg int OnCreate(LPCREATESTRUCT lpCreateStruct);
    afx_msg void OnSize(UINT nType, int cx, int cy);
    afx_msg void OnPaint();
    afx_msg BOOL OnEraseBkgnd(CDC* pDC);
    //}}AFX_MSG
    afx_msg void OnDigit(UINT nID);
    afx_msg void OnDecimalPoint();
    afx_msg void OnEquals();
    afx_msg void OnPlus();
    afx_msg void OnMinus();
    afx_msg void OnMultiply();
    afx_msg void OnDivide();
    afx_msg void OnClear();
    afx_msg void OnClearEntry();
```

The final step of the procedure is to add the functions themselves to **CCalcWnd**'s source file.

13 First, we'll provide the implementation for **OnDigit()** and **OnDecimalPoint()**:

```
void CCalcWnd::OnDigit(UINT nID)
{
    if (lstrlen(m_szInput) < MaxDigits)
    {
        TCHAR szDigit[20] = {0} ;
        _itot(nID - BaseID, szDigit, 10);
        AddDigit(m_szInput, szDigit);
```

```
        ShowCurrentValue();
        SetFocus();
    }
}

void CCalcWnd::OnDecimalPoint()
{
    if (lstrlen(m_szInput) < MaxDigits && !_tcschr(m_szInput, _T('.')))
    {
        AddDigit(m_szInput, _T("."));
        ShowCurrentValue();
        SetFocus();
    }
}
```

14 When one of the arithmetic operators is pressed, we process the previous expression (if necessary), update the display, and store the current operator. Here's the necessary code to add:

```
void CCalcWnd::OnPlus()
{
    DoCalculate();
    m_chOperator = _T('+');
    SetFocus();
}

void CCalcWnd::OnMinus()
{
    DoCalculate();
    m_chOperator = _T('-');
    SetFocus();
}

void CCalcWnd::OnMultiply()
{
    DoCalculate();
    m_chOperator = _T('*');
    SetFocus();
}

void CCalcWnd::OnDivide()
{
    DoCalculate();
    m_chOperator = _T('/');
    SetFocus();
}
```

15 Don't forget **`OnEquals()`**:

```
void CCalcWnd::OnEquals()
{
    // Save current calculation
    DoCalculate();

    // Paste into the associated window (if any)
    if (m_pwndCombo)
```

```
        m_pwndCombo->SetWindowText(m_szHold);

    // Close window
    PostMessage(WM_CLOSE);
    SetFocus();
}
```

All we do in **OnEquals()** is calculate the current result using **DoCalculate()**, and then we put it into the combo box. This method is simply the same as the user clicking back into the combo box to close the calculator window. It's provided for those people, like me, who never got the hang of those perverse (er, that's reverse) Polish notation (RPN) calculators.

16 The last two methods to add, are for **OnClear()** and **OnClearEntry()**. These clear the calculator window and the current entry:

```
void CCalcWnd::OnClear()
{
    m_szHold[0] = _T('\0');
    m_szInput[0] = _T('\0');
    m_chOperator = _T('\0');
    ShowCurrentValue();
    SetFocus();
}

void CCalcWnd::OnClearEntry()
{
    m_szInput[0] = _T('\0');
    ShowCurrentValue();
    SetFocus();
}
```

Note that we always set the focus back to the main window when we're finished processing. This is done so that the main window can trap keystrokes which are linked to keys (for example, the *1* key for entering a 1 instead of clicking on the 1 button). This leads to the next step.

17 Use ClassWizard to add a message handler to **CCalcWnd** for the **WM_CHAR** message. This message handler will allow us to process keystrokes as well as the mouse clicking on our buttons. Here's the code to add for the **OnChar()** method:

```
void CCalcWnd::OnChar(UINT nChar, UINT nRepCnt, UINT nFlags)
{
    switch (nChar)
    {
    case '0': case '1': case '2': case '3': case '4':
    case '5': case '6': case '7': case '8': case '9':
        OnDigit(BaseID + (nChar - '0'));
        break;
    case '.':
        OnDecimalPoint();
        break;
    case '+':
        OnPlus();
        break;
    case '-':
```

```
            OnMinus();
            break;
        case '*':
            OnMultiply();
            break;
        case '=': case 13:    // Pressing "Enter" works too!
            OnEquals();
            break;
        case '/':
            OnDivide();
            break;
        case 'C': case 'c':
            OnClear();
            break;
        case 'E': case 'e':
            OnClearEntry();
            break;
    }
    CWnd::OnChar(nChar, nRepCnt, nFlags);
}
```

As you can see, the **OnChar()** function simply maps keystrokes to their corresponding functions.

18 We still have a little work to do to complete the process. First, we need to write a couple of utility functions that are called from some of the other routines above. The first of these is **AddDigit()**, which simply appends the digit input to the input string:

```
void CCalcWnd::AddDigit(LPTSTR string, LPCTSTR lpszDigit)
{
    _tcscat(string, lpszDigit);
}
```

The second is the **DoCalculate()** function, which does a simple calculation based on three pieces of information: the current input string, the current calculator value, and the current operator.

```
void CCalcWnd::DoCalculate()
{
    // If we're not holding anything, just copy m_szInput into m_szHold
    if (!lstrlen(m_szHold))
    {
        lstrcpy(m_szHold, m_szInput);
        m_szInput[0] = _T('\0');
        return;
    }

    // If we are, get the value of the hold string and the current string
    double v1 = atof(m_szHold);
    double v2 = atof(m_szInput);
    double value = 0.0;

    // Do the calculation
    switch (m_chOperator)
    {
        case _T('+'):
```

```
            value = v1 + v2;
            break;
        case _T('-'):
            value = v1 - v2;
            break;
        case _T('*'):
            value = v1 * v2;
            break;
        case _T('/'):
            if (v2)
                value = v1 / v2;
            else
            {
                MessageBeep(MB_ICONEXCLAMATION);
                return;
            }
            break;
    }

    _stprintf(m_szInput, _T("%10.2lf"), value);
    ShowCurrentValue();

    // Save result into m_szHold
    lstrcpy(m_szHold, m_szInput);

    // Clear the operator
    m_chOperator = _T('\0');
    // Clear the current input string
    m_szInput[0] = _T('\0');
}
```

19 Okay, we're in the home stretch! We need to deal with only two more messages. First, we need to deal with the problem of making the calculator window go away when the user clicks on another window outside the calculator window such as clicking again on the drop-down box. Fortunately, Windows will be nice and will send us a **WM_ACTIVATE** message when the window is activated or deactivated. Deactivation means that the user has selected another window for activation. In this case, we simply want to close down our window. We can accomplish this by posting a **WM_CLOSE** message, which will do the job of closing the window and cleaning up.

Use ClassWizard to add a message handler for the **WM_ACTIVATE** message, and add the following code to the **OnActivate()** method:

```
void CCalcWnd::OnActivate(UINT nState, CWnd* pWndOther, BOOL bMinimized)
{
   CWnd::OnActivate(nState, pWndOther, bMinimized);

   // See if this is one of our buttons? Watch out, pWndOther can be NULL
   if ((pWndOther != NULL) && (pWndOther->GetParent() == this))
      return;

   if (m_hWnd && nState == WA_INACTIVE)
      PostMessage(WM_CLOSE);
}
```

20 The final step of the process is to catch the **WM_CLOSE** message to make sure that the **CCalcWnd** object itself is destroyed and the memory it occupies is deallocated. Use ClassWizard to add a new message handler for the **WM_CLOSE** message, and add the following line to **CCalcWnd::OnClose()**:

```
void CCalcWnd::OnClose()
{
    delete this;
}
```

To test the control, all you need to do is add a combo box to the main dialog in the resource editor. *Ctrl*-double-click on it to bring up ClassWizard's Add Member Variable dialog. Give the member variable a name, select Control as the Category and CCalcCombo as the Variable type, and press OK. Now add **#include "CalcCombo.h"** to the header file for the dialog, compile, and run the project.

Now, see, wasn't that simple? Oh, well, perhaps not that simple, but it surely beats writing this code several hundred times in numerous applications. These combo box calculator classes can be added to a library which is linked into your application and used in hundreds of other applications. In addition, if a bug were to be found or an enhancement requested, only one copy of the code need be changed. This is the whole idea behind components, and works quite well here.

That ends our MFC extension solution. In a matter of a few pages, we've solved two problems that plague programmers everywhere!

The ActiveX Solution: A Calendar Control

One of the more common types of input in an application is date data. Dates are required in a huge number of programs, and nearly every program has a different method for their input. Different formats, different field types, and different error messages all muddy the waters for the user and the programmer. It would be nice to create a single simple component which would allow us to input dates in a standard way and retrieve data in a standard format. For this reason, we'll consider next a control which does just that: input dates in a standard way.

When writing components, there's more to consider than simply the visual and functional aspects of the component itself. A motif is also important to the user. The motif defines the metaphor you'll use when attempting to convey to the user the type of work you're trying to accomplish. A filing cabinet motif, for example, is used in many database applications, because users are familiar with filing cabinets and associate them with large amounts of stored data. On a simpler basis, the list box is a familiar sight in many applications. Users have come to associate a list of objects with a choice selection. The most familiar motif associated with dates is the calendar.

Users know exactly what a calendar is, and most understand instantly that a calendar is to be used to select a date. For this reason, we've chosen to give our date component the look and feel of a calendar. On the following page, you can see a calendar control embedded in a dialog box. As you can see, the control is immediately recognizable as a calendar and its intent is quite obvious.

Feature List

Before we start to implement the calendar component, let's take a minute to devise a feature list for the component, just as we've done previously. The calendar component should:

- Display dates laid out in a grid like a standard calendar with seven columns, one for each day of the week.
- Display the days of the week at the top of each column to indicate to the user which day a particular date corresponds to.
- Display a full month of dates, plus the first few days of the next month and the last few days of the previous month.
- Allow a date to be selected by a single click on a day in the grid.
- Display the whole of the next or previous month in the grid if the user clicks on a date that falls outside the current month
- Indicate to the user, by appropriate use of color, which days lie in the current month, which days are in the next or previous month, and which date is currently selected.
- Let the user change months and years quickly. It would serve little purpose if we forced them to page through hundreds of months just to move forward a few years. It would also be frustrating.
- Display the correct dates. It should show the right number of days in a month, the correct day of the week for a given date, and should automatically handle leap years.
- Allow the programmer to be notified when the user has selected a new date and to determine the current date selected.
- Allow the current date to be set programmatically.
- Allow the programmer to set the earliest selectable date. In many applications a date must be after a certain day (for example, today).
- Accept and return dates using standard numbering. In other words, days go from 1–31, where appropriate, and months go from 1–12. Not many users would appreciate having to use a zero-based scheme (months going from 0-11), for example.
- Allow the font for the control to be set, so as to allow it to fit into a given dialog space.

Designing the Control

Looking at our feature list for the calendar control, our design becomes fairly straightforward. First, we need a list of properties for the control. The first property, **`Date`**, is obvious from the nature of the control, but we'd also like to be able to allow the user to individually specify elements of the date, so we should also expose **`Day`**, **`Month`**, and **`Year`** properties.

Additionally, we know that the current or selected date isn't the only date that our control will need to handle. From the requirement for an earliest selectable date, we can add **`EarliestDate`**, **`EarliestDay`**, **`EarliestMonth`**, and **`EarliestYear`** to the property list. The requirement for allowing the font to be adjusted means that we'll need to expose the **`Font`** stock property, too.

The methods for the control may not be quite so obvious, but it would be a good idea to provide **`SetDate()`**, **`GetDate()`**, **`SetEarliestDate()`**, and **`GetEarliestDate()`** methods. Why do we need these methods if we have the **`Date`** and **`EarliestDate`** properties, you might ask? For the same reason that we do anything—to make the life of whoever uses our components as easy as possible!

The **`Date`** and **`EarliestDate`** properties will accept or return a single **`DATE`**, but many users of our control will want to be able to manipulate dates in terms of their constituent parts, days, months, and years. This is why we've already supplied the **`Day`**, **`Month`**, and **`Year`** properties. If we provide methods that accept three parameters, one for the day, one for the month, and one for the year, we can replace three calls to those properties with a single one to a method. Although you may get little thanks from the users of your components by providing this sort of capability, you'd soon know about it if you didn't!

The final requirement that will affect the ActiveX control's interface, is to provide a notification to inform the programmer when the user has selected a new date. Determining when the selected date has changed is easy enough, as that is part of the basic functionality of the control, but how will we notify the programmer?

In our MFC extension classes up to this point, we have handled notification through the posting of user-defined messages. However, this isn't an ideal solution to the problem of notifications, for a number of reasons, not least of which is that some environments, such as Visual Basic, do not have an easy way to catch user-defined messages. Fortunately, ActiveX controls provide a better solution to the problem in the form of **events**. Visual C++ makes it easy to add event firing to a control, and we'll take advantage of this to satisfy the notification requirement.

In this control example, we'll add an event, **`DateChange`**, to our control which we will use to notify the programmer that the date has been changed. Since, nine times out of ten, we expect the programmer to respond to the event by requesting the new date from the control, we'll preempt this request by providing this data as parameters to the event. Hopefully, this will make the control more efficient and easier to use.

The only other design issue is how to handle the display and input of dates on the control. In our calculator example (written as an MFC extension), we used real Windows buttons to gather input from the user. In this example, we'll take a different approach by drawing the dates directly onto the control itself. There are several reasons for doing this. First, creating over forty windows for a single control is a bit excessive. Second, there's a limit of 255 controls for a single dialog box. Taking up one-sixth of them in our control would rightly be considered quite rude by other designers.

Each window also has a certain amount of overhead associated with it. There's little or no gain from using the windows, so why add to the code bloat of the world by using it? We'll use combo boxes for the display of months and years, since this is a simple control that users understand and handle well. There are only two of these controls, so their use isn't a problem in our control. In addition, this will show you how to create child windows within an ActiveX control.

Implementing the Control

To implement the control, we'll create a new OLE Control project in Visual C++, and implement the functionality of the control within that project. Follow this procedure to create the new control.

TRY IT OUT - Create a Calendar Control

1 Create a new project workspace using the OLE ControlWizard, and call the project Calendar. You can accept the default options on Step 1 of the wizard (a single control in the project without a license or a help file), but on Step 2 click the Edit Names... button and adjust some of the strings shown on the Edit Names dialog. A calendar is likely to be a popular choice for a control, so we need to try and avoid naming conflicts with other people's calendar controls.

Change the control's Type Name to Wrox Calendar Control and its Type ID to Wrox.Calendar.CalendarCtrl.1.

Change the property page's Type Name to Wrox Calendar Property Page and its Type ID to Wrox.Calendar.CalendarPropPage.1.

You can see that our type IDs take the form Company.Product.Control.Version

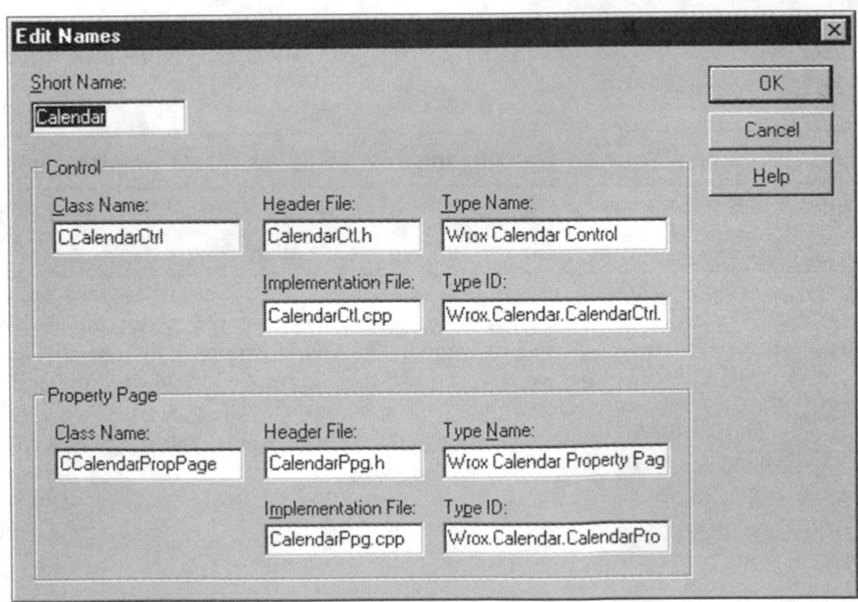

You can leave all the other options in the wizard with their default settings, and finish creating the project.

2 The first thing to do, once the project has been created, is to add the properties to the control using ClassWizard. We'll start with the single stock property, **`Font`**. Activate ClassWizard, make sure CCalendarCtrl is selected in the Class name list, and select the OLE Automation page from the property sheet. Click on Add Property.... Select Font from the drop-down list for the External name on the Add Property dialog, and click OK to add the property to the control.

3 Now select Add Property... again. Give this new property an External name of Day and the Type short. Set the Variable name field to m_nDay, leave the Notification function at OnDayChanged, and make sure that the Implementation is set to Member variable. This property will represent the currently selected day.

4 In a similar fashion, add the following properties to the control using ClassWizard. You can see the settings for each of the Add Property dialog's fields in the table below.

External name	Type	Variable name	Notification function	Implementation
Month	short	m_nMonth	OnMonthChanged	Member variable
Year	short	m_nYear	OnYearChanged	Member variable
EarliestDay	short	m_nEarliestDay	OnEarliestDayChanged	Member variable
EarliestMonth	short	m_nEarliestMonth	OnEarliestMonthChanged	Member variable
EarliestYear	short	m_nEarliestYear	OnEarliestYearChanged	Member variable

Declaring these properties also gives us the variables that we'll use to store the current and earliest dates within the class. Although we could store the dates as a single **`DATE`** or **`COleDateTime`** variable, it's easier for us to store them as separate elements.

5 The next step is to add the interface for the properties that will accept and return **`DATE`** values. So use ClassWizard's Add Property dialog to declare two more properties as shown in the table below.

External name	Type	Get function	Set function	Implementation
Date	DATE	GetDate	SetDate	Get/Set methods
EarliestDate	DATE	GetEarliestDate	SetEarliestDate	Get/Set methods

These properties are declared using Get and Set functions so that they can use the same variables as the properties that we just added. The Get functions will take the **`DATE`** they receive, and split it into a separate day, month and year for storage in the class. The Set functions will take the information from the member variables as day, month and year, and return it as a single **`DATE`** variable to whoever's requesting the value. We'll examine the implementation of these functions later.

6 Our next stage is to declare the methods available to the programmer. We'll be adding four methods to the control to get and set the earliest and the selected dates. This time, you'll need to use the Add Method... button from ClassWizard's OLE Automation page, to declare these methods. Add the methods with the settings shown in the table below:

External name	Internal name	Return type	Parameter List Name	Parameter List Type
SetDate	SetDateMethod	BOOL	nDay nMonth nYear	short short short
GetDate	GetDateMethod	void	nDay nMonth nYear	short* short* short*
SetEarliestDate	SetEarliestDateMethod	BOOL	nDay nMonth nYear	short short short
GetEarliestDate	GetEarliestDateMethod	void	nDay nMonth nYear	short* short* short*

Note that you need to append the word Method to the Internal name supplied as default, to ensure that there isn't a conflict with the functions that we declared for the **`Date`** and **`EarliestDate`** properties. The Get methods require pointers as parameters, because we need to use them to pass information back to the caller. They can't be by-value parameters.

7 While you've still got ClassWizard on screen, it's time to add the event to the control. Adding the new event is just as simple as adding a method or property. Select ClassWizard's OLE Events tab and click on the Add Event button. In the resulting dialog box, enter the name DateChange in the External Name field. Accept FireDateChange for the Internal name and add three parameters to the method, nNewDay, nNewMonth and nNewYear, all of type short. Click on the OK button. Congratulations! You have just written your first event for OCX controls.

Just like properties and methods, events are exposed through the type libraries of ActiveX controls. This means that many programming environments can provide support for the easy addition of event handlers. For example, when you add a wrapper for an ActiveX control to a Visual C++ project, ClassWizard knows all about the events that the control can fire. This is a marked improvement over the user-defined windows messages we have explored previously in MFC extension classes.

In addition to ease of use, events allow the programmer to define arguments for the event handler. Rather than having to encode everything in **`LPARAM`** and **`WPARAM`** variables, you can simply fire an event with a list of arguments, and the object which receives the fired event will receive the list as arguments to its event handler function. If you've ever programmed applications that use ActiveX or OLE controls, you'll certainly understand what I mean, but don't worry if you don't, a few examples will get you on the right track.

8 At this stage, we've almost defined the programmatic interface for our class, the only thing left to do on that front is to tidy up the **.odl** file so that it's suitable for general use. First, adjust the helpstring and library name at the top of the file, as shown below:

```
[ uuid(444AD8C0-03EE-11D0-8943-DD338433F63A), version(1.0),
  helpstring("Wrox Calendar Control"), control ]
library CalendarLib
{
```

Now, remove the Hungarian notation from the parameters to the methods and the event further down the file:

```
methods:
    // NOTE - ClassWizard will maintain method information here.
    //    Use extreme caution when editing this section.
    //{{AFX_ODL_METHOD(CCalendarCtrl)
    [id(9)] boolean SetDate(short Day, short Month, short Year);
    [id(10)] void GetDate(short* Day, short* Month, short* Year);
    [id(11)] boolean SetEarliestDate(short Day, short Month, short Year);
    [id(12)] void GetEarliestDate(short* Day, short* Month, short* Year);
    //}}AFX_ODL_METHOD

methods:
    // NOTE - ClassWizard will maintain event information here.
    //    Use extreme caution when editing this section.
    //{{AFX_ODL_EVENT(CCalendarCtrl)
    [id(1)] void DateChange(short NewDay, short NewMonth, short NewYear);
    //}}AFX_ODL_EVENT
```

None of this affects the intrinsic functionality of the control, but it should make the user of the control feel more comfortable.

9 Now we can set about providing the functionality for these properties and methods. First, we'll implement **OnDayChanged()**, **OnMonthChanged()**, and **OnYearChanged()**. Add the code highlighted below to these functions in **CalendarCtl.cpp**

```
void CCalendarCtrl::OnDayChanged()
{
    InvalidateControl();
    FireDateChange(m_nDay, m_nMonth, m_nYear);
    SetModifiedFlag();
}

void CCalendarCtrl::OnMonthChanged()
{
    UpdateCombos();
    LoadMonth();
    InvalidateControl();
    FireDateChange(m_nDay, m_nMonth, m_nYear);
    SetModifiedFlag();
}

void CCalendarCtrl::OnYearChanged()
{
    UpdateCombos();
    LoadMonth();
```

```
    InvalidateControl();
    FireDateChange(m_nDay, m_nMonth, m_nYear);
    SetModifiedFlag();
}
```

The implementation for these functions looks simple because they're calling a couple of functions that we haven't actually written yet. **UpdateCombos()** will make sure that the combo boxes in our control display the correct information, and **LoadMonth()** ensures that the correct month has been loaded so that we can use that information for painting the control. We'll see precisely how to implement those functions later.

InvalidateControl() is a function supplied by our control's base class, **COleControl**, that causes the control to redraw itself. We call this to ensure that the currently selected date is properly displayed in the grid. **FireDateChange()** is the function that we call to send the **DateChange()** event to the container of our control.

Note that we try and call as few functions as necessary to provide the correct functioning of the control. For example, there's no need to call **UpdateCombos()** or **LoadMonth()** from the **OnDayChanged()** function, since we know that the month hasn't been changed.

10 There's no need to alter the default implementation for **OnEarliestDayChanged()**, **OnEarliestMonthChanged()** or **OnEarliestYearChanged()**, so we'll go straight on to **GetDate()** and **SetDate()**.

```
DATE CCalendarCtrl::GetDate()
{
    // The zeros are for hours minutes and seconds,
    // which aren't of interest to us
    COleDateTime date(m_nYear, m_nMonth, m_nDay, 0, 0, 0);
    return (DATE) date;
}

void CCalendarCtrl::SetDate(DATE newValue)
{
    COleDateTime date(newValue);
    m_nDay = date.GetDay();
    m_nMonth = date.GetMonth();
    m_nYear = date.GetYear();

    UpdateCombos();
    LoadMonth();
    InvalidateControl();
    FireDateChange(m_nDay, m_nMonth, m_nYear);
    SetModifiedFlag();
}
```

Both of these functions are pretty straightforward, because we rely on the functionality for date manipulation supplied by MFC's **COleDateTime** class which can be easily converted to and from a **DATE**. Again, **CCalendarCtrl::SetDate()** calls **UpdateCombos()**, **LoadMonth()**, and **InvalidateControl()** to ensure that the calendar's display is updated appropriately.

11 You should provide similar implementations for **GetEarliestDate()** and **SetEarliestDate()**, but this time we don't need to worry about updating the display when the earliest date has been set.

```
DATE CCalendarCtrl::GetEarliestDate()
{
    COleDateTime dateEarliest(m_nEarliestYear, m_nEarliestMonth,
                              m_nEarliestDay, 0, 0, 0);
    return (DATE) dateEarliest;
}

void CCalendarCtrl::SetEarliestDate(DATE newValue)
{
    COleDateTime dateEarliest(newValue);
    m_nEarliestDay = dateEarliest.GetDay();
    m_nEarliestMonth = dateEarliest.GetMonth();
    m_nEarliestYear = dateEarliest.GetYear();
    SetModifiedFlag();
}
```

12 The implementations for the method functions are equally simple. Always make sure that you return or set the current date stored in **m_nDay**, **m_nMonth**, and **m_nYear** and, when the date is set, update the display and fire the event that we set up.

```
BOOL CCalendarCtrl::SetDateMethod(short nDay, short nMonth, short nYear)
{
    // If we add validation, we can return the success or failure
    // of the Set through the BOOL return type
    m_nDay = nDay;
    m_nMonth = nMonth;
    m_nYear = nYear;

    UpdateCombos();
    LoadMonth();
    InvalidateControl();
    FireDateChange(m_nDay, m_nMonth, m_nYear);
    return TRUE;
}

void CCalendarCtrl::GetDateMethod(short FAR* pDay, short FAR* pMonth,
                                  short FAR* pYear)
{
    *pDay = m_nDay;
    *pMonth = m_nMonth;
    *pYear = m_nYear;
}

BOOL CCalendarCtrl::SetEarliestDateMethod(short nDay, short nMonth,
                                          short nYear)
{
    m_nEarliestDay = nDay;
    m_nEarliestMonth = nMonth;
    m_nEarliestYear = nYear;
    return TRUE;
}
```

```
void CCalendarCtrl::GetEarliestDateMethod(short FAR* pDay, short FAR*
                                          pMonth, short FAR* pYear)
{
   *pDay = m_nEarliestDay;
   *pMonth = m_nEarliestMonth;
   *pYear = m_nEarliestYear;
}
```

13 Now let's make the properties persistent by adding some code to **CCalendarCtrl::DoPropExchange():**

```
void CCalendarCtrl::DoPropExchange(CPropExchange* pPX)
{
   ExchangeVersion(pPX, MAKELONG(_wVerMinor, _wVerMajor));
   COleControl::DoPropExchange(pPX);

   PX_Short(pPX, "Day", m_nDay, 1);
   PX_Short(pPX, "Month", m_nMonth, 1);
   PX_Short(pPX, "Year", m_nYear, 1996);
   PX_Short(pPX, "EarliestDay", m_nEarliestDay, 1);
   PX_Short(pPX, "EarliestMonth", m_nEarliestMonth, 1);
   PX_Short(pPX, "EarliestYear", m_nEarliestYear, 1980);

   if (pPX->IsLoading())
      LoadMonth();
}
```

We just use the **PX_Short()** function to make our properties persistent, saving and loading all of the properties we allow the user to modify in the resource editor. When the properties are being restored, which we check by using **CPropExchange::IsLoading()**, we also reload the month.

14 The next step is to define a couple of string arrays to help us keep our code as concise and readable as possible. Add them to **CalendarCtl.cpp**, just above the constructor for the class.

```
/////////////////////////////////////////////////////////////////////////////
// Useful Arrays
static const LPCTSTR lpszDaysOfTheWeek[] =
{
   _T("S"), _T("M"), _T("T"), _T("W"), _T("T"), _T("F"), _T("S")
};

static const LPCTSTR lpszMonthsOfTheYear[] =
{
   _T("Jan"), _T("Feb"), _T("Mar"), _T("Apr"), _T("May"), _T("Jun"),
   _T("Jul"), _T("Aug"), _T("Sep"), _T("Oct"), _T("Nov"), _T("Dec")
};
```

We'll use these strings to define the days in our grid and to fill the month combo box. We'll look at setting up the combo boxes now.

15 The first thing we need to do to get our combo boxes up and running, is to add the member variables for them to the calendar control class, so add the following code to the **// Implementation** section of the header file for **CCalendarCtrl**.

```
private:
    enum {MaxYearsInCombo = 10};
    CComboBox* m_pcboMonth;
    CComboBox* m_pcboYear;
```

The **m_pcboMonth** and **m_pcboYear** object pointers will be used to create the two combo boxes for the month and the year at the top of the control. The enumeration constant will be used to determine how many years should initially be shown in the combo box.

16 Of course, we also need to initialize these pointers in the constructor for the class:

```
CCalendarCtrl::CCalendarCtrl()
{
    InitializeIIDs(&IID_DCalendar, &IID_DCalendarEvents);

    m_pcboMonth = NULL;
    m_pcboYear = NULL;
}
```

Note the call to **InitializeIIDs()** in the constructor for the class. This call is automatically generated by ClassWizard when the class is created. It's responsible for informing the base class (**COleControl** in this case) of the interface IDs you will be using in this control. Do not remove this line because your control will not work.

17 The next step is to define the IDs for these combo boxes, so that we can create them and identify them at run time. We could just use a number to refer to them, but symbolic constants are much more readable and easily changed, so we'll create two new symbols, **IDC_COMBO_MONTH** and **IDC_COMBO_YEAR**, to represent the IDs for the combos.

This could be done in a number of ways, by declaring new integer constants or adding a **#define** to the **.cpp** file but, in this case, we'll define them as new resource symbols. Use Developer Studio's View | Resource Symbols... menu item to display the Resource Symbols dialog. Click New... to add the symbols IDC_COMBO_MONTH and IDC_COMBO_YEAR with the respective Values 101 and 102.

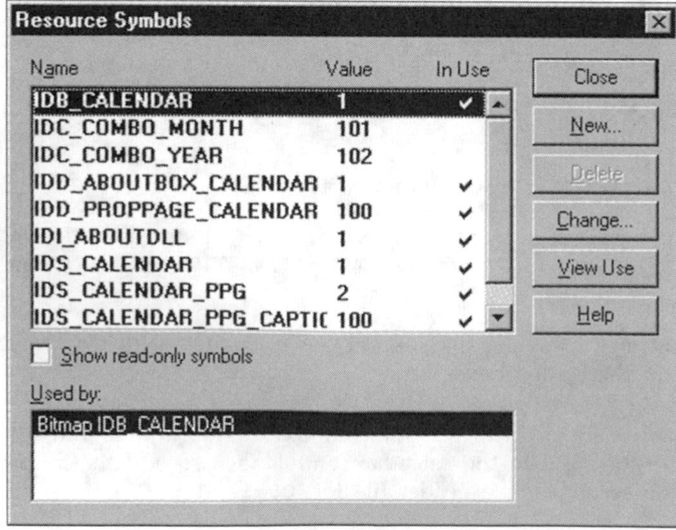

18 The next issue is how we should actually create the combo boxes. We already know that ActiveX controls can be used without having a window created for them. This is exactly what happens in the design-time environments of Developer Studio's resource editor or Visual Basic's IDE. We don't want to create the combo boxes if our control doesn't have a window to parent them, so when should we create the combos?

Fortunately, ActiveX controls follow the same sets of windows messages as normal windows, since they really *are* normal windows! For this reason, you can trap the **`WM_CREATE`** message which is sent to all windows at creation time. Creating the combo boxes in response to this message is safe, because we know that our control has a window to act as their parent. This is exactly what you'd do in a dialog class or any other type of window.

Use ClassWizard to add a message handler to **`CCalendarCtrl`** for the **`WM_CREATE`** message, and add the following code to the **`OnCreate()`** method of the calendar control:

```
int CCalendarCtrl::OnCreate(LPCREATESTRUCT lpCreateStruct)
{
   if (COleControl::OnCreate(lpCreateStruct) == -1)
      return -1;

   // Set the styles for both combos
   DWORD dwStyle = WS_BORDER | CBS_DROPDOWNLIST | WS_TABSTOP |
                   WS_VISIBLE | WS_CHILD | WS_VSCROLL;

   // Create the Month combo box
   m_pcboMonth = new CComboBox;
   CRect rectMonthCombo(5, 5, 70, 125);
   m_pcboMonth->Create(dwStyle, rectMonthCombo, this, IDC_COMBO_MONTH);
   for (int i = 0; i < 12; ++i)
      m_pcboMonth->AddString(lpszMonthsOfTheYear[i]);
   m_pcboMonth->SetCurSel(m_nMonth - 1);

   // Create the Year combo box
   m_pcboYear = new CComboBox;
   CRect rectYearCombo(90, 5, 180, 125);
   m_pcboYear->Create(dwStyle | CBS_SORT, rectYearCombo, this,
                      IDC_COMBO_YEAR);
   TCHAR szBuffer[20] = {0};
   for (i = m_nYear; i < m_nYear + MaxYearsInCombo; ++i)
   {
      _itot(i, szBuffer, 10);
      m_pcboYear->AddString(szBuffer);
   }
   m_pcboYear->SetCurSel(0);

   LoadMonth();
   UpdateCombos();
   return 0;
}
```

The creation process is pretty simple. For the month combo, we just create the control, and add the months to the list by looping through the array we set up earlier. For the year combo we do a similar thing, except we start with the current year and add as many years to the list as are specified by **`MaxYearsInCombo`**. Note that the year combo also has the **`CBS_SORT`** style set. This means that if we add years to the list later, they'll still appear in an appropriate order.

19 Don't forget to **delete** the combo boxes in the destructor.

```
CCalendarCtrl::~CCalendarCtrl()
{
    if (m_pcboMonth)
        delete m_pcboMonth;
    if (m_pcboYear)
        delete m_pcboYear;
}
```

20 Now we can add the **UpdateCombos()** function that we call whenever the date changes to ensure that the combos are displaying the correct information. Add the function declaration to the header file for **CCalendarCtrl**.

```
// Implementation
protected:
    ~CCalendarCtrl();
    void UpdateCombos();
```

Add the following implementation to the control's source file.

```
void CCalendarCtrl::UpdateCombos()
{
    // Select the current month in the combo
    m_pcboMonth->SetCurSel(m_nMonth - 1);

    // Select the current year in the combo control
    TCHAR szBuffer[20] = {0};
    _itot(m_nYear, szBuffer, 10);

    if (m_pcboYear->SelectString(-1, szBuffer) == CB_ERR)
    {
        // If we can't select it, it isn't there. Add it and select it.
        int nSel = m_pcboYear->AddString(szBuffer);
        m_pcboYear->SetCurSel(nSel);
    }
}
```

The function just uses the currently selected date, as indicated by **m_nMonth** and **m_nYear**, to select the right month and year in the combo boxes. Note that if the year doesn't currently appear in the year combo's list, we add it. This is why it was important to set the **CBS_SORT** style, so that the years wouldn't appear out of order.

21 At this stage, we're about to have to get our hands dirty with some serious date manipulation, so that we can decide precisely what we need to draw on the screen for the calendar, but, before we do that, let's take the time to add some useful helper functions to the class for this purpose. Adding some simple functions now will make the code easier to write, easier to understand and easier to modify.

The first function we'll add will take a year as input, and return a Boolean value indicating whether that year is a leap year. Add the declaration for this function to **CalendarCtl.h**.

```
protected:
    ~CCalendarCtrl();
```

```
    void UpdateCombos();
    BOOL IsLeapYear(short nYear);
```

Next, add the implementation to the source file. It might not be as straightforward as you first thought, since there's more to deciding whether a year is a leap year than just looking at its divisibility by four.

```
BOOL CCalendarCtrl::IsLeapYear(short nYear)
{
    return ((nYear % 4) == 0) &&
           ((nYear % 100) != 0 || (nYear % 400) == 0);
}
```

It's a leap year if the year is a whole multiple of 4, except it's *not* a leap year if it's a whole multiple of 100 (1900 *isn't* a leap year) unless it's also a whole multiple of 400 (but 2000 *is* a leap year). Got that? Easy, isn't it!

22 Now we'll add a function to determine whether a particular date is before the earliest date allowed by the control. Add the **protected** function declaration shown below:

```
    BOOL IsLeapYear(short nYear);
    BOOL IsBeforeEarliestDate(short nDay, short nMonth, short nYear);
```

The implementation is straightforward, since we just use **operator<()**, defined by MFC's **COleDateTime** class, to perform the test for us:

```
BOOL CCalendarCtrl::IsBeforeEarliestDate(short nDay, short nMonth,
                                         short nYear)
{
    COleDateTime dateEarliest(m_nEarliestYear, m_nEarliestMonth,
                              m_nEarliestDay, 0, 0, 0);
    COleDateTime dateTest(nYear, nMonth, nDay, 0, 0, 0);
    return (dateTest < dateEarliest);
}
```

23 Similarly, we can use the **COleDateTime** class to return the day of the week for a given date. The value returned by the function will be in the range 1–7, where 1 is Sunday, 2 is Monday, and so on. Add this declaration to **CCalendarCtrl**'s header file:

```
    BOOL IsBeforeEarliestDate(short nDay, short nMonth, short nYear);
    short DayOfWeek(short nDay, short nMonth, short nYear);
```

You can add the implementation shown to the source file.

```
short CCalendarCtrl::DayOfWeek(short nDay, short nMonth, short nYear)
{
    COleDateTime dateTest(nYear, nMonth, nDay, 0, 0, 0);
    return dateTest.GetDayOfWeek();
}
```

24 Now we'll add a further three functions to return the number of days in a month. The declarations are shown on the next page.

```
short DayOfWeek(short nDay, short nMonth, short nYear);
short DaysInMonth(short nMonth, short nYear);
short DaysInThisMonth(); // Returns the number of days in the currently
                         // selected month
short DaysInLastMonth(); // Returns the number of days in the month
                         // before the currently selected month
```

The implementations for these functions should be added to **CalendarCtl.cpp**. You can see that, although these functions are relatively simple, they'll make our lives a lot easier and also reduce the chance of errors when we write the code that needs them:

```
short CCalendarCtrl::DaysInMonth(short nMonth, short nYear)
{
   static days[] = {31, 28, 31, 30, 31, 30, 31, 31, 30, 31, 30, 31};
   if (nMonth != 2)
      return days[nMonth - 1];

   if (IsLeapYear(nYear))
      return 29;
   else
      return 28;
}

short CCalendarCtrl::DaysInThisMonth()
{
   return DaysInMonth(m_nMonth, m_nYear);
}

short CCalendarCtrl::DaysInLastMonth()
{
   // Watch out for January!
   if (m_nMonth != 1)
      return DaysInMonth(m_nMonth - 1, m_nYear);
   else
      return DaysInMonth(12, m_nYear - 1);
}
```

25 Now it's time to add a vital **private** data member to the control class.

```
CComboBox* m_pcboYear;
short m_nDayArray[42]; // This array contains the days of the previous,
                       // current and next months in the appropriate
                       // position for display.
```

This array of days will store the dates that need to be displayed in the calendar grid. We'll use the **LoadMonth()** function (that we came across earlier) to load this array with the correct dates for the current month, and then the drawing code can loop through the array to draw the dates on the control's surface. It's dimensioned to a size of 42, because this allows us to store 6 weeks worth of dates. This is enough to display the whole of the current month.

You should add some code to the class constructor to initialize this array.

```
CCalendarCtrl::CCalendarCtrl()
{
   InitializeIIDs(&IID_DCalendar, &IID_DCalendarEvents);
```

```
    m_pcboMonth = NULL;
    m_pcboYear = NULL;

    // Clear the array...
    for (int i = 0; i < 42; ++i)
       m_nDayArray[i] = 0;
}
```

26 Now we get to add the **LoadMonth()** function itself. Add the declaration to the section of the header file containing the **protected** functions we've been adding to our class:

```
short DaysInLastMonth();
void LoadMonth(); // Fills m_nDayArray[] with the days for any dates
                  // that need to be displayed
```

Now add the implementation shown below to the control's source file, **CalendarCtl.cpp**. The real work we do here is to use the values returned from **IndexOfFirst()**, **IndexOfLast()**, and **DaysInLastMonth()** to create three **for** loops that put the dates from this month, the dates from last month, and the dates for next month into the appropriate positions in the array.

```
void CCalendarCtrl::LoadMonth()
{
   // Start by clearing the array
   for (int i = 0; i < 42; ++i)
      m_nDayArray[i] = 0;

   // Now store the index of the first and last days of this month
   // and the number of days in last month
   // since we'll be using them in a loop
   int nFirstCellOfMonth = IndexOfFirst();
   int nLastCellOfMonth = IndexOfLast();
   int nDaysInLastMonth = DaysInLastMonth();

   // Fill the array with this month's dates
   for (i = nFirstCellOfMonth; i <= nLastCellOfMonth; ++i)
      m_nDayArray[i] = i - nFirstCellOfMonth + 1;

   // Go back and fill in the dates for last month
   // Loop backwards towards the start
   int j = 0;
   for (i = nFirstCellOfMonth - 1; i >= 0; --i)
   {
      m_nDayArray[i] = nDaysInLastMonth - j;
      ++j;
   }

   // Now fill the rest of the array with next month's dates
   for (i = nLastCellOfMonth + 1; i < 42; ++i)
      m_nDayArray[i] = i - nLastCellOfMonth;
}
```

Once you know that **IndexOfFirst()** returns the index of the array element that should store the first day of the current month and **IndexOfLast()** returns the index of the array element that should store the last day of the current month, it should be fairly clear how these loops work. We'll look next at the implementation of various functions relating to the array index, including the two functions just mentioned.

27 Add the declarations for the following protected functions to an appropriate position in the control's header file:

```
void LoadMonth();
int IndexOfFirst();
int IndexOfLast();
void IndexToRowCol(int nIndex, int& nRow, int& nColumn);
void IndexFromRowCol(int& nIndex, int nRow, int nColumn);
```

Now implement the functions, as shown below. **IndexOfFirst()** is easy because we just need to determine the day of the week of the first day of the current month. We subtract **1** from it because our array is zero-based, with zero corresponding to Sunday, whereas **DayOfWeek()** returns **1** for Sunday.

```
int CCalendarCtrl::IndexOfFirst()
{
   return DayOfWeek(1, m_nMonth, m_nYear) - 1;
}
```

IndexOfLast() is simple once we know **IndexOfFirst()**.

```
int CCalendarCtrl::IndexOfLast()
{
   return IndexOfFirst() + DaysInThisMonth() - 1;
}
```

The next two functions convert between an index and a row-column pair. This gives us a two-way map between an entry in **m_nDayArray** and its physical position in the calendar display. This will be very useful when it's time to draw the calendar.

```
void CCalendarCtrl::IndexToRowCol(int nIndex, int& nRow, int& nColumn)
{
   // The row and column that we will return will be zero-based
   // (i.e. the columns go from 0-6 and the rows from 0-5)
   nRow = nIndex / 7;
   nColumn = nIndex % 7;
}

void CCalendarCtrl::IndexFromRowCol(int& nIndex, int nRow, int nColumn)
{
   // The row and column are zero-based
   nIndex = nRow * 7 + nColumn;
}
```

28 We'll look at the drawing functions now. First, declare **DrawDayText()** and **DrawGridSquareText()** as shown below. These functions will be called from **CCalendarCtrl::OnDraw()** which we'll look at shortly.

```
void IndexFromRowCol(int& nIndex, int nRow, int nColumn);
// Drawing functions
void DrawDayText(CDC* pdc, int nTopOfGrid, TEXTMETRIC& tm);
void DrawGridSquareText(CDC* pdc, int nTopOfGrid, int nIndex,
                        BOOL bThisMonth, BOOL bSelected = FALSE);
```

DrawDayText() is defined to draw the column header indicating the days for our calendar. It takes three parameters, a pointer to a device context, the top of the grid containing the letters for the days, and a structure holding the metrics of the font in use:

```
void CCalendarCtrl::DrawDayText(CDC* pdc, int nTopOfGrid, TEXTMETRIC& tm)
{
   // The font will have been set by the time this is called
   // First, draw the text for each of the day letters
   CBrush brush(GetSysColor(COLOR_BTNFACE));
   CBrush* pOldBrush = pdc->SelectObject(&brush);

   for (int i = 0; i < 7; ++i)
   {
      int x = m_nCtrlLeft + 2 + i * ((2 * tm.tmMaxCharWidth) + 1);
      int y = nTopOfGrid;

      CRect rect(x, y + 1, x + 1 + 2 * tm.tmMaxCharWidth,
                 y + tm.tmHeight + 1);

      pdc->DrawText(lpszDaysOfTheWeek[i], lstrlen(lpszDaysOfTheWeek[i]),
                 &rect, DT_CENTER);
   }

   // Reset DC
   pdc->SelectObject(pOldBrush);
}
```

Essentially, the function just loops through the **lpszDaysOfTheWeek** array, drawing the text that it finds in each element of that array in the appropriate position on the control's window.

29 The **DrawGridSquareText()** function is a little more complicated. When supplied with a device context, the top of the grid that contains the dates, the index of a date to be drawn, and two boolean values indicating whether the date to be drawn is in the current month and whether it is selected, the function takes this information and draws the correct text on the calendar in the right font and at the right position.

First, it uses **nIndex** to get the corresponding date from **m_DayArray** and converts it to a string. It then determines which row and column the date should be drawn in, and uses this information to get the rectangle that the text should be drawn in. After that, it's a matter of checking the boolean parameters to determine how the text should be drawn, then calling **DrawText()** to actually draw it.

Selected dates are drawn with white text on a blue background, dates in the current month are drawn in black text, and dates in the previous or next months are drawn in gray text.

```
void CCalendarCtrl::DrawGridSquareText(CDC* pdc, int nTopOfGrid,
                 int nIndex, BOOL bThisMonth, BOOL bSelected /*=FALSE*/)
{
   // Get the date we need to draw from the array and convert it to text
   TCHAR szBuffer[10] = {0};
   _itot(m_nDayArray[nIndex], szBuffer, 10);

   // Get the row and column for the index we've been given
   int nColumn;
```

```
    int nRow;
    IndexToRowCol(nIndex, nRow, nColumn);

    CBrush brBackground(GetSysColor(COLOR_BTNFACE));
    CBrush brSelectedBackground(RGB(0, 0, 255));
    CPen npen(PS_SOLID, 1, GetSysColor(COLOR_BTNFACE));

    TEXTMETRIC tm;
    CFont* pOldFont = SelectStockFont(pdc);
    pdc->GetTextMetrics(&tm);

    int x = m_nCtrlLeft + 2 + nColumn * ((2 * tm.tmMaxCharWidth) + 1);
    int y = nTopOfGrid + nRow * (tm.tmHeight + 1);

    CRect rect(x, y, x + 1 + 2 * tm.tmMaxCharWidth, y + tm.tmHeight + 1);
    CPen* pOldPen = pdc->SelectObject(&npen);

    // Clear the background if necessary
    CBrush* pOldBrush;
    // Set the background brush
    if (bSelected == FALSE)
       pOldBrush = pdc->SelectObject(&brBackground);
    else
       pOldBrush = pdc->SelectObject(&brSelectedBackground);
    pdc->Rectangle(&rect);

    // Set the background text color
    if (bSelected == FALSE)
       pdc->SetBkColor(GetSysColor(COLOR_BTNFACE));
    else
       pdc->SetBkColor(RGB(0, 0, 255));

    // Set the text color
    if (bSelected == FALSE)
    {
       if (bThisMonth)
          pdc->SetTextColor(RGB(0, 0, 0));             // Black text
       else
           pdc->SetTextColor (RGB(128, 128, 128));      // Gray text
    }
    else
       pdc->SetTextColor(RGB(255, 255, 255));          // White text

    rect.top++;
    rect.bottom--;
    pdc->DrawText(szBuffer, lstrlen(szBuffer), &rect, DT_CENTER);

    // Reset the state of the DC.
    pdc->SelectObject(pOldPen);
    pdc->SelectObject(pOldBrush);
    pdc->SelectObject(pOldFont);
}
```

Note that, as usual, we are careful to restore the state of the device context to how it was when we found it.

It's extremely important that you always reset the state of the DC when you have finished operating on it in an ActiveX control or at any other time. If you fail to put things back the way you found them, the results will be unpredictable and can result in strange looking controls.

30 The drawing code that we have just seen is triggered in response to the **OnDraw()** function. You'll find that, when you created the control, a default implementation for this function was provided for you by AppWizard. Replace it with the code shown below.

```
void CCalendarCtrl::OnDraw(
        CDC* pdc, const CRect& rcBounds, const CRect& rcInvalid)
{
   // At this stage, we know that the m_nDayArray[] is filled with all the
   // dates that we need to draw. All we have to do is loop through it and
   // extract the numbers to draw.

   // Fill the background
   CBrush brush(GetSysColor(COLOR_BTNFACE));
   pdc->FillRect(&rcInvalid, &brush);

   // Get the size of the font used.
   TEXTMETRIC tm;
   CFont* pOldFont = SelectStockFont(pdc);
   pdc->GetTextMetrics(&tm);
   COLORREF clrOld = pdc->SetBkColor(GetSysColor(COLOR_BTNFACE));

   // And save the top left corner for drawing
    m_nCtrlTop = rcBounds.top;
    m_nCtrlLeft= rcBounds.left;

   // Get the top of the grid
   int nTopOfGrid = m_nCtrlTop + 40;

   if (m_pcboMonth)
   {
      CRect rect;
      m_pcboMonth->GetClientRect(&rect);
      nTopOfGrid = rect.bottom + 10;
   }

   // First we draw the letters for the days
   DrawDayText(pdc, nTopOfGrid, tm);

   // Set top of grid to be used in OnLButtonDown()
   m_nTopOfGrid = nTopOfGrid += (tm.tmHeight + 1) + 2;

   int nFirstCellOfMonth = IndexOfFirst();
   int nLastCellOfMonth = IndexOfLast();

   // Draw last month's dates
   for (int i = 0; i < nFirstCellOfMonth; ++i)
      DrawGridSquareText(pdc, nTopOfGrid, i, FALSE);

   // Draw this month's dates
```

```
    for (i = nFirstCellOfMonth; i <= nLastCellOfMonth; ++i)
        DrawGridSquareText(pdc, nTopOfGrid, i, TRUE);

    // Draw next month's dates
    for (i = nLastCellOfMonth + 1; i < 42; ++i)
        DrawGridSquareText(pdc, nTopOfGrid, i, FALSE);

    // Draw the selected date
    DrawGridSquareText(pdc, nTopOfGrid, nFirstCellOfMonth + m_nDay - 1,
                       TRUE, TRUE);

    // Reset the dc
    pdc->SelectObject(pOldFont);
    pdc->SetBkColor(clrOld);
}
```

What are we accomplishing here? First, we set the font based on the stock property, then determine its metrics so that we can pass this information to the **DrawDayText()** function. This is done so that we can evenly space the information across the control.

Next, we try to get the window rectangle for one of the combo boxes:

```
if (m_pcboMonth)
{
    CRect rect;
    m_pcboMonth->GetClientRect(&rect);
    nTopOfGrid = rect.bottom + 10;
}
```

The odd-looking **if** statement is there to protect us from trying to get the client rectangle of a control that doesn't exist. As we've mentioned, ActiveX controls can exist without a window and, if our control is in such a state, the combo boxes won't have been created.

The windowless state usually corresponds to design-mode, whereas we are usually supplied with a window in run-mode. How do you know if you are in design mode or run-mode? There are two solutions to this problem. First, the **m_hWnd** member of the control will be **NULL** if the control wasn't created in a window and therefore will indicate that you're in design mode. Another method of determining the mode is to call the **AmbientUserMode()** function. This will return **FALSE** if the control is in design mode, and **TRUE** if it's in run-mode. Since all we really care about is whether the combo control exists or not, we can just use a simple check on the **m_pcboMonth** pointer.

Once we've determined where to start drawing, we render the letters for the days at the top of the column with a call to **DrawDayText()**. Next, the previous month's dates (if any) are drawn at the correct positions. Following that, we draw the current month's dates then the dates for next month. All of the day rendering is done by the **DrawGridSquareText()** method. Finally, we make a single call to **DrawGridSquareText()** to draw the selected date in its highlighted form.

31 Now there are only a couple more steps to go. We simply need to add the message handlers that will allow the user to change the selected date via the control's user interface. First, we'll add handlers for the combo boxes.

Remember that we added the combo boxes with the identifiers **IDC_COMBO_MONTH** and **IDC_COMBO_YEAR**. Because ClassWizard doesn't know that these correspond to identifiers for the combo boxes, it's unable to work with the combo box notification messages for these controls. We'll need to modify the message map entries for the **CCalendarCtrl** class by hand to add message handlers for these combo boxes. To do this, add the following lines (highlighted here) to the message map in **CalendarCtl.cpp**:

```
BEGIN_MESSAGE_MAP(CCalendarCtrl, COleControl)
    //{{AFX_MSG_MAP(CCalendarCtrl)
    ON_WM_CREATE()
    ON_WM_LBUTTONDOWN()
    //}}AFX_MSG_MAP
    ON_OLEVERB(AFX_IDS_VERB_PROPERTIES, OnProperties)
    ON_CBN_SELCHANGE(IDC_COMBO_MONTH, OnMonthChange)
    ON_CBN_SELCHANGE(IDC_COMBO_YEAR, OnYearChange)
END_MESSAGE_MAP()
```

Additionally, add the function prototypes to the header file for the control in the **// Message maps** section, as shown in the following code snippet. The additions are, once again, shown highlighted:

```
// Message maps
    //{{AFX_MSG(CCalendarCtrl)
    afx_msg int OnCreate(LPCREATESTRUCT lpCreateStruct);
    afx_msg void OnLButtonDown(UINT nFlags, CPoint point);
    //}}AFX_MSG
    afx_msg void OnMonthChange();
    afx_msg void OnYearChange();
```

Add the following code to support these functions:

```
void CCalendarCtrl::OnMonthChange()
{
    int nNewMonth = m_pcboMonth->GetCurSel() + 1;

    if (nNewMonth == m_nMonth)
        return;

    if (IsBeforeEarliestDate(m_nDay, nNewMonth, m_nYear))
    {
        m_nDay = m_nEarliestDay;
        m_nMonth = m_nEarliestMonth;
        m_nYear = m_nEarliestYear;
        UpdateCombos();
        MessageBeep(MB_ICONEXCLAMATION);
    }
    else
        m_nMonth = nNewMonth;

    LoadMonth();
    InvalidateControl();
    FireDateChange(m_nDay, m_nMonth, m_nYear);
}
```

```
void CCalendarCtrl::OnYearChange()
{
```

```
    // Get the current year from the control
    CString strYear;
    m_pcboYear->GetLBText(m_pcboYear->GetCurSel(), strYear);

    // Convert to the integer year
    int nNewYear = _ttoi(strYear);

    if (nNewYear == m_nYear)
       return;

    if (IsBeforeEarliestDate(m_nDay, m_nMonth, nNewYear))
    {
       m_nDay = m_nEarliestDay;
       m_nMonth = m_nEarliestMonth;
       m_nYear = m_nEarliestYear;
       UpdateCombos();
       MessageBeep(MB_ICONEXCLAMATION);
    }
    else
       m_nYear = nNewYear;

    LoadMonth();
    InvalidateControl();
    FireDateChange(m_nDay, m_nMonth, m_nYear);
}
```

32 The final thing to do is catch the **WM_LBUTTONDOWN** message. Use ClassWizard to add a handler for this message to **CCalendarCtrl**, then modify the function as shown below.

```
void CCalendarCtrl::OnLButtonDown(UINT nFlags, CPoint point)
{
    // Select the font in order to get metrics
    CDC* pdc = GetDC();
    TEXTMETRIC tm;
    CFont* pOldFont = SelectStockFont(pdc);
    pdc->GetTextMetrics(&tm);

    // Determine which row and column this one falls in
    int nRow = -1;
    int nColumn = -1;

    for (int i = 0; i < 6; ++i)
    {
       for (int j = 0; j < 7; ++j)
       {
          int x = m_nCtrlLeft + j * ((2 * tm.tmMaxCharWidth) + 1);
          int y = m_nTopOfGrid + 1 + i * (tm.tmHeight + 1);
          CRect rect(x + 1, y + 1, x + 1 + 2 * tm.tmMaxCharWidth,
                  y + tm.tmHeight);

          if (rect.PtInRect(point))
          {
             nRow = i;
             nColumn = j;
          }
       }
    }
```

```
// If it's not in one of the cell's, nRow or nColumn will be -1
// in which case we can clear up and go home.
if (nRow == -1 || nColumn == -1)
{
   pdc->SelectObject(pOldFont);
   ReleaseDC(pdc);
   return;
}

// Now we know we're in a valid cell, find index so we can check
// whether cell is in previous, this or next month
int nIndex = 0;
IndexFromRowCol(nIndex, nRow, nColumn);

// Set up temporary values in case the date is before the earliest
int nTempDay = m_nDay;
int nTempMonth = m_nMonth;
int nTempYear = m_nYear;

// Are we in previous month?
if (nIndex < IndexOfFirst())
{
   // Get the day from the array
   nTempDay = m_nDayArray[nIndex];

   // The month is easy unless we're already in January
   if (m_nMonth != 1)
      nTempMonth = m_nMonth - 1;
   else
   {
      nTempMonth = 12;
      nTempYear = m_nYear - 1;
   }

   // Now check whether the date is before the earliest allowed
   // If it is, set selected date to earliest allowed date
   if (IsBeforeEarliestDate(nTempDay, nTempMonth, nTempYear))
   {
      m_nDay = m_nEarliestDay;
      m_nMonth = m_nEarliestMonth;
      m_nYear = m_nEarliestYear;
      MessageBeep(MB_ICONEXCLAMATION);
   }
   // Otherwise we can use the temp values that we just set up
   else
   {
      m_nDay = nTempDay;
      m_nMonth = nTempMonth;
      m_nYear = nTempYear;
   }

   LoadMonth();
   UpdateCombos();
   InvalidateControl();

}
// Are we in this month?
else if (nIndex <= IndexOfLast())
```

```
{
    // Store the current selected index for more efficient painting
    int nOriginalIndex = IndexOfFirst() + m_nDay - 1;

    // If the selected index is the same as the original,
    // clean up and go home
    if (nOriginalIndex == nIndex)
    {
        pdc->SelectObject(pOldFont);
        ReleaseDC(pdc);
        return;
    }

    // Don't need to worry about changing the month or year,
    // just check whether the proposed change is earlier
    // than the earliest allowed date
    if (IsBeforeEarliestDate(m_nDayArray[nIndex], m_nMonth, m_nYear))
    {
        m_nDay = m_nEarliestDay;
        m_nMonth = m_nEarliestMonth;
        m_nYear = m_nEarliestYear;
        MessageBeep(MB_ICONEXCLAMATION);
        nIndex = IndexOfFirst() + m_nDay - 1;
    }
    else
        m_nDay = m_nDayArray[nIndex];

    // We don't need to UpdateCombos() or LoadMonth()
    // and we can be more efficient than Invalidating the control
    // but we do need to update the display
    // Redraw the original selected cell as unselected
    DrawGridSquareText(pdc, m_nTopOfGrid, nOriginalIndex, TRUE);
    // Draw the newly selected cell
    DrawGridSquareText(pdc, m_nTopOfGrid, nIndex, TRUE, TRUE);
}
// We must be in next month
else
{
    m_nDay = m_nDayArray[nIndex];
    if (m_nMonth != 12)
        m_nMonth = m_nMonth + 1;
    else
    {
        m_nMonth = 1;
        m_nYear = m_nYear + 1;
    }

    LoadMonth();
    UpdateCombos();
    InvalidateControl();
}

FireDateChange(m_nDay, m_nMonth, m_nYear);

// Reset DC
pdc->SelectObject(pOldFont);
ReleaseDC(pdc);
```

```
    COleControl::OnLButtonDown(nFlags, point);
}
```

Essentially, this huge ream of code breaks down as follows:

- Select the font, because the size of the grid cells is dependent on it.
- Determine which cell, if any, the user has clicked in. It's easiest to determine the row and column first.
- Convert the row and column into an index in **m_nDayArray**.
- Use the value in **m_nDayArray[nIndex]** to determine what to set the current day to, but be careful because the month may need to change, too.
- Check that the new date isn't before the earliest allowed date. If it is, set the date to the earliest allowed date instead, and beep to alert the user.
- Update the display. This can be done more efficiently if the newly selected date is in the same month as the previous one, since we don't need to call **LoadMonth()** or **UpdateCombos()**.
- Fire the **DateChange** event.

You'll also need to add declarations for the **private** member variables **m_nTopOfGrid**, **m_nCtrlLeft**, and **m_nCtrlTop** to the class's header file. These get set in **OnDraw()** and used in **OnLButtonDown()** to store the coordinates for the top of the grid, and the left and top of the control rectangle.

```
short m_nDayArray[42]
int m_nTopOfGrid;
int m_nCtrlTop;
int m_nCtrlLeft;
```

That's all there is to it! Simple, wasn't it? Well, actually, it really is a fairly simple control. The problem is that the amount of code necessary to implement even a simple ActiveX control is rather staggering. Windows does tend to lend itself towards rather large applications and controls, even though the operating system itself does the lion's share of the work. We'll look at ways to combat this later in the book when we look at how ATL can help.

Here you can see the control running in the Test Container. If you compile the code now, you can test this for your self.

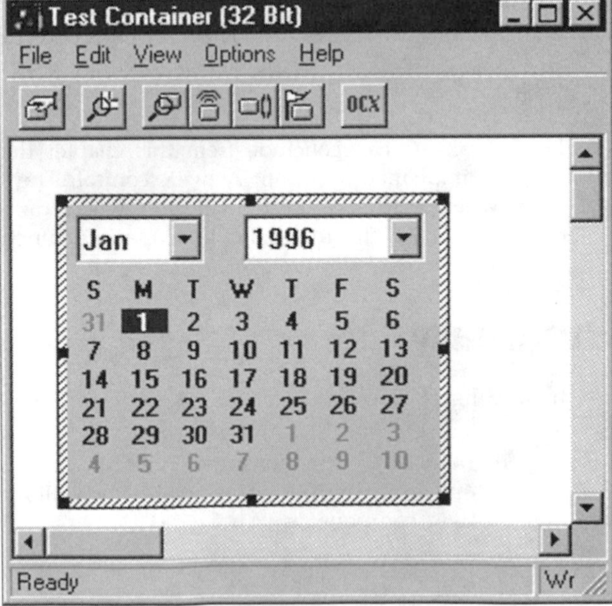

Comparing the MFC and ActiveX Solutions

Given the two solutions we came up with, what conclusions can we draw about the two kinds of approach? The first, most obvious conclusion, is that it takes a lot less code to implement an MFC extension than to solve the same sort of problem using an ActiveX control.

This is true, and it also leads to another inescapable truism about ActiveX controls. They are large. You might think that since we wrote only a few dozen lines of code (okay, maybe a few hundred), these controls really aren't that large, but take another look at all of the code generated by the AppWizard, and all of the source for the MFC classes. Code bloat in the upcoming 21st century will probably trace its roots to the day when programmers begin to write everything as an ActiveX control. The overhead necessary to implement much of what makes an ActiveX control so valuable is what makes them large as well.

Another obvious characteristic of ActiveX controls is that they are well-suited for writing end-user based components. MFC extensions suffer from the fact that they can't be directly added to a dialog as controls. They must be used through the ClassWizard (by subclassing a dialog control item) removing the direct visual link for the GUI designer. ActiveX controls can be directly added to a dialog and viewed at design time. This facility at design time becomes more and more important as programmers progress away from the actual GUI design of screens, towards simply implementing functionality of those GUI objects.

From a programming viewpoint, ActiveX controls seem to be able to do anything that MFC extensions can do. Why, then, would we choose to use the MFC drop-down calculator component over an ActiveX based one?

The biggest reason is the speed and size of MFC extensions over ActiveX solutions. The MFC extension can be moved easily into a library, eliminating the need for extra files to ship with applications. Probably the best reason to use an MFC extension, however, is shown in the first example in this chapter (the validation edit control). MFC extensions can be extended through simple C++ inheritance. We can take the validation edit control and make it into a highly specialized Social Security Number validation edit control, by simply deriving a new class and implementing the **`IsValid()`**, **`GetFormattedString()`**, and **`GetStrippedString()`** functions. ActiveX controls, on the other hand, require a new control for each new type of component you wish to implement.

In general, we can conclude from this chapter that there's nothing in an MFC extension that can't be implemented in an ActiveX control. The tradeoffs, however, favor MFC extensions in cases where size and speed matter, or where the component is intended as a base for other components which are similar in scope and function.

Summary

In looking back over the chapter, let's review what we've discovered up to this point:

- Both MFC extensions and ActiveX controls can consist of an amalgam of child windows and original code. This combination allows us to use existing bodies of code to build new components.
- MFC extensions tend to be smaller and faster than ActiveX equivalents.

- ActiveX controls allow the programmer to define properties and methods much more easily than their MFC counterparts.
- ActiveX controls allow programmers to define their own events which can be used directly in ClassWizard. MFC extensions require that the programmer post user-defined messages which can't be interpreted through ClassWizard.
- MFC extensions can be built easily around existing Windows controls to implement functionality never dreamed of in the original code. We saw an example of this in the drop-down calculator case, where the combo box was used to implement a non-list box solution.
- While Windows provides a plethora of input functionality, the ability to use either MFC extensions or ActiveX controls to get specific information from the user greatly extends the functionality and user-friendliness of applications.

Things to Try

Here are a few 'homework' assignments that you might try, to gain a fuller understanding of how ActiveX controls and MFC extensions are implemented and work.

- Derive a new class from the validation edit control to allow for the input of phone numbers.
- Modify the drop-down calculator component to allow the programmer to define their own color scheme for the buttons and background area.
- Improve the calendar in one or more of the following ways:
- Modify the calendar control to allow for the definition of special days which appear in different colors in the control. Examples of special days might include holidays, birthdays, and weekends.
- Add additional error checking to the control.
- Add the ability to validate input for the calendar. This can be accomplished now by catching date change events in the calendar, but it would be easier to reset the date if the previous setting was stored and allowed to be reset on an error condition.
- Add a property page for the control.
- Add a small amount of drawing code to show the positions of the combos at design time.
- Try improving the drawing code in general. You could add a few more checks to avoid unnecessary drawing, or try buffering the drawing. To use buffering, create a compatible off-screen device context, draw into that DC and then blit the off-screen bitmap onto the screen. This will reduce flicker as the control draws itself. There are numerous ways of improving the display for ActiveX controls, but these are mostly beyond the scope of this book, so it's up to you to seek them out!

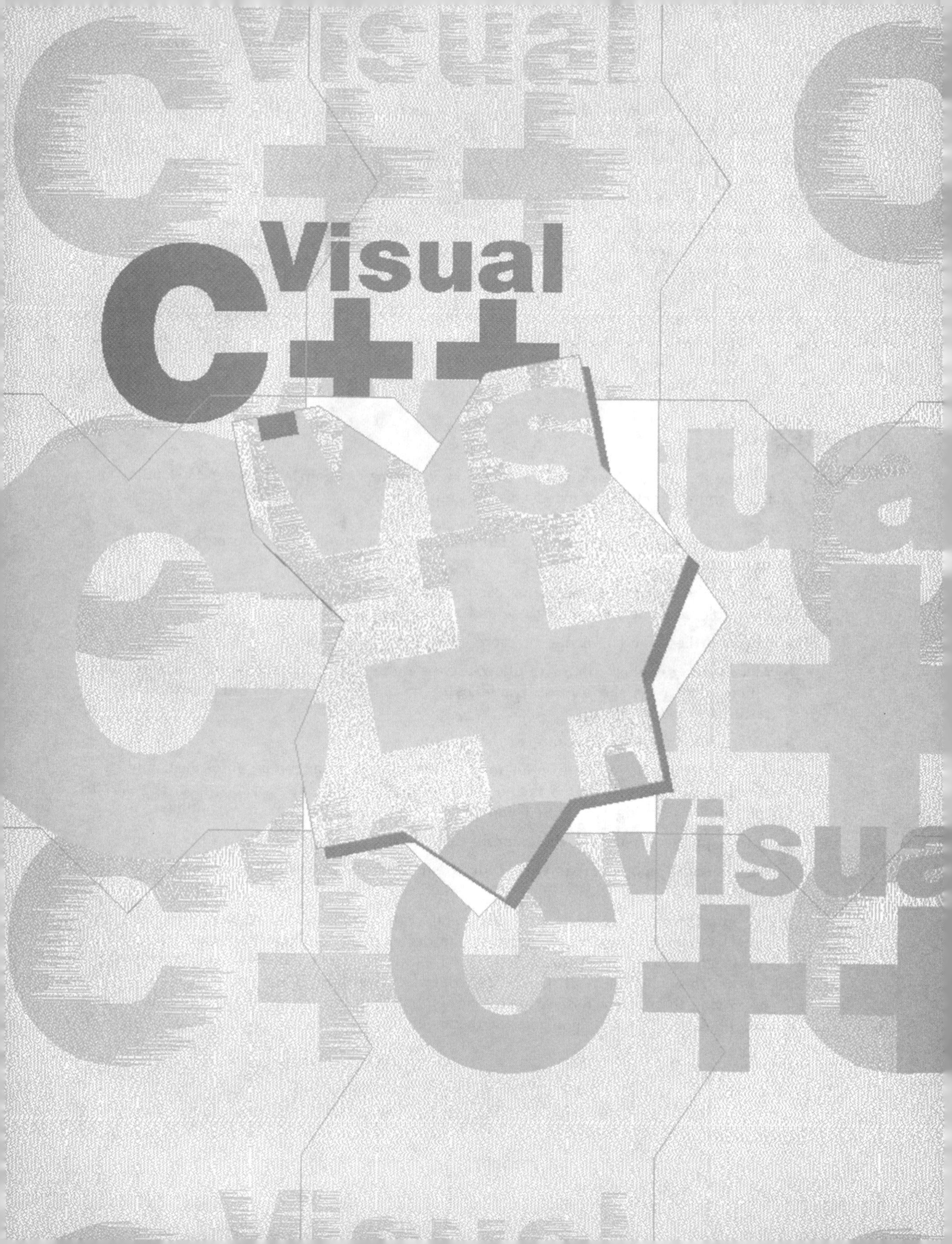
Visual
C++

List Displays

In almost every application, you'll find that you need to display lists of data. Windows provides several methods to display data in lists, but all of them suffer from some limitation or problem. If you want to display the list data in the form of multiple columns, the problems are even worse.

The Problem

If you were to examine the available list display options in Windows, and try to use them to display lists which consisted of separate fields of data (such as database records), you would find it difficult to get the available solutions to work. Although list boxes, standard Windows controls since the earliest times, can display columnar data using tab-delimited fields, they don't allow the selection of individual fields, changes of colors associated with the fields or the association of your own information with the fields.

The Windows list view control does a better job of displaying columnar information using its report view. Unfortunately, while the report view is quite good at displaying columns, it suffers in the selection and association areas. List views don't allow the selection of more than the first column of data, they can't associate information with secondary columns and, like many Microsoft controls, list views don't allow the changing of colors easily.

Visual Basic ships with a control called the **`Grid`** control, which does allow the programmer to display information in multiple columns. A version of this control also ships with Visual C++ 4.*x*, but is so hampered by inadequate documentation that it's almost useless.

What then is a programmer to do to display columnar information? In this chapter, we will look at solutions to the problem of displaying information, selecting information, and adequately dealing with record-like data in Windows.

We'll present the first solution to the list data problem as an MFC extension. This extension, a derivative of MFC's **`CListCtrl`** class, shows how to enhance the functionality of the Windows common list view control to solve the problem. This is a new direction compared with the controls we have built so far, because it relies heavily on the existing common control for most of its internal workings. Up to this point, we have focused on writing controls almost from scratch rather than building on existing components.

The second example is a simple ActiveX grid control that works much like the Microsoft effort, but with a twist. The **EGrid** is a grid control that permits three kinds of entries in its cells: static text fields, bitmaps, and—something which isn't supported by the Microsoft grid control—editable text. In this example, you will learn how to display text in a grid and allow the user to edit the text in the cell. As you will have the complete source code for the control, adding new cell types will be a snap!

The MFC Solution: Color List Control

One of the biggest problems with the Windows common list view control is that although it supports multiple columns using the report view, the extra columns are for display only. It doesn't directly support selection or the addition of user data to any column except the first, nor does it expose the display attributes (font, color, etc.) for the columns.

However, we can use subclassing, a powerful technique for 'stealing' code from Windows to use in your own applications (without breaking the law!), to create an enhanced version of the list view control with the features that we want. In this case, we will combine the concept of subclassing, which is replacing the Windows procedure for an existing Windows class, with that of owner-draw controls (something we discussed briefly in previous chapters) to form a powerful new control: the Color List control.

Feature List

The first thing we need to do before we start coding the control is to create a feature list for the desired functionality of the control. This is a simple way to do a complex job: designing a control for general use. Our new list control will have:

- All of the functionality of the **CListCtrl** class.
- Support for single or multiple selection of rows.
- Support for sorting list items within the control by clicking on a column header (and for sorting in ascending or descending order).
- The ability to reset the widths of the columns to programmer-defined values.
- The ability to select any column, row or cell in the control.
- The ability to change colors and fonts for any cell within the control.
- The ability to display grid lines in the list to make the list look like a grid if desired.
- The power to store and associate user data with each cell in the list control.

Now we have a list of the features we want to implement in the control, it's time to start deciding how we're going to do it.

Designing the Control

We've already decided that we're going to subclass **CListCtrl**. This automatically (some might say auto-magically) provides us with all of the functionality of the existing Windows common control and satisfies the first requirement of the feature list. Deriving from **CListCtrl** also allows us to support multiple selection of rows through the methods already defined in the control and provides us with a mechanism to offer automatic sorting of items. We just need to tap into the sorting mechanism and implement it in our derived class.

Setting the widths of the control's columns is also something that's provided for by **CListCtrl**, in the form of its **SetColumnWidth()** function, but **CListCtrl** doesn't provide an easy way of resetting the column widths to the values defined by the programmer. Users can change the widths of the columns at will, so it's a good idea to provide a simple way of restoring the original column widths, if necessary.

The ability to select any column, cell or row and handle the colors and fonts within the control is achieved by changing the control into an owner-draw control. Owner-draw controls allow the programmer to override the default painting which is done by the control. Since we can draw each row of the list ourselves, we can have them any way we want, including modifying the colors and fonts of the control and displaying various parts as selected.

User Data

Adding user data to the control is a more difficult problem. The default list control provides no way for the programmer to add user information to anything but the 'root' item (the item in the first column) of each row. To allow the programmer to define user data for the other columns requires a bit of thinking. We could simply implement a separate storage mechanism for the user data such that we store all of the information ourselves, but this would lead to other problems when we consider moving items around in the list via sorting, or when inserting and deleting items from the list. It also involves a higher level of complexity in making sure that the list behaves in the same fashion as the existing list control class (a requirement of our feature list).

Instead of creating more work for ourselves, it's smarter simply to extend the existing user data scheme for list controls to do what we want. Since the root item of each row must exist for the list to have additional columns, and since the list control already supports the ability to store user data along with the root control, we will use this to accomplish our goal. We will create a new class which contains within it a list of user data pointers and stores that information in the root item user data field. This new class will understand the columns associated with it and the data stored within it. As a result, we will be able to store a pointer to an allocated object of this class in the user data field. We can retrieve the object and return the information stored in it whenever the application programmer requests it.

This should give you a quick overview of what we are going to do. In short, we will derive a new class from **CListCtrl** and add the functionality we want to that derived class, while inheriting all of the base functionality from the Windows common control that **CListCtrl** encapsulates. This is the first true example of extending the functionality of an existing control that we have looked at in this book, but you can be sure it will not be the last!

Implementing the Color List Control

To implement the control, we will create a new MFC class and implement the functionality of the control within that class. Follow this procedure to create the MFC class and implement the control.

TRY IT OUT - Create a Color List View

1 Use MFC AppWizard (exe) to create a new project workspace. Call the project ColorList and select a Dialog based application on Step 1 of the AppWizard. All other options can retain their default settings.

2 Once you have created the project, activate ClassWizard and add a new class by selecting the Add Class... button and then New... from the menu. Give the new class the name **CColorListCtrl** and select **CListCtrl** as the Base class from the drop-down list. Click OK. We now have a class in which to implement the functionality of our new list control.

3 Now we'll create the class that we'll use to store the user data for each cell in the list. Create a new text file and save it as **LParamList.h** into the same directory as the rest of the project. The name of the class comes from the **LPARAM** type which is used to store user information in a list control. Add the following class definition to the newly created header file.

```
// Utility class for storing user information
#ifndef WROX_LPARAMLIST_H
#define WROX_LPARAMLIST_H

const COLORREF RGB_NORMAL = 0xFF + 1;  // 0xFF is the last valid RGB color

class CLParamList : public CObject
{
// Constructor
public:
   CLParamList(int nIndex, int nSubIndex, CString strText,
               LPARAM param = -1, COLORREF clrText = RGB_NORMAL,
               COLORREF clrBack = RGB_NORMAL);

// Attributes
public:
   int Index;
   int SubIndex;
   LPARAM lParam;
   CString Text;
   COLORREF BackColor;
   COLORREF TextColor;
   CObArray Children;

// Operations
public:
   void AddColumn(CLParamList* child);

   DECLARE_DYNAMIC(CLParamList)
};

#endif
```

As you can see, the class stores simple information for each item in a list. The information stored includes the row number (**Index**), the column number (**SubIndex**), the user data associated with the cell at that position (**lParam**), the text, and colors. The last attribute in the class is an array of children. This member is only filled for the root item in a row, and it contains **CLParamList** objects for the rest of the items in the same row. The list view control stores a single pointer to the root item's **CLParamList** object, and we can use this to get to the **CLParamList** objects for all the other cells in the same row through its **Children** member.

Don't forget to add **#include "LParamList.h"** to the top of **ColorListCtrl.h**, since we'll be using **CLParamList** from the list view class.

4 Create another new text file, save it as **LParamList.cpp** in the same directory as the rest of the project and add the file to the project. The only functions we need to add to this file are the constructor and the **AddColumn()** method (which is used to define columns) for **CLParamList**. Here's the complete text for the new file:

```
// LParamList.cpp - Implementation of CLParamList
#include "StdAfx.h"
#include "LParamList.h"

CLParamList::CLParamList(int nIndex, int nSubIndex, CString strText,
                         LPARAM param, COLORREF clrText, COLORREF clrBack)
{
  Index = nIndex;
  SubIndex = nSubIndex;
  Text = strText;
  lParam = param;
  TextColor = clrText;
  BackColor = clrBack;
}

void CLParamList::AddColumn(CLParamList* child)
{
   Children.Add(child);
}

IMPLEMENT_DYNAMIC(CLParamList, CObject)
```

As you'll see later, **AddColumn()** is called on the root item's **CLParamList** object whenever a new column is added to the list.

5 Now we'll return to the list view class. The first thing we need to do is to add some data members to support the control. Open the header file for the control (**ColorListCtrl.h**) and add the following lines to the class definition:

```
class CColorListCtrl : public CListCtrl
{
// Enumerations
public:
   enum Highlight {hiColumn, hiRow, hiCell};
   enum Grid {gridNone, gridSolid, gridDash};

...

// Implementation
public:
   virtual ~CColorListCtrl();
```

```
private:
   COLORREF m_clrText;          // The foreground text color
   COLORREF m_clrBack;          // The background text color
   COLORREF m_clrHighlight;     // The hilight color to use to display items
   CBrush* m_pbrBack;           // Brush object for holding background brush
   CFont* m_pFont;              // The font to use for displaying the text
   BOOL m_bSortAscending;       // Sort ascending flag.
   int m_nSortColumn;           // Column to sort by.
   BOOL m_bEnableSort;          // If able to sort the list ctrl.
   int m_nHighlightColumn;      // Hilighted column.
   int m_nHighlightType;        // Type of highlight.
   int m_nGridType;             // Type of grid.
   int m_nListTop;              // Top of list area in list window
   int m_nColumns;              // Number of columns.
   CDWordArray m_dwColumnWidths;    // Used to hold the initial widths,
                                    // for resetting widths.
```

The majority of the attributes should be obvious by inspection. The colors and fonts are here, as is a flag to allow enabling or disabling of sorting in the control. The **m_nColumns** attribute will hold on to the number of columns currently defined for the control. The **m_bSortAscending** flag and **m_nSortColumn** value are used for sorting the list by a given column at run time. The **m_nHighlightColumn** and **m_nHighlightType** values are used for selecting which column(s) will be highlighted in the list. These go along with the **Highlight** enumeration type which is used to define the possible ways in which we might highlight the list cells. **m_nGridType** stores the value that determines whether to draw a grid around the cells and **m_nListTop** stores the position of the top of the list; we will talk about these more as we use them. One more member is defined in the header: **m_dwColumnWidths**. This is an array that will be used to store the programmer settings for the widths of the list columns, so that they can be restored if necessary.

6 Now that we've defined the data members for the class, it would be a good idea to initialize and destroy them. Here's the code for the constructor and destructor for the class which you should add to the source file, **ColorListCtrl.cpp**:

```
CColorListCtrl::CColorListCtrl()
{
   m_clrText = RGB(0, 0, 0);           // Default text color (black)
   m_clrBack = RGB(255, 255, 255);     // Default background color (white)
   m_clrHighlight = GetSysColor(COLOR_HIGHLIGHT);
   m_pbrBack = new CBrush(m_clrBack);
   m_pFont = NULL;                     // Initialize font to be NULL

   m_bSortAscending = TRUE;          // Default sort order (ascending)
   m_nSortColumn = 0;                // Default sort column (first item)
   m_bEnableSort = TRUE;             // Default sorting option (enabled)

   m_nHighlightColumn = -1;          // Default highlighted column (none)
   m_nHighlightType = hiRow;         // Default hilight (entire row)
   m_nGridType = gridNone;           // Default grid lines (not shown)

   m_nListTop = 0;          // List top used to find bottom of grid headers
   m_nColumns = -1;                  // Number of columns in grid
   m_dwColumnWidths.RemoveAll();     // Make sure that array is clear.
}
```

```
CColorListCtrl::~CColorListCtrl()
{
   if (m_pbrBack)
      delete m_pbrBack;           // Clear background brush

   m_dwColumnWidths.RemoveAll();  // Remove all column widths
}
```

As you can see, we are simply initializing the attributes which we will be using in the control. It's always a good idea to initialize all member variables of a control which are not objects themselves. This prevents later problems caused by uninitialized values. This is especially important with Visual C++, which automatically initializes memory to **0** in debug mode but leaves it uninitialized in release mode. Failure to initialize member variables may cause problems with release versions of applications or controls that can't be duplicated in debug mode.

7 The next step in the process is to add the utility functions we will need to allow the application programmer to set the various attributes we have defined for the control. To begin with, let's add functions to allow the programmer to set the colors and fonts for the control. You can see the declarations you'll need to add to the color list view's header file below.

```
// Operations
public:
   void SetBackgroundColor(COLORREF clrBack);
   void SetFont(CFont* pFont);
   void SetTextColor(COLORREF clrText);
   void SetHighlightColor(COLORREF clrHighlight);
   void SetGridType(Grid nGridType);
   void SetHighlightType(Highlight nHilightType);
```

Now add the following code to the source file, below the message map:

```
END_MESSAGE_MAP()

/////////////////////////////////////////////////////////////////////////////
// CColorListCtrl Operations

void CColorListCtrl::SetBackgroundColor(COLORREF clrBack)
{
   m_clrBack = clrBack;                  // Reset color.
   if (m_pbrBack)
      delete m_pbrBack;                  // Free old brush.
   m_pbrBack = new CBrush(m_clrBack); // Create new brush.
   SetBkColor(m_clrBack);                // Use CListCtrl functions to set
   SetTextBkColor(m_clrBack);            // the colors of the control.
}

void CColorListCtrl::SetFont(CFont* pFont)
{
   m_pFont = pFont;
   CListCtrl::SetFont(m_pFont);
}
```

```
void CColorListCtrl::SetTextColor(COLORREF clrText)
{
   m_clrText = clrText;
   CListCtrl::SetTextColor(m_clrText);
}

void CColorListCtrl::SetHighlightColor(COLORREF clrHighlight)
{
   m_clrHighlight = clrHighlight;
}

void CColorListCtrl::SetGridType(Grid nGridType)
{
   m_nGridType = nGridType;
}

void CColorListCtrl::SetHighlightType(Highlight nHilightType)
{
   m_nHighlightType = nHilightType;
}
```

These functions are almost frighteningly straightforward. For functions that correspond to one or more functions in **CListCtrl**, we store the value passed to us in one of our own class's members, and then call the base class. If there isn't a base class equivalent (**SetHighlightColor()** or **SetGridType()**, for example), we just store the values. We need to keep track of all these values because we'll need them when it comes to drawing the control.

8 Next up, we want to provide the ability to add new columns, items, and subitems to the list view control. We'll provide four functions in all. You can see the declarations that you'll need to add to the **// Operations** section of **ColorList.h** below.

```
   void SetHighlightType(Highlight nHilightType);
   int AddColumn(CString strTitle, int nFormat = LVCFMT_LEFT,
                 int nMinWidth = -1);
   int AddItem(CString title, LPARAM param = -1,
           COLORREF clrText = RGB_NORMAL, COLORREF clrBack = RGB_NORMAL);
   int InsertAt(int nIndex, CString strTitle, LPARAM lparam = -1,
           COLORREF clrText = RGB_NORMAL, COLORREF clrBack = RGB_NORMAL);
   BOOL AddSubItem(int nItem, int nSubItem, CString title,
                   LPARAM param = -1, COLORREF clrText = RGB_NORMAL,
                   COLORREF clrBack = RGB_NORMAL);
```

9 The first implementation we'll look at is for **CColorListCtrl::AddColumn()**. This function will allow the application programmer to define the text that will appear in the header control for the column, the format (justification type) in which to display the text for the column, and the minimum width of the column itself. The column will always appear wide enough to display the text for its title, but by providing the **nMinWidth** parameter, we allow the programmer to give the column a width larger than the default value if they so choose.

```
// Method to add a new column (header) to the list.
// Does not add any data to the list.
int CColorListCtrl::AddColumn(CString strTitle,
```

```
                        int nFormat /*= LVCFMT_LEFT*/, int nMinWidth /*= -1*/)
{
   int nItem = -1;

   // If column doesn't exist and there is a string, add.
   if (!strTitle.IsEmpty())
   {
      int nWidth = GetStringWidth(strTitle) + 15;    // Check column width.

      // Make sure column width is large enough for the user.
      if (nWidth < nMinWidth)
         nWidth = nMinWidth;

      // Insert column.
      nItem = InsertColumn(++m_nColumns, strTitle, nFormat, nWidth, -1);

      if (nItem != -1)
         m_dwColumnWidths.Add(nWidth); // Save initial width.
      else
         m_nColumns--;            // Don't count column, because not added.
   }
   return nItem;
}
```

Note that the actual addition of the column is done by **`CListCtrl::InsertColumn()`**. Our function is just a wrapper for this function from the base class that uses and maintains the **`m_nColumns`** member, so that the user of our class doesn't need to keep track of the number of columns. If we succeed in adding a column, we also keep track of its width in the **`m_dwColumnWidths`** array so that the width can be restored at any time. You'll see that we provide a function for this purpose later in the chapter.

Our function will return the index of the newly inserted column, or **`-1`** if unsuccessful.

10 In order to add information to the list, we must first add the 'items', as the list control thinks of them. Items can either be added to the bottom of the list or inserted at a point in the middle. We've provided two methods for adding new items to the list: **`AddItem()`**, which adds them at the end, and **`InsertAt()`**, which inserts them at the specified position. Clearly, **`AddItem()`** is just a special case of **`InsertAt()`**, so that's exactly how we've implemented it. Here's the code for these methods:

```
int CColorListCtrl::AddItem(CString strTitle, LPARAM lparam /*= -1*/,
      COLORREF clrText /*= RGB_NORMAL*/, COLORREF clrBack /*= RGB_NORMAL*/)
{
   return InsertAt(GetItemCount(), strTitle, lparam, clrText, clrBack);
}

int CColorListCtrl::InsertAt(int nIndex, CString strTitle, LPARAM lparam,
                             COLORREF clrText, COLORREF clrBack)
{
   // Make sure something was entered
   if ((strTitle == _T("")) || (!strTitle.IsEmpty()))
   {
      LV_ITEM lv;
      memset(&lv, 0, sizeof(lv));  // Clear.
```

```
        lv.mask = LVIF_TEXT | LVIF_PARAM;
        lv.pszText = (LPTSTR)(LPCTSTR)strTitle;
        lv.cchTextMax = strTitle.GetLength();
        lv.iItem = nIndex;

        int item = InsertItem(&lv);   // Insert the item.
        if (item != -1)               // If valid insertion.
        {
           SetItemData(item, (DWORD)(new CLParamList(GetItemCount()-1, 0,
                                       strTitle, lparam, clrText,
                                       clrBack)));
           return item;
        }
     }
     return -1;
  }
```

The major work here is being done in two lines. The first is the call to **CListCtrl::InsertItem()**. This actually inserts the item into the list using the information specified in the **LV_ITEM** structure. **InsertItem()** returns the index of the newly inserted item, or **-1** if unsuccessful. The second is the call to **CListCtrl::SetItemData()**, which sets the user data for the new item. We set this data to be a pointer to a new object of our **CLParamList** class so that we can store data for all the sub-items in the row too.

You can think of adding an item as being the equivalent of adding a row to the grid, plus the data to go in the first column of that row.

11 Okay, we've seen how to add columns and rows (including adding the data for the first column in each row), but how do we actually add the data for the other columns? The answer is via **CColorListCtrl::AddSubItem()** which you can also add to **ColorListCtrl.cpp**.

```
// Method to add a sub-item to the list.
BOOL CColorListCtrl::AddSubItem(int nItem, int nSubItem, CString title,
                    LPARAM param /*= -1*/, COLORREF clrText /*= RGB_NORMAL*/,
                    COLORREF clrBack /*= RGB_NORMAL*/)
{
   BOOL item = FALSE;
   if ((title == _T("")) || (!title.IsEmpty()))
   {
      LV_ITEM lv;
      memset(&lv, 0, sizeof(lv));   // Clear.

      lv.mask        = LVIF_TEXT;
      lv.iItem       = nItem;
      lv.iSubItem    = nSubItem;
      lv.pszText     = (LPTSTR)(LPCTSTR)title;
      lv.cchTextMax = title.GetLength();

      item = SetItem(&lv);    // Set the sub-item.

      // Store the item as a child of the parent item
      CLParamList* parent = (CLParamList*)GetItemData(nItem);
      parent->AddColumn(new CLParamList(nItem, nSubItem, title, param,
```

```
                                          clrText, clrBack));
    }
    return item;
}
```

This function takes two **int** parameters, **nItem** and **nSubItem**, that determine the position of the data that is set when this function is called. **nItem** is the item that the subitem is being associated with, and is equivalent to the row that the data will appear in. **nSubItem** is the index of the subitem that is being set, and is equivalent to the column that the data will appear in. The actual addition of data is done by **CListCtrl::SetItem()**.

Note the way that user data associated with the item is stored using the **CLParamList** class. We get a pointer to the parent item's **CLParamList** object by calling **CListCtrl::GetItemData()**, then use **CLParamList::AddColumn()** to add a new **CLParamList** object to the parent's array of children.

12 The next major chunk of code that the control needs is for the actual drawing of the items. When a list control is set to owner-draw (which can be done from the Styles property page for the list control in Developer Studio's dialog editor), **CListCtrl** will call the **virtual** function **DrawItem()** each time an item (in other words, a row in the list) needs to be drawn. If we override this function in our class, we can draw whatever we choose, allowing us to change fonts, colors, and selections as we please.

We need this functionality, so we'll do exactly that. Unfortunately, ClassWizard can't help us with **DrawItem()** since it doesn't seem to know about it, so we'll have to add the function declaration by hand. Add the following code to **ColorListCtrl.h**, just below ClassWizard's **virtual** function map.

```
//}}AFX_VIRTUAL
    // Hand-coded virtual function overrides
protected:
    virtual void DrawItem(LPDRAWITEMSTRUCT lpDrawItemStruct);
```

Now add the implementation to the color list's source file.

```
/////////////////////////////////////////////////////////////////////////////
// CColorListCtrl hand-coded overrides

// Method to draw a single line of the list. Note that the list view must
// be owner-draw for this method to work!
void CColorListCtrl::DrawItem(LPDRAWITEMSTRUCT lpDrawItemStruct)
{
    CDC* pDC = CDC::FromHandle(lpDrawItemStruct->hDC);
    CBrush brHighlight(m_clrHighlight);
    CFont* pOldFont = NULL;

    if (m_pFont)
        pOldFont = pDC->SelectObject(m_pFont);

    // If this is the first item in the list, hold on to the y position of
    // the top of the rectangle for the item. This information will be used
    // for column selecting. We can check to see if a click occurs within
    // the list area or whether the user selected one of the column
```

```
   // headers.
   if (lpDrawItemStruct->itemID == 0)
      m_nListTop = lpDrawItemStruct->rcItem.top;

   CString strItemText;

   for (int i = 0; i <= m_nColumns; i++)
   {
      strItemText = GetItemText(lpDrawItemStruct->itemID, i);
      CRect rectCell = GetCellRect(lpDrawItemStruct, i);
      SetupCellColors(pDC, lpDrawItemStruct, i, rectCell, brHighlight);
      DrawCellGrid(pDC, rectCell);

      // If this is not a selected grid item, check foreground and
      // background colors.
      if (i)
      {
         if (!IsCellHighlighted(lpDrawItemStruct, i))
         {
            // Get the stored item data pointer
            CLParamList* ptr = (CLParamList*)lpDrawItemStruct->itemData;

            // If there is an object for this column, check it.
            if (ptr->Children.GetSize() > i - 1)
            {
               if (((CLParamList*)ptr->Children[i - 1])->
                                          BackColor != RGB_NORMAL)
                  pDC->SetBkColor(((CLParamList*)ptr->
                                    Children[i - 1])->BackColor);
               if (((CLParamList*)ptr->Children[i - 1])->
                                          TextColor != RGB_NORMAL)
                  pDC->SetTextColor(((CLParamList*)ptr->
                                    Children[i - 1])->TextColor);
            }
         }
      }
      // Write out the text in the rect
      pDC->DrawText(strItemText, rectCell,
                  DT_SINGLELINE | DT_LEFT | DT_VCENTER);
   }

   // Select back in the old font.
   if (pOldFont)
      pDC->SelectObject(pOldFont);
}
```

Wow! That seems like a lot of code just to display a single line in the list control, doesn't it? There's obviously a lot more going on here than simply displaying some text on a line, so let's examine the code a little more carefully.

After setting up the font for the display, we check whether we have the first item in the list by using **lpDrawItemStruct**'s **itemID** member. If this is the first item in the list, we get the position of the top of the rectangle for the item, so that we can use it later when we're checking where the user has clicked on the control. We store this value in **m_nListTop**. This will allow us to determine which items have been selected when the user clicks on the control.

Next, we loop through each column in the current row. First, we get the text for the cell using **`CListCtrl::GetItemText()`**, then the rectangle for the cell using **`CColorListCtrl::GetCellRect()`**. Once we've got the rectangle for the cell, we can call another function in our derived class, **`CColorListCtrl::SetupCellColors()`**, to set the colors and brushes in the device context ready for us to draw the text. This function checks to see whether the cell is selected so that the colors are correctly set. Then we call **`CColorListCtrl::DrawCellGrid()`** to draw the grid lines around the current cell if necessary.

Finally, we check the information in the appropriate **`CLParamList`** object to determine whether we need to set the colors individually for the cell, before drawing the text in the right place using **`CDC::DrawText()`**.

13 You might be wondering where the three functions **`GetCellRect()`**, **`SetupCellColors()`**, and **`DrawCellGrid()`** come from. The answer, of course, is that we have to write them ourselves, so let's do that now. Add the following **`protected`** function declarations to the control's header file:

```
// Implementation
public:
   virtual ~CColorListCtrl();

protected:
   CRect GetCellRect(LPDRAWITEMSTRUCT lpDrawItemStruct, int nColumn);
   void SetupCellColors(CDC* pDC, LPDRAWITEMSTRUCT lpDrawItemStruct,
                        int nColumn, CRect& rectCell,CBrush& brHighlight);
   void DrawCellGrid(CDC* pDC, CRect& rectCell);
```

14 The first function we'll look at is **`GetCellRect()`**. This returns the rectangle for the cell indicated by **`lpDrawItemStruct`** and **`nColumn`**.

```
CRect CColorListCtrl::GetCellRect(LPDRAWITEMSTRUCT lpDrawItemStruct,
                                  int nColumn)
{
   static CRect rectItem;
   static int nWidth = 0;
   static int cx = 0;

   // Get the rectangle to output the string
   if (0 == nColumn)
   {
      GetItemRect(lpDrawItemStruct->itemID, rectItem, LVIR_LABEL);
      nWidth = rectItem.Width() + 1; // Get the extra column width.
      cx = 0;
   }
   else
   {
      LV_COLUMN column;
      column.mask = LVCF_WIDTH;    // Set the mask to return only the width

      GetColumn(nColumn - 1, &column); // Get column width information.
      cx += column.cx;             // Increment for multiple column widths.

      GetColumn(nColumn, &column);
```

```
        nWidth = column.cx;
    }

    CRect rectCell = rectItem;
    rectCell.left = rectItem.left + cx;
    rectCell.right = rectCell.left + nWidth;
    return rectCell;
}
```

Each time through the loop, the **static** variables are increased to ensure the correct results. The important point here is that these variables are kept up-to-date as each call is made. The rectangle for the cell is found by adding together the total width of the cell and then using the height provided for the cell.

15 The next function uses the information supplied as its parameters to determine whether the particular cell should be drawn highlighted or not, then sets the colors and brushes of the DC accordingly.

```
void CColorListCtrl::SetupCellColors(CDC* pDC,
                        LPDRAWITEMSTRUCT lpDrawItemStruct, int nColumn,
                        CRect& rectCell,CBrush& brHighlight)
{
    if (IsCellHighlighted(lpDrawItemStruct, nColumn))
    {
        pDC->SelectObject(&brHighlight);
        pDC->SetBkColor(m_clrHighlight);
        pDC->SetTextColor(m_clrBack);
        pDC->FillRect(rectCell, &brHighlight);
    }
    else
    {
        pDC->SelectObject(m_pbrBack);
        pDC->SetBkColor(m_clrBack);
        pDC->SetTextColor(m_clrText);
        pDC->FillRect(rectCell, m_pbrBack);
    }
}
```

This function uses yet another function that we need to define, **CColorListCtrl::IsCellHighlighted()**, to determine whether the cell should be highlighted. You can see the **protected** declaration and implementation that you'll need to add for this function below:

```
    void DrawCellGrid(CDC* pDC, CRect& rectCell);
    BOOL IsCellHighlighted(LPDRAWITEMSTRUCT lpDrawItemStruct, int nColumn);
```

```
BOOL CColorListCtrl::IsCellHighlighted(LPDRAWITEMSTRUCT lpDrawItemStruct,
                                        int nColumn)
{
    if ((m_nHighlightType == hiCell &&
      nColumn == m_nHighlightColumn &&
      lpDrawItemStruct->itemState & ODS_SELECTED)
      ||
     (m_nHighlightType == hiColumn &&
      nColumn == m_nHighlightColumn)
```

```
    ||
    (m_nHighlightType == hiRow &&
     lpDrawItemStruct->itemState & ODS_SELECTED))
     return TRUE;
   else
      return FALSE;
}
```

We use a combination of the highlight type (**m_nHighlightType**), the highlight status for the column (**m_nHighlightColumn**), and the highlight status for the row (**lpDrawItemStruct->itemState**) to determine whether a particular cell should be highlighted.

16 **DrawCellGrid()** draws a line round the cell depending on the setting of **m_nGridType**.

```
void CColorListCtrl::DrawCellGrid(CDC* pDC, CRect& rectCell)
{
   // Check for grids..
   CPen penSolid(PS_SOLID, 1, RGB(0, 0, 0));
   CPen penDash(PS_DASH, 1, RGB(0, 0, 0));
   CPen* pOldPen = NULL;

   // Draw the actual grid based on the user-selected type.
   switch (m_nGridType)
   {
   case gridSolid:
      rectCell.bottom++;
      pOldPen = pDC->SelectObject(&penSolid);
      pDC->Rectangle(rectCell);
      rectCell.bottom--;
      rectCell.left++;
      rectCell.right --;
      rectCell.InflateRect(-1, -1);
      break;
   case gridDash:
      rectCell.bottom++;
      pOldPen = pDC->SelectObject(&penDash);
      pDC->Rectangle(rectCell);
      rectCell.bottom--;
      rectCell.left++;
      rectCell.right++;
      rectCell.InflateRect(-1, -1);
      break;
   case gridNone:
   default:
      break;
   }

   // Get back the old pen if one was selected.
   if (pOldPen)
      pDC->SelectObject(pOldPen);
}
```

17 The next biggest piece to the control is determining when the user clicks on a column header to indicate that they wish to sort the list by a given column. To handle this, we must first determine which column the user clicked in. Enter ClassWizard and select the

CColorListCtrl object and the **=LVN_COLUMNCLICK** message. This message will be sent to your control by Windows when the user clicks in the header control for the list. Click on the Add Function button and accept **OnColumnclick** as the name of the new message handler. Add the following code to the **CColorListCtrl::OnColumnclick()**:

```
// Method called when the user clicks in the header area on one of the
// column header buttons.
void CColorListCtrl::OnColumnclick(NMHDR* pNMHDR, LRESULT* pResult)
{
   NM_LISTVIEW* pNMListView = (NM_LISTVIEW*)pNMHDR;
   // If sorting option on.
   if (m_bEnableSort)
   {
      // Get sort column.
      m_nSortColumn = pNMListView->iSubItem;
      m_bSortAscending = !m_bSortAscending;
      SortItems(SortProcedure, (LPARAM)this);
   }
   *pResult = 0;
}
```

You can see that if sorting isn't enabled, we will do nothing in response to this message. If, on the other hand, sorting is enabled, we set the **m_nSortColumn** and **m_bSortAscending** variables with appropriate values then call **CListCtrl::SortItems()**, passing it a function pointer and the **this** pointer for the current object. **SortProcedure()** is a **static** function that will be called for each comparison that needs to be done during the sort.

18 You'll need to add to the header and source files the declaration and implementation of **CColorListCtrl::SortProcedure()**, respectively, as shown here:

```
// Implementation
public:
   virtual ~CColorListCtrl();
   static int CALLBACK SortProcedure(LPARAM item1, LPARAM item2,
                                     LPARAM ptr);
```

```
// Callback procedure for CListCtrl to use for comparing individual
// items in the list. This procedure must be defined as static in the
// header file. This is why we need to pass in the pointer to the control
// in the last parameter to the method.
int CALLBACK CColorListCtrl::SortProcedure(LPARAM item1, LPARAM item2,
                                           LPARAM ptr)
{
   int nResult = -1;
   CColorListCtrl* pCtrl = (CColorListCtrl*)ptr;

   // Make sure we have valid pointers...
   if (item1 && item2)
   {
      CLParamList* param1 = (CLParamList*)item1;
      CLParamList* param2 = (CLParamList*)item2;

      CString text1;
      CString text2;
```

```
        // If it is the first column, just use the text, otherwise we need
        // to extract the text from the internal data for the list box.
        switch (pCtrl->m_nSortColumn)
        {
        case 0: // Item
           text1 = param1->Text;
           text2 = param2->Text;
           break;
        default: // Sub-Item.
           if (param1->Children.GetSize() >= pCtrl->m_nSortColumn)
              text1 = ((CLParamList*)param1->Children[
                                            pCtrl->m_nSortColumn - 1])->Text;
           if (param2->Children.GetSize() >= pCtrl->m_nSortColumn)
              text2 = ((CLParamList*)param2->Children[
                                            pCtrl->m_nSortColumn - 1])->Text;
           break;
        }

        // Do the compare for the two items, taking into account the sorting
        // order (ascending or descending).
        if (text1 < text2)
        {
           if (pCtrl->m_bSortAscending)
              nResult = -1;
           else
              nResult = 1;
        }
        else
        {
           if (text1 > text2)
           {
              if (pCtrl->m_bSortAscending)
                 nResult = 1;
              else
                 nResult = -1;
           }
           else
              nResult = 0;
        }
     }
     return nResult;
  }
```

SortProcedure() needs to return a negative number if the first item should precede the second, a positive number if the second item should precede the first, or zero if the two items are equivalent. You can see that once we've extracted the text from the **CLParamList**, that it's a simple matter to use **CString**'s comparison operators to return the right result.

19 One more item that we need to take care of is trapping the left mouse-button clicks so that we can set the right selection status for cells in the control. We can't just use ClassWizard to add a **WM_LBUTTONDOWN** handler because the common control will 'eat' the message before it gets to us. To get round this, we need to use ClassWizard to override **CWnd**'s low-level **PreTranslateMessage()** function as follows:

```
// Method to pre-translate commands to the control before they
// are "eaten" by the Windows control. Specifically, we are interested
// in the user pressing the left mouse button to select a row/column/cell.
```

```
BOOL CColorListCtrl::PreTranslateMessage(MSG* pMsg)
{
   if (pMsg->message == WM_LBUTTONDOWN)
   {
      // Get the point.
      CPoint point(LOWORD(pMsg->lParam), HIWORD(pMsg->lParam));

      // Get the column index. Hold onto the old one for
      // comparison in case of a column select.
      int temp = m_nHighlightColumn;

      // Figure out which column we clicked in.
      m_nHighlightColumn = GetColumnIndex(point);

      // If this is a column selection, make sure we are
      // not hilighting the same column. Then invalidate the
      // control to redraw all the rows.
      if (m_nHighlightType == hiColumn && temp != m_nHighlightColumn)
         Invalidate();
   }
   return CListCtrl::PreTranslateMessage(pMsg);
}
```

The only slightly complicated thing about this function is where **GetColumnIndex()** comes from. The answer, my friend, is blowing in the wind... Actually, we have to write it ourselves.

20 First, add a function declaration for **GetColumnIndex()** to the **Implementation** section of **CColorListCtrl** as a **protected** member.

```
protected:
...
   void DrawCellGrid(CDC* pDC, CRect& rectCell);
   BOOL IsCellHighlighted(LPDRAWITEMSTRUCT lpDrawItemStruct, int nColumn);
   int GetColumnIndex(CPoint point);
```

Now add the implementation to **ColorListCtrl.cpp**.

```
// Method to get the index of the column from a user click. Used to select
// the items to be highlighted.
int CColorListCtrl::GetColumnIndex(CPoint point)
{
   int ret = -1;

   // If they clicked above the top of the list display area
   // we will not treat that as a click, rather as a column
   // selection...
   if (point.y < m_nListTop)
      return ret;

   // Make sure valid row.
   if (HitTest(point) != -1)
   {
      LV_COLUMN colInfo;
      int cx=0;
```

```
        for (int i = 0; i <= m_nColumns; i++)
        {
            colInfo.mask = LVCF_WIDTH;
            if (GetColumn(i, &colInfo)) // Get column info.
                cx += colInfo.cx;

            if (point.x <= cx)   // If less than column width, in column.
            {
                ret = i;
                break;
            }
        }
    }
    return ret;
}
```

Note that we use the **m_nListTop** member, which we set in **DrawItem()** for holding the top of the list items, to weed out any clicks on the header control. Then we use **CListCtrl::HitTest()** to determine whether the user has clicked on an item in the list. If they have, we loop through the columns to determine which column the click point would fall in.

21 There's one more matter to take care of. When the control is destroyed (because its parent window was destroyed, for example, when a dialog ends) the user data which is stored with the control must be removed to ensure that there are no memory leaks. Since application programmers get notoriously angry about library functions and objects that leak memory, we should certainly take care of that. To do this, use ClassWizard to add a message handler for the **WM_DESTROY** message. Add the following code to the **OnDestroy()** method of **CColorListCtrl**:

```
// Method called just before the windows object is destroyed. We use
// this method to free up all of the data we stored in the control item
// data before it goes away. Delete it here to avoid memory leaks.
void CColorListCtrl::OnDestroy()
{
    // Free item data blocks
    for (int i = 0; i < GetItemCount(); ++i)
    {
        CLParamList* ptr = (CLParamList*)GetItemData(i);
        // Delete all children of the array
        for (int c = 0; c < ptr->Children.GetSize(); ++c)
        {
            CLParamList* child = (CLParamList*)ptr->Children[c];
            delete child;
        }
        delete ptr;
    }
    CListCtrl::OnDestroy();
}
```

22 All that remains is to flesh out the control by adding a whole heap of utility functions. First, we'll add some **Get** functions to return useful information about the control.

Add the following code to **ColorListCtrl.h**.

```
// Attributes
public:
    LPARAM GetCellLParam(int nItem, int nSubItem);
    int GetSelectedRow();
    int GetSelectedRows(CDWordArray* pArray);
```

Now add the corresponding implementations to **ColorListCtrl.cpp**.

```
// Method used to get the lParam for any item/subitem.
LPARAM CColorListCtrl::GetCellLParam(int nItem, int nSubItem)
{
   LPARAM lparam = -1;

   // Make sure the item is valid.
   if (nItem < GetItemCount())
   {
      // Get the param inforation.
      CLParamList* pList = (CLParamList*)GetItemData(nItem);

      if (pList != NULL)           // Check for NULL
      {
         if (nSubItem == 0)
            lparam = pList->lParam; // Just want the row param.
         else
         {
            if (nSubItem > 0)      // Make sure subitem is valid
            {
               // Iterate through the list trying to find right subitem.
               for (int i=0; i < pList->Children.GetSize(); i++)
               {
                  if (((CLParamList*)pList->Children[i])->SubIndex ==
                                                               nSubItem)
                  {
                     lparam = ((CLParamList*)pList->Children[i])->lParam;
                    break;
                  }
               }
            }
         }
      }
   }
   return lparam;
}
```

The **GetCellLParam()** function is going to be used by a user who has used the **SetCellLParam()** function to associate data with the cell. What? Put in English (as opposed to whatever I was using just then), this function lets you get back the data you put into the 'back' of a cell. This is just like the data you can associate with the items of a simple list box. Perhaps it's a pointer to an object represented by the text of the list item, or maybe it's a simple index into a database of records which is shown in the list control. Whatever makes your little heart go pitter-pat.

```
int CColorListCtrl::GetSelectedRow()
{
   CDWordArray array;
```

```
    int ret = -1;

    if (GetSelectedRows(&array))
    {
        ret = array.GetAt(0);
        array.RemoveAll();
    }
    return ret;
}
```

For single select list controls, the **GetSelectedRow()** function is used to fix a long-standing grudge of mine with the list control. There's simply no way to find out what entry is currently selected by querying the control. I chose to implement this as a simple function so that the average user would have an easy method for getting back the currently selected row. Note that **GetSelectedRow()** is just a special case of **GetSelectedRows()**, so that's how I implemented it.

```
int CColorListCtrl::GetSelectedRows(CDWordArray* pArray)
{
    pArray->RemoveAll();
    int cnt = 0;

    for (int k = 0; k < GetItemCount(); k++)    // Go through list.
    {
        // If selected add to list.
        if (GetItemState(k, LVIS_SELECTED) & LVIS_SELECTED)
        {
            pArray->Add(k);
            cnt++;
        }
    }
    return cnt;
}
```

The **GetSelectedRows()** function, on the other hand, will return the total number of selected items. The indexes for these items can be found in the array which has been passed into the object. The array is a simple **CDWordArray** pointer which will be used to store the information we find in the list control. Determining whether an item is selected is by no means as simple as you might imagine. Instead, we take the brute force approach of stepping through each and every item in the list and 'asking' it if it is selected by getting the item state. If the item state has the **LVIS_SELECTED** bit set, the item is selected, otherwise it isn't (at least *that* is simple). If the item is selected, we add it to the **CDWordArray**.

One last note on this function. As currently written, it will erase the contents of the passed-in array object. It might be nice to allow a boolean flag to be passed in as well, indicating whether or not the array should be cleared before adding the new selections. This could be useful, for example, for multiple selections from different sources.

23 Now add the following functions to the control. Add the declarations to the header file under the **Operations** section, and the function bodies to **ColorList.cpp**.

```
    BOOL AddSubItem(int nItem, int nSubItem, CString title,
                    LPARAM param = -1, COLORREF clrText = RGB_NORMAL,
                    COLORREF clrBack = RGB_NORMAL);
    BOOL RemoveItem(int nID);
    BOOL RemoveAllItems();
    BOOL ChangeColumn(CString strTitle, int nCol);
    void ResetColumnWidths();

    BOOL UnselectRow(int nRow);
    BOOL UnselectAllRows();
    BOOL SelectRow(int nRow);
    BOOL SelectAllRows();

    void SetText(CString str, int nItem, int nSubItem);
    int SetCellBkColor(int nItem, int nSubItem, COLORREF clrBack);
    int SetCellTextColor(int nItem, int nSubItem, COLORREF clrText);
    int SetLParam(int nItem, LPARAM lParam);
    int SetCellLParam(int nItem, int nSubItem, LPARAM lParam);
```

```
// Remove a specific item from the list control
BOOL CColorListCtrl::RemoveItem(int nID)
{
   CLParamList* ptr = (CLParamList*)GetItemData(nID);

   // Delete all children of the array
   for (int c = 0; c < ptr->Children.GetSize(); ++c)
   {
      CLParamList* child = (CLParamList*)ptr->Children[c];
      delete child;
   }
   delete ptr;
   DeleteItem(nID); // Delete the item.

   return TRUE;
}
```

```
BOOL CColorListCtrl::RemoveAllItems()
{
   int count = GetItemCount();
   for (int k = 0; k < count; k++)
      RemoveItem(0);

   return TRUE;
}
```

```
// Method to change an existing column (header) to the list. Does not add
// or change any data in the list.
BOOL CColorListCtrl::ChangeColumn(CString strTitle, int nCol)
{
   BOOL ret = FALSE;
   // Check valid title and column
   if ((!strTitle.IsEmpty()) && (nCol <= m_nColumns))
   {
      LV_COLUMN column;
      memset(&column, 0, sizeof(column)); // Clear structure.

      // Setup information
      column.mask = LVCF_TEXT;
```

```
        column.pszText = strTitle.GetBuffer(0);
        column.cchTextMax = strTitle.GetLength();
        ret = SetColumn(nCol, &column); // Set the column information.
    }
    return ret;
}
```

```
// Method to reset column widths to default.
void CColorListCtrl::ResetColumnWidths()
{
    for (int i = 0; i <= m_nColumns; i++)   // Iterate through each column.
    {
        int nWidth = m_dwColumnWidths.GetAt(i); // Get object from the list.
        SetColumnWidth(i, nWidth);              // Set column width
    }
}
```

```
BOOL CColorListCtrl::SelectRow(int nRow)
{
    if (nRow < GetItemCount())    // Make sure valid item.
    {
        // Set the state differently.
        return SetItemState(nRow, (UINT)LVIS_SELECTED, (UINT)LVIS_SELECTED);
    }
    return FALSE;
}
```

```
BOOL CColorListCtrl::SelectAllRows()
{
    for (int i = 0; i < GetItemCount(); i++)   // Iterate through the list.
    {
        if (!SelectRow(i)) // Select the row.
            return FALSE;
    }
    return TRUE;
}
```

```
BOOL CColorListCtrl::UnselectRow(int nRow)
{
    // Set the state differently.
    return SetItemState(nRow, (UINT)~LVIS_SELECTED, (UINT)LVIS_SELECTED);
}
```

```
BOOL CColorListCtrl::UnselectAllRows()
{
    CDWordArray array;
    BOOL ret = TRUE;
    // Get the selected rows.
    if (GetSelectedRows(&array))
    {
        for (int i = 0; i < array.GetSize() && ret; i++)
            ret = UnselectRow(array.GetAt(i)); // Set the state differently.
    }
    return ret;
}
```

```
void CColorListCtrl::SetText(CString str, int nItem, int nSubItem)
```

```
{
   if (nItem < GetItemCount())    // Make sure valid item/row.
   {
      // Get the param inforation.
      CLParamList* pList = (CLParamList*)GetItemData(nItem);

      if (nSubItem == 0)
      {
         pList->Text = str; // Set text in object.
      }
      else
      {
         if (nSubItem > 0) // Make sure subitem is valid.
         {
            // Interate through the list trying to find right subitem.
            for (int i = 0; i < pList->Children.GetSize(); i++)
            {
               if (((CLParamList*)pList->Children[i])->SubIndex ==
                                                                nSubItem)
               {
                  ((CLParamList*)pList->Children[i])->Text = str;
                  break;
               }
            } // end of for
         }
      }
      SetItemText(nItem, nSubItem, str);
   }
}
```

```
int CColorListCtrl::SetCellBkColor(int nItem, int nSubItem,
                                   COLORREF clrBack)
{
   CLParamList* parent = (CLParamList*)GetItemData(nItem);
   int ret = 0;
   if (parent->Children.GetSize() >= nSubItem)
   {
      CLParamList* ptr = (CLParamList*)parent->Children[nSubItem-1];
      ptr->BackColor = clrBack;
   }
   else
      ret = -1;
   return ret;
}
```

```
int CColorListCtrl::SetCellTextColor(int nItem, int nSubItem,
                                     COLORREF clrText)
{
   CLParamList* parent = (CLParamList*)GetItemData(nItem);
   int ret = 0;
   if (parent->Children.GetSize() >= nSubItem)
   {
      CLParamList* ptr = (CLParamList*)parent->Children[nSubItem-1];
      ptr->TextColor = clrText;
   }
   else
      ret = -1;
```

```
    return ret;
}
```

```
int CColorListCtrl::SetLParam(int nItem, LPARAM lParam)
{
    CLParamList* parent = (CLParamList*)GetItemData (nItem);
    int ret = 0;
    if (parent)
        parent->lParam = lParam;
    else
        ret = -1;
    return ret;
}
```

```
int CColorListCtrl::SetCellLParam(int nItem, int nSubItem, LPARAM lParam)
{
    CLParamList* parent = (CLParamList*)GetItemData(nItem);
    int ret = 0;
    if (parent->Children.GetSize() >= nSubItem)
    {
        CLParamList* ptr = (CLParamList*)parent->Children[nSubItem-1];
        ptr->lParam = lParam;
    }
    else
        ret = -1;
    return ret;
}
```

Excellent! You just created another new control! Now you probably want to test it. Are you never satisfied?

TRY IT OUT - Test the Color List Control

1 Testing the control is simple. Open up the dialog resource for the project in Developer Studio's dialog editor and add a list control to it.

2 Double-click on the list control to bring up its property sheet and switch to the Styles page. Change the View to Report and check the Owner draw fixed check box.

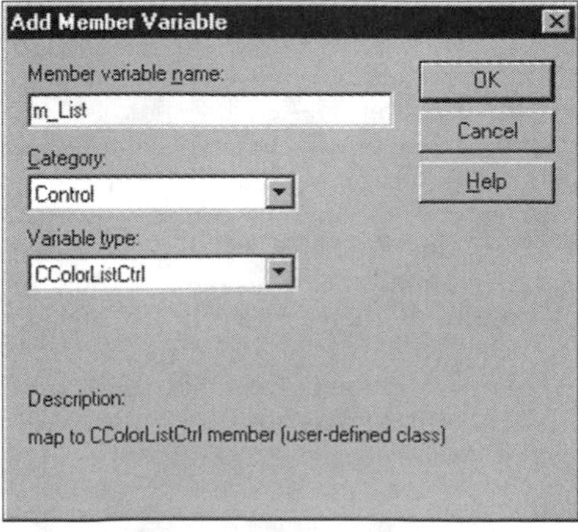

3 *Ctrl*-double-click on the control to bring up ClassWizard's Add Member Variable dialog. Set the control's Member variable name to **m_List** and set the Variable type to **CColorListCtrl**. Click OK. Add **#include "ColorListCtrl"** to the top of **ColorListDlg.h**.

4 Now add the following code to **CColorListDlg::OnInitDialog()**.

```
    // TODO: Add extra initialization here
    // Add the columns to the list
    m_List.AddColumn(_T("Column 1"));
    m_List.AddColumn(_T("Column 2"));
    m_List.AddColumn(_T("Column 3"));

    // Add some items to the list
    int idx = m_List.AddItem(_T("Blue"));
    m_List.AddSubItem(idx, 1, _T("Col2A"));
    m_List.AddSubItem(idx, 2, _T("Col3B"));
    m_List.SetCellTextColor(idx, 1, RGB(0, 0, 255));
    idx = m_List.AddItem(_T("Green"));
    m_List.AddSubItem(idx, 1, _T("Col2B"));
    m_List.AddSubItem(idx, 2, _T("Col3C"));
    m_List.SetCellTextColor(idx, 1, RGB(0, 255, 0));
    idx = m_List.AddItem(_T("Red"));
    m_List.AddSubItem(idx, 1, _T("Col2C"));
    m_List.AddSubItem(idx, 2, _T("Col3A"));
    m_List.SetCellTextColor(idx, 1, RGB(255, 0, 0));

    return TRUE;  // return TRUE  unless you set the focus to a control
}
```

You can compile and run the application at this stage. Try clicking on the list headers to order the list according to different columns. Note how you can select a row even if you don't click on the first item in the row. You could take the project from here and try some of the other facilities offered by the control. Try adding a button that resets the widths of the columns or changes the drawing of gridlines or the highlight type. It's up to you, the power is in your hands! Use it wisely.

The ActiveX Solution: The Editable Grid Control

A different kind of list solution is a true grid. A grid is really just a very simple form of the common or garden spreadsheet. For many applications, the full functionality of a spreadsheet is sheer overkill and adds additional code and resources which are detrimental to the performance of the application. In these cases, where the only real need is for some basic display and input, a grid is a valuable component.

In this example, we will explore another facet of ActiveX controls: implementing a scrollable window and handling user input through the creation of Windows controls (in this case, an edit field). Here you can see an example dialog using the grid control. It shows one cell of the grid being edited, a bitmap displayed in another cell, and yet other cells demonstrating various text display options.

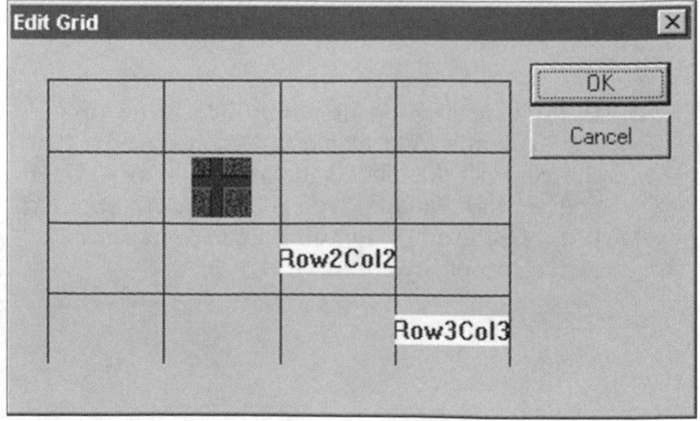

Feature List

Let's consider for a moment the sorts of features a programmer would like to see in a typical editable grid. The basic functionality of the grid would need to include:

- Resizable cells representing the grid.
- The ability to set the number of rows and columns programmatically.
- A scrollable surface, in case the number of rows and/or columns doesn't fit in the available display area.
- The ability to set the text of any cell programmatically.
- Control over text color and cell background.
- Notification if the user clicks in a cell.

In addition to the basic functionality, we also have features associated with the editable portion of the grid:

- The ability for a user to edit the text in a cell by double-clicking on the cell.
- Notification when a grid cell has been modified
- Automatic construction and destruction of a grid cell edit box when a user has selected and then deselected it.
- The ability to set a cell as editable or not.

Designing the Control

Designing the Editable Grid control is a three step process. Each step is represented by the three basic building blocks of all ActiveX controls: properties, methods, and events. Here's a quick summary of these three items:

- Properties describe attributes for ActiveX controls. They are usually persistent and can be set at either design time or run time.
- Methods are used to carry out actions on the control. They are essentially functions on the control called by the container. They have no persistency and will be used only at run time, so we don't need to worry about design-time issues.
- Events provide a means of notifying the parent of the control that something has happened, such as the user clicking in a grid cell or changing the text in the grid. Events are methods in reverse, since they are really just functions in the container called by the control. The control's container gets the information that it needs to determine what the event handler should look like from the control's type library, which gets created from `.odl` (or `.idl`) files.

Properties

The first step, then, is to look at the properties we will need. Several of these properties have already been identified directly from the requirements for the control. We must have properties for the number of rows and the number of columns of the grid. In addition, we need to implement properties for the grid background color and the default text color. Since the grid will have available cells which can contain their own background and foreground colors, it would be best if these colors were defaults that are used if no color is assigned to the cell. This would allow us to change all of the colors for a grid without having to modify each and every cell. We also need a property for the font in which the text for the grid cells will be displayed.

This gives us a total of three stock properties, **`BackColor`**, **`ForeColor`** and **`Font`**, and two custom properties, **`Rows`** and **`Cols`**.

Methods

Once the properties are out of the way, it's time to examine the real meat of the control: the methods. Methods will be used by the programmer to do all of the real work for the control, so it is important to design them for maximum flexibility and functionality. A few of the methods that we will need come directly out of the requirements definition for the control. Since the numbers of rows and columns are variable and the size of each one is also supposed to be variable, we need methods to set the height of a row and the width of a column. It would also be nice if the programmer could retrieve these values, so we'll have two corresponding methods to get back the row height and column width for a given row or column.

```
SetColumnWidth
SetRowHeight
GetColumnWidth
GetRowHeight
```

The next thing we need to deal with is setting the contents of a given cell. There are several attributes we will need to allow the programmer to modify in a cell. First, they should be able to set the type of a cell directly. Cells can contain text, bitmaps or editable fields. For text cells, we need to be able to set both the text and the text color. The same will go for editable cells, so we can consider a text cell and an editable cell to be equivalent for this purpose. For bitmap cells, we need to be able to set the bitmap for the control.

```
SetCellType
SetCellColor
SetCellText
SetCellBitmap
GetCellText
```

It would also be nice if the user was able to associate user-defined data with each cell in the grid. Methods should be available for adding and retrieving user data for each cell.

```
SetCellUserData
GetCellUserData
```

Events

The final piece of design work we need to do before we can get started in writing the control is to define the events for it. Obviously, the programmer should be notified when a grid cell has been selected and when the user has modified the data in a cell. It would also be nice to have the ability to find out when the grid is scrolling horizontally and vertically.

```
CellSelect
CellChange
```

```
VScroll
HScroll
```

Now that the preliminary design work is out of the way we'll get started in actually writing the control. Remember that in a 'real' environment, you would need to discuss the design with the potential users of the control to make sure that the design you have come up with actually satisfies their needs.

Implementing the Grid Control

To implement the control, we will create a new project workspace and implement the functionality of the control within that project. Follow this procedure to create the new control.

TRY IT OUT - Create a Grid Control

1 Create a new project workspace using the OLE ControlWizard and call the project **`EGrid`**. You can leave the settings at their default values on Step 1 of the wizard, but on Step 2, click the Edit Names... button. Use the Edit Names dialog to set the Type Name for the control to **`Wrox EGrid Control`** and the Type ID to **`Wrox.EGrid.EGridCtrl.1`**. Set the Type Name for the property page to **`Wrox EGrid Property`** Page and the Type ID to **`Wrox.EGrid.EGridPropPage.1`**. All the other options can stay at their default settings and you can finish the creation of the project.

2 Once the project has been created, we can move on to examining the additional classes we will need to write to support the control.

In order to implement the actual functionality of the control, we will need to somehow work with rows, columns, and cells. Rather than simply maintain this information in some sort of numeric array, it would be better if we implemented individual classes to represent these elements within the system. These classes could then be used in other applications for similar purposes or could be extended in this control to do such things as saving a grid to a file (an enhancement you could add at a later date).

In fact, we won't create classes for rows, columns, *and* cells since we can more easily represent a grid with just two of these classes. We will think of a grid as a one dimensional array of rows and a row as a one dimensional array of cells. This completely describes the structure of a grid without involving a separate class for columns.

First, we'll consider the cell class which will represent a single cell in the grid. A cell needs to keep certain information about itself, such as its column number, its type, the colors and fonts associated with the cell, its displayable data (textual or bitmap), and the user data which we will allow to be associated and stored with each cell.

Create a new text file and save it in the project directory as **`GridCell.h`**. This will hold the class definition for **`CGridCell`**. Here's the complete code that you should add to that file:

```
// GridCell.h - header for CGridCell

#ifndef WROX_GRIDCELL_H
```

```
#define WROX_GRIDCELL_H

class CGridCell : public CObject
{
// Enumerations
public:
   enum CellType {cellText, cellBitmap};

// Constructors
public:
   CGridCell(short nColumn, const CString& strText, long lUserData);
   CGridCell(short nColumn, CBitmap* pBitmap, long lUserData);

// Attributes
public:
   short GetColumnNumber() const;
   int GetType() const;
   void SetType(CellType nType);
   int GetText(CString& strText) const;
   int GetBitmap(CBitmap*& pBitmap);
   long GetUserData() const;

// Operations
public:
   int SetText(const CString& strText);
   int SetBitmap(CBitmap* pBitmap);
   void SetUserData(long lUserData);

// Implementation
public:
   virtual ~CGridCell();

private:
   short m_nColumn;
   CellType m_nType;
   CString m_strText;
   CBitmap* m_pBitmap;
   long m_lUserData;

   DECLARE_DYNAMIC(CGridCell)
};

#endif
```

Note that we have derived **CGridCell** from MFC's **CObject**. This will allow us to use all of the basic functionality of the **CObject** class, such as the ability to be stored in **CObArray**s or serialization, if necessary.

3 Now let's implement the methods for the **CGridCell** class so that we can use them in our new control. First, create a new text file with the name **GridCell.cpp** and insert the file into the project. Add the following code to this file:

```
// GridCell.cpp - implementation of CGridCell

#include "StdAfx.h"
#include "GridCell.h"
```

```
///////////////////////////////////////////////////////////////////////////
// CGridCell Construction and destruction

CGridCell::CGridCell(short nColumn, const CString& strText,
                     long lUserData)
{
   m_nType = cellText;          // Set the type,
   m_nColumn = nColumn;         // the column number,
   m_strText = strText;         // the text,
   m_lUserData = lUserData;     // and the user defined data
}

CGridCell::CGridCell(short nColumn, CBitmap* pBitmap, long lUserData)
{
   m_nType = cellBitmap;        // Set the type,
   m_nColumn = nColumn;         // the column number,
   m_pBitmap = pBitmap;         // the bitmap,
   m_lUserData = lUserData;     // and the user defined data
}

CGridCell::~CGridCell()
{}

///////////////////////////////////////////////////////////////////////////
// CGridCell Attributes

short CGridCell::GetColumnNumber() const
{ return m_nColumn;}

int CGridCell::GetType() const
{ return m_nType; }

void CGridCell::SetType(CellType nType)
{
     m_nType = nType;
}

int CGridCell::GetText(CString& strText) const
{
   // If this is a text cell, return the text.
   // Use the return value to indicate an error to the caller.
   if (cellText == m_nType)
      strText = m_strText;
   return m_nType;
}

int CGridCell::GetBitmap(CBitmap*& pBitmap)
{
   // If this is a bitmap cell, return the bitmap.
   // Use the return value to indicate an error to the caller.
   if (cellBitmap == m_nType)
      pBitmap = m_pBitmap;
   return m_nType;
}

long CGridCell::GetUserData() const
{ return m_lUserData; }
```

```
////////////////////////////////////////////////////////////////////////////
// CGridCell Operations

int CGridCell::SetText(const CString& strText)
{
   CellType nOldType = m_nType;
   if (cellText == m_nType)
      m_strText = strText;
   else
   {
      m_pBitmap = NULL;
      m_strText = strText;
      m_nType = cellText;
   }
   return nOldType;
}

int CGridCell::SetBitmap(CBitmap* pBitmap)
{
   CellType nOldType = m_nType;
   if (cellBitmap == m_nType)
      m_pBitmap = pBitmap;
   else
   {
      m_strText = _T("");
      m_pBitmap = pBitmap;
      m_nType = cellBitmap;
   }
   return nOldType;
}

void CGridCell::SetUserData(long lUserData)
{ m_lUserData = lUserData;    // Doesn't matter what type it is. }

IMPLEMENT_DYNAMIC(CGridCell, CObject)
```

At this point, we have a complete encapsulation of a single cell in a row. You will notice that we aren't storing the colors or fonts for the cell in this class. We'll create a new class a little later to manage that information.

4 The next class to implement is the row class, which holds information such as the row number, and the actual cells defined in the row. Since we will be storing information for each cell that is defined, this is best implemented as an array of **CGridCell** objects. As you will recall, we implemented **CGridCell** as derived from **CObject**, so now we can use MFC's **CObArray** class to store them.

Here's the class header for the grid row class. Create a new text file and save it with the name **GridRow.h** in the same directory as the rest of the project. Now add the following code to it:

```
// GridRow.h - Header for CGridRow

#ifndef WROX_GRIDROW_H
#define WROX_GRIDROW_H
```

```
#include "GridCell.h"

class CGridRow : public CObject
{
// Constuctors
public:
   CGridRow(short nRow);

// Attributes
public:
   short GetRowNumber();
   short GetNumberOfCells();
   CGridCell* GetCell(short nColumn);
   CGridCell* GetCellAt(short nIndex);

// Operations
public:
   void SetCell(short nColumn, const CString& strText, long lUserData);
   void SetCell(short nColumn, CBitmap* pBitmap, long lUserData);

// Implementation
public:
   virtual ~CGridRow();

private:
   CObArray m_Cells;
   short m_nRow;

   DECLARE_DYNAMIC(CGridRow);
};

#endif
```

5 Now, let's write the actual implementation for the **CGridRow** class. Create a new text file with the name **GridRow.cpp** and insert the file into the project:

```
// GridRow.cpp - Implementation of CGridRow
#include "StdAfx.h"
#include "GridRow.h"

///////////////////////////////////////////////////////////////////////////
// CGridRow construction and destruction

CGridRow::CGridRow(short nRow)
{
   m_nRow = nRow;
}

CGridRow::~CGridRow()
{
   for (int i = 0; i < m_Cells.GetSize(); ++i)
   {
      CGridCell* pCell = (CGridCell*)m_Cells[i];
      delete pCell;
   }
}
```

```
//////////////////////////////////////////////////////////////////////////
// CGridRow attributes

short CGridRow::GetRowNumber()
{ return m_nRow; }

short CGridRow::GetNumberOfCells()
{ return m_Cells.GetSize(); }

CGridCell* CGridRow::GetCell(short nColumn)
{
   CGridCell* pCell = NULL;
   for (int i = 0; i < m_Cells.GetSize(); ++i)
   {
      CGridCell* pTempCell = (CGridCell*)m_Cells[i];
      if (pTempCell->GetColumnNumber() == nColumn)
         pCell = pTempCell;
   }
   return pCell;
}

CGridCell* CGridRow::GetCellAt(short nIndex)
{
   if (m_Cells.GetSize() <= nIndex)
      return NULL;
   return (CGridCell*)m_Cells[nIndex];
}

//////////////////////////////////////////////////////////////////////////
// CGridRow operations

void CGridRow::SetCell(short nColumn, const CString& strText,
                       long lUserData)
{
   CGridCell* pCell = NULL;
   // Is this cell in the list?
   for (int i = 0; i < m_Cells.GetSize(); ++i)
   {
      pCell = (CGridCell*)m_Cells[i];
      if (pCell->GetColumnNumber() == nColumn)
      {
         // Yes. Just set the text and exit.
         pCell->SetUserData(lUserData);
         pCell->SetText(strText);
         return;
      }
   }
   // If we got to here we didn't find it. Add a new one.
   pCell = new CGridCell(nColumn, strText, lUserData);
   m_Cells.Add(pCell);
}

void CGridRow::SetCell(short nColumn, CBitmap* pBitmap, long lUserData)
{
   CGridCell* pCell = NULL;
   // Is this cell in the list?
   for (int i = 0; i < m_Cells.GetSize(); ++i)
   {
```

```
        pCell = (CGridCell*)m_Cells[i];
        if (pCell->GetColumnNumber() == nColumn)
        {
            // Yes. Just set the bitmap and exit.
            pCell->SetUserData(lUserData);
            pCell->SetBitmap(pBitmap);
            return;
        }
    }
    // If we got to here we didn't find it. Add a new one.
    pCell = new CGridCell(nColumn, pBitmap, lUserData);
    m_Cells.Add(pCell);
}

IMPLEMENT_DYNAMIC(CGridRow, CObject);
```

Note the defensive posture of the classes. In each case, we will try very hard to protect the programmer from bad data that's passed into the control. If the programmer asks for an invalid row or column, or tries to set data that is outside of the valid range, the control should ensure that the program isn't affected in a negative way (read: crash). This is a good habit to get into in your own programs. Make sure that you only allow valid data to pass through to get to the low-level MFC functions. A liberal usage of **ASSERT** macros could be used in debugging sessions to check for such conditions, but the final release of the product should use active error checking.

6 There are a few more utility classes we will be using in this system. Let's get them out of the way so that we can move on to implementing the functionality behind the grid control. Create a new text file and save it as **GridClasses.h**. For expediency's sake, we'll put a number of class definitions and implementations in a single file; where possible, you would normally provide two files (header and source) for every class. Add the following code to **GridClasses.h**:

```
// GridClasses.h - header file for CGridColWidth,
//                                 CGridRowHeight.
//                                 CGridCellStyle.
#ifndef WROX_GRIDCLASSES_H
#define WROX_GRIDCLASSES_H

#include "GridRow.h"

//////////////////////////////////////////////////////////////////////////////
// Enumeration for different cell types
const enum {TextCell, EditCell, ComboCell, ButtonCell};

//////////////////////////////////////////////////////////////////////////////
// CGridColWidth - Class for storage of individual column widths

class CGridColWidth : public CObject
{
// Constructors
public:
    CGridColWidth(short nColumn, short nWidth)
    {
        m_nColumn = nColumn;
        m_nWidth = nWidth;
```

```
    };

// Attributes
public:
    short GetWidth()  { return m_nWidth; };
    short GetColumn() { return m_nColumn; };

// Operations
public:
    void SetWidth(short nWidth) { m_nWidth = nWidth; };

// Implementation
public:
    ~CGridColWidth() {};

private:
    short m_nColumn;
    short m_nWidth;
};

/////////////////////////////////////////////////////////////////////////////
// CGridRowHeight - Class for storage of individual row heights

class CGridRowHeight : public CObject
{
// Construction
public:
    CGridRowHeight(short nRow, short nHeight)
    {
        m_nRow = nRow;
        m_nHeight = nHeight;
    };

// Attributes
public:
    short GetHeight() { return m_nHeight; };
    short GetRow()    { return m_nRow; };

// Operations
public:
    void SetHeight(short nHeight)
        { m_nHeight = nHeight; };

// Implementation
public:
    ~CGridRowHeight() {};

private:
    short m_nRow;
    short m_nHeight;
};

/////////////////////////////////////////////////////////////////////////////
// CGridCellStyle - Class for storage of cell colors and types

class CGridCellStyle : public CObject
{
// Construction
```

```
public:
    CGridCellStyle(short nRow, short nColumn, COLORREF clrFore,
                    COLORREF clrBack)
    {
        m_nRow = nRow;
        m_nColumn = nColumn;
        m_clrFore = clrFore;
        m_clrBack = clrBack;
        m_nType = TextCell; // Default to simple text
    };

// Attributes
public:
    short GetRow()            { return m_nRow; };
    short GetColumn()         { return m_nColumn; };
    COLORREF GetForeColor() { return m_clrFore; };
    COLORREF GetBackColor() { return m_clrBack; };
    short GetCellType()       { return m_nType; };

// Operations
public:
    void SetForeColor(COLORREF clrFore) { m_clrFore = clrFore; };
    void SetBackColor(COLORREF clrBack) { m_clrBack = clrBack; };
    void SetCellType(short nType)        { m_nType = nType; }

// Implementation
public:
    ~CGridCellStyle() {};

private:
    short m_nRow;
    short m_nColumn;
    COLORREF m_clrFore;
    COLORREF m_clrBack;
    short m_nType;
};
#endif
```

The **CGridColWidth** class is used for storing information about the column widths of the individual columns of the class. Why is this information not stored in the cell class? The answer, quite simply, is that it isn't the case that a cell object must be defined for the column to have a width. If there are no cells defined in a given column, the column still needs to be displayable for the user. For this reason, we add a secondary class that represents this information.

The **CGridRowHeight** class is used for storing information about the height of each row in the grid. Just as we don't want to force the creation of **CGridCell** objects in order for the column to have a width, we don't want to force the creation of **CGridRow** objects in order for a row to have a height.

The **CGridCellStyle** class stores information about cells in the grid. Once again, there's no requirement that a cell should have textual or bitmap information defined for it. Cells may be displayed in color without having any information that would be placed into a **CGridCell** object, and this class allows us to store the general information about the object. The **CGridCellStyle** class stores the foreground and background color for the cell, as well as the type of cell to use. We duplicate the functionality of the type between the **CGridCell** class and the **CGridCellStyle** class because they mean different things in the different classes. In this class, we're defining what the user will do with the grid cell when it's displayed. In the **CGridCell** class, we're defining the type of information stored in the object itself.

Now the utility classes have been defined, we need to add **#include "GridClasses.h"** to the top of **CEGridCtl.h**.

7 The next step is to add some member variables to the grid control to keep track of the various elements of the grid represented by the classes we've just created. Add the members shown below to the **Implementation** section of **EGridCtl.h**.

```
private:
    CObArray m_ColumnWidths;    // An array of CGridColWidths
    CObArray m_RowHeights;      // An array of CGridRowHeights
    CObArray m_CellStyles;      // An array of CGridCellStyles
    CObArray m_Rows;            // An array of CGridRows
                                // (each row keeps track of its own cells)
```

8 Now we can move on to adding the properties for this control. To do this, enter ClassWizard and select the OLE Automation page from the property sheet. Click on Add Property... for each of the stock properties, **Font**, **ForeColor**, and **BackColor**, and select their name in the External name list. Click OK to add each property to the control. Once you've done this, ClassWizard should look as shown:

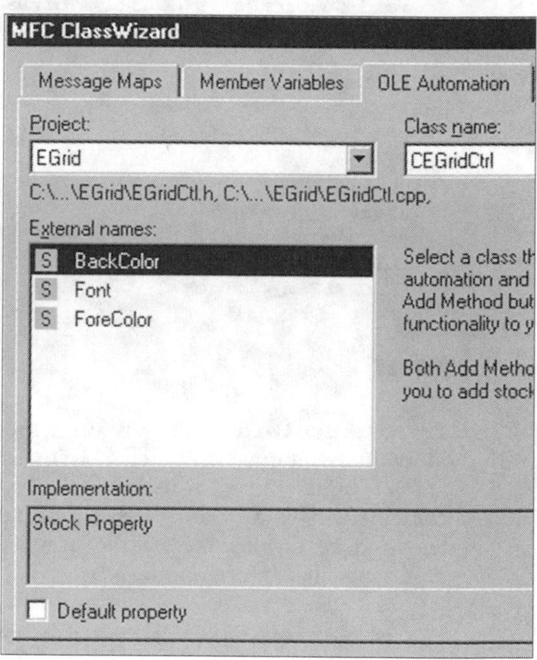

9 Now add the custom properties to the control as shown in the table below.

External name	Type	Variable name	Notification function	Implementation
Rows	short	m_nRows	OnRowsChanged	Member variable
Cols	short	m_nCols	OnColsChanged	Member variable

These properties will represent the number of rows and the number of columns, respectively, that our grid possesses. You can add the implementation of these functions to **EGridCtl.cpp** as shown here:

```
void CEGridCtrl::OnRowsChanged()
{
    InvalidateControl();
    SetModifiedFlag();
}

void CEGridCtrl::OnColsChanged()
{
    InvalidateControl();
    SetModifiedFlag();
}
```

10 Now it's time to start adding the methods to the control. Use the Add Method... button on ClassWizard's OLE Automation page to add the methods shown in this table:

External name/ Internal name	Return type	Parameter List Name	Parameter List Type
SetColumnWidth	void	nColumn nWidth	short short
SetRowHeight	void	nRow nHeight	short short
GetColumnWidth	short	nColumn	short
GetRowHeight	short	nRow	short
SetCellColor	void	nRow nColumn clrForeColor clrBackColor	short short OLE_COLOR OLE_COLOR
SetCellType	void	nRow nColumn nType	short short short

Now we'll implement these methods.

11 Start with **SetColumnWidth()** which takes two parameters, the first representing the column whose width is to be set and the second, the value for that width. Enter the following code into the function definition block in **EGridCtl.cpp**:

```
void CEGridCtrl::SetColumnWidth(short nColumn, short nWidth)
{
    // See if we already have this column in the list
    for (int i = 0; i < m_ColumnWidths.GetSize(); ++i)
    {
        CGridColWidth* cw = (CGridColWidth*)m_ColumnWidths[i];
        if (cw->GetColumn() == nColumn)
        {
            // Just set the column width in the object
```

```
            cw->SetWidth(nWidth);
            return;
        }
    }

    // If we get here we didn't find a CGridColWidth object.
    // Create a new one and add it to the array.
    CGridColWidth* cw = new CGridColWidth(nColumn, nWidth);
    m_ColumnWidths.Add(cw);

    // And redraw the whole thing to reflect the change.
    InvalidateControl();
}
```

Note the **InvalidateControl()** call at the end of the method. This is done so that if the programmer were to change the column width at run time, the control would automatically redraw itself to show the changes made.

12 The next method to implement is **SetRowHeight()**. Like the **SetColumnWidth()** method, it returns no value and takes two arguments. The first argument is the row number to set and the second argument is the height of the row. Add the following code to the body of **CEGridCtrl::SetRowHeight()**:

```
void CEGridCtrl::SetRowHeight(short nRow, short nHeight)
{
    // See if we already have this row in the list
    for (int i = 0; i < m_RowHeights.GetSize(); ++i)
    {
        CGridRowHeight* rh = (CGridRowHeight*)m_RowHeights[i];
        if (rh->GetRow() == nRow)
        {
            // Just set the row height in the object
            rh->SetHeight(nHeight);
            return;
        }
    }

    // If we get here we didn't find a CGridRowHeight object.
    // Create a new one and add it to the array.
    CGridRowHeight* rh = new CGridRowHeight(nRow, nHeight);
    m_RowHeights.Add(rh);

    // And redraw the whole thing to reflect the change
    InvalidateControl();
}
```

Again, we're determining whether we already have a row height before assigning the value. If the row height isn't found, we add it to the list. Again, the **InvalidateControl()** call at the end of the function will make sure that the control is shown properly at run time.

13 The next two methods to implement are those to retrieve the settings we just defined, **CEGridCtrl::GetColumnWidth()** and **CEGridCtrl::GetRowHeight()**. We'll look at retrieving the column width first. Add the code shown to **EGridCtl.cpp**:

```
short CEGridCtrl::GetColumnWidth(short nColumn)
{
   int nControlWidth;
   int nControlHeight;
   GetControlSize(&nControlWidth, &nControlHeight);

   int nDefaultWidth = nControlWidth;
   if (m_nCols)
      nDefaultWidth = nControlWidth / m_nCols;

   for (int i = 0; i < m_ColumnWidths.GetSize(); ++i)
   {
      CGridColWidth* cw = (CGridColWidth*)m_ColumnWidths[i];
      if (cw->GetColumn() == nColumn)
         return cw->GetWidth();
   }
   return nDefaultWidth; // Nope. Return default
}
```

Note the use of the **GetControlSize()** function. This is provided by the MFC base class of our control, **COleControl**, and returns the width and height of the control in pixels. It can be used at design or run time, which makes it a valuable function to know about. Calling **GetWindowRect()** could cause problems if the control didn't actually have a window!

Note also that we provide a default width for any column. If we can't find a **CGridColWidth** object in **m_ColumnWidths** for the specified column, we return a width based on the number of columns and the width of the control. This means that unless a column width has been set specifically, it will resize as the control changes size.

Unfortunately, it also means that even invalid columns will receive a valid width. It might have been better to have returned **0** in the case of an invalid column, but I chose not to because that could cause infinite loops in applications that tried to add them to a total width (such as the one I originally used the control for). In retrospect, this may have been a bad choice. Even professionals occasionally make mistakes! If you think this is worth rectifying, go right ahead—it'll be good practice.

14 Now we'll implement **GetRowHeight()**:

```
short CEGridCtrl::GetRowHeight(short nRow)
{
   int nControlWidth;
   int nControlHeight;
   GetControlSize(&nControlWidth, &nControlHeight);

   int nDefaultHeight = nControlHeight;
   if (m_nCols)
      nDefaultHeight = nControlHeight / m_nRows;

   for (int i = 0; i < m_RowHeights.GetSize(); ++i)
   {
      CGridRowHeight* rh = (CGridRowHeight*)m_RowHeights[i];
      if (rh->GetRow() == nRow)
         return rh->GetHeight();
```

```
    }
    return nDefaultHeight; // Nope. Return default
}
```

This looks a lot like **GetColumnWidth()** because it's doing much the same job. As you might expect, the implications of this function are that row heights will be resizable until the height for that row has been explicitly set.

15 We now need to implement the cell modification methods. First, the **SetCellColor()** method, which will simply set the colors for a given cell. Here's the code for **SetCellColor()**:

```
void CEGridCtrl::SetCellColor(short nRow, short nColumn,
                              OLE_COLOR clrForeColor, OLE_COLOR clrBackColor)
{
    // Basic sanity check. Is this a valid row/column?
    if (nRow < 0 || nRow > m_nRows - 1)
       return;
    if (nColumn < 0 || nRow > m_nCols - 1)
       return;

    COLORREF clrFore = TranslateColor(clrForeColor);
    COLORREF clrBack = TranslateColor(clrBackColor);

    // Do we already have a style object for this cell?
    CGridCellStyle* cs = GetCellStyle(nRow, nColumn);
    if (cs)
    {
       cs->SetForeColor(clrFore);
       cs->SetBackColor(clrBack);
    }
    else
    {
       cs = new CGridCellStyle(nRow, nColumn, clrFore, clrBack);
       m_CellStyles.Add(cs);
    }
    InvalidateControl();
}
```

You can see that we use the first two parameters to identify the cell that needs to have its colors set, and the last two parameters to specify the values for the colors. These color parameters are both declared as **OLE_COLOR**s which can easily be translated into **COLORREF**s using **COleControl::TranslateColor()**.

The color information is stored in an element of the **m_CellStyles** array. If there isn't an element already in existence that corresponds to the row and column specified then we create a new **CGridCellStyle** object and add it to the array.

16 The **CEGridCtrl::SetCellColor()** function uses a helper function called **GetCellStyle()** to get cell style objects. We'll create that function now. Add the member function declaration to **CEGridCtrl.h** as shown:

```
// Implementation
protected:
```

```
~CEGridCtrl();
CGridCellStyle* GetCellStyle(short nRow, short nColumn);
```

The function definition will need to go in **EGridCtl.cpp**.

```
CGridCellStyle* CEGridCtrl::GetCellStyle(short nRow, short nColumn)
{
   for (int i = 0; i < m_CellStyles.GetSize(); ++i)
   {
      CGridCellStyle* cs = (CGridCellStyle*)m_CellStyles[i];
      if (cs->GetRow() == nRow && cs->GetColumn() == nColumn)
         return cs;
   }
   return NULL;
}
```

The function just loops through the **m_CellStyles** array, checking the column and row of each of its members. If there's a match, the function will return a pointer to that object, otherwise it will return **NULL**.

This function is used internally to retrieve the information we need to display the individual cells in the grid. If no style information is available for a grid cell, we know that there's nothing 'special' about it and can continue with our lives.

17 Now we can implement the **SetCellType()** method:

```
void CEGridCtrl::SetCellType(short nRow, short nColumn, short nType)
{
   // Do we already have a style object for this cell?
   CGridCellStyle* cs = GetCellStyle(nRow, nColumn);
   if (cs)
      cs->SetCellType(nType);
   else
   {
      cs = new CGridCellStyle(nRow, nColumn,
           TranslateColor(GetForeColor()), TranslateColor(GetBackColor()));
      cs->SetCellType(nType);
      m_CellStyles.Add(cs);
   }
   InvalidateControl();
}
```

Once again, we check to see if there's already style information specified for that cell. If there is, the object is simply updated with the new information. If there's no style information defined, a new object is added to the list of cell style objects.

18 Now we'll return to ClassWizard to finish adding the methods to the control. Add the methods shown in the following table.

External name/ Internal name	Return type	Parameter List Name	Parameter List Type
SetCellText	void	nRow nColumn strText lUserData	short short LPCTSTR long
SetCellBitmap	void	nRow nColumn pBitmap lUserData	short short long long
GetCellText	BSTR	nRow nColumn	short short
SetCellUserData	void	nRow nColumn lUserData	short short long
GetCellUserData	long	nRow nColumn	short short

We'll look at implementing each of these methods in turn.

19 Here's the code you'll need to add for **SetCellText()**:

```
void CEGridCtrl::SetCellText(short nRow, short nColumn, LPCTSTR strText,
                             long lUserData)
{
   // See if we already have that column/row combination defined
   CGridRow* row = GetRow(nRow);
   if (!row)
      row = AddRow(nRow);

   // See if we have that many rows already
   if (nRow >= m_nRows)
      m_nRows = nRow + 1;

   // Do same for columns
   if (nColumn >= m_nCols)
      m_nCols = nColumn + 1;

   row->SetCell(nColumn, strText, lUserData);
   InvalidateControl();
}
```

This function is actually fairly straightforward. It gets a pointer to a **CGridRow** object and calls its **SetCell()** member to do the work. If either the row or column that has been passed as a parameter isn't part of the grid as defined by **m_nRows** and **m_nCols**, these members are increased.

However, the function does use two as yet undefined functions, **GetRow()** and **AddRow()**. We'll define them now. Add the function declarations shown to the **protected // Implementation** section of **CEgridCtrl.h**.

```
CGridCellStyle* GetCellStyle(short nRow, short nColumn);
CGridRow* GetRow(short nRow);
CGridRow* AddRow(short nRow);
```

Now add the definitions to **EGridCtl.cpp**.

```
CGridRow* CEGridCtrl::GetRow(short nRow)
{
   for (int i = 0; i < m_Rows.GetSize(); ++i)
   {
      CGridRow* row = (CGridRow*)m_Rows[i];
      if (row->GetRowNumber() == nRow)
         return row;
   }
   return NULL;
}

CGridRow* CEGridCtrl::AddRow(short nRow)
{
   CGridRow* rowNew = new CGridRow(nRow);
   m_Rows.Add(rowNew);
   return rowNew;
}
```

GetRow() searches through the list of defined rows and returns the one that matches the requested row number. If no matching row is found, a **NULL** pointer is returned instead. This is done because we do not want a row object for each available row. We are implementing a very simple spare matrix here to conserve memory and make it easier to define rows and columns after the fact. For this reason, among others, we will use the row number as a 'key' into the list of row objects, but will not store them in an array indexed by row number.

20 **SetCellBitmap()** is almost identical to **SetCellText()**.

```
void CEGridCtrl::SetCellBitmap(short nRow, short nColumn, long pBitmap,
                                long lUserData)
{
   // See if we already have that column/row combination defined
   CGridRow* row = GetRow(nRow);
   if (!row)
      row = AddRow (nRow);

   // See if we have that many rows already
   if (nRow >= m_nRows)
      m_nRows = nRow + 1;

   // Do same for columns
   if (nColumn >= m_nCols)
      m_nCols = nColumn + 1;

   row->SetCell(nColumn, (CBitmap*)pBitmap, lUserData);
   CGridCell* cell = row->GetCell(nColumn);
   if (cell)
      cell->SetType(CGridCell::cellBitmap);
   InvalidateControl();
}
```

21 Here's the code for the **GetCellText()** method:

```
BSTR CEGridCtrl::GetCellText(short nRow, short nColumn)
{
   CString strResult;
   // See if we already have that column/row combination defined
   CGridRow* row = GetRow(nRow);
   if (row)
   {
      CGridCell* cell = row->GetCell(nColumn);
      if (cell)
         cell->GetText(strResult);
   }
   return strResult.AllocSysString();
}
```

Note that if no text is defined for a given cell, the method will simply return an empty string (not **NULL**). This will avoid potential problems later in applications. By doing it this way, we can always display whatever text is available in a cell without worrying about whether that cell is defined.

22 The final two methods left to implement for the control deal with the user data associated with a cell in the grid. Here's the code for the **SetCellUserData()** method:

```
void CEGridCtrl::SetCellUserData(short nRow, short nColumn,
                                  long lUserData)
{
   // See if we already have that column/row combination defined
   CGridRow* row = GetRow(nRow);
   if (row)
   {
      CGridCell* cell = row->GetCell(nColumn);
      if (cell)
         cell->SetUserData(lUserData);
   }
}
```

Similarly, the **GetCellUserData()** function takes two **short** arguments which represent the cell row and column, and returns a **long** value which is the stored user data for that cell if any was specified. If no user data was found, **0** is returned.

```
long CEGridCtrl::GetCellUserData(short nRow, short nColumn)
{
   // See if we already have that column/row combination defined
   CGridRow* row = GetRow(nRow);
   if (row)
   {
      CGridCell* cell = row->GetCell(nColumn);
      if (cell)
         return cell->GetUserData();
   }
   return 0;
}
```

23 Okay, we're now up to the exciting part of control development—actually painting the control. This is the driving force behind all of the other functionality of the control. Here's the code for **CEGridCtrl::OnDraw()**:

```
void CEGridCtrl::OnDraw(
        CDC* pdc, const CRect& rcBounds, const CRect& rcInvalid)
{
    FillBackground(pdc, rcBounds);
    SetScrollBarHorizontal(rcBounds);
    SetScrollBarVertical(rcBounds);
    DrawGridLines(pdc, rcBounds);
    DrawData(pdc, rcBounds);
}
```

I bet you never realized drawing a grid that could contain text and bitmaps would be so easy! Unfortunately, we're going to have to implement each of these five functions ourselves and we'll also need to create a couple of other functions to support them. To make life easy, we might as well add the declarations for all these functions to **CEgridCtrl** now. You can see the code you'll need highlighted below:

```
// Implementation
protected:
    ~CEGridCtrl();
    CGridCellStyle* GetCellStyle(short nRow, short nColumn);
    CGridRow* GetRow(short nRow);
    CGridRow* AddRow(short nRow);
    void FillBackground(CDC* pDC, const CRect& rcBounds);
    long GetVirtualWidth();
    long GetVirtualHeight();
    BOOL SetScrollBarHorizontal(const CRect& rcBounds);
    BOOL SetScrollBarVertical(const CRect& rcBounds);
    long GetColumnOffset(short nColumn, const CRect& rcBounds);
    long GetRowOffset(short nRow, const CRect& rcBounds);
    void DrawGridLines(CDC* pDC, const CRect& rcBounds);
    void DrawData(CDC* pDC, const CRect& rcBounds);
```

We'll add the implementation for each of these functions in turn.

24 **FillBackground()** is designed to do nothing more than fill the control's background with the color specified by its **BackColor** property. This can be retrieved as an **OLE_COLOR** by **COleControl::GetBackColor()** so we need to use **TranslateColor()** to convert it into a **COLORREF**.

```
void CEGridCtrl::FillBackground(CDC* pDC, const CRect& rcBounds)
{
    CBrush brBack(TranslateColor(GetBackColor()));
    pDC->FillRect(&rcBounds, &brBack);
}
```

25 **GetVirtualHeight()** and **GetVirtualWidth()** return the virtual height and width of the grid. That is, they calculate how large the grid would be if it was all displayed. Since we're going to allow scrolling of the grid, the values returned by **GetVirtualHeight()** and **GetVirtualWidth()** may be larger than the dimensions of the control. In fact, we will use these functions to determine whether we need to display scroll bars.

```
long CEGridCtrl::GetVirtualWidth()
{
   long lTotalWidth = 0;
   for (int i = 0; i < m_nCols; ++i)
      lTotalWidth += GetColumnWidth(i);
   return lTotalWidth;
}

long CEGridCtrl::GetVirtualHeight()
{
   long lTotalHeight = 0;
   for (int i = 0; i < m_nRows; ++i)
      lTotalHeight += GetRowHeight(i);
   return lTotalHeight;
}
```

26 **`SetScrollBarHorizontal()`** and **`SetScrollBarVertical()`** have the responsibility of ensuring that the scroll bars in their respective direction are enabled or hidden as necessary.

```
BOOL CEGridCtrl::SetScrollBarHorizontal(const CRect& rcBounds)
{
   // Make sure the width doesn't exceed the actual bounds of the control.
   // If it DOES exceed the width, enable the horizontal scroll bar.
   // If it does NOT exceed the width, disable the horizontal scroll bar
   if (m_hWnd)
   {
      if (GetVirtualWidth() > rcBounds.Width())
      {
         EnableScrollBarCtrl(SB_HORZ, TRUE);
         SetScrollRange(SB_HORZ, 0, m_nCols - 1);
         return TRUE;
      }
      else
      {
         EnableScrollBarCtrl(SB_HORZ, FALSE);
         m_nLeftColumn = 0;
      }
   }
   return FALSE;
}

BOOL CEGridCtrl::SetScrollBarVertical(const CRect& rcBounds)
{
   if (m_hWnd)
   {
      if (GetVirtualHeight() > rcBounds.Height())
      {
         EnableScrollBarCtrl(SB_VERT, TRUE);
         SetScrollRange(SB_VERT, 0, m_nRows - 1);
         return TRUE;
      }
      else
      {
         EnableScrollBarCtrl(SB_VERT, FALSE);
         m_nTopRow = 0;
      }
   }
```

```
    return FALSE;
}
```

Each of these functions uses **CWnd::EnableScrollBarCtrl()** and **CWnd::SetScrollRange()** to set the scrollbars to appropriate values. (Remember that our control is derived from **COleControl** which is, in turn, derived from **CWnd**).

Note the member variables **m_nTopRow** and **m_nLeftColumn** that are set to **0** if the scroll bars are disabled. These hold the values of the row and column that are displayed at the top left of the control. Their values will vary as the control is scrolled and they're used for drawing the control, as you'll soon see. Since we haven't actually declared these member variables yet, we'll do that now. Add the following code to the **CEgridCtrl** header file.

```
private:
   CObArray m_ColumnWidths;     // An array of CGridColWidths
   CObArray m_RowHeights;       // An array of CGridRowHeights
   CObArray m_CellStyles;       // An array of CGridCellStyles
   CObArray m_Rows;             // An array of CGridRows
                                // (each row keeps track of its own cells)
   short m_nTopRow;             // First displayed row (used for scrolling)
   short m_nLeftColumn;         // First displayed col (used for scrolling)
```

27 The next two functions, **GetColumnOffset()** and **GetRowOffset()**, get the horizontal or vertical offset of the column or row given as a parameter.

```
long CEGridCtrl::GetColumnOffset(short nColumn, const CRect& rcBounds)
{
   // Start at left edge
   long lXOffset = rcBounds.left;
   for (int i = 0; i < nColumn; ++i)
      lXOffset += GetColumnWidth(i);
   return lXOffset;
}

long CEGridCtrl::GetRowOffset(short nRow, const CRect& rcBounds)
{
   long lYOffset = rcBounds.top;
   for (int i = 0; i < nRow; ++i)
      lYOffset += GetRowHeight(i);
   return lYOffset;
}
```

28 **DrawGridLines()** does exactly what it says. It uses a number of the functions that we've just defined to help it calculate where it should draw the lines.

```
void CEGridCtrl::DrawGridLines(CDC* pDC, const CRect& rcBounds)
{
   long lTotalHeight = GetVirtualHeight();
   long lTotalWidth = GetVirtualWidth();
   long lXOffset = GetColumnOffset(m_nLeftColumn, rcBounds);
   long lYOffset = GetRowOffset(m_nTopRow, rcBounds);

   // For each column, draw the vertical lines for the grid.
   for (int i = m_nLeftColumn - 1; i < m_nCols; ++i)
```

```
   {
      pDC->MoveTo(GetColumnOffset(i + 1, rcBounds) - lXOffset, 0);
      pDC->LineTo(GetColumnOffset(i + 1, rcBounds) - lXOffset,
                            lTotalHeight - lYOffset);
   }

   // For each row, draw the horizontal lines for the grid
   for (i = m_nTopRow - 1; i < m_nRows; ++i)
   {
      pDC->MoveTo(0, GetRowOffset(i + 1, rcBounds) - lYOffset);
      pDC->LineTo(lTotalWidth - lXOffset, GetRowOffset(i + 1, rcBounds) -
                                                          lYOffset);
   }
}
```

29 The only drawing function left to examine is **DrawData()** itself which is responsible for painting all the cells of the grid.

```
void CEGridCtrl::DrawData(CDC* pDC, const CRect& rcBounds)
{
   long lXOffset = GetColumnOffset(m_nLeftColumn, rcBounds);
   long lYOffset = GetRowOffset(m_nTopRow, rcBounds);

   // Loop through each row and get the information to display stuff.
   for (int i = m_nTopRow; i < m_nRows; ++i)
   {
      CGridRow* row = GetRow(i);

      // Get the top and bottom for this row.
      int nRowTop = GetRowOffset(i, rcBounds) - lYOffset;
      if (nRowTop > rcBounds.bottom)
         break;
      int nRowBottom = nRowTop + GetRowHeight(i);

      // Loop through the cells for this row.
      for (int j = m_nLeftColumn; j < m_nCols; ++j)
      {
         // See if we have a style defined for this cell.
         CGridCellStyle* style = GetCellStyle(i, j);

         // Determine where the cell lies.
         int nCellLeft = GetColumnOffset(j, rcBounds) - lXOffset;
         int nCellRight = GetColumnOffset(j + 1, rcBounds) - lXOffset;

         CRect rect(nCellLeft, nRowTop, nCellRight, nRowBottom);

         COLORREF clrOldBack = pDC->GetBkColor();
         COLORREF clrOldText = pDC->GetTextColor();

         if (style)
         {
            // Set the background color.
            pDC->SetBkColor(style->GetBackColor());
            // And the text color.
            pDC->SetTextColor(style->GetForeColor());

            // Fill the rectangle with the style.
```

```
                rect.DeflateRect(1, 1);
                CBrush brush(style->GetBackColor());
                pDC->FillRect (&rect, &brush);
                rect.InflateRect(1, 1);
            }

            // There may be no data for this row, continue.
            if (!row)
            {
                pDC->SetTextColor(clrOldText);
                pDC->SetBkColor(clrOldBack);
                continue;
            }

            CGridCell* cell = row->GetCell(j);

            // No cell data for this cell? Ignore it.
            if (!cell)
            {
                pDC->SetTextColor(clrOldText);
                pDC->SetBkColor(clrOldBack);
                continue;
            }

            CString strText;
            CBitmap* pBitmap = NULL;
            int nCtype = 0;
            if (style)
                nCtype = style->GetCellType();
            else
                nCtype = cell->GetType();

            switch (nCtype)
            {
            case CGridCell::cellText:
                cell->GetText(strText);
                pDC->DrawText(strText, &rect,
                           DT_VCENTER | DT_CENTER | DT_SINGLELINE);
                break;
            case CGridCell::cellBitmap:
                cell->GetBitmap(pBitmap);
                DrawBitmap(pDC->m_hDC, rect,
                       (HBITMAP)pBitmap->GetSafeHandle());
                break;
            }
            // Reset old colors in the DC.
            pDC->SetTextColor(clrOldText);
            pDC->SetBkColor(clrOldBack);
        }
    }
}
```

Although it looks like a lot of code, it really breaks down pretty simply. We use **m_nTopRow** and **m_nLeftColumn** to determine which row and column we start the drawing with and the values **m_nRows** and **m_nCols** determine where we stop. This means that we may end up drawing cells that we don't need to draw since there may be rows that are off the bottom and columns off the right of the control's display area. However, it makes life fairly simple for us, too. Feel free to optimize the code if you prefer.

First, we check if we've got a cell style defined for each row/column combination. If we have, we use the information it contains to set the back color and the text color for the device context and we fill the cell's rectangle using that information. If we don't have any style information then we do nothing. Next, we try to get a **CGridRow** object for the current row and from that a **CGridCell** object for the current column. If we can do that, we check to see what type the cell is (text or bitmap) and draw the data appropriately. Otherwise, we keep looping until we do get something to draw, or else we run out of rows and columns.

30 The data is actually displayed by two functions: **CDC::DrawText()** for the textual data and **DrawBitmap()** for the bitmaps. The second of these needs to be declared and implemented by us, so we'll do that next. Here's the code that you should add to the bottom of **GridClasses.h** to implement the **DrawBitmap()** function:

```
///////////////////////////////////////////////////////////////////////////////
// DrawBitmap - Global Function

// Prototype
BOOL DrawBitmap(HDC hdcDest, RECT rect, HBITMAP hbmNew);

// Definition
BOOL DrawBitmap(HDC hdcDest, RECT rect, HBITMAP hbmNew)
{
    HDC hdcDestMem;     // Handle of memory context to use in drawing bitmap
    HBITMAP hbmOld;
    POINT ptSize, ptOrigin;
    BITMAP bitmap;
    int nXDest, nYDest, nWidth, nHeight;

    hdcDestMem = CreateCompatibleDC(hdcDest);
    if (hdcDestMem)
    {
        // Select bitmap to be draw into memory context
        hbmOld = (HBITMAP)SelectObject(hdcDestMem, hbmNew);

        // Set the mapping mode for the memory context to match the
        // target device context.
        SetMapMode(hdcDestMem, GetMapMode(hdcDest));

        // Get the details of the bitmap being drawn
        GetObject(hbmNew, sizeof(BITMAP), &bitmap);

        // Adjust height and width for mapping mode
        ptSize.x = bitmap.bmWidth;
        ptSize.y = bitmap.bmHeight;
        DPtoLP(hdcDest, (LPPOINT)&ptSize, 1);

        // Adjust origin for mapping mode.
        ptOrigin.x = 0;
        ptOrigin.y = 0;
        DPtoLP(hdcDestMem, (LPPOINT)&ptOrigin, 1);

        // Center the bitmap in the given rectangle.
        nXDest = rect.left + (rect.right - rect.left + 1) / 2
                 - bitmap.bmWidth / 2;
        nWidth = rect.left + (rect.right - rect.left + 1) / 2
                 + bitmap.bmWidth / 2;
```

```
        nYDest = rect.top + (rect.bottom - rect.top + 1) / 2
                 - bitmap.bmHeight / 2;
        nHeight = rect.top + (rect.bottom - rect.top + 1) / 2
                  + bitmap.bmHeight / 2;

        // Draw the bitmap.
        BitBlt(hdcDest, nXDest, nYDest, nWidth, nHeight, hdcDestMem,
               ptOrigin.x, ptOrigin.y, SRCCOPY);

        // Clean up.
        SelectObject(hdcDestMem, hbmOld);
        DeleteDC(hdcDestMem);

        return TRUE;
    }
    return FALSE;
}
```

This code creates a compatible DC that we can draw on and selects the bitmap into it. Then the bitmap is 'blitted' onto the real control surface via the **`BitBlt()`** function. Finally, the DC is cleaned up and the copy destroyed. This puts the bitmap on the screen where the user can see it. Notice that the bitmap is always centered within the grid cell it resides upon.

This technique of creating a compatible DC, then blitting an image to the screen, is quite common as a means of reducing flicker when drawing and is applicable in many areas. If you feel the need, you could modify the rest of the grid's drawing code to draw to an off-screen device context before blitting the completed image to the screen.

31 Now that all of the properties and methods are defined, it would be a good time to take a trip back into ClassWizard to add the events for this control. Events are fired from the control to its container, to notify the application when certain things happen.

We will be adding four new events to this control:

`VScroll` notifies the programmer that the grid has been scrolled vertically. The parameter indicates which row is now at the top of the control.

`HScroll` notifies the programmer that the grid has been scrolled horizontally. The parameter indicates which column is now at the left of the control.

`CellChange` notifies the programmer that the user has finished editing a cell. It will be the responsibility of the programmer to determine if the string in the cell has actually changed. The parameters indicate which cell was being edited.

`Select` notifies the programmer when the user clicks in a cell. The parameters indicate which cell was clicked.

Use ClassWizard's OLE Events tab and the Add Event... button to add these events to the control according to the following table.

External name	Internal name	Parameter List Name	Parameter List Type
VScroll	FireVScroll	nNewTopRow	short
HScroll	FireHScroll	nNewLeftColumn	short
CellChange	FireCellChange	nRow nColumn	short short
Select	FireSelect	nRow nColumn	short short

32 Now we will turn our attention to implementing scrolling the control. Whenever the user scrolls the control, all we need to do is update **m_nTopRow** and **m_nLeftColumn**, then invalidate the control so that the **OnDraw()** function can handle the job of redisplaying the data properly for the new position. We also need to fire the appropriate events.

Use ClassWizard to add handlers for the **WM_HSCROLL** and **WM_VSCROLL** messages to the **CEGridCtrl** class and add the following code to the resulting functions:

```
void CEGridCtrl::OnHScroll(UINT nSBCode, UINT nPos,
                           CScrollBar* pScrollBar)
{
   COleControl::OnHScroll(nSBCode, nPos, pScrollBar);
   int nHoldColumn = m_nLeftColumn;
   switch (nSBCode)
   {
   case SB_LINEDOWN:
   case SB_PAGEDOWN:
      if (m_nLeftColumn < m_nCols - 1)
      {
         m_nLeftColumn++;
         SetScrollPos(SB_HORZ, m_nLeftColumn);
      }
      break;
   case SB_LINEUP:
   case SB_PAGEUP:
      if (m_nLeftColumn)
      {
         m_nLeftColumn--;
         SetScrollPos(SB_HORZ, m_nLeftColumn);
      }
      break;
   }
   if (nHoldColumn != m_nLeftColumn)
   {
      FireHScroll(m_nLeftColumn);
      InvalidateControl();
   }
}

void CEGridCtrl::OnVScroll(UINT nSBCode, UINT nPos,
                           CScrollBar* pScrollBar)
{
   COleControl::OnVScroll(nSBCode, nPos, pScrollBar);
   int nHoldRow = m_nTopRow;
   switch (nSBCode)
```

```
   {
   case SB_LINEDOWN:
   case SB_PAGEDOWN:
      if (m_nTopRow < m_nRows - 1)
      {
         m_nLeftColumn++;
         SetScrollPos(SB_VERT, m_nTopRow);
      }
      break;
   case SB_LINEUP:
   case SB_PAGEUP:
      if (m_nTopRow)
      {
         m_nTopRow--;
         SetScrollPos(SB_VERT, m_nTopRow);
      }
      break;
   }
   if (nHoldRow != m_nTopRow)
   {
      FireHScroll(m_nTopRow);
      InvalidateControl();
   }
}
```

As promised, you'll see the calls to **FireHScroll()** and **FireVScroll()** to notify the programmer that the grid has scrolled. Why would you want to know if the grid has scrolled? The most obvious reason is that you are maintaining a header for the grid outside of the grid itself. This header would need to be updated whenever the grid was scrolled so that the headers stayed in sync with the grid they represent. In this case, your application programmer would thank you profusely for thinking about this and adding these events.

33 Now, we'll look at editing the contents of a cell. We will allow the user to do this in response to a double-click on the cell, so we'll need a handler for the **WM_LBUTTONDBLCLK** message. Add one to **CEgridCtrl** using ClassWizard, and add the code shown below to the resulting function.

```
void CEGridCtrl::OnLButtonDblClk(UINT nFlags, CPoint point)
{
   // Determine where they clicked based on the point
   CRect rcBounds;
   int nWidth, nHeight;
   GetControlSize(&nWidth, &nHeight);

   rcBounds.top = rcBounds.left = 0;
   rcBounds.bottom = nHeight;
   rcBounds.right = nWidth;

   int lYOffset = GetRowOffset(m_nTopRow, rcBounds);
   int lXOffset = GetColumnOffset(m_nLeftColumn, rcBounds);

   for (int i = m_nTopRow; i < m_nRows; ++i)
   {
      // Define the top and bottom for this row.
      int nTop = GetRowOffset(i, rcBounds) - lYOffset;
      int nBottom = nTop + GetRowHeight(i);
```

```
      // Loop through the columns for this row.
      for (int j = m_nLeftColumn; j < m_nCols; ++j)
      {
         // Determine where the column lies.
         int nLeft = GetColumnOffset(j, rcBounds) - lXOffset;
         int nRight = GetColumnOffset(j + 1, rcBounds) - lXOffset;
         CRect rect(nLeft + 1, nTop + 1, nRight - 1, nBottom - 1);

         // If we find one, first fire the select then
         // check the type.
         if (rect.PtInRect(point))
         {
            FireSelect(i, j);
            if (m_pwndEdit)
            {
               CString strText;
               m_pwndEdit->GetWindowText(strText);
               SetCellText(m_nCurrentRow, m_nCurrentColumn, strText, 0);
               delete m_pwndEdit;
               m_pwndEdit = NULL;
            }
            m_nCurrentRow = i;
            m_nCurrentColumn = j;
            CGridCellStyle* cs = GetCellStyle(i, j);

            short ct = TextCell;
            if (cs)
               ct = cs->GetCellType();

            switch (ct)
            {
            case EditCell:
               m_pwndEdit = new CEdit;
               if (((CEdit*)m_pwndEdit)->Create(WS_CHILD | WS_VISIBLE,
                                                 rect, this, 1001))
               {
                  m_pwndEdit->ShowWindow(SW_SHOW);
                  CString strText = _T("");
                  CGridRow* row = GetRow(m_nCurrentRow);
                  if (row)
                  {
                     CGridCell* cell = row->GetCell(m_nCurrentColumn);
                     if (cell)
                        cell->GetText(strText);
                  }
                  m_pwndEdit->SetWindowText(strText);
                  m_pwndEdit->SetFocus();
               }
               break;
            case TextCell:
               break;
            default:
               break;
            }
            return;
         }
      }
   }
```

```
    COleControl::OnLButtonDblClk(nFlags, point);
}
```

The code first looks to see what cell (if any) was selected by the user. If the user *did* double-click on a cell, its cell type is retrieved. If the cell is anything other than an editable cell, the double-click is ignored, because double-clicking on other types is an undefined operation. If, on the other hand, the selected cell is editable, the control creates a new edit box (represented by **m_pwndEdit**) at the same location as the cell (using the coordinates we determined for the click area of the cell), and then gets the text for that cell. If any text was found, it's placed into the edit box using the **SetWindowText()** function. The row and column for the cell with the active edit box are maintained in **m_nCurrentRow** and **m_nCurrentColumn**.

The edit box will remain until the user clicks somewhere else in the grid. At that point, it will be destroyed and the selected text placed back into the cell for which the edit box was created, using the cell coordinates maintained in **m_nCurrentRow** and **m_nCurrentColumn**.

This function has introduced three new **private** member variables that we'll need to add to **CEGridCtrl**:

```
    short m_nLeftColumn;         // First displayed col (used for scrolling)
    CWnd* m_pwndEdit;            // The edit control for editing text
    short m_nCurrentRow;         // The row of the currently selected cell
    short m_nCurrentColumn;      // The column of the currently selected cell
```

34 The next questions are, how do we know when the user has selected a new cell, and how do we notify the programmer that the user has done this? The answers lie in the **WM_LBUTTONUP** message. Use ClassWizard to add a new handler for the **WM_LBUTTONUP** message to the **CEGridCtrl** class and add the following code to the message handler, **OnLButtonUp()**:

```
void CEGridCtrl::OnLButtonUp(UINT nFlags, CPoint point)
{
    // Determine where they clicked based on the point.
    CRect rcBounds;
    int nWidth, nHeight;
    GetControlSize(&nWidth, &nHeight);

    rcBounds.top = rcBounds.left = 0;
    rcBounds.bottom = nHeight;
    rcBounds.right = nWidth;

    long lYOffset = GetRowOffset(m_nTopRow, rcBounds);
    long lXOffset = GetColumnOffset(m_nLeftColumn, rcBounds);

    for (int i = m_nTopRow; i < m_nRows; ++i)
    {
        // Define the top and bottom for this row.
        int nTop = GetRowOffset(i, rcBounds) - lYOffset;
        int nBottom = nTop + GetRowHeight(i);

        // Loop through the cells for this row.
        for (int j = m_nLeftColumn; j < m_nCols; ++j)
```

```
        {
            // Determine where the cell lies.
            int nLeft = GetColumnOffset(j, rcBounds) - lXOffset;
            int nRight = GetColumnOffset(j + 1, rcBounds) - lXOffset;
            CRect rect(nLeft, nTop, nRight, nBottom);

            if (rect.PtInRect(point))
            {
                if (m_pwndEdit)
                {
                    CString strText;
                    m_pwndEdit->GetWindowText(strText);
                    SetCellText(m_nCurrentRow, m_nCurrentColumn, strText, 0);
                    FireCellChange(m_nCurrentRow, m_nCurrentColumn);
                    delete m_pwndEdit;
                }
                m_pwndEdit = NULL;
                FireSelect(i, j);
                m_nCurrentRow = i;
                m_nCurrentColumn = j;
                return;
            }
        }
    }
    COleControl::OnLButtonUp(nFlags, point);
}
```

First, we determine which cell was clicked on. This is done by using the utility functions **GetRowOffset()** and **GetColumnOffset()**. When we've determined the cell, the **FireCellChange()** event is called to send the application programmer a notification that the cell was selected. In addition, if the edit control has been created for a different cell in the grid, the text for that cell is updated and the edit control is deleted.

35 The final step is to make sure that everything in our control gets properly initialized and destroyed. We'll need to add some code to the constructor, the destructor and **DoPropExchange()**.

```
CEGridCtrl::CEGridCtrl()
{
    InitializeIIDs(&IID_DEGrid, &IID_DEGridEvents);
    m_nTopRow = 0;              // First displayed row (used for scrolling)
    m_nLeftColumn = 0;          // First displayed column (used for scrolling)
    m_pwndEdit = NULL;          // The edit control for editing text
    m_nCurrentRow = 0;          // The row of the currently selected cell
    m_nCurrentColumn = 0;       // The column of the currently selected cell
}
```

As usual, the **InitializeIIDs()** function is called in order to notify the base class of what identifiers will be used in the class. All of the **private** data members, except the arrays, are initialized to zero. The **CObArray** members can be safely left to initialize themselves.

```
void CEGridCtrl::DoPropExchange(CPropExchange* pPX)
{
    ExchangeVersion(pPX, MAKELONG(_wVerMinor, _wVerMajor));
```

```
    COleControl::DoPropExchange(pPX);
    PX_Short(pPX, "Rows", m_nRows, 2);
    PX_Short(pPX, "Cols", m_nCols, 2);
}
```

Adding these two lines to **DoPropExchange()** will ensure that the number of rows and columns in the grid can be saved and restored as necessary, allowing the **Rows** and **Cols** properties to be set at design time, and the values to still be usable at run time.

```
CEGridCtrl::~CEGridCtrl()
{
    for (int i = 0; i < m_Rows.GetSize(); ++i)
        delete (CGridRow*)m_Rows[i];
    for (i = 0; i < m_RowHeights.GetSize(); ++i)
        delete (CGridRowHeight*)m_RowHeights[i];
    for (i = 0; i < m_ColumnWidths.GetSize(); ++i)
        delete (CGridColWidth*)m_ColumnWidths[i];
    for (i = 0; i < m_CellStyles.GetSize(); ++i)
        delete (CGridCellStyle*)m_CellStyles[i];
    if (m_pwndEdit)
        delete m_pwndEdit;
}
```

In the destructor, we need to free up all the memory which we allocated throughout the life of the control. This includes all rows, row heights, column widths, cell styles, and edit controls.

You might like to go into the **.odl** file and tidy up the Hungarian notation and the help strings, but this isn't necessary. Compile and test the control right now; you have a complete working grid control! Here you can see the completed control running in the Test Container.

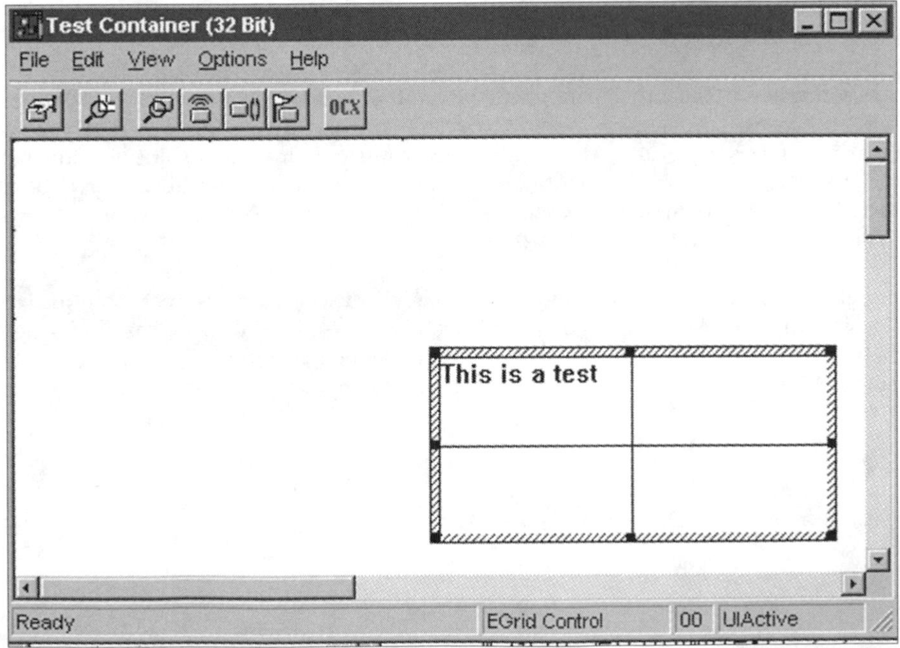

Comparing the MFC and ActiveX Solutions

The ActiveX solution is somewhat more elegant, due to the fact that it can notify the application of changes to cells and selections and text changes via the OLE event notification process. The MFC extension list control is required to make these notifications via the **`PostMessage()`** route. Fortunately, because the **`CColorListCtrl`** is a derivative of the **`CListCtrl`** object, ClassWizard understands all of the messages passed from it and allows the application programmer to catch these messages through ClassWizard.

One of the most obvious differences in approaches between the MFC extension and the ActiveX control is that of parameter types. An ActiveX control is quite limited in the type of variables it can pass back and forth. MFC objects must be cast from one type to another, or even to **`void`** pointers in order to get them to go back and forth. Because an MFC extension is just another C++ class, it can pass any type which is understood in C++.

This deficiency in ActiveX controls can cause problems when other environments are used. For example, although an ActiveX control is portable between Visual C++ and Visual Basic or Delphi, it should be obvious that by selecting a **`CBitmap`** pointer to use as a way to set bitmaps in the grid, this functionality will not translate. In this respect, our ActiveX control has become worthless as a language-independent solution. To solve this problem, you would need to use a different method to pass bitmaps between applications and the ActiveX control. One alternative would be to pass the bitmap handle (**`HBITMAP`**). This can be retrieved in Visual Basic and Delphi and could then be used in the ActiveX control. Another, better, solution would be to use an OLE picture object. This is an advanced topic, well beyond the scope of this book, but you can find more information if you look up **`OleCreatePictureIndirect()`**, **`IPicture`**, and **`IPictureDisp`** in the online help.

Another big difference between the two solutions is the ability to modify the solution. If we determined, for example, that the **`CColorListCtrl`** colors should be passed in, not as RGB values, but instead, as an index into some sort of global palette, we could quickly and easily make the modification. Applications that used the code would then 'break' when it came to compiling, but the required fixes would be fairly obvious.

ActiveX controls, on the other hand, will not automatically regenerate their wrapper classes in Visual C++. Strange problems will suddenly crop up and the program is likely to crash if a modification of this type is made. Programmers must define their solutions much more tightly in an ActiveX control than in an MFC extension. Although this is always a good goal, it can be much harder to do in the early stages of application development, when ActiveX controls are most likely to be written.

In general, therefore, we can conclude from this chapter that an ActiveX solution needs much more design than an MFC extension. Additionally, an ActiveX control has limits on the types of parameters which can be used for arguments to defined methods. Finally, MFC extensions lend themselves better to groups of similar functions, since they support inheritance.

Summary

In looking back over the chapter, let's review what we've discovered up to this point:

- Windows common controls can be extended through the use of MFC extension classes to be more powerful and flexible than the originals with relatively little work on the part of the programmer.
- ActiveX controls should be more portable between environments than MFC extensions, but require slightly more design as a result.
- MFC extensions need only worry about run-time environments, while ActiveX controls need to consider both design-time and run-time environments.
- Columnar display and entry solutions will make users happier and programs more usable.

Things to Try

Here are a few 'homework' assignments that you might try to gain a fuller understanding of ActiveX controls and MFC extensions.

- Modify **`CColorListCtrl`** to allow the programmer to display bitmaps in columns of the list. Use the **`DrawBitmap`** utility function from the **`EGrid`** project.
- Modify **`CColorListCtrl`** so that it can be serialized, allowing the list to be saved and restored from an archive.
- Modify **`CColorListCtrl`** to use the same **`CGridRow`** and **`CGridCell`** classes as the ActiveX control.
- Modify **`CEGridCtrl`** so that it uses bitmap handles rather than the **`CBitmap`** object pointers, making it more portable.

Visual
C++

Complex Data Displays

In many Windows applications, the entire approach to the program is to display a complex data structure (such as a database record) and allow the user to view, and perhaps edit, the structure. Sometimes the complex structure may be split into separate fields that can be individually viewed or edited, but often you will want to be able to display the data in a more complex format. This chapter takes two approaches toward allowing the user to view complex data in an organized fashion.

In our first example, you will learn how to create a complex MFC extension list that displays data in a columnar fashion but also allows you to use the drag-and-drop approach to editing. Data can be dragged from one columnar list to another, retaining its format. The data can be completely customized with its own colors and fonts, as well as column widths and other information. This drag-and-drop list box approach is ideally suited for data-oriented programs where the user needs to copy data from one location to another.

The second example, the Color Tree control, is an ActiveX control and is considerably more complex. The Windows common tree control has some serious limitations which make it unsuitable for many applications. In this example, you will learn how to implement a complete tree control that you will not only have complete control over but for which you will have the complete source code as well.

The Problem

Displaying data in an organized fashion is a difficult problem in any application. Data has its own internal logic and structure which often does not fit into an existing Windows control format. A database record, for example, may be best displayed as a single line of related data. Windows provides list controls for this purpose but doesn't allow the data to be easily copied from one list to another. For applications such as report writers or database backup utilities, it's essential that the user is able to see the entire record they would like to copy.

If you want to display related data in Windows, you have several options. The list control supports columns, but has limitations which we examined in the previous chapter. The tree control supports hierarchical display, but doesn't allow columns or color modifications. The regular list box supports some color modifications and bitmaps via an owner-draw display, but leaves much to be desired in the areas of data manipulation and display.

Although MFC offers **`CDragListBox`** to allow the user to reorder data in a single list, this class is still limited when it comes to dragging data between lists and displaying data in columns.

In this chapter, we examine two solutions to the complex data display problem. First, we will look at extending an existing Windows solution, the list box, and adding complex data display and handling by adding columnar display and drag-and-drop functionality.

The MFC Solution: The Drag-and-drop Columnar List Box

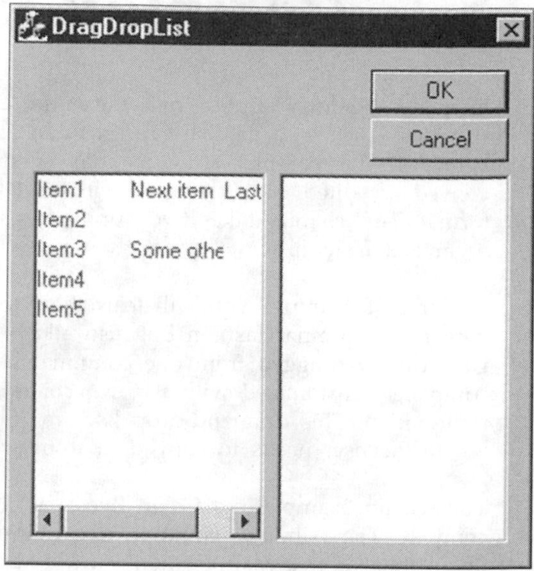

Although its name is long and unwieldy, the drag-and-drop columnar list box is anything but! This control is a complete solution to record-oriented display. The drag-and-drop part enables you to move records between multiple instances of drag-and-drop list boxes or even between a drag-and-drop list box and a normal list box. The columnar portion allows the programmer to define fixed-width columns that you can use to display fields of a record in a well-defined format.

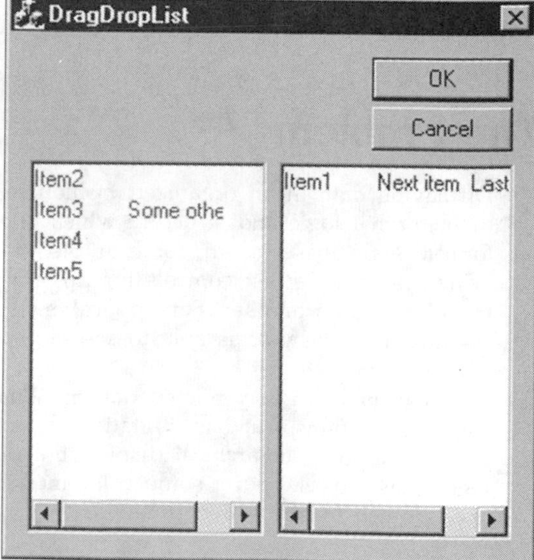

The figure opposite shows the result of dragging a list entry from one list box to another. As you can see, the resulting list maintains the columnar format of the data without any work on the part of the programmer. As an added bonus, the list box will also allow the user to drag-and-drop within a single list box, allowing the restructuring or sorting of data by the user.

Feature List

What kind of features are we going to want for our drag-and-drop columnar list box? A shorter name might be nice! Besides that, we would like at least the following functionality to be provided directly by the control:

- Drag-and-drop between our list box and any other list box, regardless of whether the other list box is a drag-and-drop list box.
- Drag-and-drop within the list box, allowing the user to modify the order of items by selecting one and dragging it to a new position in the list. This method should also retain any user data associated with items in the correct order.
- Complete control over the colors and fonts used to display the data in the list box. This information should also be available to the programmer at run time.
- Ability to define and reset columns at run time. The control should automatically update itself to allow the programmer to change column widths at run time. Any text which is too wide to display in a given column should be properly cut off, rather than running over into the next column.
- When items are copied between two drag-and-drop list boxes, the columns should be maintained, but the data should be displayed using whatever setting the new list box allows.
- The list box control should support both single and multiple selection. Multiple selections should be copied in the same order as they exist in the original list box.
- The list box should automatically support horizontal scrolling if the data displayed is wider than the physical window of the list box. Columns should be properly displayed in scrolling lists.
- Selected items should be displayed exactly as in normal list boxes, the colors being the inverse of those the programmer has selected for normal display.
- The list box should use custom cursors to show the user that a drag-and-drop operation is taking place. In addition, the list box should indicate to the user whether the area presently under the cursor is valid as a place to drop selected items.

Designing the Control

Once we have a complete feature list (in the real world, we'd have probably produced a functional design document and gone over it line by line with a design committee), we need to decide how the features are to be implemented in the real-life control. As with most MFC extensions, this control inherits most of its functionality from its base class, **`CListBox`**. Subclassing will give us most of the basic functionality of the control, requiring us to only implement the pieces of the control that aren't already provided for by a normal list box.

Columnar Display

As we saw in a previous example, an owner-draw control can be used to display individual items in a list box or list control in any format you like. By making the list box owner-draw, we can display the columns of data. The only question then is how to define columns. Defining column widths should be a simple function call. For our internal display function, however, we need a way to figure out where a text string column ends. For this class, we will implement this functionality by embedding a tab character in the string at the position between fields. There are two reasons why you should use a tab character. First, the normal Windows list box uses a tab stop to delimit columns, and second, it's simple to construct a **CString** from a database record by separating fields with a tab character.

If the normal list box supports tab stops, why are we doing all of this extra work to display columns? The answer is that normal list boxes do not implement true column display when displaying tab stops. Instead, they display fields at the nearest tab stop which means that, when a field is too large for a column, it will be displayed wider than fields in previous records. This is unacceptable for a columnar display.

At this point, we know that we can display a simple list box using columns and whatever fonts and colors we would like by implementing an owner-draw list box. The next problem is the drag-and-drop portion of the list box control.

Inter-list Drag-and-drop

Drag-and-drop is generally a matter of intercepting three Windows messages which are sent during the process: one corresponding to the mouse button press, one to the mouse movement and one to the button release. First, we need to catch the **WM_LBUTTONDOWN** message, which will be sent to our list box window when the user presses the mouse button within the list box client area. If the user selects a list box item and clicks the mouse, it will generate the left mouse button down message. Catching this message will allow us to know when to start the drag-and-drop process.

Once the drag-and-drop process has started, we need to monitor where the mouse is moving while the user is trying to drag it somewhere. This means we must catch the **WM_MOUSEMOVE** message as it is sent to us by Windows. Although Windows will send us mouse-move messages while the user is moving the mouse within our window, it will not normally send them once the mouse is outside of the window. How then can we find out where the selected entries have been dropped?

SetCapture() helps us here. **SetCapture()** tells Windows that we want to be notified of all mouse messages until we tell it otherwise (by calling **ReleaseCapture()**). By calling **SetCapture()** after the left mouse button message is detected, we can continue to follow the mouse all around the screen until the user releases the left mouse button. Now we can find out when the drag-and-drop operation starts, and follow it while the user decides where to drop the selections.

By catching the **WM_LBUTTONUP** message, we can determine when the user decides to drop the selections. Because we have captured the mouse messages, we will be notified when the user releases the mouse button. This will terminate the drag process and will allow us to move the selections to the new location.

Two problems still exist, however. First, we need to be able to determine whether the mouse is over a valid place on which we can drop the selected items from the list box. Second, we have to be able to actually drop the selected items and add them to the new list box.

The first problem is the more complex of the two, so let's tackle that one first. To know whether we can drop something onto whatever the mouse is over, we need to know what kind of window we're dealing with. To find this out, we need to know where the mouse is on the screen. This information is actually given to us during the mouse move process. As the mouse moves across the screen, Windows will send us mouse-move messages (**WM_MOUSEMOVE**). Each of these messages contains the point at which the mouse was when the message was generated. Unfortunately, the position is given in terms of the client area of the list box we are dragging from. In order to find another window on the screen, we need to know the screen coordinates of the point.

The Win32 API provides a function called **ClientToScreen()** that will 'translate' a client coordinate into a screen coordinate. We will call this function as the mouse moves to determine where on the screen we can find the mouse. Once we have the position of the mouse on the screen (really the desktop), we can find the window underneath the mouse by using **WindowFromPoint()**, which is a **static** member function of the **CWnd** class in MFC.

When the mouse moves, we can determine, using these two functions, what window is underneath the mouse cursor at any given time. Once we know this, we can determine the kind of window underneath the mouse by using **CObject::IsKindOf()**. This retrieves the information stored in the extra bytes of the window and can be retrieved for each MFC window. If the **IsKindOf()** function indicates that the window is a derivative of **CListBox**, the selected items can be dropped onto it. In this case, we set the cursor to a form that indicates to the user that dropping is allowed. If the window isn't a derivative of **CListBox**, the cursor is changed to the universal 'not allowed' sign (a circle with a line through it) and dropping is disabled for that window.

Note that this approach limits the drag-and-drop functionality to list boxes within a single application since there's no way of knowing what classes were used for list boxes in another application, or even whether C++ was used at all.

Once the user releases the mouse, we can use the same process to determine if the window can be dropped upon. If it can, we use the **CListBox** functions to add the strings and user data for the selected items to the new list box. Since we know that the window under the mouse cursor must be a list box, we can simply cast the window pointer that was returned from **WindowFromPoint()** to a **CListBox** class object. This gives us the ability to use the **CListBox** functions to add strings and data to the new list box. At that point, we then use the functions of the current list box to remove them from the list.

Intra-list Drag-and-drop

This will all work well if the window is a different list box within the same application. In our requirements, however, we also specified that the user must be able to drag-and-drop within the same list box. How are we to accomplish this?

It isn't very hard to determine whether the window the cursor starts in and the window the cursor ends in are the same. Although the pointers returned from the **WindowFromPoint()** and the **this** pointer for the object will be different, the window handles for the two objects will be the same. If this is true, there's very little difference in handling for the two objects. We need to be a little more careful with copying the selected item before deleting it and moving the user data around, but this isn't a major problem. We will also be nice and check to see if the starting and ending points are the same. If so, we will assume that the user didn't really mean to move things. Finally, we will not allow multiple selection movement within the same list box. This is simply reasonable behavior, since it would be difficult to guess where they wanted multiple items to fall inside the same list.

Horizontal Scrolling

The only remaining issue for the list box is that of horizontal scrolling. If you have worked with list boxes before, you will know that horizontal scrolling is allowed for list boxes and will be handled by the control itself. The only catch is that the horizontal scrolling works only if you set the maximum length of a line in the list box. What this means is that we need to keep track of the columns in the list that is being displayed and use this information to set the length for scrolling, using the **`SetHorizontalExtent()`** function of the list box.

Now that all of the design issues are worked out, it's time to roll up our sleeves and start coding! To implement the control, we will create a new MFC class and implement the functionality of the control within that class. Follow this procedure to create the MFC class and implement the control:

TRY IT OUT - Create a Drag-and-drop Columnar List Box

1. Use MFC AppWizard (exe) to create a new project. Give the project the name DragAndDropList and save it to the directory of your choice. Create a Dialog based application. You can leave all the other options at their default settings.

2. In ClassWizard, add a new class by selecting the Add Class... button and selecting New... from the list. Give the new class the name CDragDropListBox. Select CListBox from the Base class drop-down list and click Create.

3. The first step toward implementing the new control is to add some new member variables to this class. To do this, add the following lines to the header file for the class, **`DragDropListBox.h`**. As usual, the lines that you need to add are shaded:

```
// Implementation
public:
   virtual ~CDragDropListBox();
private:
   HCURSOR m_hcurDrop;
   HCURSOR m_hcurNoDrop;
   int m_nCurrentItem;
   CPoint m_ptButtonDown;
   int* m_pFieldLengths;
   int m_nFields;
   COLORREF m_clrFore;
   COLORREF m_clrBack;
```

The **`HCURSOR`** variables will be used to hold on to the custom cursors we will create to indicate the drag-and-drop effect in action.

The **m_nCurrentItem** and **m_ptButtonDown** variables are used to keep track of where we started in the process. This information is used to decide whether the user really wanted to drag-and-drop.

The **m_pFieldLengths** and **m_nFields** variables are used to store the information for the column widths to display in the list box. This information can be set by the programmer at run time.

Finally, the **m_clrBack** and **m_clrFore** variables hold the background and foreground colors for the control.

4 Once we have added the new members, we can now initialize them in the constructor:

```
CDragDropListBox::CDragDropListBox()
{
   m_hcurDrop = ::LoadCursor(AfxGetInstanceHandle(),
                              MAKEINTRESOURCE(IDC_DROP));
   m_hcurNoDrop = ::LoadCursor(AfxGetInstanceHandle(),
                              MAKEINTRESOURCE(IDC_NODROP));
   m_nFields = 0;
   m_pFieldLengths = NULL;
   m_clrFore = RGB(0, 0, 0);          // Default to black
   m_clrBack = RGB(255, 255, 255);    // Default to white
}
```

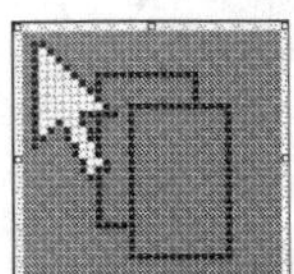
IDC_DROP

You can choose the look of the two cursors which are displayed during a drag operation. **IDC_DROP** is displayed when the object can be dropped, and **IDC_NODROP** when the object can't. Visual C++ provides you with a cursor resource called **IDC_NODROP** that's suitable for our needs, but you may feel that you need to create your own cursor for **IDC_DROP**. However you decide to create the cursor resources, you'll need to make sure that they are added to your application.

IDC_NODROP

While we are at it, here is the destructor for the class, which frees up all the memory allocated by the class:

```
CDragDropListBox::~CDragDropListBox()
{
   if (m_pFieldLengths)
      delete [] m_pFieldLengths;
}
```

5 Now, we need to implement the functions to set the field lengths, as well as the foreground and background colors. First add the declarations for the following functions to **DragDropListBox.h**.

```
// Operations
public:
   void SetFieldLength(int nFields, int* pFieldLengths);
```

```
    void SetTextColor(COLORREF clrText);
    void SetBackColor(COLORREF clrBack);
```

Now add the definitions to **DragDropListBox.cpp**.

```
void CDragDropListBox::SetFieldLength(int nFields, int* pFieldLengths)
{
   m_pFieldLengths = new int[nFields];
   for (int i = 0; i < nFields; ++i)
      m_pFieldLengths[i] = pFieldLengths[i];
   m_nFields = nFields;
}

void CDragDropListBox::SetTextColor(COLORREF clrText)
{
   m_clrFore = clrText;
}
void CDragDropListBox::SetBackColor(COLORREF clrBack)
{
   m_clrBack = clrBack;
}
```

6 The **DrawItem()** routine will make use of a couple of functions that we'll look at now. Add the declarations for these functions to the header file for **CDragDropListBox**.

```
// Implementation
public:
   virtual ~CDragDropListBox();
   int GetField(LPTSTR lpszString, LPTSTR lpszBuffer);
   BOOL IsMultipleSelect();
private:
```

The first function, **GetField()**, extracts a single column of data from an input string:

```
int CDragDropListBox::GetField(LPTSTR lpszString, LPTSTR lpszBuffer)
{
   for (int i = 0; i < lstrlen(lpszString); ++i)
   {
      if (lpszString[i] == _T('\t'))
         break;
      lpszBuffer[i] = lpszString[i];
   }
   lpszBuffer[i] = 0;
   return i + 1;
}
```

In addition, we need to implement the function to determine whether the list box is a multiple, or extended, selection list box:

```
BOOL CDragDropListBox::IsMultipleSelect()
{
   long lStyle = GetWindowLong(m_hWnd, GWL_STYLE);
   if (lStyle & LBS_MULTIPLESEL || lStyle & LBS_EXTENDEDSEL)
      return TRUE;
   return FALSE;
}
```

As you can see, this function works by examining the window style of the list box to see if the multiple selection or extended selection bits are set. Multiple selection indicates that the list box allows you to select more than one item at a time by clicking your choices. Extended selection list boxes support the more familiar *Shift*-click and *Ctrl*-click combinations to select ranges and multiple individual items in the list.

7 The next item of interest is the handling of the owner-draw functionality for the list box. There are actually three member methods that will need to be overridden for an owner-draw list box. First, we need to do the actual drawing of the item. To do this, use ClassWizard to add an override for DrawItem to **CDragDropListBox**. Add the following code to **DrawItem()**:

```
void CDragDropListBox::DrawItem(LPDRAWITEMSTRUCT lpDrawItemStruct)
{
CString strText;

   // If there are no list box items, skip this message.
   if (lpDrawItemStruct->itemID == -1)
      return;

   switch (lpDrawItemStruct->itemAction)
   {
   case ODA_SELECT:
   case ODA_DRAWENTIRE:
      GetText(lpDrawItemStruct->itemID, strText);
      if (lpDrawItemStruct->itemState & ODS_SELECTED)
      {
         ::SetTextColor(lpDrawItemStruct->hDC, m_clrBack);
         ::SetBackColor(lpDrawItemStruct->hDC, m_clrFore);
         CBrush brushFore(m_clrFore);
         FillRect(lpDrawItemStruct->hDC, &(lpDrawItemStruct->rcItem),
                  (HBRUSH)brushFore.GetSafeHandle());
      }
      else
      {
         ::SetTextColor(lpDrawItemStruct->hDC, m_clrFore);
         ::SetBackColor(lpDrawItemStruct->hDC, m_clrBack);
         CBrush brushBack(m_clrBack);
         FillRect(lpDrawItemStruct->hDC, &(lpDrawItemStruct->rcItem),
                  (HBRUSH)brushBack.GetSafeHandle());
      }

      // Get and display the text for the list item
      TCHAR szTemp[256] = {0};
      TCHAR szBuffer[80] = {0};
      memset(szTemp, 0, 256);
      lstrcpyn(szTemp, strText, 256);

      // Loop through the text, looking for tab characters
      TEXTMETRIC tm;
      GetTextMetrics(lpDrawItemStruct->hDC, &tm);
      int nStart = 0;
      int nFld = 0;
      int y = (lpDrawItemStruct->rcItem.bottom +
               lpDrawItemStruct->rcItem.top - tm.tmHeight) / 2;
      int x = lpDrawItemStruct->rcItem.left;

      while (nStart < lstrlen(szTemp) && nFld < m_nFields)
```

```
        {
            nStart += GetField(szTemp+nStart, szBuffer);

            // Calculate the end position of this field
            CRect rect = lpDrawItemStruct->rcItem;
            rect.left  = x;
            rect.right = x + m_pFieldLengths[nFld];

            ::ExtTextOut(lpDrawItemStruct->hDC, x, y,
                         ETO_CLIPPED | ETO_OPAQUE, &rect,
                         szBuffer, lstrlen(szBuffer), NULL);
            x += m_pFieldLengths[nFld];
            nFld++;
        }

        if (lpDrawItemStruct->itemState & ODS_FOCUS)
            DrawFocusRect(lpDrawItemStruct->hDC,
                          &(lpDrawItemStruct->rcItem));
        break;
    }
    int nMaxWidth = 0;
    for (int c = 0; c < m_nFields; ++c)
        nMaxWidth += m_pFieldLengths[c];
    SetHorizontalExtent(nMaxWidth);
}
```

What's going on here? When you take on the responsibility for drawing a control, Windows passes you a pointer to a structure of type **DRAWITEMSTRUCT**, which gives you the information you need in order to be able to draw the control properly. We'll see various members of this structure in use as we look at this routine. First, we check to see whether there are any items in the list box. If there aren't, the ID of the list box item which we're drawing will be set to **-1**, and in that case we can exit.

Next, we check the action type: if the item is being selected or we're drawing the entire list, then we want to handle it. Assuming that this is what we want, we retrieve the text associated with the item. We have foreground and background colors set for the list box, and we're going to need to use them either normally or reversed, depending on whether the item is selected or not. The next code section sets the colors accordingly, and draws a filled rectangle, using the bounding rectangle for the list item, **lpDrawItemStruct->rcItem**, which was thoughtfully provided for us in the **DRAWITEMSTRUCT**.

The next step is to draw the text, after first expanding it into columns. The **ExtTextOut()** API call is used to draw the text, clipped to the dimensions of the column.

8 Windows also requires us to override the **MeasureItem()** method for owner-draw list boxes. This method will indicate how tall any given item is in the list. Since we aren't allowing variable height entries, this is pretty simple. Just use ClassWizard to add an override for MeasureItem to the **CDragDropListBox** class:

```
void CDragDropListBox::MeasureItem(
                                    LPMEASUREITEMSTRUCT lpMeasureItemStruct)
{
    CDC* dc = GetDC();
    TEXTMETRIC tm;
```

```
    dc->GetTextMetrics(&tm);
    lpMeasureItemStruct->itemHeight = tm.tmHeight;
    ReleaseDC(dc);
}
```

Finally, the list box requires us to override the **CompareItem()** function. Repeat the ClassWizard override process to add a new method for CompareItem and add the following code:

```
int CDragDropListBox::CompareItem(LPCOMPAREITEMSTRUCT lpCompareItemStruct)
{
    // TODO: Add your code to determine sorting order of specified items
    // return -1 = item 1 sorts before item 2
    // return 0 = item 1 and item 2 sort the same
    // return 1 = item 1 sorts after item 2

    return _tcscmp((TCHAR*)lpCompareItemStruct->itemData1,
                   (TCHAR*)lpCompareItemStruct->itemData2);
}
```

9 Once the attributes are set and the owner-draw functionality is handled, we need to start working on the implementation of the drag-and-drop functionality. First, we will handle the user pressing the mouse button while over the list. To do this, add a new message handler to the **CDragDropListBox** in ClassWizard for the **WM_LBUTTONDOWN** message. Add the following code to **CDragDropListBox::OnLButtonDown()**.

```
void CDragDropListBox::OnLButtonDown(UINT nFlags, CPoint point)
{
    // Do default handling so we can get the current item number
    CListBox::OnLButtonDown(nFlags, point);

    // Get the current selected item
    if (!IsMultipleSelect())
    {
        m_nCurrentItem = GetCurSel();

        // If no item, get out of here
        if (m_nCurrentItem == LB_ERR)
            return;
    }

    m_ptButtonDown = point;

    // And capture all subsequent mouse messages
    SetCapture();
}
```

Note that we're tracking the current item in the list only if there's no multiple selection allowed for the list. In either case, we hold on to the point at which the mouse cursor was when the button was pressed and then start the tracking of mouse movements using the **SetCapture()** function. If they are working in a single select list box, we will allow them to select and deselect single items and move them around. In this case, we check to see if there is an item selected. Note that we make sure to call the default **CListBox::OnLButtonDown()** *before* we do the processing, so that the selection is made. If there are no items currently selected, we don't bother to do any more processing and leave the function.

10 Once the user has selected an item in the list box, the next step is to watch them move the mouse around the screen and notify them of whether the current location is a valid place to drop things. This is handled via the **WM_MOUSEMOVE** message. Use ClassWizard to add a new handler for the **WM_MOUSEMOVE** message to **CDragDropListBox** and add the following code to the new function:

```
void CDragDropListBox::OnMouseMove(UINT nFlags, CPoint point)
{
   if (GetCapture() == this)
   {
      // Get the window under the point
      ClientToScreen(&point);
      CWnd* pWnd = CWnd::WindowFromPoint(point);

      if (!pWnd || !pWnd->IsKindOf(RUNTIME_CLASS(CListBox)))
         SetCursor(m_hcurNoDrop);
      else
         SetCursor (m_hcurDrop);
   }
   else
      CListBox::OnMouseMove(nFlags, point);
}
```

What is going on here? First, we check to be sure that we are actually tracking mouse movements. This is done by the **GetCapture()** call, which returns a pointer to the window that currently has the capture. If the returned pointer is to our list box window, we get the screen coordinates of the mouse cursor point via the **ClientToScreen()** function. This is necessary for the next step, which is to get the window underneath the mouse cursor.

The function which does this job is the **static** member function of the **CWnd** class, **WindowFromPoint()**. This function takes a point in screen coordinates, so we need to do the conversion to get the right window. Once we have obtained a pointer (or **NULL** if the mouse was over the desktop) to the window under the mouse cursor, we examine the window pointer to see if it is a kind of window that we know how to deal with. We decide whether it is by using two MFC functions called **IsKindOf()** and **RUNTIME_CLASS()**. The **RUNTIME_CLASS()** macro will return a unique identifier for each class. The **IsKindOf()** function will look at this identifier and determine whether the requested type is the same as the object for which it was invoked.

IsKindOf() checks for all derivatives from the level at which it was requested. Thus, **IsKindOf(RUNTIME_CLASS(CListBox))** will return **TRUE** if it was invoked for either a **CListBox** or any class which is derived from **CListBox**. It would return **FALSE** if the window in question was a button or combo box. However, if the window under the mouse cursor is, in fact, a list box or derivative we will set the cursor to be indicative of the fact that this window can be dropped upon. If the window under the mouse cursor was not a list box, we would set the cursor to a no-drop version.

11 Just one last message to process, **WM_LBUTTONUP**. To handle this message, add a message handler for **WM_LBUTTONUP** to **CDragDropListBox** in ClassWizard. Add the following code to the new method:

```
void CDragDropListBox::OnLButtonUp(UINT nFlags, CPoint point)
{
```

```
// Do default handling so we can get the current item number
CListBox::OnLButtonUp(nFlags, point);

// If we're not capturing the mouse, we don't need to do anything
if (GetCapture() == this)
{
   CPoint ptOriginal = point;
   // Get the window under the mouse...
   ClientToScreen(&point);
   CWnd* pWnd = CWnd::WindowFromPoint(point);

   // If the window isn't a CListBox, we don't need to do anything
   if (pWnd && pWnd->IsKindOf(RUNTIME_CLASS(CListBox)))
   {
      // If we're multiselect and dropping to the same list,
      // we don't need to do anything except release the mouse
      CListBox* pList = (CListBox*)pWnd;
      if (IsMultipleSelect() && pList->m_hWnd == m_hWnd)
      {
         ReleaseCapture();
         return;
      }

      // Get the currently selected item
      TCHAR szBuffer[256] = {0};
      DWORD dwItemData;

      if (!IsMultipleSelect())
      {
         GetText(m_nCurrentItem, szBuffer);
         dwItemData = GetItemData(m_nCurrentItem);
      }

      // See if we can figure out where to put it...
      // First, get the DC for the other list box.
      CDC* pDC = pList->GetDC();
      TEXTMETRIC tm;
      pDC->GetTextMetrics(&tm);
      pList->ReleaseDC(pDC);

      int nHeight = tm.tmHeight;

      if (pList->GetCount())
      {
         CRect rect;
         pList->GetItemRect(0, &rect);
         nHeight = rect.bottom - rect.top;
      }

      // See what row this might be...
      int nRow = pList->GetTopIndex() + (ptOriginal.y / nHeight);

      // If this is our list box and the row and starting point are
      // the same, ignore it. It means they didn't really mean to
      // move the item
      if (pList->m_hWnd != m_hWnd || nRow != m_nCurrentItem)
      {
         if (!IsMultipleSelect())
```

```
                NotMultiSel(pList, nRow, szBuffer, dwItemData);
            else
                MultiSel(pList, nRow, szBuffer, dwItemData);
        }
        GetParent()->PostMessage(LBN_DRAGFROM, 0, 0);
        pList->GetParent()->PostMessage(LBN_DRAGTO, 0, 0);
    }
  }
  ReleaseCapture();
}
```

You'll also need to add a couple of helper functions, so that the handler doesn't get too unwieldy. Add the function declarations to the class header as shown:

```
   BOOL IsMultipleSelect();
protected:
   void NotMultiSel(CListBox* pList, int nRow,
                    LPTSTR lpszBuffer, DWORD dwItemData);
   void MultiSel(CListBox* pList, int nRow,
                 LPTSTR lpszBuffer, DWORD dwItemData);
```

Now add the implementation for these functions to **DragDropListBox.cpp**:

```
/////////////////////////////////////////////////////////////////////////////
// OnMouseMove helpers

void CDragDropListBox::NotMultiSel(CListBox* pList, int nRow,
                                   LPTSTR lpszBuffer, DWORD dwItemData)
{
   // If this is our list box delete the old string first
   if (pList->m_hWnd == m_hWnd)
      DeleteString(m_nCurrentItem);

   // If it is greater than the number of items, just add it.
   int nIndex;
   if (nRow > pList->GetCount() - 1)
      nIndex = pList->AddString(lpszBuffer);
   else
      nIndex = pList->InsertString(nRow, lpszBuffer);

   // And set any data that might have been with it
   pList->SetItemData(nIndex, dwItemData);

   // And remove it from our list
   if (pList->m_hWnd != m_hWnd)
      DeleteString(m_nCurrentItem);
}

void CDragDropListBox::MultiSel(CListBox* pList, int nRow,
                                LPTSTR lpszBuffer, DWORD dwItemData)
{
   // Get the selected items
   int nSelCount = GetSelCount();
   int* pSelections = new int[nSelCount];
   GetSelItems(nSelCount, pSelections);
```

```
    // For each one, add/insert it into new list box
    for (int i = 0; i < nSelCount; ++i)
    {
        // Get the text for this entry
        GetText(pSelections[i], lpszBuffer);
        dwItemData = GetItemData(pSelections[i]);

        // If it is greater than the number of items, just add it.
        int nIndex;
        if (nRow > pList->GetCount() - 1)
            nIndex = pList->AddString(lpszBuffer);
        else
            nIndex = pList->InsertString(nRow, lpszBuffer);

        // And set any data that might have been with it
        pList->SetItemData(nIndex, dwItemData);

        // Delete that string
        DeleteString(pSelections[i]);

        // Update the list with correct numbers
        for (int j = 0; j < nSelCount; ++j)
            if (pSelections[j] > pSelections[i])
                pSelections[j]--;
    }

    // Now delete them from our list
    delete [] pSelections;
}
```

Once again, we check to be sure that the window under the mouse is a valid list box to drop onto. If not, we ignore the process and get out of the function. Once we have determined that the window is a list box, the next step is to ensure that, if this is the same window we dragged from, it is not a multiple select list box. If it is, we again ignore the request. If it is the same list box and not multiple select, we then delete the original string before adding the string at its new position. We then either add or append the string to the list box at the new position. If the user dropped the mouse outside of the available number of list items, we will append new data to the end. We reset the user data to be correct and exit. This takes care of the single selection case.

For the multiple selection case, the problem is more complex. We need to handle the selected strings one at a time, because the position of the items will change as we delete them. As a result, as soon as we have deleted the string from the list box, we will then update the selected list by subtracting one from the selection index. This works because the selected items are always returned in numeric order from smallest to largest.

The final step is to notify the list boxes' parent windows that they have been modified by the user. This is a courtesy and it releases the parents from the need to inquire of each list box whether or not it has changed each time it needs that information. The notification is done by posting a message to the parent windows of the two list boxes. Here are the definitions of the list box notification messages which you should add to the header file:

```
/////////////////////////////////////////////////////////////////////////////
// CDragDropListBox messages
```

```
const UINT LBN_HSCROLL = 8;
const UINT LBN_DRAGFROM = 9;
const UINT LBN_DRAGTO = 10;
```

12 Oops! We almost forgot one of our requirements—the ability to scroll the list box horizontally. Although the list box itself will handle the scrolling part, we need to make sure that the display is correct. Add a new handler for the **WM_HSCROLL** message to the **CDragDropListBox** class in ClassWizard. Add the following code to **OnHScroll()**:

```
void CDragDropListBox::OnHScroll(UINT nSBCode, UINT nPos,
                                 CScrollBar* pScrollBar)
{
   int nMin, nMax;
   GetScrollRange(SB_HORZ, &nMin, &nMax);

   int nScrollPos = GetScrollPos(SB_HORZ);

   switch (nSBCode)
   {
   case SB_LINEDOWN:
      if (nScrollPos >= nMax - 1)
         return;
      GetParent()->PostMessage(LBN_HSCROLL, nSBCode,
                               MAKELPARAM(nPos, GetDlgCtrlID()));
      break;

   case SB_LINEUP:
      if (nScrollPos == 0)
         return;
      GetParent()->PostMessage(LBN_HSCROLL, nSBCode,
                               MAKELPARAM(nPos, GetDlgCtrlID()));
      break;
   }
   CListBox::OnHScroll(nSBCode, nPos, pScrollBar);
}
```

All we will be doing here is posting a message to the parent indicating the position of the scroll in the window to make sure that it's up-to-date. That's all the code necessary to implement the class.

TRY IT OUT - Test the Drag-and-drop List Box

1 Open up the main dialog resource, **IDD_DRAGANDDROPLIST_DIALOG**, in Developer Studio's dialog editor, and add two list boxes to it. Give the list boxes the IDs **IDC_LIST1** and **IDC_LIST2**, and set their properties so that:

- The Owner Draw property is Fixed (so it knows we're going to draw it, and every row is the same height).
- The Has Strings check box is ticked.
- The Sort and Notify check boxes are unchecked.
- Scrollbars can be included if required.

2 Now we need to make sure that the controls in the dialog are handled by our new list box class. *Ctrl*-double-click on each of the list boxes in the dialog editor and use ClassWizard's Add Member Variables dialog to add control members to the dialog class as shown.

List Box ID	Member variable name	Category	Variable type
IDC_LIST1	m_DragList1	Control	CDragDropListBox
IDC_LIST2	m_DragList2	Control	CDragDropListBox

Make sure that you add **#include "DragDropListBox.h"** to the top of **DragAndDropListDlg.h**.

3 The next step is to set up the list boxes, and add some data to them. The obvious place to do this is in the dialog's **InitDialog()** function, so modify **CDragAndDropListDlg::OnInitDialog()** as shown. This will initialize the lists with suitable data.

```
   // TODO: Add extra initialization here
   int nFields[] = { 50, 50, 50 };

   m_DragList1.SetFieldLength(3, nFields);
   m_DragList2.SetFieldLength(3, nFields);

   m_DragList1.SetTextColor(RGB(255, 0, 0)); // Red
   m_DragList2.SetTextColor(RGB(0, 0, 255)); // Blue

   m_DragList1.AddString(_T("Item1\tNext item\tLast item"));
   m_DragList1.AddString(_T("Item2"));
   m_DragList1.AddString(_T("Item3\tSome other item"));
   m_DragList1.AddString(_T("Item4"));
   m_DragList1.AddString(_T("Item5"));
   return TRUE;  // return TRUE  unless you set the focus to a control
```

When you build and run the project, you should see a dialog similar to the following, which allows you to drag and drop the list box items:

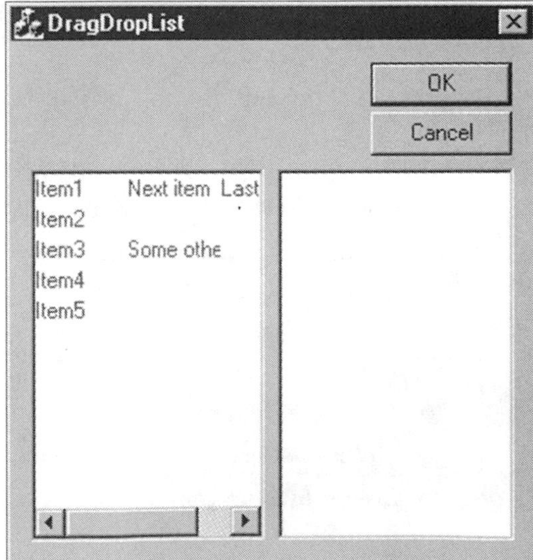

That completes the drag-and-drop list box.

The ActiveX Solution: The Color Tree Control

The next control we will consider is by far the most ambitious project in the entire book. We will write, from scratch, a complete tree control that supports multiple modifiable bitmaps, different colors, multiple selection, programmatic control, extended selection, user-defined data and many other features.

A tree control is a complex data-display device which can display a hierarchical tree of items. Our tree control supports multiple columns, which means that each line of the tree can contain multiple columns of data as well as children that support multiple columns. Each item is fully configurable in terms of color and bitmap. The bitmaps for the expanded and contracted nodes can be changed. Tree nodes may have their own color scheme or can inherit from the tree settings.

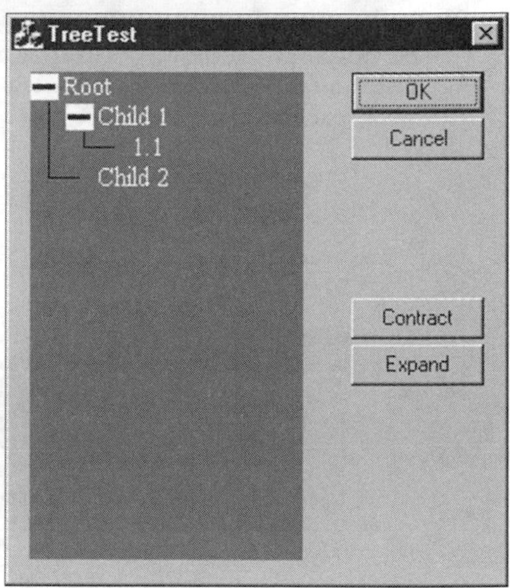

In short, we're designing a completely customizable tree control that you can use in Visual C++ dialogs, form views, or other windows and allow the programmer complete control over their look, feel, and behavior. Events will be provided for selection changes, expansion and contraction of nodes, double-clicking of nodes, and other information. Make no mistake, this is a major-league control, and here it is in all its glory:

Feature List

Features for the color tree control will be as follows:

- Ability to add, delete or update nodes in the tree.
- Complete control over color for each node of the tree.
- Multiple columns per node.
- Multiple root-level items.
- Programmatic control over all features in the tree including expansion, contraction, and visibility of nodes.
- Bitmaps for nodes and fully configurable expansion (+) and contraction (-) buttons.
- Multiple selection, including extended selection using *Ctrl*-click and *Shift*-click.
- Events fired to parent window for node selection, expansion, and contraction.

- Ability to define all parts of display including space between bitmaps and text, indent distance for nodes from parents, whether or not to draw lines connecting nodes, whether or not to allow multiple selection.
- Ability to associate user data with any node in the tree and to retrieve it.
- Ability to retrieve the number of selected nodes and the node numbers of selected nodes.
- Ability to save node numbers as unique identifiers that will persist for the life of the tree.
- Ability to force a node to be displayed.
- Ability to show 'tips' on nodes whose text is too wide to fit on the tree window. This will allow the user to view very long text strings by holding the mouse over the node text for a brief period of time. A pop-up window will then be displayed over the spot allowing the user to view the text. When the mouse moves away from the node, the pop-up will be destroyed.
- Ability to store user settings for tree values persistently in a resource file or Visual Basic form file.

Designing the Control

Designing such a large-scale control as this will be extremely good practice for writing large mission-critical controls of your own, but how do you go about it? The most important thing is that the design is complete enough so that anyone reading the specification will understand what it is that the control is intended to do and whether the features outlined are enough for the user's needs.

First, what is a tree control? Simply put, a tree is a hierarchical representation of data showing a parent/child relationship by indentation. Parent nodes are shown on the left-most side of the tree control window, while child nodes are indented one level from their parents (the actual distance will be user-defined in our case). Child nodes can be parents too, so a node might be indented four or five levels down from a root-level parent.

Each node in the tree can be assigned a bitmap which is simply a graphical representation of the item. For example, if you had a tree which represented different kinds of files shown in the system, documents might have one kind of bitmap while executable files would have another. Bitmaps are optional additions to nodes.

Node Information

This brings up the first level of design. What sort of information do we need to have in a node? From what we have already discussed, you can see that a node needs the text to be displayed, the colors in which to display the text, an optional bitmap and an optional parent. A node which doesn't have a parent is referred to as a root node. We also mentioned that nodes can have user data assigned to them. Finally, a node needs a unique identifier which represents a number that the programmer can use at any time to refer to it. Since you can move a node about a tree by inserting or deleting other nodes, this identifier mustn't change.

The first cut at a design for the node structure might lead you towards storing the information in an internal B-tree or other tree structure. B-trees by themselves will not work since there can be more than two children for any parent. A normal tree structure would work, but it is difficult to traverse and locating an arbitrary node is a slow process. Our internal method of storing the tree structure will be a simple array. In fact, we will use two arrays: the first array will represent the complete tree and will have entries for every node in the tree; the second will represent only those nodes which are visible.

This second array is implemented purely for reasons of efficiency. The tree control needs very quick access to node information for displayed nodes since these are accessible to the user. Clicking on the node or expanding the nodes can be done only if the node is visible, and since the number of visible nodes will probably be much smaller than the total number of nodes, it makes sense to duplicate this information so that it can be more easily searched.

The array structure lends itself well to the tree for other reasons. Since finding the parent level of a node is a matter of simply going backwards through the array until we find a node with a different parent, this will make expansion and contraction (where we need to find the parent node) very quick.

Once we have decided on the design of the node structure itself and the way in which the nodes will be stored, the remainder of the tree design falls out quite quickly. Expanding a node is simply a matter of marking a node as open or visible. This leads to more information that needs to be kept in each node element. We need both the parent of the node and a flag indicating whether or not the node is visible.

Actually, on further examination, there are quite a few items of information that need to be stored in the node that we haven't considered yet. Looking back at the feature list, we note that nodes can be selected, so this is another bit of information that needs to go in the node. Again, referring to the feature list, we see that nodes need to have colors and that if no color is defined for the node, it will inherit its color from the tree itself. In this case, we need to store not only the color information for the node but also flags indicating whether or not the color has been set. The final bit of information comes from the fact that nodes support multiple columns. That column information must be stored somewhere! Since it is 'per node' information, we will store all of the column text and information in the node itself.

Selecting, Expanding, and Contracting

We seem to have taken care of the node and how it will be implemented. The next issue is how to deal with selection, expansion, and contraction of nodes in the tree. Obviously, clicking on the plus or minus in the node will expand or contract it. The question is, how do we know where the user clicked in the tree? Since we will require all nodes to be the same height, determining the node which was clicked upon is fairly easy. First, what about the indentation level of the node? Do we need to store this information? Remember that the nodes are stored in an array and finding the parent of a node is simply a matter of backtracking until we hit a root node. Since the total number of levels of indentation is probably small, there doesn't seem to be a compelling reason to store the indentation level, since we can calculate it on the fly.

Once we know where the node is displayed on a line, we can determine what the user clicked on. If the node has children, the first thing to be displayed is going to be the plus/minus bitmap. If the node has a bitmap which is associated with it, that will be displayed next. Finally, the text for the node will be displayed. Since all of the items have fixed size, we can figure out which piece the user clicked on. Clicking on the plus/minus bitmap will do the expansion or contraction. Clicking anywhere else on the line will select the item.

Is it enough to allow the user to expand, contract or select the node via the mouse? Quite honestly, no. All controls which use the mouse should also provide a keyboard interface to allow the user to work in the fashion to which he or she is most accustomed. The 'standard' for working with tree controls is to move up and down through the tree using the up and down cursor keys. Expansion is generally done through the right arrow key and contraction through the left arrow key. Selection should be done via the *Shift*-down/up or *Ctrl*-down/up key combinations. We will look at some of the problems associated with using cursor keys in ActiveX controls in this example as well.

Display

Now let's take a look at the overall process for displaying the tree. When the control is displayed, it needs to determine the starting position of the first node on the screen. This implies that we will keep track of which node is on top. Why would this node change? Vertical scrolling, of course! Since the programmer will probably add more nodes than will fit on the screen at one time, the user will need to scroll vertically to view all of the nodes. We will keep an internal variable which represents the top node of the viewable area.

We perform the same process for each node in the tree. The indentation level of the node is found by determining how many parents the node has and multiplying that level by the indentation amount. If the node has children, the plus or minus bitmap will then be displayed. If the node has an associated bitmap, that's the next thing to be displayed. Finally, the text for the node and any columns for the node are displayed. This process is repeated until we either run out of nodes or reach the bottom of the displayable area. Note that, in each case, we need to set the colors for the node depending on what the node settings are (background and foreground color, selection).

User Interaction

Once the display has been taken care of, the next issue is user interaction. There are basically five things the user can do with the tree control:

- Select and deselect nodes
- Move the mouse around the control window
- Expand and contract nodes
- Scroll vertically
- Double-click on a node

First, let's consider selecting or deselecting nodes. This will be done either by clicking on the textual part of the node or by using the keyboard. In either case, we should follow the same process: if the node is selected and the user clicks on it, deselect it, otherwise select it.

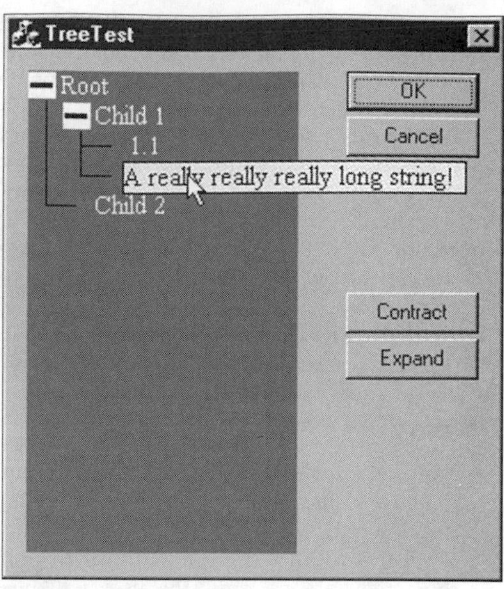

The second action the user might take is to move the mouse around the control window. Although you might think that there is little that moving the mouse might accomplish, we would like to display a pop-up window for node strings that are too wide for the displayable area, so we need to respond to mouse movement. If the mouse is over a node and the text is too wide, a pop-up window will be displayed over the area.

The third action a user can take is to expand or contract a node. This involves identifying all of the children of the node and marking them as open. Once we have identified all the now-visible nodes, we invalidate the control and let the paint routine update the display with the new nodes.

Next up in the user action parade is vertical scrolling. In our case, handling vertical scrolling is a simple action. We update the top node of the control and redisplay it. If the user scrolls up, for example, we subtract one from the top node, update the scrollbar with the new position and invalidate it. There is a question that arises though: how does the scrollbar know what the range of valid items is? Well, the paint routine bases its enabling and disabling of the scrollbar on whether the number of displayable nodes in the list would overflow the viewable area of the control.

The final user action is double-clicking on a node in the control. The only things to do in this case are to find out which node was double-clicked, notify the parent window that the action took place and expand or contract that node if it's a parent.

It all seems rather simple and straightforward, doesn't it. If this were so, wouldn't you think that there would be hundreds of tree controls available for public consumption? As you will see by the massive body of code necessary to implement the features we have discussed, it is never as easy as it looks.

TRY IT OUT - Implement the Color Tree Control

To implement the control, we will create a new project and implement the functionality of the control within that project. Follow this procedure to create the new control.

1 Create a new project workspace using the OLE ControlWizard. Give the project the name ColorTree and place the control wherever you would like to have it reside. The only options that you need to change from their default settings are on Step 2 of ControlWizard behind the Edit Names... button. Change the control's Type Name to Wrox ColorTree Control and its Type ID to Wrox.COLORTREE.ColorTreeCtrl.1. Change the property page's Type Name to Wrox ColorTree Property Page and its Type ID to Wrox.COLORTREE.ColorTreePropPage.1. You can leave the rest of the settings as they are and finish creating the project.

2 The next step is to add the OLE properties to the control. We'll start by adding the stock properties, **ForeColor**, **BackColor** and **Font**, to the control. Remember that you need to start ClassWizard, select **CColorTreeCtrl** from the Class name list and go to the OLE Automation tab, which is where we add properties and methods. For each stock property, click on the Add Property... button, select its name from the External Name list and click OK.

ForeColor will represent the default text color used in the tree; **BackColor** will represent the default background color of the tree and any nodes which don't define their own background colors. **Font** will be the style of text used for the whole tree. Although we will allow the color of the text to be set for each node, the style will be the same throughout the tree.

3 Now we'll add the custom properties, all of which can be implemented as member variables. Use ClassWizard to add the properties shown in the table below.

External name	Type	Variable name	Notification function
IndentDistance	short	m_nIndentDistance	OnIndentDistanceChanged
BitmapSpacing	short	m_nBitmapSpacing	OnBitmapSpacingChanged
DrawNodeLines	BOOL	m_bDrawNodeLines	OnDrawNodeLinesChanged

IndentDistance represents the distance that each level of the tree will be indented from its parent.

BitmapSpacing will represent the user-defined space between the bitmaps for a node and the text of the node.

DrawNodeLines is a flag that is set to **TRUE** if the user wants the lines connecting the nodes to be drawn and **FALSE** if they do not wish node lines to appear on the control.

Changing any of these properties will require the control to be redrawn so you should add **InvalidateControl()** to each of the notification functions as shown below.

```
void CColorTreeCtrl::OnIndentDistanceChanged()
{
   InvalidateControl();
   SetModifiedFlag();
}

void CColorTreeCtrl::OnBitmapSpacingChanged()
{
   InvalidateControl();
   SetModifiedFlag();
}
```

```
void CColorTreeCtrl::OnDrawNodeLinesChanged()
{
    InvalidateControl();
    SetModifiedFlag();
}
```

We also want these properties to be persistent, so add the following code to **DoPropExchange()**:

```
void CColorTreeCtrl::DoPropExchange(CPropExchange* pPX)
{
    ExchangeVersion(pPX, MAKELONG(_wVerMinor, _wVerMajor));
    COleControl::DoPropExchange(pPX);
    PX_Short(pPX, "IndentDistance", m_nIndentDistance, 10);
    PX_Short(pPX, "BitmapSpacing", m_nBitmapSpacing, 2);
    PX_Bool(pPX, "DrawNodeLines", m_bDrawNodeLines, TRUE);
}
```

That takes care of the properties for the control. The majority of the work for this control will be in the design of the methods, rather than the properties. We will begin adding those methods now.

4 Let's add some of the variables we're going to need to the control class header file right away. Add these to the class definition, and we'll see what they mean as we go on:

```
// Implementation
protected:
    ~CColorTreeCtrl();
private:
    long m_lTopNodeID;
    long m_lCurrentItem;
    CBitmap* m_pbmpPlus;
    CBitmap* m_pbmpMinus;
    CObArray m_DisplayedNodes;
    CObArray m_NodeList;
    CDWordArray m_ColumnWidths;
    CTreeNode* m_pLastNode;
    CPopupTip* m_pDispWnd;
    CString m_strPopupClassName;
    BOOL m_bMultiSelect;
    long m_lAnchorPoint;
```

5 We're going to be adding quite a few methods to the control, so it will save time if we use ClassWizard to add them in chunks, then we'll go through the implementation for each of the methods before adding the next lot of methods. Use ClassWizard to add the methods shown in the table below:

External name/ Internal name	Return type	Parameter List Name	Parameter List Type
AddNode	long	lParentNodeID strText	long LPCTSTR
SetNodeBackColor	void	lNodeID clrNodeBack	long OLE_COLOR

Table Continued on Following Page

External name/ Internal name	Return type	Parameter List Name	Parameter List Type
SetNodeTextColor	void	lNodeID clrNodeText	long OLE_COLOR
SetNodeBitmap	void	lNodeID pBitmap	long LPUNKNOWN
SetNodeUserData	void	lNodeID lUserData	long long
GetNodeUserData	long	lNodeID	long

6 The first method we're going to implement is, quite naturally, the method to add a new node to the tree. Without this method, and the nodes that it adds, the user can't do much with the tree. If there are no nodes, there's nothing to display and little to work with!

Here is the code for the **AddNode()** method:

```
long CColorTreeCtrl::AddNode(long lParentNodeID, LPCTSTR strText)
{
   // Create a new node object
   CTreeNode* pNewNode = new CTreeNode(strText, lParentNodeID);

   // Default the node colors to the tree colors
   pNewNode->SetBackColor(TranslateColor(GetBackColor()));
   pNewNode->SetTextColor(TranslateColor(GetForeColor()));

   // If the parent node parameter is NOT -1, insert after the last child
   if (lParentNodeID != -1)
   {
      CTreeNode* pParentNode = GetNodeById(lParentNodeID);
      if (pParentNode == 0)
         return -1;

      // Make sure the parent knows it has children.
      pParentNode->AddChild();

      // Find the parent in the list
      int nIndex = GetPositionOfNode(lParentNodeID);

      // Loop through all those following this id
      for (int i = nIndex + 1; i < m_NodeList.GetSize(); ++i)
      {
         CTreeNode* pTestNode = (CTreeNode*)m_NodeList[i];

         // Is this a child of the parent?
         if (!IsParent(lParentNodeID, pTestNode->GetNodeId()))
            break;
      }

      if (i < m_NodeList.GetSize())
         m_NodeList.InsertAt(i, pNewNode);
      else
         m_NodeList.Add(pNewNode);
   }
   else
```

```
        // No parent, append to the end of the array
        m_NodeList.Add(pNewNode);

    long lNewNodeID = m_NodeList.GetSize() - 1;
    pNewNode->SetNodeId(lNewNodeID);

    InvalidateControl();

    return lNewNodeID;
}
```

The parameters for this method are the ID of the node to use as a parent (this should be set to **-1** if the new node is intended as a root item) and the text to be displayed for the node. This is all that's necessary to define a basic node in the system.

Let's take a look at what's going on here. Don't worry about all of the variables and methods that are used here but not yet defined. We will get to them all in good time. First, we create a new **CTreeNode** object. We haven't defined this class yet, but it just stores all the settings necessary for a node. We then set the colors of the new node from the current tree settings.

Next, we check to see whether the user intends to add this node as a root node or as a child node. If this is to be a root node, we won't worry about its parent and we can just add the new node to **m_NodeList**, which is the control's array of nodes. If the parent node value is not **-1**, this is a child node and we need to associate the node with its parent. This is done by finding the parent node using the **GetNodeById()** method.

If the proposed parent exists, we look for the node in the list of defined nodes. Once we find it, we will scan through the list from that point and look for all nodes which also have this node as a parent. The node will then be added to the end of the list of nodes which have the same parent. Thus all new nodes are added to the end of the parent node list. If there is no parent for the node it's simply appended to the node list.

Finally, we define the unique identifier for the node by getting the number of nodes defined in the list. This is set as the identifier for the node and returned to the user as the new node's ID.

7 Once the node is added, the next thing to do is to implement the methods for setting the various attributes of the node. These methods are all very straightforward. They each take the node ID passed in as the first parameter and use **GetNodeById()** to get a pointer to a **CTreeNode** object. They then store the data passed as the second parameter in that object.

```
void CColorTreeCtrl::SetNodeBackColor(long lNodeID, OLE_COLOR clrNodeBack)
{
    CTreeNode* pNode = GetNodeById(lNodeID);
    if (pNode == NULL)
        return;
    // Set the color
    pNode->SetBackColor(TranslateColor(clrNodeBack));
}
```

```
void CColorTreeCtrl::SetNodeTextColor(long lNodeID, OLE_COLOR clrNodeText)
{
   CTreeNode* pNode = GetNodeById(lNodeID);
   if (pNode == NULL)
      return;
   // Set the color
   pNode->SetTextColor(TranslateColor(clrNodeText));
}

void CColorTreeCtrl::SetNodeBitmap(long lNodeID, LPUNKNOWN pBitmap)
{
   CTreeNode* pNode = GetNodeById(lNodeID);
   if (pNode == NULL)
      return;

   pNode->SetBitmap((CBitmap*)pBitmap);
}

void CColorTreeCtrl::SetNodeUserData(long lNodeID, long lUserData)
{
   CTreeNode* pNode = GetNodeById(lNodeID);
   if (pNode == NULL)
      return;
   // Store the data
   pNode->SetUserData(lUserData);
}
```

Once again, we've put the control users' needs above our own by providing the ability to associate user data with each node. In fact, it wasn't at all hard to provide this capability and the control's users will thank us for it. Of course, they'll only thank us if we also supply a way for them to get the data back again, so add the code shown below to **GetNodeUserData()**:

```
long CColorTreeCtrl::GetNodeUserData(long lNodeID)
{
   CTreeNode* pNode = GetNodeById(lNodeID);
   if (pNode == NULL)
      return 0L;
   return pNode->GetUserData();
}
```

You could add **Get** methods for the node's other attributes, but we'll leave that as an exercise.

8 Now we need to go back to ClassWizard and add some more methods to our control. Add those shown in this table:

External name/ Internal name	Return type	Parameter List Name	Parameter List Type
Contract	void	lNodeID	long
Expand	void	lNodeID	long
SetVisible	void	lNodeID	long

The first two methods simply take the node represented by the node ID passed as a parameter and store the expanded or contracted state in the **CTreeNode** object. They then invalidate the control so that it redraws itself with the new information. This will cause the child items of the node to appear if the node is expanded or disappear if the node is contracted.

```
void CColorTreeCtrl::Contract(long lNodeID)
{
   CTreeNode* pNode = GetNodeById(lNodeID);
   if (pNode == NULL)
      return;
   pNode->SetContracted();
   InvalidateControl();
}

void CColorTreeCtrl::Expand(long lNodeID)
{
   CTreeNode* pNode = GetNodeById(lNodeID);
   if (pNode == NULL)
      return;
   pNode->SetExpanded();
   InvalidateControl();
}
```

SetVisible() takes the node ID passed as its only parameter, makes sure that node is expanded, then calls **SetVisible()** using the parent node's ID. This continues until a root node is hit. This ensures that the node identified by the client's call to **SetVisible()** and all its parents are expanded, thus making the original node visible.

```
void CColorTreeCtrl::SetVisible(long lNodeID)
{
   // Make sure this node's parents are visible
   CTreeNode* pNode = GetNodeById(lNodeID);
   if (pNode)
   {
      // Have we reached a root?
      if (pNode->GetParent() == -1)
      {
         pNode->SetExpanded();
         InvalidateControl();
         return;
      }
      pNode->SetExpanded();
      SetVisible(pNode->GetParent());
   }
}
```

9 Now use ClassWizard to add all the methods relating to the selection of nodes in the control:

External name/ Internal name	Return type	Parameter List Name	Parameter List Type
SetMultiSelect	void	bMultiSelectFlag	BOOL
SetNodeSelected	void	lNodeID bSelectNode	long BOOL
ClearAllSelections	void	-	-
GetNumSelectedNodes	long	-	-
GetSelectedNodes	long	pSelectedNodes lMaxNumber	long* long
IsNodeSelected	BOOL	lNodeID	long

The **SetMultiSelect()** method will set the multiple selection flag of the tree control to indicate whether the user can make single or multiple selections in the control.

```
void CColorTreeCtrl::SetMultiSelect(BOOL bMultiSelectFlag)
{
   m_bMultiSelect = bMultiSelectFlag;
}
```

SetNodeSelected() is a method which will programmatically select a given node. The method takes two arguments: a node ID which identifies the node we want to select or deselect, and a flag indicating whether we are selecting (**TRUE**) or deselecting (**FALSE**) the node. If you try to select an already selected node (or deselect an already deselected node), nothing will happen.

```
void CColorTreeCtrl::SetNodeSelected(long lNodeID, BOOL bSelectNode)
{
   CTreeNode* pNode = GetNodeById(lNodeID);
   if (pNode)
   {
      if (m_bMultiSelect == FALSE)
         ClearAllSelections();
      pNode->Select(bSelectNode);
      InvalidateControl();
   }
}
```

The method first tries to find the given node identifier. If the node isn't found, nothing will happen; there is nothing to be gained by throwing an error, for example, since there's little the programmer could do about it. Once the node is found, the control then checks the multiple selection flag. If the flag isn't set, indicating that the control is a single selection control, all other selections are cleared. It's necessary to do this since we don't know whether any other selections are set. Once all of the selections are cleared, we select this node in the tree and repaint the control to reflect the changes for the user.

The **ClearAllSelections()** method is also exposed to the user. This is a good example of simple code reuse within a single control. This single method is used internally within the control to clear all of the selections as well as being exposed to the programmer to do the same job. Why write two methods when a single one will do?

```
void CColorTreeCtrl::ClearAllSelections()
{
   for (int i = 0; i < m_NodeList.GetSize(); ++i)
   {
      CTreeNode* pNode = (CTreeNode*)m_NodeList[i];
      pNode->Select(FALSE);
   }
}
```

The next three methods, **GetNumSelectedNodes()**, **GetSelectedNodes()** and **IsNodeSelected()**, can tell the programmer the number of selected nodes, the IDs of the selected nodes, and whether a given node is selected.

```
long CColorTreeCtrl::GetNumSelectedNodes()
{
   long lCount = 0;
   for (int i = 0; i < m_NodeList.GetSize(); ++i)
   {
      CTreeNode* pNode = (CTreeNode*)m_NodeList[i];
      if (pNode->IsSelected())
         lCount ++;
   }
   return lCount;
}
```

The second method, **GetSelectedNodes()**, returns a type **long** (which represents the number of nodes found) and takes two arguments. The first is a pointer to a **long** which represents an array that will be filled with the IDs of the selected nodes. The second argument represents the maximum number of entries which may be placed in the array. The programmer who calls this function is responsible for ensuring that the maximum number of allowed entries is not greater than the size of the array. Here's the code:

```
long CColorTreeCtrl::GetSelectedNodes(long FAR* pSelectedNodes,
                                      long lMaxNumber)
{
   long lCount = 0;
   for (int i = 0; i < m_NodeList.GetSize(); ++i)
   {
      CTreeNode* pNode = (CTreeNode*)m_NodeList[i];
      if (pNode->IsSelected())
      {
         if (lCount < lMaxNumber)
         {
            pSelectedNodes[lCount] = pNode->GetNodeId();
            lCount ++;
         }
      }
   }
   return lCount;
}
```

IsNodeSelected() just takes a node ID and returns a **BOOL** indicating whether the node is selected or not. If the node isn't found it isn't considered selected.

```
BOOL CColorTreeCtrl::IsNodeSelected(long lNodeID)
{
   // Get this node and make sure it exists.
   CTreeNode* pNode = GetNodeById(lNodeID);
   if (pNode)
   {
      // Tell caller whether it is currently selected.
      if (pNode->IsSelected())
         return TRUE;
   }
   return FALSE;
}
```

10 Now we'll finish off the addition of methods by using ClassWizard to add these methods:

External name/ Internal name	Return type	Parameter List Name	Parameter List Type
RemoveNode	void	lNodeID bDeleteChildren	long BOOL
RemoveAllNodes	void	-	-
AddNodeColumn	void	lNodeID strText	long LPCTSTR
SetColumnWidth	void	lColumn lWidth	long long

RemoveNode() takes two arguments, the ID of the node to delete and a **BOOL** value which indicates whether or not to remove any children from the node if it is a parent. If the node is a parent and the flag isn't set, the children will become children of the parent of the deleted node (that is, orphaned nodes will be adopted by their grandparents). If the deleted node was a root node, all of its children will become root nodes. Here's the code for the **RemoveNode()** method:

```
void CColorTreeCtrl::RemoveNode(long lNodeID, BOOL bDeleteChildren)
{
   // We need to get the parent of this node first
   CTreeNode* pNode = GetNodeById(lNodeID);
   if (pNode == NULL)
      return;

   long lParentID = pNode->GetParent();

   // Now loop through all nodes and look for any that
   // have this node as a parent. If so, assign them
   // the parent of this node, unless they wanted them
   // deleted
   if (bDeleteChildren == FALSE)
   {
      for (int i = 0; i < m_NodeList.GetSize(); ++i)
      {
         CTreeNode* pChildNode = (CTreeNode*)m_NodeList[i];
         if (pChildNode->GetParent() == lNodeID)
            pChildNode->SetParent(lParentID);
```

```
        }
    }
    else
    {
        int i = 0;
        while (i < m_NodeList.GetSize())
        {
            CTreeNode* pChildNode = (CTreeNode*)m_NodeList[i];
            if (pChildNode->GetParent() == lNodeID)
            {
                delete pChildNode;
                m_NodeList.RemoveAt(i);
            }
            else
                i++;
        }
    }

    // Get the position in the array
    long lIndex = GetPositionOfNode(lNodeID);

    // Remove that index from the array
    m_NodeList.RemoveAt(lIndex);

    // Delete the pointer
    delete pNode;

    // And redraw the control
    InvalidateControl();
}
```

The next issue is that of completely clearing the tree of nodes. This can be done simply by adding the following code to the **RemoveAllNodes()** method:

```
void CColorTreeCtrl::RemoveAllNodes()
{
    // Blow away all the nodes
    for (int i = 0; i < m_NodeList.GetSize(); ++i)
    {
        CTreeNode* pNode = (CTreeNode*)m_NodeList[i];
        delete pNode;
    }
    m_NodeList.RemoveAll();
    InvalidateControl();
}
```

The next two methods deal with columns. The first method, **AddNodeColumn()**, adds a new column of text to an existing node. Its first argument is the ID of the node to which the column should be added, and the second argument is the text to add to the column. Column information is for display only: users may not select a column separately from the node, nor may they modify the column information.

```
void CColorTreeCtrl::AddNodeColumn(long lNodeID, LPCTSTR strText)
{
    // Get the node
    CTreeNode* pNode = GetNodeById(lNodeID);
```

```
    if (pNode == NULL)
       return;

    // Add this column
    pNode->AddColumn(strText);
    InvalidateControl();
}
```

Along with the column text, the width of the column is also of interest to the programmer. While the text is a part of each node, the column width is actually a part of the control as a whole. Every node will be displayed with the same column width.

SetColumnWidth() takes two arguments: the number of the column whose width is being set, and the width itself. The default text for a node is considered to be held in column 0, all other columns fall to the right of that and are numbered from 1 upward.

```
void CColorTreeCtrl::SetColumnWidth(long lColumn, long lWidth)
{
    // Do we already have one of these?
    if (lColumn < m_ColumnWidths.GetSize())
    {
       m_ColumnWidths[lColumn] = lWidth;
       InvalidateControl();
       return;
    }

    if (m_ColumnWidths.GetSize() < lColumn)
    {
       for (int i = 0; i < lColumn; ++i)
          m_ColumnWidths.Add(50);
    }
    m_ColumnWidths.Add(lWidth);
    InvalidateControl();
}
```

You'd probably also want to be able to modify the text in a column. Although not a particularly difficult job, this modification is left as an exercise for the reader.

11 That accounts for all of the exposed external methods we need to implement. Before we add any more functions, let's add the OLE events to our control that we'll use to notify the user. Adding events to an ActiveX control is very easy, because we don't have to do any coding at all. An event is a function that the control calls in its client, in order to tell it that something has happened. The control provides the prototype of the event-handling function, but it is up to the client to implement the function.

We'll notify the client of four events: when a node is expanded, when a node is contracted, when one has been double-clicked, and when the selection has changed. All of these events will send the ID of the node this event refers to as their only parameter.

Start ClassWizard and select the OLE Events tab. For each event, click the Add Event... button and fill in the fields as shown on the next page.

External name	Internal name	Parameter List Name	Parameter List Type
ExpandNode	FireExpandNode	lNodeID	long
ContractNode	FireContractNode	lNodeID	long
DoubleClick	FireDoubleClick	lNodeID	long
SelectionChanged	FireSelectionChanged	lNodeID	long

Note that the **DoubleClick** event that we add to the control isn't the same as the stock **DblClick** event, since we need to pass the ID of the node that has been clicked. You'll see precisely where each of these events gets fired as we go through the rest of the code.

12 At this point, we need to start implementing the actual functionality of the class. The best place to start this process is at the beginning, with the constructor for the class:

```
CColorTreeCtrl::CColorTreeCtrl()
{
   InitializeIIDs(&IID_DColorTree, &IID_DColorTreeEvents);

   m_lTopNodeID = 0;

   // Create the bitmaps and load them
   m_pbmpPlus = new CBitmap;
   m_pbmpPlus->LoadBitmap(IDB_PLUS);

   m_pbmpMinus = new CBitmap;
   m_pbmpMinus->LoadBitmap(IDB_MINUS);

   m_pLastNode = NULL;
   m_lCurrentItem = -1;
   m_bMultiSelect = FALSE;
   m_lAnchorPoint = 0;
   m_pDispWnd = NULL;
   m_strPopupClassName = ::AfxRegisterWndClass(CS_SAVEBITS,
                          ::AfxGetApp()->LoadStandardCursor(IDC_ARROW));
   // Set initial property values
   m_nIndentDistance = 10;
   m_nBitmapSpacing = 2;
   m_bDrawNodeLines = TRUE;
}
```

The first thing that we do is to initialize the top node pointer. This internal variable (**m_lTopNodeID**) is used to store the ID of the node at the top of the tree display. We need this variable to allow scrolling so that we know which node to start drawing from.

Next, we load the open and close (plus and minus) bitmaps. You'll need to create a couple of small bitmaps and add them to the project's resources with the IDs **IDB_PLUS** and **IDB_MINUS**, if you want to see these buttons.

Finally, the member variables of the class need to be initialized. We will talk about these as we get to them.

Perhaps the most interesting thing going on in the constructor is the call to **AfxRegisterWndClass()** which registers a new window name for the pop-up window we will use for the display of long text strings. Note that the **CS_SAVEBITS** flag is used so that Windows will automatically save the background of the window when it's created. This will ensure that we have a very fast refresh of the window under the pop-up—we don't want to repaint the entire tree. We won't be talking much about the pop-up window used in this example. We'll talk about it in more detail in the next chapter.

13 At this point, we're ready to begin the real work of writing the control. The code we have written up to this point will set the attributes for the control, and allow the user to call methods within the control. Unfortunately, none of those attributes or methods will have any impact unless we start dealing with the realities of working with Windows. The first of those realities is to make the control display itself on the screen. As usual, this is accomplished through **OnDraw()**. Here's the code to add to **CColorTreeCtrl::OnDraw()**:

```
void CColorTreeCtrl::OnDraw(
        CDC* pdc, const CRect& rcBounds, const CRect& rcInvalid)
{
   // Remove all displayed nodes. Since we will attempt to redraw all
   // of the nodes regardless of whether they are really drawn or not
   // this will keep the display in sync with the list.
   m_DisplayedNodes.RemoveAll();

   // Clear the background of the tree
   CBrush brBack(TranslateColor(GetBackColor()));
   CRect rect = rcBounds;
   pdc->FillRect(&rect, &brBack);

   // Loop through the nodes starting at the top one and
   // moving through all "open" nodes.
   CFont* pOldFont = SelectStockFont(pdc);
   TEXTMETRIC tm;
   pdc->GetTextMetrics(&tm);
   CFont* pFont = pdc->SelectObject(pOldFont);

   CPoint bp = rcBounds.TopLeft();
   CPoint ep = rcBounds.BottomRight();
   int y = bp.y;

   BOOL bScrollFlag = FALSE;

   for (int i = m_lTopNodeID; i < m_NodeList.GetSize(); ++i)
   {
      if (!DrawNode(pdc, i, y, tm, ep))
      {
         bScrollFlag = TRUE;
         break;
      }
   }

   // If we ran past the bottom OR we aren't at the start of the
   // list, enable the scrollbar.
   if (bScrollFlag || m_lTopNodeID != 0)
   {
      // Only enable scrollbar if we are in running mode.
      if (m_hWnd)
```

```
            EnableScrollBarCtrl(SB_VERT, TRUE);
    }
    else
        if (m_hWnd)
            EnableScrollBarCtrl(SB_VERT, FALSE);
}
```

This function is pretty simple because most of the hard work is done in the helper function **DrawNode()**, which we'll add to the class shortly. All that's really happening here is that we remove all the nodes from **m_DisplayedNodes**, fill in the background for the control, get the **TEXTMETRIC** for the current font, then loop through each node calling **DrawNode()**. Finally, we enable the scroll bars if necessary.

You might be wondering exactly what the **m_DisplayedNodes** array is for and why we're removing all of its contents. The array maintains the nodes which are currently displayed on the control window. This is different to the array of all nodes in the tree (**m_NodeList**), which is constant (ignoring little things like adding or removing tree nodes). The displayed nodes represent the 'window' into the total list which is currently visible to the user. The array serves several purposes: first, it makes it easier to determine which node the user clicks on when they are selecting a node from the tree. Second, the array makes it a snap to move to the next or previous node in response to a keyboard cursor key press. Finally, the list can be used to figure out what is currently showing, so that we know what colors to use.

14 Now we need to add the **DrawNode()** function itself. Add the declaration for this function to **ColorTreeCtl.h** as shown:

```
// Implementation
protected:
    ~CColorTreeCtrl();
    BOOL DrawNode(CDC* pdc, int nNodeID, int& y, TEXTMETRIC& tm,
                  CPoint ptEnd);
```

Now add the implementation to **ColorTreeCtl.cpp**:

```
BOOL CColorTreeCtrl::DrawNode(CDC* pdc, int nNodeID, int& y,
                               TEXTMETRIC& tm, CPoint ptEnd)
{
    CTreeNode* pNode = (CTreeNode*)m_NodeList[nNodeID];

    // Is this node open?
    if (IsVisible(pNode) == FALSE)
        return TRUE;

    CFont* pOldFont = SelectStockFont(pdc);
    // Get the x-offset of this child...
    int x = GetNodeOffset(pNode);

    // Does the node have children?
    if (pNode->HasChildren())
    {
        // If it is open draw the '-' otherwise draw the '+'
        if (IsExpanded(pNode) == FALSE)
            DrawBitmap(pdc, m_pbmpPlus, x, y + 1, tm.tmMaxCharWidth,
```

```
                tm.tmHeight - 2);
        else
            DrawBitmap(pdc, m_pbmpMinus, x, y + 1, tm.tmMaxCharWidth,
                tm.tmHeight - 2);
    }

    // Add in the padding space
    x += m_nBitmapSpacing;

    // And move over by the width of the bitmap.
    x += tm.tmMaxCharWidth;

    // See if the node has a bitmap associate with it. If so,
    // draw the bitmap in front of the text
    if (pNode->GetBitmap())
    {
        // Draw the bitmap at that location...
        DrawBitmap(pdc, pNode->GetBitmap(), x, y + 1, tm.tmMaxCharWidth,
                tm.tmHeight - 2);
        x += tm.tmMaxCharWidth;
        x += m_nBitmapSpacing;
    }

    // Yes, set the colors for the node and draw the text
    if (pNode->IsSelected() == FALSE)
    {
        pdc->SetTextColor(pNode->GetTextColor());
        pdc->SetBkColor(pNode->GetBackColor());
    }
    else
    {
        pdc->SetTextColor(pNode->GetBackColor());
        pdc->SetBkColor(pNode->GetTextColor());
        if (pNode->NumColumns())
        {
            CBrush br(pNode->GetTextColor());
            CRect r(x, y, x + GetColumnWidth(0), y + tm.tmHeight);
            pdc->FillRect(&r, &br);
        }
    }

    // Draw the node text.
    CRect rectText(x, y, x + GetColumnWidth(0), y + tm.tmHeight);
    pdc->DrawText(pNode->GetText(), &rectText, DT_LEFT);

    // Check for multiple columns here...
    int nOff = GetColumnWidth(0);

    for (int c = 0; c < pNode->NumColumns(); ++c)
    {
        CRect r(nOff, y, nOff + GetColumnWidth(c + 1), y + tm.tmHeight);
        nOff += GetColumnWidth(c + 1);

        CBrush br(pNode->GetTextColor());
        if (pNode->IsSelected())
            pdc->FillRect(&r, &br);
        pdc->DrawText(pNode->GetColumnText(c), &r, DT_LEFT);
    }
```

```
      // Draw the line connecting to parent node here...
      DrawNodeLines(pdc, pNode, y, y + tm.tmHeight,
                    tm.tmMaxCharWidth + m_nBitmapSpacing);

      // Increment the vertical position by the font height.
      y += tm.tmHeight;

      // And add this node to the displayed list
      m_DisplayedNodes.Add(pNode);

      // Are we at the bottom yet?
      if (y >= ptEnd.y)
      {
         pdc->SelectObject(pOldFont);
         return FALSE;
      }

      pdc->SelectObject(pOldFont);
      return TRUE;
}
```

Although it looks complicated, the function actually breaks down quite simply, as follows:

```
* Is the node visible?
   * Yes - Continue
   * No - Exit and return TRUE
* Is this node a parent?
   * Yes - display the open or closed bitmap (depending on state)
   * No - do not display an open or closed bitmap
* Does this node have a bitmap associated with it?
   * Yes - draw the bitmap for the node
   * No - continue
* Is this node selected?
   * No - Use node colors
   * Yes - Use reverse colors
* Draw the text for the item
* Draw the text for each column
* Draw the node lines
* Is this node at the bottom of the display?
   * Yes - Exit and return FALSE
   * No - Exit and return TRUE
```

15 Now we need to add the **DrawNodeLines()** function used by **DrawNode()**. Add the **protected** function declaration shown below to **CColorTreeCtrl.h**:

```
   BOOL DrawNode(CDC* pdc, int nNodeID, int& y, TEXTMETRIC& tm,
                 CPoint ptEnd);
   void DrawNodeLines(CDC* pdc, CTreeNode* node, int y1, int y2,
                      int nWidth);
```

Implement the function as shown. It's used to draw the connecting lines for the individual nodes.

```
void CColorTreeCtrl::DrawNodeLines(CDC* pdc, CTreeNode* node, int y1,
                                   int y2, int nWidth)
{
   // Make sure we are supposed to draw lines in this
   // tree before we do anything with it...
   if (m_bDrawNodeLines == FALSE)
      return;

   CTreeNode* pNode = node;

   // Loop through and draw each parent line...
   while (pNode->GetParent() != -1)
   {
      int x_line = GetNodeOffset(pNode) - (m_nIndentDistance / 2);
      int mid_y = y1 + (y2 - y1) / 2;

      // If this is the last child of its parent, only draw the
      // bottom of the line to the child itself, instead of its
      // next line down.
      long pos = GetPositionOfNode(node->GetNodeId());
      BOOL bFlag = FALSE;

      // This only applies to the innermost node. Outermost nodes
      // will still draw a complete line.
      if (pNode == node)
      {
         // The last one is obviously the end...
         if (pos == m_NodeList.GetSize() - 1)
            bFlag = TRUE;
         else
         {
            CTreeNode* nextChild = (CTreeNode*)m_NodeList[pos + 1];

            // If the next one doesn't have the same parent and
            // the next one is not a child of this one...
            if (nextChild->GetParent() != pNode->GetParent() &&
                nextChild->GetParent() != node->GetNodeId())
               bFlag = TRUE;
         }
      }
      pdc->MoveTo(x_line, y1);
      if (!bFlag)
         pdc->LineTo(x_line, y2);
      else
         pdc->LineTo(x_line, mid_y);

      // If this the first one, draw the cross bar
      if (!pNode->HasChildren())
      {
         pdc->MoveTo(x_line, mid_y);
         pdc->LineTo(x_line + nWidth, mid_y);
      }
      pNode = GetNodeById(pNode->GetParent());
   }
}
```

16 The next step is to deal with the user clicking in the control. Here we will check for node selection, expansion, and contraction of parents, and multiple node selection problems. To deal with the user clicking on the control, we'll add a new message handler for the **WM_LBUTTONUP** message.

> *We're using the left mouse 'button up' message, rather than 'button down'. This is for a very good reason: processing a left mouse 'button down' message in the control will often lead to problems with the control 'eating' messages. For whatever reason, try to rely on 'up', rather than 'down', messages.*

Use ClassWizard to add a new handler for the **WM_LBUTTONUP** message to **CColorTreeCtrl**. Add the following code to the handler:

```
void CColorTreeCtrl::OnLButtonUp(UINT nFlags, CPoint point)
{
   CDC* pdc = GetDC();
   CFont* pOldFont = SelectStockFont(pdc);
   TEXTMETRIC tm;
   pdc->GetTextMetrics(&tm);
   CFont* pFont = pdc->SelectObject(pOldFont);
   ReleaseDC(pdc);

   // Which entry did we land on?
   int nWhich = point.y / tm.tmHeight;

   // If they landed on one, select it.
   if (m_DisplayedNodes.GetSize() > nWhich)
   {
      // See if we need to reset anchor point.
      if (!(nFlags & MK_SHIFT))
         m_lAnchorPoint = nWhich + m_lTopNodeID;

      CTreeNode* pNode = (CTreeNode*)m_DisplayedNodes[nWhich];

      // Figure out where the bitmap will be displayed.
      int x = GetNodeOffset(pNode);

      // Is this hit inside the bitmap?
      if (point.x >= x &&
          point.x <= x + tm.tmMaxCharWidth &&
          pNode->HasChildren())
      {
         // If we get here we clicked in bitmap AND it has children.
         // If it is currently expanded, contract it otherwise
         // expand it
         if (pNode->IsExpanded())
         {
            FireContractNode(pNode->GetNodeId());
            pNode->SetContracted();
         }
         else
         {
            FireExpandNode(pNode->GetNodeId());
            pNode->SetExpanded();
         }
      }
      else
```

```
        {
            if (pNode->IsSelected())
                HandleSelectedNode(pNode, nFlags, nWhich);
            else
                HandleUnselectedNode(pNode, nFlags, nWhich);
        }
        InvalidateControl();
    }
    COleControl::OnLButtonDown(nFlags, point);
}
```

This handler makes use of a couple of helper functions to stop the routine getting too long. You'll need to add the **protected** function declarations to the header file **ColorTreeCtl.h**, and the implementations to **ColorTreeCtl.cpp**:

```
    void DrawNodeLines(CDC* pdc, CTreeNode* node, int y1, int y2,
                       int nWidth);
    void HandleSelectedNode(CTreeNode* pNode, UINT nFlags, int nWhich);
    void HandleUnselectedNode(CTreeNode* pNode, UINT nFlags, int nWhich);
```

```
void CColorTreeCtrl::HandleSelectedNode(CTreeNode* pNode, UINT nFlags,
                                        int nWhich)
{
    // If this is NOT multiselect clear the selection
    m_pLastNode = NULL;
    if (!m_bMultiSelect)
        pNode->Select(FALSE);
    else
    {
        // This IS multi-select. Clear all selections
        // then Select this one UNLESS the control key
        // is pressed (and the shift key is not pressed).
        if (!(nFlags & MK_CONTROL) && !(nFlags & MK_SHIFT))
        {
            ClearAllSelections();
            pNode->Select(TRUE);
        }
        else
        {
            // If the SHIFT key is not set, just
            // clear this entry.
            if (!(nFlags & MK_SHIFT) || !m_bMultiSelect)
                pNode->Select(FALSE);
            else
            {
                // Shift key set. Select everything
                // between anchor point and this one.
                if (m_lAnchorPoint < nWhich)
                {
                    ClearAllSelections();
                    for (int i = m_lAnchorPoint; i <= nWhich + m_lTopNodeID;
                         ++i)
                    {
                        CTreeNode* pNode = (CTreeNode*)m_NodeList[i];
                        pNode->Select(TRUE);
                    }
                }
```

```
            else
            {
               ClearAllSelections();
               for (int i = nWhich + m_lTopNodeID; i <= m_lAnchorPoint;
                  ++i)
               {
                  CTreeNode* pNode = (CTreeNode*)m_NodeList[i];
                  pNode->Select(TRUE);
               }
            }
         }
      }
   }
   FireSelectionChanged(pNode->GetNodeId());
}

void CColorTreeCtrl::HandleUnselectedNode(CTreeNode* pNode, UINT nFlags,
                                           int nWhich)
{
   // Deselect the last selected node(s).
   if (!m_bMultiSelect || !(nFlags & MK_CONTROL))
      ClearAllSelections();
   if (!(nFlags & MK_SHIFT) || !m_bMultiSelect)
      pNode->Select(TRUE);
   else
   {
      // Shift key set. Select everything
      // between anchor point and this one.
      if (m_lAnchorPoint < nWhich)
      {
         ClearAllSelections();
         for (int i = m_lAnchorPoint; i <= nWhich + m_lTopNodeID; ++i)
         {
            CTreeNode* pNode = (CTreeNode*)m_NodeList[i];
            pNode->Select(TRUE);
         }
      }
      else
      {
         ClearAllSelections();
         for (int i = nWhich + m_lTopNodeID; i <= m_lAnchorPoint; ++i)
         {
            CTreeNode* pNode = (CTreeNode*)m_NodeList[i];
            pNode->Select(TRUE);
         }
      }
   }
   m_pLastNode = pNode;
   FireSelectionChanged(pNode->GetNodeId());
}
```

The first thing we do here is determine where the user clicked in the control. After all, if they clicked in an unused portion of the control, such as a line that doesn't contain an entry, it would not make sense to process anything. We calculate the line clicked on by the user by dividing the *y* coordinate of the point by the font height we have used to display all of the lines. Since in this version of the control we only use a single font for all nodes, this will always tell us what line the user clicked on.

Once we know which line was selected, the next step is to determine what the user was trying to accomplish by selecting a line. Basically, this can be broken down into three different options:

- The user was trying to select a single line in the tree. We would know this because the click would fall outside of the open/close bitmap for the node and somewhere to the right of where the text begins for the node.
- The user was trying to expand a parent node to view all of its children. This would be true if the click was within the border of the first bitmap displayed, the node was a parent, and that node was presently closed.
- The user was trying to contract a parent node to hide all of its children. We could determine this if the click was within the border of the first bitmap displayed, the node was a parent and that node was presently open.

Looking at the code, we can see that there is actually more going on here than just this. First of all, we need to consider multiple selection within the tree. All of the lines which check for **MK_SHIFT** or **MK_CONTROL** are checking to see if the user pressed the *Shift* key or *Ctrl* key respectively. If these keys are down, we need to treat the selection differently than if the user simply clicks in a line. For single clicks with no modifiers, all existing selections are cleared. For clicks with *Shift* or *Ctrl* down, the current line (and others in the case of a *Shift*) is selected in addition to the other selected lines.

In either case, the node is selected by calling **Select()** on it, with a flag indicating if the node is to be selected (**TRUE**) or cleared (**FALSE**). The control notifies its container that the selection has been changed by calling **FireSelectionChanged()**. Finally, the control is invalidated, allowing the paint routine to update the display with the user's changes.

17 Like the mouse button press, we also need to handle the user double-clicking within the control. To do this, use ClassWizard to add a handler for the **WM_LBUTTONDBLCLK** message to **CColorTreeCtrl**. Add the following code to the handler:

```
void CColorTreeCtrl::OnLButtonDblClk(UINT nFlags, CPoint point)
{
   CDC* pdc = GetDC();
   CFont* pOldFont = SelectStockFont(pdc);
   TEXTMETRIC tm;
   pdc->GetTextMetrics(&tm);
   CFont* pFont = pdc->SelectObject(pOldFont);
   ReleaseDC(pdc);

   // Which entry did we land on?
   int nWhich = point.y / tm.tmHeight;

   // If they landed on one, select it.
   if (m_DisplayedNodes.GetSize() > nWhich)
   {
      CTreeNode* pNode = (CTreeNode*)m_DisplayedNodes[nWhich];

      // Just tell the user what they clicked on...
      FireDoubleClick(pNode->GetNodeId());

      // Figure out where the bitmap will be displayed.
```

```
        int x = GetNodeOffset(pNode);

        // Is this hit inside the bitmap?
        if (point.x >= x &&
            point.x <= x + tm.tmMaxCharWidth &&
            pNode->HasChildren())
        {
            // If we get here we clicked in bitmap AND it has children.
            // If it is currently expanded, contract it otherwise
            // expand it
            if (pNode->IsExpanded())
            {
                FireContractNode(pNode->GetNodeId());
                pNode->SetContracted();
            }
            else
            {
                FireExpandNode(pNode->GetNodeId());
                pNode->SetExpanded();
            }
            // Either way, select it
            pNode->Select(FALSE);
        }
        else
        {
            // If it has children, either expand or contract it
            if (pNode->HasChildren())
            {
                if (pNode->IsExpanded())
                    pNode->SetContracted();
                else
                    pNode->SetExpanded();
            }
            pNode->Select(FALSE);
        }
    }
    COleControl::OnLButtonDblClk(nFlags, point);
}
```

The process here is exactly the same as for a mouse button up message; only the results differ. If the selected line was a parent and it was already expanded, the parent node will be contracted. Likewise, if the parent was contracted, it will be expanded. In any case, the control's container is notified via one of the events **FireContractNode()** or **FireExpandNode()**.

18 Because we have insisted that the user be allowed to use the keyboard to perform actions just like the mouse, we need to add another handler for the tree control. Use ClassWizard to add a new handler for the **WM_KEYDOWN** message and add the following code for the handler:

```
void CColorTreeCtrl::OnKeyDown(UINT nChar, UINT nRepCnt, UINT nFlags)
{
    // Get the state of the shift and control keys...
    BOOL bShift = GetKeyState(VK_SHIFT) < 0;
    BOOL bControl = GetKeyState(VK_CONTROL) < 0;
    switch (nChar)
```

```
   {
   case VK_DOWN:    // Next item (if any)
      CaseDown(nChar, nRepCnt, nFlags, bShift, bControl);
      break;

   case VK_UP:    // Previous item (if any)
      CaseUp(nChar, nRepCnt, nFlags, bShift, bControl);
      break;

   case VK_RIGHT:    // Expand current node
      if (m_pLastNode && m_pLastNode->HasChildren())
      {
         if (!m_pLastNode->IsExpanded())
         {
            FireExpandNode(m_pLastNode->GetNodeId());
            m_pLastNode->SetExpanded();
            InvalidateControl();
         }
      }
      break;

   case VK_LEFT:
      if (m_pLastNode && m_pLastNode->HasChildren())
      {
         if (m_pLastNode->IsExpanded())
         {
            FireContractNode(m_pLastNode->GetNodeId());
            m_pLastNode->SetContracted();
            InvalidateControl();
         }
      }
      break;

   case VK_RETURN:    // Select current node
      if (m_pLastNode)
         FireDoubleClick(m_pLastNode->GetNodeId());
      break;

   case VK_F1:    // Help for control...
      break;
   }
   COleControl::OnKeyDown(nChar, nRepCnt, nFlags);
}
```

We've split out the up and down cases to prevent the function from becoming too unwieldy and difficult to read. You should add the declarations for the **`protected`** functions **`CaseDown()`** and **`CaseUp()`** to **`ColorTreeCtl.h`**:

```
   void CaseDown(UINT nChar, UINT nRepCnt, UINT nFlags, BOOL bShift,
                 BOOL bControl);
   void CaseUp(UINT nChar, UINT nRepCnt, UINT nFlags, BOOL bShift,
               BOOL bControl);
```

Now add their implementations to **`ColorTreeCtl.cpp`**.

```
void CColorTreeCtrl::CaseDown(UINT nChar, UINT nRepCnt, UINT nFlags,
                              BOOL bShift, BOOL bControl)
{
   if (m_pLastNode)
   {
      // Get the position of this one...
      long lPosition = GetPositionOfNode(m_pLastNode->GetNodeId());

      while (lPosition < m_NodeList.GetSize() - 1)
      {
         lPosition++;
         CTreeNode* pTempNode = (CTreeNode*)m_NodeList[lPosition];
         if (IsVisible(pTempNode))
         {
            if (!m_bMultiSelect || (!bControl && !bShift))
            {
               if (m_pLastNode->IsSelected())
                  m_pLastNode->Select(FALSE);
               else
                  m_pLastNode->Select(TRUE);
            }
            m_pLastNode = (CTreeNode*)m_NodeList[lPosition];

            if (!m_pLastNode->IsSelected())
               m_pLastNode->Select(TRUE);
            else
               m_pLastNode->Select(FALSE);

            // If this node would not be visible, increase
            // the top node ptr.
            BOOL bFlag = FALSE;

            for (int i = 0; i < m_DisplayedNodes.GetSize(); ++i)
            {
               CTreeNode* pNode = (CTreeNode*)m_DisplayedNodes[i];
               if (pNode->GetNodeId() == m_pLastNode->GetNodeId())
               {
                  bFlag = TRUE;
                  break;
               }
            }
            if (bFlag == FALSE)
               m_lTopNodeID++;

            InvalidateControl();
            break;
         }
      }
   }
}

void CColorTreeCtrl::CaseUp(UINT nChar, UINT nRepCnt, UINT nFlags,
                            BOOL bShift, BOOL bControl)
{
   if (m_pLastNode)
   {
      // Get the position of this one...
      long lPosition = GetPositionOfNode(m_pLastNode->GetNodeId());
```

```
        while (lPosition > 0)
        {
           lPosition--;
           CTreeNode* pTempNode = (CTreeNode*)m_NodeList[lPosition];
           if (IsVisible(pTempNode))
           {
              if (!m_bMultiSelect || (!bControl && !bShift))
                 if (m_pLastNode->IsSelected())
                    m_pLastNode->Select(FALSE);
                 else
                    m_pLastNode->Select(TRUE);
              m_pLastNode = (CTreeNode*)m_NodeList[lPosition];
              if (!m_pLastNode->IsSelected())
                 m_pLastNode->Select(TRUE);
              else
                 m_pLastNode->Select(FALSE);


              // If this node would not be visible, decrease
              // the top node ptr.
              BOOL bFlag = FALSE;

              for (int i = 0; i < m_DisplayedNodes.GetSize(); ++i)
              {
                 CTreeNode* pNode = (CTreeNode*)m_DisplayedNodes[i];
                 if (pNode->GetNodeId() == m_pLastNode->GetNodeId())
                 {
                    bFlag = TRUE;
                    break;
                 }
              }
              if (bFlag == FALSE)
                 m_lTopNodeID--;

              InvalidateControl();
              break;
           }
        }
     }
  }
```

The keys used in the tree control are listed in the following table:

Key	Purpose
Right Arrow	Expand current node (if possible)
Left Arrow	Contract current node (if possible)
Up Arrow	Move current node up one (scrolling tree if necessary)
Down Arrow	Move current node down one (scrolling tree if necessary)

The tree doesn't currently support *Page Up* or *Page Down* keys, but adding support for them would not be difficult and is left as an exercise for the reader.

If you were to implement the control using the code we've just discussed and try the resulting control in the Test Container or in a dialog, you would discover that the tree will not respond to the keys. Why should this be? We added a handler for the **WM_KEYDOWN** message like we are supposed to. We wrote a handler that dealt with the keys as they should be sent to us. Why, then, doesn't it work?

The answer lies in message reflection for ActiveX controls. Because of the way Microsoft chose to implement message reflection, cursor keys (and other non-character keys) never reach the control itself. Instead they are 'reflected' to the parent window of the control. Rather than have this happen, we would prefer to capture the keys in our control. To do this, we need to catch the messages before they are sent on to the parent window.

19 Use ClassWizard to add an override for the **PreTranslateMessage() virtual** function and modify it as follows:

```
BOOL CColorTreeCtrl::PreTranslateMessage(MSG* pMsg)
{
    switch (pMsg->message)
    {
    case WM_KEYDOWN:
    case WM_KEYUP:
        switch (pMsg->wParam)
        {
        case VK_UP:
        case VK_DOWN:
        case VK_LEFT:
        case VK_RIGHT:
            SendMessage(pMsg->message, pMsg->wParam, pMsg->lParam);
            return TRUE;
        }
        break;
    }
    return COleControl::PreTranslateMessage(pMsg);
}
```

This method will force the tree to respond to keystrokes by sending those messages to itself directly. This will allow us to catch the messages before they are routed to the parent. Note that if you add **case**s for any other keystrokes in the **OnKeyDown()** handler, you need to add similar ones here as well. If you don't, they will never reach your message handler.

20 Another of the Windows messages we need to deal with for this control is the **WM_MOUSEMOVE** message. This message will be sent to the control whenever the user moves the mouse inside the control itself. Why would we need to worry about the user moving the mouse around? Because we would like to add the ability to view longer strings than the size of the control would normally allow, without forcing the user to scroll across the control. This was one of the features we wrote about at the design phase, and it's now time to implement it.

First, use ClassWizard to add a handler for **WM_MOUSEMOVE** to **CColorTreeCtrl**. Modify the handler as shown:

```
void CColorTreeCtrl::OnMouseMove(UINT nFlags, CPoint point)
{
```

```
if (m_hWnd == NULL)
{
   COleControl::OnMouseMove(nFlags, point);
   return;
}
// If the point is outside of the window, clear the popup(if it exists)
// and release the capture for the window. Don't forget to clear the
// "current" item so that it will display again when we are finished.
CRect rectClient;
GetClientRect(&rectClient);

if (!rectClient.PtInRect(point))
{
   COleControl::OnMouseMove(nFlags, point);
   if (m_pDispWnd)
   {
      m_pDispWnd->DestroyWindow();
      m_pDispWnd = NULL;
   }
   ReleaseCapture();
   m_lCurrentItem = -1;
   return;
}

CRect rectWindow;
GetWindowRect(&rectWindow);
CDC* pDC = GetDC();
CFont* pOldFont = SelectStockFont(pDC);
TEXTMETRIC tm;
pDC->GetTextMetrics(&tm);
CFont* pFont = pDC->SelectObject(pOldFont);

// Which entry did we land on?
int nWhichItem = point.y / tm.tmHeight;

// If they landed on one, select it.
if (m_DisplayedNodes.GetSize() > nWhichItem)
{
   SetCapture();

   if (m_lCurrentItem != nWhichItem)
   {
      // See if we need to destroy old pop-up window
      if (m_pDispWnd)
      {
         m_pDispWnd->DestroyWindow();
         m_pDispWnd = NULL;
      }

      // Get the text for this item
      CTreeNode* pNode = (CTreeNode*)m_DisplayedNodes[nWhichItem];

      CString strNodeText = pNode->GetText();
      CString strExt = pNode->GetText() + _T("0");

      pDC->SelectObject(pFont);
      CSize sizeText = pDC->GetTextExtent(strExt, strExt.GetLength());
      pDC->SelectObject(pOldFont);
```

```
            int x = GetNodeOffset(pNode) + tm.tmMaxCharWidth;

            // See if the pNode has a bitmap associated with it.
            if (pNode->GetBitmap())
            {
               x += tm.tmMaxCharWidth;
               x += m_nBitmapSpacing;
            }

            // See if the string would extend beyond the extent of the window
            // client area and if the node is visible
            if (x + sizeText.cx > rectClient.Width() && IsVisible(pNode))
            {
               // Okay, create a new window in this place.
               m_pDispWnd = new CPopupTip(m_strPopupClassName, this);
               m_pDispWnd->SetFont(pFont);
               m_pDispWnd->SetDisplay(strNodeText);

               // And display the item at the window point for the start of
               // this list box item.
               CPoint ptPopup(rectWindow.left + x - 2, rectWindow.top +
                                    nWhichItem * tm.tmHeight);
               m_pDispWnd->PopItUp(ptPopup, TTIPS_SQUARESTYLE);
            }
            m_lCurrentItem = nWhichItem;
         }
      }
      else
         if (m_pDispWnd)
         {
            m_pDispWnd->DestroyWindow();
            m_pDispWnd = NULL;
            m_lCurrentItem = -1;
         }

      // Remember to free DC!
      ReleaseDC(pDC);

   COleControl::OnMouseMove(nFlags, point);
}
```

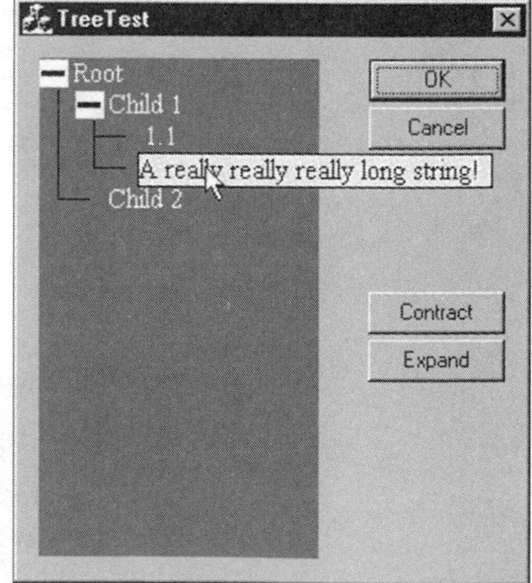

Although the code for this handler looks complex, it isn't really that bad. First, we find out where the mouse is at the moment. This happens in the same way that we found the information in the single- and double-click cases.

Next, we see whether there's a node under the mouse. If there is an item at that position, we get the text for that node and see whether the string is too wide for the control. If it is too wide, you will see a window appear over the item showing the complete string. This uses a special window class that we'll look at shortly.

If the area under the mouse isn't the current item, or it isn't a long string, we simply destroy the old pop-up window (assuming one existed) and set the pointer to **NULL** to indicate that the window isn't visible anymore.

21 Now we'll add the pop-up window class to the code. We'll examine this class in much more detail in the next chapter, but for now we'll just show the complete code for it so that you can get this example to compile.

Create two new text files and save them in the project directory as **PopupTip.h** and **PopupTip.cpp**. Insert **PopupTip.cpp** into the project so that it will get compiled along with everything else and add **#include "PopupTip.h"** to the top of **ColorTreeCtl.h**. Now add the following text to **PopupTip.h**:

```
// PopupTip.h : header file
//

#define TTIPS_SQUARESTYLE    0
#define TTIPS_ROUNDSTYLE     1

/////////////////////////////////////////////////////////////////////////////
// CPopupTip window

class CPopupTip : public CWnd
{
// Construction
public:
   CPopupTip(CString& strClass, CWnd* pParent);

// Attributes
public:

// Operations
public:
   void SetDisplay(const CString &strDisplay);
   void SetFont(CFont* pFont);
   void SetSelected(BOOL bSelected);
   BOOL PopItUp(POINT point, UINT nNewStyle);

// Overrides
   // ClassWizard generated virtual function overrides
   //{{AFX_VIRTUAL(CPopupTip)
   protected:
   virtual BOOL PreCreateWindow(CREATESTRUCT& cs);
   virtual void PostNcDestroy();
   //}}AFX_VIRTUAL

// Implementation
public:
   virtual ~CPopupTip();

private:
   UINT m_nStyleFlag;
   CWnd* m_pParent;
   BOOL m_bSelected;
   CFont* m_pFont;
   CString m_strDisplay;
```

```
    CString m_strClass;

    // Generated message map functions
protected:
    //{{AFX_MSG(CPopupTip)
    afx_msg void OnPaint();
    afx_msg BOOL OnEraseBkgnd(CDC* pDC);
    afx_msg void OnLButtonDblClk(UINT nFlags, CPoint point);
    afx_msg void OnLButtonDown(UINT nFlags, CPoint point);
    afx_msg int OnMouseActivate(CWnd* pDesktopWnd, UINT nHitTest, UINT message);
    //}}AFX_MSG
    DECLARE_MESSAGE_MAP()
};

/////////////////////////////////////////////////////////////////////////////
```

The code that needs to go into **PopupTip.cpp** looks like this:

```
// PopupTip.cpp : implementation file
//

#include "stdafx.h"
#include "ColorTree.h"
#include "PopupTip.h"

#ifdef _DEBUG
#define new DEBUG_NEW
#undef THIS_FILE
static char THIS_FILE[] = __FILE__;
#endif

/////////////////////////////////////////////////////////////////////////////
// CPopupTip

CPopupTip::CPopupTip(CString& strClass, CWnd* pParent)
{
    m_strClass = strClass;
    m_pParent = pParent;
    m_bSelected = FALSE;
    m_pFont = NULL;
}

CPopupTip::~CPopupTip()
{ }

BEGIN_MESSAGE_MAP(CPopupTip, CWnd)
    //{{AFX_MSG_MAP(CPopupTip)
    ON_WM_PAINT()
    ON_WM_ERASEBKGND()
    ON_WM_LBUTTONDBLCLK()
    ON_WM_LBUTTONDOWN()
    ON_WM_MOUSEACTIVATE()
    //}}AFX_MSG_MAP
END_MESSAGE_MAP()

/////////////////////////////////////////////////////////////////////////////
// CPopupTip hand-coded functions
```

```
BOOL CPopupTip::PopItUp(POINT point, UINT nNewStyle)
{
   if (nNewStyle < TTIPS_SQUARESTYLE || nNewStyle > TTIPS_ROUNDSTYLE)
      nNewStyle = TTIPS_SQUARESTYLE;

   int  nBorder = 2;

   // Get the width and height of the window based on length of text
   CWindowDC dc(NULL);
   CFont* pOldFont = dc.SelectObject(m_pFont);
   CString strExt = m_strDisplay + "0";
   CSize sizeText = dc.GetTextExtent(strExt, strExt.GetLength());
   dc.SelectObject(pOldFont);

   // See of the box is off the screen to the right.  If it is,
   // move it back onto the screen.
   int nScreenRight = GetSystemMetrics(SM_CXSCREEN);
   if (point.x + sizeText.cx > nScreenRight - 6)
      point.x = nScreenRight - sizeText.cx - 6;

   if (CreateEx(0, m_strClass, NULL, WS_POPUP,
               point.x, point.y, sizeText.cx, sizeText.cy + 2,
               m_pParent->m_hWnd, 0))
   {
      ShowWindow(SW_SHOWNOACTIVATE);
      m_nStyleFlag = nNewStyle;
      return TRUE;
   }
   else
      return FALSE;
}

void CPopupTip::SetDisplay(const CString &strDisplay)
{ m_strDisplay = strDisplay; }

void CPopupTip::SetFont(CFont* pFont)
{ m_pFont = pFont; }

void CPopupTip::SetSelected(BOOL bSelected)
{ m_bSelected = bSelected; }

/////////////////////////////////////////////////////////////////////////////
// CPopupTip message handlers

void CPopupTip::OnPaint()
{
   CPaintDC dc(this); // device context for painting
   CRect rectClient;
   GetClientRect(&rectClient);

   // Draw the rectangle box for the tip
   CBrush brYellow(RGB(255, 255, 128));  // Standard tool tip yellow
   CBrush brSelected(::GetSysColor(COLOR_HIGHLIGHT));  // Usually blue
   CBrush* pOldBrush;

   if (m_bSelected)
      pOldBrush = dc.SelectObject(&brSelected);
   else
```

```
      pOldBrush = dc.SelectObject(&brYellow);

   if(m_nStyleFlag == TTIPS_ROUNDSTYLE)
   {
      CPoint ptEllipse(5, 10);
      dc.RoundRect(&rectClient, ptEllipse);
   }
   else
      dc.Rectangle(&rectClient);
   dc.SelectObject(pOldBrush);

   CFont* pOldFont = NULL;
   if (m_pFont)
      pOldFont = dc.SelectObject(m_pFont);

   // Force colors
   int nBkMode = dc.SetBkMode(TRANSPARENT);

   COLORREF clrText;
   if (!m_bSelected)
      clrText = dc.SetTextColor(RGB(0, 0, 0));
   else
      clrText = dc.SetTextColor(::GetSysColor(COLOR_HIGHLIGHTTEXT));

   dc.DrawText(m_strDisplay, -1, &rectClient,
               DT_LEFT | DT_VCENTER | DT_SINGLELINE);

   dc.SetTextColor(clrText);
   dc.SetBkMode(nBkMode);

   if (pOldFont)
      dc.SelectObject(pOldFont);

   // Do not call CWnd::OnPaint() for painting messages
}

BOOL CPopupTip::OnEraseBkgnd(CDC* pDC)
{ return TRUE; }

BOOL CPopupTip::PreCreateWindow(CREATESTRUCT& cs)
{ return TRUE; }

void CPopupTip::PostNcDestroy()
{ delete this; }

void CPopupTip::OnLButtonDblClk(UINT nFlags, CPoint point)
{
   m_pParent->GetParent()->PostMessage(WM_COMMAND,
                     MAKEWPARAM(m_pParent->GetDlgCtrlID(), LBN_DBLCLK),
                     (LPARAM)m_pParent->m_hWnd);
   CWnd::OnLButtonDblClk(nFlags, point);
}

void CPopupTip::OnLButtonDown(UINT nFlags, CPoint point)
{
   m_pParent->SendMessage(WM_LBUTTONDOWN, nFlags,
                           MAKEWORD(point.x, point.y));
   CWnd::OnLButtonDown(nFlags, point);
```

```
}

int CPopupTip::OnMouseActivate(CWnd* pDesktopWnd, UINT nHitTest,
                               UINT message)
{ return MA_NOACTIVATE; }
```

22 The final Windows message our control needs to handle is the **WM_VSCROLL** message. This will allow the user to navigate through the tree when that tree is longer than the window it is displayed in. Since this is a fairly common occurrence, we need to deal with it. In our paint routine, we handled enabling and disabling the scrollbar based on whether there were enough entries to warrant a scrollbar, so in the **OnVScroll()** handler we can just scroll the window as necessary.

Use ClassWizard to add a handler to **CColorTreeCtrl** for the **WM_VSCROLL** message. Modify the handler as shown:

```
void CColorTreeCtrl::OnVScroll(UINT nSBCode, UINT nPos,
                               CScrollBar* pScrollBar)
{
   CDC* pdc = GetDC();
   CFont* pOldFont = SelectStockFont(pdc);
   TEXTMETRIC tm;
   pdc->GetTextMetrics(&tm);
   CFont* pFont = pdc->SelectObject(pOldFont);
   ReleaseDC(pdc);

   switch (nSBCode)
   {
   case SB_LINEDOWN:
      if (m_lTopNodeID < m_NodeList.GetSize())
      {
         m_lTopNodeID ++;
         ScrollWindow(0, -tm.tmHeight);
      }
      break;
   case SB_LINEUP:
      if (m_lTopNodeID)
      {
         m_lTopNodeID--;
         ScrollWindow(0, tm.tmHeight);
      }
      break;
   }
   UpdateWindow();
   COleControl::OnVScroll(nSBCode, nPos, pScrollBar);
}
```

In this handler, we determine the kind of scrolling done. If the user wants to scroll the window up, we will receive a **SB_LINEDOWN** message (intuitive, isn't it?). In this case, we determine if the top line displayed is the last line of the tree. If not, we increment the starting line (top line) and scroll the window up one line.

Alternatively, the user could desire the window to scroll backwards, in which case the window receives a **SB_LINEUP** message. In this case, we simply check to see if we are already at the top. If not, the top line is decremented and the tree window scrolled down one line.

23 Once we have handled the scroll messages, we're done processing the Windows messages to be sent to the control. As far as the control class is concerned, that only leaves writing the utility functions we need to process the information, search through the nodes and do the things that need to be done.

The first routine we will write is a generic function that will permit you to draw a bitmap at a given location in a window. Create a new file called **DrawBitmap.h** and save it in the same directory as the rest of the project. Add **#include "DrawBitmap.h"** to the top of **ColorTreeCtl.h**.

Add the code for the **DrawBitmap()** function into **DrawBitmap.h**:

```
void DrawBitmap(CDC* pdc, CBitmap* pBitmap, int x, int y, int w, int h)
{
   // Create a compatible dc
   CDC dc;

   dc.CreateCompatibleDC(pdc);
   dc.SelectObject(pBitmap);

   // Get the dimensions of the bitmap
   BITMAP bm;
   pBitmap->GetObject(sizeof(BITMAP), (LPTSTR)&bm);

   // Now, draw the pBitmap at the specified location
   pdc->StretchBlt(x, y, w, h, &dc, 0, 0, bm.bmWidth, bm.bmHeight,
                   SRCCOPY);
}
```

The function is quite straightforward and should work with anything that needs to have a bitmap drawn (including buttons, list boxes, form views, and other MFC windows). The caller passes in a pointer to a device context, a pointer to a bitmap object and four values representing the rectangle in which to display the bitmap. A new device context is created which is compatible (number of colors, bit planes, color or monochrome and so forth) with the desired device context. The bitmap object is then 'selected' into the device context, effectively making the device context a large bitmap containing the desired image. Finally, the bitmap is stretched into the requested size on the original window device context using the **StretchBlt()** function.

24 Now for a bunch of utility functions. Add the following **protected** function declarations to the **ColorTreeCtl.h** file:

```
   CTreeNode* GetNodeById(long lNodeID);
   long GetPositionOfNode(long lNodeID);
   BOOL IsParent(long lParentNodeID, long lNodeID);
   int GetNodeOffset(CTreeNode* node);
   BOOL IsVisible(CTreeNode* pNode);
   BOOL IsExpanded(CTreeNode* pNode);
   int GetColumnWidth(int nColumn);
   void SetPlusBitmap(LPUNKNOWN pBitmap);
   void SetMinusBitmap(LPUNKNOWN pBitmap);
```

We'll look at each of these functions in turn. The first function returns a pointer to a given tree node identified by its ID.

```
CTreeNode* CColorTreeCtrl::GetNodeById(long lNodeID)
{
   for (long i = 0; i < m_NodeList.GetSize(); ++i)
   {
      CTreeNode* pNode = (CTreeNode*)m_NodeList[i];
      if (pNode->GetNodeId() == lNodeID)
         return pNode;
   }
   return NULL;
}
```

GetPositionOfNode() returns the index into the **m_NodeList** array for a given node identified by its ID.

```
long CColorTreeCtrl::GetPositionOfNode(long lNodeID)
{
   for (long i = 0; i < m_NodeList.GetSize(); ++i)
   {
      CTreeNode* pNode = (CTreeNode*)m_NodeList[i];
      if (pNode->GetNodeId() == lNodeID)
         return i;
   }
   return -1;
}
```

We use these functions to find a given node in the object at run time, so that we can modify or retrieve its attributes.

The next function we will define is interesting because it's a recursive function. If you recall from your computer science school days, a recursive function is one which calls itself repeatedly until a desired end result is found. Although recursive functions can be dangerous (due to the potential lack of an exit and the rate at which they consume memory) they can also be extremely useful under the right circumstances. Here's an example of such a circumstance and the code which implements the function:

```
// Determines if a given node is (at any level) a parent of this node
// WARNING: This method is recursive.
BOOL CColorTreeCtrl::IsParent(long lParentNodeID, long lNodeID)
{
   CTreeNode* pNode = GetNodeById(lNodeID);

   // Have we reached a root?
   if (pNode->GetParent() == -1)
      return FALSE;

   // Is this the parent?
   if (pNode->GetParent() == lParentNodeID)
      return TRUE;

   // Nope. Back up a level and check again
   return IsParent(lParentNodeID, pNode->GetParent());
}
```

As you can see, the function simply tracks backward through the node list until it encounters a node which is either the parent of the requested node, or its root node. In either case, that node will be marked and the result returned.

We'll implement a simple utility function next, **GetNodeOffset()**. This function returns the indent distance at which to display a given node. The node is examined and its parent found. Once there are no more parents for a node, we are at a root node. The number of parents found between the original node and the root node multiplied by the indent distance determines where to start the requested node.

```
int CColorTreeCtrl::GetNodeOffset(CTreeNode* node)
{
   // How does this work? Easy. Keep examining the parent node
   // of the child until we find the beginning. That number is
   // is used to determine the x-offset
   int nOffsets = 0;
   int nParent = node->GetParent();

   while (nParent != -1)
   {
      nOffsets ++;

      // Get parent node
      CTreeNode* pNode = GetNodeById(nParent);

      nParent = pNode->GetParent();
   }

   return nOffsets * m_nIndentDistance;
}
```

Next up are two simple methods that simply indicate whether a given node ID is visible on the tree and whether or not a given node is expanded.

```
BOOL CColorTreeCtrl::IsVisible(CTreeNode* pNode)
{
   // Root nodes are always visible
   if (pNode->GetParent() == -1)
      return TRUE;

   // Otherwise, it depends on whether our parent is contracted
   return IsExpanded(GetNodeById(pNode->GetParent()));
}

BOOL CColorTreeCtrl::IsExpanded(CTreeNode* pNode)
{
   // Is the node contracted?
   if (pNode->IsContracted())
      return FALSE;

   // No. If it has a parent, check it
   if (pNode->GetParent() != -1)
      return IsExpanded(GetNodeById(pNode->GetParent()));

   // Nope. Must be open
   return TRUE;
}
```

Our next utility method is the routine which is called to retrieve the current width of a given column for multicolumn display nodes. This routine checks to see if a given column is defined yet, and if not returns a default value for the column width.

```
int CColorTreeCtrl::GetColumnWidth(int nColumn)
{
   if (m_ColumnWidths.GetSize() <= nColumn)
   {
      if (nColumn == 0) // First column
         return 150;
      else              // Any other column
         return 50;
   }
   return m_ColumnWidths[nColumn];
}
```

Note that we have temporarily set the width of the first column to 150 pixels and all other columns to 50 pixels.

The final two functions necessary are the ones to allow the user to add a plus or minus bitmap of their own. In this case, we need to do two things. First, we need to get rid of the existing bitmap if we allocated one. This is necessary to avoid memory leaks. If the user previously set a bitmap, we don't want to get rid of it here, or later in the destructor, since we don't want to kill off memory that doesn't belong to us. The second thing we need to do is to assign the new bitmap and make sure that it won't get killed off later. Here's the code for the function to set the new bitmap for a 'closed' (plus) node, **SetPlusBitmap()**:

```
void CColorTreeCtrl::SetPlusBitmap(LPUNKNOWN pBitmap)
{
   // Do we still have our allocated bitmap
   if ( m_bPlusBitmap )
   {
      // Yes. Delete it
      if (m_pbmpPlus)
         delete m_pbmpPlus;
   }

   // Now use the one that the user passes in
   m_pbmpPlus = (CBitmap *)pBitmap;

   // Make sure we don't try to delete it
   m_bPlusBitmap = FALSE;
}
```

In this case, we check to see if we already have an assigned bitmap from the user. If we do, the flag **m_bPlusBitmap** will be set to **FALSE**. If not, this is our own bitmap and we should delete it to avoid the memory leak. Here, similarly, is the **SetMinusBitmap()** function:

```
void CColorTreeCtrl::SetMinusBitmap(LPUNKNOWN pBitmap)
{
   // Do we still have our allocated bitmap
   if ( m_bMinusBitmap )
   {
```

```
        // Yes. Delete it
        if (m_pbmpMinus)
            delete m_pbmpMinus;
    }

    // Now use the one that the user passes in
    m_pbmpMinus = (CBitmap *)pBitmap;

    // Make sure we don't try to delete it
    m_bMinusBitmap = FALSE;
}
```

In order to accommodate the changes for the bitmap changes, add the following lines to the private section of your header file:

```
    BOOL m_bPlusBitmap;
    BOOL m_bMinusBitmap;
```

And it's probably a good idea to initialize these variables at the start of the source file, too:

```
    // Create the bitmaps and load them
    m_pbmpPlus = new CBitmap;
    m_pbmpPlus->LoadBitmap(IDB_PLUS);
    m_bPlusBitmap = TRUE;

    m_pbmpMinus = new CBitmap;
    m_pbmpMinus->LoadBitmap(IDB_MINUS);
    m_bMinusBitmap = TRUE;
```

25 And finally, modify the destructor for the class to read as follows:

```
CColorTreeCtrl::~CColorTreeCtrl()
{
    if (m_bPlusBitmap && m_pbmpPlus)
        delete m_pbmpPlus;
    if (m_bMinusBitmap && m_pbmpMinus)
        delete m_pbmpMinus;
    RemoveAllNodes();
    m_ColumnWidths.RemoveAll();
}
```

26 That takes care of all of the code for the control itself. The only remaining issue is the **CTreeNode** object we have been referring to all along. We will create that class now. First, create a new text file and save it as **TreeNode.h**. Add **#include "TreeNode.h"** to the top of **ColorTreeCtl.h**.

To make life simple, we'll add the complete definition for this class and all its functions in the header file. Since the functions are all very simple, it's OK that they will all be implicitly **inline**, but this way of laying out your code is far from ideal. If you intend to adapt or extend this example, you should probably take the time to split this class into a proper source and header file. Here's the code that needs to be in **TreeNode.h**:

```
#ifndef WROX_TREENODE_H
#define WROX_TREENODE_H

// This class implements a single node in the tree.
class CTreeNode : public CObject
{
private:
   COLORREF m_clrBack;  // Background color of node
   COLORREF m_clrText;  // Text color of node
   CString m_strText;   // Text of node
   CBitmap* m_pBitmap;  // Bitmap to display for node.
   BOOL m_bSelected;    // Flag to indicate if this node is selected
   BOOL m_bExpanded;    // Flag to indicate if children are expanded
   int m_nChildren;     // Number of children for node
   long m_lParentNodeID;// Number of parent node for this node
   long m_lNodeID;      // Identifier for this node.
   long m_lUserData;    // User data associated with this node
   CStringArray m_ColumnText;  // Column text

public:
   CTreeNode(const CString& strText, long lParentNodeID = -1)
   {
      m_strText = strText;              // Set text for this node
      m_clrBack = RGB(255, 255, 255);   // Default is white
      m_clrText = RGB(0, 0, 0);         // Default is black
      m_pBitmap = NULL;                 // No specialized bitmap to display
      m_bSelected = FALSE;              // Default to NOT selected
      m_nChildren = 0;                  // Default to leaf node
      m_lParentNodeID = lParentNodeID; // Parent node.
      m_bExpanded = TRUE;               // Assume starting out expanded
      m_lUserData = 0;
   }

   // Destructor for class
   virtual ~CTreeNode()
   {
   }

   // Method to set background color of node
   void SetBackColor(COLORREF clrBack)
   { m_clrBack = clrBack; }

   // Method to set foreground color of node
   void SetTextColor(COLORREF clrText)
   { m_clrText = clrText; }

   // Method to change text of node
   void SetText(CString& strText)
   { m_strText = strText; }

   // Method to set a bitmap for the node
   void SetBitmap(CBitmap* pBitmap)
   { m_pBitmap = pBitmap; }

   // Method to return the parent number node of this node
   long GetParent()
   { return m_lParentNodeID; }
```

```
// Method to assign a new parent to a node
void SetParent(long lParentNodeID)
{ m_lParentNodeID = lParentNodeID; }

// Method to indicate if this node has children
BOOL HasChildren()
{
   if (m_nChildren)
      return TRUE;
   else
      return FALSE;
}

// Method to return the text for the node
CString& GetText()
{ return m_strText; }

// Method to return the current foreground color
COLORREF GetTextColor()
{ return m_clrText; }

COLORREF GetBackColor()
{ return m_clrBack; }

// Method to return the current bitmap for this node
CBitmap* GetBitmap()
{ return m_pBitmap; }

// Method to add a child to this node
void AddChild()
{ m_nChildren++; }

// Method to remove a child from this node
void RemoveChild()
{ m_nChildren--; }

void SetNodeId(long lNodeID)
{ m_lNodeID = lNodeID; }

long GetNodeId()
{ return m_lNodeID; }

BOOL IsSelected()
{ return m_bSelected; }

void Select(BOOL bFlag)
{ m_bSelected = bFlag; }

BOOL IsExpanded()
{  return m_bExpanded; }

void SetExpanded()
{ m_bExpanded = TRUE; }

BOOL IsContracted()
{ return !m_bExpanded; }

void SetContracted()
```

```
    { m_bExpanded = FALSE; }

    void SetUserData(long lUserData)
    { m_lUserData = lUserData; }

    long GetUserData()
    { return m_lUserData; }

    void AddColumn(const CString& strText)
    { m_ColumnText.Add(strText); }

    CString& GetColumnText(int nColumn)
    { return m_ColumnText[nColumn]; }

    int NumColumns()
    {  return m_ColumnText.GetSize(); }

};
#endif
```

27 That's all you need do for a fully functioning tree. You could use the control now, but we'll just round out our implementation by adding the property pages to the control. This will allow programmers to modify the control's properties more easily at design time. We'll add controls and code to handle three properties: the indent distance, bitmap padding, and whether lines are drawn between nodes.

Open the dialog resource with the ID **`IDD_PROPPAGE_COLORTREE`**, and delete the static text item. Add two edit controls, **`IDC_INDENT`** and **`IDC_SPACING`**, and give them suitable labels. Also add a checkbox, **`IDC_DRAWLINES`**; you should end up with a dialog resource looking like this:

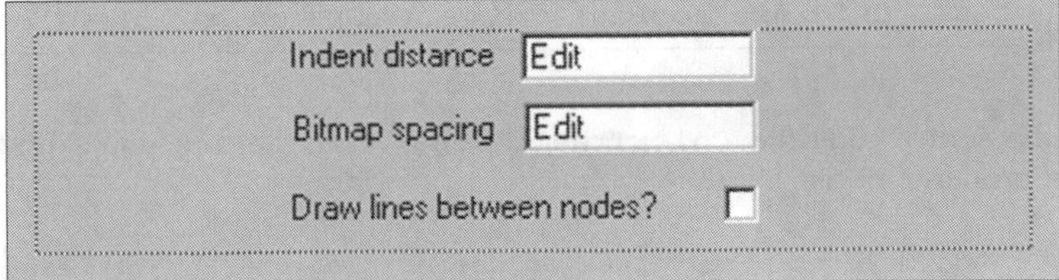

We next need to add exchange member variables for these controls to connect them with the properties of our control. To do this, *Ctrl*-double-click on each of the controls in the dialog editor (not the static text fields) to open ClassWizard's Add Member Variables dialog. Fill in the fields as shown in the table below:

Control ID	Member variable name	Category	Variable type	Optional OLE property name
`IDC_INDENT`	m_nIndentDistance	Value	short	IndentDistance
`IDC_SPACING`	m_nBitmapSpacing	Value	short	BitmapSpacing
`IDC_DRAWLINES`	m_bDrawNodeLines	Value	BOOL	DrawNodeLines

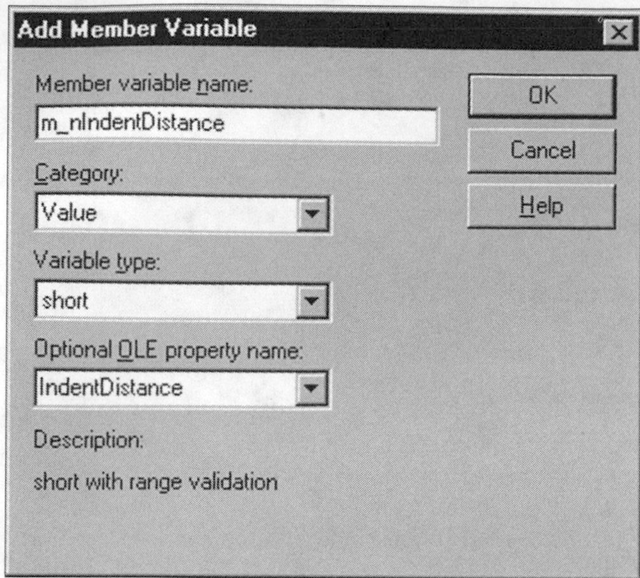

That's all we need to do for our custom properties, but let's not forget to add pages for the stock properties that we added to the control.

28 There are three stock property pages, which are available for use by any control:

Property Page ID	Description
CLSID_CColorPropPage	Page to allow setting of color properties
CLSID_CFontPropPage	Page to allow font selection
CLSID_CPicturePropPage	Page to set picture properties

Open the source code file **ColorTreeCtl.cpp**. Near the top, you'll find the code which sets up the property pages for the control:

```
// TODO: Add more property pages as needed. Remember to increase the count
BEGIN_PROPPAGEIDS(CCTreeCtrl, 1)
    PROPPAGEID(CCTreePropPage::guid)
END_PROPPAGEIDS(CCTreeCtrl)
```

The **BEGIN_** and **END_PROPPAGEIDS** macros are used to surround one or more **PROPPAGEID** declarations, each of which defines a property page which will be used by this control. The default is to have just one page, the one created by ControlWizard.

In order to add another one, add a new **PROPPAGEID** declaration, giving it the ID of one of the stock property pages. Remember to increment the count in the **BEGIN_PROPPAGEIDS** macro. We'll actually add two property pages, one for the **ForeColor** and **BackColor** properties, and one for the **Font** property.

```
BEGIN_PROPPAGEIDS(CColorTreeCtrl, 3)
    PROPPAGEID(CColorTreePropPage::guid)
```

```
    PROPPAGEID(CLSID_CFontPropPage)
    PROPPAGEID(CLSID_CColorPropPage)
END_PROPPAGEIDS(CColorTreeCtrl)
```

When you display the control's property pages at design time, you should now see all these pages displayed on the property sheet.

Now that we've built the control, let's develop a simple application to show it in action.

TRY IT OUT - Test the Color Tree Control

1 Start Developer Studio and generate a new project workspace using MFC AppWizard (exe). Call the application TreeTest and save it wherever you like. Choose to create a Dialog based application on Step 1 of the wizard and make sure that you check the option for OLE controls support on Step 2, otherwise you'll find it pretty hard to compile the test application! You can leave all the other options and finish creating the application.

If you need to add OLE control support to a previously created application, you can use the component called OLE Control containment, which you'll find in the Component Gallery, to add it for you. Note that using Component Gallery to add OLE controls to your project will not automatically add the OLE support that you need to get your project to compile.

2 Now we need to create the wrapper classes for our ColorTree control, so activate Component Gallery and switch to its OLE Controls page. The OLE Controls page will display all the registered OLE/ActiveX controls on your system. Since the build process for controls also registers them, you should find all the Wrox controls that you have built through the course of this book.

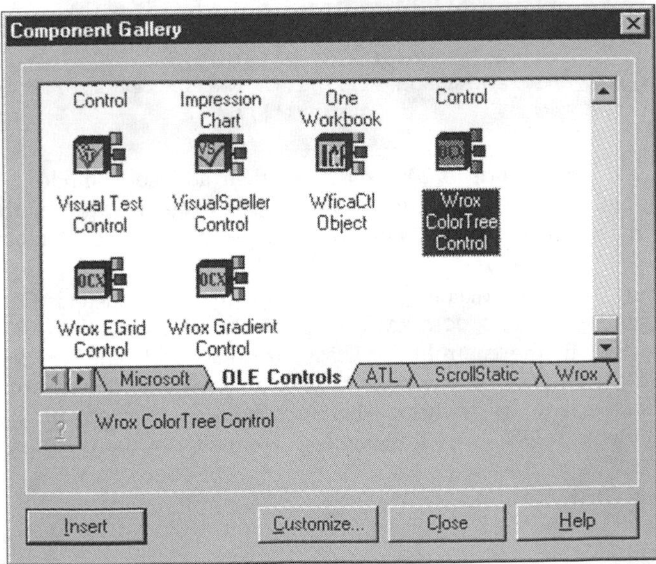

Select the Wrox ColorTree Control from the list and press Insert. The Gallery will ask you to confirm the classes that you want added to the project. Press OK, and close the Gallery.

Why has the Component Gallery added these classes? ActiveX controls talk to their containers using OLE automation, and that means using the **IDispatch** COM interface in general, and the **Invoke()** method in particular. What the Component Gallery does is to add a class which wraps all the automation methods you can use for communicating with the control, so that you don't have to get involved with the low-level COM stuff (or even the low-level MFC stuff!). This makes using a control seem just like using any other C++ class.

3 Now open up the **IDD_TREETEST_DIALOG** resource. You'll notice that a new button has been added to the dialog editor's control palette, representing our control. Click on the button, and use it to place a control on the dialog.

As it stands, the control is invisible when not selected. We can change the properties of the control, such as background color, by right-clicking on it, and selecting Properties from the menu which pops up. You will see the property pages for the control, which you can use to define many of the control's properties at run time. By selecting the Colors tab and BackColor in the Property Name combo box, you can select a background color for the control. When you dismiss the property sheet, you should see the control displaying in your chosen color.

4 Now add a variable to the dialog class to represent the control. The easiest way to do this is to *Ctrl*-double-click on the control in the dialog editor and fill in the Add Member Variable dialog. Give the variable the name **m_ctlTree**.

5 We want to add code to the dialog to fill the control with data, so add some code to **CTreeTestDlg::OnInitDialog()**. Use the following code as a guide:

```
// TODO: Add extra initialization here
m_ctlTree.SetIndentDistance(20L);
m_lRootID = m_ctlTree.AddNode(-1, _T("Root"));
long l1 = m_ctlTree.AddNode(m_lRootID, _T("Child 1"));
long l2 = m_ctlTree.AddNode(m_lRootID, _T("Child 2"));
long l3 = m_ctlTree.AddNode(l1, _T("1.1"));
long l4 = m_ctlTree.AddNode(l1, _T("A really really really long
                                   string!"));
```

We set the indent distance to 20 pixels, and then add some nodes. You'll also need to add the **long** member variable **m_lRootID** as a **private** member of the dialog class. We store this value in the class as we'll want to use it from a couple of other functions.

6 Add two buttons to the dialog, give them captions Expand and Contract, and set their IDs to **IDC_EXPAND** and **IDC_CONTRACT** respectively. We'll use these buttons to expand and contract the tree in the control. Use ClassWizard to add handlers for the button click events of each of these (the quickest way is to *Ctrl*-double-click on each of the buttons in the dialog editor). What we'll do is to check whether a node is selected. If so, we'll operate on that one. If nothing is selected, we'll expand or contract the root.

```
void CTreeTestDlg::OnContract()
{
    long lNodeID;

    // See how many nodes are selected. For a single selection tree,
    // it will be 0 or 1
    long nSel = m_ctlTree.GetNumSelectedNodes();

    // Contract either the root, or the selected node
    if (nSel == 0)
        m_ctlTree.Contract(m_lRootID);
    else
    {
        long l = m_ctlTree.GetSelectedNodes(&lNodeID, 1);
        m_ctlTree.Contract(lNodeID);
    }
}

void CTreeTestDlg::OnExpand()
{
    long lNodeID;

    // See how many nodes are selected. For a single selection tree,
    // it will be 0 or 1
    long nSel = m_ctlTree.GetNumSelectedNodes();

    // Expand either the root, or the selected node
    if (nSel == 0)
        m_ctlTree.Expand(m_lRootID);
    else
    {
        long l = m_ctlTree.GetSelectedNodes(&lNodeID, 1);
        m_ctlTree.Expand(lNodeID);
    }
}
```

Now you can build and test the application, and check that you can manipulate the tree control. Try out some other tests on it before using it in your own applications.

Comparing the MFC and ActiveX Solutions

The most interesting relationship between the two solutions given in this chapter must be the fact that both a tree control and a list control are provided as standard with Windows, yet we've still found a need for functionality that they don't provide. In the first case, we extended the functionality of the common list box by adding a drag-and-drop feature to it. In the second case, however, our tree control represents a complete rewrite of the common tree control with extra features.

If it's so easy to extend an existing control, why didn't we simply subclass the common tree control to add the functionality we wanted? The answer is that it's quite easy to extend a list box to do considerably more than the original programmer intended. This shows how flexible the controls built into Windows can be.

Certainly the programmer who wrote the original list box never even thought of the idea of dragging and dropping data between list boxes, otherwise they would have added it to the control. On the other hand, the control was open-ended and allowed us 'hooks' into its internals which allowed the extension to be possible.

Sadly, some other common controls are not as well thought out. Microsoft was rushed into delivering some of the functionality of Windows and it shows badly in the common control area. The tree control and, as we saw in the last chapter, the list control do not lend themselves well to extension. We had to rewrite the entire tree control from scratch to accomplish what we needed.

If there's one thing you should take from this book, it is the knowledge that you can be a hero (or at least a well-liked programmer) in the eyes of those that come after you if you allow them to extend the things you have done with minimal effort. Hopefully, by placing the source code for this tree control in the hands of those that have to use it, we will do our bit towards eliminating the problem once and for all.

Summary

Let's review what we have discovered up to this point:

- While some Windows common controls can be extended to do more than they were originally intended to, others require more work to extend than to rewrite from scratch.
- Controls should be designed and implemented for maximum reuse and allow as much flexibility as possible in order to extend their usefulness and usability.
- Utility functions, such as drawing a bitmap, should be as simple and easy to use as possible and should be placed in a library for reuse.
- Ease of use and flexibility of display are as important to users as functionality. If a user can't figure out how to use a control or how to make it do what he or she wants, then that user will find another control to use.

Things to Try

Here are a few 'homework' assignments that you might try to gain a fuller understanding of how ActiveX controls work.

- Modify the drag-and-drop list box to support different colors for each list entry.
- Modify the drag-and-drop list box to allow items to be dropped into other window types, such as edit boxes. You will probably want to simply allow the windows which support the **`SetWindowText()`** function call to be used.
- Modify the tree control to allow columns to be resized by the user. You might consider using the Windows header control and resize the columns when the user resizes the header.
- Modify the tree control to allow modifiable fonts for each node of the tree. You will also need to modify the code which determines which node is selected. This might be a good time to write another method for the control.

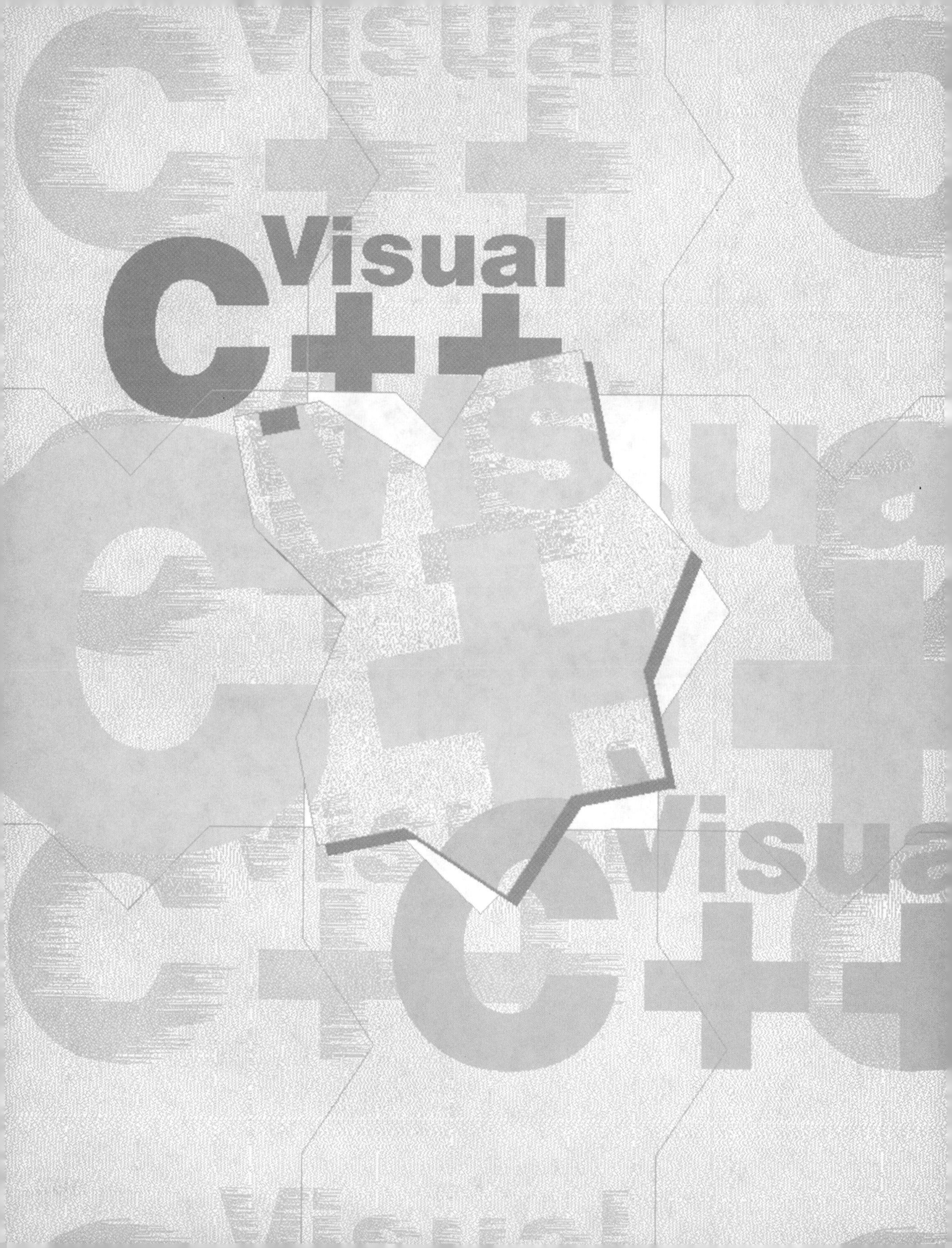
Visual
C++

Total Quality Applications

The biggest difference between programs written today and those written ten years ago is in the area of user interface design. While a program once needed to be only functional to gain a huge following, programs today need to be more than just functional, they also need to provide a complete user-interface solution.

When we talk about a complete user interface, we're talking about more than just applying the common Windows controls to a dialog. Even the simplest Windows controls, such as the list box or edit box, can be extended by programmers to be both more usable and more aesthetically pleasing. Excellent examples can be found in the Microsoft Developer Network Library and Intuit's Quicken program. Both of these programs provide a higher level of user interface by extending simple controls in more usable and pleasing fashions.

In this chapter we'll examine two simple controls that you can add to your own applications to make them more user-friendly. First, we'll look at a control similar to the MSDN table of contents control. If you have never used the Microsoft Developer Network CD, the table of contents is displayed in a simple list tree. This tree, however, contains many entries that are far too wide for the display of the text. Rather than having the list box entries wrap-around, which makes the display unreadable, or forcing the reader to use a horizontal scrollbar to scroll the text (which is annoying and still makes it hard to read long entries), Microsoft chose to display a small pop-up window over the position of the list entry whenever the user's mouse is held over such a list item.

We will base our example on the standard Windows list box. This sort of control extension is an excellent example. The list box behaves like a normal list because the control is really just a subclassed Windows list box, programmers can simply use the new control anywhere they would use a normal list box. This leads to better programs and more reuse without any pain or large overhead.

The second control we will examine in this chapter is a gradient control. You have seen hundreds of examples of color gradients in installation programs. The color gradient is used for the background of the installation window, giving it the appearance of a graduated background which 'fades' from blue to black down the window. We will provide a control to create this effect. Gradient controls are quite easy to write and provide a wonderful way to make the screen look prettier and more professional at little cost to the programmer.

The most important thing to take away from this chapter is the fact that the user is no longer satisfied with a boring screen. In today's marketing-driven world you have to be more sensitive to the look and feel of your applications, even as you develop their functionality.

The Problem

One of the largest problems facing programmers in today's world is the need to provide applications which not only do the job, but also look good doing it. Unfortunately, the realities of software development mean that there's no extra time available for developing pretty user interfaces without sacrificing functional development time. Since users will not purchase a program that doesn't do the job, and that doesn't have a modern look, what is a programmer to do (without working hundreds of hours of unpaid overtime)?

There are many individual solutions to this problem, but the most basic one is to enhance simple applications with modern controls that add to the look of an application without detracting from the functionality of the program. With the advent of code generators and dialog design programs, a programmer's job will rely more and more on his ability to develop usable applications in less and less time.

The MFC Solution: The Contents List

One of the nicest features of the MSDN Library product is the Contents List. It provides a fixed-size list box which can display a 'tip' window when the string for the list box is wider than the list box window. This allows the user to maximize usable window space while still maintaining the ability to see all of the information in the list.

In this case, we're going to implement a list box which supports this tip-window display functionality. You can use a list box anywhere you would use a normal list box. A list box will not require a horizontal scrollbar to view extended strings, and the list box window will not need to be resized to view the entire string. Text wrapping isn't done in the Contents List box as the string can be viewed in its entirety on a single line on the desktop.

Probably the most important aspect of this list box is that it looks and behaves exactly like a standard Windows control. This means that it must properly handle colors, fonts and keyboard entries as a normal list box does. Single and multiple selection must work in the same way. In short, we wish to simply add existing functionality to the standard Windows list box (via the subclassing technique we've discussed previously) without in any way modifying the behavior that users have come to expect from a Windows list box.

Here you can see the list box we're going to create along with a string which is much longer than the width of the list box to which it belongs. The user has placed the mouse cursor over the long item in the list and the list box has popped up a window over the item to display the extended string.

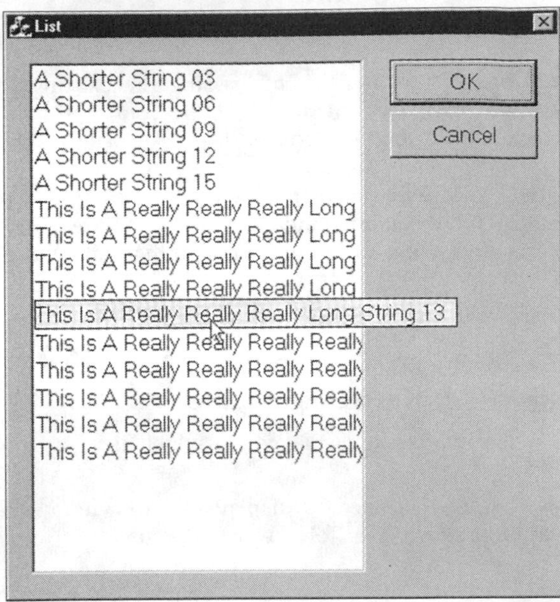

If you were to look at the resource file for the dialog shown above, you would see that the control is in all ways a normal Windows list box. No extra information is stored in the resource file, and there's no need for any special actions to be taken in the resource editor.

Feature List

What sorts of things do we want to support in our Contents List box? Obviously an important requirement is that the new control does everything that the existing list box supports. With this as a given, we would also like to able to do the following:

- Display a pop-up tip window when the user moves the mouse cursor over a list box item which is too wide to be displayed in the list box window.
- Have the tip window appear directly over the text of the list box entry for which it is displayed. In addition, it should use the same font as the existing list box.
- Use a color for the tip window that's different from the standard color of the list box so that the user's eye is immediately drawn to the pop-up window.
- Work with either the keyboard or the mouse. However, the control should only display the pop-up window if the mouse pointer is over the item. This is to ensure that the user will not be distracted when using the keyboard to navigate through the list.
- Maintain the normal operation of the list box control. In addition, the pop-up window should disappear as soon as the user moves the mouse away from the item in the list.
- Require no extra work on the part of the programmer beyond adding a member variable of the correct type for the contents list.

Designing the Control

The Contents List box will be implemented by subclassing the existing MFC list box class, **CListBox**. This will take care of the requirement that the control should work exactly like the basic list box, since the control will *be* a list box (just as long as we don't break anything!).

Clearly we will need to track the mouse cursor as it travels across our control so that we can display a pop-up tip window for the item under the mouse pointer. In order to show the pop-up window at the right place we need to know several things about the state of the system:

- Which item in the list, if any, is the mouse pointer over?
- Whether the string for that item is too wide to view without the aid of a tip window.
- Whether a tip window is already being displayed.
- If a tip window is already being displayed, to which item is it attached?

This information will tell us when we need to display the tip window, in what position to display it and what the appropriate text is for the list box item.

When you're faced with the problem of implementing specific behavior in a Windows application, the first things you should consider are the facilities already provided by MFC and the Windows API. For example, we can quickly determine at this point that the best way to keep track of the user's mouse cursor on the screen (or the list box) is to capture the **WM_MOUSEMOVE** message. You've undoubtedly done this several times in the past and should be able to learn from your past work. This is a small example of *knowledge reuse.*

Once we know the mouse is over a given point, we need to find the item which resides at that location. There are several methods that we could use to determine the item number under the mouse. Probably the easiest is to rely on the fact that the font in a list box is fixed for all items in the list box. This means that all items in the list are the same height. Given a position within the list box window, we can determine which item is under the mouse by dividing the y-coordinate of the mouse position by the height of the font used in the list box window. This will give us an index relative to the first visible item in the list box.

Since the list could have been scrolled, we will add to that index the index of the first visible item in the list box. **CListBox::GetTopIndex()** returns this information very easily (although you could get it by sending the message **WM_GETTOPINDEX** to the list box via the **SendMessage()** API function if you want to do things the hard way).

We will now know that the mouse is over a given item and the index of that given item in the list. To determine the width of the string at that index, you need two bits of information. First, you must determine the string in the list at that index which can be retrieved via **CListBox::GetText()**. Second, you need to know how wide this string will be when displayed in the list. To do this, we will first get the font for the list box and use it in conjunction with **CDC::GetTextExtent()** to find the width of the string as displayed in the list box. This width (in pixels) will then be compared to the width of the actual list box on the dialog.

If the list box entry under the mouse isn't wider than the window, nothing will happen. On the other hand, if the list box entry *is* wider than the window, we will create a new instance of the pop-up window class and set the text of that window to be the string we retrieved earlier. The pop-up window will then be responsible for coloring itself, displaying the text and determining where to position itself relative to the list box entry. How do we find out where the list box entry starts? We use the height of the font to find the top of the entry on the screen and then offset slightly from the left-hand side of the list box window.

As we just implied, the pop-up window itself will be a separate class. Since the programmer will not be required to implement any functionality besides simply adding a variable of the right type, the control must do all of the work of registering window classes and creating and destroying pop-up windows itself.

At this point, you might be asking why we don't simply use the tree view control (wrapped by MFC's **CTreeCtrl)** that ships with all 32-bit Windows systems now. This control provides exactly the tooltip functionality that we're looking for without requiring any coding effort on our part. This is a good question that deserves a good answer.

The answer is simply that the tree view control is often massive overkill for a simple program. Programmers really prefer simple controls for simple circumstances such as the ones we're discussing here. The tree control is certainly capable of doing the job, it's just that it is much like using a sledgehammer to swat a fly. It works, but often there isn't enough left of the fly to tell us that it worked! The point is that there are times when you don't want the full power of the tree control. When all you need is a list of items, just use a list box. After all, if the tree control was perfect for all situations, why would we still have the list box in Windows at all?

A better case, however, could probably be made for using the tooltip control that ships with Windows 95 and Windows NT (wrapped by **CToolTipCtrl**) rather than the proprietary pop-up window class that we're designing. In this case, I plead for your forgiveness. The tooltip control doesn't exist in Windows 3.1 (nor, for that matter does the tree control) and I am often required to write 16-bit code for clients. Rather than create two versions for different environments, it's simpler for me (and I hope it will be simpler for you) to keep this control in one piece for both the 32-bit and 16-bit environments.

This design is all well and good but it needs to be translated into something that the computer can understand before we can reap the rewards of our labors. At this point we'll move on to the implementation phase of the project.

Implementing the Contents List

To implement the control, we will create two new MFC classes and implement the functionality of the control within them. Follow this procedure to create the MFC class and implement the control:

TRY IT OUT - Create a Contents List

1 Use MFC AppWizard (exe) to create a new project workspace called **List**. Choose to create a Dialog based application from Step 1 of the wizard, leave all other options at their default settings and finish creating the project.

2 Use ClassWizard to add a new class by selecting the Add Class... button and selecting New... from the menu. Give the new class the name **CContentsList**. Select **CListBox** as the Base class from the drop-down list. Click OK. We've now created the basic class structure for our new Contents List box, all we need to do is to add the extended functionality.

Note that if you do intend to use this control with 16-bit Visual C++, you will need to use the standard DOS 8.3 naming convention when you create the files in this example.

3 The first thing we will add to the control is its data members. Add the following code to the class definition in **ContentsList.h**.

```
// Implementation
public:
    virtual ~CContentsList();
private:
    int m_nCurrentItem;
    CPopupTip* m_pPopupTip;
    CString m_strPopupTipClassName;
```

We also need to ensure that these members are set to proper default values at the time of instantiation of the object. To accomplish this, add the following code to the constructor for the class, **CContentsList::CContentsList()**.

```
CContentsList::CContentsList()
{
    m_nCurrentItem = -1;
    m_pPopupTip = NULL;
    m_strPopupTipClassName = ::AfxRegisterWndClass(CS_SAVEBITS | CS_DBLCLKS,
                             ::AfxGetApp()->LoadStandardCursor(IDC_ARROW));
}
```

The **m_nCurrentItem** member is used to keep track of the item in the list for which we are currently displaying a pop-up window. Since the list is zero-based, we use a value of **-1** to indicate that no item has a pop-up. We will use this value to check whether a new item that needs a pop-up is, in fact, the same as the current item. If this is the case, we can do nothing. Without this variable, we'd be constantly creating and destroying pop-up windows unnecessarily.

The **m_pPopupTip** is a pointer to the pop-up tip window. Since we will test this variable against **NULL** to determine whether we're currently displaying a pop-up tip, it's very important that we set it to **NULL** in the constructor.

The final member, **m_strPopupTipClassName**, is necessary so that we can register multiple pop-up windows with the same name.

4 We only need to add two message handlers to the entire window class to accomplish our task. The first message handler you will need to add to your source code is for the **WM_MOUSEMOVE** message, so use ClassWizard to add a handler to **CContentsList**. Add the following code to the **OnMouseMove()** message handler for the **CContentsList** class:

```
void CContentsList::OnMouseMove(UINT nFlags, CPoint point)
{
    // If the point is outside of the window, destroy popup if necessary
    // and let SafeDestroyPopupTip() clean up
    CRect rectClient;
    GetClientRect(&rectClient);
```

```
if (!rectClient.PtInRect(point))
{
   SafeDestroyPopupTip();
   CListBox::OnMouseMove(nFlags, point);
   return;
}

CRect rect;
GetWindowRect(&rect);
// Figure out how tall a given item is.
CDC* pDC = GetDC();
CFont* pOldFont = pDC->SelectObject(GetFont());
TEXTMETRIC tm;
pDC->GetTextMetrics(&tm);
pDC->SelectObject(pOldFont);

int nItemHeight = tm.tmHeight;
// Now that we have the height of an item, which item is this?
int nOverItem = point.y / nItemHeight;
nOverItem += GetTopIndex();   // Add top index of list box

if (nOverItem < GetCount())
{
   if (m_nCurrentItem == nOverItem) // If we're still over same item,
   {                                // clean up and leave
      ReleaseDC(pDC);
      CListBox::OnMouseMove(nFlags, point);
      return;
   }

   SafeDestroyPopupTip();  // Destroy old pop-up window

   // Get the text for this item
   CString strItem;
   GetText(nOverItem, strItem);

   CString strExt = strItem + "0";
   CFont* pOldFont = pDC->SelectObject(GetFont());
   CSize sizeText = pDC->GetTextExtent(strExt, strExt.GetLength());
   pDC->SelectObject(pOldFont);

   if (sizeText.cx > rect.Width())
   {
      SetCapture();           // Capture subsequent mouse events
      // Okay, create a new window in this place.
      m_pPopupTip = new CPopupTip(m_strPopupTipClassName, this);
      m_pPopupTip->SetFont(GetFont());
      m_pPopupTip->SetDisplay(strItem);

      if (nOverItem == GetCurSel())
         m_pPopupTip->SetSelected(TRUE);
      else
         m_pPopupTip->SetSelected(FALSE);

      // And display the item at the window point for the start of
      // this list box item.
      CPoint pointStart(rect.left + 3,
                rect.top + (nOverItem - GetTopIndex()) * nItemHeight);
```

```
            m_pPopupTip->PopItUp(pointStart, TTIPS_SQUARESTYLE);
        }
        m_nCurrentItem = nOverItem;
    }
    else
        // If nOverItem is larger than number of items in list and there's
        // an active tip, destroy it
        SafeDestroyPopupTip();

    // Remember to free DC!
    ReleaseDC(pDC);
    CListBox::OnMouseMove(nFlags, point);
}
```

This is a lot to digest in a single chunk so let's look at this code in pieces to get an idea of what's going on here. The first segment of the code deals with determining if the mouse is currently in the window of our control. This is done by getting the client rectangle for the control and checking, using **PtInRect()**, whether the position of the mouse pointer, given as a parameter to the message handler, is within that rectangle.

If the point is outside the control rectangle, we just call **SafeDestroyPopupTip()**, then the base class handler before returning. **SafeDestroyPopupTip()** performs all the clean up necessary to destroy a pop-up tip window. It does it safely by ensuring that there's a window there to destroy in the first place. You should add the code for this function to the header and source files for **CContentsList** as shown below.

```
public:
    virtual ~CContentsList();
protected:
    void SafeDestroyPopupTip();
private:
    int m_nCurrentItem;
```

```
inline void CContentsList::SafeDestroyPopupTip()
{
    if (m_pPopupTip)
    {
        m_pPopupTip->DestroyWindow(); // CPopupTip deletes itself
        m_pPopupTip = NULL;           // Re-initialze the pointer
        m_nCurrentItem = -1;          // Re-initialize the current item
        ReleaseCapture();      // If there was a tooltip, we must have been
                               // capturing the mouse, so release it
    }
}
```

Keeping all the clean up code in one place like this minimizes the chances of missing anything. Note that we don't need to explicitly **delete** the **m_pPopupTip** pointer as the **CPopupTip** class, which we'll examine later, does this itself. Note also the call to **ReleaseCapture()**. The correct functioning of the pop-up tips relies on us calling **SetCapture()** when we display a tip, so we must make sure to call **ReleaseCapture()** when a tip is destroyed.

Going back to the **OnMouseMove()** code, the next piece of the solution is to determine which item the mouse is currently over in the list box. Since each list box item is the same height, we can determine the current item by figuring out how many items the mouse pointer is below the item displayed at the top of the list. This offset is added to the list index for the top item, obtained with a call to **CListBox::GetTopIndex()**, to give us the actual list box entry index of the item under the pointer. If this index is larger than the number of items in the list, we don't do anything since there's nothing to be done for a blank entry.

If the mouse cursor is over a valid entry in the list, we need to next check whether this is a new entry. The user could have simply moved the mouse along the entry they are looking at. Replacing the same entry each time the mouse moves would cause an annoying flickering effect, so we avoid that by checking the new item against the current item. If they're the same, we don't do anything except call the base class handler.

If the current entry is new, we need to first get rid of the old pop-up window and clear all the appropriate settings. This is done with a call to **SafeDestroyPopupTip()**. Once the old window is gone, we retrieve the text for the list box entry under the mouse cursor using the **CListBox::GetText()**. When we have the text for the entry, we retrieve the actual length of the text as it would be displayed using the device context for the list box and calling the **GetTextExtent()** method. This method will return the actual length of the string in pixels as it would be displayed on the screen using the current settings (such as font and color) of the DC.

If the total width of the control is less than the width of the string, we need to display a pop-up. We first capture all subsequent mouse events then create the new pop-up window, passing it the class name we defined in the constructor and a pointer to the list box window for which it is to be a child. We then call two new methods of the pop-up class, **SetFont()** and **SetDisplay()** which set the font to use when drawing the string and the text to use to display in the window. **SetSelected()** tells the pop-up whether it should draw itself as a selected item. Finally, we pop-up the tip window by calling **CPopupTip::PopItUp()** with the position (the top left corner of the list box entry) at which to display itself.

Lastly, we make sure that the DC is released so that we don't run out of them. Whenever you call **GetDC()** for a window, be very sure to call **ReleaseDC()** for every subsequent exit point in that function. If you fail to properly release device contexts, your application will probably crash randomly in functions other than the one causing the problem. The true source of the trouble can be difficult to track down.

5 The last message handler we need to add to **CContentsList** is a handler for the **WM_LBUTTONDOWN** message, so use ClassWizard to add this. This message will be sent to the control when the user presses the left mouse button while in the control. In our case, we need to display the pop-up window (if it's present) in a selected state when the user clicks on it. This will satisfy our requirement that the pop-up window must behave exactly like the normal list box. Here's the code to add for the new message handler:

```
void CContentsList::OnLButtonDown(UINT nFlags, CPoint point)
{
   CListBox::OnLButtonDown(nFlags, point);
   if (m_pPopupTip)
   {
```

```
        if (m_nCurrentItem == GetCurSel())
            m_pPopupTip->SetSelected(TRUE);
        else
            m_pPopupTip->SetSelected(FALSE);
        m_pPopupTip->Invalidate();
    }
}
```

Note that we call the base class handler before we try to use **GetCurSel()** to determine the current selection. I hope you can see that trying it the other way round will not produce the desired results.

Note that in extended or multiple select mode, the only pop-up window to be displayed as selected will be the one for the last item to have been selected. Consider this a feature of the control which you can fix up yourself if you choose.

6 That takes care of the **CContentsList** class. All we need to implement now is the pop-up window class. This isn't a hard task and we should tackle it right away. First, use ClassWizard to create a new class. Call the class **CPopupTip** and use **generic CWnd** as the Base class.

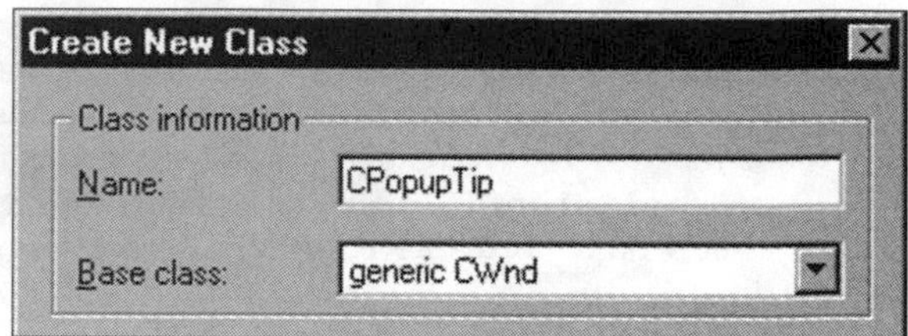

7 Open the header file, **PopupTip.h**, for the **CPopupTip** class and make the following modifications. Changes to the file are shown highlighted:

```
// PopupTip.h : header file
//

#define TTIPS_SQUARESTYLE   0
#define TTIPS_ROUNDSTYLE    1

/////////////////////////////////////////////////////////////////////////////
// CPopupTip window

class CPopupTip : public CWnd
{
// Construction
public:
   CPopupTip(CString& strClass, CWnd* pParent);

// Attributes
public:

// Operations
public:
   void SetDisplay(const CString &strDisplay);
   void SetFont(CFont* pFont);
   void SetSelected(BOOL bSelected);
   BOOL PopItUp(POINT point, UINT nNewStyle);
```

```
// Overrides
    // ClassWizard generated virtual function overrides
    //{{AFX_VIRTUAL(CPopupTip)
    protected:
    //}}AFX_VIRTUAL

// Implementation
public:
    virtual ~CPopupTip();

private:
    UINT m_nStyleFlag;
    CWnd* m_pParent;
    BOOL m_bSelected;
    CFont* m_pFont;
    CString m_strDisplay;
    CString m_strClass;

    // Generated message map functions
protected:
    //{{AFX_MSG(CPopupTip)
    //}}AFX_MSG
    DECLARE_MESSAGE_MAP()
};
```

Any further changes to the header file will be added by ClassWizard when we add message handlers and virtual function overrides.

8 The first step toward implementing the class is to add the code for the constructor to initialize the member variables we added to the header file. Here's the constructor for the class:

```
CPopupTip::CPopupTip(CString& strClass, CWnd* pParent)
{
    m_strClass = strClass;
    m_pParent = pParent;
    m_bSelected = FALSE;
    m_pFont = NULL;
}
```

Here, we hold on to the information that was sent to us by the caller of this function. We will use the class name and parent window pointer when we call **`CreateEx()`** to create the pop-up tip window in response to a call to **`PopItUp()`**. We also initialize the other two members, **`m_bSelected`** and **`m_pFont`**, to sensible default values.

9 The next step is to implement the Set functions. These are straightforward:

```
void CPopupTip::SetDisplay(const CString &strDisplay)
{
    m_strDisplay = strDisplay;
}

void CPopupTip::SetFont(CFont* pFont)
{
    m_pFont = pFont;
```

```
}

void CPopupTip::SetSelected(BOOL bSelected)
{
   m_bSelected = bSelected;
}
```

10 When the calling application wants to create the new pop-up window, it must call **`CPopupTip::PopItUp()`**. This method is responsible for creating the actual window using the proper settings and background information. Add this code to the source file:

```
BOOL CPopupTip::PopItUp(POINT point, UINT nNewStyle)
{
   if (nNewStyle < TTIPS_SQUARESTYLE || nNewStyle > TTIPS_ROUNDSTYLE)
      nNewStyle = TTIPS_SQUARESTYLE;

   int  nBorder = 2;

   // Get the width and height of the window based on length of text
   CWindowDC dc(NULL);
   CFont* pOldFont = dc.SelectObject(m_pFont);
   CString strExt = m_strDisplay + "0";
   CSize sizeText = dc.GetTextExtent(strExt, strExt.GetLength());
   dc.SelectObject(pOldFont);

   // See if the box is off the screen to the right. If it is, move it
   // back onto the screen.

   int nScreenRight = GetSystemMetrics(SM_CXSCREEN);
   if (point.x + sizeText.cx > nScreenRight - 6)
      point.x = nScreenRight - sizeText.cx - 6;

   if (CreateEx(0, m_strClass, NULL, WS_POPUP,
               point.x, point.y, sizeText.cx, sizeText.cy + 2,
               m_pParent->m_hWnd, 0))
   {
      ShowWindow(SW_SHOWNOACTIVATE);
      m_nStyleFlag = nNewStyle;
      return TRUE;
   }
   else
      return FALSE;
}
```

As you can see, we pop up the window based on the length of the string that's stored in the class. The window size is calculated by getting the current font and selecting it into a device context.

This provides us with something of a problem. How can we use a device context if we don't yet have a window? We solve this by using a **`NULL`** in the place of a window for the CDC constructor. This creates a compatible screen device context which can be used to determine the width of the string using the **`GetTextExtent()`** method. We use the width and height to set the rectangle for the window and then to create it on the fly.

11 Now we need to use ClassWizard to create a message handler for **WM_PAINT**; this will display the window at run time. Here's the code for **OnPaint().**

```
void CPopupTip::OnPaint()
{
   CPaintDC dc(this); // device context for painting
   CRect rectClient;
   GetClientRect(&rectClient);

   // Draw the rectangle box for the tip
   CBrush brYellow(RGB(255, 255, 128));  // Standard tool tip yellow
   CBrush brSelected(::GetSysColor(COLOR_HIGHLIGHT));  // Usually blue
   CBrush* pOldBrush;

   if (m_bSelected)
      pOldBrush = dc.SelectObject(&brSelected);
   else
      pOldBrush = dc.SelectObject(&brYellow);

   if(m_nStyleFlag == TTIPS_ROUNDSTYLE)
   {
      CPoint ptEllipse(5, 10);
      dc.RoundRect(&rectClient, ptEllipse);
   }
   else
      dc.Rectangle(&rectClient);
   dc.SelectObject(pOldBrush);

   CFont* pOldFont = NULL;
   if (m_pFont)
      pOldFont = dc.SelectObject(m_pFont);

   // force colors
   int nBkMode = dc.SetBkMode(TRANSPARENT);

   COLORREF clrText;
   if (!m_bSelected)
      clrText = dc.SetTextColor(RGB(0, 0, 0));  // use black for text
   else
      clrText = dc.SetTextColor(::GetSysColor(COLOR_HIGHLIGHTTEXT));

   dc.DrawText(m_strDisplay, -1, &rectClient,
               DT_LEFT | DT_VCENTER | DT_SINGLELINE);

   dc.SetTextColor(clrText);
   dc.SetBkMode(nBkMode);

   if (pOldFont)
      dc.SelectObject(pOldFont);

   // Do not call CWnd::OnPaint() for painting messages
}
```

All we're really doing in this paint function is to draw a filled rectangle as the total area of the window with the correct color. We then add the text representing the window pop-up information. We selected yellow for the pop-up tip color background and black for the window text. These are simply standard colors for the Windows operating system.

12 The second Windows message we will handle is the **WM_ERASEBKGD** message. This message is sent by Windows whenever the window background needs to be erased and colored with the window background color. Since we're already setting the background color in the paint function, this method doesn't really need to do anything except notify Windows that the background has been 'cleared'. Use ClassWizard to add a new handler for the **WM_ERASEBKGD** message to the **CPopupTip** class. Add the following code for the message handler:

```
BOOL CPopupTip::OnEraseBkgnd(CDC* pDC)
{
    return TRUE;
}
```

This message handler prevents the background of the window from clearing itself since we have already handled this in **CPopupTip::OnPaint()**. In this way we limit the amount of clearing and painting that needs to be done so that the control looks like a simple pop-up window.

13 Now we need to override a couple of window-related functions, **PreCreateWindow()** and **PostNcDestroy()**. Use ClassWizard to add overrides for these two functions to **CPopupTip**.

PreCreateWindow() is called by Windows to register the window with the proper information. Since we want to display the window ourselves at the proper time, we don't want MFC to do anything during this process. Add the following line to the source file to accomplish this:

```
BOOL CPopupTip::PreCreateWindow(CREATESTRUCT& cs)
{
    return TRUE;
}
```

Now we need to modify the **PostNcDestroy()** function. This is the last chance a Windows control will get to handle anything since it is sent at the time of the window's destruction. We handle this message to make sure that the memory occupied by the pop-up tip is released when the window is destroyed:

```
void CPopupTip::PostNcDestroy()
{
    delete this;
}
```

14 Finally, we need to make sure that our pop-up window never receives focus. If we allowed that to happen, there would be lots of flashing of the title bar of any dialog that contained our list box as focus shifted between the dialog and the pop-up tips. To prevent that, you use ClassWizard to add a handler for **WM_MOUSEACTIVATE** to **CPopupTip**. Now add the code shown below to the handler.

```
int CPopupTip::OnMouseActivate(CWnd* pDesktopWnd, UINT nHitTest,
                               UINT message)
{
    return MA_NOACTIVATE;
}
```

By returning **`MA_NOACTIVATE`**, we ensure that the pop-up tip window won't be activated when the user clicks on it. It will, however, still receive mouse messages so we need to ensure that, if necessary, these are passed back to the list window.

15 Use ClassWizard to add a new handler for the **`WM_LBUTTONDOWN`** message. This message is sent whenever the user presses the left mouse button down within the window. Here's the code for the new handler.

```
void CPopupTip::OnLButtonDown(UINT nFlags, CPoint point)
{
    m_pParent->SendMessage(WM_LBUTTONDOWN, nFlags,
                           MAKEWORD(point.x, point.y));
    CWnd::OnLButtonDown(nFlags, point);
}
```

We just pass the message directly to the **`CContentsList`** object represented by **`m_pParent`**.

16 Now use ClassWizard to add a handler for the **`WM_LBUTTONDBLCLK`** message, which is sent when the user double-clicks the tip window. Add the following code to the new handler

```
void CPopupTip::OnLButtonDblClk(UINT nFlags, CPoint point)
{
    m_pParent->GetParent()->PostMessage(WM_COMMAND,
                          MAKEWPARAM(m_pParent->GetDlgCtrlID(), LBN_DBLCLK),
                          (LPARAM)m_pParent->m_hWnd);
    CWnd::OnLButtonDblClk(nFlags, point);
}
```

Here we are 'simulating' a double-click to a list box item and sending that message to the parent of the tip window's parent, in other words to the dialog or window that contains the list box.

That's all there is to it! We're now in a position to test the control by embedding it in an application and trying it out with a list box that contains both short and long strings.

TRY IT OUT - Test the Contents List

1 Open the project's main dialog resource, **`IDD_LIST_DIALOG`**, in Developer Studio's dialog editor.

2 Add a new list box to the dialog and *Ctrl*-double-click on it to bring up ClassWizard's Add Member Variable dialog. Fill in the fields as shown to add a control variable for the list to the class.

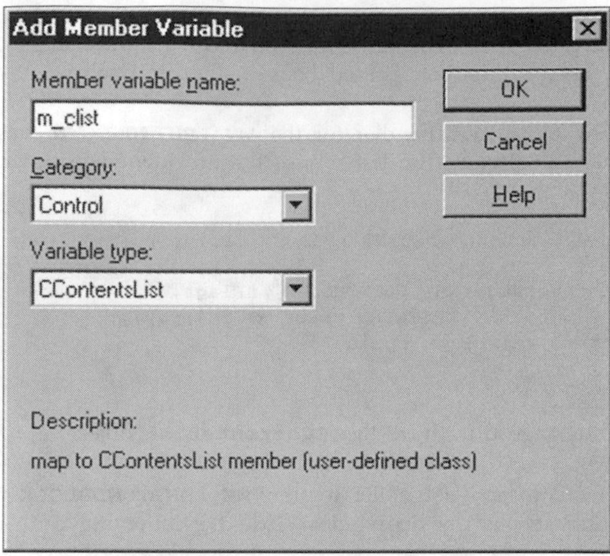

3 Add **#include "ContentsList.h"** to the top of the header file for the dialog, **ListDlg.h**.

4 Now add some strings to the list by adding code to **CListDlg::OnInitDialog()** as shown here:

```
// TODO: Add extra initialization here
m_clist.AddString(_T("This Is A Really Really Really Long String 01"));
m_clist.AddString(_T("This Is A Really Really Really Really Long
                  String 02"));
m_clist.AddString(_T("A Shorter String 03"));
m_clist.AddString(_T("This Is A Really Really Really Long String 04"));
m_clist.AddString(_T("This Is A Really Really Really Really Long
                    String 05"));
m_clist.AddString(_T("A Shorter String 06"));
m_clist.AddString(_T("This Is A Really Really Really Long String 07"));
```

You can compile and run the project at this stage. See whether the control behaves as advertised. Try changing the size of the list box in the dialog editor or changing its sort order to check whether everything still works. Once you're satisfied that it does, you can add it to your own applications, or use it as a basis for your own version of a Contents List box.

The ActiveX Solution: A Gradient Control

Many Windows installation programs make use of a color gradient to improve the appearance of the installation screen. A gradient is simply a smooth progression of colors moving gradually from one shade to the next. For example, a blue gradient displays all of the possible shades of blue, from one end of the blue spectrum to the other. Although a color gradient by itself isn't very useful, when combined with other, more functional controls, it provides a professional touch to a program. We'll examine how to create an ActiveX control that displays a color gradient.

Feature List

The features for the gradient control are really quite simple. We want to be able to display a complete rainbow consisting of all of the shades of a given color in the full control window. The only real question is how much control we give to the end programmer to determine what's displayed. Since gradient controls will only work well in the three basic color bands (red, green and blue), we will allow the programmer only those three options when setting the control properties. This isn't such a limitation as most of the other options wouldn't look particularly professional on screen.

Designing the Control

Our feature 'list' tells us that the only property that we'll need for the gradient control is the base color setting. We'll call this setting **`BaseColor`**. There are no methods for the control, since all it needs to do is redraw itself when necessary using the defined color. This is by far and away the simplest control from both the user's and the programmer's perspective, yet it meets a real need. This might well be the perfect reusable component.

In order to actually do the job of displaying a gradient, however, there's a bit more that must go on behind the scenes. We need internal information just as much as we need external information for the control. The first thing we'll need is to know how many intensity levels are supported. As it turns out, using 256 levels works just fine on all monitors. Windows will replace any non-supported levels with the previous or next level, leaving us with equally spaced bands. What we'll do is to simply fill in 1/256th of the total vertical space available in the control with each color band. This gives a smooth transition of colors down the control and makes it easy to program. We'll get the color for each band using the **`RGB()`** macro, iterating through a single parameter (red, green, or blue) from 0 to 255.

That's really all there is to the control, so let's get stuck into the code.

Implementing the Gradient Control

Follow this procedure to create the new control.

TRY IT OUT - Create a Gradient Control

1 Create a new project workspace called Gradient using the OLE ControlWizard. The only options that you need to change from their default settings are on Step 2 of ControlWizard behind the Edit Names... button. Change the control's Type Name to Wrox Gradient Control and its Type ID to Wrox.Gradient.GradientCtrl.1. Change the property page's Type Name to Wrox Gradient Property Page and its Type ID to Wrox.Gradient.GradientPropPage.1. You can leave the rest of the settings as they are and finish creating the project.

2 The first thing we're going to add to the control is the property representing the color we want to use as the base for the gradient spectrum. To do this, activate ClassWizard and go to the OLE Automation page. Add a new property by selecting the Add Property... button. Set the property up like this:

External name	Type	Variable name	Notification function	Implementation
BaseColor	short	m_nBaseColor	OnBaseColorChanged	Member variable

3 The next thing we need to do is to enhance our **.odl** file to make using our control as easy as possible. Just as we did with the **ShadeText** control, we will add an enumeration to the type library so that the users of our control can more easily choose an appropriate value for the property.

```
[ uuid(BC29E880-0CC8-11D0-AB39-0020AF71E433), version(1.0),
  helpstring("Wrox Gradient Control"), control ]
library GradientLib
{
   importlib(STDOLE_TLB);
   importlib(STDTYPE_TLB);

typedef [ uuid(BC29E899-0CC8-11D0-AB39-0020AF71E433),
            helpstring("BaseColor constants") ]
            enum {
                   [helpstring("Red")]      wrxBaseRed = 0,
                   [helpstring("Green")]    wrxBaseGreen,
                   [helpstring("Blue")]     wrxBaseBlue,
                   } BaseColorConstants;

   //  Primary dispatch interface for CGradientCtrl
   [ uuid(BC29E881-0CC8-11D0-AB39-0020AF71E433),
     helpstring("Dispatch interface for Wrox Gradient Control"), hidden ]
   dispinterface _DGradient
   {
      properties:
         // NOTE - ClassWizard will maintain property information here.
         //    Use extreme caution when editing this section.
         //{{AFX_ODL_PROP(CGradientCtrl)
         [id(1)] BaseColorConstants BaseColor;
         //}}AFX_ODL_PROP
```

FYI

When adding enumerations to your own .odl files you should use the GUID Generator component to create the uuid values.

We've also changed the **helpstring** for the library to make it easier to find Wrox controls. You'll notice that the various different containers use different items to identify controls to users. For example, Visual Basic 4.0 shows a list of controls to users that displays the type library **helpstring** for each control, whereas the Test Container uses the control's type name that we set when we created the project. It's a good idea to set these two items identically to avoid confusion.

4 The next step is to add a similar enumeration to **CGradientCtrl** in the header file for the control, **GradientCtl.h**.

```
// Enumerations
public:
    enum BaseColor {baseRed, baseGreen, baseBlue};
```

5 Now we can make sure that the property for the control can be persistently set and that it has a sensible default value by adding a line of code to **CGradientCtrl::DoPropExchange()**.

```
void CGradientCtrl::DoPropExchange(CPropExchange* pPX)
{
    ExchangeVersion(pPX, MAKELONG(_wVerMinor, _wVerMajor));
    COleControl::DoPropExchange(pPX);
    PX_Short(pPX, "BaseColor", m_nBaseColor, baseBlue);
}
```

Always give the most commonly used setting as the default value for that property. In the case of a gradient control, the most commonly used setting is blue (as witnessed by the many installation programs that use the blue gradient background).

Remember that the **OnResetState()** function is called whenever the control needs to be reinitialized. The default implementation of that function simply uses the code supplied in **DoPropExchange()** to reset the values. This is sufficient for this control, but sometimes you may need to override **OnResetState()**; for example, if you need to initialize values that you don't wish to make persistent.

6 The last bit of code before we get to draw our control is the code that will force the control to redraw itself when the **BaseColor** property is changed. Here's the code to add to **CGradientCtrl::OnBaseColorChanged()**:

```
void CGradientCtrl::OnBaseColorChanged()
{
    InvalidateControl();
    SetModifiedFlag();
}
```

7 The final piece of the puzzle is the control's **OnDraw()** function. Here's where we will do all of the work of actually displaying the gradient. Here's the code for **CGradientCtrl::OnDraw()**:

```
void CGradientCtrl::OnDraw(
        CDC* pdc, const CRect& rcBounds, const CRect& rcInvalid)
{
   CRect rectFill;             // Rectangle for filling band
   float fltStep;              // How large is each band?
   int nBand;                  // Loop index

   // Determine how large each band should be in order to cover the
   // client with 256 bands (one for every color intensity level)
   fltStep = (float)rcBounds.Height() / 256.0f;

   // Start filling bands
   for (nBand = 0; nBand < 256; nBand++)
   {
      // Set the location of the current band
```

```
        SetRect(&rectFill,
                rcBounds.left,                              // Upper left X
                rcBounds.top + (int)(nBand * fltStep),      // Upper left Y
                rcBounds.right,                             // Lower right X
                rcBounds.top + (int)((nBand + 1) * fltStep));  // Lower rt Y
        // Create a brush with the appropriate color for this band
        short nRed = 0;
        short nGreen = 0;
        short nBlue = 0;

        switch (m_nBaseColor)
        {
        case baseRed:
           nRed = (255 - nBand);
           break;
        case baseGreen:
           nGreen = (255 - nBand);
           break;
        case baseBlue:
           nBlue = (255 - nBand);
           break;
        }

        CBrush brush(RGB(nRed, nGreen, nBlue));
        pdc->FillRect(&rectFill, &brush);
    }
}
```

Looking at the code, you can see that it's really quite simple. The control window rectangle is divided up into 256 bands of equal height. Each band is then filled in by creating a brush and filling a rectangle. The brush is created using the **RGB()** macro which creates a color value in Windows by setting the red, green, and blue components of the color. Since our colors are all one of red, green or blue, we simply vary the intensity of the color from brightest (255) to darkest (0 which is actually black). This color is then used to fill the rectangle, creating the color gradient.

8 Now we have a fully functional control that you could compile and use. There's just one more thing to do though, and that's create the property sheet for the control. Again, this is much the same as the one we created for the **ShadeText** control.

Use Developer Studio's resource editor to open the dialog property sheet, **IDD_PROPPAGE_GRADIENT**. Change the static field that's already on the dialog so that it says Base Color: then add a combo box to the dialog. Double-click on the combo to bring up its property sheet and add three items to the list that says Enter listbox items: 0 - Red, 1 - Green, 2 - Blue. Now switch to the Styles page and set the combo's type to Drop List. Finally, *Ctrl*-double-click on the combo and add a member variable to the property page according to the settings shown below.

Member variable name	Category	Variable type	Optional OLE property name
m_nBaseColor	Value	int	BaseColor

Now if you compile and test the control, you should see a property page similar to the one shown here:

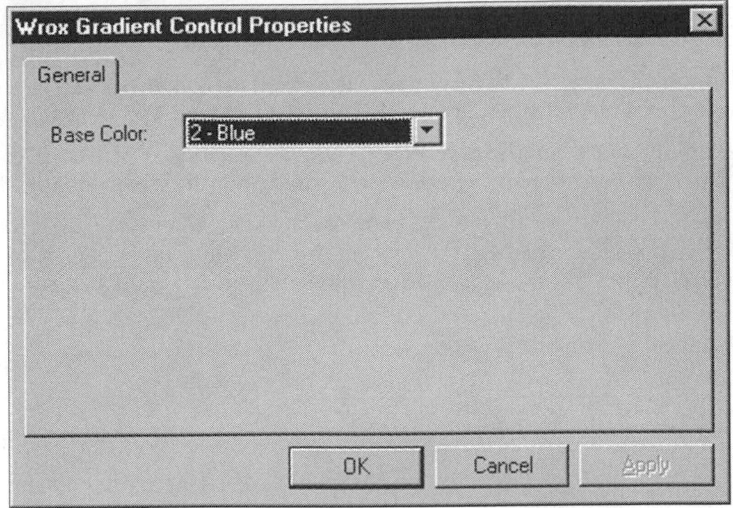

Summary

Let's look back over the chapter and review what we've discovered:

- A complete and polished user interface is an important consideration in designing and implementing professional programs. Users have come to expect certain features and it is encumbent upon programmers to implement those features in their programs. These features often add little in the way of raw functionality to the application, but they make users happier and the applications easier to use.
- Existing Windows controls can be extended to make them easier and more efficient without adding much overhead. As in the Contents List box, the programmer can often make better use of limited screen space without sacrificing the ability to display data.
- A feature which is implemented in nearly all installation programs is the color gradient background. A color gradient makes a screen prettier and distracts the user during what can be a lengthy process.
- A good design plan for a control beats superior optimization in code one hundred times out of one hundred. Although we didn't actually learn this in this example, this has been a cornerstone of the whole book and should be stressed at least once!
- Before implementing any control or component, consider what the user will get out of it. If the control is being implemented solely for the benefit of the programmer, why is it being implemented at all?

Things to Try

Here are a few 'homework' assignments that you might try to gain a fuller understanding of component programming.

- Consider adding a few new features to the Contents list box. One you could think about is setting the background color for the pop-up window.
- Add a 'time-out' value for the Contents list box that will make the control vanish after a fixed period of time, whether or not the user has moved the mouse.
- Add the ability to the gradient control to use a 'rainbow' of different colors banding the screen. This can be extremely effective in certain 'splash' screen dialogs.
- Add a double-click event to the gradient control that allows the user to display another kind of splash screen. This sort of 'hidden' functionality, often called an Easter egg, can garner your application more free advertising than you would believe possible.

Visual
C++

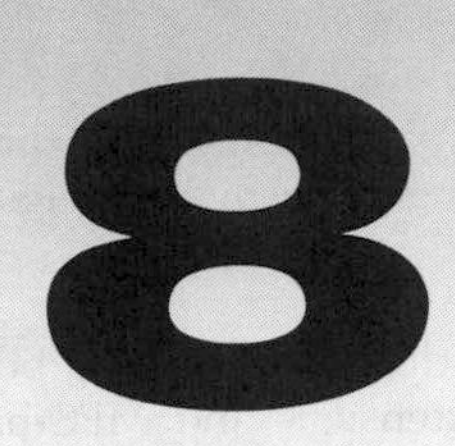

Custom AppWizards

Since this book is built on the assumption that you know how to use the Visual C++ wizards, I won't explain what an AppWizard can do for you. You've already seen it several times in this book as we used MFC AppWizard (exe) (usually referred to as *the* AppWizard) and the OLE ControlWizard to create the skeletons of new projects based on options you choose. You may not have realized, however, that it's not just Microsoft and their special friends who can create AppWizards. You can too, and it's easy!

Suppose your company often created DLLs that had a common foundation. Wouldn't it be rather nice to be able to generate a simple skeleton for the DLL through an AppWizard clone and then simply add the code to implement specific features? It certainly would! Fortunately for my sanity, Microsoft has already realized that programmers are going to want to be able to do this and has provided a relatively simple mechanism for it. Instead of having to write a complete application that loops through dialog boxes and displays confirmation pages before doing a great deal of string manipulation in order to generate the skeleton applications, you can use the Custom AppWizard AppWizard to help you create new AppWizards! You'll see how through the rest of this chapter.

Before we get into AppWizards, though, let's have a little chat about the use of controls in the Internet environment.

The Future of Components

If there's one thing that's certain about the future, it is that things will change. Some of the newest technologies exist in a stable form and some are still being developed. When I started writing these chapters, Visual C++ 4.1 was the latest version of the compiler, the ActiveX Template Library didn't have a version number, and both the ActiveX SDK and Internet Explorer 3.0 were in beta. Now, Visual C++ 4.2 has been released (and the patch to version 4.2a is in beta), ATL is at version 1.1 and both the ActiveX SDK and Internet Explorer have been released. These changes represent significant advances in a short time and they aren't the only things that Microsoft have been working on!

Given the huge rate of change in the areas that we're about to discuss, it's possible that things may change again between the writing of this chapter and the time you get to read it. Please don't hold me personally responsible for this—blame it on Microsoft! (Now that sounds like a catch phrase for the 90s.) Seriously, although we are now able to discuss released technologies, with the exception of the VC++ 4.2a patch, remember that the future is an uncertain place. As the saying goes, the more things change, the more things break your code (or something like that). Caution over.

This chapter also marks a change in the format of the book. Up to this point, we have developed similar controls as MFC extensions and MFC-based ActiveX controls. We've provided complete implementations and compared the development methodologies that created them. From this point on, however, we'll move the focus away from purely MFC-based components towards wider horizons. In this chapter, for example, we will first implement a custom AppWizard and then use that custom AppWizard in the next chapter to implement a spanking new SDK-based ActiveX control for your own use!

Creating a Custom AppWizard

Put simply, a custom AppWizard is a specialized DLL. It must have the **.awx** extension and it must reside in a special directory. Actually, it can reside in one of two special directories, **\Msdev\Bin\Ide** or **\Msdev\Template**, but you should only use the second of these for your own AppWizards. **\Msdev\Bin\Ide** is used by Microsoft for holding all things relating to the Developer Studio. If you're curious, you can look through its contents to see Microsoft's AppWizards. **\Msdev\Template** is used to hold any enhancements that the user makes to the environment, including resource templates, custom AppWizards and, one of the other great mysteries of life, the Component Gallery database, **Gallery.dat**.

The combination of the file extension and its location are enough for Visual C++ to 'know' that the file is a custom AppWizard and attempt to load it. Of course, if it isn't really an AppWizard, then nothing much will happen, so the real question is, how do we create a genuine custom AppWizard? Let's go through the process and find out.

Throughout this book, I have simply assumed that you can generate a skeleton application or component using the wizards. At this point, however, because writing custom AppWizards is not a normal function of life, we will examine the process in a little more detail.

TRY IT OUT - Create the Custom AppWizard Skeleton

1 To start out, fire up Developer Studio and choose to create a new project workspace. You will then see the New Project Workspace dialog shown. The Type list will display the available AppWizards on your system. Select Custom AppWizard from this list, give the project the name ActiveXGen (for **ActiveX** Control **Gen**erator) and set the Location to wherever you want to store the project. Click Create...

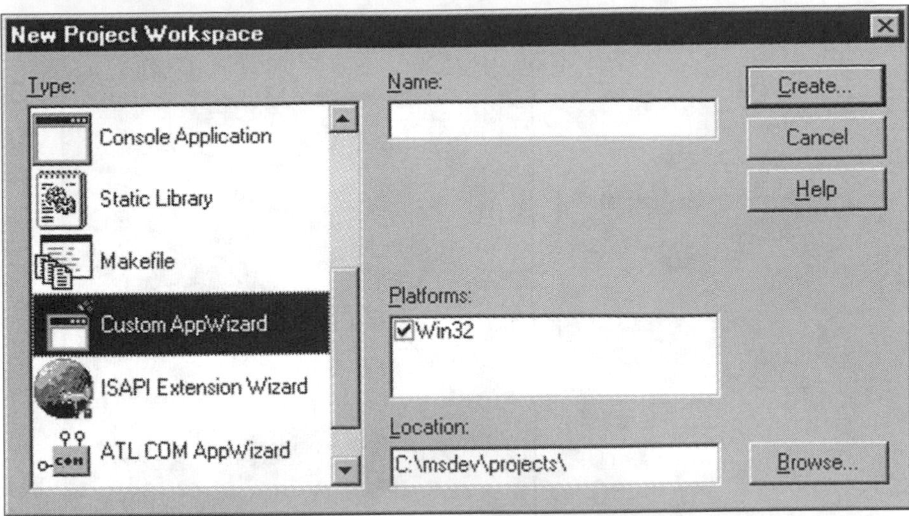

2 The next dialog you will see is labeled Custom AppWizard - Step 1 of 2. On this screen you can select what kind of wizard you would like to create. Since we don't have a project on which to base the wizard, and we don't want a wizard based on the standard AppWizard, you should select Your own custom steps as the starting point. Note how the title of the dialog changes when you do this to Custom AppWizard - Step 1 of 1. Changing the option has reduced the number of steps in the dialog and the title of the current step has updated accordingly.

There's no need to change the name of the wizard shown in the edit field; ActiveXGen AppWizard is fine unless you want to change it. This is the name that will appear in the Type list on the New Project Workspace dialog.

The final thing you need to decide is how many custom steps to give the wizard. The answer to this will determine how many pages the custom AppWizard is going to display to the user. Obviously, you have to give some forethought to creating the wizard before using this tool!

In our case, the custom ActiveXGen wizard will have two custom steps. As you will see later, the wizard doesn't really *need* two steps, it could get by quite well with only one, but we'll go ahead and add a second page to it anyway. This will allow room for you to add your own customizations later, when you understand more about the controls we will generate with the wizard.

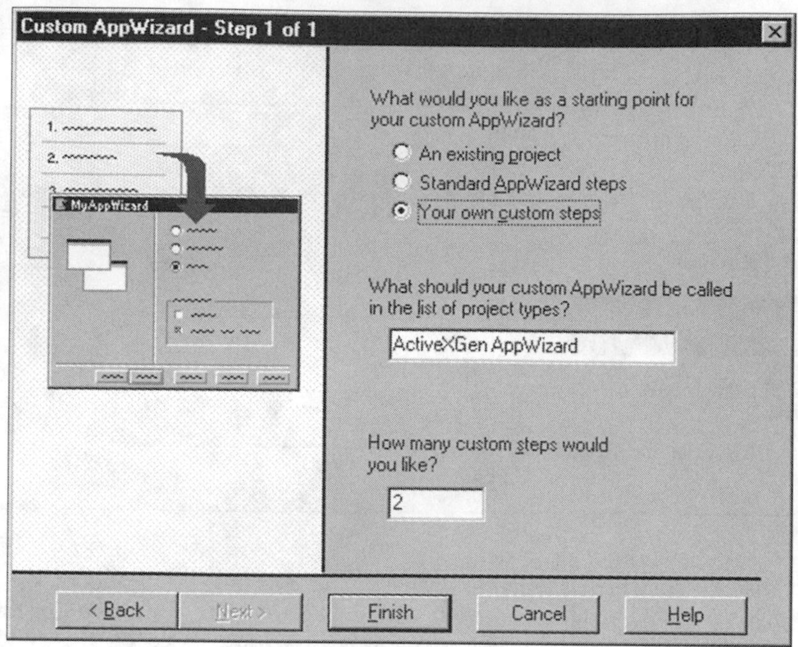

3 When you have finished entering the information for this dialog, click Finish. You should see a New Project Information dialog which looks much like the one shown. If you're using Visual C++ 4.2, the note it contains is very important for the continued success of this example. You won't see this note in other versions of VC++. Once you've read the information, you can press OK to finish the creation of the project.

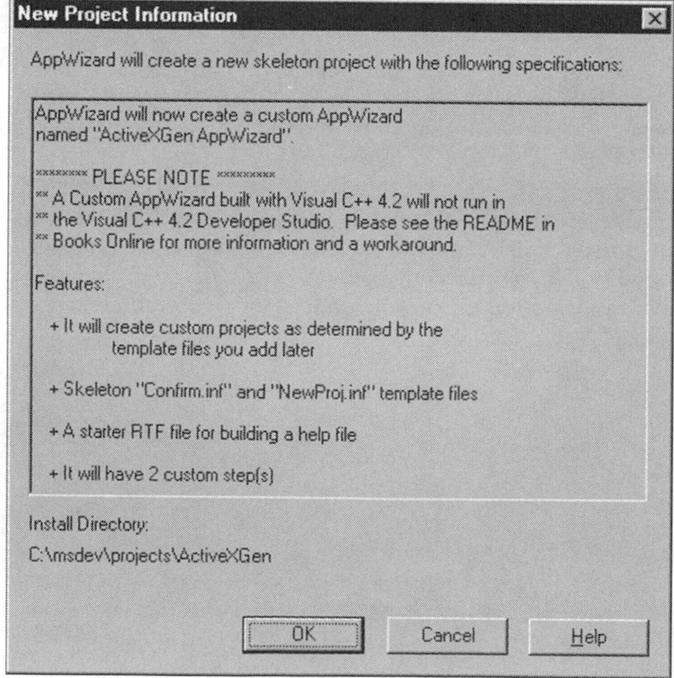

If you are using Visual C++ 4.2, you must build the custom AppWizard using the libraries from Visual C++ 4.1. You can find out the steps that you need to take by reading the relevant section of **`Vcread.wri`** *which you can find in your* **`\Msdev`** *directory.*

So, you have just generated a complete custom AppWizard! Why not compile it now? There's a custom build step that will copy the compiled AppWizard into the **`\Template`** directory so, once the build is complete, you can try out creating a new project workspace based on the AppWizard. Isn't that a wonderful feeling?

It would probably feel a whole lot better if the custom AppWizard actually did something, though. Before we can begin to implement the functionality behind the AppWizard, however, we need to go back to the custom AppWizard that was generated for us and understand it a little better. We'll start by looking at the classes that were generated for our own custom wizard.

Generated Classes

If you take a look at the ClassView in Developer Studio, you'll see that the Custom AppWizard AppWizard has created a number of classes for us, most of which look pretty unfamiliar. Let's take a quick look through them to see what we can learn.

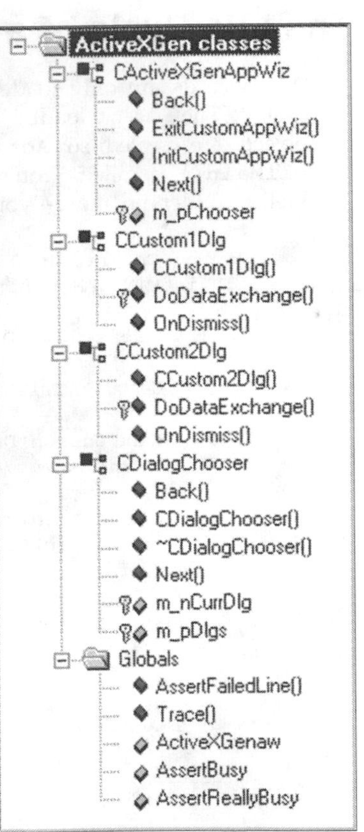

CActiveXGenAppWiz

First up, we've got **`CActiveXGenAppWiz`** and the associated global object **`ActiveXGenaw`**. This object is the only occurrence of the class in this DLL and is used to implement all of the global code for the DLL. Developer Studio will load the DLL and then look for this object. Since **`CActiveXGenAppWiz`** is derived from **`CCustomAppWiz`**, Developer Studio can simply invoke known methods in the global object and let the implementation of the specific AppWizard class determine what to do.

CCustomxDlg

Following that, we've got a couple of dialog classes, **`CCustom1Dlg`** and **`CCustom2Dlg`**. You probably won't be surprised to learn that when you create a custom AppWizard, you will find one of these custom dialog classes for each step that you decide to have. You will also find a corresponding dialog in the resource file. Note that these steps will actually form part of a larger dialog. The buttons and title bar of the AppWizard are provided by Developer Studio. The steps only need to contain the controls specific to that AppWizard.

If you take a look at the header for these classes you'll see that they are actually derived from **CAppWizStepDlg**. **CAppWizStepDlg** derives from **CDialog** and apart from the **OnDismiss()** function, it doesn't really add a lot of functionality that we need to worry about. **OnDismiss()** will be called whenever a step is dismissed, so that we can handle whatever validation needs doing. We'll look at this in more detail later.

CDialogChooser

The last class is **CDialogChooser**. The chooser in a custom AppWizard is the object which decides which wizard page is displayed next in response to the user choosing the Back or Next buttons. You can see that it's pretty simple, with just two functions (**Back()** and **Next()**) to respond to the user navigating through the wizard, a member **m_nCurrDlg** to keep track of the current dialog and an array, **m_pDlgs**, of pointers to the dialog steps.

We'll examine each of these classes in more detail as we implement the AppWizard. First, let's run quickly through the life of a custom AppWizard.

The Life Cycle of a Custom AppWizard

AppWizards are only loaded when the user clicks on their name in the New Project Workspace dialog. They aren't loaded until they're needed. First, as in any DLL or application, the global objects are created, so **ActiveXGenaw** is alive through the whole life of the AppWizard. Next, **DllMain()** is called. You're probably wondering where the AppWizard's **DllMain()** is hiding. Well, wonder no more—you can find it in **ActiveXGen.cpp**:

```
extern "C" int APIENTRY
DllMain(HINSTANCE hInstance, DWORD dwReason, LPVOID lpReserved)
{
    if (dwReason == DLL_PROCESS_ATTACH)
    {
        TRACE0("ACTIVEXGEN.AWX Initializing!\n");

        // Extension DLL one-time initialization
        AfxInitExtensionModule(ActiveXGenDLL, hInstance);

        // Insert this DLL into the resource chain
        new CDynLinkLibrary(ActiveXGenDLL);

        // Register this custom AppWizard with MFCAPWZ.DLL
        SetCustomAppWizClass(&ActiveXGenaw);
    }
    else if (dwReason == DLL_PROCESS_DETACH)
    {
        TRACE0("ACTIVEXGEN.AWX Terminating!\n");
    }
    return 1;   // ok
}
```

This function initializes the custom AppWizard in the same way for all wizards. First, the MFC extension module is initialized by calling **AfxInitExtensionModule()**. This is a one-time initialization done when the DLL is first loaded (as the comment indicates). Next, the DLL is inserted into the resource chain. This is done by the call to **new CDynLinkLibrary()**. Basically, this allocation allows the DLL to be used as a resource by itself and by applications (such as Developer Studio). Finally, a curious function called **SetCustomAppWizClass()** is called. This function links our custom AppWizard into Developer Studio itself, identifying it as a valid AppWizard and ensuring that it's displayed in the Type list of the New Project Workspace dialog. This is also how Developer Studio gets a pointer to the **ActiveXGenaw** object so that it can call its functions when necessary.

CActiveXGenAppWiz::InitCustomAppWiz() is called as soon as the custom AppWizard is fully loaded. If you need to do any system-wide initialization, checking, or other pre-startup code you should implement that code here. The default implementation looks like this.

```
void CActiveXGenAppWiz::InitCustomAppWiz()
{
   // Create a new dialog chooser; CDialogChooser's constructor
   // initializes  its internal array with pointers to the steps.
   m_pChooser = new CDialogChooser;

   // Set the maximum number of steps.
   SetNumberOfSteps(LAST_DLG);

   // TODO: Add any other custom AppWizard-wide initialization here.
}
```

It just creates a new chooser and sets the number of steps of the dialog. You can find the definition of **LAST_DLG** in **Chooser.h**. The constructor for the chooser just creates new objects based on the dialog step classes and stores them in its list.

The next thing to happen is that the user will click Create in the New Project Workspace dialog to create a new project based on your wizard. At this stage, Developer Studio will call **CCustomAppWiz::Next()**. This function will also be called every time the user moves through the AppWizard's steps using the Next button. The return value of this function must be a pointer to the next step dialog to display. By default, **CCustomAppWiz::Next()** just calls **CDialogChooser::Next()** which simply steps forward through its array of dialogs and returns the next one.

From here on, the user can step backwards and forwards through the dialogs using the Back and Next buttons. Each time, a call will be made to **CCustomAppWiz::Next()** or **CCustomAppWiz::Back()**, which just delegates that call to the corresponding **CDialogChooser** function. Each time a dialog is dismissed, its **OnDismiss()** function is called to allow it to perform any validation necessary.

The user won't be able to go beyond the number of steps that actually exist because Developer Studio uses the number passed by the call to **SetNumberOfSteps()** to disable the Next button if the last step has been reached, and to keep the Step *x* of *y* information in the title bar up to date.

Eventually, the Finish button will be pressed and the AppWizard will be unloaded. Just before this happens, **CActiveXGenAppWiz::ExitCustomAppWiz()** will be called, allowing the AppWizard to clean up any resources. The default implementation just **delete**s the chooser that it created. The chooser destructor, in turn, **delete**s all the step dialogs that it created.

Producing Files

Okay. So we've seen how to navigate through the steps of a wizard, we know that we don't need to supply the buttons to do this and, if we don't need to do anything special, we can just leave it up to **`CDialogChooser`** to determine which dialog to display. We can add controls to the dialogs associated with the steps and validate the input in **`OnDismiss()`**.

There's only one thing missing: the files that the AppWizard should create. Where do they come from, and how do we alter them based on the user's input? Maybe we should start by looking at the standard AppWizards to find out where they store their files.

If you look through the directory in which AppWizards are stored, you won't find any source files. They don't appear in any other directory on your hard-drive or CD-ROM, either. Where is Microsoft putting the things? The surprising answer is that the files are actually stored *inside* the AppWizard as custom resources (called **`"TEMPLATE"`** resources in custom AppWizards). This is a powerful technique that you could use in your own applications as well.

> ***Consider using custom resources when you need to create files or databases during the normal execution of your programs.***

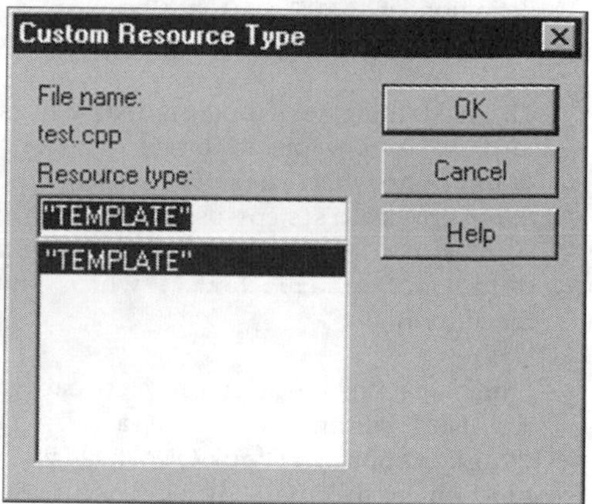

In order to store a file in your custom AppWizard, you first open the resource editor, right-click on the folder that says "TEMPLATE" in the list of resources, and click on the Import... menu item. Select the file that you want to import, make sure that the Open as list says Custom and click the Import button.

This will bring up the Custom Resource Type dialog. You can just select "TEMPLATE" from the list and click OK to add the file as a **`"TEMPLATE"`** resource. The resource editor will load the file into a binary format in your resource script (**`.rc`** file) and the resource will then be available to your custom AppWizard to load when it's time to generate the files.

> ***WARNING: The file generator can't handle files which contain end-of-file markers put there by DOS editors. If you use such an editor (e.g. the DOS version of Brief), you will need to load the file into the internal Developer Studio editor and remove the file marker, which will be a strange looking box at the very end of the file. If you do not do this, you will get weird error messages when the custom AppWizard tries to generate the file from the template.***

If you look at the "TEMPLATE" resources for the custom AppWizard project, you will see that there are already two resources there, "CONFIRM.INF" and "NEWPROJ.INF". These resources, based on the files of the same names (which you can find in the **\Template** directory under the project directory for your custom AppWizard), are vital to the functioning of an AppWizard, so we'll consider them next.

NewProj.inf

There's a lot more to getting the custom AppWizard to add files to the projects it creates than just adding them to the resources. We also need to supply entries for them in the **NewProj.inf** file. If you open the file now, you'll see the contents shown below.

```
$$// newproj.inf = template for list of template files
$$//  format is 'sourceResName' \t 'destFileName'
$$//    The source res name may be preceded by any combination of '=',
$$//                                                         '+', and/or '*'
$$//       '=' => the resource is binary
$$//       '+' => the file should be added to the project
$$//       '*' => bypass the custom AppWizard's resources when loading
$$//   if name starts with / => create new subdir
```

Believe it or not, it's pretty straightforward once you've deciphered the cryptic comments. The first thing you need to understand is that, if you add files to the **"TEMPLATE"** resources, you should surround their names with quote marks, but when you give the resource name in the **NewProj.inf** file, you should give the name of the resource without the quotes.

The second thing to watch out for is that you don't have your editor options set to convert tabs to spaces when you edit the **NewProj.inf** file. It really does want a tab (i.e. the result of pressing the *Tab* key) between the resource name and the filename.

You also need to understand what the **=** and **+** signs do. If you put **=** in front of the resource name, that resource will not be **processed** before a file is produced from it. We haven't looked at how files can be processed by AppWizard yet, but AppWizard can use a form of macro substitution to adapt the output files based on settings that the user has chosen. If you have files that don't need to be processed, you should precede the resource name with an **=** sign. Note that the **NewProj.inf** file is itself processed for macros.

The **+** sign means that the file produced from the resource should be added to the makefile (**.mak**) for the project. This will be handled for you automatically.

Confirm.inf

Confirm.inf is the standard file that is used to display the confirmation page for the AppWizard when the user clicks the Finish button. This file will always be processed for macros and there's no need to put an entry for it into **NewProj.inf**, since we don't want to actually create it as a separate file when the user finishes using our custom AppWizard.

Macro Substitution

As we've just mentioned, the files that are emitted from the AppWizard based on the resources it stores are processed by Developer Studio's built-in AppWizard macro processor (unless they are preceded by an **=** sign in the **NewProj.inf** file). But what do macros actually look like when they're in the files? How are they separated from normal text that shouldn't be converted into something else?

The answer is that they simply consist of a name surrounded by double dollar signs, for example **$$MACRO_NAME$$**. When processing takes place, all occurrences of **$$MACRO_NAME$$** will be replaced by the value of that macro. That leads us to the second question: how do we give macros values?

That's pretty simple. Macro values are stored in a dictionary. This dictionary is actually a **CMapStringToString** member, called **m_Dictionary**, of the main custom AppWizard object (in our case, **ActiveXGenaw**). This just maps the macro name to another string value which is used to replace the macro when processing occurs (i.e. when the user has clicked Finish and confirmed their choices).

You can add macros to the dictionary and set their values using syntax like this:
ActiveXGenaw.m_Dictionary["MACRO_NAME"]="A macro was here";
or you can remove macros from the dictionary using **RemoveKey()** like this:
ActiveXGenaw.m_Dictionary.RemoveKey("MACRO_NAME");
Note that in both cases the macro name is surrounded by quotes, but not double dollars.

There are also a number of predefined macros which you can use in your custom AppWizard. **ROOT** and **Root** are used quite regularly. These represent, respectively, the project name (without the extension) in uppercase and in the case entered by the user. You can find the complete list of predefined or standard macros in the online help.

Well, that's quite enough theory for one day. Let's get down to creating a working custom AppWizard.

TRY IT OUT - A Simple Custom AppWizard

1 First, create a new text file and save it as **Test.txt** in the **\Template** directory of the custom AppWizard project. Add the following text to it:

```
// This file has been produced by a custom AppWizard
Control Name:           $$ControlName$$
Short Control Name:     $$ShortName$$
Company Name:           $$CompanyName$$
Standard Macros:
$$FULL_DIR_PATH$$
$$ROOT$$
$$Root$$
$$root$$
$$SAFE_ROOT$$

```

This will serve to demonstrate that macro substitution does work.

> *Note the extra blank line at the bottom of the file. Sometimes, AppWizard parsing can behave a little strangely. If you make sure that all files that need to be processed have a blank line at the end, you will find fewer problems.*

2 Now switch to Resource View, right-click on the "TEMPLATE" folder and select Import... from the pop-up menu. Use the resulting Import Resource dialog to select the **Test.txt** file, set Open as to Custom and click Import. Now select "TEMPLATE" as the custom resource type and the file will be imported. Bring up the properties for the new resource and change its ID to "TEST.TXT".

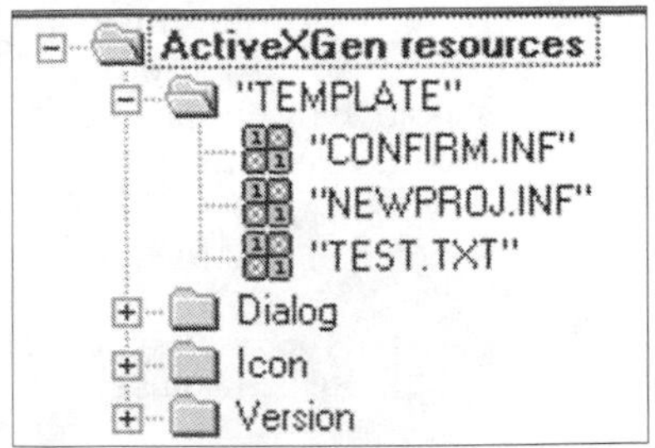

3 Now open **NewProj.inf** and add the following line to it. (Again, note the blank line.)

```
+Test.txt    $$ControlName$$.txt
```

4 The next step is to modify the dialogs that will be displayed for each step of the custom AppWizard, so use the resource editor to modify the custom dialog **IDD_CUSTOM1** to look as shown. This will become the first page of our custom AppWizard, and will be displayed to the user to input the name of a control as well as a shorter, internal name.

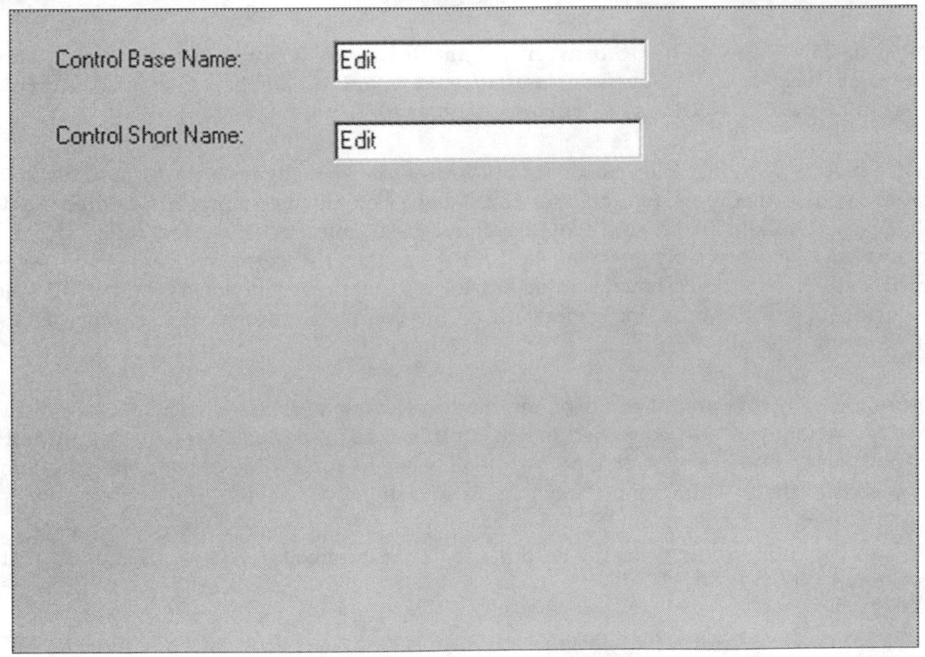

Similarly, you can add an edit box to the second dialog which will accept a company name.

5 The next step is to add data variables for these edit controls to the dialog classes. *Ctrl-*double-click on each of the edit boxes to bring up the Add Member Variable dialog. All the members should be of Category: Value and Variable type: CString. Give them the names **m_strControlName**, **m_strShortControlName**, and **m_strCompanyName**.

6 Now comes the fun part! We need to copy the new values of these variables into the global object, **ActiveXGenaw**, which keeps track of all of the settings for the new project. This should be done in the **OnDismiss()** methods of the dialog classes. Make the following modifications to the **CCustom1Dlg::OnDismiss()** and **CCustom2Dlg::OnDismiss()**:

```
BOOL CCustom1Dlg::OnDismiss()
{
   if (!UpdateData(TRUE))
      return FALSE;

   ActiveXGenaw.m_Dictionary["ControlName"] = m_strControlName;
   ActiveXGenaw.m_Dictionary["ShortName"] = m_strShortControlName;
   return TRUE;    // return FALSE if the dialog shouldn't be dismissed
}

BOOL CCustom2Dlg::OnDismiss()
{
   if (!UpdateData(TRUE))
      return FALSE;

   ActiveXGenaw.m_Dictionary["CompanyName"] = m_strCompanyName;
   return TRUE;    // return FALSE if the dialog shouldn't be dismissed
}
```

We just set up the mapping between the macro names (**ControlName**, **ShortName**, **CompanyName**) and whatever the user entered in the dialog boxes (**m_strControlName**, **m_strShortControlName**, **m_strCompanyName**).

7 When you're working with custom AppWizards, it isn't always safe to assume that the values you wished to have the user input have actually been input. Required fields should always be checked to be sure that they have been entered before the code can be generated. In our case, it's probably not realistic to assume that the company name will always be initialized. If you don't have a value set for a component/dictionary entry, the system will generate an error during the generation of the completed project if that entry is used in one of the template files.

You should always initialize all of the values in your system and check them when entered. We aren't going to add any checking to **OnDismiss()** because we can simply initialize the macro values and leave it at that. We don't need to force the user to enter anything, but if they didn't, there wouldn't be much point in using the wizard.

This sort of initialization should be done in **InitCustomAppWiz()** so modify that function as shown below.

```
void CActiveXGenAppWiz::InitCustomAppWiz()
{
   // Create a new dialog chooser; CDialogChooser's constructor
   // initializes its internal array with pointers to the steps.
   m_pChooser = new CDialogChooser;

   // Set the maximum number of steps.
   SetNumberOfSteps(LAST_DLG);
```

```
    m_Dictionary["ControlName"] = "ControlName";
    m_Dictionary["ShortName"] = "Name";
    m_Dictionary["CompanyName"] = "My Company Inc.";
}
```

8 Now compile the AppWizard and create a new project based on it. You'll see that the new project will contain a single text file with whatever name you gave as the control's name. If you open that file, you'll see that the macros have indeed been expanded. The confirmation dialog won't have been much to look at, but we'll fix that when we go on to implement a more functional version of the AppWizard.

The ActiveXGen AppWizard

Hopefully, you now have an understanding of what's happening when you generate a project with AppWizard. To recap, it's a macro substitution scheme. You supply information in the Wizard steps which are then inserted into the files stored as resources in the Wizard DLL.

Now we are able to extend this to the complete ActiveX generator project. As with any code generated with an AppWizard, there's more than a single file generated. For an ActiveX control we'll need code to initialize the control, code for the control itself, code for the property pages, **.def** and **.odl** files, a makefile, various headers and, of course, a resource file. Here's the complete listing of the **Newproj.inf** file that we will be using in this ActiveX generator. We will then examine each of the files in the list and show you what's going on.

A word of warning: as you can see below, there's a lot of code coming up. Unlike making modifications to generated files, you need to enter the whole project from scratch. We also need all the files to be present before we can actually create any projects that are meaningful. So, you may want to grab the source code from the Wrox Press web site (http://www.wrox.com/download.htm#0499).

```
$$// newproj.inf = template for list of template files
$$//  format is 'sourceResName' \t 'destFileName'
$$//    The source res name may be preceded by any combination of '=', '+', and/or
'*'
$$//       '=' => the resource is binary
$$//       '+' => the file should be added to the project
$$//       '*' => bypass the custom AppWizard's resources when loading
$$//   if name starts with / => create new subdir
```

```
+tmpl.cpp    $$ControlName$$.cpp
+tmplctl.cpp    $$ControlName$$Ctl.cpp
+tmplctl.h    $$ControlName$$Ctl.h
+tmplppg.cpp    $$ControlName$$Ppg.cpp
+tmplppg.h    $$ControlName$$Ppg.h
+tmpl.def    $$ControlName$$.def
+tmpl.odl    $$ControlName$$.odl
+tmplinte.h    $$ControlName$$Interfaces.h
+makefile    Makefile
+guids.cpp    guids.cpp
```

```
+guids.h    guids.h
+localobj.h    localobj.h
+dispids.h    dispids.h
+dwWinVers.h    dwWinVers.h
+resource.h    resource.h
+tmpl.rc    $$ControlName$$.rc
+test.txt    Readme.txt
```

Obviously, you don't want to type in all of this code without testing it along the way. Unfortunately, the only thing you can really test is that the substitution is working as expected. To do this, simply place **$$//** before every line except for the file you want to test, compile the custom AppWizard and use it. You can then check the resulting file to make sure the code is what you expected.

At the end of the chapter, we'll give some tips on to how to make building custom AppWizards easier.

Tmpl.cpp

Let's start at the top. This is actually the main entry point for an ActiveX control generated by our custom AppWizard. Create a new source file in Visual C++, add the following code to the file and save it as **Tmpl.cpp**:

```
//=--------------------------------------------------------------------------=
// $$ControlName$$.Cpp
//=--------------------------------------------------------------------------=
//
// Company:  $$CompanyName$$
//
// various routines etc. that aren't in a file for a particular automation
// object, and don't need to be in the generic ole automation code.
//
#define INITOBJECTS                    // define the descriptions for our objects

#include "IPServer.H"
#include "LocalSrv.H"


#include "LocalObj.H"
#include "CtrlObj.H"
#include "Globals.H"
#include "Util.H"
#include "Resource.H"

#include "$$ControlName$$Ctl.H"
#include "$$ControlName$$PPG.H"

// needed for ASSERTs and FAIL
//
SZTHISFILE

//=--------------------------------------------------------------------------=
```

```
// our Libid.  This should be the LIBID from the Type library, or NULL if you
// don't have one.
//
const CLSID *g_pLibid = &LIBID_$$ControlName$$Objects;


//=--------------------------------------------------------------------------=
// Localization Information
//
// We need the following two pieces of information:
//    a. whether or not this DLL uses satellite DLLs for localization.  if
//       not, then the lcidLocale is ignored, and we just always get resources
//       from the server module file.
//    b. the ambient LocaleID for this in-proc server.  Controls calling
//       GetResourceHandle() will set this up automatically, but anybody
//       else will need to be sure that it's set up properly.
//
const VARIANT_BOOL    g_fSatelliteLocalization =  FALSE;
LCID             g_lcidLocale = MAKELCID(LANG_USER_DEFAULT, SORT_DEFAULT);


//=--------------------------------------------------------------------------=
// your license key and where under HKEY_CLASSES_ROOT_LICENSES it's sitting
//
const WCHAR g_wszLicenseKey [] = L"";
const WCHAR g_wszLicenseLocation [] = L"";


WNDPROC g_ParkingWindowProc = NULL;

//=--------------------------------------------------------------------------=
// This Table describes all the automatible objects in your automation server.
// See AutomationObject.H for a description of what goes in this structure
// and what it's used for.
//
OBJECTINFO g_ObjectInfo[] = {
    CONTROLOBJECT($$ControlName$$),
    PROPERTYPAGE($$ControlName$$General),
    EMPTYOBJECT
};

const char g_szLibName[] = "$$ControlName$$";

//=--------------------------------------------------------------------------=
// IntializeLibrary
//=--------------------------------------------------------------------------=
// called from DllMain:DLL_PROCESS_ATTACH.  allows the user to do any sort of
// initialization they want to.
//
// Notes:
//
void InitializeLibrary(void)
{
    // TODO: initialization here.  control window class should be set up in
    // RegisterClassData.
}

//=--------------------------------------------------------------------------=
```

```
// UninitializeLibrary
//=--------------------------------------------------------------------------=
// called from DllMain:DLL_PROCESS_DETACH.  allows the user to clean up anything
// they want.
//
// Notes:
//
void UninitializeLibrary(void)
{
    // TODO: uninitialization here.  control window class will be unregistered
    // for you, but anything else needs to be cleaned up manually.
    // Please Note that the Window 95 DLL_PROCESS_DETACH isn't quite as stable
    // as NT's, and you might crash doing certain things here ...
}


//=--------------------------------------------------------------------------=
// CheckForLicense
//=--------------------------------------------------------------------------=
// users can implement this if they wish to support Licensing.  otherwise,
// they can just return TRUE all the time.
//
// Parameters:
//    none
//
// Output:
//    BOOL            - TRUE means the license exists, and we can proceed
//                      FALSE means we're not licensed and cannot proceed
//
// Notes:
//     - implementers should use g_wszLicenseKey and g_wszLicenseLocation
//       from the top of this file to define their licensing [the former
//       is necessary, the latter is recommended]
//
BOOL CheckForLicense(void)
{
    // TODO: decide whether or not your server is licensed in this function.
    // people who don't want to bother with licensing should just return
    // true here always.  g_wszLicenseKey and g_wszLicenseLocation are
    // used by IClassFactory2 to do some of the licensing work.
    //
    return TRUE;
}

//=--------------------------------------------------------------------------=
// RegisterData
//=--------------------------------------------------------------------------=
// lets the inproc server writer register any data in addition to that in
// any other objects.
//
// Output:
//    BOOL            - false means failure.
//
// Notes:
//
BOOL RegisterData(void)
{
    // TODO: register any additional data here that you might wish to.
```

```
    //
    return TRUE;
}

//=-------------------------------------------------------------------------=
// UnregisterData
//=-------------------------------------------------------------------------=
// inproc server writers should unregister anything they registered in
// RegisterData() here.
//
// Output:
//    BOOL            - false means failure.
//
// Notes:
//
BOOL UnregisterData(void)
{
    // TODO: any additional registry cleanup that you might wish to do.
    //
    return TRUE;
}


//=-------------------------------------------------------------------------=
// CRT stubs
//=-------------------------------------------------------------------------=
// these two things are here so the CRTs aren't needed. this is good.
//
// basically, the CRTs define this to suck in a bunch of stuff.  we'll just
// define them here so we don't get an unresolved external.
//
// TODO: if you are going to use the CRTs, then remove this line.
//
extern "C" int __cdecl _fltused = 1;

extern "C" int _cdecl _purecall(void)
{
  FAIL("Pure virtual function called.");
  return 0;
}

BOOL       CheckLicenseKey(LPWSTR wszCheckme)
{
   return TRUE;
}

BSTR       GetLicenseKey(void)
{
   return NULL;
}
```

As you can see, we perform only eight substitutions in the file. Most of the contents of this file are completely generic to any ActiveX project. There's one very important thing to note about the file: the large quantity of comments. When you create a custom AppWizard you're generating code that other people will be modifying. You therefore need to add **TODO** comments, and explain why they are there. Without these, your generated code would be very difficult for someone else to use.

As before, this file needs to be added to the **ActiveXGen** project resources. In the ResourceView, right-click on the "TEMPLATE" folder and select Import... from the pop-up menu. Use the resulting Import Resource dialog, select the **Tmpl.cpp** file, set Open as to Custom and click Import. Now select "TEMPLATE" as the custom resource type and the file will be imported. Bring up the properties for the new resource and change its ID to "TMPL.CPP".

Tmplctl.cpp

The next file we are going to look at is the **Tmplctl.cpp** file. This is the main control implementation file and contains all of the support code for ActiveX controls. We will discuss this file in considerably more depth when we actually implement a new control using this wonderful new custom AppWizard we're creating:

```
#include "IPServer.H"

#include "Guids.H"
#include "LocalObj.H"
#include "Util.H"
#include "Globals.H"
#include "Resource.H"
#include "$$ControlName$$ctl.H"

// for ASSERT and FAIL
//
SZTHISFILE

WCHAR wsz$$ShortName$$ [] = L"$$ShortName$$";


const GUID *rg$$ControlName$$PropPages [] = {
    &CLSID_$$ControlName$$GeneralPage
};

IUnknown *C$$ControlName$$Control::Create(IUnknown *pUnkOuter)
{
    // make sure we return the private unknown so that we support aggegation
    // correctly!
    //
    C$$ControlName$$Control *pNew = new C$$ControlName$$Control(pUnkOuter);
    return pNew->PrivateUnknown();
}

#pragma warning(disable:4355)  // using 'this' in constructor
C$$ControlName$$Control::C$$ControlName$$Control(IUnknown *pUnkOuter)
: CInternetControl(pUnkOuter, OBJECT_TYPE_CTL$$ControlName$$, (IDispatch *)this)
{
}
#pragma warning(default:4355)  // using 'this' in constructor

C$$ControlName$$Control::~C$$ControlName$$Control ()
{
}

BOOL C$$ControlName$$Control::RegisterClassData()
{
    WNDCLASS wndclass;
```

```
    // TODO: register any additional information you find interesting here.
    //       this method is only called once for each type of control
    //
    memset(&wndclass, 0, sizeof(WNDCLASS));
    wndclass.style          = CS_VREDRAW | CS_HREDRAW | CS_DBLCLKS | CS_OWNDC;
    wndclass.lpfnWndProc    = COleControl::ControlWindowProc;
    wndclass.hInstance      = g_hInstance;
    wndclass.hCursor        = LoadCursor(NULL, IDC_ARROW);
    wndclass.hbrBackground  = (HBRUSH)(COLOR_WINDOW + 1);
    wndclass.lpszClassName  =
WNDCLASSNAMEOFCONTROL(OBJECT_TYPE_CTL$$ControlName$$);

    return RegisterClass(&wndclass);
}

void C$$ControlName$$Control::BeforeCreateWindow()
{
}

BOOL C$$ControlName$$Control::AfterCreateWindow()
{
   return TRUE;
}

HRESULT C$$ControlName$$Control::InternalQueryInterface(REFIID  riid,void
**ppvObjOut)
{
    IUnknown *pUnk;

    *ppvObjOut = NULL;

    // TODO: if you want to support any additional interrfaces, then you should
    // indicate that here.  never forget to call COleControl's version in the
    // case where you don't support the given interface.
    //
    if (DO_GUIDS_MATCH(riid, IID_I$$ControlName$$)) {
        pUnk = (IUnknown *)(I$$ControlName$$ *)this;
    } else{
        return COleControl::InternalQueryInterface(riid, ppvObjOut);
    }

    pUnk->AddRef();
    *ppvObjOut = (void *)pUnk;
    return S_OK;
}

STDMETHODIMP C$$ControlName$$Control::LoadTextState(IPropertyBag
*pPropertyBag,IErrorLog*pErrorLog)
{
    VARIANT v;

    VariantInit(&v);

    v.vt = VT_BSTR;
    v.bstrVal = NULL;

    HRESULT hr = S_OK;
    // try to load in the property.  if we can't get it, then leave
```

```
    // things at their default.
    //
    pPropertyBag->Read(::wsz$$ShortName$$, &v, pErrorLog);

    return hr;
}
const DWORD STREAMHDR_MAGIC = 12345678L;

STDMETHODIMP C$$ControlName$$Control::LoadBinaryState(IStream *pStream)
{
    DWORD     sh;
    HRESULT     hr;

    // first read in the streamhdr, and make sure we like what we're getting
    //
    hr = pStream->Read(&sh, sizeof(sh), NULL);
    RETURN_ON_FAILURE(hr);

    // sanity check
    //
    if (sh != STREAMHDR_MAGIC )
      return E_UNEXPECTED;

    return 0;
}

STDMETHODIMP C$$ControlName$$Control::SaveTextState(IPropertyBag
*pPropertyBag,BOOL fWriteDefaults)
{
    HRESULT hr = 0;

    return hr;
}

STDMETHODIMP C$$ControlName$$Control::SaveBinaryState(IStream *pStream)
{
    DWORD sh = STREAMHDR_MAGIC;
    HRESULT hr;

    // write out the stream hdr.
    //
    hr = pStream->Write(&sh, sizeof(sh), NULL);
    RETURN_ON_FAILURE(hr);

    return hr;
}
HRESULT C$$ControlName$$Control::OnDraw(DWORD dvAspect, HDC hdcDraw, LPCRECTL
prcBounds, LPCRECTL prcWBounds,
    HDC       hicTargetDevice, BOOL fOptimize )
{
    // TODO: Draw control here

    return S_OK;
}
HRESULT C$$ControlName$$Control::OnProgress(DISPID propId, ULONG progress, ULONG
themax,
      ULONG   statusFlag,
      LPCWSTR   statusString)
```

```
{
   // TODO: put custom progress UI notification code here. The default action
   //    (shown below) is to fire an OnProgress event to the host

   return(FireProgress(themax ? (progress * 100)/themax : 0));
}

LRESULT C$$ControlName$$Control::WindowProc(UINT  msg,WPARAM wParam,LPARAM lParam)
{

    // TODO: handle any messages here, like in a normal window
    // proc.  note that for special keys, you'll want to override and
    // implement OnSpecialKey.
    //

    return OcxDefWindowProc(msg, wParam, lParam);
}

void C$$ControlName$$Control::AboutBox(void)
{
}

HRESULT C$$ControlName$$Control::OnData(DISPID propId,DWORD grfBSCF,IStream *strm,
   DWORD      dwSize)
{
   return 0;
}
```

To conserve space in this book, all of the comment header blocks before the code have been removed. The complete version of each file can be found on the Wrox Press web site, and all generated code will contain the complete header source blocks. After all, I just got through ranting and raving for several chapters about writing documentation. Did you really think I would leave it out now?

Class and Variable Names

Apart from what the code actually does (we'll discuss that in a moment), the main thing to note about this file is the use of the substitution mechanism to generate a class name based on the control name, in the same way that Custom AppWizard AppWizard did for us. So the line

```
HRESULT C$$ControlName$$Control::OnData(DISPID propId, DWORD grfBSCF,
                                          IStream *strm, DWORD dwSize)
```

would expand to

```
HRESULT CMyControlControl::OnData(DISPID propId, DWORD grfBSCF, IStream *strm,
                                                          DWORD dwSize)
```

if the user of the **ActiveXGen** AppWizard entered **MyControl** for the control's name. Now, here's an important point. When you're designing your custom AppWizard, you must make sure that all the classes and variables that you generate with the substitution will be unique where they need to be. Consider the following situation: your control has an About dialog associated with it, so somewhere in the generated project you define a **C$$ControlName$$About** class. Your version of the About dialog has a button that shows a dialog about the company, so you also define a **C$$CompanyName$$About** class. Everything will be fine and dandy, until someone generates an Wrox control for Wrox.

So, make sure that it's impossible for the AppWizard user to enter some information during the steps that can lead to this situation. You can do this either by validating the information as it is entered, in this case making sure the **ControlName** and **CompanyName** can never be the same, or by using only one macro to generate all the classes and variables within the project, as we have done.

The Purpose Behind Tmplctl.cpp

Getting back to our custom AppWizard, after entering the above file and saving it as **Tmplctl.cpp**, you need to add this file as a "TEMPLATE" resource in the resource file.

Now, let's take a look at some of the high points of the **Tmplctl.cpp** file. This file represents the actual ActiveX interface for the control. All control drawing, input, output, and property selection takes place through this interface. Let's look at the big picture by taking the code apart in methods and examining them. The table below shows the complete list of methods and what they do:

Method	Purpose
Create()	This method creates the actual ActiveX object. It'sautomatically generated and probably will not need to be changed by the users of your Wizard.
Constructor	The normal C++ constructor for the object. This is a good place to put one-time initialization for the object and member variable settings.
RegisterClassData()	This method registers the window class for this control. Any specialized window settings should be done here.
BeforeCreateWindow()	After the control object is created (but before the actual control window is created), this method is called. This is a good place to put startup code for drawing.
AfterCreateWindow()	This method is called after the control window is created.
InternalQueryInterface()	This method is called to find out what interfaces are supported by the ActiveX control. Normally, you will not modify this method unless you are adding new interfaces to the control. Multiple interface controls are not discussed in this book.
LoadTextState()	This method is one of the ways that properties can be loaded into the control. We will discuss this method a little later in the chapter.
LoadBinaryState()	This is the other method for retrieving properties in a control in a binary state. It should be used to load complete structures.
SaveTextState()	This is a method used for object persistence to write out changed or new attributes or properties.
SaveBinaryState()	This is the binary equivalent for writing out object data to support object persistence.

Table Continued on Following Page

Method	Purpose
OnDraw()	The main rendering method for the object. This is where all rendering of the ActiveX control on the client canvas takes place. There will be more discussion of this method a little later.
OnProgress()	Called when the object is downloading data, this method allows the programmer to display custom progress indicators to indicate how far along the download is.
AboutBox()	A simple utility method called to allow the programmer to display an About dialog for this control. This is actually the first example of a true object method in the control.
WindowProc()	Just like a normal Windows window procedure, this method is used to handle special processing of Windows messages (mouse clicks, keyboard entries, etc.).
OnData()	Called to load data for the control.

The above table provides a fairly comprehensive list of the available methods when using the ActiveX control objects. Some of the methods are fairly obvious in design, such as the **OnDraw()** method. This method is used to draw the control. Other methods are less obvious, such as the **LoadTextState()** method. This method is how you will load data from the HTML page on which you are running, via property settings embedded in the page. We will take a look at how to do this in our first sample control later in this chapter.

The **RegisterClassData()**, **BeforeCreateWindow()** and **AfterCreateWindow()** methods are entry points for your users' own customization. In these functions, we have put the minimum amount of code for the generated ActiveX control to work, then left **TODO** comments for them.

Tmplctl.h

For completeness (and so you can get things to compile), here is the **Tmplctl.h** header file (don't forget to add it as a new "TEMPLATE" type resource in your custom AppWizard):

```
//=--------------------------------------------------------------------------=
// $$ControlName$$Ctl.H
//=--------------------------------------------------------------------------=
//
// class declaration for the $$ControlName$$ control.
//
#ifndef _$$ControlName$$CONTROL_H_

#include "IPServer.H"
#include "CtrlObj.H"
#include "Internet.h"
#include "$$ControlName$$Interfaces.H"
#include "Dispids.H"


#include "DibCls.H"

typedef struct tag$$ControlName$$CTLSTATE {

    // TODO: Replace with real state variables
```

```
    short TEMP;

} $$ControlName$$CTLSTATE;

//=--------------------------------------------------------------------------=
// C$$ControlName$$Control
//=--------------------------------------------------------------------------=
// our control.
//
class C$$ControlName$$Control : public CInternetControl,
                                public I$$ControlName$$,
                                public ISupportErrorInfo
{

  public:
    // IUnknown methods
    //
    DECLARE_STANDARD_UNKNOWN();

    // IDispatch methods
    //
    DECLARE_STANDARD_DISPATCH();

    // ISupportErrorInfo methods
    //
    DECLARE_STANDARD_SUPPORTERRORINFO();

    // I$$ControlName$$ methods
    //
    //
    STDMETHOD_(void, AboutBox)(THIS) ;

    // OLE Control stuff follows:
    //
    C$$ControlName$$Control(IUnknown *pUnkOuter);
    virtual ~C$$ControlName$$Control();

    // static creation function.  all controls must have one of these!
    //
    static IUnknown *Create(IUnknown *);

  private:
    // overridables that the control must implement.
    //
    STDMETHOD(LoadBinaryState)(IStream *pStream);
    STDMETHOD(SaveBinaryState)(IStream *pStream);
    STDMETHOD(LoadTextState)(IPropertyBag *pPropertyBag, IErrorLog *pErrorLog);
    STDMETHOD(SaveTextState)(IPropertyBag *pPropertyBag, BOOL fWriteDefault);
    STDMETHOD(OnDraw)(DWORD dvAspect, HDC hdcDraw, LPCRECTL prcBounds, LPCRECTL
prcWBounds, HDC hicTargetDev, BOOL fOptimize);
    virtual LRESULT WindowProc(UINT msg, WPARAM wParam, LPARAM lParam);
    virtual BOOL    RegisterClassData(void);

    virtual HRESULT InternalQueryInterface(REFIID, void **);
    virtual void    BeforeCreateWindow(void);

    virtual BOOL    AfterCreateWindow(void);
```

```
    //   Internet specific callbacks:
    //
    ///   OnData is called asynchronously as data for an object or property
arrives...
    virtual HRESULT OnData( DISPID id, DWORD grfBSCF,IStream * bitstrm, DWORD
amount );

    //   OnProgess is called to allow you to present progess indication UI
    virtual HRESULT OnProgress( DISPID, ULONG progress, ULONG themax, ULONG,
LPCWSTR);


     // private state information.
     //

    HDC                m_dc;

};

extern const GUID    *rg$$ControlName$$PropPages [];
DEFINE_CONTROLOBJECT($$ControlName$$,
     &CLSID_$$ControlName$$,
     "$$ControlName$$Ctl",
     C$$ControlName$$Control::Create,
     1,
     &IID_I$$ControlName$$,
     "$$ControlName$$.HLP",
     &DIID_D$$ControlName$$Events,
     OLEMISC_SETCLIENTSITEFIRST|OLEMISC_ACTIVATEWHENVISIBLE|
            OLEMISC_RECOMPOSEONRESIZE|OLEMISC_CANTLINKINSIDE|OLEMISC_INSIDEOUT,
    0,
     RESID_TOOLBOX_BITMAP,
     "$$ControlName$$WndClass",
     1,
     rg$$ControlName$$PropPages,
     0,
     NULL);

#define _$$ControlName$$CONTROL_H_
#endif // _$$ControlName$$CONTROL_H_
```

Tmplppg.cpp

Moving right along with the files, we come to the property page for the control. This will display the standard OCX property page for controls when in a suitable container object (such as Visual Basic or Test Container). Here's the source file for the **Tmplppg.cpp** source file which you should add to the "TEMPLATE" resources. Once again, the comments have been stripped out of the source file to save space in the book.

```
//=---------------------------------------------------------------------------=
// $$ControlName$$PPG.Cpp
//=---------------------------------------------------------------------------=
//
// property page implementations for $$ControlName$$ control.
//
#include "IPServer.H"
```

```
#include "LocalObj.H"
#include "$$ControlName$$PPG.H"
#include "$$ControlName$$Ctl.H"
#include "Resource.H"
#include "Util.H"


// for ASSERT and FAIL
//
SZTHISFILE


IUnknown *C$$ControlName$$GeneralPage::Create
(
    IUnknown *pUnkOuter
)
{
    return (IUnknown *)new C$$ControlName$$GeneralPage(pUnkOuter);
}

C$$ControlName$$GeneralPage::C$$ControlName$$GeneralPage
(
    IUnknown *pUnkOuter
)
: CPropertyPage(pUnkOuter, OBJECT_TYPE_PPG$$ControlName$$GENERAL)
{
    // initialize local variables here.
}

C$$ControlName$$GeneralPage::~C$$ControlName$$GeneralPage()
{
    // clean up
}

BOOL C$$ControlName$$GeneralPage::DialogProc
(
    HWND   hwnd,
    UINT   msg,
    WPARAM wParam,
    LPARAM lParam
)
{
    HRESULT     hr;
    I$$ControlName$$ *p$$ControlName$$;
    IUnknown    *pUnk;
    DWORD       dwDummy;
    VARIANT    var;

    switch (msg) {

      case WM_COMMAND:
        break;
    }

   return(FALSE);
}
```

Once again, let's take a look at the methods available in the property page class for the ActiveX control.

Method	Purpose
`Create()`	Creates an instance of the property page object for the control.
Constructor	Called when the object is instantiated, this method is best for one-time initialization of property page data.
Destructor	Called to clean up any allocated memory within the property page run.
`DialogProc()`	Analogous to the **`WindowProc()`** method of the control itself, this is the dialog procedure used to handle messages to the dialog. We will discuss this method in depth shortly.

Tmplppg.h

Let's look at the header file for the property page, **`Tmplppg.h`**:

```
//=--------------------------------------------------------------------------=
// $$ControlName$$PPG.H
//=--------------------------------------------------------------------------=
//
// class declaration for $$ControlName$$'s property pages.
//
#ifndef _$$ControlName$$PROPPAGE_H_


// kinda need these
//
#include "PropPage.H"
#include "Resource.H"
#include "Guids.H"

class C$$ControlName$$GeneralPage : public CPropertyPage {

  public:
    static IUnknown *Create(IUnknown *pUnkOuter);

    // constructor and destructor
    //
    C$$ControlName$$GeneralPage(IUnknown *pUnkOuter);
    virtual ~C$$ControlName$$GeneralPage();

  private:
    virtual BOOL DialogProc(HWND, UINT, WPARAM, LPARAM);

};

DEFINE_PROPERTYPAGEOBJECT($$ControlName$$General,
    &CLSID_$$ControlName$$GeneralPage,
    "$$ControlName$$ General Propery Page",
    C$$ControlName$$GeneralPage::Create,
    IDD_PROPPAGE_$$ControlName$$GENERAL,
    IDS_$$ControlName$$_GENERALPAGETITLE,
```

```
        IDS_$$ControlName$$_GENERALDOCSTRING,
        "vb.hlp",
        0);

#define _$$ControlName$$PROPPAGE_H_
#endif // _$$ControlName$$PROPPAGE_H_
```

Not too much is exciting here. The **DEFINE_PROPERTYPAGEOBJECT** is a macro used to identify the property page by name and ID to the system, and give it the proper values so that it can be loaded later. That's why there's so much substitution occurring.

Tmpl.def

The next file to examine is the **Tmpl.def** module definition file. It's neither exciting nor informative, but it's necessary.

```
; ------------------------------------------------------------------------
; $$ControlName$$.Def - Module definition file for $$ControlName$$.Ocx (win32)
; ------------------------------------------------------------------------
;

LIBRARY         $$ControlName$$
PROTMODE

DESCRIPTION
'Test Control'

CODE            PRELOAD MOVEABLE DISCARDABLE
DATA            PRELOAD MOVEABLE SINGLE

EXPORTS         DllRegisterServer
EXPORTS         DllUnregisterServer
EXPORTS         DllCanUnloadNow
EXPORTS         DllGetClassObject
```

As you can see, the primary purpose of the module definition file is to export the four required interface functions for the control:

- **DLLRegisterServer** will register this control with the system so that it can be found and loaded.
- **DLLUnregisterServer** will unload this control from the system registry so that it can be replaced or deleted.
- **DLLCanUnloadNow** is a query method to see if this DLL control can be unloaded from memory.
- **DLLGetClassObject** returns the object for which the control is implemented.

In fact, it would be a rare circumstance if this file ever needed to be edited by the user of your Wizard, but then this is exactly the reason for us including it in the "TEMPLATE" resource; you are removing the need for the user to write or alter code which will never change from project to project.

Tmpl.odl

Unlike the module definition file, which is boring, the **.odl** (OLE description language file) is really quite interesting. Let's take a quick look at it, and highlight, the important points to be found in the file:

```
//=--------------------------------------------------------------------------=
// $$ControlName$$.ODL
//
// ODL file for the control(s) and automation object(s) in this inproc server
//
#include <olectl.h>
#include <idispids.h>
#include <internet.h>
#include "dispids.h"

// can't include oaidl.h, so this will have to do
//
#define DISPID_NEWENUM -4


//=--------------------------------------------------------------------------=
// the libid for this type libray
//
[
    uuid(b92bb5c0-2e73-11cf-b6cf-00aa00a74daf),
    helpstring("$$ControlName$$ Control Library"),
    lcid(0x0000),
    version(1.0)
]
library $$ControlName$$Objects {

    // standard imports
    //
    importlib("STDOLE32.TLB");
    importlib(STDTYPE_TLB);
    importlib("datapath.tlb");

    // primary dispatch interface for C$$ControlName$$ control
    //
    [
        uuid(bb1a1840-2e73-11cf-b6cf-00aa00a74daf),
        helpstring("$$ControlName$$ Control"),
        hidden,
        dual,
        odl
    ]
    interface I$$ControlName$$ : IDispatch {

        // properties
        //

        // methods
        //
        [id(DISPID_ABOUTBOX)]
            void AboutBox(void);

    };
```

```
        // event interface for C$$ControlName$$ controls ...
        //
        [
            uuid(bbcb18c0-2e73-11cf-b6cf-00aa00a74daf),
            helpstring("Event interface for $$ControlName$$ control"),
            hidden
        ]
        dispinterface D$$ControlName$$Events {

            properties:

            methods:

            [id(DISPID_PROGRESS)]
                void OnProgress(long percentDone);

        };

        // coclass for C$$ControlName$$ controls
        //
        [
            uuid(bd11a280-2e73-11cf-b6cf-00aa00a74daf),
            helpstring("$$ControlName$$ control")
        ]
        coclass $$ControlName$$ {
            [default]          interface I$$ControlName$$;
            [default, source] dispinterface D$$ControlName$$Events;
        };
    };
```

This file contains all sorts of goodies, so let's begin by looking through it for pearls of wisdom. To begin with, the **.odl** file is used by the **mktyplib** utility program to create a **.tlb** file. This **.tlb** file represents a **type library** which can be used by external applications such as Visual C++ and Visual Basic to identify ActiveX controls in order to use them. This type library file contains binary information used to list the methods, properties, and interfaces of the control.

Within the specific example listed above, we define a class (given the name we define in the wizard) and the interfaces for that class.

```
coclass $$ControlName$$ {
    [default]          interface I$$ControlName$$;
    [default, source] dispinterface D$$ControlName$$Events;
```

This class is not to be confused with the C++ class it represents. When the **mktyplib** program is run, a corresponding C++ class and header will be generated for this class, which is a wrapper around the OLE control we're defining here.

To understand more about the .odl file and what it represents, get a good book on OLE and read it thoroughly. Then read it again and try to make some sense of it. Finally, throw it away and dig into some more OLE code.

As you can (hopefully) see from the above example, our class defines a single dispatch method for the **AboutBox()** method we defined in the class header. Where are all of the rest of the methods we defined with the **STDMETHOD** macro in the control? The answer is that they are defined in the base class for the control and are imported into the **.odl** file via the import statements at the top of the file. When a class inherits from another class in OLE, you need not redefine the methods which are inherited, even if they are overridden in the child class.

The **helpstring** markers denote strings which are used by the container object for this control to display help information about the particular bits they are defined for. For the UUID of the control, for example, the help string **$$ControlName$$ control** is defined, indicating that this is the actual control class we're defining, rather than the property page or wrapping DLL class.

Tmplinte.h

The next few files we'll be discussing are the same for each ActiveX file you define. The first is the **Tmplinte.h** file, which contains the interface information for the control. Here's the file itself:

```
/* This header file machine-generated by mktyplib.exe */
/* Interface to type library: $$ControlName$$Objects */

#ifndef _$$ControlName$$Objects_H_
#define _$$ControlName$$Objects_H_

DEFINE_GUID(LIBID_$$ControlName$$Objects,0xB92BB5C0L,0x2E73,0x11CF,
                  0xB6,0xCF,0x00,0xAA,0x00,0xA7,0x4D,0xAF);
#ifndef BEGIN_INTERFACE
#define BEGIN_INTERFACE
#endif

DEFINE_GUID(IID_I$$ControlName$$,0xBB1A1840L,0x2E73,0x11CF,0xB6,
                  0xCF,0x00,0xAA,0x00,0xA7,0x4D,0xAF);

/* Definition of interface: I$$ControlName$$ */
#undef INTERFACE
#define INTERFACE I$$ControlName$$

DECLARE_INTERFACE_(I$$ControlName$$, IDispatch)
{
BEGIN_INTERFACE
#ifndef NO_BASEINTERFACE_FUNCS

     /* IUnknown methods */
     STDMETHOD(QueryInterface)(THIS_ REFIID riid, LPVOID FAR* ppvObj) PURE;
     STDMETHOD_(ULONG, AddRef)(THIS) PURE;
     STDMETHOD_(ULONG, Release)(THIS) PURE;

     /* IDispatch methods */
     STDMETHOD(GetTypeInfoCount)(THIS_ UINT FAR* pctinfo) PURE;

     STDMETHOD(GetTypeInfo)(
       THIS_
       UINT itinfo,
       LCID lcid,
```

```
        ITypeInfo FAR* FAR* pptinfo) PURE;

      STDMETHOD(GetIDsOfNames)(
        THIS_
        REFIID riid,
        OLECHAR FAR* FAR* rgszNames,
        UINT cNames,
        LCID lcid,
        DISPID FAR* rgdispid) PURE;

      STDMETHOD(Invoke)(
        THIS_
        DISPID dispidMember,
        REFIID riid,
        LCID lcid,
        WORD wFlags,
        DISPPARAMS FAR* pdispparams,
        VARIANT FAR* pvarResult,
        EXCEPINFO FAR* pexcepinfo,
        UINT FAR* puArgErr) PURE;
  #endif

      /* I$$ControlName$$ methods */
      STDMETHOD(get_ReadyState)(THIS_ long FAR* thestate) PURE;
      STDMETHOD_(void, AboutBox)(THIS) PURE;
  };

  DEFINE_GUID(DIID_D$$ControlName$$Events,0xBBCB18C0L,0x2E73,0x11CF,0xB6,
                0xCF,0x00,0xAA,0x00,0xA7,0x4D,0xAF);

  /* Definition of dispatch interface: D$$ControlName$$Events */
  #undef INTERFACE
  #define INTERFACE D$$ControlName$$Events

  DECLARE_INTERFACE_(D$$ControlName$$Events, IDispatch)
  {
  BEGIN_INTERFACE
  #ifndef NO_BASEINTERFACE_FUNCS

      /* IUnknown methods */
      STDMETHOD(QueryInterface)(THIS_ REFIID riid, LPVOID FAR* ppvObj) PURE;
      STDMETHOD_(ULONG, AddRef)(THIS) PURE;
      STDMETHOD_(ULONG, Release)(THIS) PURE;

      /* IDispatch methods */
      STDMETHOD(GetTypeInfoCount)(THIS_ UINT FAR* pctinfo) PURE;

      STDMETHOD(GetTypeInfo)(
        THIS_
        UINT itinfo,
        LCID lcid,
        ITypeInfo FAR* FAR* pptinfo) PURE;

      STDMETHOD(GetIDsOfNames)(
        THIS_
        REFIID riid,
        OLECHAR FAR* FAR* rgszNames,
        UINT cNames,
```

```
        LCID lcid,
        DISPID FAR* rgdispid) PURE;

      STDMETHOD(Invoke)(
        THIS_
        DISPID dispidMember,
        REFIID riid,
        LCID lcid,
        WORD wFlags,
        DISPPARAMS FAR* pdispparams,
        VARIANT FAR* pvarResult,
        EXCEPINFO FAR* pexcepinfo,
        UINT FAR* puArgErr) PURE;
#endif

      /* D$$ControlName$$Events methods:
      void OnReadyStateChange(long newState);
      void OnProgress(long percentDone);
      */
};

DEFINE_GUID(CLSID_$$ControlName$$,0xBD11A280L,0x2E73,0x11CF,0xB6,
                  0xCF,0x00,0xAA,0x00,0xA7,0x4D,0xAF);

#ifdef __cplusplus
class $$ControlName$$;
#endif

#endif
```

This file simply represents the **mktyplib** output from the **.odl** file we discussed last. It will be regenerated by **mktyplib** whenever the **.odl** file changes, but we need to include it into the project initially, as it's required for the project to compile... which is a nice segue into the next section.

Makefile

In order to compile the project, we need to specify the building of the executable and all other files. This takes place in the **Makefile** for the application, which is the next file to create. Here's the **Makefile**, in all of its glory:

```
dll = 1

Proj = $$ControlName$$


# These are "extra" libs beyond the standard set that inetsdk.mak will
#  append to the libs set

libs=uuid2.lib uuid3.lib urlmon.lib urlhlink.lib wininet.lib ocx96.lib shell32.lib
oleaut32.lib cap.lib


# Static libs have to be treated specially.
# Notice that this particular one is built from the ..\framewrk directory
```

```
STATICLIBS= ..\lib\CtlFwD32.lib


# Commands to be added to the compile line... in this case to locate headers

cDefines= -I..\Include
RFLAGS= -I..\Include


# pull in the master SDK makefile that defines all of the macros
#  and all of the build rules
#
# TODO: you may need to change this path so that it points to where
#       you have installed the Internet SDK

!include <c:\inetsdk\include\inetsdk.mak>


all: $(ObjDir)\$(Proj).ocx REGISTER


# itemize all of the required object files

OBJS=$(ObjDir)\Guids.Obj    \
     $(ObjDir)\$$ControlName$$.Obj     \
     $(ObjDir)\$$ControlName$$Ctl.Obj \
     $(ObjDir)\$$ControlName$$PPG.Obj \
     $(Proj).res


# after the ocx is built, register it

REGISTER: $(ObjDir)\$(Proj).ocx
  regsvr32 /s $(ObjDir)\$(Proj).ocx

# special case the odl file since the output header has a special name

$(Proj)Interfaces.h: $(Proj).odl
  mktyplib /DWIN32 -I..\Include /h $(Proj)Interfaces.h /o $(Proj).log /tlb
$(Proj).tlb $(Proj).odl

# and finally, just define the dependencies

$(ObjDir)\$(Proj).ocx: $(OBJS) $(ObjDir)\$(Proj).Exp $(STATICLIBS)

$(ObjDir)\$(Proj).Exp: $(Proj).def $(STATICLIBS)

$(ObjDir)\guids.obj: guids.cpp $(Proj)Interfaces.h
```

As you can see, this isn't a standard Visual C++ makefile. Rather, it's a command-line-oriented makefile. The reason for this is that the system must be setup just so for the ActiveX library to be compiled and linked correctly. All of the makefiles for the ActiveX SDK are already command-line-oriented, so this doesn't seem like much of a hardship. Compiling from the command line is also much faster than the IDE, and since the internal tools (ClassWizard, resource editor, etc.) really can't be used with these projects (because the ActiveX SDK doesn't have the correct information for them to work) you aren't losing much. Enter this file and save it as **Makefile**. Don't forget to add it as a "TEMPLATE" resource in the custom AppWizard project. Put the file with all of the others in the template directory of the project you created for the custom AppWizard.

Guids.cpp

The next two files to create are for the GUIDs in the system. GUID stands for Globally Unique Identifier and is intended to be a 128-byte identifier which is global across all of space and time. The chances of two GUIDs having the same value in two controls are... actually quite good. Since we are not generating new identifiers for each control, the controls will always have the same identifier.

> *You can fix this by generating a new GUID each time the ActiveXGen AppWizard is used. We'll leave this as an exercise for you to do, but as a little clue (actually it's a huge clue), have a look in **CoCreateGuid()**.*

Here's the **Guids.cpp** file:

```
//=---------------------------------------------------------------------------=
// Guids.Cpp
//=---------------------------------------------------------------------------=
//
// contains the guids we will define ourselves.
//


#define INITGUID                          // define all the guids.
#include "IPServer.H"

#include "Guids.H"
#include "olectl.h"
#include "datapath.h"
#include "docobj.h"
#include "$$ControlName$$Interfaces.H"
```

And here's the header file, **Guids.h**:

```
//=---------------------------------------------------------------------------=
// Guids.H
//=---------------------------------------------------------------------------=
//
// guids that we define locally
//
#ifndef _GUIDS_H_

// for each property page this server will have, put the guid definition for it
// here so that it gets defined ...
//
DEFINE_GUID(CLSID_$$ControlName$$GeneralPage, 0xbe508b20, 0x2e73, 0x11cf,
                0xb6, 0xcf, 0x00, 0xaa, 0x00, 0xa7, 0x4d, 0xaf);


#define _GUIDS_H_
#endif // _GUIDS_H_
```

If the user of your Wizard needs to add new property pages to their control or new interfaces, they will need to modify this file. One option you have is to get them to define the number of pages and interfaces in one of the Wizard steps. The substitution process actually caters for loops and branches, so you build up a list of GUIDs and insert them into **Guids.h**. This is beyond the scope of this book, so we'll leave our Wizard with a single property page.

Localobj.h

The next file we'll consider is also quite small. It holds the identifiers for the control numbers such as property pages and controls. Give this file the name **Localobj.h**:

```
//=--------------------------------------------------------------------------=
// LocalObj.H
//=--------------------------------------------------------------------------=
//
// this file is used by automation servers to delcare things that their objects
// need other parts of the server to see.
//
#ifndef _LOCALOBJECTS_H_

//=--------------------------------------------------------------------------=
// these constants are used in conjunction with the g_ObjectInfo table that
// each inproc server defines.  they are used to identify a given  object
// within the server.
//

#define OBJECT_TYPE_CTL$$ControlName$$ 0
#define OBJECT_TYPE_PPG$$ControlName$$GENERAL 1

#define _LOCALOBJECTS_H_
#endif // _LOCALOBJECTS_H_
```

When you're adding new properties or methods to the control, you will do so through a combination of the **.odl** file and the header and source files for the control object. When you're doing this, you will often find yourself trying to determine the last ordinal number of the control method or property you defined. We'll look at this in detail in the next section, when we actually create a new control using the wizard. For now, just take my word for it.

Dispids.h

The control identifiers are better created as defined values, using constants defined in a separate file. In the case of ActiveX controls, this file is the **Dispids.h** file:

```
//=--------------------------------------------------------------------------=
// Dispids.H
//=--------------------------------------------------------------------------=
//
// dispids for use in an automation or control object.
//
#ifndef _DISPIDS_H_

//=--------------------------------------------------------------------------=
// properties & methods
//
```

```
// events
//


#define _DISPIDS_H_
#endif // _DISPIDS_H_
```

As you can see, there's nothing presently in the file. That's because when a control is generated, there are no properties or events; the Wizard users must add these themselves. You'll see this when we cover it later on.

Tmpl.rc

The next big file to consider is the resource script file for the object. This file will be called **`Tmpl.rc`** and looks like this:

```
//////////////////////////////////////////////////////////////////////////////
// $$ControlName$$.Rc
//
// contains the resources for our DLL, including the TypeLib, error strings,
// and versioning information.
//
#include "Resource.H"
#include "Windows.H"

#define IDC_STATIC -1

//////////////////////////////////////////////////////////////////////////////
//
// Bitmap and Icons that are not localized
//

//////////////////////////////////////////////////////////////////////////////
//
// Our Non-Localized Type Library
//
1 TYPELIB $$ControlName$$.TLB



//////////////////////////////////////////////////////////////////////////////
// EVERYTHING FROM HERE UNTIL THE VERSION RESOURCES IS LOCALIZABLE          //
//////////////////////////////////////////////////////////////////////////////



//////////////////////////////////////////////////////////////////////////////
//
// String tables with Exception Information, etc.
//
STRINGTABLE DISCARDABLE
BEGIN
    IDS_PROPERTIES,                         "$$ControlName$$ Properties"
    IDS_$$ControlName$$_GENERALPAGETITLE,         "General Properties"
    IDS_$$ControlName$$_GENERALDOCSTRING,         "General properties for the
$$ControlName$$ control"
```

```
END

////////////////////////////////////////////////////////////////////////////
//
// Property Page Dialog
//

IDD_PROPPAGE_$$ControlName$$GENERAL DIALOG DISCARDABLE  0, 0, 195, 127
STYLE WS_CHILD | 0x4
FONT 8, "MS Sans Serif"
BEGIN
    RTEXT           "Image URL:",-1,6,42,51,11
    EDITTEXT        IDC_URL,9,59,178,14,ES_AUTOHSCROLL
END


////////////////////////////////////////////////////////////////////////////
// Version Information
////////////////////////////////////////////////////////////////////////////
//
#include "dwWinVers.h"
#include <winver.h>

VS_VERSION_INFO VERSIONINFO

FILEVERSION    04,00,vusVersNumf2,vusVersNuml2 //<----- This is used by setup!
PRODUCTVERSION    04,00,vusVersNumf2,vusVersNuml2


FILEFLAGSMASK   VS_FFI_FILEFLAGSMASK
#ifdef DEBUG
FILEFLAGS   VS_FF_DEBUG
#else
FILEFLAGS   0L
#endif

FILEOS       VOS_NT_WINDOWS32

FILETYPE   VFT_DLL
FILESUBTYPE   0
{
    BLOCK "StringFileInfo"
    {
        BLOCK "040904B0" // Language and character set identifiers.
        {
            VALUE "CompanyName",       "$$CompanyName$$"
            VALUE "FileDescription", "$$ControlName$$"
            VALUE "FileVersion",      vszVersNumAll
            VALUE "InternalName",      "$$ControlName$$.Ocx\0"
            VALUE "LegalCopyright",  vszCopyright
            VALUE "LegalTrademarks", "Put Legal TradeMarks here ...\0"
            VALUE "ProductName",       "$$ControlName$$ Object Library\0"
            VALUE "ProductVersion",  vszVersNumAll
            VALUE "Comments",          vszMakeDate
            VALUE "OLESelfRegister", "\0"
        }
    }
    BLOCK "VarFileInfo"
```

```
        {
            VALUE "Translation" ,0x409, 0x4b0
        }
    }
```

Resource.h

To go along with the resource script, there are two utility files that must be included as well. Create a new file called **Resource.h** and add the following lines to it:

```
//=--------------------------------------------------------------------------=
// Resource.H
//=--------------------------------------------------------------------------=
//
// resource IDs.
//
#ifndef _RESOURCE_H_

#define RESID_TOOLBOX_BITMAP 1


//=--------------------------------------------------------------------------=
// Strings
//
#define IDS_PROPERTIES                   1000              // this MUST be 1000 !!!
#define IDS_$$ControlName$$_GENERALPAGETITLE 2003
#define IDS_$$ControlName$$_GENERALDOCSTRING 2004
#define IDS_$$ControlName$$_ABOUTBOXVERB     2005


//=--------------------------------------------------------------------------=
// Dialog Stuff
//
#define IDD_PROPPAGE_$$ControlName$$GENERAL 2000

#define IDC_URL   101

#define _RESOURCE_H_
#endif // _RESOURCE_H_
```

dwWinVers.h

And finally, add the following lines to a new file called **dwWinVers.h**:

```
#define vszMakeDate    "May 19, 1996\0\0"
#define vszMakeVers    "Version 1 - RELEASE - ntfs-e\0\0"
#define vszVersNum   "1\0"
#define vszVersNumAll    "1.00.10\0"
#define vusVersNuml2    8
#define vusVersNumf2   25
#define vszCopyright    "Copyright 1996 $$CompanyName$$\0\0"
#define VBA_VERHI   0x30000
#define VBA_VERLO   0x170F
```

These are simply the default settings for the version information to be stored with each control. Storing version information is a wonderful way to track changes to controls as well as a way to identify a control as belonging to yourself or your company. You should always add version information to any control you create so that it can be readily identified later.

Confirm.inf

That's all of the source code and related files that need to be added to the wizard. If you were to generate a new project with it, the project would compile and run fine. The problem is that when you came to the end of the wizard process (pressing the Finish button in the custom AppWizard), you would be presented by a blank confirmation page. The confirmation page is the page which displays the settings for the control and asks the user if this is really what they want. In the normal AppWizard application, the confirmation page displays whether the generated application is to be single or multiple document interface based, the OLE settings, the Database settings, and the names of the main classes. It would be nice if our custom AppWizard had something of the sort, rather than a simple screen that says very little.

The confirmation page information is simply another templated file which was generated by the AppWizard when you told it that you wanted a custom AppWizard application. This file is called **Confirm.inf**. Modify the **Confirm.inf** file (which is already listed in the resource file as a "TEMPLATE" resource) as follows:

```
ActiveX Control $$ROOT$$:
Target:
   Win32

Classes to be created:
   Main Entry Point:      $$ControlName$$.CPP
   Control File:          $$ControlName$$Ctl.CPP
   Property Page File:    $$ControlName$$Ppg.CPP

Features:
    + ActiveX Control
```

This will result in a display which shows the end user the name of the control, the name of the files that were generated, and the features for the control (which in our case is simply that the application is an ActiveX control). Once you have completed this step, your resources should look like the display shown on the next page. If your screen looks like this screen, you're all set!

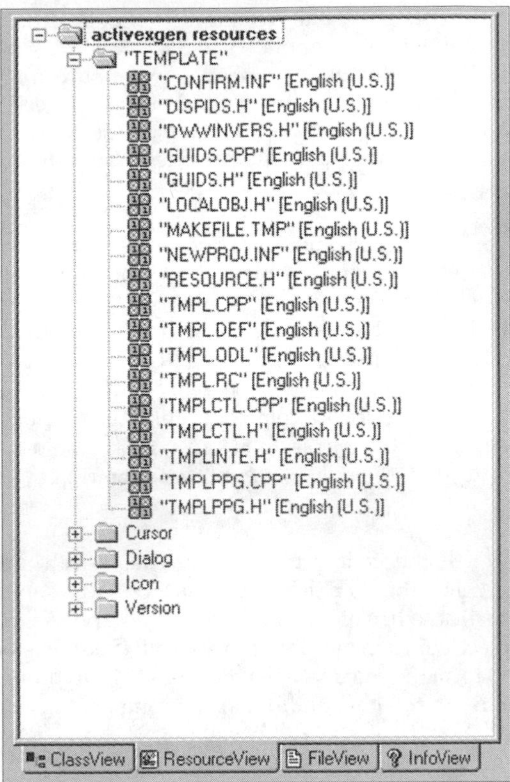

All that's really left to do is compile the application and try it out, which we'll do in the next chapter.

Tips on Creating Custom AppWizards

Before we get on to using our custom AppWizard, we did promise to give you some tips on creating custom AppWizards. As you have seen from reading this chapter, we have really assumed that you know in advance what files are needed so that you can create the "TEMPLATE" resource for the AppWizard. This is rarely the case though. It would be almost impossible to start from the Custom AppWizard AppWizard and work forwards. Instead, you should start from a complete, compilable project and work backwards to the "TEMPLATE" resources required—this is the key to success.

Normally, you would only consider generating your own custom AppWizard if you regularly code applications that have some commonality between them, which of course is why you use AppWizard in the first place. A good example would be if you used a particular class library above and beyond, or instead of, MFC. In this case, you would want to generate projects that already included the right headers into the right places in your source files and linked in the right libraries. This can have an added benefit if the libraries are written in-house—you would know that your programmers were always using the correct versions.

The question is, then, how do you go about creating the "TEMPLATE" resources? Well, let's assume that you have a fully functioning application. The first thing you'll have to do is remove all the functionality from it. When you do, you should make sure that you put in **`TODO`** comments that indicate what the function is there for. You'll also need to make sure that the functions return something meaningful. The idea behind this is to reduce the application into a state where you only have a skeleton which still compiles. Once done, you're half way to getting your "TEMPLATE" resources.

The next stage is to start replacing class and variable names. This is where things start to get a little complicated. Remember that you don't actually have to change any names in the project at all; this would just mean that all projects created with your custom AppWizard would contain the same names. This could be fine, but then again, it could lead to problems. For example, what happens if you try to combine two projects? Your code won't compile! If you were to follow Microsoft's scheme, class names should be based on the project name. To this I would add that global functions which have **`TODO`** comments in should also be based on the project name. After you have made your decision as to what names should change, go through the source code, changing them to something like **`CProjNameAboutDlg`**, etc. You should then make sure the project still compiles.

The final stage is to go through the code replacing **`ProjName`** with **`$$ProjName$$`**. Once done, your files are ready to insert into the "TEMPLATE" resource. You should do a similar thing with the filenames themselves, so that when you use the custom AppWizard, the created project has filenames based on the project name. Now you can compile your custom AppWizard and try it out. The best way to check to make sure you haven't missed anything is to create a project called **`ProjName`**. You can then use the Windiff tool to compare the created project with the files used to create the template. As a final check, reinstate all the functionality that you removed from the original project and make sure you can compile the source, and that it works as the original. If it does, you're done!

Summary

Custom AppWizards are really a separate variety of component, and deserve a bit of attention for that reason. Components are intended to save you time and reduce duplication by allowing you to write a single component that does the work in multiple places. AppWizards are components that allow you to create new components (usually programs) by reusing a standard bed of code. They can be used to 'customize' your application development by standardizing the naming of files, headers within files, and all utilities which are normally included in your 'standard' applications.

By creating a custom AppWizard for the ActiveX controls, I hope that you will find it easier to concentrate on the 'hard' work of actually implementing some functionality in the control, rather than worrying about the donkey work of creating the framework for the control in the first place. This is the real power of a custom AppWizard. By allowing you to zoom in on the job at hand, and not on the pieces that need to be in place for your masterpiece to work, custom AppWizards allow programmers to spend more time on the 'good' stuff: programming!

In the next chapter, now that we have got the difficult bits out of the way, we'll show you how to use your custom AppWizard to generate one of these much talked about Internet ActiveX controls, and how you can use it in your own web pages.

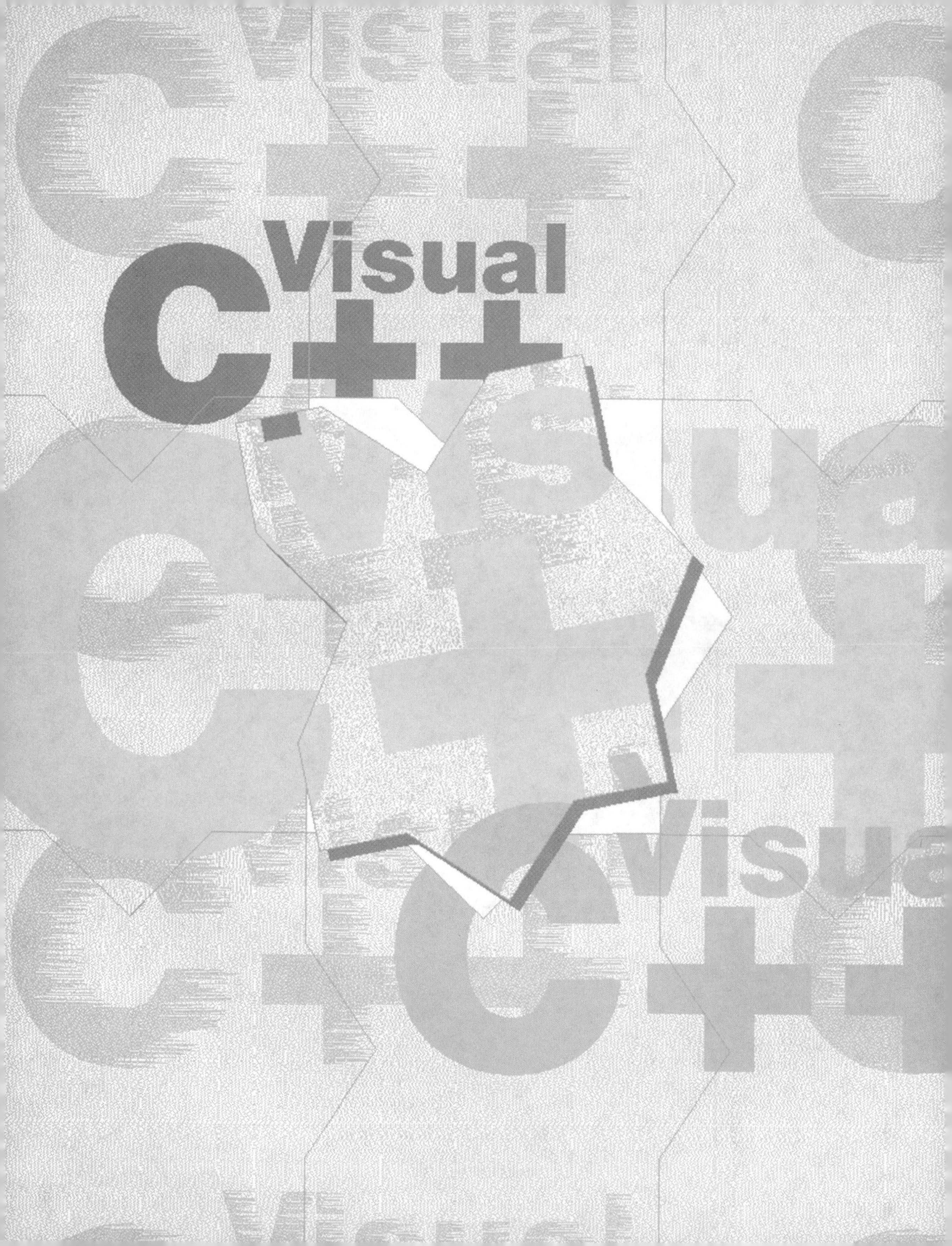
Visual
C++

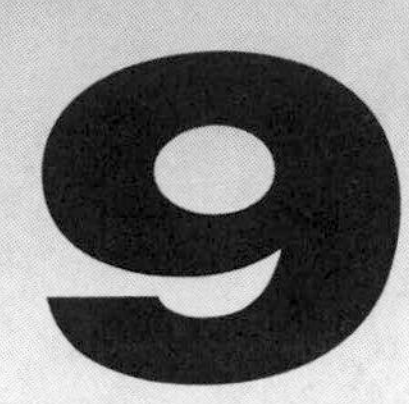

Internet ActiveX Controls

In the last chapter, we spent some time developing a custom AppWizard to generate projects based around the Internet SDK. These projects are Internet ActiveX controls, which are cut down versions of the controls we've been writing up to now. They are cut down because, being part of the Internet, you don't want to be downloading the huge amounts of code which tend to make up normal controls. Let's follow Microsoft's lead and start activating the Web.

Using the New Custom AppWizard

Our test of the new custom AppWizard for this chapter will be a quite simple control that displays text 'Times Square' style. The effect is a rotating color display around the edge of a control box, with the text of the control displayed in varying colors within the center of the control. In this section, we will learn the following new things:

- How to use a custom AppWizard to generate a new ActiveX control
- How to create an ActiveX control that implements a simple display
- How to create an HTML page in which to display and test your ActiveX control
- How to use embedded properties in an HTML page for your ActiveX control
- How to use the Internet Explorer 3.0 to display and test your control
- Where you can go from here (don't take this badly!)

Are we all set? Good! Let's do it.

TRY IT OUT - Using Our Custom AppWizard

Before you can begin to add new functionality to an ActiveX control and get it to work on an HTML page, you need to create at least the skeleton application to work with.

1 To do this, select the New... menu item from the Visual C++ menu. Select Project Workspace from the list box that is displayed. You should then see a dialog box much like that shown on the following page. Notice the selected icon on the left-hand side of the dialog, indicating that this will be an ActiveXGen generated application. Select your version of this icon.

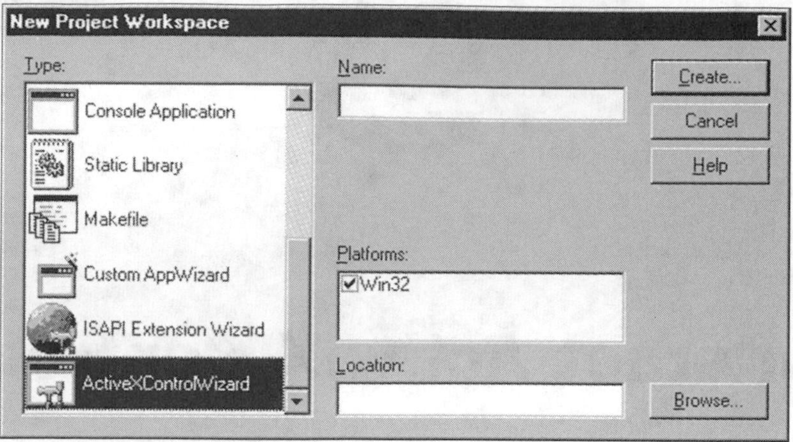

2 Enter the name **`TSText`** for the name of the new control. This is short for **`TimesSquareText`** and represents the fact that:

- I am originally from New York and remember Times Square fondly.
- Times Square is quite famous for its gaudy and garish signs which often contain moving text and lights.
- Well, hey, there has to be some reason for calling it this, doesn't there? Choose to save the control in whatever directory you would like and click on the Create... button.

3 The next dialog to be displayed (shown below) is the first page of our custom AppWizard. This page should be filled in as shown, with a control name of **`TSText`** and a short name of **`TS`**. When you've finished entering the data, click on the Next button to take you to the next step.

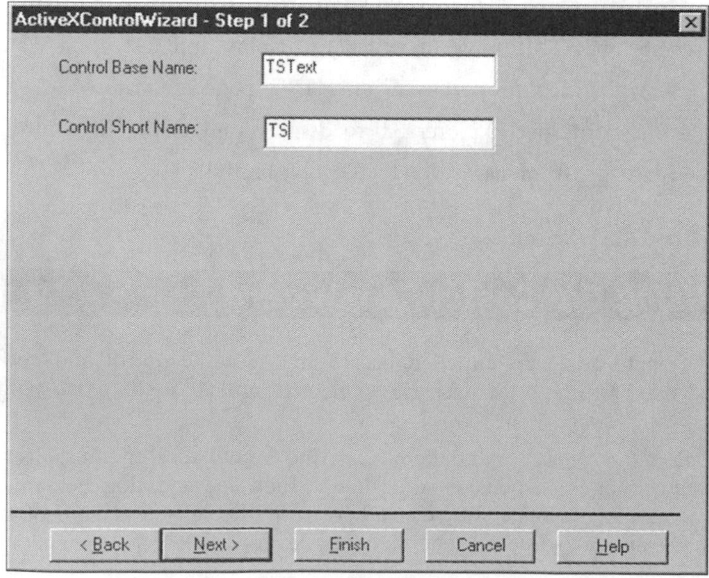

4 The second dialog page shown displays only a single entry, that of the company name for this control. In the case of the control we are creating, you can enter any company name that you like (or none at all). When you have finished entering the company name, click on the Finish button to generate the skeleton application from your input.

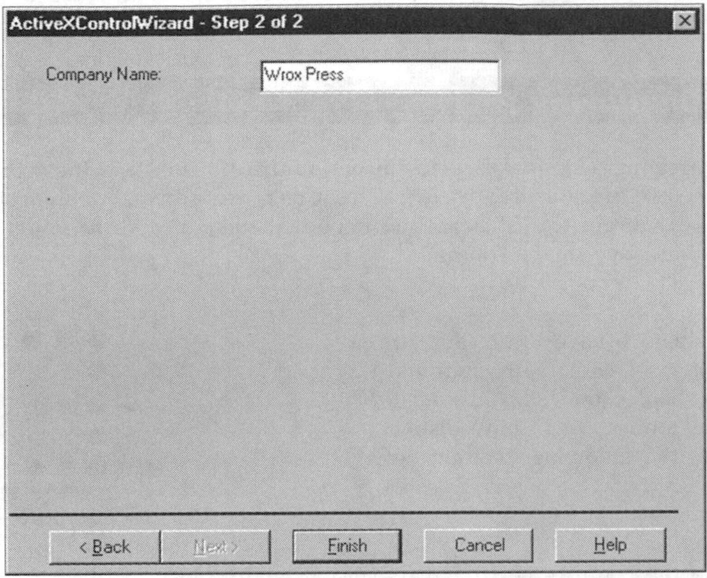

When you've finished entering all of the data and generated the skeleton application, you will have a new directory full of files. Here's a list of the files you should expect to see in that directory:

```
TSText.cpp
TSTextCtl.cpp
TSTextCtl.h
TSTextPpg.cpp
TSTextPpg.h
TSText.def
TSText.odl
TSTextInterfaces.h
makefile
guids.cpp
guids.h
localobj.h
dispids.h
resource.h
TSText.rc
dWinVers.h
```

We could now compile the control and use it; however, as we haven't added any functionality, it would be a pretty boring control to add to any web page.

In this particular example, we're most concerned with the **`TSTextCtl`** files (**`.cpp`** source file and **`.h`** header file) and the **`TsText.odl`** object description language file. These files will be modified to allow our control to display the text and rotating text blocks for the 'Times Square' effect on your HTML web pages.

Adding some Functionality

For the first 'cut' of the control, we won't worry about adding a rotating block of colors, the properties, or methods, or anything else. We'll concentrate on the important part of the control, the display. This is a simple text string in the middle of the control. We'll worry about the aspects of the control that make it useful to other people later.

TRY IT OUT - Displaying Text

All the actual drawing action takes place in the **OnDraw()** function (now there's a surprise), so this will be the first function that we'll modify. Don't worry about defining the member variables at this point, we will get to that next. The important thing here is to understand what's going on in the drawing stage of the control.

1 The first thing we have to do, apart from fill in the control with the background color, is to display the lights around the edge of the control. We'll draw distinct lights, as in the following diagram:

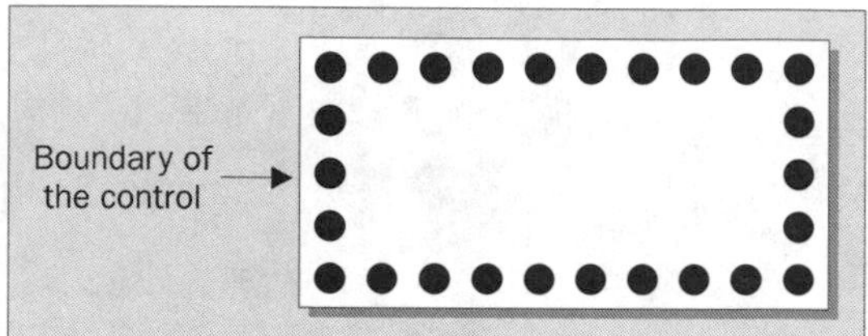

We'll divide the control's horizontal dimension by 10, the vertical by 5, and take the smallest of these as being the diameter of the lights (we'll limit the diameter to a maximum of 10 pixels). Here's the code to do this:

```
HRESULT CTsTextControl::OnDraw(DWORD dvAspect,
    HDC hdcDraw,
    LPCRECTL prcBounds,
    LPCRECTL prcWBounds,
    HDC      hicTargetDevice,
    BOOL     fOptimize)
{
   // First, fill the entire rectangle with the background color
   HBRUSH br = CreateSolidBrush ( GetBkColor( hdcDraw ) );
   RECT wr;
   wr.top = rcBounds.top;
   wr.bottom = rcBounds.bottom;
   wr.right = rcBounds.left;
   wr.left = rcBounds.right;

   FillRect( hdcDraw, &wr, br );

   // Next, draw the lights
   RECT rcBounds;

   rcBounds.left = 0;
   rcBounds.top = 0;
   rcBounds.bottom = (prcBounds->bottom - prcBounds->top);
   rcBounds.right = (prcBounds->right - prcBounds->left );

   HBRUSH b1 = CreateSolidBrush( m_color1 );
```

```
    HBRUSH b2 = CreateSolidBrush( m_color2 );

    // Divide the bounding rectangle horizontally by 10,
    // and vertically by 5.
    float width =  rcBounds.right / 10.0f;
    float height = rcBounds.bottom / 5.0f;

    // Find the minimum of these and make sure it's not more than 10
    int diameter = (int)min(width, height);
    diameter = min(diameter, 10);

    // Do the horizontal rows of lights
    int voffset1 = int(height/2.0) - diameter/2;
    int voffset2 = voffset1 + int(height*4.0);
    int hoffset1, hoffset2;
    for(int lights = 0; lights < 10; lights ++)
    {
       hoffset1 = int(width/2.0) - diameter/2 + int(lights*width);
       if((lights + start_brush) % 2 == 0)
          SelectObject(hdcDraw, b1);
       else
          SelectObject(hdcDraw, b2);
       Ellipse(hdcDraw, hoffset1, voffset1, hoffset1 + diameter, voffset1 +
diameter);
       Ellipse(hdcDrwaw, hoffset1, voffset2, hoffset1 + diameter, voffset2 +
diameter);
    }

    // Do the vertical rows of lights (we actaully only need the center 3
    hoffset1 = int(width/2.0) - diameter/2;
    hoffset2 = hoffset1 + int(width*9.0);
    for(lights = 1; lights < 4; lights ++)
    {
        voffset1 = int(height/2.0) - diameter/2 + int(lights*height);
       if((lights + start_brush) % 2 == 0)
          SelectObject(hdcDraw, b1);
       else
          SelectObject(hdcDraw, b2);
       Ellipse(hdcDraw, hoffset1, voffset1, hoffset1 + diameter, voffset1 +
diameter);
       if((lights + start_brush) % 2 == 0)
          SelectObject(hdcDraw, b2);
       else
          SelectObject(hdcDraw, b1);
       Ellipse(hdcDraw, hoffset2, voffset1, hoffset2 + diameter, voffset1 +
diameter);
    }

    // Draw the text
    RECT r;
    r.top = prcBounds->top;
    r.bottom= prcBounds->bottom;
    r.right = prcBounds->right;
    r.left = prcBounds->left;

    SetTextColor ( hdcDraw, RGB(m_red, m_green, m_blue) );
    if ( m_text )
       DrawText( hdcDraw, m_text, strlen(m_text),
```

```
            &r, DT_SINGLELINE | DT_VCENTER | DT_CENTER );

    // Free up the memory allocated
    DeleteObject ( br );
    DeleteObject ( b2 );
    DeleteObject ( b1 );
    return S_OK;
}
```

The first thing you're likely to notice about this listing is that no MFC objects have been used to implement any of the drawing code. There's no **CDC** object to draw the control, nor is there a **CRect** object to maintain the boundaries of the control drawing area. All of the code for working with this (and all other) ActiveX controls is done using the Win32 SDK functions. That means using **TextOut()**, **SetTextColor()**, and so forth, on the actual device context handle that is passed in.

It's possible to use MFC when writing Internet controls, but it's counterproductive. Not only would you need a way to initialize the MFC when the control was loaded, but you would also be stuck with the massive overhead of the MFC dynamic-link libraries (or worse, the static library) when the control was downloaded from an Internet server into a user's web page. Remember that these controls are intended to be very small and very fast for purposes of making the web page download as quickly as possible. For this reason, you should learn to stick with the functions made available to you by the Windows Win32 SDK and not worry about MFC. In addition, if you learn to use the SDK functions within the simple framework of the ActiveX control library, you will find that you'll become a better Windows programmer in general.

An understanding of low-level code is a must when writing high-level code.

That aside, what's going on here? The **OnDraw()** method of the control is called whenever the control needs to be refreshed onto the web page. This method is not guaranteed to be called within the framework of a window, a concern that we will deal with a little later. The code itself is dealing with three different aspects of the drawing code. First, the whole control is filled with the background color, effectively deleting the previously drawn control. Next, the horizontal lights are drawn, swapping between the two colors, then the vertical lights. Finally, the color is varied and the text for the control is drawn in the center of the box for the control. The number of lights is fixed, not for any particular reason, but rather because 5 lights down and 10 lights across happen to look nice. There isn't always a scientific reason for the things we do.

2 You will notice that several variables are used in the drawing code. There are color variables set, text variables used, and some sort of flag is used to indicate which lights should be drawn in which colors. The first thing we'll need to do (besides defining all of these things) is to initialize the variables. We do this in the constructor for the object, as follows:

```
CTsTextControl::CTsTextControl(IUnknown  *pUnkOuter)
: CInternetControl(pUnkOuter, OBJECT_TYPE_CTLTsTextControl,
                  (IDispatch *)this)
{
    start_brush = 0;
```

```
    m_color1 = RGB(255,0,0);
    m_color2 = RGB(0,255,0);

    m_red = 0;
    m_green = 0;
    m_blue = 0;

    pCtrl  = this;
    m_text = "This is a test";
}
```

As you can see, we're initializing all of the variables to set values without any concern for what the poor user might want. We will always be displaying the text 'This is a test', for example, without allowing any change to that text. It seems like a poor compromise, but there you are.

3 One thing that might be concerning you about now is how the control is repainting itself to make the lights appear to rotate. I know it worried me, and I wrote the code! Fortunately, I looked further into the problem and discovered the secret. When the control is first initialized, several functions will be invoked by the container object for the control. The first of these is the constructor, which is actually called before the control itself exists on the HTML page. The constructor is called as soon as the user calls **CreateObject()** (or whatever method is used to create the object indirectly) to instantiate our control on the page.

Following the constructor call, the **BeforeCreateWindow()** method of the control will be called. It's certainly possible for us to initialize values in this method, but in this case we used the constructor instead. After the **BeforeCreateWindow()** method (in spite of how strange that sounds), the **AfterCreateWindow()** method is called. In this method, we know that there is, in fact, a window available for us and that our drawing code is likely to be called shortly thereafter. For this reason, we want to make sure that our control gets repainted regularly to give the illusion of the rotating colored boxes.

In Windows, you can't simply sit in a loop and ask the system to keep repainting. The reason is quite simple: there's nowhere you could put such code. If you placed it in, say, the **OnDraw()** method, then you would never exit it. From Windows' point of view, you haven't finished processing the Windows message which caused this method to be called. All other messages get queued up waiting for that message to complete, including the message to close; basically, you hang the task. (Under Windows 3.11, you would have hung the system, as Windows expected the task to return control back to it once the message had been processed.) How, then, can we force Windows to repaint our window at regular intervals?

In the back of the room, I can see several experienced programmers waving their hands and murmuring, "Timers...". This is not a good thing to do. People who wander around murmuring to themselves are often carted off to rooms with very soft walls. In spite of this, the answer is correct. Windows implements a timer mechanism that allows the programmer to specify that his or her task should be 'woken' regularly by the posting of a special message (called a timer message) to the task. This is exactly how we will implement the illusion for this control. Add the following code to the **AfterCreateWindow()** method:

```
BOOL CTSTextControl::AfterCreateWindow()
{
    // Create a timer
    m_timer = ::SetTimer( NULL, 123, 200, (TIMERPROC)TimerFunc );
    return TRUE;
}
```

Interestingly, the `AfterCreateWindow()` method returns a boolean value. In the original version of the ActiveX SDK, `AfterCreateWindow()` had a void return type and didn't return anything. I can only assume that Microsoft decided that conditions might arise whereby a control needed to abort itself during the initial display.

In the **`AfterCreateWindow()`** method, we're implementing a new Windows timer by calling the Win32 SDK function **`SetTimer()`**. This method takes several arguments which are worth examining now.

The first is a window handle to which messages should be sent. Normally, when operating within the scope of a Windows control, this argument would be the handle of the window. In our case, however, there is the problem of not necessarily having a window on which to operate. ActiveX controls can operate in a 'passive' mode, in which they are 'drawn', but they aren't real windows. For this reason, we will use an alternate form of the **`SetTimer()`** function.

The second argument is the timer identifier. We're passing **`123`**, but you could use pretty much any value you wanted here.

The third argument is the number of milliseconds that should pass between posting of timer messages. In our case we want the control to repaint often, but not instantaneously (because you wouldn't see anything happening except a slight flicker). I chose 200 milliseconds as a good compromise value.

4 The final argument to **`SetTimer()`** is an optional pointer to a function to be called during the timer intervals, instead of the default action which is posting messages. This is an ideal solution for us, since our function will always be around, but there is no guarantee that we will have a window around to receive messages. We will pass the **`TimerFunc`** function to the **`SetTimer()`** function and let it deal with the problem. Here's the code for the **`TimerFunc`** function:

```
void CALLBACK TimerFunc(HWND hWnd, UINT uMsg, UINT idEvent, DWORD dwTime)
{
    pCtrl->MoveLights();
    pCtrl->IncrementColors();
    pCtrl->OcxInvalidateRect(NULL, TRUE);
}
```

As you can see, this function simply calls three methods of an object. The first two, **`MoveLights()`** and **`IncrementColors()`**, we'll talk about in a moment. The third method, **`OcxInvalidateRect()`** is a new method invented solely for ActiveX controls. This method will invalidate the drawing area of an ActiveX control and force a repaint of the control area that is invalidated (by passing in **TRUE** as the second argument). It's very much like the standard Windows function **InvalidateRect()** or the MFC method **Invalidate()**.

5 We now need to cause the lights to change color. If you remember, we use the variable **start_brush** to indicate which of the two possible colors the light can have:

```
if((lights + start_brush) % 2 == 0)
   SelectObject(hdcDraw, b1);
else
   SelectObject(hdcDraw, b2);
```

As we're only seeing if the sum of **lights** and **start_brush** is even, to rotate the lights we simply have to increment **start_brush**. We could alternate **start_brush** between **0** and **1**, but there would be little point; the extra code required to do this is exactly what we're trying to avoid. The **MoveLights()** method looks like this:

```
// Method to rotate lights
inline void MoveLights()
{
   start_brush++;
}
```

MoveLights() is responsible for making the blocks appear to move by varying the starting color of the first block drawn. Since the color of the first block oscillates between red and green in this example, the blocks appear to 'move' round the control's outside edge. You could improve the illusion of movement by the use of three colors, but that can be left as an exercise for you to try later on.

6 Here's the **IncrementColors()** method:

```
inline void IncrementColors(void)
{
   if ( m_red < 255 )
      m_red += 32;
   else
       if ( m_green < 255 )
          m_green += 32;
      else
         if ( m_blue < 255 )
            m_blue += 32;
         else
         {
            m_red = 0;
            m_green = 0;
            m_blue = 0;
         }
}
```

IncrementColors() is responsible for changing the color of the text displayed in the center of the control (now permanently defined as 'This is a test'). This method is called each time the control is to be updated so that the text appears to change color regularly.

As you can see, we've made both **MoveLights()** and **IncrementColors()** inline functions. They're only small, and doing so will make the code quicker.

7 The **pCtrl** object used in **TimerFunc()** was set in the constructor for the control by setting it to the **this** pointer at that time (have a look at step 2 again). We need to define this pointer as a global pointer within the scope of this file by placing the following definition at the top of the source code in this file:

```
CTSTextControl *pCtrl = NULL;
```

This will initialize the variable to a preset (**NULL**) state and allow the **TimerFunc()** function, which isn't a method of the object, to call it. This is necessary because Windows will not allow us to use member functions as arguments to the **SetTimer()** function. The reason for this is that it is impossible for Windows to know what object the **SetTimer()** function was invoked in, and therefore you can't pass a **this** pointer to the method (which is necessary for the method to work properly).

8 The final bit to add to the **.cpp** file is the destructor for the control. When you create a new Windows timer using the **SetTimer()** function, it's important that you get rid of that timer using the **KillTimer()** function. We will accomplish this in the destructor:

```
CTsTextControl::~CTsTextControl ()
{
   KillTimer( NULL, m_timer );
}
```

9 The last thing to do is to update the header file for the control so that it will compile properly. Here's the complete header file with all changes shown highlighted:

```
//=--------------------------------------------------------------------------=
// TsTextCtl.H
//=--------------------------------------------------------------------------=
//
// class declaration for the TsText control.
//
#ifndef _TsTextCONTROL_H_

#include "IPServer.H"
#include "CtrlObj.H"
#include "Internet.h"
#include "TsTextInterfaces.H"
#include "Dispids.H"


#include "DibCls.H"

typedef struct tagTsTextCTLSTATE {

   // TODO: Replace with real state variables

   short TEMP;

} TsTextCTLSTATE;

//=--------------------------------------------------------------------------=
// CTsTextControl
//=--------------------------------------------------------------------------=
```

```
// our control.
//
class CTsTextControl : public CInternetControl,
                       public ITsText,
                       public ISupportErrorInfo
{
public:
   // IUnknown methods
   //
   DECLARE_STANDARD_UNKNOWN();

   // IDispatch methods
   //
   DECLARE_STANDARD_DISPATCH();

   // ISupportErrorInfo methods
   //
   DECLARE_STANDARD_SUPPORTERRORINFO();

   // ITSText methods
   //
   //
   STDMETHOD(get_ReadyState)(THIS_ long FAR* thestate);
   STDMETHOD_(void, AboutBox)(THIS) ;

   // OLE Control stuff follows:
   //
   CTSTextControl(IUnknown *pUnkOuter);
   virtual ~CTSTextControl();

   // static creation function.  all controls must have one of these!
   //
   static IUnknown *Create(IUnknown *);

   // Method to rotate lights
   inline void MoveLights();
   inline void IncrementColors(void);

private:
   // overridables that the control must implement.
   //
   STDMETHOD(LoadBinaryState)(IStream *pStream);
   STDMETHOD(SaveBinaryState)(IStream *pStream);
   STDMETHOD(LoadTextState)(IPropertyBag *pPropertyBag,
                            IErrorLog *pErrorLog);
   STDMETHOD(SaveTextState)(IPropertyBag *pPropertyBag,
                            BOOL fWriteDefault);
   STDMETHOD(OnDraw)(DWORD dvAspec, HDC hdcDraw, LPCRECTL prcBounds,
                     LPCRECTL prcWBounds,
        HDC hicTargetDev, BOOL fOptimize);
    virtual LRESULT WindowProc(UINT msg, WPARAM wParam, LPARAM lParam);
    virtual BOOL    RegisterClassData(void);

    virtual HRESULT InternalQueryInterface(REFIID, void **);
    virtual void    BeforeCreateWindow(void);

    virtual BOOL    AfterCreateWindow(void);
```

```
    // Internet specific callbacks:
    //
    // OnData is called asynchronously as data for an object or property
                                                                  arrives...
    virtual HRESULT OnData(DISPID id, DWORD grfBSCF,IStream * bitstrm,
                          DWORD amount);

    //  OnProgess is called to allow you to present progess indication UI
    virtual HRESULT OnProgress(DISPID, ULONG progress, ULONG themax,
                              ULONG, LPCWSTR);


    // private state information.
    //
    HDC              m_dc;

    // Actual properties
    // The colors to display the moving lights in

    COLORREF m_color1;
    COLORREF m_color2;
    char    *m_text;

    // A flag to deal with the illusion of movement
    int       start_brush;

    // Timer id
    UINT      m_timer;

    // Text Colors
    short     m_red;
    short     m_green;
    short     m_blue;
};

extern const GUID     *rgTSTextPropPages [];
DEFINE_CONTROLOBJECT(TsText,
    &CLSID_TsText,
    "TSTextCtl",
    CTSTextControl::Create,
    1,
    &IID_ITSText,
    "TSText.HLP",
    &DIID_DTsTextEvents,
    OLEMISC_SETCLIENTSITEFIRST|OLEMISC_ACTIVATEWHENVISIBLE|
                              OLEMISC_RECOMPOSEONRESIZE|
                              OLEMISC_CANTLINKINSIDE|
                              OLEMISC_INSIDEOUT,
    0,
    RESID_TOOLBOX_BITMAP,
    "TSTextWndClass",
    1,
    rgTSTextPropPages,
    0,
    NULL);


#define _TsTextCONTROL_H_
#endif // _TsTextCONTROL_H_
```

10 We're now ready to compile the control.

> *At the time of writing, the following instructions were valid for the compilation of ActiveX controls. Things may very well have changed, as the area is rather volatile. Check with your ActiveX SDK documentation for up-to-the-minute details.*

To compile the ActiveX control, you must have at least the following:

The ActiveX SDK

Microsoft Visual C++ 4.x

It's also nice to have the Win32 SDK. The ActiveX control will compile without the newest Win32 SDK (since most of it is in Visual C++) but you will get a bunch of silly warnings. The newest MIDL compiler is also available with the SDK and is needed for the controls we will develop in the next chapter using the ActiveX Template Library.

To compile the controls, first set the environment variables for the Visual C++ compiler. These are found in the **Bin** subdirectory of the Visual C++ environment. If you're using the professional edition of the compiler, this batch file will be called **Msvcvars.bat**. If you're using the 'standard' edition of the compiler, the batch file will be called **Vcvars32.bat**. In either case, run the batch file for Visual C++ first.

For the ActiveX SDK, the batch file is generally called **Setenv.bat** (although this also may have changed). In addition to the settings in this file, you will also need to add the include directory for the samples base control directory as well. If you did a standard install of the ActiveX SDK, this directory will be found in **\Inetsdk\Samples\Basectl\Include**. Add this to your include list by either modifying the batch file (**Setenv.bat**) or by typing:

```
set include = %include%;\inetsdk\samples\basectl\include
```

at the command prompt. You're now ready to compile the new control by typing

```
nmake
```

from the directory that contains the control source code. That's all there is to it. If you haven't made any errors in typing in the code, the control will be compiled, linked and registered with the operating system ready for your use! The only thing left is testing the control so that we can see whether it works!

Now we'll have a look at creating the HTML page. There are a variety of ways to implement an HTML page with which you can test your ActiveX controls. Two of the simplest are typing in the HTML page in your favorite text editor, or using a program specially designed for ActiveX controls. At the time of writing, the newest and easiest way to add ActiveX controls, text, and other controls to HTML pages is Microsoft's utility application, the ActiveX Control Pad editor. This program, which is really just a wrapper around the new Internet Explorer control, allows you to design and edit HTML pages and include registered ActiveX controls.

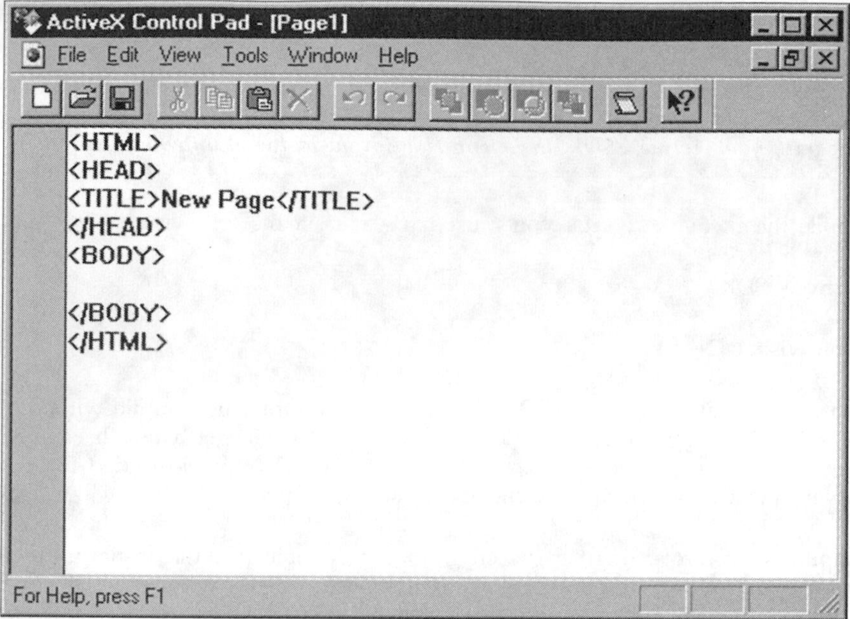

To implement a test HTML page for this control, you can either type in the HTML by hand, or, if you have a copy of the ActiveX Control Pad editor (which was free at the time of writing), you can simply use this to embed the control in a page. Once you've done this, you will end up with the following HTML page (listed in HTML format):

```
<HTML>
<HEAD>
<TITLE>New Page</TITLE>
</HEAD>
<BODY>
This is a test of the emergency broadcast system.
This system was invented to show off a control.
<OBJECT ID="TSTextControl1" WIDTH=100 HEIGHT=51
  CLASSID="CLSID:BD11A280-2E73-11CF-B6CF-00AA00A74DAF">
     <PARAM NAME="_ExtentX" VALUE="2646">
     <PARAM NAME="_ExtentY" VALUE="1349">
</OBJECT>
</BODY>
</HTML>
```

The above listing shows the simplest version of the control. The name of the object (shown in the **OBJECT** tag) is **TSTextControl1**. This name can be modified by the programmer to be anything you want. In the HTML code, you would simply edit the name directly in the text. In the Pad, you would bring up the properties for the control and modify the name to suit your fancy.

The **WIDTH** and **HEIGHT** parameters are used by the container of the control to position the control properly when the page is displayed. You will not need to know these parameters within your control, since they will be a part of the rectangle passed into your **OnDraw()**

method. These parameters define the clipping area of the control within the page when the control is in passive mode (no window) or the actual rectangle of the window when the control is in active mode (window handle is valid).

The next parameter listed is **CLASSID**. This parameter specifies the CLSID (or GUID) identifier which, theoretically, uniquely identifies this control to the world at large. The number which follows this tag is the same number you'll find in the **.odl** file for the control.

```
// coclass for CTsTextControl controls
//
[
    uuid(bd11a280-2e73-11cf-b6cf-00aa00a74daf),
            helpstring("TsTextControl control")
]
coclass TsTextControl {
    [default]        interface ITsTextControl;
            [default, source] dispinterface DTsTextControlEvents;
};
```

If you examine the highlighted line and compare it to the GUID listed in the HTML script file, you'll find that the two numbers are the same. This GUID is used to find the control on the system and to link it directly into the HTML container object. The Internet Explorer, for example, uses this number to load the control and verify that all of the parameters passed are valid. In addition, it creates an instance of this control to place on its display region.

To test the control, bring up the Microsoft Internet Explorer 3.0 and enter the filename of the HTML file directly into the URL area of the viewer. This would then bring up the page (probably asking you if it is safe for you to download an ActiveX control) and display it on the screen, running your control in the process. Using Microsoft Internet Explorer 3.0, you would see the following on the screen:

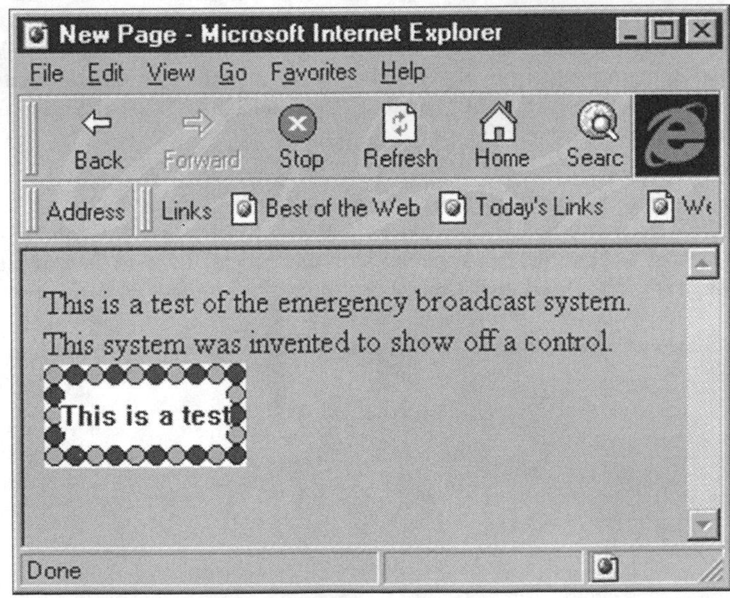

That's really all there is to loading and displaying an ActiveX control.

> *At the time of writing, it was not possible to use the Test Container to verify the running of ActiveX controls designed for the Internet. Test Container doesn't properly pass in device contexts to the control and so will display a silly error message. If you're willing to ignore this error message and continue, the control will often display itself but may not work properly. Do not test your controls if you get this error display.*

Adding Properties to Our Control

It's certainly all well and good to display a simple control on an HTML page. It would be nicer, however, if we could allow the page designer to actually have some input into how the text on our control was displayed. After all, it seems unlikely that a large number of pages really need a text box that reads 'This is a test' in the middle of them. We would be better serving the net community if we allowed the page designer to decide what text they would like to add to the page.

The job of getting information from the outside world is a matter of implementing **properties** for your control. Properties are settings which your control uses to determine the display and other behavior of the control while it's running. Properties can be used to set text (in our case), colors, or other things such as how the control reacts when the mouse is clicked in it. For this example, we will add a simple property to the control which allows us to input the text to be displayed in the control at run time.

TRY IT OUT - Adding a Text Property

In order to add our new property, we will need to modify several files in the control. First, we will need to add a new property to the header file for the application to hold the input text. Actually, since we want to add a new text property we will simply use the existing **m_text** variable to hold the input text. Normally, however, you would need to add the property to the header file as a new variable. Second, we will need to modify the source file for the control to be able to load the property from the HTML file as a parameter to the control. Like the **HEIGHT**, **WIDTH**, and other properties that appeared in the control **OBJECT** tag in the HTML file, this property will be added as well.

1 Let's call the new property **AXText** for ActiveX text. This property will be a simple string, or in OLE terms a **BSTR**. In order to read the new property in from the file, we need to override the **LoadTextState()** method of the control to read in our new property from the HTML file. Here's the updated **LoadTextState()** method of the control:

```
STDMETHODIMP CTsTextControl::LoadTextState(IPropertyBag *pPropertyBag,
                                           IErrorLog *pErrorLog)
{
   VARIANT v;

   VariantInit(&v);

   v.vt = VT_BSTR;
   v.bstrVal = NULL;
```

```
    HRESULT hr = S_OK;
    // try to load in the property.  if we can't get it, then leave
    // things at their default.
    //
    pPropertyBag->Read(::wszAX, &v, pErrorLog);
    if (v.bstrVal) {
        // Get the property as a "real" string
        MAKE_ANSIPTR_FROMWIDE(psz, v.bstrVal);

        if ( m_text )
            delete m_text;
        m_text = new char[strlen(psz)+1];
        strcpy ( m_text, psz );
    }

    return hr;
}
```

Let's take a look at what's going on here. The first thing that happens is that we declare a new variable of type **VARIANT**. A variant data type is used by OLE to input any type of data that you want to use, that will conform to one of the standard OLE types in some way. This is necessary because all of the internal functions are written to use **VARIANT** types as parameters. In this case, our variant type is really a pointer to a string, or a **BSTR** (**BSTR** comes from Binary String which is really a UNICODE, or multibyte string). Once we've defined the type, we try to read in a block from the input stream. The container object for our control, which is Internet Explorer in our example, will define the stream and set it up for the control to read. We need to tell the container that we're looking for a particular piece of information in the string, which is defined by the **::wszAX** parameter in the **Read()** function (we'll get to the definition of this in a bit).

If an entry is found, the value will be copied into the variant structure, **v**. If the string isn't found, we'll simply be content with knowing that we did our best to load data and if the user really doesn't want any text displayed in the center of our box, that is their own fault!

Assuming that the user really wanted text displayed, the variant string is then copied into our member variable by using the **MAKE_ANSIPTR_FROMWIDE** macro. Don't go looking through the source code convinced that you missed a line to input. There really is no definition for the **psz** variable in the entire source file. Instead, this macro will define it and copy the value of the string as a character pointer into the variable now known as **psz**.

At this point, we check to see if the **m_text** variable already had some value and if so, delete it. This is necessary since we might already have initialized **m_text** to point to an allocated block. The new string is copied into our member variable and the function returns a successful value to the container indicating that its job was done well. If you had multiple tags that you wished to read in, you would repeat the process. The variant would be initialized to a new type and the property 'bag' interrogated for the next piece. This would continue until either a fatal error occurred or all of the data that you needed was loaded. For some controls, this can be a rather extensive process of searching through the tags looking for data until all of the necessary pieces are retrieved. For our control, on the other hand, this was a fairly simple (though informative) process.

2 At the top of your source file, you need to add the following line:

```
WCHAR wszAX [] = L"AXText";
```

This defines a simple wide text string which will have the value **AXText**. This is the name of the property that we're looking for in the **OBJECT** tag.

3 It isn't enough, however, simply to allow the user to input data from the HTML file. There are other ways to get data into a control and we should really support them. The most important, in all likelihood, is to support the property **set** and **get** methods. Implementing the methods themselves is quite easy, just add the following code to the bottom of your source file:

```
STDMETHODIMP   CTSTextControl::get_Text(BSTR * text)
{
     BSTR * pbstrText = text;
     *pbstrText = (m_text) ? BSTRFROMANSI(m_text) : SysAllocString(L"");
     return (*pbstrText) ? S_OK : E_OUTOFMEMORY;
}

STDMETHODIMP   CTSTextControl::set_Text(BSTR text)
{
     BSTR& bstrText = text;

     //
     // get an ANSI pointer
     //

     MAKE_ANSIPTR_FROMWIDE(pszText, bstrText);
     m_text = new char[strlen(pszText)+1];
     strcpy ( m_text, pszText );
     return S_OK;
}
```

The first method, **get_Text()**, will return the text currently in the control to the calling program. When will this method ever be used? Basically, this brings us into the realm of scripting languages and ActiveX controls, which is a far wider topic than this book could ever consider. If you're interested in using scripting languages for Internet web pages, please feel free to look into Java or VBScript as possible answers. We will examine a very simple VB interface in the next chapter, which should whet your appetite for this subject.

In addition to the **get** method, there's a corresponding **set** method which stores new text in the control. Like the original text load, this method copies the data from an input wide character string into a local character buffer (**psz**) and then copies it from there into the **m_text** member variable so that the string gets displayed.

4 If the world were a programmer-friendly place, all you would then need to do would be to add the following lines to the header file for the control for everything to work perfectly:

```
     STDMETHOD(get_Text)(THIS_ BSTR FAR* text) ;
     STDMETHOD(put_Text)(THIS_ BSTR text) ;
```

5 Unfortunately, things rarely work as easily as we might like them to. Instead of simply defining the methods and allowing everything to work itself out, we will need to 'inform' the outside world of our methods as well. This is often called 'publishing' methods and properties, and takes place within the object description language for the control within the **.odl** file.

Here's the updated **.odl** file with the new lines marked in bold print and missing some of the lines that remain the same (marked by the **...**):

```
//=--------------------------------------------------------------------------=
// TsText.ODL
//=--------------------------------------------------------------------------=
//
// ODL file for the control(s) and automation object(s) in this inproc server
//
#include <olectl.h>
#include <idispids.h>
#include <internet.h>
#include "dispids.h"

// can't include oaidl.h, so this will have to do
//
#define DISPID_NEWENUM -4


//=--------------------------------------------------------------------------=
// the libid for this type libray
//
[
   uuid(b92bb5c0-2e73-11cf-b6cf-00aa00a74daf),
   helpstring("TsText Control Library"),
   lcid(0x0000),
   version(1.0)
]
library TsTextObjects {

   // standard imports
   //
   importlib("STDOLE32.TLB");
   importlib(STDTYPE_TLB);
   importlib("datapath.tlb");

   // primary dispatch interface for CTsText control
   //
   [
      uuid(bb1a1840-2e73-11cf-b6cf-00aa00a74daf),
      helpstring("TsText Control"),
      hidden,
      dual,
      odl
   ]
   interface ITsText : IDispatch {

      // properties
      //
      [id(101), propget]
         HRESULT Text([out, retval] BSTR * text);
      [id(101), propput]
         HRESULT Text([in] BSTR text);

 ...

   };
 };
```

6 Finally, we need to modify the HTML document so that the control will display the text we want. Within the **OBJECT** tag, we add a new tag indicating we want to specify a new parameter of the control, what the parameter is and its value:

```
<HTML>
<HEAD>
<TITLE>New Page</TITLE>
</HEAD>
<BODY>
This is a test of the emergency broadcast system.
This system was invented to show off a control.
<OBJECT ID="TsTextControl1" WIDTH=100 HEIGHT=51
 CLASSID="CLSID:BD11A280-2E73-11CF-B6CF-00AA00A74DAF">
    <PARAM NAME="_ExtentX" VALUE="2646">
    <PARAM NAME="_ExtentY" VALUE="1349">
    <PARAM NAME="AXText" VALUE = "Hi There!">
</OBJECT>
</BODY>
</HTML>
```

If you run the Internet Explorer 3.0 and load in the file shown above, you will end up with a page displayed similar to that opposite.

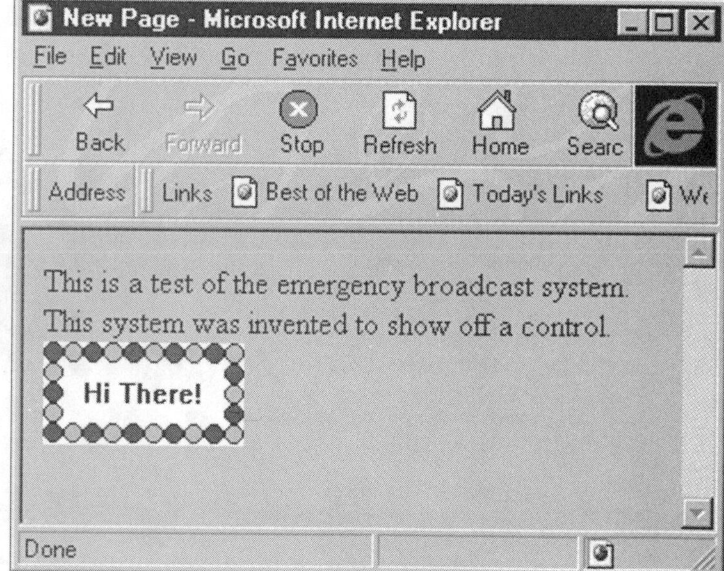

Where You Can Go from Here

This is where I get to tell you where to go, but don't worry—I'll be nice about it. What you have seen in this simple example is a fairly complete ActiveX control for the purposes of display. It doesn't add any user interface functionality. One thing *you* could do is add some of that functionality.

Let's add a simple method to the ActiveX control that we can call internally in response to the mouse being clicked in the control. While we're at it, let's also add a way for an external routine (VBScript or Java) to call this method inside our control in order to accomplish some (rather nebulous, I'm afraid) functionality. This isn't the best possible example of exposing functionality to the outside world, but it will do for our purposes here.

The problem breaks down into three parts:

- What is it that we want to accomplish in the control?
- How do we respond to mouse clicks within the control?
- How do we expose the functionality (whatever it turns out to be) to the outside world?

The first problem is simple. Since we're adding functionality for a control that displays text within a colored rotating border, the new method should affect either the text being displayed or the colors used to display the border. We've already taken care of modifying the text of the control by adding a parameter to the control and **get/set** methods to modify it. That leaves the matter of the rotating colors to work with in the functionality of our new method. Problem solved!

We'll examine how to respond to mouse clicks in more detail as we begin to implement the solution. The basic intention, though, is to be able to 'catch' any valid Windows message or command and deal with it. Keystrokes, cut and paste, and so forth, are all handled the same way, so you can use this solution generically later.

The final problem is actually the easiest of the three, since we've already solved it. When we added functionality to the **.odl** and source files to implement the **get/set** methods of the text for the control, we exposed the method of adding new functionality to the control. That same method will be used to add new functionality to the control here.

Stalking the Elusive Windows Message

The **WindowProc()** method is probably the most likely (after **OnDraw()**) to be customized by the programmer. This method is similar to the standard Windows window procedure for handling any messages that are sent to the control window. It's usually implemented as a standard **switch** statement, with **case**s set for each Windows message you wish to handle. You can also handle specialized ActiveX messages here. ActiveX controls don't support the standard MFC message map handling system directly through ClassWizard or in code, so you must do things the 'old fashioned' way. As we will see in the next chapter though, ActiveX is a vast improvement for the programmer over ATL (Active Template Library) code, which doesn't even allow the use of MFC code within it unless you do so explicitly.

ActiveX controls can use most of the utility functions of the MFC. **CString**, **CMapStringToString**, **CBitmap**, and so forth, are available to you as a programmer. By the same token, the base control for the ActiveX controls, **COleControl**, offers only rudimentary Windows MFC support, that you may have taken for granted up to this point. Couple this with the need to worry about whether your control is really a window, or simply a bitmap on a drawn page, and you begin to understand some of the complexity of working with ActiveX controls. In spite of these limitations, however, ActiveX is an extremely powerful programming tool which will only get bigger and more important as Internet access becomes a more standard part of all applications.

The first thing you will need to know when you're trying to capture various Windows messages (such as mouse clicks) is how the ActiveX control processes messages. Many messages are simply translated into one of the internal functions, such as the **WM_PAINT** message being dispatched to the **OnDraw()** handler.

For the majority of non-processed Windows messages, such as **WM_LBUTTONDOWN** for a mouse click, the message itself is dispatched to the **WindowProc()** procedure. This procedure, which was automatically generated by the custom AppWizard earlier, can be used to trap pretty much any message and deal with it as you see fit.

Let's take a look at the **WindowProc()** as it was originally generated for our application by the custom AppWizard:

```
LRESULT CTSTxtControl::WindowProc(UINT  msg,WPARAM wParam,LPARAM lParam)
{

    // TODO: handle any messages here, like in a normal window
    // proc.  note that for special keys, you'll want to override and
    // implement OnSpecialKey.
    //

    return OcxDefWindowProc(msg, wParam, lParam);
}
```

The comments in the code make it seem likely that we would implement our handler for the mouse messages here. The question is, how do we implement a new handler?

TRY IT OUT - Adding a Message Handler

The first step towards the new handler is to capture the mouse message that we would like to handle and then dispatch it to whatever code we want to use to handle it. In our case, the message to be handled would be **WM_LBUTTONDOWN**. What we would like to do is to change the color of the rotating boxes which are displayed around the outside of the text box to be different each time the mouse is clicked. In addition to this, we would like to allow the user to change the color of these boxes (the user, in this case, being the HTML page author).

1. First things first. Let's add a simple handler that changes the rotating text block color back and forth between the wonderful green and red that's currently displayed and an even more spectacular blue and yellow display. No, I'm not color blind, and I don't lack color sense. These are simply the easiest colors to implement without worrying about what colors a monitor shows, whether dithering will take place, how the colors blend together, and so forth. Here's the code to implement the simple color change. This code will switch the colors back and forth in response to the user clicking the mouse (actually just pressing the mouse button will do it—no need to release) within the control:

```
LRESULT CTsTextControl::WindowProc(
    UINT  msg,
    WPARAM wParam,
    LPARAM lParam)
{
    switch ( msg )
    {
        case WM_LBUTTONDOWN:
            // Set color here.
            if ( m_color1 == RGB(255,0,0) )
            {
                m_color1 = RGB(0,0,255);
                m_color2 = RGB(255,255,0);
            }
```

```
            else
            {
               m_color1 = RGB(255,0,0);
               m_color2 = RGB(0,255,0);
            }
            break;
   }
   return OcxDefWindowProc(msg, wParam, lParam);
}
```

Note that there's nothing really very fancy going on here. The color scheme is changed and the next time the timer goes off, the control will repaint itself using those colors.

2 Our next step is to implement true 'methods' which can be called from external programs (VBScript applications, for example) to set the colors for the control. As you might remember from our discussion about implementing the text functionality, this is best done by using property **set/get** routines in the **.odl** file. Here's the modified **.odl** file with the new methods highlighted and some of the code replaced by **...** to conserve trees:

```
//=------------------------------------------------------------------------=
// TsText.ODL
//=------------------------------------------------------------------------=
//
// ODL file for the control(s) and automation object(s) in this inproc server
//
#include <olectl.h>
#include <idispids.h>
#include <internet.h>
#include "dispids.h"

// can't include oaidl.h, so this will have to do
//
#define DISPID_NEWENUM -4


//=------------------------------------------------------------------------=
// the libid for this type libray
//
[
   uuid(b92bb5c0-2e73-11cf-b6cf-00aa00a74daf),
   helpstring("TsText Control Library"),
   lcid(0x0000),
   version(1.0)
]

library TsTextObjects {

   // standard imports
   //
   importlib("STDOLE32.TLB");
   importlib(STDTYPE_TLB);
   importlib("datapath.tlb");

   // primary dispatch interface for CTsText control
   //
```

```
[
    uuid(bb1a1840-2e73-11cf-b6cf-00aa00a74daf),
    helpstring("TsText Control"),
    hidden,
    dual,
    odl
]
interface ITsText : IDispatch {

    // properties
    //
    [id(101), propget]
       HRESULT Text([out, retval] BSTR * text);
    [id(101), propput]
       HRESULT Text([in] BSTR text);
    [id(102), propget]
       HRESULT Color1([out, retval] OLE_COLOR *clr);
    [id(102), propput]
       HRESULT Color1([in] OLE_COLOR clr);

    // methods
    //
    [id(DISPID_ABOUTBOX)]
       void AboutBox(void);
};

...

};
```

3 Next, modify **TSTextCtl.h** to read as follows (changes shown highlighted):

```
class CTSTextControl :          public CInternetControl,
                                public ITsText,
                                public ISupportErrorInfo
{

public:
    // IUnknown methods
    //
    DECLARE_STANDARD_UNKNOWN();

    // IDispatch methods
    //
    DECLARE_STANDARD_DISPATCH();

    // ISupportErrorInfo methods
    //
    DECLARE_STANDARD_SUPPORTERRORINFO();

    // ITsText methods
    //
    //
    STDMETHOD_(void, AboutBox)(THIS) ;
    STDMETHOD(get_Text)(THIS_ BSTR FAR* path) ;
    STDMETHOD(put_Text)(THIS_ BSTR text) ;
    STDMETHOD(get_Color1)(THIS_ OLE_COLOR FAR* clr) ;
```

```
    STDMETHOD(set_Color1)(THIS_ OLE_COLOR clr) ;
    STDMETHOD(get_Color2)(THIS_ OLE_COLOR FAR* clr) ;
    STDMETHOD(set_Color2)(THIS_ OLE_COLOR clr) ;

...

}
```

4 Finally, add the four new methods to the source file for the control (**TSTextCtl.cpp**) as follows:

```
STDMETHODIMP   CTsTextControl::get_Color1(OLE_COLOR * clr)
{
    *clr = (OLE_COLOR)m_color1;
    return S_OK;
}

STDMETHODIMP   CTsTextControl::set_Color1(OLE_COLOR clr)
{
    m_color1 = OleTranslateColor ( clr, NULL, NULL );
    return S_OK;
}

STDMETHODIMP   CTsTextControl::get_Color2(OLE_COLOR * clr)
{
    *clr = (OLE_COLOR)m_color2;
    return S_OK;
}

STDMETHODIMP   CTsTextControl::set_Color2(OLE_COLOR clr)
{
    m_color2 = OleTranslateColor ( clr, NULL, NULL );
    return S_OK;
}
```

Congratulations! You have just added two new methods to an existing control. Want to know how they work? I thought so. The **OleTranslateColor()** function will take an **OLE_COLOR** value and translate it into a 'normal' (**COLORREF**) value. **OLE_COLOR** values are really just **COLORREF**s with the high bit set to indicate that they are **OLE_COLOR**s. Why this is necessary is beyond me, but it works. Translating back, of course, is simply a matter of adding that high bit, which is done by casting it into a **OLE_COLOR**. Once this has been done the control knows about the color, the user knows about the color, and the world is a better place.

What Have We Learned in this Chapter?

Quite a bit, actually. This chapter introduces a new form of control, called an ActiveX Internet control. You will find that ActiveX has become a catch phrase for any kind of control that can be embedded in an HTML form. ActiveX controls include the specialized lightweight COM controls (COM stands for Component Object Model) as well as OCXs (OLE Control extensions), COM DLLs, and any other form of control (such as Java classes) that are understood by Web browsers. In spite of this little bit of confusion, ActiveX controls are *really* controls which conform to the ActiveX SDK standards, which we have implemented here.

In our next chapter, we will examine not only some more about ActiveX controls, but also a different 'flavor' of ActiveX, the ActiveX Template Library (ATL for short) which allows even lighter-weight objects to be created when the overhead of visual components isn't needed.

Visual
C++

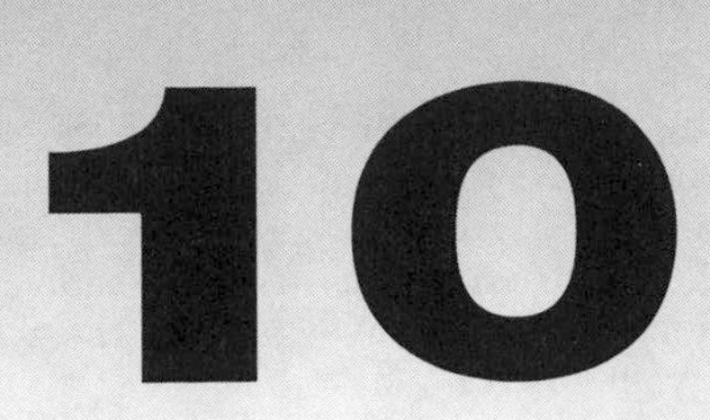

The Cutting Edge of Components

In the previous chapter, we began to look at the true 'cutting edge' as far as component technology is concerned. Custom AppWizards, ActiveX Internet controls and other components make up the forefront of Windows development technology. In this chapter, we'll expand on the ActiveX technology by examining the ActiveX component not only as a web control, but also as an OLE extension. In addition, we'll explore **ATL**, a new technology that represents the 'bleeding edge' of technology at the moment.

By bleeding-edge we mean the pain endured by you, the developer, working a little too close to the cutting edge of technology! You may be working without the benefit of existing documentation, examples, or any sort of 'safety net' in development terms. To work with bleeding-edge technology takes a will of steel, a lot of luck, and increases the likelihood of a developer suffering a heart attack.

The first component we'll look at in this chapter will be an ATL component. This sort of component is useful for implementing technology not only for web pages, but also for simple extensions to Visual Basic. In this case, we'll examine a control which validates, and extracts information from, input ISBN (International Standard Book Number) strings.

The second component we'll create in this chapter will be a new ActiveX component which supports the `IDropTarget` interface standard. Don't worry if you don't understand what `IDropTarget` is, or even what an interface is—all will be explained. Without further ado, let's move on to actually implementing these components.

ATL Controls

Imagine, for a moment, that your boss walks up to your desk one day. "You're doing a great job <fill-in-your-name-here>," he beams. Your guard goes up instantly and you start to think of words like 'downsizing'. Then it gets worse....

"What we need is an OLE control. Just a normal, common or garden, everyday OLE control that we can use from web pages or our Visual Basic applications." You start to relax for a moment, but he goes on. "Oh yeah, it needs to be invisible!" Well, that doesn't sound too bad. After all, the MFC `COleControl` doesn't need to be visible, and it can be used from VB. For just a moment, the sun starts shining again in your world.

Then the boss finishes thinking and says, "Oh yeah. We need it to be small, real small. Can't use that MFC library either. Got to be small enough to download quickly. Make it able to take an input string and validate it for ISBN entries." Your heart sinks. No MFC? This is going to take weeks. Got to learn OLE, got to write 'interfaces' (whatever they are), got to test the thing with any number of applications, probably have to write the whole stupid thing in C. Visions of weeks of agony run through your brain.

The boss pokes his head round the door again. "Oh, one more thing," he says, "I promised the guys in marketing that they could have it next week." The rest of whatever he has to say is lost as it is drowned out by the sound of your head hitting the floor.

Welcome to programming in the 90s. More buzzwords than ever, less time to learn, and higher and higher expectations. Of course, it's reasonable to assume that a small shop programmer can keep up with the hundreds of programmers at a huge software giant like Microsoft. Lightweight OLE controls with no required MFC DLLs? How hard can something like that be? Maybe you should consider another career choice. Something with a future to it, like used-car sales.

Surprise! It's easy to implement simple, lightweight OLE controls without dragging in the huge bulk of the entire MFC library. You don't even have to write the whole thing in pure C either. I'd be lying if I said that you don't have to make a few sacrifices of course, but we're not at the goats and chickens level.

The first thing you need to do is to run (don't walk) to your local web server and connect to the Microsoft Internet site. There, you will discover, lies a wondrous treasure which is truly priceless. In the midst of games and Internet browsers and other things that are fun to play with, you will find the **ActiveX Template Library** (ATL for short).

What is the ATL?

Put simply, the ATL is a set of classes, combined with a custom AppWizard (much like we built in the previous chapter), which will allow you to write simple, non-visible, COM controls. These components are simple in that they support a bare minimum of interfaces. Compared to OCX or true ActiveX controls, components developed with the ATL system are poor cousins indeed. The ActiveX Template library is just what it sounds like: a library of **templates**. A template is simply a 'boilerplate' version of a simple object which can be enhanced by customizing it for a given application. In the case of the ATL, the template is the basic support necessary for a COM object and the customization is the adding of any functionality that you want the COM interface to support. Got all that? I didn't think so.

Let's get the bad news out of the way first. Here are the low points of developing controls using the ATL component system:

- ATL doesn't intrinsically support visible COM controls. Unlike ActiveX controls, they aren't derived from **`COleControl`** and have no built-in niceties such as **`OnDraw()`** and **`WindowProc()`** for handling output to the user and input from the world of Windows.
- ATL can't create ActiveX controls without a considerable amount of coding. An ATL control is normally created as either a stand-alone executable (**`.exe`**) file or as a loadable dynamic-link library (**`.dll`**) file.
- ATL doesn't normally (and as we shall see, probably should never) include MFC support. ATL components are written in C++, but any interface to the Windows environment needs to be done through the SDK.

- There's no ClassWizard support for ATL controls. All methods and properties for the control need to be done 'by hand'. As you will see when we begin to develop the actual component, this can lead to some tedious cutting and pasting between files.

So, given all of these problems with ATL components, why would anyone want to use them? Actually, there are two basic reasons for wanting to use the ATL: size and speed. ATL components are very small, fully functional, COM objects. Where a true ActiveX control might weigh in at 50–60K plus the MFC libraries behind it, an ATL control is likely to be very much smaller and not require the MFC libraries (or dynamic-link libraries) at all. This makes them ideal for Internet web pages.

Speed is another important issue in Internet web page design and implementation. Things are bad enough today with the huge graphic images embedded in many pages. Imagine how long downloading a web page would take if it contained several large ActiveX controls! Speed of execution is equally important. Because ATL components are stripped down to bare bones implementations of COM controls, they will execute more quickly than their MFC-bloated cousins.

The final argument for ATL is, believe it or not, simplicity. Because an ATL control doesn't support a visible object in web pages, you can simply concentrate on implementing the underlying functionality of the control that you're concerned with, rather than worrying about visual aspects, user input, sizes of displays, parameters passed, and so forth.

All this said, why would you want a non-visible control on something as fundamentally visual as a web page? Isn't that much like implementing a color selection dialog for an application that supports only monochrome monitors? The answer to this conundrum is that as web pages become more and more complex, and the functionality required of those pages increases, so too does the need for more 'behind the scenes' processing. Web pages today require searching, validation, and other functionality that was once the sole province of application development environments. In short, web pages are becoming programs in their own right. Much like Visual Basic grew from a simple 'front end for databases' language into a full-blown application development environment, the next few years will see the same process occur with web pages and the Internet.

A Real-world Problem

Throughout this book, I have tried to focus on developing real-world solutions (or at least as real as things get in the computer industry) to real-world problems. I considered, for the ATL example, just cobbling together a simple ATL control that illustrated all of my points without dealing with the issues that go along with a real problem (like actually doing something!). This seemed like a good idea at the time, if for no other reason than it would give my editor something to gripe about. A note to budding authors: always give your editor something to gripe about. They are going to find something anyway and if you aim them in a specific direction, they might leave the rest of your writing alone. Just kidding folks!

After reconsidering the issue, and with much 'help' from the nice people at Wrox, I decided on a real-world problem to solve using the ATL system. Since there are a large number of publishers on the net who love to sell books, an ATL component which would help publishers out would be quite useful (actually, a happy publisher is really a very scary thing). One of the biggest problems in the publishing world, besides authors I mean, is the need to identify the books which people are trying to order. Many books have similar titles, and authors' names are often forgotten or mangled in the translation process between buyer and publisher. I mean, really, a simple name like 'Telles' (as an example, of course). Six letters, none hidden or silent, a normal number of vowels and consonants, you would think that this would be easy, right? You should see the mangled addresses on the mail I get....

Returning to the problem at hand, publishers need a way to identify their books uniquely to the general book-buying public. Much akin to the government's use of Social Security Numbers (SSNs) to uniquely identify people, publishers use a number called an ISBN to identify each book. ISBNs have a standard format and you can find them on the inside or back cover of every book printed today. The problem with ISBNs, as with all other fixed format numbers (like SSNs), is making sure that the number you're given is at least realistic. It isn't enough to verify that the ISBN contains the proper number of digits and dashes. ISBNs have a fixed format and a built-in checksum property which can be used to validate them. In addition, the digits in the ISBN represent three separate components: the group the book belongs to, the publisher of the book, and the identifier for the particular title.

ISBNs are ten digits long and are always split into four sections, but the widths of those sections aren't fixed. For example, the following are all valid ISBNs:

```
0-7897-0687-3
1-55615-695-2
0-672-30620-4
```

The first digit represents the book group, the next section is the publisher identifier, and the third part of the number is assigned to a particular book (or edition of a book). The final digit is a computer check digit calculated from the preceding nine.

We're going to create a brand new ATL control which will accomplish several things:

- **Validate ISBN entries.** The entire purpose of the control is to allow all web page designers to embed the invisible control inside their pages and for our control to validate various entries on the associated HTML form.
- **Retrieve the components of the ISBN entry.** This is really provided as a convenience to the user who might want to check the individual pieces of the entry. For example, a validation check before ordering might be to verify that the publisher number entered as part of the ISBN entry is, indeed, the publisher of the book (and therefore the web page).
- **Allow the control to validate multiple different input sources.** By allowing our control to be non-visible, we can call the object from different sources within the script of the HTML page. By using VBScript within the form, for example, we would be able to validate any sort of entry to ISBN edit fields within a single instance of the control.

The general design of the control requires that we have at least four methods. First, we want a method called **`Validate()`**. This method will accept as input a string containing a supposed ISBN entry and will return from it a Boolean flag indicating whether the entry was, in fact, a valid ISBN string.

The second method we will need will be called **`GetPublisherCode()`**. This method will take as input an ISBN string (we don't want to store any information in the control between calls so that it can be re-entrant for multiple calls). If the string is valid, it should extract and return the publisher code portion of the string. If the input string isn't valid, the returned publisher code will not be modified and an error code will be returned.

The third method of the control will be called **`GetBookGroup()`**. This method will take an ISBN string as well. If the ISBN string is valid it will, as you might expect, return the book group portion of the input string. If the input string isn't valid, the method shouldn't modify the book group string and should instead return an error code to the calling function.

The fourth and final method of the control should be called **`GetBookID()`**. As usual, it will validate an input ISBN string and, if the string is valid, return the book identifier portion of the string. For invalid input, the usual error codes will be returned.

TRY IT OUT - Create Your First ATL Control: The ISBN Control

Before you start, you need to ensure that you have the ATL correctly installed into Visual C++. If you don't already have it, you should download the ATL installation from the Microsoft WWW site (`http://www.microsoft.com`).

This chapter was written using ATL version 1.1; there were considerable differences between versions 1.0 and 1.1, and it's likely that if you're using a later version, there may be significant differences between the procedures presented here, and what you may need to do.

1 First, bring up the custom ATL COM AppWizard. This is accomplished by selecting the File | New... item from the Visual C++ IDE menu and then selecting Project Workspace from the list box in the resulting dialog. At this point, you will see the screen (or at least a reasonable facsimile of it) shown below:

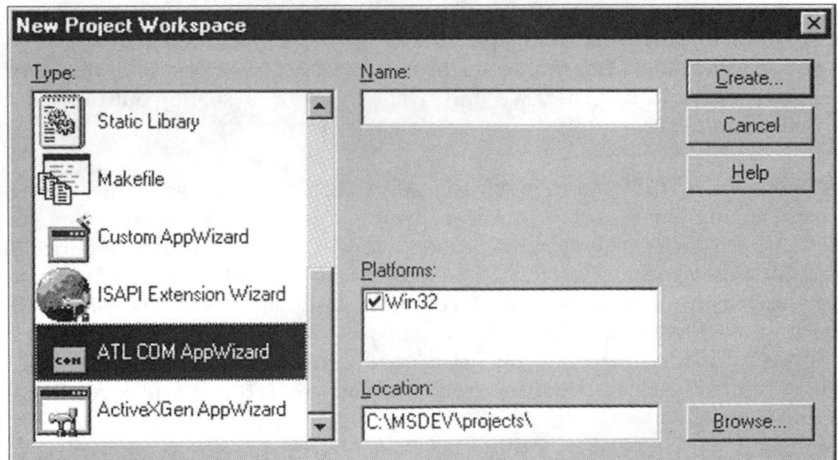

As shown in the above figure, select the ATL COM AppWizard option from the Type list in the AppWizard list. Enter **`ISBNCtl`** for the name of the new project in the Name: edit field. Finally, select a directory in which to store your control source code as you would for any normal AppWizard-generated project.

This will bring you to the next screen, labeled ATL COM AppWizard - Step 1 of 2, as shown:

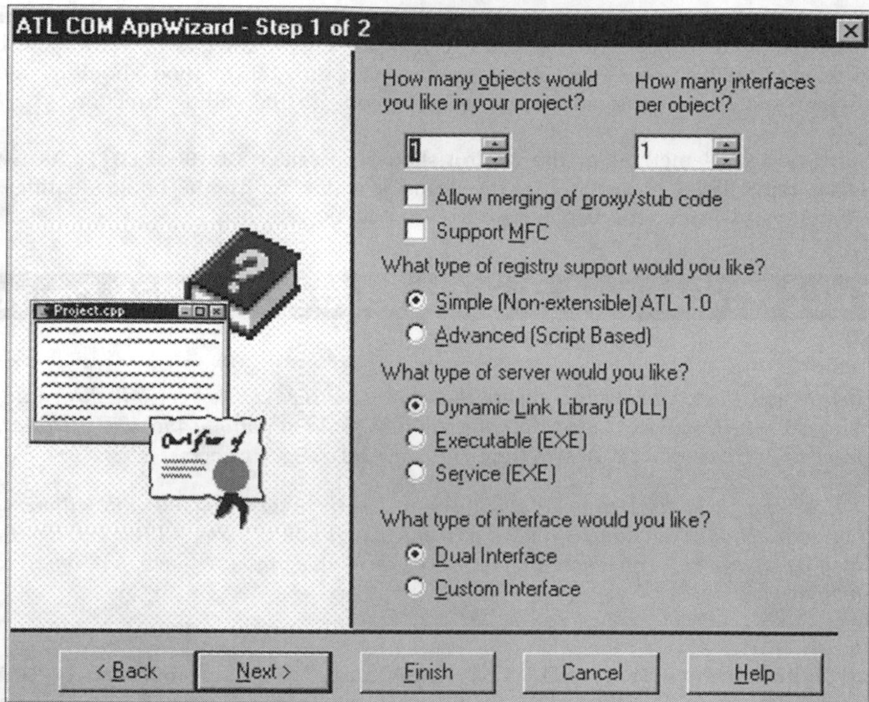

2 The first question you're faced with is, How many objects would you like in your project? When you create a DLL (or executable) for COM objects, you can store multiple objects in the single file (**.dll** or **.exe**). Among other things, this allows you to cut down on the number of files to ship with your application. By default, the objects will be named (in this case) **ISBNCtl1**, **ISBNCtl2**, and so forth, until **ISBNCtl*n*** where *n* is the number you select in this spin control. In our case, we only want to create a single control, so leave the spin control setting at 1.

3 You are then asked, How many interfaces per object? An interface is a set of methods that allows you to implement certain functionality for a control. There are many kinds of interface and an object may support one or more of them. Unless you understand a fair amount about the workings of COM and how to implement new interfaces for your object, leave this spin control at 1, as well. A complete, in-depth description of interfaces and how they are implemented is well beyond the scope of this book. If you wish to understand the matter more fully, I recommend you get a good book and read up on them. COM/OLE isn't a simple subject to tackle, so get yourself nice and comfortable while you read it.

4 The next choice is a checkbox labeled Allow merging of proxy/stub code. Leave this box unchecked as well.

5 Following the first checkbox is a second checkbox labeled Support MFC. If you recall, I told you that ATL controls don't normally support MFC. Actually, I lied. If you check this box, two things will happen. First, the application will allow you to use MFC functionality. This will be accomplished by placing a main **WinApp**-derived class in your DLL to make it MFC-compliant. This changes the DLL from the equivalent of a generic DLL into an MFC extension DLL. The second thing that will happen if you check this box is that your control will become bloated beyond belief! If you really want to use the MFC in COM controls, please stick to ActiveX controls. ATL is for those who are willing to make the sacrifice of suffering through low-level coding techniques to gain the advantages of size and speed. Trust me. Really. Go ahead and ignore this checkbox.

6 The next option you will face is the type of registry entry that you want for this control. The two options shown are Simple (Non-extensible) ATL 1.0 and Advanced (Script Based). The more complex Script Based registry entries are beyond the scope of this book. If you don't understand something on these pages, your best bet is to leave the default, which in this case is the Simple choice.

7 Following the registry entry is the type of server you want for your ATL control. Your options here are Dynamic Link Library (DLL), Executable (EXE) and Service (EXE). Once again, the default choice is the easiest, a simple DLL, so that's what we'll choose. For applications where you would prefer that your ATL control be a complete executable module, you would most likely choose Executable. The Service option appears to be a thing for the future.

8 Following these choices comes the next, strange-looking question: What type of interface would you like? I'll make your life easier and extinguish what I am sure is a raging debate burning inside of you. Check the Dual Interface option and be done with it. Custom interfaces are beyond the scope of this book.

Guess what? You have now finished the first screen. At this point, there's bad news and there's good news. The bad news is that the dialog title up there reads Step 1 of 2. The good news is that the second page is a lot easier than the first. Click on the Next button and you will see what I mean. You should see another page that looks just like this:

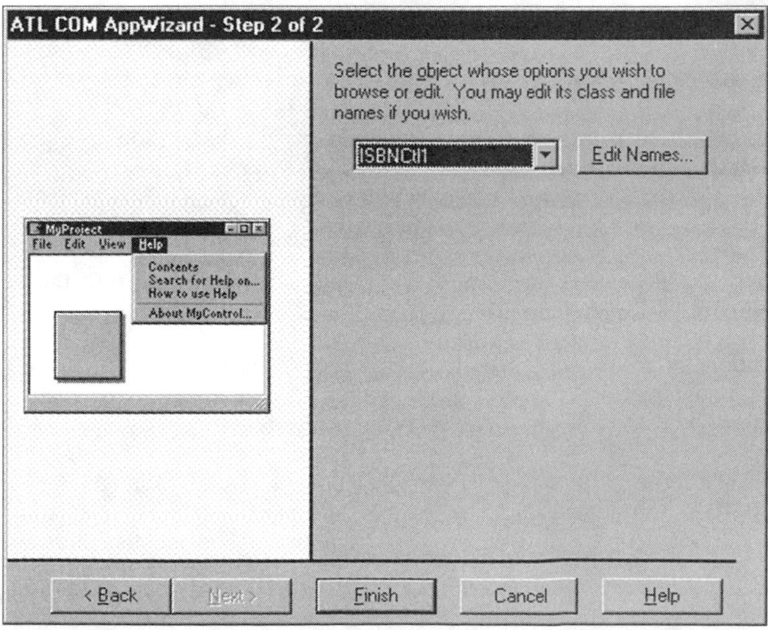

9 As you can see, the whole second page of the wizard dialog consists of the phrase Select the object whose options you wish to browse or edit. You may edit its class and file names if you wish. Next to that innocent looking phrase is a combo box which contains (if you have followed directions correctly up to this point) the single string **`ISBNCtl1`**. If you have a great yen to do so, you can certainly click this button and look at, or even change, the names listed for the class and filenames for the control, but there's no particular reason to do so. Click on Finish when you've finished browsing and/or editing the class and filenames.

At this point, you should probably do a complete project build to verify that everything works properly. That way you will know that everything's fine before we begin the next step: implementing the actual control. Take a deep breath, get something to drink and relax. The real work is about to begin!

> ***When I upgraded from ATL 1.0 to 1.1, I had all sorts of problems with things not compiling properly, not linking, and so forth. If you have such problems, and are using Visual C++ 4.2, it may help to install the patch to Visual C++ 4.2a, available from the Microsoft WWW site.***

10 So, now we have an ATL control that will, theoretically at least, compile into a fully working lightweight ActiveX control. Further, you can embed that control in a web page or Visual Basic form (yes, they work there too—we'll even discover how later) of your choosing and access its methods to extend the functionality of our applications. The only remaining issue, then, is how do we add methods to our new control that actually make it something worth using?

In fact, the method for adding new methods to an ATL control is almost exactly the same as the method we used for adding new methods to an ActiveX control. Furthermore, since ATL controls are even simpler than 'normal' ActiveX controls (having no visual components), it's usually easier to install new functionality in an ATL control that it would be to add the same functionality to an ActiveX control.

Adding new methods to an ATL control is a three-step process:

- Modify the existing IDL file to contain the new declarations for the methods you wish to add to the control.
- Run the MIDL compiler to regenerate the OLE interface files (**`.c`** and **`.h`** files that were defined as the output from MIDL in the custom build steps).
- Copy the generated function (actually method) prototypes into the header files and source files for the control.

In addition, of course, once you've added the skeleton bodies of the new methods for the control, you have to actually implement the functionality of those methods. That sort of goes without saying, but I'll say it anyway for completeness.

Let's take a look at an example by adding the **`Validate()`** method to our new ISBN control. The control, you might remember, is intended to take in a string from some external source (VBScript or Visual Basic code) and return a Boolean flag indicating whether the input string is (**`TRUE`**) or is not (**`FALSE`**) a valid ISBN string. If you were to implement a method in C++ to do this, you might expect it to look something like this:

```
BOOL Validate(LPTSTR lpszStr)
{
   if (isValid(lpszStr))      // Valid string
      return TRUE;
   return FALSE;              // Not a valid string
}
```

Guess what? The ATL version looks nothing at all like this! If you're surprised, you shouldn't be; I warned you that ActiveX was a strange beast. Let's examine the differences step by step as we follow the process to implement the **Validate()** method.

11 The modifications you need to make to the IDL file, **ISBNCtl.idl**, to add the new **Validate()** method to the ISBN control are highlighted here:

```
// ISBNCtl.idl : IDL source for ISBNCtl.dll
//

// This file will be processed by the MIDL tool to
// produce the type library (ISBNCtl.tlb) and marshalling code.

   [
      object,
      uuid(C7B876A2-0636-11D0-A73A-444553540000),
      dual,
      helpstring("IISBNCtl1 Interface"),
      pointer_default(unique)
   ]
   interface IISBNCtl1 : IDispatch
   {
      import "oaidl.idl";
      HRESULT Validate([in]BSTR str, [out,retval] boolean* retval);
   };


[
   uuid(C7B876A0-0636-11D0-A73A-444553540000),
   version(1.0),
   helpstring("ISBNCtl1 1.0 Type Library")
]
library ISBNCTLLib
{
   importlib("stdole32.tlb");

   [
      uuid(C7B876A6-0636-11D0-A73A-444553540000),
      helpstring("ISBNCtl1 Class")
   ]
   coclass CISBNCtl1
   {
      [default] interface IISBNCtl1;
   };

};
```

There are some interesting features of this line, so let's examine it a bit further before we go on to the next step in the process. The **HRESULT** return type is the standard return type from any OLE method in an ActiveX control. **Validate()** is, of course, the name of the method itself. What's all that funky stuff before the next comma, though?

When you're defining parameters, there are several strange rules you will need to follow. Each parameter should be prefaced by either an **[in]** or an **[out]** statement indicating whether the function is receiving (in) or returning (out) a value in that parameter. If you wish to have a parameter which is both input to the method and returning a new value from the method, you should use the **[in,out]** syntax.

> *If your parameter contains the* **[out]** *keyword, you must make the type of the parameter a pointer or MIDL will generate an error.*

Following the directional information is the type of parameter you would like passed into (or out of) your new method. In OLE Automation (which this is, by the way), there are a fairly limited number of valid argument types that you can use. For strings, you will typically get a **BSTR**. These allow for UNICODE (multibyte) entries and can be converted to and from most standard character strings (**LPTSTR**, wide character strings, even **CStrings** in MFC). In this case, we're passing in the string and don't expect it to be modified (actually, we prohibit the modification of the value) by specifying the **BSTR** argument with the **[in]** direction. Had we desired to modify the string as well, we would have specified the **[in,out]** direction and made the type **BSTR*** (a pointer to a **BSTR**).

Why does OLE only allow certain types? Because OLE is intended not only to be multilanguage (callable from Visual C++, Visual Basic, Internet Explorer, HTML pages, Java, and so forth) but also eventually multiplatform (Windows 95, Windows NT, UNIX, and so on), some restrictions were necessary to make compatibility possible. If you wish more information on the subject, pick up a good book on OLE and marshaling.

Before we sidetracked, we were about to discuss the second, even odder looking, parameter to the method. The second argument is listed as **[out,retval] boolean* retval**. What does all of this gobbledygook mean? Well, the **[out** portion of the direction indicates that this parameter will be modified, as we discovered a few paragraphs earlier. The **,retval]** portion of the string indicates that this parameter is the return value from the method.

OLE methods can have two return values. One is a return value to the OLE system indicating whether or not the method was called properly. This is the **HRESULT** return type. This return type should be set to **S_OK** if the method was called correctly, if all memory was allocated properly, and if in general the calling sequence was successful. This return value doesn't indicate that the return from the method (in this case, a Boolean value) was right or wrong, just that nothing went wrong in the actual processing. The second, optional, return value of the method is the programmer-defined return value from the function. In our case, the second return type is a Boolean value (**TRUE** or **FALSE**) and indicates that the string is (**TRUE**) or is not (**FALSE**) valid. It's normal for your function to set the return type to **FALSE** (indicating that the passed in string wasn't a valid ISBN string) and return a value of **S_OK** to the calling container object.

> *Regardless of whether the* **[out]** *parameter is an argument to the method or whether it's a return value from the method (using the* **[retval]** *syntax), it must be defined as a pointer type.*

12 Once we have the IDL entries defined, we can move on to step two of the process: generating the new copies of the **ISBNCtl.h** and **ISBNCtl_i.c** files. There are two ways to do this. First, you can simply try compiling the project within the Visual C++ IDE. This will run the MIDL compiler, as you want, but it will also try to build the remainder of the project as well. Since we haven't yet defined the **Validate()** method (that's the point of the present exercise), it won't be able to find the definition of the method and you will get several strange C++ compiler errors about instantiating an abstract class. This is owing to the fact that the IDL file produces the interface class from which the **CISBNCtl1** class (our actual control) is derived. Since all IDL methods are defined as **pure** in the interface class, the compiler will find a pure virtual C++ method defined in the interface class and no override in the **CISBNCtl1** class. This is an error in C++ and the IDE generates the error messages for you.

The other alternative is to run the MIDL compiler by hand by typing

> **{path}\midl /ms_ext /c_ext ISBNCtl.idl**

and pressing the *Return* key on the command line. In this example, the **{path}** variable should be replaced with the actual path of your **Midl.exe** executable if, and only if, the executable program isn't in your path. In fact, if you haven't got **Midl.exe** in your path, it would be a good idea to run the **Vcvars32.bat** batch file, which you'll find in the same directory as **Midl.exe**, to set the path and environment variables correctly. Unless you do this your compilation is unlikely to be successful.

When you've finished, and assuming there are no compiler errors which need to be taken care of, you will be able to look at the **ISBNCtl.h** file. Here's a listing of the **ISBNCtl.h** header file, which implements the interface for our new COM control:

```
/* this ALWAYS GENERATED file contains the definitions for the interfaces */


/* File created by MIDL compiler version 3.00.15 */
/* at Thu Sep 05 08:55:16 1996
 */
/* Compiler settings for isbnctl.idl:
    Os, W1, Zp8, env=Win32, ms_ext, c_ext
    error checks: none
*/
//@@MIDL_FILE_HEADING(  )
#include "rpc.h"
#include "rpcndr.h"
#ifndef COM_NO_WINDOWS_H
#include "windows.h"
#include "ole2.h"
#endif /*COM_NO_WINDOWS_H*/

#ifndef __isbnctl_h__
#define __isbnctl_h__
```

```
#ifdef __cplusplus
extern "C"{
#endif

/* Forward Declarations */

#ifndef __IISBNCtl1_FWD_DEFINED__
#define __IISBNCtl1_FWD_DEFINED__
typedef interface IISBNCtl1 IISBNCtl1;
#endif    /* __IISBNCtl1_FWD_DEFINED__ */


/* header files for imported files */
#include "oaidl.h"

void __RPC_FAR * __RPC_USER MIDL_user_allocate(size_t);
void __RPC_USER MIDL_user_free(void __RPC_FAR *);

#ifndef __IISBNCtl1_INTERFACE_DEFINED__
#define __IISBNCtl1_INTERFACE_DEFINED__

/****************************************
 * Generated header for interface: IISBNCtl1
 * at Thu Sep 05 08:55:16 1996
 * using MIDL 3.00.15
 ****************************************/
/* [unique][helpstring][dual][uuid][object] */


EXTERN_C const IID IID_IISBNCtl1;

#if defined(__cplusplus) && !defined(CINTERFACE)

    interface IISBNCtl1 : public IDispatch
    {
    public:
        virtual HRESULT STDMETHODCALLTYPE Validate(
            /* [in] */ BSTR str,
            /* [retval][out] */ boolean __RPC_FAR *retval) = 0;
    };

#else   /* C style interface */

    typedef struct IISBNCtl1Vtbl
    {
        BEGIN_INTERFACE

        HRESULT ( STDMETHODCALLTYPE __RPC_FAR *QueryInterface )(
            IISBNCtl1 __RPC_FAR * This,
            /* [in] */ REFIID riid,
            /* [out] */ void __RPC_FAR *__RPC_FAR *ppvObject);

        ULONG ( STDMETHODCALLTYPE __RPC_FAR *AddRef )(
            IISBNCtl1 __RPC_FAR * This);

        ULONG ( STDMETHODCALLTYPE __RPC_FAR *Release )(
            IISBNCtl1 __RPC_FAR * This);
```

```
        HRESULT ( STDMETHODCALLTYPE __RPC_FAR *GetTypeInfoCount )(
            IISBNCtl1 __RPC_FAR * This,
            /* [out] */ UINT __RPC_FAR *pctinfo);

        HRESULT ( STDMETHODCALLTYPE __RPC_FAR *GetTypeInfo )(
            IISBNCtl1 __RPC_FAR * This,
            /* [in] */ UINT itinfo,
            /* [in] */ LCID lcid,
            /* [out] */ ITypeInfo __RPC_FAR *__RPC_FAR *pptinfo);

        HRESULT ( STDMETHODCALLTYPE __RPC_FAR *GetIDsOfNames )(
            IISBNCtl1 __RPC_FAR * This,
            /* [in] */ REFIID riid,
            /* [size_is][in] */ LPOLESTR __RPC_FAR *rgszNames,
            /* [in] */ UINT cNames,
            /* [in] */ LCID lcid,
            /* [size_is][out][in] */ DISPID __RPC_FAR *rgdispid);

        /* [local] */HRESULT ( STDMETHODCALLTYPE __RPC_FAR *Invoke )(
            IISBNCtl1 __RPC_FAR * This,
            /* [in] */ DISPID dispidMember,
            /* [in] */ REFIID riid,
            /* [in] */ LCID lcid,
            /* [in] */ WORD wFlags,
            /* [in] */ DISPPARAMS __RPC_FAR *pdispparams,
            /* [out][in] */ VARIANT __RPC_FAR *pvarResult,
            /* [out] */ EXCEPINFO __RPC_FAR *pexcepinfo,
            /* [out] */ UINT __RPC_FAR *puArgErr);

        HRESULT ( STDMETHODCALLTYPE __RPC_FAR *Validate )(
            IISBNCtl1 __RPC_FAR * This,
            /* [in] */ BSTR str,
            /* [retval][out] */ boolean __RPC_FAR *retval);

        END_INTERFACE
    } IISBNCtl1Vtbl;

    interface IISBNCtl1
    {
        CONST_VTBL struct IISBNCtl1Vtbl __RPC_FAR *lpVtbl;
    };


#ifdef COBJMACROS


#define IISBNCtl1_QueryInterface(This,riid,ppvObject)    \
    (This)->lpVtbl -> QueryInterface(This,riid,ppvObject)

#define IISBNCtl1_AddRef(This)    \
    (This)->lpVtbl -> AddRef(This)

#define IISBNCtl1_Release(This)    \
    (This)->lpVtbl -> Release(This)


#define IISBNCtl1_GetTypeInfoCount(This,pctinfo)    \
```

```
    (This)->lpVtbl -> GetTypeInfoCount(This,pctinfo)

#define IISBNCtl1_GetTypeInfo(This,itinfo,lcid,pptinfo)    \
    (This)->lpVtbl -> GetTypeInfo(This,itinfo,lcid,pptinfo)

#define IISBNCtl1_GetIDsOfNames(This,riid,rgszNames,cNames,lcid,rgdispid)    \
    (This)->lpVtbl -> GetIDsOfNames(This,riid,rgszNames,cNames,lcid,rgdispid)

#define  IISBNCtl1_Invoke(This,dispidMember,riid,lcid,wFlags,pdispparams,
                                        pvarResult,pexcepinfo,puArgErr)    \
    (This)->lpVtbl -> Invoke(This,dispidMember,riid,lcid,wFlags,pdispparams,
                                            pvarResult,pexcepinfo,puArgErr)


#define IISBNCtl1_Validate(This,str,retval)    \
    (This)->lpVtbl -> Validate(This,str,retval)

#endif /* COBJMACROS */


#endif    /* C style interface */


HRESULT STDMETHODCALLTYPE IISBNCtl1_Validate_Proxy(
    IISBNCtl1 __RPC_FAR * This,
    /* [in] */ BSTR str,
    /* [retval][out] */ boolean __RPC_FAR *retval);


void __RPC_STUB IISBNCtl1_Validate_Stub(
    IRpcStubBuffer *This,
    IRpcChannelBuffer *_pRpcChannelBuffer,
    PRPC_MESSAGE _pRpcMessage,
    DWORD *_pdwStubPhase);


#endif    /* __IISBNCtl1_INTERFACE_DEFINED__ */



#ifndef __ISBNCTLLib_LIBRARY_DEFINED__
#define __ISBNCTLLib_LIBRARY_DEFINED__

/****************************************
 * Generated header for library: ISBNCTLLib
 * at Thu Sep 05 08:55:16 1996
 * using MIDL 3.00.15
 ****************************************/
/* [helpstring][version][uuid] */



EXTERN_C const IID LIBID_ISBNCTLLib;

#ifdef __cplusplus
EXTERN_C const CLSID CLSID_CISBN1;

class CISBN1;
```

```
#endif
#endif /* __ISBNCTLLib_LIBRARY_DEFINED__ */

/* Additional Prototypes for ALL interfaces */

unsigned long __RPC_USER  BSTR_UserSize(unsigned long __RPC_FAR*, unsigned long,
                                        BSTR __RPC_FAR*);
unsigned char __RPC_FAR * __RPC_USER  BSTR_UserMarshal(unsigned long __RPC_FAR *,
                                        unsigned char __RPC_FAR*, BSTR __RPC_FAR*);
unsigned char __RPC_FAR * __RPC_USER  BSTR_UserUnmarshal(unsigned long __RPC_FAR*,
                                        unsigned char __RPC_FAR*, BSTR __RPC_FAR*);
void __RPC_USER  BSTR_UserFree(unsigned long __RPC_FAR*, BSTR __RPC_FAR*);

/* end of Additional Prototypes */

#ifdef __cplusplus
}
#endif

#endif
```

13 Notice the highlighted lines. Copy these lines into your header file (**ISBNCtl1.h**) and, modifying them slightly, place the result in the blank public section at the very end of the definition of **CISBNCtl1**. You will end up with the following declaration as a new prototype for your method, as shown in the following code:

```
class CISBNCtl1 :
   public CComDualImpl<IISBNCtl1, &IID_IISBNCtl1, &LIBID_ISBNCTLLib>,
   public ISupportErrorInfo,
   public CComObjectRoot,
   public CComCoClass<CISBNCtl1,&CLSID_CISBNCtl1>
{
public:
   CISBNCtl1() {}
BEGIN_COM_MAP(CISBNCtl1)
   COM_INTERFACE_ENTRY(IDispatch)
   COM_INTERFACE_ENTRY(IISBNCtl1)
   COM_INTERFACE_ENTRY(ISupportErrorInfo)
END_COM_MAP()
//DECLARE_NOT_AGGREGATABLE(CISBNCtl1)
// Remove the comment from the line above if you don't want your object to
// support aggregation.  The default is to support it

DECLARE_REGISTRY(CISBNCtl1, _T("ISBNCtl.ISBNCtl1.1"), _T("ISBNCtl.ISBNCtl1"),
                 IDS_ISBNCTL1_DESC, THREADFLAGS_BOTH)
// ISupportsErrorInfo
   STDMETHOD(InterfaceSupportsErrorInfo)(REFIID riid);

// IISBNCtl1
public:
   HRESULT __stdcall Validate(BSTR str, boolean __RPC_FAR* retval);
};
```

You can now simply copy this line into your source file for the control object (**ISBNCtl1.cpp**) and use it as the starting point for implementing the new method. That takes care of the third step of our process. (As an aside, you now know everything there is to know about the ISO9000 standard. It says you simply define a process and follow it. Aren't you glad to know that we're ISO9000-compliant?)

14 Once you've finished all of the groundwork for the control, it's time to move on to the 'fun' part: implementing the functionality behind the control method. The algorithm for validating an ISBN number isn't exactly a state secret, nor is it very complex, so we can show it here in its entirety. Place all of the following code at the top of the **ISBNCtl1.cpp** file:

```
/////////////////////////////////////////////////////////////////////////////
//

STDMETHODIMP CISBNCtl1::InterfaceSupportsErrorInfo(REFIID riid)
{
    static const IID* arr[] =
    {
        &IID_IISBNCtl1,
    };

    for (int i=0;i<sizeof(arr)/sizeof(arr[0]);i++)
    {
        if (InlineIsEqualGUID(*arr[i],riid))
            return S_OK;
    }
    return S_FALSE;
}
```

```
#include <ctype.h>

#ifdef UNICODE
    #define FROM_OLE_STRING(str) str
    #define TO_OLE_STRING(str) str
#else
    #define FROM_OLE_STRING(str) ConvertToAnsi(str)
    LPTSTR ConvertToAnsi(OLECHAR FAR* szW);
    #define TO_OLE_STRING(str) ConvertToUnicode(str)
    OLECHAR* ConvertToUnicode(char FAR* szA);
    // Maximum length of string that can be converted between Ansi & Unicode
    #define STRCONVERT_MAXLEN 300
#endif

#ifdef WIN32

    #ifndef UNICODE
        LPTSTR ConvertToAnsi(OLECHAR FAR* szW)
        {
            static TCHAR chA[STRCONVERT_MAXLEN];

            WideCharToMultiByte(CP_ACP, 0, szW, -1, chA, STRCONVERT_MAXLEN, NULL,
                                                                          NULL);
            return chA;
        }

    OLECHAR* ConvertToUnicode(char FAR* szA)
    {
        static OLECHAR achW[STRCONVERT_MAXLEN];

        MultiByteToWideChar(CP_ACP, 0, szA, -1, achW, STRCONVERT_MAXLEN);
```

```
      return achW;
   }
   #endif

#endif


// Method to strip characters from a given string
void stripCharacters (LPTSTR lpszBuffer, TCHAR chToStrip)
{
   // Allocate a new buffer of the maximum size
   LPTSTR lpszTemp = new TCHAR[lstrlen(lpszBuffer)+1];
   int pos = 0;

   // Loop through and copy everything that isn't the character to strip
   for (int i=0; i<(int)lstrlen(lpszBuffer); ++i)
      if (lpszBuffer[i] != chToStrip)
         lpszTemp[pos++] = lpszBuffer[i];

   // NULL terminate temp string
   lpszTemp[pos] = 0;

   // Copy it back to original (losing deleted characters)
   lstrcpy (lpszBuffer, lpszTemp);

   // Free the memory we allocated
   delete lpszTemp;
}

// Method to validate a given input ISBN string
int IsValidISBN(LPTSTR szBuffer)
{
   // Remove all hyphens.
   stripCharacters (szBuffer, '-');

   // Check length of string...
   if (lstrlen(szBuffer) != 10)
      return 0;

   // Okay, length checks out. Check each character
   int nCheckSum = 0;

   for (int i=0; i<(int)lstrlen(szBuffer); ++i)
   {
      //ISBN's may only contain digits. If this isn't a digit, it is an error.
      if (!isdigit(szBuffer[i]))
         return 0;

      // Do checksum calculation here...
      int nT = (10-i) * (int)(szBuffer[i]-'0');
      nCheckSum += nT;
   }

   // In order to be valid, check sum MUST be an even multiple of 11.
   if (nCheckSum % 11 != 0)
      return 0;

   // Sanity check: An all zero ISBN is invalid
```

```
    if (nCheckSum == 0)
       return 0;

    return 1;        // Default: It must be valid!
}

HRESULT __stdcall CISBNCtl1::Validate(BSTR str, boolean __RPC_FAR* retval)
{
    LPTSTR lpszT = FROM_OLE_STRING(str);
    *retval = IsValidISBN(lpszT);
    return S_OK;
}
```

The general algorithm for validating an ISBN entry is as follows:

Each number in the string is multiplied by 11 minus its position number, where the left-most is position number 1. (In C++ these will be 10 and 0 because of the numbering conventions used.) The numbers are then totaled to an overall result.

If the result is evenly divisible by 11, the input string is a valid ISBN entry.

If it isn't evenly divisible (found by using the mod **%** operator in C++), then the input string isn't valid.

I have extracted the validation function from the actual **Validate()** method because it will be used in all of the other methods as well. Each of the other functions of the control (**GetPublisherCode()**, **GetBookGroup()**, and **GetBookID()**) will call this single function before doing any extraction of the string. One other thing about ISBNs: although they include dashes (**-**) in the strings, these dashes aren't used either in calculating the validity of the data, or in extracting the data from the string.

15 Here are the changes to make to the IDL file, **ISBNCtl.idl**, to add the new functions. As you can see, they are quite similar to the existing **Validate()** function, simply adding a new output parameter called **str**. Note that you need to modify the existing entry for **Validate()**, in order to add the dispatch ID to the start.

```
interface IISBNCtl1 : IDispatch
{
   import "oaidl.idl";
   [id(1)] HRESULT Validate([in] BSTR str, [out, retval] boolean* retval);
   [id(2)] HRESULT GetPublisherCode([in] BSTR isbn, [out]BSTR* str,
                  [out, retval] boolean* retval);
   [id(3)] HRESULT GetBookGroup([in] BSTR isbn, [out]BSTR* str,
                  [out, retval] boolean* retval);
   [id(4)] HRESULT GetBookID([in] BSTR isbn, [out]BSTR* str,
                  [out, retval] boolean* retval);
};
```

As before, open a DOS window and run the MIDL compiler by hand, to regenerate the **ISBNCtl.h** file. Once this has run, use the function definitions in the **IISBNCtl1** interface definition to provide prototypes for the new functions:

```
interface IISBNCtl1 : public IDispatch
    {
    public:
        virtual /* [id] */ HRESULT STDMETHODCALLTYPE Validate(
            /* [in] */ BSTR str,
            /* [retval][out] */ boolean __RPC_FAR *retval) = 0;

        virtual /* [id] */ HRESULT STDMETHODCALLTYPE GetPublisherCode(
            /* [in] */ BSTR isbn,
            /* [out] */ BSTR __RPC_FAR *str,
            /* [retval][out] */ boolean __RPC_FAR *retval) = 0;

        virtual /* [id] */ HRESULT STDMETHODCALLTYPE GetBookGroup(
            /* [in] */ BSTR isbn,
            /* [out] */ BSTR __RPC_FAR *str,
            /* [retval][out] */ boolean __RPC_FAR *retval) = 0;

        virtual /* [id] */ HRESULT STDMETHODCALLTYPE GetBookID(
            /* [in] */ BSTR isbn,
            /* [out] */ BSTR __RPC_FAR *str,
            /* [retval][out] */ boolean __RPC_FAR *retval) = 0;

    };
```

Modifying these as before will give you the prototypes, which you should add to the **ISBNCtl1.h** header file:

```
class CISBNCtl1 :
   public CComDualImpl<IISBNCtl1, &IID_IISBNCtl1, &LIBID_ISBNCTLLib>,
   public ISupportErrorInfo,
   public CComObjectRoot,
   public CComCoClass<CISBNCtl1,&CLSID_CISBNCtl1>
{
public:
   CISBNCtl1() {}
BEGIN_COM_MAP(CISBNCtl1)
   COM_INTERFACE_ENTRY(IDispatch)
   COM_INTERFACE_ENTRY(IISBNCtl1)
   COM_INTERFACE_ENTRY(ISupportErrorInfo)
END_COM_MAP()
//DECLARE_NOT_AGGREGATABLE(CISBNCtl1)
// Remove the comment from the line above if you don't want your object to
// support aggregation.  The default is to support it

DECLARE_REGISTRY(CISBNCtl1, _T("ISBNCtl.ISBNCtl1.1"), _T("ISBNCtl.ISBNCtl1"),
IDS_ISBNCTL1_DESC, THREADFLAGS_BOTH)
// ISupportsErrorInfo
   STDMETHOD(InterfaceSupportsErrorInfo)(REFIID riid);

// IISBNCtl1
public:
   HRESULT __stdcall Validate(BSTR str, boolean __RPC_FAR* retval);
   HRESULT __stdcall GetPublisherCode(BSTR isbn, BSTR* str,
                                      boolean __RPC_FAR* retval);
   HRESULT __stdcall GetBookGroup(BSTR isbn, BSTR* str,
                                  boolean __RPC_FAR* retval);
   HRESULT __stdcall GetBookID(BSTR isbn, BSTR* str, boolean __RPC_FAR* retval);
};
```

16 Here's the code for the three new functions, which you should add to **ISBNCtl1.cpp**:

```
HRESULT __stdcall CISBNCtl1::GetPublisherCode(BSTR isbn, BSTR* str,
                                              boolean __RPC_FAR* retval)
{
   LPTSTR lpszT = FROM_OLE_STRING(isbn);
   TCHAR  szTemp[256];

   // Make a temporary copy to validate it.
   lstrcpy (szTemp, lpszT);

   *retval = IsValidISBN(szTemp);

   // If the string is valid, extract the first part - the publisher code
   if (*retval)
   {
      TCHAR szPubCode[20];

      // Extract the publisher code
      memset (szPubCode, 0, 20);

      // Look for first - in string
      for (int i=0; i<(int)lstrlen(lpszT); ++i)
         if (lpszT[i] == '-')
            break;

      i ++;               // Skip over -
      int nStart = 0;

      for (; i<(int)lstrlen(lpszT) && lpszT[i] != '-'; i++)
         szPubCode[nStart++] = lpszT[i];

      szPubCode[nStart] = 0;

      // Now, copy the string into the output string
      *str = SysAllocString(TO_OLE_STRING(szPubCode));
   }
   return S_OK;
}


HRESULT __stdcall CISBNCtl1::GetBookGroup(BSTR isbn, BSTR* str,
                                          boolean __RPC_FAR* retval)
{
   LPTSTR lpszT = FROM_OLE_STRING(isbn);
   TCHAR  szTemp[256];

   // Make a temporary copy to validate it.
   lstrcpy (szTemp, lpszT);
   *retval = IsValidISBN(szTemp);

   // If the string is valid, extract the book code from the string
   if (*retval)
   {
      TCHAR szBookGroup[20];

      // Extract the book group
      memset (szBookGroup, 0, 20);
```

```
      // Look for first - in string
      for (int i=0; i<(int)lstrlen(lpszT); ++i)
      {
         if (lpszT[i] == '-')
            break;

         szBookGroup[i] = lpszT[i];
      }
      szBookGroup[i] = 0;

      // Now, copy the string into the output string
      *str = SysAllocString(TO_OLE_STRING(szBookGroup));
   }
   return S_OK;
}


HRESULT __stdcall CISBNCtl1::GetBookID(BSTR isbn, BSTR* str,
                                       boolean __RPC_FAR* retval)
{
   LPTSTR lpszT = FROM_OLE_STRING(isbn);
   TCHAR  szTemp[256];

   lstrcpy (szTemp, lpszT);
   *retval = IsValidISBN(szTemp);

   if (*retval)
   {
      TCHAR szBookID[20];

      // Extract the book ID
      memset (szBookID, 0, 20);

      // Look for second - in string
      int nCnt = 0;
      for (int i=0; i<(int)lstrlen(lpszT); ++i)
      {
         if (lpszT[i] == '-')
            nCnt ++;
         if (nCnt == 2)
            break;
      }

      i++;        // Skip over -
      int nStart = 0;

      for (; i<(int)lstrlen(lpszT) && lpszT[i] != '-'; i++)
         szBookID[nStart++] = lpszT[i];
      szBookID[nStart++] = 0;

      // Now, copy the string into the output string
      *str = SysAllocString(TO_OLE_STRING(szBookID));
   }
   return S_OK;
}
```

At this point, barring any typographical or editing errors, your control should be able to compile. If all goes well, and the control compiles and links, you will see the message shown in the following picture, indicating that the control was successfully registered.

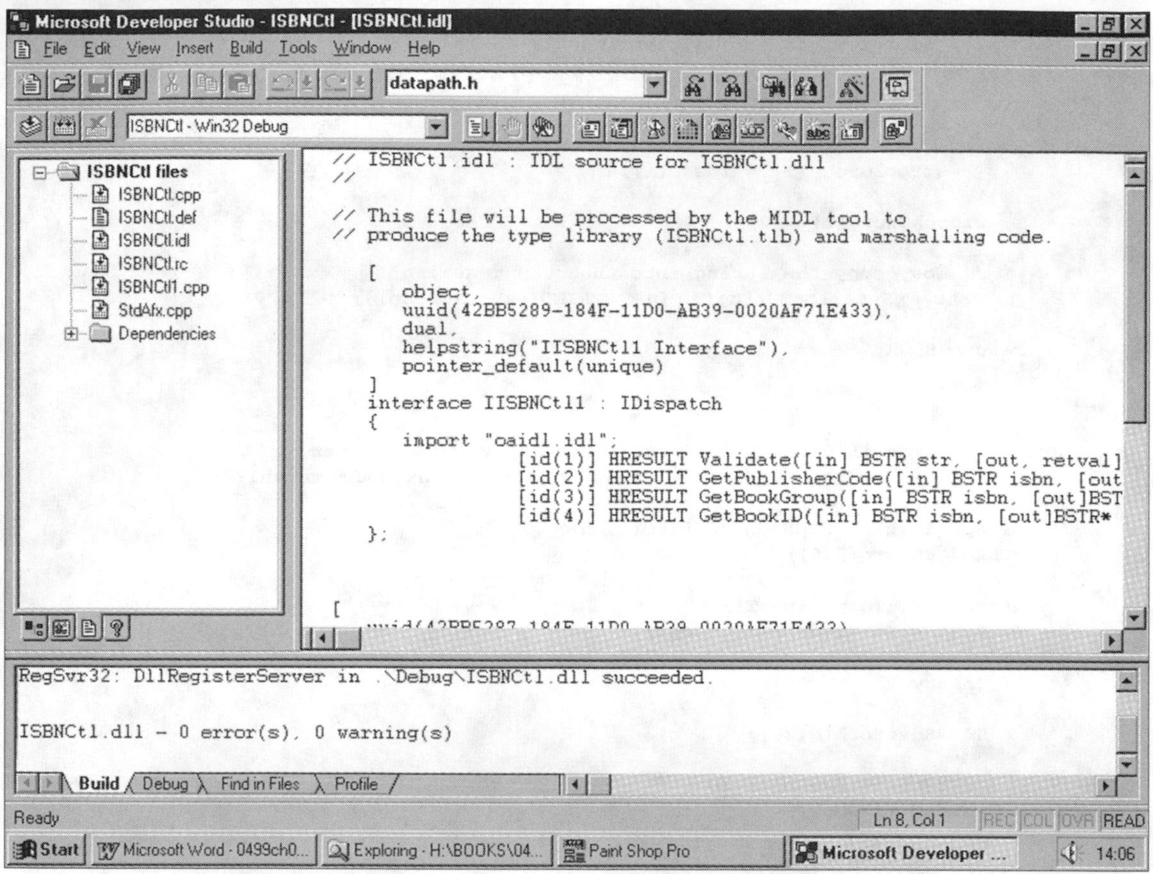

TRY IT OUT - Testing the ISBN Control

1 So, you have this fancy new ISBN Validation object with its brilliantly written **`Validate()`** method. How, exactly, are you going to test it? There are a couple of ways that you can test a simple ActiveX COM control. Remember that the control has no user interface, so you can't simply use the Test Container to test it. You can, however, create a complete web page, register the control, add the control to the page, add some VBScript or Java to call the control method, and then try to figure out what went wrong without using a debugger.

The alternative to this nightmarish scenario is to use **Visual Basic**! You really shouldn't be surprised; Visual Basic, or VB as it's affectionately known, was one of the first true OLE container objects available for testing OLE/COM controls. Visual Basic 4.0 (VB4) now sports support (say that three times fast) for OLE controls, COM controls, and a host of other stuff. The only tricky part is getting VB4 to *find* our control!

The problem with simple COM controls is that they are simple. They aren't ActiveX controls and have no built-in support to insert themselves into new applications and containers. They *do* know how to register themselves and, most importantly, they have type libraries. You might remember that we spent quite a bit of time discussing IDL files and how they created header files and method prototypes and interface files. They are also responsible for another, more important, output: the type library (**`.tlb`**) file.

Visual Basic can directly reference controls via their type libraries. This is done by referencing the TLB file for the control. Within this control file, VB finds all of the information that it needs to load and use the methods of the control. Once you have referenced a type library for a control, you can use it just like any other object in the system. We will take a look at how you use the control in VB in a moment (or at least a page or two). First, though, let's examine the problem of 'teaching' Visual Basic about our new ISBN control.

2 Using Visual Basic 4.0, you can add new objects to the system by 'referencing' them. To accomplish this, fire up VB4 and select the Tools | References menu item. You should see some version of the dialog shown below. Don't worry if your list doesn't look exactly like mine, the list is a factor of which controls and what software you have installed on your system. Since most people don't have exactly the same programs installed, the controls in the list will vary.

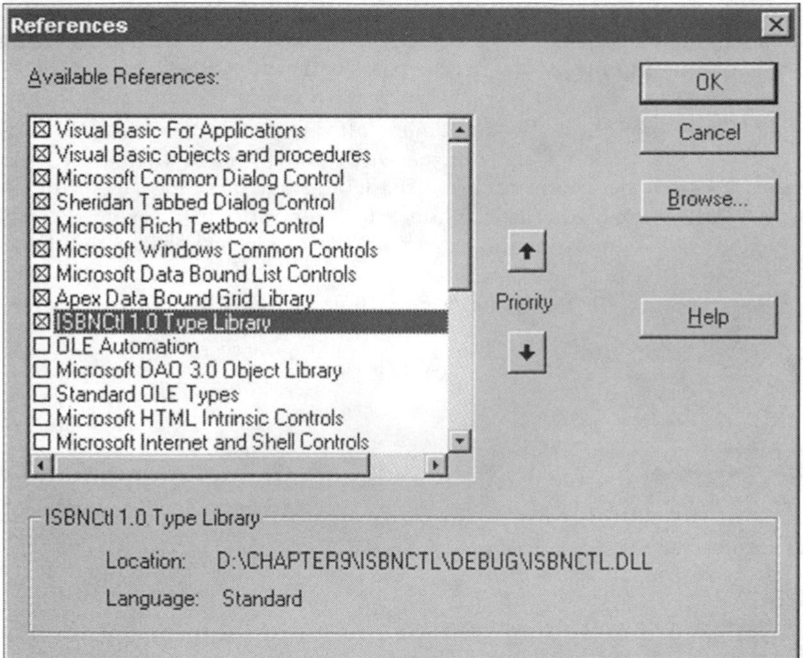

Check the objects listed in your version of the list box. If your control compiled and registered itself properly, there will be an entry called **`ISBNCtl 1.0 Type Library`**, or something similar. For the moment, though, we will assume that your control isn't shown. This will happen if you compile the control on one machine and then move it over to another, for example. From the above dialog, select the Browse button and navigate to the directory where the type library (**`ISBNCtl.tlb`**) is stored. If, for example, you created the control in a directory called **`Chapter9\ISBNCtl`**, then you are probably as strange as I am. In spite of that, the **`.tlb`** file would be found in either **`Chapter9\ISBNCtl\Debug`** or

Chapter9\ISBNCtl\Release, depending on whether you had last created the debug or release version of the project to build. By default, the debug version of the control will normally be built.

Once the control is selected (or if this is the same machine on which it was built), the name of the control will appear in the checklist box on the left-hand side of the dialog. You can then include this control in your project by simply checking the checkbox for the control. In the case of our control, the name is **ISBNCtl 1.0 Type Library**. It's important that you update the version information in your control if you change its behavior, since projects that rely on the control will have no other way to know that they aren't using it correctly.

Once the type library has been registered with VB4 and the control included in a project, you can create instances of the control the same way you would create anything else in VB. Here's a small code fragment that shows how you would create a new instance of an **ISBNCtl** object in your Visual Basic application:

```
Dim Isbn as New IsbnCtlObj
```

Once this is done, you can refer to the **Isbn** object to call the methods for the object: **Validate()**, **GetPublisherCode()**, and so forth. Visual Basic, which knows the names of the methods and the types of the arguments, will do its usual fine job of syntax and type checking for the arguments you try to pass to the methods.

3 All right, that's enough of this academic stuff. Let's build a simple VB form that will let you play with the ISBN control and call the **Validate()** method that we worked so laboriously to create. Create a new form in Visual Basic and add a single label with the caption Enter ISBN Number:. Next to the label, place a text control with the name **Text1** (the default). Finally, place two buttons on the form with the captions Validate and Exit.

Add a new handler for the first (Validate) button and add the following code to the button click handler:

```
Private Sub Command1_Click()
   Dim ISBN As New ISBNCtl
   Dim PubCode As String
   Dim BookGroup As String
   Dim BookID As String

   If (ISBN.Validate(Text1.Text)) Then
      MsgBox "Valid ISBN Entry"
   Else
      MsgBox "Not Valid ISBN Entry"
   End If
End Sub
```

4 Next, add another handler, this time for the second button (Exit). Add the following line of code to the handler for the Exit button:

```
Private Sub Command2_Click()
   End
End Sub
```

5 Try out the program by selecting Run | Start from the main menu. You should now see a screen that looks much like this one:

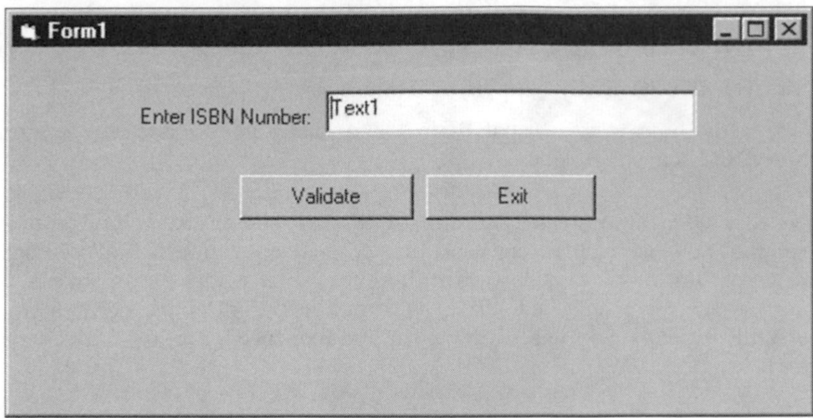

Enter a valid ISBN number in the edit box and click on the Validate button. You should, assuming that you typed in the number correctly, see a message box which reads Valid ISBN Number appear. Where can you get a valid ISBN number, you ask? A good place to start might be the back of this particular book!

6 Let's next add some code to retrieve the pieces of the ISBN entry and display them for the user. Add the following code to the Validate button handler (the new code is shown in bold print):

```
Private Sub Command1_Click()
   Dim ISBN As New ISBNCtl
   Dim PubCode As String
   Dim BookGroup As String
   Dim BookID As String

   If (ISBN.Validate(Text1.Text)) Then
      MsgBox "Valid ISBN Entry"
   Else
      MsgBox "Not Valid ISBN Entry"
   End If

   ISBN.GetPublisherCode Text1.Text, PubCode
   ISBN.GetBookGroup Text1.Text, BookGroup
   ISBN.GetBookID Text1.Text, BookID

   MsgBox PubCode
   MsgBox BookGroup
   MsgBox BookID
End Sub
```

Congratulations! You have now written a completely functional COM control that uses the ATL library. At this point, let's take a moment to review everything that we've learned so far in this chapter:

- We've learned how to implement a simple ATL control using the ATL COM custom AppWizard.

- How to add new methods to an ActiveX control using the IDL files.
- How to send and receive binary (BSTR) strings.
- That Visual Basic uses OLE/COM controls via their type libraries.
- That ATL creates simple, lightweight OLE/COM controls.
- That ATL doesn't easily support user interfaces or user input.
- And, lastly, how to use Visual Basic 4.0 to load and test our new control via its type library and some VB code.

Once you've learned a little about OLE and COM, you will probably find yourself quite interested in the 'how to' of OLE construction. Or perhaps you will find yourself never wanting to hear the term OLE again outside of a bull-fighting arena. One never knows. In spite of that, to learn more about the whole OLE thing, with our next control we delve more deeply into the concepts of OLE by exploring one of the more common needs for an ActiveX control: drag-and-drop support.

The Drop Target ActiveX Control

With the advent of Internet technology and the massive proliferation of web pages sending out and gathering information, it's inevitable that people (well, users anyway) want drag-and-drop support for their web pages. Actually, it isn't the 'dragging' that they want so much as the 'dropping'. Basically, people want to be able to select text in their Microsoft Word documents (for example) and drop them onto a web form as data. This brings us to the purpose of the next (actually the last) control we will develop: the ActiveX Drop Target control.

The Drop Target control will implement a drop target interface within a web page, allowing the user to 'drop' data (we will only support text, but it could be easily modified to support other types) onto the control, which can then be queried by other controls on HTML forms to get data from it.

What exactly is a drop target, and why would we want one? Although it sounds like a military term ("Approaching the drop target, sir." "Very good Johnson, drop the bomb."), it actually belongs to OLE. To be more exact, a drop target is a specific OLE interface.

An OLE interface is simply a protocol for 'talking' to an OLE object. Consider a C++ object, which has a set of methods you can call (or invoke) and properties (usually called member variables for C++ classes) which you can set. OLE/COM objects are the same, but different. In the C++ model, a class exposes a certain set of methods which is static for the life of the class. For example, if we had a C++ class like this:

```
class Foo
{
   public:
      int Print();
      int Open();
      int Close();
};
```

We could say that the **Foo** interface consists of three methods, named **Print()**, **Open()** and **Close()**. No matter what **Foo** object you had, you could always rely on the fact that the object would support these methods. In C++, a class which was derived from **Foo** would also automatically inherit the ability to support the **Print()**, **Open()**, and **Close()** methods as well.

An OLE interface is quite similar to the **Foo** class. The difference is that OLE always has a base set of methods (called the **IUnknown** interface methods) which exist for every valid OLE object, but may or may not contain any other methods. The major difference between the C++ model and the OLE model is that while a C++ class contains a specified set of methods, an OLE object (which is analogous to the C++ class) contains a specified set of interfaces. An object may expose one or more interfaces that a calling application may use. If an object doesn't support a given interface, there's no compile time error to let you know that fact, as there is in C++. Rather, you must deal with the fact that the interface isn't supported at run time.

Here's another difference between an interface and a set of methods: an interface can exist outside an OLE object. In fact, rather than implementing an OLE object by inheriting from interfaces, you can instead implement it by embedding an object which deals with a given interface within an OLE object, and not expose that functionality to the outside world.

In the OLE world, the **IUnknown** interface must be supported by all objects. We've mentioned this before, but it's important to understand why this is so. In order to get at any other interfaces supported by a given object, you must first obtain the **IUnknown** interface and query it for a different interface. This is why the **IUnknown** interface must be supported. If it were not, there would be no way to get at any other interfaces supported by a given object.

In C++, you would model such a system by inheritance, and that's exactly the way that OLE works as well. In our **Foo** class, for example, the interface would be described as:

```
class Foo : public IUnknown // Make the Foo class an interface
{
   // Methods for IUnknown implemented for Foo

   // method for Foo interface
};
```

Unlike C++, however, interfaces can be separated from the objects they belong to in certain ways. In this example, we will create a stand-alone class to encapsulate the functionality of a certain OLE interface (**IDropTarget**, in this case) and use that object to encapsulate the implementation of the interface for our ActiveX control. Don't worry a great deal if you didn't understand the slightest bit of what I just said. All will be explained shortly in nice, easy to understand code (if that itself isn't an oxymoron).

The first thing we need to decide, of course, is what we want the ActiveX control to do. A drop target control will be used in web browsers to allow the end user (the person using the browser, in this case) to 'drag' text from other applications, such as Microsoft Word or Excel, and 'drop' that text onto the control space. This control can then be queried by other parts of the form or application in which the control is running for data to be used elsewhere. The ActiveX control can be used in HTML Forms, Visual Basic forms, and Visual C++ applications (at some point in the future, at least)—in fact, pretty much anywhere.

From the description above, you can (hopefully) see that the control has two major responsibilities to the outside world. First of all, the control needs to be able to accept dropped text from other applications or other outside sources. Secondly, the control needs to be able to be 'queried' for that text at a later time by other controls and/or applications. The second half of the equation is really pretty easy to implement. By storing the text that's dropped into the control in a member variable of the ActiveX control object, we can then expose that information to the outside world via methods. Since we will know whether any data has been dropped onto our control area, we can easily determine whether there's any text to return.

It's the first half of the problem which requires a bit of thought. How do you support drag-and-drop of text from any arbitrary application? In the 'good old days' of Windows 3.*x* programming, such a transfer would have been accomplished either by a messy cut and paste operation (mark some text, copy it to the clipboard, switch to the other application, select the control and paste the text) or by a DDE link between the two applications. Both solutions have problems in our Windows 95 ActiveX solution. Cut and paste requires that the control supports user input into the control. The whole purpose of having drag-and-drop is to avoid the problems of having users type in data more than once. To let the user 'paste' things into our control we would most likely have to allow them to type into it as well. A DDE solution, on the other hand, requires that both sides 'know' about each other in order to establish a link between them. This limitation violates the requirement that the control works with any arbitrary application which can drag text to us. How, then, are we to implement a solution to the problem?

By now, you've probably guessed two things. First, that there's probably a solution to the problem, otherwise why bother to talk about such a control in the first place? Second, that the solution to the problem lies in the aforementioned OLE interface strategy. You are, of course, correct in both realizations.

Getting into Your Interface

The first thing we should probably examine in our quest would be the methods needed to implement the **IDropTarget** interface correctly. This table lists the necessary methods. Notice that the methods listed include the standard **IUnknown** interface (marked with an asterisk):

Method Name	Description
***QueryInterface()**	**IUnknown** method to get any other interfaces defined for this interface.
***AddRef()**	**IUnknown** method to increment the reference count of this object, so that it will not be deleted when **Release** is called.
***Release()**	**IUnknown** method called to release a reference counter so that the object can be deleted (when the reference count is zero).
DragEnter()	Called when the mouse is dragged into our window.
DragOver()	Called when the mouse is moved over our window. Allows us to set the cursor and indicate if the drop is in a valid location
DragLeave()	Called when the mouse moves out of our window.
Drop()	Called when a drag operation terminates by releasing the mouse button inside of our window.
QueryDrop()	Called when the mouse is inside our window to check the keyboard state and whether this is a move or copy operation.

Okay. Now you know what things you need to implement. How do you make that phenomenal leap between the OLE interface specification and a working C++ class that handles dropped text for us?

The first thing to understand about OLE interfaces is that all of the 'standard' ones are already implemented—in ODL! As you probably remember from our discussion on ActiveX (last chapter), when you compile an IDL file using the MIDL compiler, you will get two output files. The first of these two output files is a header file which describes a C++ class that does the job specified in the IDL file (or at least is a skeleton for the job). The second output file is the source file for that implemented object. The standard OLE interfaces are already represented in IDL files that describe the methods in the previous table listed (in this case, the **IUnknown** interface). In addition, each standard interface is implemented in a C++ wrapper that has the same name. Therefore, for the **IDropTarget** interface, we already have a C++ class, **IDropTarget**, to work with.

It can't be *that* easy, can it? Of course not. The **IDropTarget** class has no useful implementation for our class. In fairness, there's no way that it could have one. Instead of using the actual **IDropTarget** class, we need to derive a new class from **IDropTarget** and implement the methods the way we want them to work. After all, had Microsoft implemented the **IDropTarget** class so that it did all things for all programmers, it would be bloated beyond belief. Instead, they left the implementation up to the programmer who knows what he or she wants and merely implemented the 'standard' for the interface so that all drop target objects understand the same methods.

TRY IT OUT - Create a DropTarget Object for ActiveX

1 Let's take a look at the class which implements the **IDropTarget** interface methods. If you don't have any desire to know how it works or how it was implemented, just skip to the next section after typing in this code (or downloading it from the Wrox web site). We'll create the Visual C++ application in a short while. For now, create a directory called **DragDrop**, and put the following code in a file called **IDragDrop.h**:

```
#ifndef _IDRAGDROP_H_
#define _IDRAGDROP_H_

#include "DragDropctl.H"

class CDragDrop : public IDropTarget
{
private:
   CDragDropControl* m_myParent;
public:
   CDragDrop(CDragDropControl *pParent);

   /* IUnknown methods */
   STDMETHOD(QueryInterface)(REFIID riid, void FAR* FAR* ppvObj);
   STDMETHOD_(ULONG, AddRef)(void);
   STDMETHOD_(ULONG, Release)(void);

   /* IDropTarget methods */
   STDMETHOD(DragEnter)(LPDATAOBJECT pDataObj, DWORD grfKeyState, POINTL pt,
                                                LPDWORD pdwEffect);
   STDMETHOD(DragOver)(DWORD grfKeyState, POINTL pt, LPDWORD pdwEffect);
   STDMETHOD(DragLeave)();
   STDMETHOD(Drop)(LPDATAOBJECT pDataObj, DWORD grfKeyState, POINTL pt, LPDWORD
                                                          pdwEffect);

   /* Utility function to read type of drag from key state */
```

```
   STDMETHOD_(BOOL, QueryDrop)(DWORD grfKeyState, LPDWORD pdwEffect);

private:
   ULONG m_refs;
   BOOL m_bAcceptFmt;
};

#endif
```

2 That wasn't so bad, was it? Enter this next block into **IDragDrop.cpp**:

```
#include "IPServer.H"
#include "LocalSrv.H"

#include "LocalObj.H"
#include "CtrlObj.H"
#include "Globals.H"
#include "Util.H"
#include "Resource.H"
#include "idragdrop.h"

// Constructor for class

CDragDrop::CDragDrop(CDragDropControl*  pParent)
{
   m_refs = 1;
   m_bAcceptFmt = FALSE;
   m_myParent= pParent;
}

//---------------------------------------------------------------------
//                      IUnknown Methods
//---------------------------------------------------------------------

STDMETHODIMP
CDragDrop::QueryInterface(REFIID iid, void FAR* FAR* ppv)
{
   if(iid == IID_IUnknown || iid == IID_IDropTarget)
   {
      *ppv = this;
      AddRef();
      return NOERROR;
   }
   *ppv = NULL;
   return ResultFromScode(E_NOINTERFACE);
}

STDMETHODIMP_(ULONG)
CDragDrop::AddRef(void)
{
   return ++m_refs;
}

STDMETHODIMP_(ULONG)
CDragDrop::Release(void)
{
   if(--m_refs == 0)
```

```
    {
       delete this;
       return 0;
    }
    return m_refs;
}

//---------------------------------------------------------------------
//                    IDropTarget Methods
//---------------------------------------------------------------------

STDMETHODIMP
CDragDrop::DragEnter(LPDATAOBJECT pDataObj, DWORD grfKeyState, POINTL pt, LPDWORD
pdwEffect)
{
    FORMATETC fmtetc;

    fmtetc.cfFormat = CF_TEXT;
    fmtetc.ptd      = NULL;
    fmtetc.dwAspect = DVASPECT_CONTENT;
    fmtetc.lindex   = -1;
    fmtetc.tymed    = TYMED_HGLOBAL;

    // Does the drag source provide CF_TEXT, which is the only format we accept.
    m_bAcceptFmt = (NOERROR == pDataObj->QueryGetData(&fmtetc)) ? TRUE : FALSE;

    QueryDrop(grfKeyState, pdwEffect);
    return NOERROR;
}

STDMETHODIMP
CDragDrop::DragOver(DWORD grfKeyState, POINTL pt, LPDWORD pdwEffect)
{
    QueryDrop(grfKeyState, pdwEffect);
    return NOERROR;
}

STDMETHODIMP
CDragDrop::DragLeave()
{
    m_bAcceptFmt = FALSE;
    return NOERROR;
}

STDMETHODIMP
CDragDrop::Drop(LPDATAOBJECT pDataObj, DWORD grfKeyState, POINTL pt, LPDWORD
pdwEffect)
{
    FORMATETC fmtetc;
    STGMEDIUM medium;
    HGLOBAL hText;
    LPTSTR lpszText;
    HRESULT hr;

    if (QueryDrop(grfKeyState, pdwEffect))
    {
       fmtetc.cfFormat = CF_TEXT;
       fmtetc.ptd = NULL;
```

```
      fmtetc.dwAspect = DVASPECT_CONTENT;
      fmtetc.lindex = -1;
      fmtetc.tymed = TYMED_HGLOBAL;

      // User has dropped on us. Get the CF_TEXT data from drag source
      hr = pDataObj->GetData(&fmtetc, &medium);
      if (FAILED(hr))
         goto error;

      // Display the data and release it.
      hText = medium.hGlobal;
      lpszText = (LPTSTR)GlobalLock(hText);
      m_myParent->SetText(pszText);
      GlobalUnlock(hText);
      ReleaseStgMedium(&medium);
   }
   return NOERROR;

error:
   *pdwEffect = DROPEFFECT_NONE;
   return hr;
}

#define OleStdGetDropEffect(grfKeyState)      \
   ((grfKeyState & MK_CONTROL) ?              \
      ((grfKeyState & MK_SHIFT) ? DROPEFFECT_LINK : DROPEFFECT_COPY) :  \
      ((grfKeyState & MK_SHIFT) ? DROPEFFECT_MOVE : 0))

STDMETHODIMP_(BOOL) CDragDrop::QueryDrop(DWORD grfKeyState, LPDWORD pdwEffect)
{
   DWORD dwOKEffects = *pdwEffect;

   if (!m_bAcceptFmt)
      goto dropeffect_none;

   *pdwEffect = OleStdGetDropEffect(grfKeyState);
   if (*pdwEffect == 0)
   {
      // No modifier keys used by user while dragging. Try in order: MOVE, COPY.
      if (DROPEFFECT_MOVE & dwOKEffects)
         *pdwEffect = DROPEFFECT_MOVE;
      else if (DROPEFFECT_COPY & dwOKEffects)
         *pdwEffect = DROPEFFECT_COPY;
      else goto dropeffect_none;
   }
   else
   {
      // Check if the drag source application allows the drop effect desired
      // by user. The drag source specifies this in DoDragDrop
      if (!(*pdwEffect & dwOKEffects))
         goto dropeffect_none;

      // We don't accept links
      if (*pdwEffect == DROPEFFECT_LINK)
         goto dropeffect_none;
   }
   return TRUE;
```

```
dropeffect_none:
    *pdwEffect = DROPEFFECT_NONE;
    return FALSE;
}
```

3 Remember, I told you that if you didn't care how this all works, you should skip this section. Okay, you were warned! Let's examine the methods of the **CDragDrop** class on a method-by-method basis.

The first method that you will encounter in the source file (**IDragDrop.cpp**) is the constructor for the object. There's very little remarkable here except the sole parameter to the method, **pParent**. This parameter will represent the pointer to our ActiveX Control window. Remember that the **CDragDrop** class itself is *not* a window. Rather, it's a protocol object which is attached to a window. In just a few minutes, we'll examine exactly how the OLE system knows about our protocol object but for now just keep it in mind. The reason that we pass the object pointer to our protocol object is that we need a way to communicate any text dropped on the object to the window which is to hold that text.

The next three methods for the class are **QueryInterface()**, **AddRef()**, and **Release()**. These three methods represent the **IUnknown** portion of the OLE interface. As mentioned previously, these three methods are *required* to be implemented by any OLE interface (or control) object. In our case, we simply verify that the requested interface (in **QueryInterface()**) is either **IUnknown** or **IDropTarget** and return a pointer to the object itself. Note that the way you query for an interface is via the interface's GUID, which is defined in the ODL file for the interface object. For any other requested interface, we simply return a **NULL** pointer for the interface and indicate the error condition (**E_NOINTERFACE**) reporting that this object doesn't support the requested interface. This will allow the calling application to 'degrade' gracefully to the interfaces which we do support. The **AddRef()** and **Release()** methods, on the other hand, are extremely simple implementations of **reference counting** for the object.

Reference counting is a way to ensure that the object isn't deleted 'out from under you'. Basically, the reference counting system makes sure that as long as someone has a pointer to an OLE object (obtained by either the **QueryInterface()** or by making a copy of a pointer and calling **AddRef()** on the pointer), that object won't be deleted. For this reason, it's extremely important that you call **AddRef()** whenever you obtain a pointer to an OLE object and **Release()** when you're done with it. Failure to call **AddRef()** will result in a program crash through access to an invalid pointer, while failure to call **Release()** will result in a program memory leak.

> ***Compared to the C++ implementation of pointers, the OLE system is actually quite ingenious. In C++, many errors are caused because one method deletes a pointer which another method is still referring to. In OLE, you never call the delete method directly, but instead rely on the OLE object to delete itself when everyone is through with it.***

Once we have implemented the required **IUnknown** methods, we come to the first of the **IDropTarget** methods, **DragEnter()**. This method is called when the user drags a selection within the bounds of our window object (in this case, the ActiveX control window).

When **DragEnter()** is called, the OLE subsystem calls this method to see whether we will allow the requested dragged object to be dropped on our window. In our case, all that we care about is that the dragged object can be displayed in text format (**CF_TEXT**). No other format matters to us, since text is the only format that we 'understand'. To accomplish this, we 'ask' the object if it supports text format. If it does, we indicate to the OLE system that this object is acceptable for dropping onto our window.

The next method in the source file is the **DragOver()** method. This method is called as the mouse moves across our window during a drag operation. All that happens here is that we check to see what keys the user is holding down (in the **DragQuery()** method) to see what cursor type to show during the process. Similarly, the **DragLeave()** method does nothing, since we didn't do any processing during either the **DragEnter()** or **DragOver()** methods.

The **Drop()** method of the interface is where all of the interesting stuff happens. Basically, when this method is invoked, the OLE system will pass us a pointer to the object which is being 'dropped' onto the window (called **pDataObj** in the code) which contains the information to 'drop' into our control. We then get the textual information from the object by calling the **GetData()** method of the object with the proper flags set up. The returned structure (called **medium** in the code) contains a handle to the globally allocated block holding the selected text to drop into our window. We call **GlobalLock()** (an API function) to get a pointer to the data itself (rather than the handle to the memory) and pass that data to our parent control object via the **SetText()** method (we'll look into this shortly). The handle is then unlocked and released back to the system.

So, we have received some text when the user dragged the mouse into our window holding some text and then released the mouse button. The only real problems at this point are, first, that we don't have a window and, second, that we don't have an application. Let's do something about that right now.

4 To create our new ActiveX control application in which to place all of that wonderful code we just wrote (or copied, as the case may be) we will use the custom AppWizard that we developed in the previous chapter. Fire up the AppWizard main screen and select the ActiveX custom wizard from the wizard list. Enter **DragDrop** for the name of the control and **DD** for the short name. Enter whatever you choose for the remaining options (directory, company name, and so forth) and then click on the Finish button to generate the new project.

5 The first step to modifying the project to do what we want is to change the makefile for the project to add our new interface class files. Remember that the makefile isn't a Visual C++ IDE project makefile, and you can't use the IDE to modify them (via the Insert Files Into Project menu option). Instead, load the makefile into your favorite text editor and make the following changes which we've highlighted here:

```
dll = 1

Proj = DragDrop

# These are "extra" libs beyond the standard set that inetsdk.mak will
#  append to the libs set

libs=uuid2.lib uuid3.lib urlmon.lib urlhlink.lib wininet.lib ocx96.lib shell32.lib
oleaut32.lib cap.lib
```

```
# Static libs have to be treated specially.
# Notice that this particular one is built from the ..\framewrk directory

STATICLIBS= c:\inetsdk\samples\basectl\lib\CtlFwD32.lib

# Commands to be added to the compile line... in this case to locate headers

cDefines= -I..\Include
RFLAGS= -I..\Include

# pull in the master SDK makefile that defines all of the macros
#  and all of the build rules

!include <c:\inetsdk\include\inetsdk.mak>

all: $(ObjDir)\$(Proj).ocx $(Proj).tlb REGISTER

# itemize all of the required object files

OBJS=$(ObjDir)\Guids.Obj    \
     $(ObjDir)\DragDrop.Obj     \
     $(ObjDir)\DragDropCtl.Obj \
     $(ObjDir)\DragDropPPG.Obj \
     $(ObjDir)\IDragDrop.Obj \
     $(Proj).res

# after the ocx is built, register it

REGISTER: $(ObjDir)\$(Proj).ocx
   regsvr32 /s $(ObjDir)\$(Proj).ocx

# special case the odl file since the output header has a special name

$(Proj)Interfaces.h: $(Proj).odl
   mktyplib /DWIN32 -I..\Include /h $(Proj)Interfaces.h /o $(Proj).log /tlb
$(Proj).tlb $(Proj).odl

$(Proj).tlb: $(Proj).odl
   mktyplib /DWIN32 -I..\Include /h $(Proj)Interfaces.h /o $(Proj).log /tlb
$(Proj).tlb $(Proj).odl

# and finally, just define the dependencies

$(ObjDir)\$(Proj).ocx: $(OBJS) $(ObjDir)\$(Proj).Exp $(STATICLIBS) idragdrop.h

$(ObjDir)\$(Proj).Exp: $(Proj).def $(STATICLIBS)

$(ObjDir)\guids.obj: guids.cpp $(Proj)Interfaces.h
```

Once the makefile has been updated with the changes shown, the next thing you should probably do is to run a full build of the application to be sure that there are no errors in the code you just typed in (or the code that was generated, but that seems unlikely). This is always a good idea, as it gives you a starting point for finding problems or compile errors that might crop up later.

6 Adding the new interface to the control is a two-step process. First, you need to add the member variables and include files needed to the header file for the control. To do this, edit **DragDropCtl.h** and make the following modifications to the header file:

```
//=--------------------------------------------------------------------------------=
// DragDropCtl.H
//=--------------------------------------------------------------------------------=
//
// class declaration for the DragDrop control.
//
#ifndef _DragDropCONTROL_H_

#include "IPServer.H"
#include "CtrlObj.H"
#include "Internet.h"
#include "DragDropInterfaces.H"
#include "Dispids.H"

#include "DibCls.H"

typedef struct tagDragDropCTLSTATE {

   // TODO: Replace with real state variables

   short TEMP;

} DragDropCTLSTATE;

//=--------------------------------------------------------------------------------=
// CDragDropControl
//=--------------------------------------------------------------------------------=
// our control.
//
class CDragDropControl :        public CInternetControl,
                                public IDragDrop,
                                public ISupportErrorInfo
{
   public:
   // IUnknown methods
   //
   DECLARE_STANDARD_UNKNOWN();

   // IDispatch methods
   //
   DECLARE_STANDARD_DISPATCH();

   // ISupportErrorInfo methods
   //
   DECLARE_STANDARD_SUPPORTERRORINFO();

   // IDragDrop methods
   //
   //
   STDMETHOD_(void, AboutBox)(THIS) ;

   // OLE Control stuff follows:
   //
```

```
    CDragDropControl(IUnknown* pUnkOuter);
    virtual ~CDragDropControl();

    // static creation function.  all controls must have one of these!
    //
    static IUnknown *Create(IUnknown*);

    // Method for interface to call to set our text.

    void SetText(LPTSTR lpszText);

    private:
    // overridables that the control must implement.
    //
    STDMETHOD(LoadBinaryState)(IStream* pStream);
    STDMETHOD(SaveBinaryState)(IStream* pStream);
    STDMETHOD(LoadTextState)(IPropertyBag* pPropertyBag, IErrorLog* pErrorLog);
    STDMETHOD(SaveTextState)(IPropertyBag* pPropertyBag, BOOL fWriteDefault);
    STDMETHOD(OnDraw)(DWORD dvAspect, HDC hdcDraw, LPCRECTL prcBounds,
            LPCRECTL prcWBounds, HDC hicTargetDev, BOOL fOptimize);
    virtual LRESULT WindowProc(UINT msg, WPARAM wParam, LPARAM lParam);
    virtual BOOL    RegisterClassData(void);

    virtual HRESULT InternalQueryInterface(REFIID, void**);
    virtual void    BeforeCreateWindow(void);

    virtual BOOL    AfterCreateWindow(void);

    // Internet specific callbacks:
    //
    // OnData is called asynchronously as data for an object or property arrives...
    virtual HRESULT OnData(DISPID id, DWORD grfBSCF, IStream* bitstrm,
            DWORD amount);

    // OnProgess is called to allow you to present progess indication UI
    virtual HRESULT OnProgress(DISPID, ULONG progress, ULONG themax,
            ULONG, LPCWSTR);

    // private state information.
    //

    HDC                 m_hDC;
    LPTSTR              m_pStr;
    LPDROPTARGET        m_pDropTarget;
};

extern const GUID* rgDragDropPropPages[];
    DEFINE_CONTROLOBJECT(DragDrop,
    &CLSID_DragDrop,
    "DragDropCtl",
    CDragDropControl::Create,
    1,
    &IID_IDragDrop,
    "DragDrop.HLP",
    &DIID_DDragDropEvents,
    OLEMISC_SETCLIENTSITEFIRST | OLEMISC_ACTIVATEWHENVISIBLE |
       OLEMISC_RECOMPOSEONRESIZE | OLEMISC_CANTLINKINSIDE | OLEMISC_INSIDEOUT,
    0,
```

```
    RESID_TOOLBOX_BITMAP,
    "DragDropWndClass",
    1,
    rgDragDropPropPages,
    0,
    NULL);

#define _DragDropCONTROL_H_
#endif // _DragDropCONTROL_H_
```

Note that not only have we added the actual interface variable (**m_pDropTarget**) to the file, but also the text variable (**m_pStr**) and the method (**SetText()**). All of these are needed to support the drop action for the control.

7 Our next step is to actually instantiate the interface and connect it to the window of the ActiveX control itself. To accomplish this task, we need to delve a bit into the mysteries of the **WindowProc()** method of the **CDragDropCtl** class.

In many ways, you can consider the **WindowProc()** method to be like a centralized post office. Messages are all sent to a single location (the **WindowProc()**) which dispatches the messages to their appropriate addresses (message handlers). For example, when the control is created, the world at large (actually Windows 95) sends a **WM_CREATE** message to the control. When **WindowProc()** gets such a message, it has three choices on what to do with it. First, it can ignore the message and allow the message to be delivered to the 'dead letter office' (**OcxDefWindowProc()**). Messages sent to the dead letter office aren't handled by the main ActiveX control at all, they are 'dumped' to the base class **COleControl** which handles them as it sees fit.

The second option for an ActiveX control **WindowProc()** message is to be handled entirely by the control itself. If you wanted, for example, to not allow mouse messages (button up, button down, and mouse movement) you might have code such as the following in your **WindowProc()** method:

```
switch (msg)
{
   case WM_LBUTTONDOWN:
   case WM_LBUTTONUP:
   case WM_MOUSEMOVE:
   return 1L;
}
```

The final option for a message in **WindowProc()** is to be both processed and sent on to the base **COleControl** for further processing. This is the option we will be exploring in our drop target handler. Here, in fact, is the code for the **CDragDrop::WindowProc()**.

```
LRESULT CDragDropControl::WindowProc(UINT msg, WPARAM wParam, LPARAM lParam)
{
   switch (msg)
   {
      case WM_CREATE:
         // Create new interface for Drag/Drop
         m_pDropTarget = (LPDROPTARGET)new CDragDrop(this);

         // Force the object to remain loaded and make it a drag/drop
```

```
        // enabled target
        CoLockObjectExternal((IUnknown*)m_pDropTarget, TRUE, TRUE);
        RegisterDragDrop(m_hwnd, m_pDropTarget);
        break;

    case WM_CLOSE:
        // Remove this window from drag/drop enabled list
        RevokeDragDrop(m_hwnd);

        // Free up our interface object
        m_pDropTarget->Release();

        // And let it go away.
        CoLockObjectExternal(m_pDropTarget, FALSE, TRUE);
        break;
    }
    return OcxDefWindowProc(msg, wParam, lParam);
}
```

What's going on here? First of all, there are two separate conditions being handled: **WM_CREATE** and **WM_CLOSE**. **WM_CREATE** is a Windows message which will be sent to your ActiveX control window when it's initially created, before it's actually displayed. **WM_CLOSE**, on the other hand, is the last message your window will get (as far as we're concerned; **WM_NCDESTROY** is the very final message any window will receive). Let's look at each message in turn and what happens in response to them.

In the case of **WM_CREATE**, we're interested in two things. First, we want to instantiate a copy of the interface code we just wrote. Once the interface object is successfully instantiated, we need to hook up the interface code with the window to make it accept dropped text. Instantiating the interface code object is accomplished by simply creating a new instance of the **CDragDrop** class using the new operator. The **this** pointer of the ActiveX control is passed into the constructor to become the parent object we talked about earlier for the **CDragDrop** class. The return is cast to an **LPDROPTARGET** pointer because it is this, base, class which all other functions expect to see. We could have simply cast each call with this object to an **LPDROPTARGET** parameter, but that would have made the code much more cluttered. This is simpler, since we don't actually do much with this pointer in our ActiveX control source code.

One last point—don't forget to add the **m_hwnd** member variable to the header file for the application:

```
private:
    HWND    m_hwnd;
```

Once the **LPDROPTARGET** has been created, there's a interesting chunk of code which reads:

```
// Force the object to remain loaded and make it a drag/drop enabled target
CoLockObjectExternal((IUnknown*)m_pDropTarget, TRUE, TRUE);
```

The **CoLockObjectExternal()** function is used to force an object to remain loaded in memory. If you don't do this, the object will eventually go out of memory and leave you with an invalid pointer. The first **TRUE** argument to the function indicates that the object is to be locked (**FALSE** would indicate that the object was to be unloaded from memory or unlocked). The second **TRUE** argument for the function indicates that this is the final lock of the chain of calls to the object. If you don't pass **TRUE** for this argument, the object may not be properly released by a second call to the **CoLockObjectExternal()** function.

9 The final piece of the creation code handler is to call **RegisterDragDrop()** with the handle of our ActiveX control window and the pointer to our **IDropTarget** interface object. This is the actual connection (See? I told you it was there somewhere.) between the 'real' window handle and the interface object. Once this function successfully returns, all drop-related functionality for our ActiveX control will be relayed through our interface object automatically.

10 Now let's handle what happens when the window closes. A window receives the **WM_CLOSE** message when it's going away, and in the case of an ActiveX control window, the window is usually closed when the page on which it resides is closed or destroyed. A **WM_CLOSE** message, therefore, is the signal for us to shut down our connection with the outside world and terminate the drop processing.

The first thing we need to do is to notify the operating system that we will no longer be accepting dropped items from other applications or windows. This is accomplished by calling the **RevokeDragDrop()** function, specifying the handle to our window as the sole parameter. Following the termination of the connection, we release our **DragDrop** interface object, decrementing the reference count (to account for incrementing it earlier). Finally, we call the **CoLockObjectExternal()** function of the system again, this time passing a **FALSE** as the second argument. This tells the function we're unlocking the object from memory and that it's now okay to delete the object and free any memory associated with it. At this point, the **m_pDropTarget** object pointer is no longer valid and shouldn't be used.

You should never call **delete** on an OLE/COM object. Instead, call **release()** to allow the object to delete itself if and only if it's safe to do so (i.e. no other objects have a pointer to it).

11 At this point we have a complete interface object. It has been allocated, given a parent object, and hooked into the drag-and-drop system for the ActiveX control. If you were to compile and link the object (assuming all went well), you could create this object in an HTML form, and then drag text from external sources, such as Microsoft Word, onto the object and paste the text into the control.

Actually, that's not quite true. If you've been following along (or if you actually tried to compile and link the control), you will have noticed that the **SetText()** method of the control is missing. In addition, there's a small bit of initialization that needs to be done in the constructor for the ActiveX control **CDragDropCtl** for it to work properly. Here are those additions:

```
#pragma warning(disable:4355)  // using 'this' in constructor
CDragDropControl::CDragDropControl(IUnknown* pUnkOuter)
: CInternetControl(pUnkOuter, OBJECT_TYPE_CTLDragDrop, (IDispatch*)this)
{
   m_pStr = NULL;
   m_pDropTarget = NULL;
}
```

```
#pragma warning(default:4355)  // using 'this' in constructor

void CDragDropControl::SetText(LPTSTR lpszStr)
{
   if (m_pStr)
      delete m_pStr;
   m_pStr = new TCHAR[lstrlen(lpszStr)+1];
   lstrcpy (m_pStr, lpszStr);
}
```

12 Now, at last, we have a fully implemented control, right? Technically, the control is complete at this point. It allows you to drag text onto it from other sources and stores that text internally. It will accept a drag-and-drop operation from any drop source interface which supports the **CF_TEXT** data format. So, in that regard, the control is complete. Unfortunately, from a usability standpoint, our control is sadly lacking in two critical areas: feedback and data access.

By *feedback*, I mean that the control must in some way show the user that the drag-and-drop operation was successful at the receiving end. It isn't enough for the text to disappear (in the case of a move-type drag) or become unhighlighted (in the case of a copy-type drag)—the text needs to reappear somewhere as well. The problem isn't particularly difficult to solve, as we're already storing the text in the **SetText()** method. To solve this problem, first modify the **SetText()** method as follows:

```
void CDragDropControl::SetText(LPTSTR lpszStr)
{
   if (m_pStr)
      delete m_pStr;
   m_pStr = new TCHAR[lstrlen(lpszStr)+1];
   lstrcpy (m_pStr, lpszStr);
   OcxInvalidateRect(NULL, TRUE);
}
```

Next, modify the **OnDraw()** method of the **CDragDropCtl** object so that the text stored in the control is displayed in the control. Here's the new **OnDraw()** method for the **CDragDropCtl** class:

```
HRESULT CDragDropControl::OnDraw(DWORD dvAspect, HDC hdcDraw, LPCRECTL prcBounds,
                                 LPCRECTL prcWBounds, HDC hicTargetDevice,
                                 BOOL fOptimize)
{
   RECT rcBounds;

   rcBounds.left = 0;
   rcBounds.top = 0;
   rcBounds.bottom = (prcBounds->bottom - prcBounds->top);
   rcBounds.right = (prcBounds->right - prcBounds->left);
   if (m_pStr)
      DrawText(hdcDraw, m_pStr, lstrlen(m_pStr),
         &rcBounds, DT_SINGLELINE | DT_VCENTER | DT_CENTER);

   return S_OK;
}
```

13 In addition to feedback, we also wanted to address the problem of *data access*. By which, I mean that outside sources need to be able to inquire whether the control has had any text dropped onto it and, if so, what that text looks like.

To make these two capabilities possible, we need to add two new methods to the control. The first method, **HasText()**, will be a simple function that returns **TRUE** if data has been dragged and dropped onto the control and **FALSE** if data has not yet been dropped onto the control. The second method, **GetText()**, will return the text dropped onto the control (only if there actually was any text dropped, of course).

14 To add new functionality to our drop target control, we will need to do several things. First of all we will modify the ODL file, but in addition we will add the new methods to the **CDragDropCtl** header and source files. Finally, of course, we will implement the actual functionality of the methods in the source code for the control. To implement the methods in the ODL file, we need to know what parameters the methods have and what types they should be.

The **HasText()** method is pretty simple. It doesn't really need any parameters and returns a simple Boolean **TRUE/FALSE** value. Here is the ODL-style definition for **HasText()**:

```
[id(101)] HRESULT HasText([out, retval] boolean* retv);
```

Note again that, although we want to return the Boolean value from the function, we define **HasText()** to return an **HRESULT** value to the OLE system and define the 'real' return value as an output parameter with the special (**[retval]**) keyword, indicating that it is the return value for the method to external sources.

The **GetText()** method is similar, in that it also needs to return a Boolean value. It differs in that it needs to return the text in the control (if there is any) as well. A method can have only one return value (how would you call it otherwise?), so we need to decide which parameter is to be the return value and which will be a simple output parameter. Conventionally, the return value of a method is used to indicate the status of the operation. In this case (as we normally do), we'll adhere to that convention and use this definition:

```
[id(102)] HRESULT GetText([out]BSTR* pBstr, [out,retval]boolean* retv);
```

15 Remember that all output parameters in ODL must be *pointers* to a type. OLE provides no support for C++ style references which change the value of a parameter without passing in the address of a parameter. Here's the relevant section of the ODL file showing the new methods in our standard highlighting:

```
...

    interface IDragDrop : IDispatch {

        // properties
        //

        // methods
        //
        [id(DISPID_ABOUTBOX)]
        void AboutBox(void);
```

```
        [id(101)] HRESULT HasText([out, retval]boolean* retv);
        [id(102)] HRESULT GetText([out] BSTR* pBstr, [out, retval]boolean* retv);
    };
...
```

16 The next step toward implementing the complete functionality of the new methods is to add the prototypes for the new methods to the header file for the control and to add the skeleton methods to the source file. Here's where to insert the new methods in the header file for the control:

```
...
{
   public:
      // IUnknown methods
      //
      DECLARE_STANDARD_UNKNOWN();

      // IDispatch methods
      //
      DECLARE_STANDARD_DISPATCH();

      // ISupportErrorInfo methods
      //
      DECLARE_STANDARD_SUPPORTERRORINFO();

      // IDragDrop methods
      //
      //
      STDMETHOD_(void, AboutBox)(THIS) ;

      HRESULT __stdcall HasText(boolean __RPC_FAR* retval);
      HRESULT __stdcall GetText(BSTR* pBstr, boolean __RPC_FAR* retval);

      // OLE Control stuff follows:
...
```

17 Finally, we need to add the method skeletons to the source file and add the code necessary to make them work. First, the simpler **`HasText()`** method. This code simply checks to see if the **`m_pStr`** variable is **`NULL`** (indicating that it has never been assigned any text) and returns that information to the calling application. Here's the complete code for the **`HasText()`** method:

```
HRESULT __stdcall CDragDropControl::HasText(boolean __RPC_FAR* retval)
{
   if (m_pStr)
      *retval = TRUE;
   else
      *retval = FALSE;
   return S_OK;
}
```

The **GetText()** method does the same thing and just a little more. If there's no text in the internal buffer (in other words, **m_pStr** is **NULL**), **GetText()** does nothing more than **HasText()**. If there is text in the internal buffer (**m_pStr** is not **NULL**), **GetText()** uses the text to allocate a buffer and copies that buffer into the output string. Here's the code for **GetText()**:

```
HRESULT __stdcall CDragDropControl::GetText(BSTR* str, boolean __RPC_FAR* retval)
{
    if (m_pStr)
    {
        *retval = TRUE;
        *str = SysAllocString(TO_OLE_STRING(m_pStr));
    }
    else
        *retval = FALSE;

    return S_OK;
}
```

18 That's all there is to it. Save all of the files and compile the result. If you haven't made any compile errors in typing, you will have a complete drop target ActiveX control.

TRY IT OUT - Testing the ActiveX DropTarget Object

To try it out, create an HTML form with a drag-and-drop control embedded in it. The easiest way to do this is to use the Microsoft Control Pad utility to create the HTML file. Here's a listing of such a form, if you would rather do the job by hand (or if you don't have a copy of the Control Pad tool):

```
<HTML>
<HEAD>
<TITLE>New Page</TITLE>
</HEAD>
<BODY>
<OBJECT ID="DragDrop1" WIDTH=100 HEIGHT=51
 CLASSID="CLSID:BD11A280-2E73-11CF-B6CF-00AA00A74DAF">
    <PARAM NAME="_ExtentX" VALUE="2646">
    <PARAM NAME="_ExtentY" VALUE="1323">
</OBJECT>
<OBJECT>
</OBJECT>
<OBJECT>
</OBJECT>
</BODY>
</HTML>
```

Remember to substitute the GUID of your control in place of the one given above!

The following screenshot shows the form running in Internet Explorer, along with an instance of Microsoft Word. In this example, I have just finished dragging the text shown highlighted in Word to the drop-target control which now displays the text.

To copy text into the control from Word, you must hold down the control key while doing the text drag. If you don't do this, you will remove the text from the Word document.

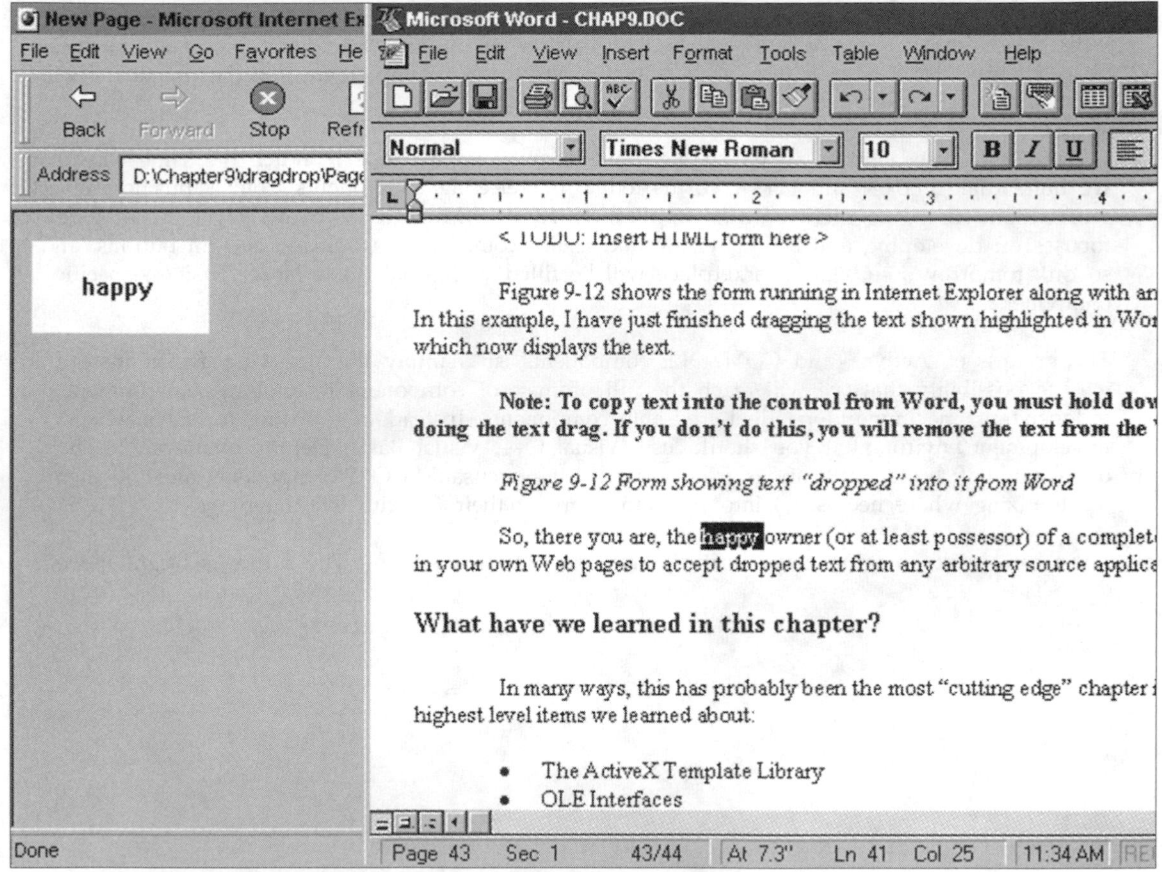

So, there you are. You're the happy owner (or at least possessor) of a complete ActiveX control you can use in your own web pages to accept dropped text from any arbitrary source application. Mission accomplished!

What Have We Learned in this Chapter?

In many ways, this has probably been the most forward-looking chapter in this book. To cover just the highest level items, we learned about:

- The ActiveX Template Library
- OLE interfaces
- Drag-and-drop

- ODL implementations of exportable methods
- Using Internet Explorer to test ActiveX controls
- Using OLE/COM object in Visual Basic

It's the first control that we covered, however, that should garner the most excitement. In the ISBN validation component, we scratched the surface of the most exciting topic of all: business objects. This software niche presents a way for businesses to implement specific functionality in small objects and then reuse (and resell) those objects.

I, for one, foresee a future in which we build business applications in much the same way that we build dialog boxes and HTML forms today: by selecting components from a 'business object toolbox' and dragging them onto an application 'canvas'. Much as software development today focuses on developing and selling visual and utility components (toolbars, custom buttons, and so on), tomorrow's software marketplace will be filled with small (and large) business-specific components.

The promise of ActiveX and COM/OLE components isn't simply the 'gee-whiz' factor. Instead, it's the possibility that we will reach the full promise of component technology: environment-independent, machine-independent, reusable components. Instead of debating for days which development environment you should use (Visual C++, Visual Basic, Delphi, whatever), each developer will build applications from a stock list of reusable COM components and 'fit' them (customizing where necessary) into the framework of their favorite IDE/language.

I just can't wait. Imagine never writing another accounting system! The future is bright indeed.

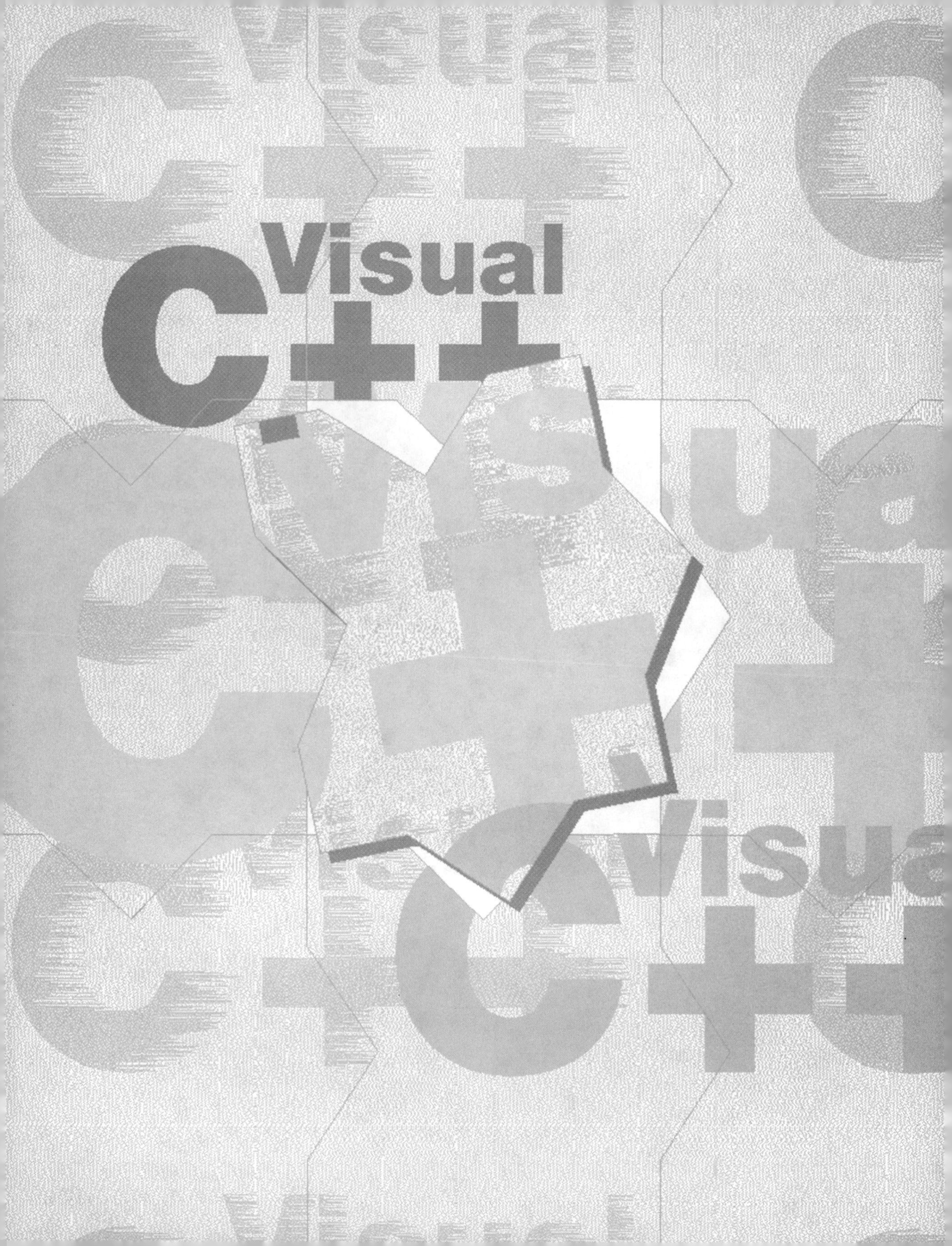
Visual
C++

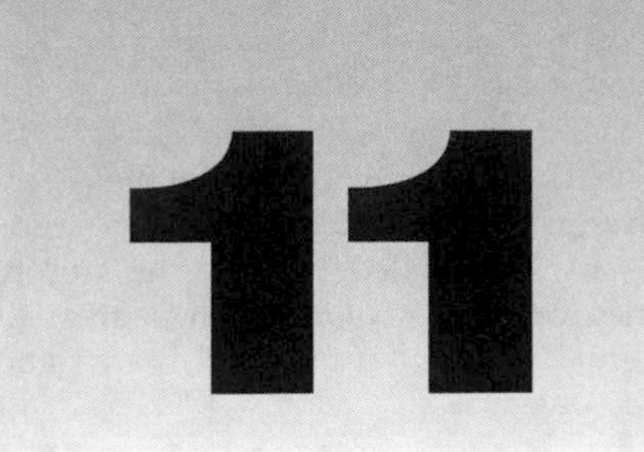

The Project

As I promised you at the beginning of the book, this chapter ties everything together in a Gordian knot (look it up). All programming books have at least one project developed in their pages—it's a tradition, or an old charter, or something. However, the project in this book differs in one fundamental way from those you will find in most other books.

Generally, the project phase of a computer book is where the most complex, esoteric, or instructional code (or any combination of the three) can be found. Projects are usually the largest body of code in a computer book, used to illustrate the points that the author has been trying to make. If you have been paying attention so far, however, you should recognize that my point is that we should all be writing *less* code and reusing it *more.*

The project in this book is at least nominally useful (I hope). It's a hypertext (HTML) viewer that allows the user to 'browse' through the documentation for the various components we have developed in the book. It can be easily extended to allow you to add your own custom component information, or even information about other things, such as applications written by a company. In short, it's a document viewer that supports HTML documents. It's also a fairly minimal coding exercise. In fact, I think you will find that we talk more about concepts and their application than we do about writing code.

The purpose of this project is twofold. First, as with all good applications, I hope to provide you with a useful tool that you can use for yourself. Second, the project is designed to show off the power of component technology and to demonstrate how that technology can be used to improve the software development world.

The HTML Component

When I first thought about the design of this project, the one sticking point in my mind was the HTML display. Although I had written an HTML parser and display module at one point in my career (I lead a strange life, what can I say?), I was reluctant to place that code here. An HTML parser is a good-sized body of code that would 'eat up' the pages allocated to this book in a hurry. Also, it would detract from the underlying concept of component reuse. Finally, my technical editor would throw a fit if he had to test something so wide-open. I put the project on a back burner while I thought about the problem some more.

Imagine my surprise, then, when I was lightly browsing the Microsoft Corporation web site (a pastime I highly recommend: **`http://www.microsoft.com`**) and discovered that Microsoft had released to the general public a package called the Internet Control Pack. Scanning through the description of the package, I discovered that along with a great deal else it contained, wonder of wonders, a complete HTML component that could load, parse and display HTML pages. It seemed that my problems were solved!

Proving My Point

At the time I found the Internet Control Pack, about a third of this book was already written. Just to satisfy my own curiosity, I tried to apply my own concepts and criteria to the HTML component in the Control Pack. Somewhat surprisingly (at least to me; I have always believed that programmers generally release good stuff), I found that the control failed miserably.

The initial release of the HTML component crashed regularly, used incomprehensible method names and properties with undocumented types, and came with no documentation apart from a **`Readme.txt`** file that told me what to avoid doing with the control (or else it would crash). I was not a happy puppy. Once again, I put the project aside and tried to think of what I was going to do to illustrate the power of component development.

A month or so went by. Once again, I happened to find myself on the Microsoft web site. (Funny things like that happen when you start web surfing. You never really know where you are going to end up. It's not unlike software development in that respect.) Lo and behold, there was a new version of the Internet Control Pack. I downloaded the new package and installed it. Either Microsoft had been reading preliminary drafts of this book or (somewhat more likely), many complaints had been heard in the halls of Redmond concerning the first release of the product. The new Internet Control Pack (still in beta form at the time of writing) features a vastly more solid construction, decent documentation, and a number of good examples that pick up where the documentation leaves off. I was saved!

Some people might ask why, in a book that deals with component development, I would feature so prominently a component that was not developed in its pages. If you think about it for a few moments, however, you will realize that I am simply putting my money (figuratively, I hope) where my mouth is. Why should I put time and effort into developing something that already exists? By promoting Microsoft's HTML component, I hope to lend weight to the whole reusability thing that we keep talking about in the development community but never get round to doing anything about. If you are the sort of person who believes that a component that doesn't come with source code isn't reusable, you probably never even read this far anyway!

A Bit of Detail

By this point, it should come as no surprise when I tell you that I'll focus on the requirements and design phase before digging into the application code. You have your hang-ups and I have mine. Buy me a good beer and I will tell you stories that will explain why I formed my opinions (some may even curl your hair). That notwithstanding, let's take a couple of minutes to look at what it is that we are developing here.

The end product is intended to be a document viewer that allows you to view HTML documents about components, view details about those components, and add new components (or other things) to your viewable list. Although it's intended primarily for use with components and controls (the two aren't synonymous) such as C++ and ActiveX controls, there's no actual requirement for it to be used for this purpose. Anything which has a description and a detailed view of its information could use this interface: a project management system perhaps, or even (hint, hint) a requirements definition system for your company.

The project (getting back to it at last) will be implemented as a Visual C++ project using MFC running under Windows 95 (and Windows NT). It will have a single main window which will contain a list of items, and an HTML viewer which will bring up descriptive documents about the selected item in the list. In addition, support dialogs will be available to view details about the selected topic as well as to add new viewable topics. At this point, to save time and space in the book, printing of the documents will not be supported.

The figure below shows the main window for the application. The left-hand side (or pane) of the window will have a list of viewable items. The right-hand side will display the HTML pages describing the topic (component selected).

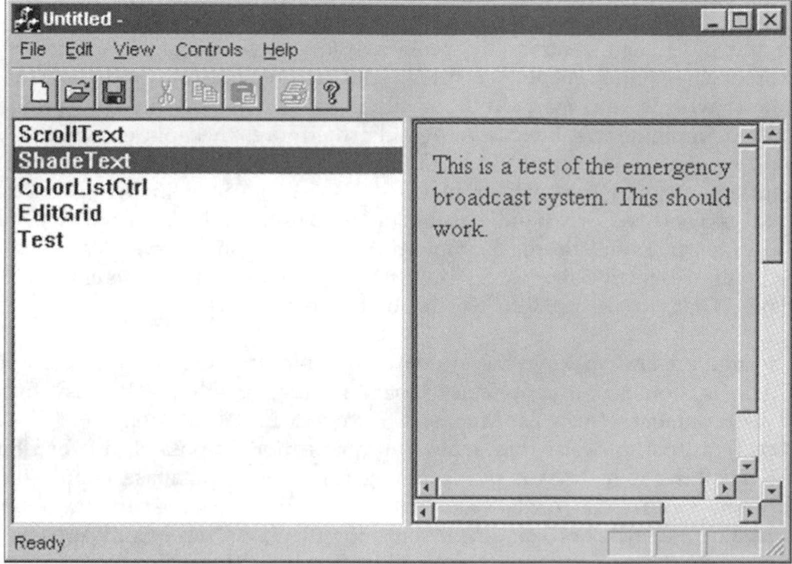

Here are the major requirements for the project:

- Allow browsing of topics and display HTML documentation for those topics.
- Allow display of topic details in a programmer-defined method without the need to recompile.
- Allow addition of new topics without any recompiling.
- Require minimum coding abilities. The code should be as simple as possible within the framework of the MFC architecture.
- Use only standard MFC implementations (no shelling off of other applications, digging into ActiveX internals, or use of VB forms).
- Don't reinvent the wheel!

More importantly, perhaps, here are the issues we need to solve:

- How to support the split-screen main window.
- How to display HTML pages without massive coding and without requiring access to a network or a phone line.
- How to store the information for the topics such that it may be retrieved easily with the minimum of coding.
- How to make the system easily extensible by the end user without requiring coding changes.
- How to make best use of existing functionality to avoid writing a lot of code.
- Determining which (available) components best solve which problems.

Getting Started

Rather than going on at length about the problems, let's begin to tackle the issue of the solutions. The first two requirements we listed, split-screen windows and the HTML display, can be solved without writing any major code at all. The MFC library already provides **`CSplitterWnd`** to implement splitter windows. Furthermore, the splitter window is an option during the code generation process of AppWizard. We will look at the considerations involved in fitting our requirements into the MFC framework as a whole in a moment. The second issue, the display of HTML pages, we will handle using the Microsoft control, of course, but that leads immediately to other potential problems. How do we embed an ActiveX control in our view window? How will view window resizing (a necessity on differing systems) affect the control and the display? What do we need to watch out for in the process?

Storing the information and making the system extensible are two other important, related issues. If the data is stored in a proprietary binary format, it will not be easy to add to it. If the data is stored in a database (such as Microsoft Access using the Jet engine, for example) the overhead of the required software may make the application impossible to distribute and install easily. Imagine installing a huge system containing a complete database engine on a small laptop! In addition, proprietary formats and databases require a substantial amount of code to retrieve data, update records, and modify layouts for display. This would appear to violate the dictum that we "Keep it simple, stupid!" (the KISS principle that all programmers should keep holy). Worse, it would violate my own requirement that the code written is kept to a minimum. A text format would be the ideal solution, since it's easy to maintain and even easier to understand. The difficulty with text formats, however, is the need to read in and parse the data. This leads to problems with error handling, and complex code to deal with extracting the data we need from the text we read in. How then are we to solve the problem of storing simple data without writing a lot of code?

Everything Old Is New Again

"A long, long time ago, but I can still remember when..." (with apologies to Don McLean), **initialization files** ruled the Windows world. In the days of Windows 3.*x*, the standard method of storing persistent information for programs was not the registry (as it is in Windows 95 today) but the lowly initialization file (known affectionately as an **`.ini`** file). Windows itself used two major **`.ini`** files, **`Win.ini`** and **`System.ini`**, for managing nearly all of the complex information needed to load and run Windows.

Microsoft no longer officially sanctions the initialization file, of course. Everything today should be stored in the Windows registry under Windows 95 and Windows NT. Like vinyl records and stick-shift cars, however, initialization files are still used and, mostly for backward-compatibility reasons, still supported by the Windows 95 (and NT) operating systems. In addition to acknowledging their existence, Windows 95 also provides functionality for retrieving and updating data in these files.

As a review (or an introduction for those who have never used them), let's take a moment to talk about initialization files. Basically, initialization files have three major components: **topics**, **keys**, and **key values**.

Topics are major entries in the file. A topic is a heading for a group of keys and key values. An example of a topic might be printers. Printers are a major area that contain many subtopics (called keys), which contain more detailed information about the topic. Topics can be thought of in the same way as dividers in a bound notebook. Each subject in the notebook (History, Science, Mathematics, English, etc.) is a topic which contains multiple pages.

Keys are analogous to the pages within the section dividers. Each page might represent a different kind of entry (perhaps the day's notes) in that subject. Going back to the example of printers, we might have key values for the number of printers installed on the system, the ports on which the printers are installed, and the characteristics of each printer on each port in the system.

The actual value of the keys is known (surprise!) as the key value. Within the topic of printers, for example, we said we had a key which represented the number of printers installed on the system. The key value of this key is an integer value such as five (5). Thus, the complete entry has a topic named 'Printers', a key of 'Number of Printers', and a key value of 5. In a 'real' initialization file, this would be represented by an entry that looked like this:

```
[Printers]
NumberOfPrinters = 5
```

That is, each topic in the initialization file is enclosed in square brackets **[]**, every key entry is followed by an equals sign **=**, and each key value follows the equals sign on the same line as the key entry to which it is assigned. This simple format makes it an easy matter for us to write some code to read the file, wouldn't you think?

But I'm playing Devil's Advocate. Why would you write code to do something that's obviously an operating system level task? If Windows itself uses the initialization file system structure to store information, wouldn't you think that there would exist a function to read the entries from the file? You would think so, and you would be right. Windows provides two major functions to deal with initialization files, **GetPrivateProfileString()** and **WritePrivateProfileString()**, for retrieving and adding or updating data respectively.

Why *private* profile strings? Aren't initialization files supposed to be very public? Well, yes, they are. And yes, there are functions called **GetProfileString()** and **WriteProfileString()**. (Don't ask why they aren't called **GetProfileString()** and **SetProfileString()**, or even **ReadProfileString()** and **WriteProfileString()**. Nobody knows.) These functions, however, operate on the system initialization file, **Win.ini**. Private initialization files are simply those that belong to an application, not to the system. For example, if you had a program named **Fred.exe**, the normal naming scheme would mean the name of the initialization file would be **Fred.ini**.

Back to the subject at hand, however. The **GetPrivateProfileString()** API function has the following syntax:

```
int GetPrivateProfileString(lpszSection, lpszEntry, lpszDefault,
                            lpszReturnBuffer, cbReturnBuffer, lpszFileName)
LPCTSTR lpszSection;
LPCTSTR lpszEntry;
LPCTSTR lpszDefault;
LPTSTR lpszReturnBuffer;
int cbReturnBuffer;
LPCTSTR lpszFileName;
```

What exactly do all of these parameters mean? You were thinking that this would be easy, weren't you? Actually, it *is* easy. The first parameter, **lpszSection** is the topic you are looking for in the **.ini** file. Using our notebook analogy, this parameter informs Windows which 'tab' of the notebook to flip to. The **lpszEntry** parameter is the key value you're looking for. For our printers example, the **lpszSection** would be 'Printers', and the **lpszEntry** entry would be 'Number of Printers'.

The next three parameters (**lpszDefault**, **lpszReturnBuffer**, and **cbReturnBuffer**) are used to get back information about the specified topic and entry. The first specifies an optional default value to return if the entry isn't found in the file. The return buffer parameter is the string in which the value found will be returned. If no topic and key entry were found, the buffer would be the same as the default entry. **cbReturnBuffer** is simply the size, in bytes, of the buffer passed in as **lpszReturnBuffer**.

The final parameter of the function, **lpszFileName**, is the actual name of the initialization file from which to extract data. This will be the file that's searched for the topic and key values, and can be found in the Windows directory, the Windows system directory, or another directory which lies in the file search path for Windows.

How Initialization Files Can Help

All this background information is very well and good, but unless it has some relevance to our current project it's just so much useless trivia. Can initialization files and their access functions help us with our data storage problems or not? Hopefully, you'll have spotted what I'm working up to by now. We're storing certain information (keys) for a number of components (topics) which have some given settings (key values). In general, our initialization file for the project will look like this,

```
[<component name>]
HTMLFile = <HTML file name>
DetailFile  = <Detail file name>
```

where the **<component name>** represents the entry we want to see in the left-hand list box of our main window. Unsurprisingly, the **<HTML file name>** represents the fully qualified path name of the HTML file to display in the right-hand side of the main window when the corresponding component is selected by the user.

This brings us to the **<Detail file name>** portion. As mentioned in the requirements section of the project, we would like to be able to display not only a generalized documentation file for the component containing a simple list of all its **public** methods, but also a detailed view listing all of the member variables, **public** methods and **protected** or **private** methods for the component as well.

We've done it once, so we can do it again. The detail file can be another initialization file with topics corresponding to the highest level of detail we want to see. Example topics in this file might be **public** methods, **private** methods, member variables, **protected** methods, overridables, and so forth. If this hierarchical list suggests to you a tree control, you are on exactly the right track!

So, now you know how we're going to store the information. You know how the detail file will be constructed. You even know more than you ever thought you'd need to know about initialization files and how to access them through Windows API functions. The question you might be asking now is, "Where do we go from here?" The answer to this one, you'll be happy to hear, is that it's time to write some code—although not too much. Remember the project requirements!

Creating the Project

The first thing to do is to generate the skeleton application for our project. Fire up the AppWizard, follow me and I will show you how it's done. In order to create a really 'excellent' application, the first thing you will need to come up with is a really great name. Without a truly fabulous name, application development projects are doomed to wither and die on the vine. The project name should say something about the entire scope of the application and convey a sense of what, exactly, the program will do for the end user.

For this reason, I have carefully considered the issue and come up with the brilliant name... 'Chapter11'. It's succinct, easy to remember, and particularly appropriate as it appears in the eleventh chapter of this book. With that monumental decision made, we can move on to the less important things in life, like deciding all of the basic attributes of the project.

Although AppWizard is really a pretty nice little application that saves a monumental amount of time, it suffers from several obvious problems. Probably the biggest is what I refer to as the 'one way' problem, which is that several decisions you make in AppWizard are irrevocable later on in the project's life. If you choose, for example, that you want an ActiveX server application, there's no way, short of changing all the files manually, that you can go back later and change the application to a dialog-based application with no ActiveX support. While it's unlikely that you would want to make that drastic a change (who, pray tell, was responsible for the requirements definition of *that* project?), other, less severe decisions can be just as hard to alter later on.

After we've chosen an MFC AppWizard (exe) project (and given it a name, of course) we choose whether to make the application single document (SDI) or multiple document (MDI) interface based. This decision is one of those irrevocable ones I talked about, so it's rather important to make the right choice here first time. In the case of the Chapter11 project, I have chosen to go with the SDI approach. This decision is based on several factors, but is basically because our viewer will never operate on more than one input file at a time (initialization files will be considered as the input files for the application). Since there really is no reason for the user to view multiple screens at once, a multiple document interface would just lead to confusion for the user. Also, since the application is a document viewer, screen real estate is important. It's difficult to imagine viewing documentation in anything other than a maximized window, so what would we gain by using MDI?

Once the MDI/SDI debate is settled, a few other options fall out of the combination of that decision's consequences and the project requirements. Since this entire application is intended to showcase the ActiveX and MFC components developed in this book, we will need to include support for ActiveX controls in the application skeleton. In Step 3, therefore, check the box marked OLE controls. Also, because we specifically stated that this product would not support printing of documents or other information, we can eliminate print previews from our list of options required by the application.

Splitter Windows Aren't so Tough

In the 'Scribble' example given in the MFC tutorial that comes with Visual C++, an entire chapter is devoted to using a splitter window within the application. The tutorial goes into excruciating detail concerning modifying the header files, adding methods to certain classes, and changing the entire flow of the application to accommodate the changes that result from the addition of the splitter window. Can it really be all that hard? Since we are adding a splitter window as part of the initial design, shouldn't it be easier to add splitter window support?

Fortunately, the answer to this question is a resounding "Yes." In the Step 4 screen of the AppWizard (which lets you specify the features you wish to include in your application), you will find a small, innocuous button labeled Advanced.... Clicking on this button will lead you to the Advanced Options dialog.

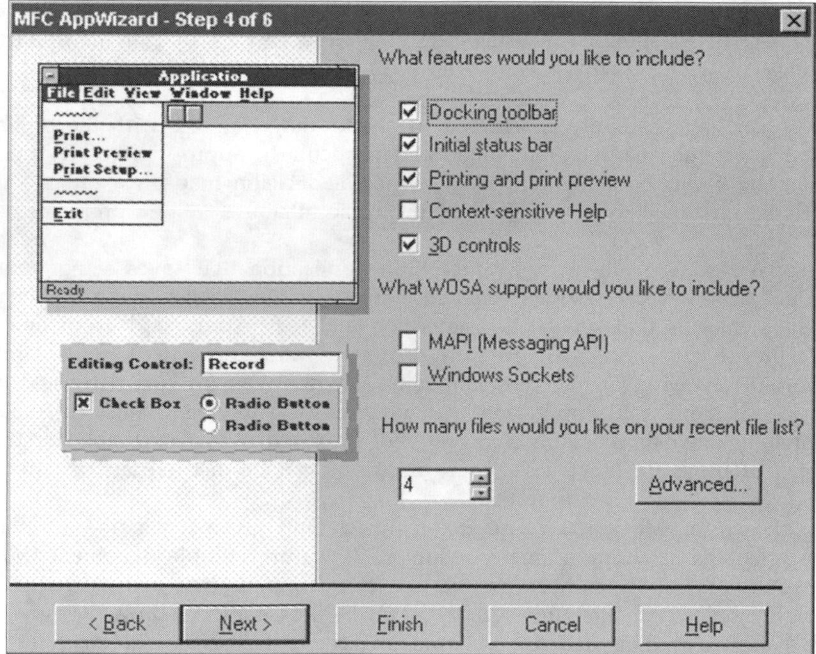

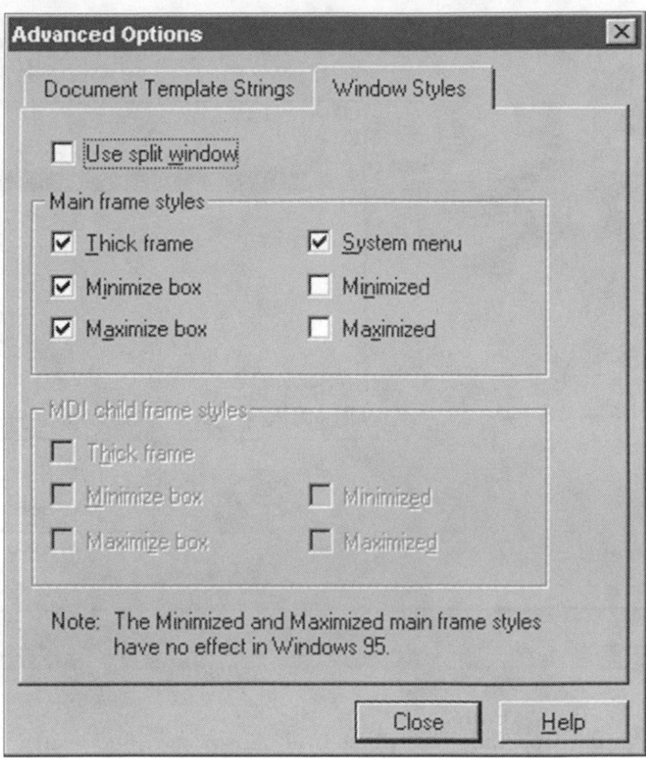

There, tucked away under the Window Styles tab, you'll find a little checkbox that reads Use split window. If you check that box, you will find that the generated application will have a splitter window in its main window. The generated code isn't perfect and, as you will see, we'll need to modify a good chunk of it. It does, however, remove much of the donkey work necessary to implement splitter windows. Since the goal of our implementation is to reuse as much code as possible, having AppWizard do the job instead of us seems like a good idea. I hope you agree!

The only remaining thing to do in the initial code generation phase of the application is to deal with the view class. By default, the view class generated will be called **`CChapter11View`**. We will actually need two view classes for our application: one to display the list of controls to select from, and one to display the HTML documentation for selected controls. AppWizard, however, will only allow us to generate a single view class. The second view class will need to be added later using ClassWizard.

For the 'default' view class for our application, we will simply select the first view that will be used. In this case, the first view class will be the control list view. Modify the generated name of the view class for the application to **`CCtrlListView`**, and the associated file names to **`CCtrlListView.h`** and **`CCtrlListView.cpp`**. Leave the rest of the settings for the view and document classes alone as there's no compelling reason to change them. After all these modifications have been made, you should see the wizard page, as shown on the next page.

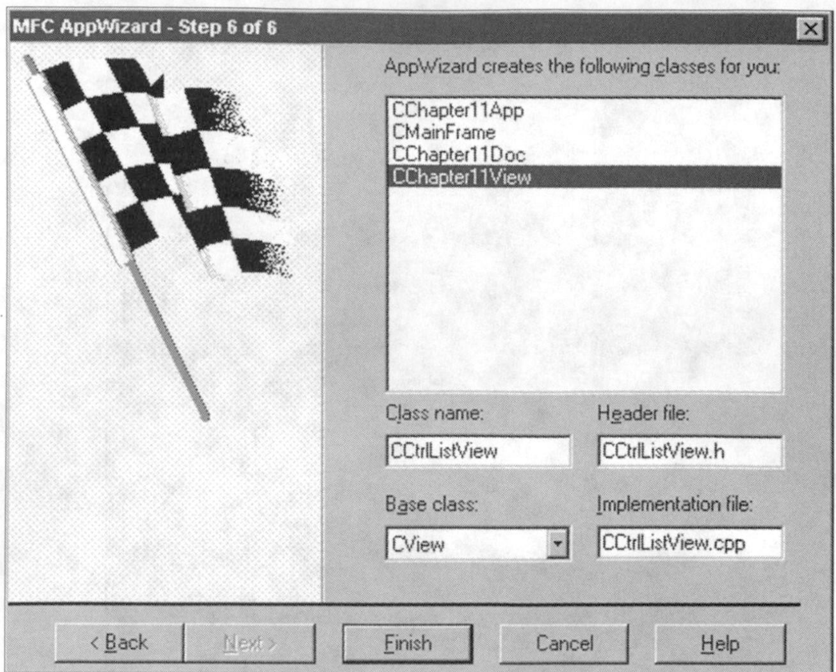

At this point, you can click on the Finish button of AppWizard and watch the code generator do its magic. The application code will be written for you and be ready for the next step, which will be to add some real code to actually do something in the application.

Adding a Second View

Now the application skeleton is in place, it's time to start fleshing it out. As mentioned in our previous discussion, the first order of business is to add a new view class to handle the HTML display. There's no default view class to do this, but we do have the HTML control provided in the Internet Control Pack. Creating an ActiveX control in a **`CView`** isn't the easiest job, however. There's a bit of initialization that needs to be done, connections that need to be established, and so forth. Placing an ActiveX control in an MFC dialog, on the other hand, is simple: just drop it onto the dialog template, create a dialog class, and add a member variable for the ActiveX control in the resulting C++ class. Visual C++ and the ClassWizard take care of creating a wrapper class for the ActiveX control, handling the initialization of the system, and handling the connection between the member variable of the C++ dialog class and the actual implementation of the ActiveX object. It's a shame that we can't just forget the whole idea of a view for the HTML documentation display and use a simple dialog instead, isn't it?

Maybe things aren't quite as bad as they seem. The MFC provides a class known as **`CFormView`**, which implements a view based on a dialog template. Furthermore, ClassWizard understands all about **`CFormView`**s and 'knows' that ActiveX controls can be used within them. Maybe, just maybe, this whole component reusability thing can be used to our advantage? As it turns out, this approach will work just fine!

Implementing the CHTMLView Class

In order to create the new **`CHTMLView`** class (as I have named it) in our application as a **`CFormView`**, we need first to create a dialog template upon which to operate. Let's take care of that little problem right now.

TRY IT OUT - Create a Dialog Template

1 Click on the resource tab of the project and click on the Dialog entry in the tree control shown in the new view. Right click on the dialog list and select Insert Dialog from the pop-up menu that appears. A new, simple, dialog will appear in the edit window. This dialog has both an OK and a Cancel button, but no other controls are displayed.

2 Bring up the properties of the dialog, select the Style tab and change the Style: drop-down list to Child, and the Border: drop down to None. You can avoid this step by using the Insert | Resource... menu option and inserting an IDD_FORMVIEW dialog.

3 Get rid of the OK and Cancel buttons, since our form view will not permit the user to exit this way. Select both controls by holding down the *Shift* key and clicking on first one of the buttons and then the other. Press the *Delete* key or select the Delete option from the Edit menu. You will now have a blank dialog to work from.

4 Add the HTML control to the dialog template. Right click within the dialog edit window and select Insert OLE Control... from the resulting pop-up menu. A dialog will appear like the one shown opposite. Don't worry if your control list doesn't look exactly like mine; my system probably has a lot more diverse and bizarre controls than yours does. This is normal and has no effect on the final result.

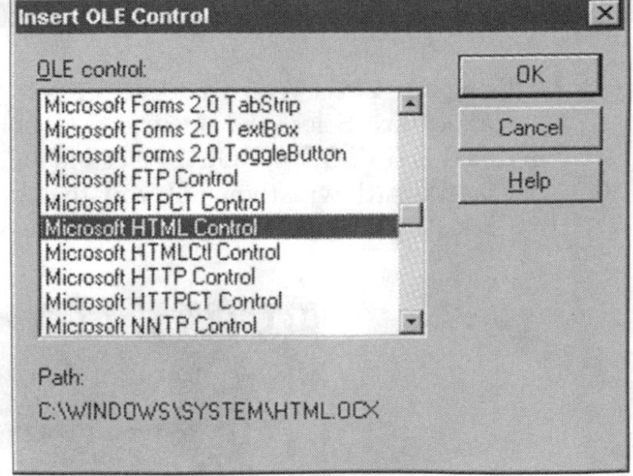

*If **Microsoft HTML Control** doesn't show up in the list, you haven't installed the Internet Control Pack. Go to **`http://www.microsoft.com/msdownload`** to download it. Once you've done that, running the executable will install the new controls.*

Select Microsoft HTML Control from the list and click on the OK button. The dialog will close and a small white box will appear in the upper-left corner of the dialog. Select the control by clicking on it, and make it bigger by grabbing the bottom-right corner and dragging it towards the bottom right corner of the dialog. Don't worry too much about the exact size and placement of the control within the dialog. As you'll see shortly, we will deal with those during the run-time operation of the thing. While we're here, we can give the control a name. Double-click inside the control to bring up its properties, and in the ID: edit box enter the name HTMLCONTROL1.

5 Once you have the dialog template completed, it's time to actually generate a C++ class to work with the dialog. Right-click on the dialog edit window and select ClassWizard... from the pop-up menu that's displayed. Accept the Create a new class selected option from the dialog which appears and click on the OK button. Give the new class the name **CHTMLView** and the base class **CFormView**. Turn off the Add to Component Gallery checkbox unless you really want your component gallery cluttered with one-time classes. Click on the Create button to generate the class from ClassWizard.

Dealing with the HTML Control

Before you can actually work with the HTML control in the newly generated **CHTMLView** class, you first need access to it in a form that you know how to deal with. Since ActiveX controls are a bit harder to interface to than so-called 'normal' controls (edit fields, list boxes, combo boxes, and so forth), the easiest way to work with them is through a member variable (rather than using **GetDlgItem()**, for example). Let's go ahead and add a new member variable for the HTML control to the **CHTMLView** class.

TRY IT OUT - Interface with the HTML Control

1 Bring up ClassWizard and select the **CHTMLView** class from the Class name: drop-down combo box. Select the Member Variables tab. There should be a single line in the list box called HTMLCONTROL1. Select that line and then click the Add Variable... button. The ClassWizard will then tell you that no wrapper class has been generated for the control yet. Click OK in the dialog shown below, and generate the control wrapper:

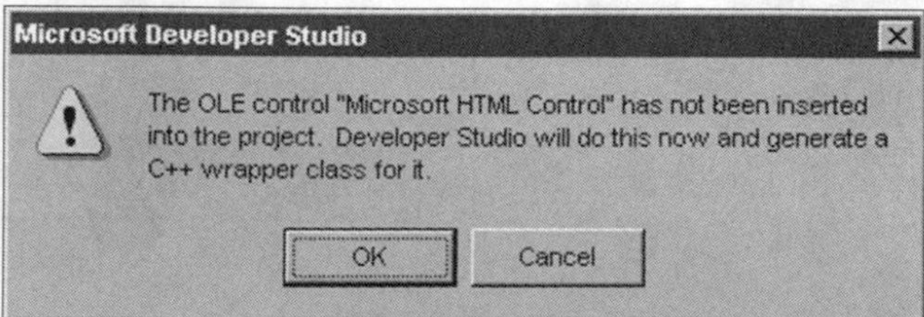

This will then give us a class that encapsulates all the functionality of Microsoft's HTML control. As you will see, we won't be using very much of that functionality, but at least you will know that the functions are available to you in the future should you ever need them.

2 All that aside, the next question that ClassWizard will ask you is the name of the variable. Enter **m_HTML** for the name and press *Enter* or click on the OK button.

At this point, we have a complete form view which encapsulates the HTML viewer dialog. This dialog contains an HTML control which is referenced by our **m_HTML** member variable. This member variable allows you access to all of the ClassWizard-generated wrapper classes for the control. This game summary was brought to you by... just kidding.

3 Our next task is to make the HTML control take up the full size of the view window. As you may remember, I promised that you needn't worry about sizing or aligning the HTML control in the dialog editor because that would be taken care of later. Well, now's the time. Start ClassWizard, select the Message Maps tag and the **CHTMLView** object from the Class name combo box. Select it again in the Object IDs list, along with the **WM_SIZE** message. If you prefer, you can simply select the **htmlview.cpp** source file, load it into the editor, and then select the **WM_SIZE** message from the message combo box at the top of the source file editor. In either case, add a new handler for the **WM_SIZE** message and add the following code to it:

```
void CHTMLView::OnSize(UINT nType, int cx, int cy)
{
   CFormView::OnSize(nType, cx, cy);

   if ( m_HTML.GetSafeHwnd() )
      m_HTML.MoveWindow(0,0,cx,cy);
}
```

This handler is really pretty simple. It verifies that the HTML control has been created using the **GetSafeHwnd()** function, then resizes the control window (assuming it's valid) to the full size of the view window. The window validity check is necessary because the **OnSize()** handler will be called immediately after the view is created, but before the control window is created. If you don't check the window handler to be sure that it's OK, you will get a nasty assertion error in debug mode and a program crash in release mode. Better safe than sorry!

Creating and Adding the Views

The point of doing all this work to define the individual views is, of course, so that we can then display those views for the user to look at. So far, all we have on the screen is a single main frame window which contains a blank splitter window. It's time to do something about that blank part. If you were to examine the **Mainfrm.cpp** source file, you would find a method called **OnCreateClient()**. The generated code for the **OnCreateClient()** method looks like this:

```
BOOL CMainFrame::OnCreateClient( LPCREATESTRUCT /*lpcs*/,
   CCreateContext* pContext)
{
   return m_wndSplitter.Create( this,
      2, 2,                // TODO: adjust the number of rows, columns
      CSize( 10, 10 ),     // TODO: adjust the minimum pane size
      pContext );
}
```

The code shown above creates a splitter window (which is initially a single pane) taking up the entire width and height of the view window, which can be split into four distinct views showing two rows and two columns. All these panes will be filled with instances of **CCtrlListView** (the default view for the application which we specified in AppWizard).

For our application, however, this code presents numerous problems. First of all, we don't want four panes of views, we only want two panes. More specifically, we don't want two rows and two columns of the same view. Rather, we want *one* row with two columns, each containing a separate view (**CCtrlListView** and **CHTMLView**). In addition, we really don't want the end user to be able to add new panes to the splitter—the number must remain fixed at two. In order to do all of this, we need to learn a little about the types of splitter windows MFC supports (since we most certainly don't want to write our own splitter window class) and how to use them.

A Short Course in Splitter Windows

Microsoft introduced the splitter window to solve a specific need: multiple views without multiple frames. The concept behind the splitter window is certainly old enough. MS-DOS applications such as Brief allowed you to split the screen into multiple panes (or windows) which operated independently of one another.

There are two distinct types of splitter windows. **Dynamic splitters** allow the user to resize each pane by dragging a horizontal or vertical bar across the window to set the width and/or height of each child pane. In addition to resizing, however, dynamic splitters also allow the end user to add new panes by defining which pane they want to split and how (horizontally or vertically) they wish to do so. Dynamic splitters generally only support a single view type within the panes. They are very useful for occasions where the user wants to look at two different parts of the same document. With dynamic splitters, the number of panes visible is under the end user's control.

Static splitter windows, on the other hand, are used in cases where two (or more) different view types need to be supported. **Static splitters** allow the user to resize the panes in the frame by dragging a horizontal or vertical bar, but generally do not allow the user to add new panes to (or remove any existing panes from) the screen directly. Because the number of panes doesn't change, the windows are referred to as *static*. Since the number and types of views are fixed in a static splitter, all of the individual panes must be added before the window is initially displayed. This is the major difference between static and dynamic splitter windows.

In our application we need two different view types: the **`CCtrlListView`** (to display a list of components for the user to select from) and the **`CHTMLView`** (to display HTML documentation for the component selected in the list). It makes no sense to add or remove panes from the display, since it would remove the basic functionality of the application. For this reason, we will use a static splitter window in our main frame window.

Modifying the Splitter Window

In order to create a new, static splitter window in the frame, we need to modify the **`OnCreateClient()`** method of the **`CMainFrame`** class. Let's look at the modifications first, then I'll take a shot at explaining how the modified code will work. If you don't care how the code works, or just trust me (always a mistake, ask my wife and children), feel free to skip the explanation. Here is the source code for the **`Mainfrm.cpp`** file with the highlighted changes:

```
// MainFrm.cpp : implementation of the CMainFrame class
//

#include "stdafx.h"
#include "Chapter11.h"

#include "MainFrm.h"
#include "Chapter11Doc.h"
#include "CCtrlListView.h"
#include "HTMLView.h"
```

```
#ifdef _DEBUG
#define new DEBUG_NEW
#undef THIS_FILE
static char THIS_FILE[] = __FILE__;
#endif

/////////////////////////////////////////////////////////////////////////////
// CMainFrame

IMPLEMENT_DYNCREATE(CMainFrame, CFrameWnd)

BEGIN_MESSAGE_MAP(CMainFrame, CFrameWnd)
   //{{AFX_MSG_MAP(CMainFrame)
      // NOTE - the ClassWizard will add and remove mapping macros here.
      //    DO NOT EDIT what you see in these blocks of generated code !
   //}}AFX_MSG_MAP
END_MESSAGE_MAP()

static UINT indicators[] =
{
   ID_SEPARATOR,           // status line indicator
   ID_INDICATOR_CAPS,
   ID_INDICATOR_NUM,
   ID_INDICATOR_SCRL,
};

/////////////////////////////////////////////////////////////////////////////
// CMainFrame construction/destruction

CMainFrame::CMainFrame()
{
   // TODO: add member initialization code here

}

CMainFrame::~CMainFrame()
{
}

int CMainFrame::OnCreate(LPCREATESTRUCT lpCreateStruct)
{
   if (CFrameWnd::OnCreate(lpCreateStruct) == -1)
      return -1;

   if (!m_wndToolBar.Create(this) ||
      !m_wndToolBar.LoadToolBar(IDR_MAINFRAME))
   {
      TRACE0("Failed to create toolbar\n");
      return -1;      // fail to create
   }

   if (!m_wndStatusBar.Create(this) ||
      !m_wndStatusBar.SetIndicators(indicators,
        sizeof(indicators)/sizeof(UINT)))
   {
      TRACE0("Failed to create status bar\n");
      return -1;      // fail to create
   }
```

```
    // TODO: Remove this if you don't want tool tips or a resizeable toolbar
    m_wndToolBar.SetBarStyle(m_wndToolBar.GetBarStyle() |
       CBRS_TOOLTIPS | CBRS_FLYBY | CBRS_SIZE_DYNAMIC);

    // TODO: Delete these three lines if you don't want the toolbar to
    //  be dockable
    m_wndToolBar.EnableDocking(CBRS_ALIGN_ANY);
    EnableDocking(CBRS_ALIGN_ANY);
    DockControlBar(&m_wndToolBar);

    return 0;
}

BOOL CMainFrame::OnCreateClient( LPCREATESTRUCT /*lpcs*/,
    CCreateContext* pContext)
{
    BOOL ret = m_wndSplitter.CreateStatic( this, 1, 2,
                             WS_CHILD | WS_VISIBLE, AFX_IDW_PANE_FIRST );
    if (ret)
    {
       CRect r;
       GetClientRect(&r);
       CSize s(r.Width()/2, r.Height());
       m_wndSplitter.CreateView( 0, 0, RUNTIME_CLASS(CCtrlListView), s,
                                 pContext);
       m_wndSplitter.CreateView( 0, 1, RUNTIME_CLASS(CHTMLView), s,
                                 pContext);
    }

    return ret;
}

BOOL CMainFrame::PreCreateWindow(CREATESTRUCT& cs)
{
    // TODO: Modify the Window class or styles here by modifying
    //  the CREATESTRUCT cs

    return CFrameWnd::PreCreateWindow(cs);
}

/////////////////////////////////////////////////////////////////////////////
// CMainFrame diagnostics

#ifdef _DEBUG
void CMainFrame::AssertValid() const
{
    CFrameWnd::AssertValid();
}

void CMainFrame::Dump(CDumpContext& dc) const
{
    CFrameWnd::Dump(dc);
}

#endif //_DEBUG

/////////////////////////////////////////////////////////////////////////////
// CMainFrame message handlers
```

As you can see, we are now creating a static splitter window (using the **CreateStatic()** method call in **OnCreateClient()**) with one row and two columns. This will give the appearance of the simple 'split screen' that we talked about during the design phase. What about the next part, though? The **CreateView()** method does what you would expect of it, creating a new view within one of the panes of the splitter window. The question is, where is the view object actually being created? First of all, let's take a look at the definition for the **CreateView()** method:

```
virtual BOOL CreateView( int row, int col, CRuntimeClass* pViewClass,
                         SIZE sizeInit, CCreateContext* pContext );
```

The row and column parameters are straightforward. These define which pane in the splitter window the view will appear in. The **CRuntime** object, however, deserves a little bit of explanation.

Run-time Type Identification and MFC

One of the handiest built-in features of the Microsoft Foundation Classes is that of **run-time type identification** (RTTI). This feature, although not (yet) the same as the RTTI specified in the C++ standard, allows the system (and thus the programmer) to determine, at run time, what class a given object belongs to, provided that object is derived from the base MFC object, **CObject**. This allows the programmer to safely determine whether an object is of a given type (class) before it's cast to that class by the programmer.

In the MFC implementation of RTTI, however, there's an additional benefit. By using the MFC **RUNTIME_CLASS** macro, you can create instances of a class dynamically. This ability is what allows the entire document template architecture to function. In the document template, for example, there's one **CRuntimeClass** pointer to a document class and one to a view class (that is, a class derived from **CDocument** and a class derived from **CView**). At run time, the MFC internals create new documents and views by using the **CreateObject()** method of the **CRuntimeClass**. In this way, the internals of the system don't need to 'know' about the derived classes (normally a requirement to use the **new** operator) in order to create new instances of them.

What this means to you as a programmer is this: it's possible to create new objects of a class indirectly, that is, without directly invoking the **new** operator within your program. I'm not entirely sure why Microsoft chose this approach over instantiating objects and passing them into methods such as **CreateView()**, but there you are.

In the **CreateView()** method, for example, we pass in the **CRuntimeClass** pointer representing the view class we want to appear in that window pane. How do we get this pointer? The **RUNTIME_CLASS** macro will, given the name of a class, return a **CRuntimeClass** pointer. It can accomplish this because all of the RTTI information is stored within the class as static member data and can therefore be called without a real instance of the class.

Is this magic? Or is it some brilliant new coding technique at Microsoft, or perhaps a new extension to the compiler? Where does all this static member data come from for a class, without any work on the part of the programmer? Actually, you don't do the work. ClassWizard does it for you. Take a look at the generated header file for the **CCtrlListView** class:

```
// CCtrlListView.h : interface of the CCtrlListView class
//
/////////////////////////////////////////////////////////////////////////////
```

```
class CCtrlListView : public CView
{
protected: // create from serialization only
    CCtrlListView();
    DECLARE_DYNCREATE(CCtrlListView)

// Attributes
public:
    CChapter10Doc* GetDocument();

// Operations
public:

// Overrides
    // ClassWizard generated virtual function overrides
    //{{AFX_VIRTUAL(CCtrlListView)
    public:
    virtual void OnDraw(CDC* pDC);  // overridden to draw this view
    virtual BOOL PreCreateWindow(CREATESTRUCT& cs);
    protected:
    //}}AFX_VIRTUAL

// Implementation
public:
    virtual ~CCtrlListView();
#ifdef _DEBUG
    virtual void AssertValid() const;
    virtual void Dump(CDumpContext& dc) const;
#endif

protected:

// Generated message map functions
protected:
    //{{AFX_MSG(CCtrlListView)
        // NOTE - the ClassWizard will add and remove member functions here.
        //    DO NOT EDIT what you see in these blocks of generated code !
    //}}AFX_MSG
    DECLARE_MESSAGE_MAP()
};

#ifndef _DEBUG  // debug version in CCtrlListView.cpp
inline CChapter10Doc* CCtrlListView::GetDocument()
   { return (CChapter10Doc*)m_pDocument; }
#endif

/////////////////////////////////////////////////////////////////////////////
```

You wouldn't think that there was any magic going on here, would you? The header file seems pretty straightforward and simple; there doesn't appear to be any extra member data defined. But looks can be deceptive. That one highlighted line up there does a lot of the work. Because the class is defined with the **DECLARE_DYNCREATE** macro (and a corresponding **IMPLEMENT_DYNCREATE** macro in the source file for the class), it's capable of dynamically creating itself at run time.

Hopefully, you now understand at least why the **CreateView()** doesn't require you to create instances of the view objects. If you learned more than that, well, more power to you! The last change you will need to make to the **MainFrm.cpp** source file (remember that?) is to include the header files at the top, so that the compiler can find the definitions for the **CCtrlListView** and **CHTMLView** classes. These files should be **CCtrlListView.h** and **HTMLView.h**, respectively.

You now have the main window up on the screen and the two views displayed in splitter window panes. The HTML view has been implemented to create the HTML control and it's been resized to fit in the window pane to which it's assigned. It's time to implement the **CCtrlListView** window and place some data into it so that the user can actually select something.

Implementing the CCtrlListView Class

The **CCtrlListView** view pane of the splitter window is intended to display a list of component names for the user to select from in order to view documentation for those components. The problem with this pane is that the user is allowed to resize it. Like the HTML control view, therefore, we will need to resize it as we change the window size. Unlike the Microsoft HTML control, however, a list box does not 'wrap' the strings which appear in it so that they are completely visible.

Instead, a list box requires that the programmer implements code to enable and set limits on the horizontal scroll bar for the list-box window. Once the scrollbar is created, the user then has to scroll the text horizontally to see what each string in the list box contains. If that string is too long to fit in the list box window, then at no time can the user actually view all the data for a given string. There *must* be a better way, and fortunately for us, there is: the Contents List.

Earlier in this book, we developed the Contents List component. This enhanced list box component, modeled after the list box on the MSDN CD-ROM, allows the user to view very wide strings in a list box by displaying a pop-up window over the list box item which is wide enough to show the whole string at once. Wouldn't this be an excellent way to reuse the code in a real application, even if it *was* hideously contrived in the first place?. By simply creating a Contents List object, rather than a standard list-box object, we automatically get the functionality we want with absolutely no code changes to our application.

TRY IT OUT - Reuse the Contents List

1 To accomplish the goal of adding the Contents List to your project, we need to do a few things in preparation. First, copy the source files for the Contents List project: **ContentsList.cpp**, **ContentsList.h**, **PopupTip.cpp** and **PopupTip.h**. Insert into our Chapter11 project the **.cpp** files (**ContentsList.cpp** and **PopupTip.cpp**). This will make the files available for the compiler and linker and allow us to use the functionality in this application.

> *You may very well find yourself creating a library or DLL to hold all the MFC extensions developed in this book. Not only is this OK, it's actually a very good idea. You might, for example, create a new library called **MFCComponents** and store all the header files in a single, centrally located, directory. This will allow you to reuse these components in multiple applications without needing to copy the source and header files into each and every application you develop. It saves disk space too!*

2 Let's look at the changes needed to create the **CContentsList** object in the **CCtrlListView**. Use the ClassWizard to add a handler for the **WM_CREATE** message to the **CCtrlListView.cpp** source file, and this is what you get:

```
//////////////////////////////////////////////////////////////////////////////
// CCtrlListView message handlers

int CCtrlListView::OnCreate(LPCREATESTRUCT lpCreateStruct)
{
   if (CView::OnCreate(lpCreateStruct) == -1)
      return -1;

   CRect r(0,0,0,0);

   m_List.Create( WS_CHILD | WS_VISIBLE | LBS_NOTIFY, r, this,
_APS_NEXT_CONTROL_VALUE );

   return 0;
}
```

3 Once you've added the highlighted code to the source file, you will also need to add the definition of the member variable to the header file:

```
#include "ContentsList.h"
...
private:
   CContentsList m_List;
```

4 We also have to make a change to the application header **Chapter11.h**. The reason for this is the **_APS_NEXT_CONTROL_VALUE** we used to specify as the ID for the Contents List. This define is specific to the resource editor and is used to assign the next available ID when you insert a control. We are using it for exactly this reason, we don't want to fix the Contents List ID in case we add new controls later in the project's life. The problem with **_APS_NEXT_CONTROL_VALUE** is that it's protected by **#ifdef**s in **Resource.h**. So to get around this, we'll cheat a bit and set the required **#define**s so that we can use them ourselves. Therefore, you should add the following lines to **Chapter11.h**:

```
// Chapter11.h : main header file for the CHAPTER11 application
//

#ifndef __AFXWIN_H__
   #error include 'stdafx.h' before including this file for PCH
#endif

#define APSTUDIO_INVOKED
#undef  APSTUDIO_READONLY_SYMBOLS

#include "resource.h"       // main symbols

#undef APSTUDIO_INVOKED
#define APSTUDIO_READONLY_SYMBOLS
...
```

5 Add a handler, **`OnSize()`**, for the **`WM_SIZE`** message exactly as you did for the **`CHTMLView`** class and put the following code into it. This will handle making the list box the same size as the view (just as it did for the HTML control in the HTML view).

```
void CCtrlListView::OnSize(UINT nType, int cx, int cy)
{
   CView::OnSize(nType, cx, cy);

   if ( m_List.GetSafeHwnd() )
      m_List.MoveWindow(0,0,cx,cy);
}
```

Initializing the Contents List

Once the Contents List has been successfully created and resized, the next issue is to load it with a list of components which are viewable. We've already agreed that an initialization file will contain the information for the component list. Let's take a look at a sample initialization file for some of the components we have developed in this book up to this point:

```
[ScrollText]
File=d:\chapter3\scrltxt.htm
ListFile=d:\chapter3\scrltxt.lst

[ShadeText]
File=d:\chapter3\shdtxt.htm
ListFile=d:\chapter3\shdtxt.lst

[ColorListCtrl]
File=d:\chapter5\clrlist.htm
ListFile=d:\chapter5\clrlist.lst

[EditGrid]
File=d:\chapter5\editgrid.htm
ListFile=d:\chapter5\editgrid.lst
```

> *The actual path names used would, of course, be different on your system.*

Each entry in the **`.ini`** file enclosed in square brackets (e.g. **`[ShadeText]`**) will appear in the list. The other entries will be used to display information in either the HTML view or the forthcoming detail screen. It should be a simple matter, then, to write some code to search through the initialization file for all entries which begin with **`[`** and end with **`]`**, and parse out the component name string in between the two.

Wait a minute! "...write some code to search..."? Didn't we just get through talking about how we would use initialization files because we didn't need to write additional code for them? Did we go through all of this for nothing? Is there, in fact, no way to get back the topics from the **`.ini`** file without knowing what they are up front? Would Microsoft do something like this to us?

Of course not. It's actually quite easy to get back all of the topics in an initialization file without knowing anything about them. It's not exactly intuitive, but it's easy. Let's take a look at the code that does the job (to be added to the **`OnCreate()`** method), then talk a little bit about how it works (and, yes, this *is* documented behavior!).

```
int CCtrlListView::OnCreate(LPCREATESTRUCT lpCreateStruct)
{
   if (CView::OnCreate(lpCreateStruct) == -1)
      return -1;

   CRect r(0,0,0,0);

   m_List.Create( WS_CHILD | WS_VISIBLE | LBS_NOTIFY, r, this,
_APS_NEXT_CONTROL_VALUE );

   char RetString[8196];
   char * word;

   DWORD numChars = ::GetPrivateProfileString( NULL, "", "", RetString,
                                             8196, "docview.ini");

   int processedChars = 0;
   int wordLen;

   while ( processedChars < (int)numChars )
   {
      word = RetString + processedChars;
      wordLen = strlen ( word );
      if ( wordLen )
         m_List.AddString ( word );
      processedChars += wordLen + 1;
   }
   return 0;
}
```

What's happening here isn't quite apparent until you check the documentation for the **GetPrivateProfileString()** API function. This function normally takes as its first argument the topic entry for which you are trying to retrieve a key value. If, however, **NULL** is passed as the first argument, **GetPrivateProfileString()** will return a list of all of the topics found in the initialization file. Each topic is null terminated, which explains why we look for the string length of the returned string multiple times in the above code. We simply scan through the list of returned topics until we reach the end of the list, which is determined by counting the number of characters we scan until we hit the number of characters in the returned buffer. This total number of characters is the return value (DWORD) of the function.

Once a string has been extracted from the returned buffer, it's placed into the Contents List using the **AddString()** method inherited from the base class **CListBox**. At this point, all of the topic entries will be loaded into the list box, which will then be displayed when the splitter window is painted. Isn't life great?

Finding Out about those Changes

Now we actually have the Contents List displayed in the **CCtrlListView** pane, we want, once a list item has been selected, to display the corresponding HTML page in the HTML control in the other pane. Before we concern ourselves about that, though, we first need to worry about how to determine that the user has actually made a selection in the list box.

Normally, if you had a list box in a dialog, you would just use ClassWizard to add a new handler to the list box for the **LBN_SELCHANGE** message. This message is sent whenever the selection index in a list box is changed, either by the end user or by programmatic modification.

In this case, however, there are a few problems with that approach. First, ClassWizard doesn't 'know' about our list box because we created it dynamically. This makes it difficult to add a message map entry. Second, of course, this isn't a dialog. How do we get around these problems?

> *At this point, some of you may be wondering why I didn't simply make the* **`CCtrlListView`** *a* **`CFormView`***-derived class, and then add a list box to the dialog template as I did with the* **`CHTMLView`** *class. In fact, in the initial design for the view, I did exactly that. It occurred to me, however, that this point might come up in your own applications and now seemed like a good time to show you how to fix it. I guess you could say I was showing off. I prefer to think of it as 'instructing'.*

As it turns out, a **`CListBox`** object window (the underlying Windows list box control for the Contents List) doesn't care whether its parent is a dialog window or a **`CDialog`** window. It will happily post a **`LBN_SELCHANGE`** message to it regardless of what it is. It also turns out that MFC doesn't care whether a message map entry is added by ClassWizard or whether you add the whole thing by hand. It works the same either way. As a result, the solution to the problem is simply to add a message handler by hand for the message from the list box. Here's how you do it.

TRY IT OUT - Add a Message Handler by Hand

1 Add a message map entry to the **`CCtrlListView`** class by adding the following line (shown highlighted) to the **`CtrlListView.cpp`** source file:

```
BEGIN_MESSAGE_MAP(CCtrlListView, CView)
    //{{AFX_MSG_MAP(CCtrlListView)
    ON_WM_CREATE()
    ON_WM_SIZE()
    //}}AFX_MSG_MAP
    ON_LBN_SELCHANGE( _APS_NEXT_CONTROL_VALUE, OnListChange )
END_MESSAGE_MAP()
```

2 Add a new method description to the header file for the class **`CCtrlListView.h`**. The modified line is shown highlighted again:

```
// Generated message map functions
protected:
    //{{AFX_MSG(CCtrlListView)
    afx_msg int OnCreate(LPCREATESTRUCT lpCreateStruct);
    afx_msg void OnSize(UINT nType, int cx, int cy);
    //}}AFX_MSG
    afx_msg void OnListChange(void);
    DECLARE_MESSAGE_MAP()
```

3 Add the actual code to do the work once the message is received. This can simply be typed into the source file (**`CtrlListView.cpp`**) at the bottom of the file:

```
void CCtrlListView::OnListChange()
{
    GetParent()->PostMessage(WM_COMMAND, CONTROL_CHANGE);
}
```

This method simply posts a message to its parent indicating that the list has been selected. It will now be up to the parent window (the **CMainFrame** window) to deal with the problem at this point. That will be the next thing we'll tackle.

4 Before that, let's define the message we post, **CONTROL_CHANGE**. We do this by adding the following declaration to the top of the **CCtrlListView.h** source file:

```
const CONTROL_CHANGE = WM_USER+1;
```

This is also necessary for adding a message map entry which we'll come to next. The message map macros don't handle entries such as **WM_USER+1** very easily, and anyway, the declaration makes the message map cleaner.

Modifying the MainFrame

Adding the new handler to **CMainFrame** for the message posted to the Control List view is the same problem as handling the **LBN_SELCHANGE** method was for **CCtrlListView**. Because ClassWizard knows nothing about the specialized message (**CONTROL_CHANGE**) we are sending, it can't be used to add a handler to it. Some days you have to do all of the work yourself. Oh well, maybe the next version of the software...

TRY IT OUT - Add another Message Handler

1 Add a message map entry for the new message handler to the **MainFrm.h** header file:

```
// Generated message map functions
protected:
    //{{AFX_MSG(CMainFrame)
    afx_msg int OnCreate(LPCREATESTRUCT lpCreateStruct);
    //}}AFX_MSG
    afx_msg void OnControlChange(void);
    DECLARE_MESSAGE_MAP()
```

2 You should also add the following line to the message map in **MainFrm.cpp**:

```
BEGIN_MESSAGE_MAP(CMainFrame, CFrameWnd)
    //{{AFX_MSG_MAP(CMainFrame)
    ON_WM_CREATE()
    //}}AFX_MSG_MAP
    ON_COMMAND(CONTROL_CHANGE, OnControlChange)
END_MESSAGE_MAP()
```

3 Add the actual code to do the work when the message is received. Place this new method at the bottom of the **MainFrm.cpp** source file:

```
void CMainFrame::OnControlChange(void)
{
    // Get the views
    CCtrlListView *listView = (CCtrlListView *)m_wndSplitter.GetPane(0,0);
    CHTMLView *htmlView = (CHTMLView *)m_wndSplitter.GetPane(0,1);
```

```
    // Get the control name from the list view
    CString cName;
    listView->GetCurrentControl(cName);

    // Get the file name from the INI file
    char fName[_MAX_PATH];

    ::GetPrivateProfileString( cName, "File", "", fName, _MAX_PATH,
                               "docview.ini");

    // And set the HTML control to point to it
    htmlView->SetHTMLPage(fName);
}
```

4 Adding this new method will require that you add new methods to both the **CCtrlListView** and **CHTMLView** classes as well. Let's look at those changes:

```
void CCtrlListView::GetCurrentControl(CString& cName)
{
    // Get the currently selected item
    m_List.GetText( m_List.GetCurSel(), cName );
}
```

```
void CHTMLView::SetHTMLPage( const CString& fName )
{
    CString realName = "file:///" + fName;
    m_HTML.RequestDoc(realName);
}
```

What's going on here? We got a selection from the list control and somehow turned it into an HTML display in the HTML view. How exactly did this happen? First, the **CCtrlListView** class is notified of the user making a selection by receiving an **LBN_SELCHANGE** message. The list view then posts a message to its parent window (which is actually the splitter window) but since that doesn't process the message, it 'bubbles up' to the **CMainFrame** class object. **CMainFrame** deals with this message by doing several things:

- Pointers to the 'real' view classes are obtained by getting the view from each pane of the splitter window and casting that pointer to the appropriate class type (**CCtrlListView** or **CHTMLView**).
- The name of the selected component is extracted by querying the **CCtrlListView** object for the item currently selected in the list via the **GetCurrentControl()** method. The list view retrieves this name by getting the text of the currently selected list box item.
- The HTML file name associated with that component is acquired by retrieving the appropriate entry from the initialization file using the component name as the topic.
- The new file name is passed to the **CHTMLView** class via the **SetHTMLPage()** method of that class.
- The **CHTMLView** class object then uses the filename passed to it to build a URL (Uniform Resource Locator) to pass to the HTML control to display the document via the **RequestDoc()** method of that class.

You have probably noticed the rather strange syntax of building the URL to display the HTML document in the HTML control. The control, written by Microsoft, recognizes a 'device name' of **`file:///`** to represent a local file. If you don't pass the filename in this format, the HTML control will try to load the file via the Internet. This will result in the currently defined network access program (TCP/IP stack) being loaded and (assuming you connect via the phone line) the number of your local Internet provider being dialed. This is obviously not the solution we're looking for in a system that might very well be used on a laptop computer.

So, what is our project status? Actually, at this point, all of the major features we talked about during the requirements phase of the project (with one exception that we will talk about next) have been completed. We can load an initialization file, read the individual components from the file, load them into the contents list control and allow the user to select from them. The HTML file for the selected component is then loaded into the HTML control (in the secondary HTML view pane) and viewed by the user.

You have in your possession a genuine example of the power of component technology. You've written about two dozen lines of code, and you have a powerful HTML document viewer. Amazing, isn't it?

The Nitty Gritty Details

The only major requirement still missing from our initial project design is the ability to display a detailed view of the major implementation pieces of the component. We would like to display a structured view of the details of the selected component: **`public`** methods, **`private`** methods, member variables, and any other information (notes, perhaps) that the component designer would like to see in the detail screen. Because wanting to view the details will be less common than viewing the overall documentation for a given component, we won't attempt to implement the detail screen as a view in its own right. Instead, we will create a brand new dialog in which to display the detail.

Our discussion up to this point has focused on the hierarchical nature of the detail information for the components. It should come as no surprise, therefore, that we will use the tree control developed earlier in the book to display those details. Let's look at how to construct a dialog to display the information in the tree.

TRY IT OUT - Build the Detail Dialog

1 Create a new dialog in the resource editor. Move the OK and Cancel buttons to the bottom of the dialog, and make the whole thing bigger (the actual size is a matter of personal preference, but people do need to be able to read it).

2 Right-click within the dialog and select Insert OLE control... from the resulting pop-up menu. From the list of controls installed on your system, locate and select the **`ColorTree`** control. The new control will then be displayed as a blank box at the upper-left corner of the dialog window. Select the new control and make it larger (taking up most of the available space in the dialog). Change the title of the dialog to **`Detail Dialog`** by double-clicking on the title bar of the new dialog and entering that text into the Caption.

3 The next step is to generate a new C++ dialog class for the dialog. Right-click on the dialog editor window and select ClassWizard... from the pop-up menu. Give the new class the name **CDetailDlg**. Turn off the Add to Component Gallery checkbox and make sure that the base class is **CDialog** (it should be by default, but it never hurts to check these things). Click on the Create button to generate the new class header and source files.

4 Now we have a new dialog class, it's time to do something with it. In order for us to work efficiently with the tree control object, we need to have a wrapper class defined for it. Select the Member Variables tab in ClassWizard and then the tree control ID (it should be the only one that isn't **IDOK** or **IDCANCEL**), and click on the Add Variable... button. Answer Yes when ClassWizard asks you if you want to generate a wrapper class for the control. Once the generation process is complete, give the new variable the name **m_Tree**.

5 There really isn't a great deal that we need to 'do' with this dialog. It's intended for display only. For this reason, all we need to do is add some data to the tree control for the user to view. In order to do this, however, we need to tell the dialog which component we wish to view detailed information about. Rather than passing in a component name and thus tying this dialog irrevocably to our original initialization file, let's simply give it a filename which directly represents an initialization file from which it is to get its information to display. Modify the constructor for the **CDetailDlg** class (in the file **DetailDlg.cpp**) as follows:

```
CDetailDlg::CDetailDlg(char *fName, CWnd* pParent /*=NULL*/)
   : CDialog(CDetailDlg::IDD, pParent)
{
   //{{AFX_DATA_INIT(CDetailDlg)
      // NOTE: the ClassWizard will add member initialization here
   //}}AFX_DATA_INIT
   m_fileName = fName;
}
```

6 In addition, you will need to make a few simple modifications to the header file for the class (shown highlighted):

```
// DetailDlg.h : header file
//

/////////////////////////////////////////////////////////////////////////////
// CDetailDlg dialog
//{{AFX_INCLUDES()
#include "colortree.h"
//}}AFX_INCLUDES

class CDetailDlg : public CDialog
{
public:
   CString m_fileName;

// Construction
public:
   CDetailDlg(char *fName, CWnd* pParent = NULL);   // standard constructor

// Dialog Data
   //{{AFX_DATA(CDetailDlg)
   enum { IDD = IDD_DIALOG2 };
```

```
    CColorTree  m_Tree;
    //}}AFX_DATA

// Overrides
    // ClassWizard generated virtual function overrides
    //{{AFX_VIRTUAL(CDetailDlg)
    protected:
    virtual void DoDataExchange(CDataExchange* pDX);    // DDX/DDV support
    //}}AFX_VIRTUAL

// Implementation
    // Generated message map functions
    //{{AFX_MSG(CDetailDlg)
       // NOTE: the ClassWizard will add member functions here
    //}}AFX_MSG
    DECLARE_MESSAGE_MAP()
};
```

7 Now we're ready to put the information from the requested initialization file into the tree control. Add a new handler for the **WM_INITDIALOG** message and add the following code to the **OnInitDialog()** method of **CDetailDlg**:

```
BOOL CDetailDlg::OnInitDialog()
{
    CDialog::OnInitDialog();

    char RetString[8196];
    char Ret2String[8196];
    char * word;

    // Set the width to show the whole text
    m_Tree.SetColumnWidth(0, 250);

    DWORD numChars = ::GetPrivateProfileString( NULL, "", "", RetString,
                                                 8196, m_fileName);

    int processedChars = 0;
    int wordLen;
    int idx;

    while ( processedChars < (int)numChars )
    {
       word = RetString + processedChars;
       wordLen = strlen ( word );
       if ( wordLen )
       {
          idx = m_Tree.AddNode ( -1, word );

          // Add the sub-topics for this topic
          DWORD nChars = ::GetPrivateProfileString(word, NULL, "",
                              Ret2String, 8196, m_fileName);

          AddSubTopics(nChars, Ret2String, idx);
       }
       processedChars += wordLen + 1;
    }
```

```
    return TRUE;  // return TRUE unless you set the focus to a control
                  // EXCEPTION: OCX Property Pages should return FALSE
}
```

8 In case you're wondering where the **AddSubTopics()** function comes from, well, that's one of ours as well. Insert this code right above the **OnInitDialog()** method:

```
void CDetailDlg::AddSubTopics(DWORD numChars, char *RetString, long idx)
{
    int i = 0;
    int wordLen;
    char * word;

    int processedChars = 0;

    while ( processedChars < (int)numChars )
    {
        // Get each "word" from the string
        word = processedChars + RetString;
        wordLen = strlen ( word );

        if ( wordLen )
            m_Tree.AddNode ( idx, word );
        processedChars += wordLen + 1;
    }
}
```

9 That's all of the code we need to implement the new dialog, but if your aesthetic sensibilities are anything like mine, you might still think there's something missing. If you look at the dialog for the detail view, you will notice something about it. Most glaringly, it's boring! All that battleship gray color makes it look dull and unattractive. Let's do something to spice it up a bit, shall we?

Open the dialog in the resource editor. Right-click on the dialog and select Insert OLE Control... from the pop-up menu. Select the Gradient control from the dialog list and click on the OK button. The Gradient control, showing itself in bright blue splendor, will appear at the top-left corner of the dialog. Resize the control so that it takes up the whole dialog. Your complete dialog should then look like the this:

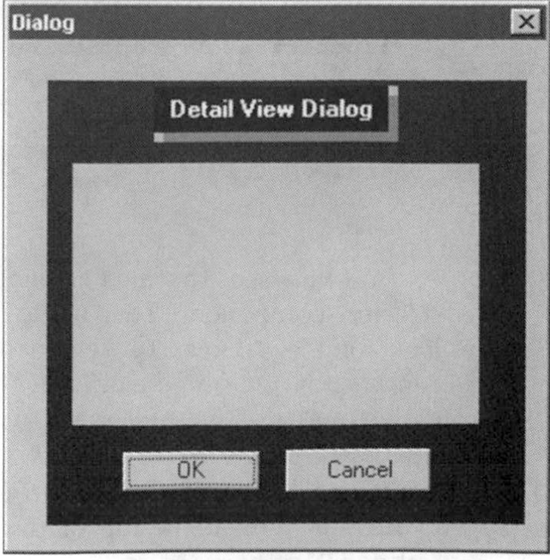

Note that no coding changes are necessary to add the gradient control to the dialog. You don't need to add any member variables nor generate any wrapper classes for the control. In short, you have a much prettier dialog at the total expense of a few mouse clicks and drags.

10 Once the new dialog is created, the final step to putting it into the application is to write some code to actually display the thing. This is a two-step process. First, add a new menu command for the user to select the detail dialog. Second, add a menu handler for the new menu command to display the dialog for the currently selected component.

Add a new menu using the resource editor like this: select the menu item in the resource list, then select the **IDR_MAINFRAME** menu (hopefully the only one present). Double-click on the 'empty' menu item and give the new menu the caption Controls. In the new submenu that appears, enter the text Detail View for the item caption and **ID_DETAIL_VIEW** for the menu identifier. Close the menu edit window.

11 The second step is to add a new menu handler for the new command which will display our new dialog. Enter ClassWizard and select the **CMainFrame** object from the drop-down combo box. Select the **ID_DETAIL_VIEW** object from the Object IDs list and the **COMMAND** message from the Messages list. Click on the Add Function... button. Give the new function the name **OnDetailView()**. This will be our 'callback' method when the user selects the View Details menu item.

12 All that remains is to actually write the code to do the job. Add the following to the **OnDetailView()** method of **CMainFrame**:

```
void CMainFrame::OnDetailView()
{
   // Get the view
   CCtrlListView *listView = (CCtrlListView *)m_wndSplitter.GetPane(0,0);

   // Get the control name from the list view
   CString cName;
   listView->GetCurrentControl(cName);

   // Get the file name from the INI file
   char fName[_MAX_PATH];

   ::GetPrivateProfileString( cName, "ListFile", "", fName, _MAX_PATH,
                              "docview.ini");

   CDetailDlg dlg(fName, this);
   dlg.DoModal();
}
```

As you can see, the method simply interrogates the list view for the name of the currently selected component. That name is then used as a key into the initialization file topic. We look for the **ListFile** key for the topic and then pass the returned filename to the constructor for our dialog. We then use the dialog's **DoModal()** method to display the dialog and do the rest of the work.

13 Only one little thing left to do (honest!). Add the include file for our dialog class to the list of include files at the top of the **MainFrm.cpp** source file. In this case, that's going to be **DetailDlg.h**.

That takes care of all of the major requirements for the project! We have implemented a fairly complete document viewer for HTML pages with just a few dozen lines of code (and a bit of help from the Visual C++ wizards and our previously developed components).

Adding Utility Functions to the Application

Although the code we have written so far is functionally complete and fulfills the requirements for the project, there are still a few problems to sort out. First, the editing functions that most people would expect for this sort of an application are missing: you can't add or remove components from the list of displayable entries. We did say that the entry list had to be easily modifiable, after all.

The second, more obvious, error is the fact that the project was designed to showcase the components we developed in this book. We need more components used! You should get used to this, as real-world programming often works this way. The boss sees a 'neat' new package and has to have all of the wonderful new features incorporated into the next release of your product. So, welcome to the real world!

The first utility function we will look at is deleting items from the displayable list. Basically, we're faced with the problem of dealing with a list of items currently included in the component list and extracting and removing those items (one or more) that the user wants out of it.

Implementing the Delete Dialog

This is a perfect opportunity to reuse another of the components we worked with earlier in the book: the Drag-and-drop List Box. As you'll no doubt recall, this is another simple MFC extension that allows the user to drag items from one list to another. It automatically handles the problem of deleting the entries from the 'from' list and inserting the selected items into the 'to' list. Isn't it amazing how well it fits into this application? Please, no applause, just throw money (or beer, but only if it's still in the bottle)!

TRY IT OUT - More Component Reuse

1 In order to implement the dialog to delete items from the list, we first need to define a dialog template for the class. Create a new dialog template in the resource editor of Visual C++. Move the OK and Cancel buttons to the bottom of the dialog. Add two list boxes to the dialog, side by side, horizontally centered.

2 Place a static text field (or even better a ShadeText control) above the first list box and set the text of the control to be Entries In File:. The advantage of the ShadeText control is that we could then set the text color to, say, blue, to indicate that the list items are already there. Now, add a second ShadeText control above the second list box. Set the text of this control to be Entries To Remove: and set the text color to red (to indicate these entries will be deleted!). Change the title of the dialog to Remove Entries. You should now see the dialog shown opposite (without the box contents, of course).

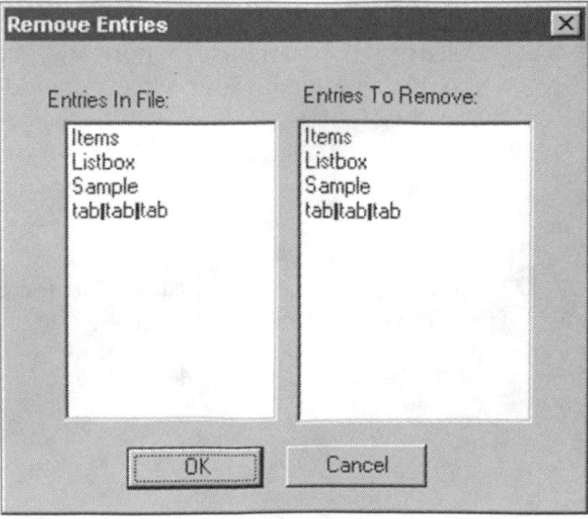

3 Use ClassWizard to generate a dialog class for the new dialog template as we have done so many times before. Give the new class the name **CDeleteDlg**. Add two member variables for the two list boxes in the dialog. For the first list box (the 'from' list), give the member variable the name **m_FromList**. For the second list (the 'to' list), give the member variable the name **m_ToDeleteList**.

4 It's now time to copy in the selected files from the DragAndDropList project. You will need the **DragDropListBox.cpp** source file and **DragDropListBox.h** header file. Add the **DragDropListBox.cpp** source file to the project by selecting Insert | Files Into Project... from the Visual C++ IDE main menu.

As **DragDropListBox.cpp** uses resources, we must make sure that it has the resource defines available to it, otherwise it won't compile. To do this, simply replace the **#include "DragDropList.h"** line with:

```
// DragDropListBox.cpp : implementation file
//

#include "stdafx.h"
#include "chapter11.h"
#include "DragDropListBox.h"
...
```

5 There's one further job we need to do. In addition to the source and header files, this component requires two custom cursors to do its job. Open the resource file for the DragAndDropList project in Visual C++. To do this, select File | Open..., and navigate to the resource script file (**.rc**) for that project. Open the resource tab on the Chapter11 project. Open the Cursor entry on the DragAndDropList project and highlight the **IDC_DROP** and **IDC_NODROP** cursors by holding down the control key and clicking on each. While still holding the control key down, 'drag' the entries over into the Chapter11 project resource tab. Release the left mouse button and the resources should be copied. Your screen should now look like this:

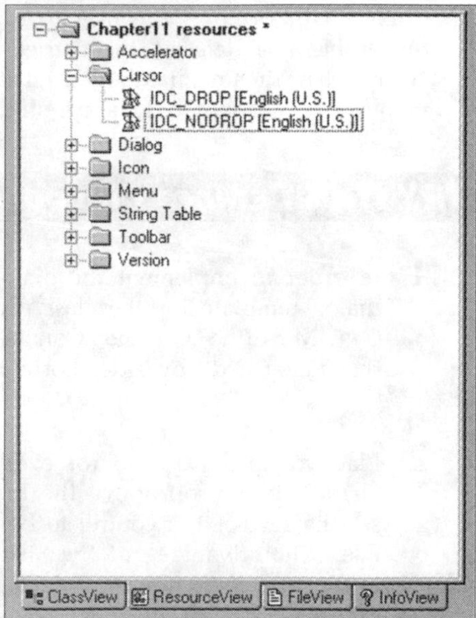

6 Modify the generated header file for the **CDeleteDlg** class to use the new drag-and-drop list boxes as follows:

```
// DeleteDlg.h : header file
//

/////////////////////////////////////////////////////////////////////////////
// CDeleteDlg dialog
```

```
#include "DragDropListBox.h"

class CDeleteDlg : public CDialog
{
// Construction
public:
   CDeleteDlg(CWnd* pParent = NULL);   // standard constructor

// Dialog Data
   //{{AFX_DATA(CDeleteDlg)
   enum { IDD = IDD_DIALOG3 };
   CDragDropListBox   m_ToDeleteList;
   CDragDropListBox   m_FromList;
   //}}AFX_DATA

// Overrides
   // ClassWizard generated virtual function overrides
   //{{AFX_VIRTUAL(CDeleteDlg)
   protected:
   virtual void DoDataExchange(CDataExchange* pDX);    // DDX/DDV support
   //}}AFX_VIRTUAL

// Implementation
protected:

   // Generated message map functions
   //{{AFX_MSG(CDeleteDlg)
      // NOTE: the ClassWizard will add member functions here
   //}}AFX_MSG
   DECLARE_MESSAGE_MAP()
};
```

7 In order to deal with the deletion of data, we first need to put data into the list box for the end users to operate upon. Add a new message handler for the **WM_INITDIALOG** message to the **CDeleteDlg** class. Add the following code to the **OnInitDialog()** method of **CDeleteDlg**:

```
BOOL CDeleteDlg::OnInitDialog()
{
   CDialog::OnInitDialog();

   char RetString[8196];
   char * word;

   DWORD numChars = ::GetPrivateProfileString( NULL, "", "", RetString,
                                               8196, "docview.ini");

   int processedChars = 0;
   int wordLen;

   while ( processedChars < (int)numChars )
   {
      // Get each "word" from the string
      word = RetString + processedChars;
      wordLen = strlen ( word );
      if ( wordLen )
         m_FromList.AddString ( word );
```

```
        processedChars += wordLen + 1;
    }

    return TRUE;   // return TRUE unless you set the focus to a control
                   // EXCEPTION: OCX Property Pages should return FALSE
}
```

8 The only remaining issue, apart from displaying the dialog, is to actually delete the entries from the initialization file when the user finishes selecting them. The user will be presented with a list of items or component names in the In File list. They can then drag those entries that they would like to delete over to the To Remove list. The **DragDropListBox** class will handle all the work of moving the items back and forth for us. All we need to do is to deal with the final result, when the user actually commits to the changes. In our case, that commitment comes when the user selects the OK button (by either clicking on the button directly or pressing the *Enter* key within the dialog).

Let's add the new handler for the OK button and look at the code. Then we can figure out how it all works. Select the **CDeleteDlg** class from the drop-down combo box in ClassWizard. Click on the **IDOK** object and the **BN_CLICKED** message. Click on the Add Function... button and accept **OnOK()** as the name of the new function. Here's the code for the **OnOK()** method for **CDeleteDlg**:

```
void CDeleteDlg::OnOK()
{
    // For each selected item we find in the
    // "to" list, delete the item.
    for ( int i=0; i<m_ToDeleteList.GetCount(); ++i )
    {
        CString s;
        m_ToDeleteList.GetText(i, s);

        // Delete the item by writing a NULL key for it
        ::WritePrivateProfileString(s,NULL,NULL,"docview.ini");
    }
    CDialog::OnOK();
}
```

The secret to this process is another poorly understood but documented function of the Windows API. The **WritePrivateProfileString()** function normally updates an initialization file topic and key by inserting or updating a given key with a given key value. For example, the function call:

```
WritePrivateProfileString( "Printers", "Number Of Printers", "5",
                           "printers.ini" );
```

will create an entry (or update the entry if it already exists) of the form

```
[Printers]
Number Of Printers=5
```

in the initialization file **Printers.ini**. If, however, you specify **NULL** in the place of the key parameter (**Number of Printers** in the above example) then the *entire topic* (Printers) and all of its keys will be deleted from the **Printers.ini** file.

In our **OnOK()** method, therefore, we simply iterate through all of the entries that were 'dropped' into the delete list, obtain the text of the entries, and then delete all keys for the topic by using the text as a topic name and **NULL** for the key.

9 Finally, add another item on the Edit menu, Delete, and add a handler for the **COMMAND** message with ClassWizard. In the function, place the following code:

```
void CMainFrame::OnEditDelete()
{
   CDeleteDlg dlg;
   dlg.DoModal();
}
```

remembering to add **#include "DeleteDlg.h"** to the top of the file, so that the compiler knows about **CDeleteDlg**.

10 Okay, I lied. Step 9 isn't the last one. The reason would be obvious if you compiled the code at this point and tried it out. You would see that the dialog works as advertised, and that if you deleted an item and then went back into the delete dialog, the item would not be there anymore. However, our splitter doesn't get updated! Oops.

To get this to work, we'll first add a new function to our **CCtrlListView**, **RefreshList()**. Most of the code for this comes from the **OnCreate()** member; in fact, cut out the code from there and replace it with a call to **RefreshList()**:

```
int CCtlListView::OnCreate(LPCREATESTRUCT lpCreateStruct)
{
   if (CView::OnCreate(lpCreateStruct) == -1)
      return -1;

   CRect r(0,0,0,0);

   m_List.Create( WS_CHILD | WS_VISIBLE | LBS_NOTIFY, r, this,
_APS_NEXT_CONTROL_VALUE );
   RefreshList();

   return 0;
}
```

11 Add **RefreshList()** to the class by using the Add Function... option from the context menu in ClassView, inserting the code:

```
void CCtrlListView::RefreshList()
{
   //Clear list contents
   m_List.ResetContent();

   char RetString[8196];
   char * word;

   DWORD numChars = ::GetPrivateProfileString( NULL, "", "", RetString,
                                               8196, "docview.ini");

   int processedChars = 0;
```

```
    int wordLen;
    while (processedChars < (int)numChars)
    {
        //strcpy(word, RetString+processedChars);
        word = RetString + processedChars;
        wordLen = strlen(word);

        if ( wordLen )
            m_List.AddString ( word );
        processedChars += wordLen + 1;
    }
}
```

12 Again, finally (this time for real), we need to modify our menu handler so that it calls **RefreshList()** after the dialog is closed:

```
void CMainFrame::OnEditDelete()
{
    CDeleteDlg dlg;
    dlg.DoModal();
    CCtlListView *listView = (CCtlListView *)m_wndSplitter.GetPane(0,0);
    listView->RefreshList();
}
```

That's all there is to the delete case. Another fine mess cleared up through the use of components!

Adding New Entries to the File

The very last (promise!) function we will add to the application will allow you to add new entries to the file. This isn't a particularly difficult feature to implement. All we need is the name of the component and a valid HTML and detail file name to add to the initialization file.

Ah, that validity thing! How can we make sure that the input from the user is valid? There are two basic approaches here that will work. We could display the Open File dialog box, get the name of the HTML file, then display another Open File dialog box to get the name of the detail file name. Finally, we would need somehow to get the name of the component from the user, probably using yet another dialog. Although this approach will work and does promote component reuse (the Open File dialog is a component in its own right, after all), it seems a rather unwieldy thing for the user to work with. As it stands, if they make a mistake in selecting a file, or change their mind at the component name stage, they would need to cancel the process and start over from scratch. Besides, it doesn't show off any of the work we have done in the book.

The second approach to making sure the input is valid is simply to validate it as the user enters it. That's right: we're talking about the ValidationEdit control!

TRY IT OUT - Create the Add Dialog

1 The first step toward implementing the new dialog is, as usual, to create the dialog template on which to base all of the rest of the work. Let's do that first, shall we? Enter the resource editor and create a new dialog. Move the OK and Cancel buttons to the bottom of the dialog. Add three new edit fields to the dialog, vertically aligned on the left edge.

2 On the left of each edit field, add a static text field. Give the first static text field the caption Component Name:. The second edit field label (second static text field from the top) should get the caption HTML Filename:, while the third should be called Detail Filename:. When you're finished, you should have a dialog box that looks like this:

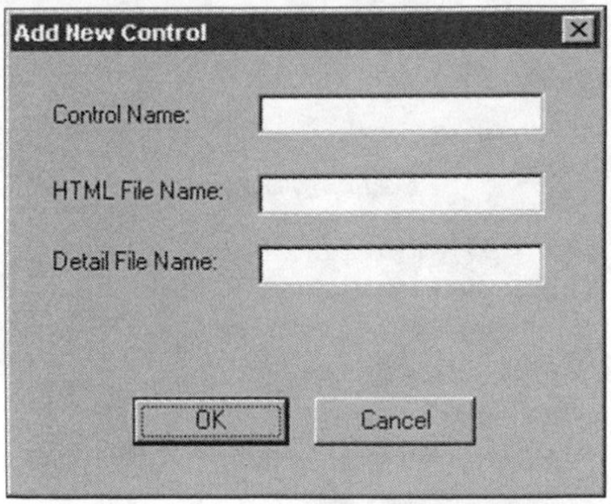

Add New Control

Control Name:

HTML File Name:

Detail File Name:

OK Cancel

3 The next step is to generate a C++ class for the dialog template we just finished. Right-click on the dialog template in the resource editor and select ClassWizard from the pop-up menu. Accept the offer of creating a new dialog class. Give the new dialog the name **CAddDlg** (well, what did you expect? Fred?) and remove the Add To Component Gallery check.

4 We have the framework for the dialog in place; now we need to bring the ValidationEdit component into play. The first part of the job is easy: just copy the **ValidationEdit.cpp** and **ValidationEdit.h** files over from the code you wrote in Chapter 4. The next step is a little (but not much) tougher: creating a new validation class based on **CValidationEdit**.

In order to actually implement file validation, we need to do a simple derivation of the **CValidationEdit** class that 'knows' how to validate file names. In order to do this, we need to override the **IsValid()** method of the class in our new, derived, class.

5 The easiest way to create the derived class, is to let ClassWizard do all the hard work for us. The problem is, ClassWizard doesn't know about **CValidateEdit**. This shouldn't stop us though. In ClassWizard, click the Add Class... button and create a class named **CFileEdit**, based on generic CWnd. Now we have to change the base class from **CWnd** to **CValidateEdit**. The modifications to **FileEdit.h** are highlighted here:

```
// FileEdit.h : header file
//

/////////////////////////////////////////////////////////////////////////////
// CFileEdit window

#include "ValidationEdit.h"

class CFileEdit : public CValidationEdit
{
// Construction
public:
   CFileEdit();

// Attributes
public:

// Operations
```

```
public:

// Overrides
    // ClassWizard generated virtual function overrides
    //{{AFX_VIRTUAL(CFileEdit)
    //}}AFX_VIRTUAL

// Implementation
public:
    virtual ~CFileEdit();

    // Generated message map functions
protected:
    virtual BOOL IsValid(void) const;
    //{{AFX_MSG(CFileEdit)
        // NOTE - the ClassWizard will add and remove member functions here.
    //}}AFX_MSG
    DECLARE_MESSAGE_MAP()
};
/////////////////////////////////////////////////////////////////////////////
```

6 In **FileEdit.cpp** we have to change the Message Map macros so that the map points to the right parent:

```
BEGIN_MESSAGE_MAP(CFileEdit, CValidationEdit)
    //{{AFX_MSG_MAP(CFileEdit)
        // NOTE - the ClassWizard will add and remove mapping macros here.
    //}}AFX_MSG_MAP
END_MESSAGE_MAP()
```

7 Now we can implement the override of **IsValid()**:

```
BOOL CFileEdit::IsValid(void) const
{
    // To be valid, we need only get the file's status
    CString strFileName;
    GetWindowText(strFileName);

    CFileStatus status;
    return CFile::GetStatus( strFileName, status )
}
```

As you can see, our 'validation' consists of nothing more than trying to get the file's status using the static version of **CFile::GetStatus()** which requires the file name and a **CFileStatus** to store the status in. We simply return the value the **GetStatus()** returns.

8 In order to validate the input from the dialog, we'll use the **CFileEdit** class we just created. To do this, fire up the old ClassWizard and select the **CAddDlg** class. Move to the Member Variables tab and select the second edit field (**IDC_EDIT2**). This field is supposed to contain the HTML filename. Add a new variable by clicking on the Add Variable... button.

Enter the name **m_HTMLFile** for the name of the new member variable. Select Control for the type of the variable and leave **CEdit** as the type selected. We will modify this class setting shortly. Repeat the process for the **IDC_EDIT3** entry, giving it the name **m_DetailFile**. Lastly, add a variable for the **IDC_EDIT1** entry. Give it the name **m_ComponentName** and leave the settings at variable of type **CString**.

9 Make the following modifications to the **AddDlg.h** header file. The changes to be made are all shown highlighted, in keeping with convention:

```
// AddDlg.h : header file
//

/////////////////////////////////////////////////////////////////////////////
// CAddDlg dialog

#include "FileEdit.h"

class CAddDlg : public CDialog
{
// Construction
public:
   CAddDlg(CWnd* pParent = NULL);   // standard constructor

// Dialog Data
   //{{AFX_DATA(CAddDlg)
   enum { IDD = IDD_DIALOG3 };
   CFileEdit   m_DetailFile;
   CFileEdit   m_HTMLFile;
   CString   m_ControlName;
   //}}AFX_DATA


// Overrides
   // ClassWizard generated virtual function overrides
   //{{AFX_VIRTUAL(CAddDlg)
   protected:
   virtual void DoDataExchange(CDataExchange* pDX);   // DDX/DDV support
   //}}AFX_VIRTUAL

// Implementation
protected:

   // Generated message map functions
   //{{AFX_MSG(CAddDlg)
      // NOTE: the ClassWizard will add member functions here
   //}}AFX_MSG
   DECLARE_MESSAGE_MAP()
};
```

Believe it or not, the dialog will now automatically validate the input filenames! When the user tries to leave one of the file edit fields, the field will be validated via the **IsValid()** method. If the filename can't be found or opened, the error message Invalid Entry will be displayed and the focus will be returned to that field.

10 We aren't quite done yet, but we are getting pretty close. All that is left to do is to handle adding the new entry when the user clicks the OK button or presses *Enter* in the dialog. Let's do this last task. Using ClassWizard, add a new handler for the **IDOK** button clicked message. Add the following code to the generated **OnOK()** method for **CAddDlg**:

```
void CAddDlg::OnOK()
{
    CString dFileName, hFileName;

    m_DetailFile.GetWindowText(dFileName);
    m_HTMLFile.GetWindowText(hFileName);

    // Do some validation
    if ( dFileName.IsEmpty() )
    {
        MessageBox("The detail file name is required!", "Error" );
        return;
    }

    if ( hFileName.IsEmpty() )
    {
        MessageBox("The HTML file name is required!", "Error" );
        return;
    }

    UpdateData(TRUE);
    if ( m_ComponentName.IsEmpty() )
    {
        MessageBox("The component name is required!", "Error" );
        return;
    }

    WritePrivateProfileString(m_ComponentName, "File", hFileName, "docview.ini" );
    WritePrivateProfileString(m_ComponentName, "ListFile", dFileName, "docview.ini"
);

    CDialog::OnOK();
}
```

The dialog is now functionally complete. All we need to do is to hook the dialog into a new menu item command (so that the user can actually get to it) and the application will finally be finished.

11 In the application's menu resource, add a new menu item with the caption Add... to the end of the Edit menu we created previously. Give the new menu item the identifier **ID_ADD_DLG**. Save the menu item and close the menu editor.

12 Bring up ClassWizard and select the **CMainFrame** class. Select the **ID_ADD_DLG** object and the **COMMAND** message. Click on the Add Function... button and give the new method the name **OnAddDlg()** (as suggested by the wizard). Add the following code to the **OnAddDlg()** method of **CMainFrame**:

```
void CMainFrame::OnEditAdd()
{
    CAddDlg dlg;
    dlg.DoModal();
     CCtlListView *listView = (CCtlListView *)m_wndSplitter.GetPane(0,0);
    listView->RefreshList();
}
```

13 Last of all, add the include file **AddDlg.h** to the top of the **MainFrm.cpp** include file list... and that does the job! The project is finished.

In Summation

At this point, you have a fully working implementation of an HTML documentation viewer. You can add or delete entries, as well as viewing details on individual entries. In addition to the experience of writing a complete working application (not something that every programmer can say they have), you've gained valuable experience in working with components to piece together an application.

I hope you had some fun with this book and learned a little something along the way. If you apply only a fraction of what you learned here, I assure you that you will do pretty well in the software development industry. Besides, even if you only reuse one of the components in the book in one of your own applications, you will save the cost of the book several times over!

Enjoy, and happy componenting!

Visual
C++

Beginning Visual C++ Components

Symbols

A

D

E

F

G

H

I

K

L

M

N

O

T

U

V

W

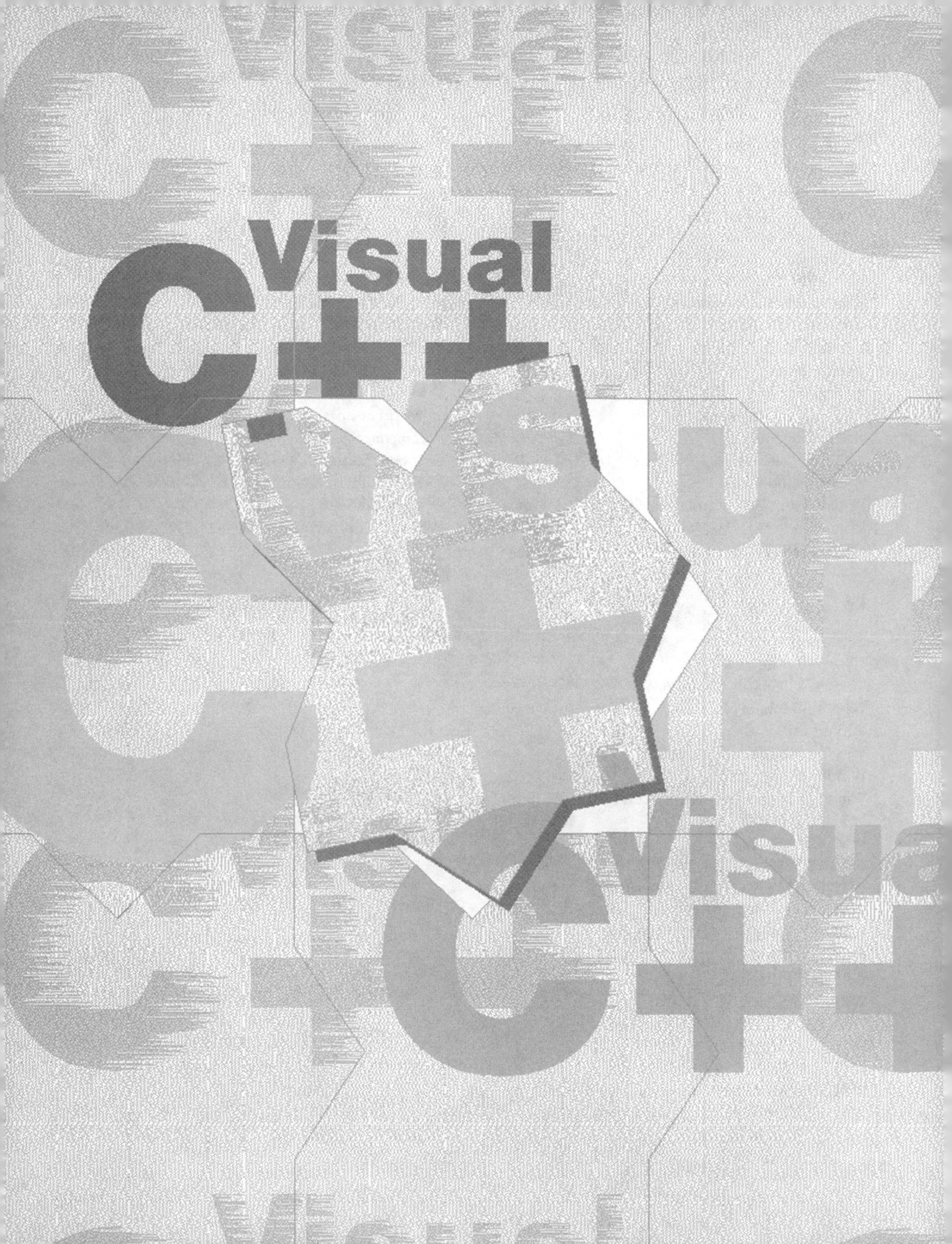

Visual
C++

Beginning WordBasic Programming

Author: Alex Homer ISBN: 1874416869
Price: $39.95 C$55.95 £37.49

Starting with an introduction to WordBasic, macros and templates, the first section of the book goes on to look at the language elements of WordBasic. We cover everything from statements, functions and control structures to communicating with your users using dialog boxes. There are clear discussions on the complex issues of the dynamic dialog!

In the second section of the book we look at Word in the workplace covering topics such as creating wizards and add-ins for using Word in a business environment. We show you how to manage large documents and how to automate some of the tasks faced by publishing companies such as controlling changes to documents, creating indexes and tables of contents and improving Word's printing options. We then go into detail on creating Help systems and HTML pages for the Internet. The book takes time out to look at Word Macro viruses and the complexities of DDE with Excel and Access.

All the source code from the book is included on the disk.

Visual C++ 4 MasterClass

Authors: Various ISBN: 1874416443
Price: $49.95 C$69.95 £46.99

The book starts by covering software design issues related to programming with MFC, providing tips and techniques for creating great MFC extensions. This is followed by an analysis of porting issues when moving your applications from 16 to 32 bits.

The next section shows how you can use COM/OLE in the real world. This begins with an examination of COM technologies and the foundations of OLE (aggregation, uniform data transfer, drag and drop and so on) and is followed by a look at extending standard MFC OLE Document clients and servers to make use of database storage.

The third section of the book concentrates on making use of, and extending, the features that Windows 95 first brought to the public, including the 32-bit common controls, and the new style shell. You'll see how to make use of all the new features including appbars, file viewers, shortcuts, and property sheets.

The fourth section of the book provides a detailed look at multimedia and games programming, making use of Windows multimedia services and the facilities provided by the Game SDK (DirectX).

The final section covers 'net programming, whether it's for the Internet or the intranet. You'll see how to make the most of named pipes, mailslots, NetBIOS and WinSock before seeing how to create the corporate intranet system of your dreams using WinINet and ActiveX technology.

Beginning Linux Programming

Authors: Neil Matthew, Richard Stones

ISBN: 187441680

Price: $36.95 C$51.95 £33.99

The book is unique in that it teaches UNIX programming in a simple and structured way, using Linux and its associated and freely available development tools as the main platform. Assuming familiarity with the UNIX environment and a basic knowledge of C, the book teaches you how to put together UNIX applications that make the most of your time, your OS and your machine's capabilities.

Having introduced the programming environment and basic tools, the authors turn their attention initially on shell programming. The chapters then concentrate on programming UNIX with C, showing you how to work with files, access the UNIX environment, input and output data using terminals and curses, and manage data. After another round with development and debugging tools, the book discusses processes and signals, pipes and other IPC mechanisms, culminating with a chapter on sockets. Programming the X-Window system is introduced with Tcl/Tk and Java. Finally, the book covers programming for the Internet using HTML and CGI.

The book aims to discuss UNIX programming as described in the relevant POSIX and X/Open specifications, so the code is tested with that in mind. All the source code from the book is available under the terms of the Gnu Public License from the Wrox web site.

Revolutionary Guide to Visual Basic 4 Professional

Author: Larry Roof ISBN: 1874416370

Price: $44.95 C$62.95 £49.99

This book focuses on the four key areas for developers using VB4: the Win32 API, Objects and OLE, Databases and the VB development cycle. Each of the areas receives in-depth coverage, and techniques are illustrated using rich and complex example projects that bring out the real issues involved in commercial VB development. It examines the Win32 API from a VB perspective and gives a complete run-down of developing multimedia apps. The OLE section includes a help file creator that uses the Word OLE object, and we OLE automate Netscape Navigator 2. The database section offers complete coverage of DAO, SQL and ODBC, finishing with a detailed analysis of client/server database systems. The final section shows how to design, code, optimize and distribute a complete application. The book has a CD including all source code and a hypertext version of the book.

Future Titles from Wrox Press

Instant VBScript

Authors: Alex Homer, Darren Gill ISBN: 1861000448 Price: $25.00 C$34.95 £22.99

This is the guide for programmers who already know HTML and another programming language and want to waste no time getting up to speed. This book takes developers right into the code, straight from the beginning of Chapter 1. The first object is to get the programmer to create their own 'reactive' web pages as quickly as possible while introducing the most important HTML and ActiveX controls. This new knowledge is quickly incorporated into more complex examples with a complete sample site built early in the book.

As Internet Explorer is the browser that introduced VBScript, we also take a detailed look at how to use VBScript to access different objects within the browser. We create our own tools to help us with the development of applications, in particular a debugging tool to aid error-trapping. Information is provided on how to build your own controls and sign them to secure Internet download. Finally we take a look at server side scripting and how with VBScript you can get the clients and server communicating freely. The book is supported by our web site which contains all of the examples in the book in an easily executable form.

Professional Java Fundamentals

Authors: Shy Cohen, Tom Mitchell, Andres Gonzalez, Larry Rodrigues, Kerry Hammil
ISBN: 1861000383 Price: $35.00 C$49.00 £32.49

Professional Java Fundamentals is a high-level, developer's book that gives you the detailed information and extended coverage you need to program Java for real, making the most of Java's potential.

It starts by thoroughly recapping the basics of Java, providing a language reference, looking at object-oriented programming issues and then at Java's fundamental classes. The book then details advanced language features, such as multithreading, networking, file I/O and native methods. There are five Abstract Windowing Toolkit chapters which provide in-depth coverage of event handling, graphics and animation, GUI building blocks and layout managers. Lastly, the book shows you how to design and implement class libraries in Java.

The book is supported by the Wrox web site, from which the complete source code is available.

Future Titles from Wrox Press

Instant HTML

Author: Steve Wright ISBN: 1861000766 Price: $15.00 C$21.00 £13.99

This book is a fast paced guide to the latest version of the HTML language, including the extensions to the standards added by Netscape and Microsoft. Aimed at programmers, it assumes a basic knowledge of the Internet. It starts by looking at the basics of HTML including document structure, formatting tags, inserting hyperlinks and images and image mapping, and then moves on to cover more advanced issues such as tables, frames, creating forms to interact with users, animation, incorporating scripts (such as JavaScript) into HTML documents, and style sheets.

The book includes a full list of all the HTML tags, organised by category for easy reference.

Professional ISAPI Programming in C++

Author: Michael Tracy ISBN: 1861000664 Price: $40.00 C$56.00 £36.99

This is a working developer's guide to customizing Microsoft's Internet Information Server, which is now an integrated and free addition to the NT4.0 platform. This is essential reading for real-world web site development and expects readers to already be competent C++ and C programmers. Although all techniques in the book are workable under various C++ compilers, users of Visual C++ 4.1 will benefit from the ISAPI extensions supplied in its AppWizard.

This book covers extension and filter programming in depth. There is a walk through the API structure but not a reference to endless calls. Instead, we illustrate the key specifications with example programs.

HTTP and HTML instructions are issued as an appendix. We introduce extensions by mimicking popular CGI scripts and there's a specific chapter on controlling cookies. With filters we are not just re-running generic web code - these are leading-edge filter methods specifically designed for the IIS API.

Wrox Press Developer's Journal

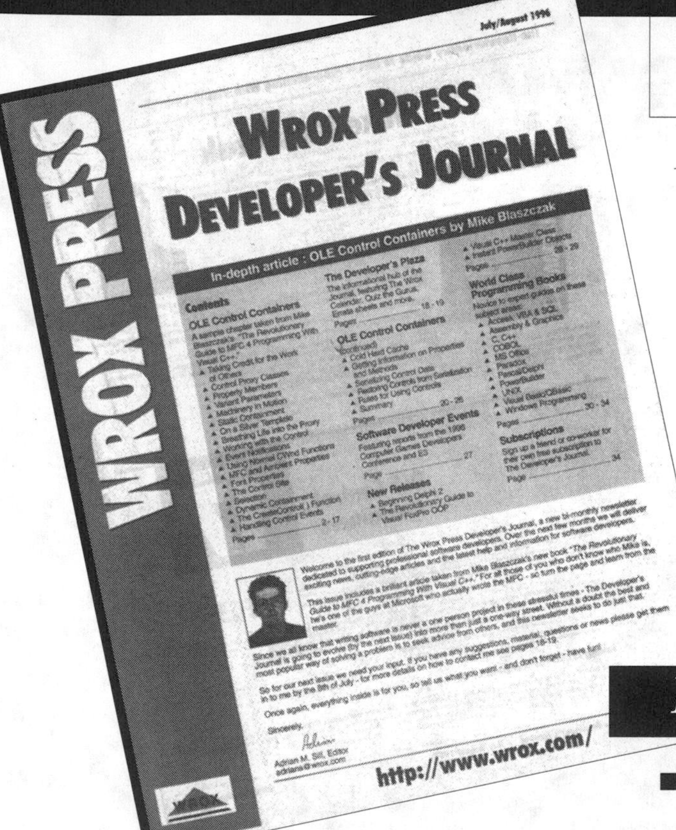

Free subscription

A 40-page bi-monthly magazine for software developers, The Wrox Press Developer's Journal features in-depth articles, news and help for everyone in the software development industry. Each issue includes extracts from our latest titles and is crammed full of practical insights into coding techniques, tricks and research.

In forthcoming editions

- Articles on Unix, SQL Server 6.5, WordBasic, Java, Internet Information Server, Visual Basic and lots, lots more.
- Hard hitting reports from cutting edge technical conferences from around the world.
- Full and extensive list of all Wrox publications including a brief description of contents.

To Subscribe:

Please send in your full name and address to Wrox Press and receive the next edition of the Wrox Press Developer's Journal.

- Wrox Press, 30 Lincoln Rd, Olton, Birmingham, B27 6PA, UK.
  Contact: Gina Mance, +44 121 706 6826
- Wrox Press, 2710, W. Touhy, Chicago, IL 60645, USA.
  Contact: Kristen Schmitt, +1 312 465 3559

or e-mail us on devjournal@wrox.com